SECOND EDITION

# ACCOUNTING
## Principles & Practices

### Module 1

**THE ACCOUNTING CYCLE:**
Service and Merchandising Businesses
(Chapters 1-14)

L. Paden Neeley, PhD, CPA

Executive Director,
Professional Development Institute
North Texas State University

Frank J. Imke, PhD, CPA

Professor of Accounting
The University of Texas at Arlington

*Published by*

A42 **SOUTH-WESTERN PUBLISHING CO.**

CINCINNATI WEST CHICAGO, ILL. DALLAS PELHAM MANOR, N.Y. PALO ALTO, CALIF.

ISBN: 0-538-01420-2

Library of Congress Catalog Card Number: 81-85013

3 4 5 6 7 8 9 K 0 9 8 7 6 5

Printed in the United States of America

# PREFACE

The purpose of *Accounting: Principles and Practices* is to provide students with a basic understanding of accounting. Emphasis is placed on the fundamentals of accounting in an effort to give the student a strong foundation for entry into and development within a business environment.

The title of the text is indicative of its approach to the study of accounting; namely, the explanation of accounting principles (the "why" of accounting) with examples of the related accounting practices (the "how" of accounting). It is essential that the accounting student know why certain practices and procedures are necessary. It is equally important for the student to know how to apply basic accounting principles. The "why" and the "how" reinforce each other in a very significant way in the study of accounting.

To meet the needs of accounting classes with varying curricular patterns and proficiency standards, *Accounting: Principles and Practices* is available in two modules. Each module is a combined text-workbook. The consecutive use of both modules constitutes the coverage of the first full year of accounting study. For shorter courses, an abridged edition (Module 1A) covering Chapters 1–10 of Module 1 is available. An individual module may be used for either one quarter or one semester, depending upon the students' abilities.

An accounting simulation is available with each of the two modules. The simulation for Module 1 may also be used for Module 1A. These simulations are intended to give the students the most realistic experience possible in an academic environment by providing transactions documents, books of account, and other accounting-related records.

Module 1, *The Accounting Cycle: Service and Merchandising Businesses*, covers the basic accounting cycle for service and merchandising businesses in Chapters 1–9. The accounting cycle for the service enterprise includes journalizing, posting, preparation of the work sheet and financial statements, adjusting and closing entries, and the post-closing trial balance. Special journals are utilized in the coverage of the accounting cycle for a merchandising business.

Chapters 10–14 include payroll accounting, internal control and use of the voucher system, accruals and deferrals, receivables and payables, merchandise inventory, and plant assets and depreciation.

Accounting Simulation 1 is of one month's duration and covers the accounting cycle for a merchandising business that utilizes special journals and includes payroll accounting.

Module 2, *Partnerships and Corporations: Cost Accounting*, covers partnership and corporate accounting, financial statement analysis, the statement of changes in financial position, departmental accounting, cost accounting systems, managerial accounting topics, federal income taxes, and data processing. Accounting Simulation 2 is of one month's duration and pertains to the cost accounting system of a manufacturing business organized as a corporation.

Each chapter in the modules is divided into easily readable parts, normally covering one major topic per part. At the end of each part, Questions for Discussion are presented to aid in developing the students' comprehension of the topic presented. Short exercises, new to this revision, are also included at the end of each part to allow coverage of individual concepts presented in the chapters.

At the end of each part, the students are directed to the appropriate assignment in the workbook section of the text. Each assignment contains objective-type questions which are designed to review the terminology and concepts presented in the chapter. The balance of each assignment consists of accounting problems for which ruled forms are provided to facilitate the learning process and to minimize the required completion time. Supplementary problems, located at the end of the workbook section of the text, are provided for each chapter to enable the students to obtain additional problem-solving practice. Inasmuch as these supplementary problems are not accompanied by working papers, the students can gain practical experience in developing accounting forms while preparing the solutions.

The practical, straight-forward presentation of this material provides students with the foundation that will allow them to obtain employment and perform successfully in positions requiring basic accounting knowledge. Additionally, completion of both modules should provide a strong background for those students who wish to pursue further accounting study.

L. Paden Neeley

Frank J. Imke

# CONTENTS

Chapter **1**

# THE STRUCTURE AND NATURE OF ACCOUNTING

This textbook provides an introduction to the area of knowledge known as accounting. *Accounting* is a very broad field and includes activities such as recording, summarizing, reporting, and interpreting financial data. The sequence of activities beginning with the recording of the transactions of a business and ending with the reporting of financial data is known as the *accounting cycle*.

The process of recording and classifying the transactions of a business is called *bookkeeping*. An accountant usually plans the record keeping system which the bookkeeper maintains, summarizes the information obtained from the system, and prepares and interprets accounting reports. The clerical function of the bookkeeper is increasingly being performed by data processing equipment. In this textbook, both the bookkeeping and other accounting processes will be considered. Emphasis, however, will be placed upon the reporting and interpreting of the information obtained from the accounting system.

In our society, no entity can function efficiently without accounting. An entity may be a family, a shoe store, a restaurant, a church, or a manufacturer, for example. Regardless of the type of entity, financial information is needed to plan and control the use of resources. Families, for example, cannot maximize the enjoyment of resources available to them, nor can they function as responsible citizens without using accounting information in a variety of ways. It is also true that no business entity can survive for very long in our economic environment without the aid of reliable accounting information.

## PART A PROPERTY AND RIGHTS TO PROPERTY

Persons owning property for the purpose of conducting a business operation do so with the expectation of increasing the value of their property. To accomplish this objective, they use their property to produce goods or services that are demanded in the marketplace. They sell their products and use the amounts received to buy other properties which are, in turn, used to produce more goods or services. Manufacturers use property such as buildings and machinery to produce goods that can be sold to wholesalers or retailers. To be successful, they must sell their products for an amount greater than the cost of producing, marketing, and delivering them to their customers. Retail merchants also use property in operating their businesses. They purchase merchandise from manufacturers and wholesalers. To bring the merchandise to the attention of prospective customers, retailers may use display equipment to exhibit the merchandise in a store building. These are just a few examples of the kinds of properties used by businesses.

## PROPERTY AND PROPERTY RIGHTS

The properties used in the operation of a business are called *assets*. The owner's right to the properties is called the *owner's equity* or *capital*. If there are no claims against the assets other than those of the owner, the relationship of the owner's equity to the assets may be expressed by the following equation:

**PROPERTY = PROPERTY RIGHTS**

**or**

**ASSETS = OWNER'S EQUITY**

Most business people find that they are unable to conduct their businesses satisfactorily using only the property which they invest in the business. They often borrow money from others to buy assets which they need to operate the business. They also may obtain property on credit by giving a promise to pay at some future date. Those from whom business people borrow or buy on credit are known as *creditors*. The creditors have a claim to the property of the business until they are paid by the owner. These claims, which are the property rights of creditors, are called *liabilities*.

If Ron Fike borrows $400 from Ann Wall, Wall is a creditor of Fike. Wall has a claim against the assets of Fike until the $400 is paid. If Fike purchases supplies from the Ace Company, and he promises to pay for the supplies in 30 days, the Ace Company is also a creditor of Fike. If Fike fails to pay, the Ace Company can enforce its claim by legal action. The claim of each creditor against the assets of Fike represents a liability to Fike.

From the above discussion, it is apparent that assets (properties) are subject to two kinds of claims (property rights), those arising from the rights of creditors (liabilities) and those arising from the rights of the owner (owner's equity). The sum of the rights of creditors and the rights of the owner is equal to the value of the assets. This fact may be expressed by the *accounting equation:*

**ASSETS = LIABILITIES + OWNER'S EQUITY**

The total of the owner's equity can be determined at any time by subtracting the liabilities from the assets. This can be expressed by rearranging the equation as follows:

**ASSETS − LIABILITIES = OWNER'S EQUITY**

If Fike is using $11,000 of assets in operating a business, and he has liabilities of $1,500, his equity is $9,500. This condition is shown in equation form at the top of the next page.

| ASSETS | = | LIABILITIES | + | OWNER'S EQUITY |
|---|---|---|---|---|
| $11,000 | | $1,500 | | $9,500 |

or

| ASSETS | – | LIABILITIES | = | OWNER'S EQUITY |
|---|---|---|---|---|
| $11,000 | | $1,500 | | $9,500 |

The relationship between assets, liabilities and owner's equity is basic to the understanding of accounting. All business property is subject to property rights. This concept is fundamental to understanding double-entry accounting. *Double-entry accounting* is the technique used to assure that the dollar amount of the property will at all times equal the dollar amount of the property rights. Business transactions may result in changes to both property and property rights. Sometimes a transaction may involve only the exchange of one type of property for another type or the change from one type of property right to another type. Recording such events still requires double-entry accounting since the transaction must be recorded in two places. The amount of a transaction must be added to one type of property or property right and subtracted from another.

## EFFECT OF BUSINESS OPERATIONS ON PROPERTY AND PROPERTY RIGHTS

Business people are continually buying and selling commodities and services. The buying and selling process produces changes in both the nature and the amount of the property used in conducting a business.

Clare Rivera has $10,000 that she decides to use in the operation of a telephone answering service. The business assets and equity are shown by the following equation:

| ASSETS | = | OWNER'S EQUITY |
|---|---|---|
| $10,000 | | $10,000 |

Rivera buys office supplies for $300 cash. This purchase decreases the asset, cash, but creates a new asset, office supplies. Note that Rivera's equity was unaffected by the transaction. The equation now is:

| ASSETS | | | = | OWNER'S EQUITY |
|---|---|---|---|---|
| Cash | + | Office Supplies | = | Clare Rivera, Capital |
| $9,700 | | $300 | | $10,000 |

Rivera buys equipment from the Decatur Equipment Company for $15,000 *on account* (on credit). This transaction increases the assets of the business and also increases the liabilities by the same amount. The equation now is:

| ASSETS | | | | | = | LIABILITIES | + | OWNER'S EQUITY |
|---|---|---|---|---|---|---|---|---|
| Cash | + | Office Supplies | + | Office Equipment | = | Accounts Payable | + | Clare Rivera, Capital |
| $9,700 | | $300 | | $15,000 | | $15,000 | | $10,000 |

As should always be the case, the assets (properties) still equal the sum of the liabilities and owner's equity (property rights).

## EFFECT OF BUSINESS OPERATIONS ON OWNER'S EQUITY

In operating the business, Rivera receives money from clients and she pays business expenses. The money collected from clients increases the assets of the business and increases the owner's equity. An increase in assets resulting from the sale of merchandise or services is called *revenue*. For example, if collections for the day total $420, both cash and owner's equity are increased by $420 as shown in the following equation:

| ASSETS | | | | | = | LIABILITIES | + | OWNER'S EQUITY |
|---|---|---|---|---|---|---|---|---|
| Cash | + | Office Supplies | + | Office Equipment | = | Accounts Payable | + | Clare Rivera, Capital |
| $ 9,700 | | $300 | | $15,000 | | $15,000 | | $10,000 |
| +420 | | | | | | | | +420 |
| $10,120 | | $300 | | $15,000 | | $15,000 | | $10,420 |

Expenses incurred by Rivera, if paid in cash, reduce the assets of the business and also reduce her equity. If utilities totaling $100 for the month are paid, the effect on the equation is as follows:

| ASSETS | | | | | = | LIABILITIES | + | OWNER'S EQUITY |
|---|---|---|---|---|---|---|---|---|
| Cash | + | Office Supplies | + | Office Equipment | = | Accounts Payable | + | Clare Rivera, Capital |
| $10,120 | | $300 | | $15,000 | | $15,000 | | $10,420 |
| −100 | | | | | | | | −100 |
| $10,020 | | $300 | | $15,000 | | $15,000 | | $10,320 |

If Rivera incurs an expense on account, this has no effect on the assets of the business, but it increases the liabilities and reduces the owner's equity by the amount of the expense incurred. For example, if Rivera advertises the answering service in the local newspaper during the month and receives a bill for $80 from the Evening News at the end of the month, the changes in the equation are as follows:

| ASSETS | | | | | = | LIABILITIES | + | OWNER'S EQUITY |
|---|---|---|---|---|---|---|---|---|
| Cash | + | Office Supplies | + | Office Equipment | = | Accounts Payable | + | Clare Rivera, Capital |
| $10,020 | | $300 | | $15,000 | | $15,000 | | $10,320 |
| | | | | | | +80 | | −80 |
| $10,020 | | $300 | | $15,000 | | $15,080 | | $10,240 |

If Rivera withdraws $400 cash from the business for personal use, the effect is a decrease in assets and a corresponding decrease in equity, as shown in the following equation:

| ASSETS | | | | | = | LIABILITIES | + | OWNER'S EQUITY |
|---|---|---|---|---|---|---|---|---|
| Cash | + | Office Supplies | + | Office Equipment | = | Accounts Payable | + | Clare Rivera, Capital |
| $10,020 | | $300 | | $15,000 | | $15,080 | | $10,240 |
| −400 | | | | | | | | −400 |
| $ 9,620 | | $300 | | $15,000 | | $15,080 | | $ 9,840 |

If $2,500 is paid on the liability incurred with the Decatur Equipment Company, the assets and the liabilities are decreased by the same amount and there is no effect on the owner's equity.

| ASSETS | | | | | = | LIABILITIES | + | OWNER'S EQUITY |
|---|---|---|---|---|---|---|---|---|
| Cash | + | Office Supplies | + | Office Equipment | = | Accounts Payable | + | Clare Rivera, Capital |
| $9,620 | | $300 | | $15,000 | | $15,080 | | $9,840 |
| −2,500 | | | | | | −2,500 | | |
| $7,120 | | $300 | | $15,000 | | $12,580 | | $9,840 |

Other transactions that Rivera performs in the operation of the business will produce similar changes in the property and the rights to the property.

## NEED FOR ACCOUNTING INFORMATION

In order to operate a business effectively, the owner should be informed as to the nature and amount of each asset, each liability, and the amount of owner's equity. For purposes of planning and controlling business operations, the owner should also know when, why, and how frequently changes occur in the various assets, liabilities, and the owner's equity of the business.

There are others, in addition to the owner, who are interested in and entitled to information concerning the operations of the business. If the owner desires to borrow money from a bank, the loan officer will require information which allows the bank to determine the owner's ability to repay the loan. The business will also be required to file various reports with government agencies — federal, state, and local — concerning income taxes, property and sales taxes, and information on salaries paid to employees.

Without written records, business owners are not able to keep track of the nature and the amount of the assets, liabilities, and owner's equity and the changes that occur in their composition. A good record keeping system is usually essential to provide the necessary information. This system of record keeping should show the effect of each transaction on the assets, liabilities, and owner's equity of the business.

### QUESTIONS FOR DISCUSSION

1. Name three kinds of property that could be used in each of the following entities: (a) a dress shop, (b) a bakery, and (c) a hospital.
2. Margaret Baker invests $9,500 cash in an interior decorating business. She finds that she needs $5,000 of additional property to conduct the business properly. In what two ways may she secure this property?
3. Give two transactions that result in an increase in owner's equity and two that result in a decrease in owner's equity.
4. Don Pali, a TV repairer, has assets amounting to $17,000, liabilities of $6,500, and owner's equity of $10,500. He completes a transaction that produces a change in the nature of his assets but not in their total. (a) Does this transaction result in any change in the total of his liabilities and owner's equity? Why or why not? (b) Give two examples of such a transaction.

5. Ron Henson, a free-lance artist, has assets totaling $9,000, liabilities of $3,000, and owner's equity of $6,000. He completes a transaction that results in an increase of $300 in his total assets. What change, if any, does this transaction produce in the total of his liabilities and owner's equity? Explain your answer.

6. At the beginning of business on April 1, Jim Kim, a plumber, has total assets of $18,000, total liabilities of $8,000, and owner's equity of $10,000. His first transaction of the day results in an increase of $400 in total assets. (a) If liabilities remain unchanged, what effect does this transaction have on owner's equity? Explain your answer. (b) Give an example of such a transaction.

## EXERCISES

1. On September 1, the financial condition of Betty Wilson, owner of a carpet cleaning company, is shown by the following equation:

| ASSETS | | | | | LIABILITIES | | OWNER'S EQUITY |
|---|---|---|---|---|---|---|---|
| Cash | + Cleaning Supplies | + | Cleaning Equipment | = | Accounts Payable | + | Betty Wilson, Capital |
| $1,300 | $450 | | $2,600 | | $800 | | $3,550 |

Using the above properties and property rights:

(a) Describe two transactions that Wilson may complete, each of which will result only in a change in the nature of the assets and will not affect the total amount of the assets, the liabilities, or the owner's equity.

(b) Describe two transactions, each of which will decrease the total assets and the owner's equity by the same amount.

(c) Describe two transactions, each of which will increase the total assets and the owner's equity by the same amount.

(d) Describe a transaction that will decrease the total assets and decrease the liabilities by the same amount.

(e) Describe a transaction that will increase the total assets and increase the liabilities by the same amount.

2. Determine the missing amount in each of the following equations:

| | ASSETS | – | LIABILITIES | = | OWNER'S EQUITY |
|---|---|---|---|---|---|
| a. | 1,230 | – | 410 | = | ______ |
| b. | 2,180 | – | ______ | = | 1,340 |
| c. | ______ | – | 775 | = | 1,050 |
| d. | ______ | – | 1,720 | = | 3,660 |
| e. | 4,125 | – | 2,890 | = | ______ |

## ASSIGNMENT 1-A

**Tear out pages 329–332 and complete Assignment 1-A. Follow the instructions given for each section. An understanding of the principles developed in the preceding discussion is needed to complete this assignment. If necessary, review the textbook discussion. After completing the assignment, continue with the textbook discussion until Assignment 1-B is required.**

## PART B FINANCIAL STATEMENTS

One of the main purposes of the accounting records is to show in summary form the effects of the business transactions on the assets, liabilities, and owner's equity. It is not feasible for the owner to determine the effect of each transaction immediately after its occurrence because this would normally involve the consideration of a tremendous amount of detail, since even small firms may complete hundreds of transactions each day. For this reason accounting reports known as *financial statements* are prepared periodically to inform the owner, creditors, and other interested parties as to the financial condition and operating activities of the business.

### THE BALANCE SHEET

The financial statement which shows the amount and nature of the business assets, liabilities, and owner's equity as of a specific point in time, usually the last day of a month or year, is called a *balance sheet*. It is also known as a *statement of financial position* or a *statement of financial condition*. By analyzing the balance sheet, the present financial condition of the business can be determined. If compared with previous balance sheets, the effects of business operations on the assets, liabilities, and owner's equity can also be measured. As stated above, it is usually sufficient for the owner, creditors, and other interested outsiders to receive a balance sheet periodically, usually monthly or annually.

A balance sheet in its simplest form is a statement of the basic accounting equation and shows only the totals of the assets, liabilities, and owner's equity. If Clare Rivera, a small business owner, has $22,420 in assets and $12,580 in liabilities, her financial condition can be expressed by the following equation:

| ASSETS | = | LIABILITIES | + | OWNER'S EQUITY |
|---|---|---|---|---|
| $22,420 | | $12,580 | | $9,840 |

This equation, however, does not provide sufficient information about Rivera's business. It does not show the nature or composition of the assets and liabilities. It does not indicate whether she has enough cash to meet current obligations or sufficient facilities to satisfy the demands of customers. The statement does not indicate the amount of equipment being used in business operations. All of this information is important, for if she has invested too much in one form of asset and too little in another, the business may not be as profitable as it could be. An examination discloses the following facts about the assets and the liabilities of Clare Rivera. The assets consist of:

| | |
|---|---|
| Cash | $ 7,120 |
| Office Supplies | 300 |
| Office Equipment | 15,000 |

The liabilities consist of:

Accounts payable:

| | |
|---|---|
| Decatur Equipment Company | $12,500 |
| Evening News | 80 |

The above information for Clare Rivera's business was shown in equation form on page 5. This information can be more conveniently read and understood if prepared in the following form:

| ASSETS | | LIABILITIES | |
|---|---|---|---|
| Cash | $ 7,120 | Accounts payable: | |
| Office supplies | 300 | Decatur Equipment Company | $12,500 |
| Office equipment | 15,000 | Evening News | 80 |
| | | OWNER'S EQUITY | |
| | | Clare Rivera, capital | 9,840 |
| Total assets | $22,420 | Total liab. and owner's equity | $22,420 |

## Balance Sheet Format

The major sections of a balance sheet are (**1**) the heading, (**2**) the assets, (**3**) the liabilities, and (**4**) the owner's equity. The heading for a balance sheet should contain the name of the company, the title of the statement, and the date of the statement. The balance sheet shows the financial position of a business *as of a specific date*. Assuming the preceding information was prepared on December 31, 1982, the balance sheet for Rivera's Answering Service on that date would appear as shown below.

Rivera's Answering Service
Balance Sheet
December 31, 1982

| Assets | | Liabilities | |
|---|---|---|---|
| Cash | 7120 00 | Accounts payable: | |
| Office supplies | 300 00 | Decatur Equip. Co. | 12500 00 |
| Office equipment | 15000 00 | Evening News | 80 00 |
| | | Total liabilities | 12580 00 |
| | | Owner's Equity | |
| | | Clare Rivera, capital | 9840 00 |
| Total assets | 22420 00 | Total liab. + owner's equity | 22420 00 |

***Account Form Balance Sheet — Rivera's Answering Service***

The balance sheet format shown above is known as the *account form*. Sometimes the balance sheet is prepared in the format shown on page 9 which is known as the *report form*.

The two balance sheets present the same information, only the arrangement is different. The account form more closely follows the format of the accounting equation. In the report form, the information is rearranged; liabilities and owner's equity are placed below the assets section. Both forms are commonly used.

| Rivera's Answering Service<br>Balance Sheet<br>December 31, 1982 | | |
|---|---|---|
| **Assets** | | |
| Cash | 7120 00 | |
| Office supplies | 300 00 | |
| Office equipment | 15000 00 | |
| Total assets | | 22420 00 |
| **Liabilities** | | |
| Accounts payable: | | |
| Decatur Equipment Company | 12500 00 | |
| Evening News | 80 00 | |
| Total liabilities | | 12580 00 |
| **Owner's Equity** | | |
| Clare Rivera, capital | | 9840 00 |
| Total liabilities and owner's equity | | 22420 00 |

***Report Form Balance Sheet — Rivera's Answering Service***

## Definition of Balance Sheet Items

The various asset, liability, and owner's equity items should be presented on the balance sheet in a manner which is easily understandable to balance sheet users. Some of the terms most frequently used to identify common types of assets are defined as follows:

*Cash* includes the monetary items available to meet current obligations. Bank deposits available for immediate withdrawal, coins, currency, checks, and money orders are examples of items properly included as cash on the balance sheet.

*Accounts receivable* represent claims against the property of a customer of the business. Usually such claims arise through the sale of merchandise or the performance of services for which the customer will pay in the future.

*Notes receivable* also represent claims against the property of a customer, but in contrast to an account receivable, a note receivable is evidenced by a note which is a formal written promise to pay a definite sum of money at a specified future time.

*Store supplies* are items used while performing selling activities and include wrapping paper, paper sacks, twine, and similar items.

*Office supplies* include typewriter ribbons, stationery, file folders, and similar items used in performing administrative and clerical functions.

*Land* refers to the earth's surface and includes building sites, parking areas, and yards.

*Buildings* include the various structures that are affixed to the land. They also include fixtures and equipment that are permanently attached to the building structures such as loading docks, heating systems, and elevators.

*Equipment* includes properties such as trucks, automobiles, typewriters, and adding machines used in conducting business operations.

*Furniture and fixtures* include items needed in a business office such as desks, tables, chairs, and file cabinets.

Two very common forms of liabilities are identified as follows:

*Accounts payable* are creditors' claims against the business that generally arise through the purchase of goods or services on account.

*Notes payable* are formal written promises to pay a definite sum of money at a specified future time. Notes payable are often created when cash is borrowed from a bank or other financial institution. Notes are also created when goods are purchased on credit from a supplier who requires that a note be given as evidence of indebtedness.

*Proprietorship, capital,* and *net worth* are other terms used to identify owner's equity.

## THE INCOME STATEMENT

The *income statement*, sometimes called a *profit and loss statement* or an *operating statement*, is a formal financial statement that summarizes operating activities (revenue and expenses) *for a specific period of time*, usually a month or a year. A twelve-month period covered by an income statement is known as a *fiscal year*. The fiscal year of a business need not agree with the calendar year (January 1 to December 31). Any period for which an income statement is prepared, be it month, year, or other, is called a *fiscal period*.

If operations have been successful, a business will have earned a profit (often called *net income*) and the owner's equity will have increased. If operations have not been successful, a business will have incurred a loss (*net loss*) and the owner's equity will have decreased. By comparing the amount of owner's equity on balance sheets prepared at different dates, it can be determined whether equity has increased or decreased during a period of time. However, these comparative balance sheets do not reflect the causes of the increases or decreases and provide no details concerning revenue and expenses associated with operations for the period of time. The purpose of the income statement is to provide such information.

### Income Statement Format

The major components of an income statement are (**1**) the heading, (**2**) the revenue section, (**3**) the expense section, and (**4**) the final determination of net income or net loss. The heading for the income statement should contain the name of the company, the title of the statement, and the period covered by the statement. If during the month of January, 1983, Rivera's Answering Service had revenue of $2,900 and expenses of $1,545, the income statement for the month's operations in its simplest form would appear as shown on page 11.

| Rivera's Answering Service<br>Income Statement<br>For Month Ended January 31, 1983 | | |
|---|---|---|
| Revenue | | 2900 00 |
| Expenses | | 1545 00 |
| Net income | | 1355 00 |

This simplified income statement would be of only limited value to the owner of the business or any other interested reader such as a banker or creditor. The statement is much more informative if the various sources of revenue and types of expenses are shown separately.

## Definition of Income Statement Items

The two terms used most often in the income statement are "revenue" and "expenses." *Revenue* is the gross increase in owner's equity resulting from the operations of the business. It results from the sale of goods or services to customers. It also includes items such as rental income on property and interest income on money loaned.

The sources of revenue for the answering service would probably be limited to fees received from clients. Many businesses have more than one source of revenue. For example, the owner of an automobile dealership would probably want a breakdown of the company's revenues by (1) new car sales, (2) used car sales, and (3) service department billings.

*Expenses* are the costs of goods and services consumed in the operation of the business. Supplies, salaries, advertising, utilities, and rental of the building are examples of expenses which Rivera might incur in the operation of the business. If the expenses reported for the month of January, 1983, were office supplies, $90; salaries, $670; advertising, $80; utilities, $275; and rent expense, $430, the income statement would appear as shown below.

***Income Statement — Rivera's Answering Service***

| Rivera's Answering Service<br>Income Statement<br>For Month Ended January 31, 1983 | | |
|---|---|---|
| Revenue from clients | | 2900 00 |
| | | |
| Expenses: | | |
| Salary expense | 670 00 | |
| Rent expense | 430 00 | |
| Utilities expense | 275 00 | |
| Office supplies expense | 90 00 | |
| Advertising expense | 80 00 | |
| Total expenses | | 1545 00 |
| Net income | | 1355 00 |

There is no required order in which individual expenses must be listed on the income statement. Expenses are often listed by dollar amount with the largest expense first and the others following in descending order. A common exception is that Miscellaneous Expense is normally listed last regardless of its amount.

## THE CAPITAL STATEMENT

A third formal financial statement, the *capital statement*, is often prepared to report all of the changes in owner's equity that occur during a fiscal period. In addition to the change in owner's equity that results from operations, other changes in equity occur when additional investments are made by the owner or when personal withdrawals are made from the business. Such withdrawals of assets by the owner, called *drawings*, may be made as advance withdrawals of business profits with no intention of reducing the owner's investment in the business. The owner could, for example, withdraw $950 a month for personal living expenses.

### Capital Statement Format

The major components of a capital statement are (1) the heading, (2) the owner's capital balance at the beginning of the period, (3) the increases and decreases in owner's capital during the period, (4) the net effect of these increases and decreases, and (5) the owner's capital balance as of the end of the period. The heading for the capital statement should contain the name of the company, the title of the statement, and the period covered by the statement. If during the month of January, 1983, Rivera withdrew $950 for personal use and the income earned for the month was $1,355, as computed earlier, the capital statement would appear as illustrated on page 13. The capital balance on January 31, 1983, $10,245, is the amount shown in the owner's equity section of the balance sheet prepared on the same date as the capital statement.

## SEQUENCE OF PREPARING FINANCIAL STATEMENTS

The capital statement serves as the connecting link between the income statement and the balance sheet. The net income reported on the income statement is added to the beginning capital balance along with any additional investment made by the owner during the period. After deducting withdrawals, the amount of owner's equity to be shown on the balance sheet is determined. Because of this relationship of data between the financial statements, the necessary sequence of preparing the financial statements is as follows:

1. Prepare the income statement to determine the net income (or loss) to be used in preparing the capital statement.
2. Prepare the capital statement to determine the amount of owner's equity to be shown on the balance sheet.
3. Prepare the balance sheet.

To illustrate this sequence of preparation, the financial statements for Rivera's Answering Service for the month of January, 1983, are presented below.

**Rivera's Answering Service**
**Income Statement**
**For Month Ended January 31, 1983**

| | | |
|---|---|---|
| Revenue from clients | | 2900 00 |
| Expenses: | | |
| Salary expense | 670 00 | |
| Rent expense | 430 00 | |
| Utilities expense | 275 00 | |
| Office supplies expense | 90 00 | |
| Advertising expense | 80 00 | |
| Total expenses | | 1545 00 |
| Net income | | 1355 00 |

**Rivera's Answering Service**
**Capital Statement**
**For Month Ended January 31, 1983**

| | | |
|---|---|---|
| Capital, January 1, 1983 | | 9840 00 |
| Net income for the month | 1355 00 | |
| Less withdrawals | 950 00 | |
| Increase in capital | | 405 00 |
| Capital, January 31, 1983 | | 10245 00 |

**Rivera's Answering Service**
**Balance Sheet**
**January 31, 1983**

| | | |
|---|---|---|
| **Assets** | | |
| Cash | 7615 00 | |
| Office supplies | 210 00 | |
| Office equipment | 15000 00 | |
| Total assets | | 22825 00 |
| **Liabilities** | | |
| Accounts payable: | | |
| Decatur Equipment Company | 12500 00 | |
| Evening News | 80 00 | |
| Total liabilities | | 12580 00 |
| **Owner's Equity** | | |
| Clare Rivera, capital | | 10245 00 |
| Total liabilities and owner's equity | | 22825 00 |

*Interrelationship of Financial Statements — Rivera's Answering Service*

## SUMMARY OF FINANCIAL STATEMENTS

All financial statements should be identified by a proper heading which includes the name of the business, the name of the statement, and the date or period covered. The income statement presents information concerning the operations of a business and the effect of operations on capital. This is done by summarizing the revenue and the expenses for the period and reporting the net income or loss.

The capital statement serves as the connecting link between the income statement and the balance sheet. It uses the net income obtained from the income statement along with the additional investments and withdrawals by the owner to determine the owner's equity to be shown on the balance sheet.

The financial history of a business may be found by comparing the balance sheets prepared at the end of each year. The balance sheet reports the financial position of the business as of a particular date by listing the business's assets, liabilities, and owner's equity on that date. It normally is prepared as of the close of business on the last day of the accounting period.

The life of a business may be expressed graphically by a horizontal line representing time. The relationship of the financial statements to time may then be expressed as shown below.

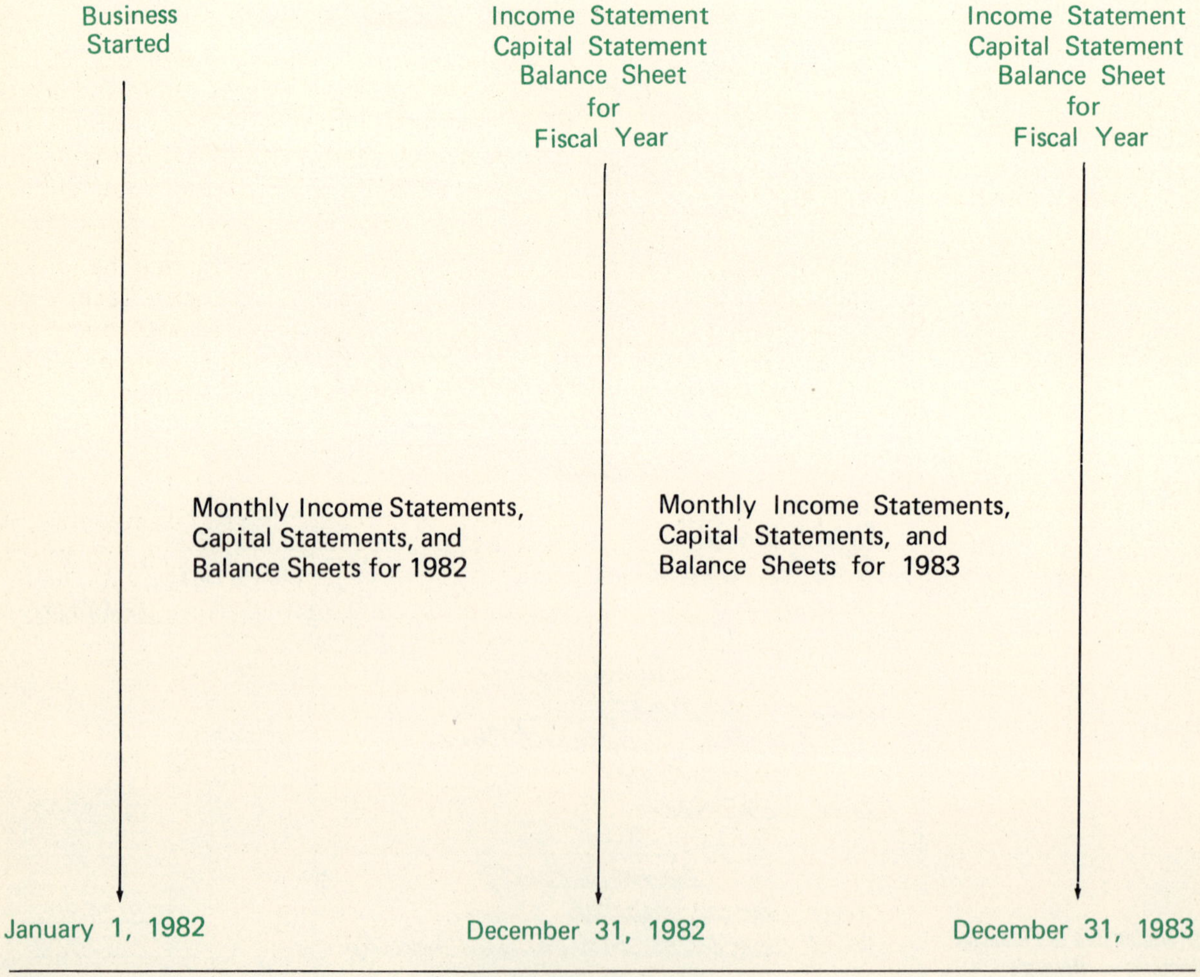


THE LIFE OF A BUSINESS

## QUESTIONS FOR DISCUSSION

1. What are the three financial statements prepared for a business owned by an individual?
2. (a) What is the purpose of the balance sheet? (b) In what two forms may the balance sheet be prepared?
3. What three items are included in the heading of the balance sheet?
4. What is the purpose of an income statement?
5. How does the heading of an income statement differ from the heading of a balance sheet?
6. What is the connecting link between the income statement and the balance sheet?
7. In what sequence should the financial statements be prepared? Why?
8. Indicate whether each of the following items would be classified as asset, liability, owner's equity, revenue, or expense: (a) fees received, (b) notes payable, (c) rent on building used, (d) accounts receivable, (e) investment by owner, (f) office furniture.

## EXERCISES

1. During the month of August, the Locy Company had revenues of $4,400 and the following expenses: salaries, $820; rent, $400; utilities, $350; insurance, $40; and miscellaneous, $25. Determine Locy's net income or loss for the month of August.
2. On January 1, Hazel Lucas opens a beauty salon by investing $7,000 in cash. During the year she invests an additional $4,000. At the end of the period, the assets of the business are $18,300 and the liabilities are $4,900. Lucas made no withdrawals during the period. (a) Compute the increase in owner's equity during the period. (b) Determine the amount of net income as shown on the income statement.
3. Carlos McCloud, the owner of McCloud Towing Service, had the following account balances on December 31 of the current year: Cash, $670; Office Supplies, $90; Equipment, $1,650; Truck, $4,700. McCloud owed $600 to Dean Suppliers and $2,200 to Smiley Motors. Prepare a balance sheet in report form for McCloud Towing Service on December 31.

## ASSIGNMENT 1-B

**Tear out pages 333–336 and complete Assignment 1-B according to the instructions given. If you have any difficulty completing this assignment, review the material discussed in this chapter. After completion, you may proceed to the study of Chapter 2 until the next assignment is required.**

Chapter **2**

# RECORDING BUSINESS TRANSACTIONS

As illustrated in Chapter 1, every transaction performed by a business produces a change in one or more elements of the accounting equation. Successful business owners know the value of maintaining a continuous and accurate record of the effect of each of these changes on the assets, liabilities, and owner's equity of the firm. This information will then be readily available for the preparation of the financial statements at the end of the fiscal period.

In every transaction performed by a business, the information is recorded in at least two places. Based on the mathematical expression of the accounting equation, Assets = Liabilities + Owner's Equity, it is apparent that a change in any asset, liability, or in the owner's equity requires an equal and offsetting change in one or more of these elements. For example, when the owner invests cash in the business, there is an increase in the asset cash and an equal increase in owner's equity. Many times a transaction affects two items within the same element. For example, if supplies are purchased for cash, the only element affected is assets, but two assets are involved: supplies are increased and cash is decreased.

The requirement that every transaction must be recorded in at least two places, as mentioned above, has created what is commonly known as the *double-entry system* of accounting. The term "double-entry" means that the dual effect which each transaction has on the accounting equation is recorded in the books in order to maintain the equality of the accounting equation. It does not mean that each transaction is recorded twice.

The double-entry system of accounting has been in use for several centuries in essentially the same form as it is used today. The major advantage of this system is that it provides for the organization of the financial data of a business in an orderly fashion. Also, the self-balancing nature of the accounting elements, as expressed by the accounting equation, promotes accuracy and makes the discovery of certain types of errors easier. For example, if one half of a transaction is recorded and the other half is not, the equation will not balance.

## PART A BALANCE SHEET ACCOUNTS

It is apparent that the effect of business transactions could be recorded directly on the balance sheet. For example, the balance sheet of Bill Penny, a printer, at the beginning of business on June 1, 1982 is presented at the top of the next page.

Balance Sheet — Bill Penny, Printer

| Bill Penny, Printer<br>Balance Sheet<br>June 1, 1982 | | | |
|---|---|---|---|
| **Assets** | | **Liabilities** | |
| Cash | 1 540 00 | Accounts payable: | |
| Printing supplies | 700 00 | Dow Paper Co. | 1 200 00 |
| Printing equipment | 16 000 00 | | |
| | | **Owner's Equity** | |
| | | Bill Penny, capital | 17 040 00 |
| Total assets | 18 240 00 | Total liab. + owner's equity | 18 240 00 |

If Penny decides that $800 in additional capital is needed for operating his business and he makes this cash investment, Cash is increased by $800 and Bill Penny, Capital is increased by $800. The balance sheet, without headings, would appear as follows:

| Assets | | Liabilities | |
|---|---|---|---|
| Cash | $2,340 | Accounts payable: | |
| Printing supplies | 700 | Dow Paper Co. | $1,200 |
| Printing equipment | 16,000 | | |
| | | **Owner's Equity** | |
| | | Bill Penny, capital | 17,840 |
| Total assets | $19,040 | Total liabilities and owner's equity | $19,040 |

If he purchases additional supplies costing $200 from the Dow Paper Co. on account, the asset, Printing Supplies, is increased by $200, and the liability, Accounts Payable — Dow Paper Co., is also increased by $200. The balance sheet, without headings, immediately following this transaction would be:

| Assets | | Liabilities | |
|---|---|---|---|
| Cash | $ 2,340 | Accounts payable: | |
| Printing supplies | 900 | Dow Paper Co. | $ 1,400 |
| Printing equipment | 16,000 | | |
| | | **Owner's Equity** | |
| | | Bill Penny, capital | 17,840 |
| Total assets | $19,240 | Total liabilities and owner's equity | $19,240 |

If Penny pays $400 on his liability to Dow Paper Co., Cash is decreased by $400 and Accounts Payable — Dow Paper Co. is reduced by the same amount. The balance sheet would appear as follows:

| Assets | | Liabilities | |
|---|---|---|---|
| Cash | $ 1,940 | Accounts payable: | |
| Printing supplies | 900 | Dow Paper Co. | $ 1,000 |
| Printing equipment | 16,000 | | |
| | | **Owner's Equity** | |
| | | Bill Penny, capital | 17,840 |
| Total assets | $18,840 | Total liabilities and owner's equity | $18,840 |

This procedure for recording transactions demands an unreasonable amount of work. It requires that a new balance sheet be prepared each time a transaction is recorded even though the transaction usually affects only two items on the balance sheet.

## BALANCE SHEET ACCOUNTS IN THE LEDGER

A more convenient procedure is to maintain a separate record for each item on the balance sheet and to show in this record the increases and decreases to the item during the accounting period. The balance for the item at the end of the period is determined by adding the dollar increases and subtracting the dollar decreases during the period from the amount of the item at the beginning of the period. This final balance would then appear on the balance sheet prepared at the end of the period. This form of individual record is known as an *account*. A group of accounts is called a *ledger*. The most common ledger, and the one that will be discussed in the early chapters, is called the *general ledger*.

The types of account forms used will vary, depending on the specific needs of each business. Some may be in the form of bound books, others may be in loose-leaf binders or on large cards maintained in a file drawer or portable rack. Computers may be used to store the information and to print out this information when needed.

The standard two-column ledger account form, so called because it has two amount columns, is presented below:

*Standard Two-Column Ledger Account Form*

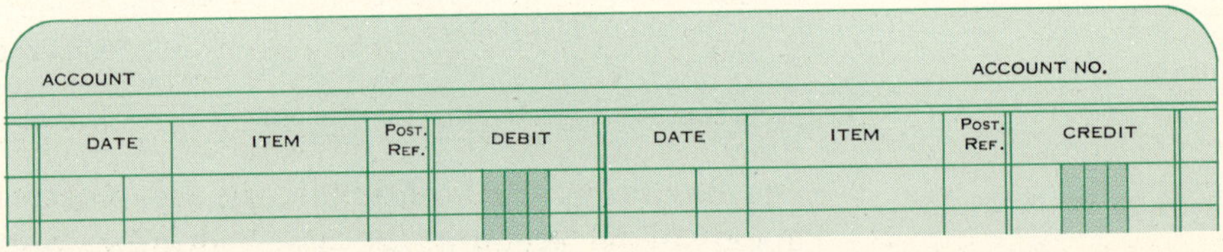


A ledger account form should always provide space at the top for the account title, (for example, Cash) and the account number (which will be discussed in Chapter 3). The form presented above is divided into two sides: the left side, which is called the *debit* side, and the right side, which is called the *credit* side. Each side of the ledger account has four columns. The Date column is used to record the date on which the transaction occurred. The Item column is used to write a short explanation of the entry if necessary. The Posting Reference column is used for posting references which will be discussed in Chapter 3. The last column on each side of the account is used to record the dollar amount of the transaction. The amount column on the left side is entitled Debit, (abbreviated Dr.), and the amount column on the right side is entitled Credit, (abbreviated Cr.).

The balance of an account can be determined at any time by totaling the amounts in the debit column, totaling the amounts in the credit column, and then subtracting to find the difference between the two. This difference is called the *balance* of the account.

For illustration purposes, a skeleton outline of an account is frequently used. This skeleton form is drawn like a large letter "T" and is commonly called a *T-account*. This form provides the same basic data as any standard ledger account: **(1)** the account title, **(2)** the debit information, and **(3)** the credit information.

*T-Account Form*

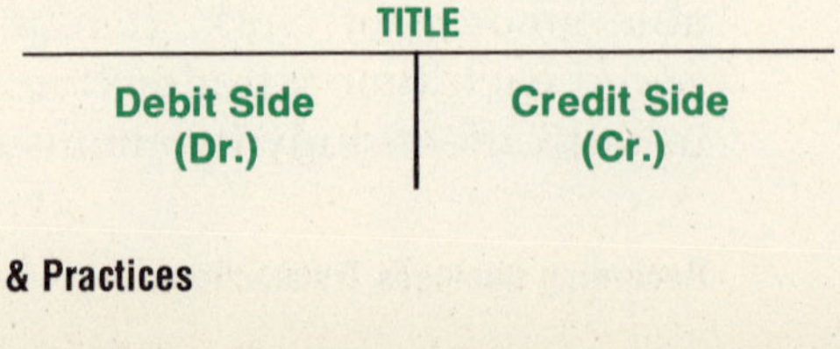

## Construction of Accounts

The relationship between the construction of the ledger accounts and the balance sheet can best be observed by superimposing the basic accounting equation over a T-account:

| ASSETS | = LIABILITIES + OWNER'S EQUITY |
|---|---|
| Debit Side | Credit Side |

Assets, which appear on the left side of the accounting equation, are entered on the left (debit) side of the T-account. Since asset balances are entered on the debit side of an account, increases to asset accounts are recorded as debits and decreases are recorded as credits. Liabilities and owner's equity appear on the right side of the accounting equation and are entered on the right (credit) side of the T-account. Since liability and owner's equity balances are entered on the credit side of an account, increases to liability and owner's equity accounts are recorded as credits and decreases are recorded as debits.

The above illustration can be expanded to reflect the debit and credit rules for each balance sheet element as follows:

| ASSETS | | = LIABILITIES + OWNER'S EQUITY | | | |
|---|---|---|---|---|---|
| Normal Balance — Debit | | Normal Balance — Credit | | | |
| CASH | | DOW PAPER CO. | | BILL PENNY, CAPITAL | |
| Debit | Credit | Debit | Credit | Debit | Credit |
| increases | decreases | decreases | increases | decreases | increases |

The account serves as an arithmetical device for showing increases and decreases in balances. When items are to be added, they are placed on the same side of an account as its normal balance; when they are to be subtracted, they are placed on the opposite side. Since asset balances are shown on the debit side of the account, it may be said that assets have a *normal debit balance*. The balance of an asset account then would logically be increased by a debit and decreased by a credit. To complete the system mathematically, the liability and owner's equity accounts are to the right of the equals sign. Therefore, the mathematical signs change; that is, they are the opposite of assets. Consequently, liability and owner's equity accounts are shown on the credit side of the account and have a *normal credit balance*. This credit balance is increased with additional credits and decreased by debits.

Basic understanding of the rules of debit and credit will be made easier by learning that a debit is an entry to the left side of an account and a credit is an entry to the right side of an account. Good or bad connotations should not be associated with the words "debit" and "credit"; a credit to an account is not always a desirable result and a debit to an account is not always undesirable, and vice versa. The two words are accounting terminology with very specific meanings; that is, debit means left side and credit means right side.

Recording increases and decreases to the accounts in this manner reflects the basic equality of assets to liabilities and owner's equity. It also maintains equality between the total amounts debited to all accounts and the total amounts credited.

When an account has a balance that is other than its normal balance, this balance is indicated by entering it in red in the account or by entering it in the normal manner and placing a circle around the amount. For example, if an account payable of $230 is erroneously paid as $320, this creates an abnormal debit balance in the liability account. This debit balance to a liability account (which normally has a credit balance) would be as shown below:

**ACCOUNTS PAYABLE**

| Dr. | | Cr. |
|---|---|---|
| | 320 | 230 |
| Balance | (90) | |

***Abnormal Account Balance***

## Relationship of the Ledger to the Balance Sheet

The relationship of the general ledger accounts to the balance sheet is illustrated below and on page 21. The ledger accounts of Bill Penny at the beginning of business on June 1, 1982, are presented, followed by his balance sheet. The word "Balance" (Bal.) is written next to each amount to distinguish the beginning amount in an account from the amounts relating to transactions recorded during the month.

The ledger contains a separate account for each item on the balance sheet. For illustration purposes, only the basic T-account form is used here. It should be noted that total assets equal liabilities plus owner's equity. Also, since all asset accounts have debit balances and all liability and owner's equity accounts have credit balances, total debits equal total credits.

Subsequent increases in Bill Penny's assets will be entered on the debit side of the asset accounts, and decreases will be entered on the credit side. Subsequent increases in the liabilities or in owner's equity will be entered on the credit side and decreases will be entered on the debit side of the liability or capital account respectively.

**GENERAL LEDGER**

**CASH**

| Dr. | | Cr. |
|---|---|---|
| June 1 Bal. | 1,540 | |

**ACCOUNTS PAYABLE — DOW PAPER CO.**

| Dr. | Cr. | |
|---|---|---|
| | June 1 Bal. | 1,200 |

**PRINTING SUPPLIES**

| Dr. | | Cr. |
|---|---|---|
| June 1 Bal. | 700 | |

**PRINTING EQUIPMENT**

| Dr. | | Cr. |
|---|---|---|
| June 1 Bal. | 16,000 | |

**BILL PENNY, CAPITAL**

| Dr. | Cr. | |
|---|---|---|
| | June 1 Bal. | 17,040 |

Bill Penny, Printer
Balance Sheet
June 1, 1982

| Assets | | Liabilities | |
|---|---|---|---|
| Cash | 1540 00 | Accounts payable: | |
| Printing supplies | 700 00 | Dow Paper Co. | 1200 00 |
| Printing equipment | 16000 00 | | |
| | | Owner's Equity | |
| | | Bill Penny, capital | 17040 00 |
| Total assets | 18240 00 | Total liab. + owner's equity | 18240 00 |

Balance Sheet — Bill Penny, Printer

## Recording Transactions in the Balance Sheet Accounts

The following transactions relate to Penny's business for the month of June.

**Transaction:** June 2. Penny invested an additional $800 in cash. The transaction is recorded in the ledger as follows:

**CASH**

| Debit | | Credit | |
|---|---|---|---|
| June 1 Bal. | 1,540 | | |
| 2 | 800 | | |

**BILL PENNY, CAPITAL**

| Debit | | Credit | |
|---|---|---|---|
| | | June 1 Bal. | 17,040 |
| | | 2 | 800 |

**Analysis:** The result of this transaction is an increase in Cash and an increase in Bill Penny, Capital. The cash account now totals $2,340, the sum of the two debits in the account. The capital account shows that owner's equity is now $17,840, the sum of the two credits in the account. The amount of the transaction, $800, was entered as both a debit and a credit and the ledger therefore remains in balance, that is, the sum of all debits is equal to the sum of all credits.

**Transaction:** June 9. Penny purchased additional printing supplies for $200 from the Dow Paper Co. on account.

**PRINTING SUPPLIES**

| Debit | | Credit | |
|---|---|---|---|
| June 1 Bal. | 700 | | |
| 9 | 200 | | |

**ACCOUNTS PAYABLE — DOW PAPER CO.**

| Debit | | Credit | |
|---|---|---|---|
| | | June 1 Bal. | 1,200 |
| | | 9 | 200 |

**Analysis:** This transaction results in an increase of $200 in the asset Printing Supplies and an increase in the liability to Dow Paper Co. by the same amount. The printing supplies account now has total debits of $900. Accounts Payable — Dow Paper Co. now shows total credits of $1,400, which represents Penny's liability to this company.

All transactions recorded in the accounts up to this time resulted in *additions* to assets, liabilities, and capital. Many transactions, however, result in *reductions* in the individual accounts. Since assets have normal debit balances and are increased by debits, reductions are shown as credits to the individual asset accounts. Liability and owner's equity accounts, which have normal credit balances and are increased by credits, are reduced by debits.

**Transaction:** June 20. Penny mailed $400 to Dow Paper Co. in partial payment of the liability.

| CASH | | | |
|---|---|---|---|
| June 1 Bal. | 1,540 | June 20 | 400 |
| 2 | 800 | | |

| ACCOUNTS PAYABLE — DOW PAPER CO. | | | |
|---|---|---|---|
| June 20 | 400 | June 1 Bal. | 1,200 |
| | | 9 | 200 |

**Analysis:** This payment decreases Cash by $400 and decreases the liability to Dow Paper Co. by $400. The balance in the cash account is computed by subtracting the credit of $400 from the total debits of $2,340. The result is a debit balance of $1,940. The liability to Dow Paper Co. would likewise be determined by subtracting the $400 debit from the total credits of $1,400, leaving a credit balance of $1,000. Since the transaction resulted in an equal reduction in assets and liabilities, the ledger is still in balance.

## THE TRIAL BALANCE

Because of the large number of transactions recorded daily in most businesses, it is cumbersome to determine the balance in each account after each transaction. It is also unnecessary to determine that the ledger is in balance after each transaction. Totaling the accounts and determining the balances in the ledger is normally done at periodic intervals, that is, weekly or monthly. It *must* be completed before financial statements can be prepared.

Under the double-entry system of accounting, the record of each transaction consists of debits and credits that are equal in amount and that are entered on opposite sides of the ledger. If the original record of each transaction is made correctly, the ledger should at all times be in balance; that is, the total dollar amount of all the debits in the ledger should equal the total dollar amount of all the credits. It is possible to test the accuracy of the ledger by comparing the total debits with the total credits to see if they are equal. This test is known as a *trial balance*. A *trial balance* is a list of all the accounts appearing in the ledger with the dollar amount of the debit or credit balance of each.

### Footing the Accounts

Before preparation of the trial balance, it is customary to total the debit and credit entries to each account and to place the total of each in small pencil figures just below the last debit and credit entry. This practice of securing a column total is known as *footing*. If an account has both debits and credits, the balance of the account is written in small pencil figures in the explanation column of the side with the larger total. The accounts Cash and Accounts Payable — Dow Paper Co. on page 23 are examples of accounts whose balances have been determined by this procedure.

If the total debits in an account equal the total credits, the account is said to be in balance (has a zero balance) and is omitted from the trial balance. The illustration below shows the ledger of Bill Penny after the accounts have been footed. None of the accounts were in balance, so none are omitted from the trial balance.

ACCOUNT *Cash* ACCOUNT NO.

| Date | | Item | Post. Ref. | Debit | Date | | Item | Post. Ref. | Credit |
|---|---|---|---|---|---|---|---|---|---|
| 1982 June | 1 | Balance | | 1540 00 | 1982 June | 20 | | | 400 00 |
| | 2 | | | 800 00 | | | | | |
| | | 1,940.00 | | 2340 00 | | | | | |

ACCOUNT *Printing Supplies* ACCOUNT NO.

| Date | | Item | Post. Ref. | Debit | Date | | Item | Post. Ref. | Credit |
|---|---|---|---|---|---|---|---|---|---|
| 1982 June | 1 | Balance | | 700 00 | | | | | |
| | 9 | | | 200 00 | | | | | |
| | | | | 900 00 | | | | | |

ACCOUNT *Printing Equipment* ACCOUNT NO.

| Date | | Item | Post. Ref. | Debit | Date | | Item | Post. Ref. | Credit |
|---|---|---|---|---|---|---|---|---|---|
| 1982 June | 1 | Balance | | 16000 00 | | | | | |

ACCOUNT *Accounts Payable—Dow Paper Co.* ACCOUNT NO.

| Date | | Item | Post. Ref. | Debit | Date | | Item | Post. Ref. | Credit |
|---|---|---|---|---|---|---|---|---|---|
| 1982 June | 20 | | | 400 00 | 1982 June | 1 | Balance | | 1200 00 |
| | | | | | | 9 | | | 200 00 |
| | | | | | | | 1,000.00 | | 1400 00 |

ACCOUNT *Bill Penny, Capital* ACCOUNT NO.

| Date | | Item | Post. Ref. | Debit | Date | | Item | Post. Ref. | Credit |
|---|---|---|---|---|---|---|---|---|---|
| | | | | | 1982 June | 1 | Balance | | 17040 00 |
| | | | | | | 2 | | | 800 00 |
| | | | | | | | | | 17840 00 |

***General Ledger After Footing Accounts***

## Preparing a Trial Balance

A trial balance of the ledger illustrated is shown on page 24. The trial balance was prepared on June 30, 1982, with the assumption that the three transactions previously illustrated were the only ones which occurred during the month of June. The trial balance shows that the debit and credit totals are equal in amount. Since total debit balances equaled total credit balances as indicated by the June 1 balance sheet, the trial balance as of June 30 indicates that in recording the

Bill Penny, Printer
Trial Balance
June 30, 1982

| | | |
|---|---|---|
| Cash | 1940 00 | |
| Printing Supplies | 900 00 | |
| Printing Equipment | 16000 00 | |
| Accounts Payable — Dow Paper Co. | | 1000 00 |
| Bill Penny, Capital | | 17840 00 |
| | 18840 00 | 18840 00 |

*Trial Balance – Bill Penny, Printer*

three transactions for the month of June the total debits were equal to the total credits.

If the total debits in the trial balance equal the total credits, the trial balance is said to be in balance. But the fact that the trial balance is in balance does not necessarily prove the complete accuracy of the accounting records. For example, if the supplies purchased on June 9 had been recorded in the printing equipment account by mistake, the total debits in the ledger would still have been $18,840 and the error would not have been revealed by the trial balance. The trial balance is positive proof of only one fact concerning the accuracy of the work, namely, that the debits and credits in the ledger are equal.

A trial balance is not a formal financial statement such as the balance sheet, income statement, or capital statement. It will probably never be seen by anyone except the accountant or bookkeeper. It serves primarily as an arithmetical device used to test the equality of the debits and credits in the ledger. It also provides summary data which are useful in preparing the financial statements at the end of the period. To illustrate, Penny could easily prepare the following balance sheet as of June 30 from the trial balance above.

Bill Penny, Printer
Balance Sheet
June 30, 1982

| | | |
|---|---|---|
| Assets | | |
| Cash | 1940 00 | |
| Printing supplies | 900 00 | |
| Printing equipment | 16000 00 | |
| Total assets | | 18840 00 |
| | | |
| Liabilities | | |
| Accounts payable: | | |
| Dow Paper Co. | | 1000 00 |
| | | |
| Owner's Equity | | |
| Bill Penny, capital | | 17840 00 |
| Total liabilities and owner's equity | | 18840 00 |

*Balance Sheet – Bill Penny, Printer*

## QUESTIONS FOR DISCUSSION

1. What is meant by double-entry accounting?
2. Why do businesses use a ledger in their accounting systems?
3. Name the three major parts of a standard ledger account.
4. Is it possible to have a transaction that decreases an asset account but does not decrease a liability or owner's equity account? Explain.
5. Does a debit always increase an account?
6. Will a debit to a liability account have the same effect on the account as a debit will have on an asset account? Explain.

## EXERCISES

1. Indicate how each of the following accounts are increased (debited or credited) and decreased (debited or credited), and indicate the normal balance (debit or credit) for each account: (a) Accounts Payable; (b) Office Supplies; (c) Land; (d) Owner's Capital; (e) Accounts Receivable; (f) Cash; (g) Delivery Equipment.
2. The cash account below is for the Andra Company. (a) Determine the account balance as of the end of the month. (b) Assuming the April 12 entry was in payment of an account payable to Mim Company and the April 20 entry was an additional investment in the business by the owner, Mike Andra, list the accounts that would have been debited and credited to record these transactions.

ACCOUNT **Cash** ACCOUNT NO.

| DATE | | ITEM | POST. REF. | DEBIT | DATE | | ITEM | POST. REF. | CREDIT |
|---|---|---|---|---|---|---|---|---|---|
| 1982 | | | | | 1982 | | | | |
| Apr. | 1 | Balance | | 1 400 00 | Apr. | 12 | | | 400 00 |
| | 20 | | | 500 00 | | | | | |

3. You are given the following account balances for the Wing Company as of August 31 of the current year: Equipment, $2,500; Cash, $630; Accounts Payable — AMI, $1,100; Sam Wing, Capital, $2,340; Office Supplies, $310. Prepare a trial balance as of August 31 for the Wing Company.

## ASSIGNMENT 2-A

Tear out pages 337–340 and complete Assignment 2-A. After completing the assignment, continue with the following reading material until the next assignment is required.

# PART B INCOME STATEMENT ACCOUNTS

The most important reason for individuals to invest their time, property, and talent in a business is the desire to benefit from the profit generated by a successful business. In addition to providing a livelihood for themselves and increasing their personal wealth, proprietors may be motivated by other factors, such as a desire for independence or personal creativity which they could not enjoy as employees. Profit, however, must be the central motivation, because none of the other objectives, regardless of their importance to the individual, can be attained if the business ceases to exist because it was not profitable.

## EFFECT OF REVENUE AND EXPENSES ON OWNER'S EQUITY

As was discussed in Chapter 1, net income is achieved in a business when the revenue earned from operations during a period exceeds the expenses incurred during that period. If the expenses incurred exceed the revenue for any given period, the business has suffered a net loss. Net income for the period increases owner's equity, whereas a net loss decreases owner's equity.

Revenue may be earned in a variety of ways, such as by selling merchandise, by performing services for customers or clients, by renting property, and by earning interest on money invested or loaned. In most instances, the increase in owner's equity through revenue results from an increase in assets without any change in liabilities. For example, if a service such as repairing an automobile is performed for a customer and the amount of the bill is $80, this transaction increases either the asset cash, if the bill is paid when presented, or the asset accounts receivable, if it is not paid immediately. In either case, the result of the transaction is an increase in owner's equity.

Expenses are the costs, measured by the money spent or the liability incurred, of supplies or services used in the process of producing revenue. When an expense is incurred, either the liabilities are increased or the assets are reduced. For example, the owner of a garage may record a liability of $25 for salary owed to an employee but not yet paid or reduce the asset cash by $40 to buy parts used for repairs. In both situations the owner's equity is reduced.

Transactions involving revenue and expenses always cause a change in the owner's equity. It is necessary to maintain a record of the operations of the business so that the effect of individual revenue and expenses on the owner's equity can be determined from time to time.

## REVENUE AND EXPENSE ACCOUNTS

It is possible to record all revenue by increasing the owner's capital account directly. In the repair of the automobile, the revenue earned could have been recorded as a debit to Cash or Accounts Receivable and a credit to Capital. The expenses incurred could have been recorded as a debit to Capital and a credit to Cash or Accounts Payable, depending upon whether the expenses were paid immediately or charged.

If this practice were followed by a business which had many revenue and expense transactions, the owner's capital account would require a great deal of analysis to determine the amount of income or loss for the period and the reasons for this income or loss.

Another problem involved in recording all revenue and expense transactions in the capital account is that additional investments by the owner, which are not revenue, are also recorded directly to the capital account as a credit. Similarly, any decrease in capital, such as the withdrawal of assets from the business for the owner's personal use, is recorded directly to the capital account as a debit.

With all this information recorded in the owner's capital account, it would appear at the end of the period as follows:

**OWNER'S CAPITAL**

| Debit | Credit |
|---|---|
| **Decreases** | **Increases** |
| **Expenses** | **Revenue** |
| **Withdrawals** | **Additional Investments** |

It is more convenient and less cluttered to set up individual accounts for the revenue and expenses. These revenue and expense accounts are called *temporary* or *nominal* accounts because they represent a subdivision of the owner's capital account during the accounting period. At the end of the period, after the income or loss has been determined and an income statement prepared, the balances in these revenue and expense accounts are transferred to the capital account. The process of transferring these revenue and expense balances into the capital account is known as *closing the books* and will be discussed in detail in Chapter 4.

## Revenue and Expense Accounts in the Ledger

It is important to remember that revenue and expense accounts are temporary capital accounts and that the rules of debits and credits are applied to these accounts based on the effect they will ultimately have on the capital account. For example, the capital account has a normal credit balance and is therefore increased by a credit and decreased by a debit. Revenues *increase* capital and are therefore recorded as credits and have normal credit balances. Expenses, on the other hand, *decrease* capital and are recorded as debits and have normal debit balances. This relationship of the revenue and expense accounts to the capital account may be illustrated as follows:

**OWNER'S CAPITAL**

| Debit | | Credit | |
|---|---|---|---|
| **Decreases** | | **Increases** | |
| **Expense Account** | | **Revenue Account** | |
| **Dr.** | **Cr.** | **Dr.** | **Cr.** |
| (+) | (−) | (−) | (+) |

A separate account should be kept for each type of revenue and expense. When a transaction involves a revenue, it is recorded as a credit to the appropriate revenue account. If a transaction involves an expense, the amount of the expense is recorded as a debit to the specific expense account.

### Recording Transactions in the Revenue and Expense Accounts

To illustrate the process of recording revenue and expenses in the ledger, the transactions for Bill Penny for the month of July will be analyzed and recorded in the proper accounts. These transactions represent a continuation of the earlier illustration of Penny's business. The balances in the ledger accounts were obtained from the June 30 trial balance appearing on page 24.

**Transaction:** July 3. Penny completed a printing job and received $8,000 from a customer.

| CASH | | | |
|---|---|---|---|
| July 1 Bal. | 1,940 | | |
| 3 | 8,000 | | |

| REVENUE FROM PRINTING | | | |
|---|---|---|---|
| | | July 3 | 8,000 |

**Analysis:** This transaction is recorded as an increase to the asset Cash by a debit of $8,000 and an increase to owner's equity which is recorded in the revenue account, Revenue from Printing, by a credit of $8,000.

**Transaction:** July 29. Penny paid monthly salaries of $5,000 to his employees.

| CASH | | | |
|---|---|---|---|
| July 1 Bal. | 1,940 | July 29 | 5,000 |
| 3 | 8,000 | | |

| SALARY EXPENSE | | | |
|---|---|---|---|
| July 29 | 5,000 | | |

**Analysis:** This transaction reduces the asset cash by $5,000 and reduces the owner's equity by $5,000, which is recorded in the expense account, Salary Expense.

**Transaction:** July 31. Penny paid $500 for advertising for the month of July.

| CASH | | | |
|---|---|---|---|
| July 1 Bal. | 1,940 | July 29 | 5,000 |
| 3 | 8,000 | 31 | 500 |

| ADVERTISING EXPENSE | | | |
|---|---|---|---|
| July 31 | 500 | | |

**Analysis:** This transaction has the same effect as the previous one, reducing cash and owner's equity because it represents the payment of an expense. The expense account, Advertising Expense, is debited.

All the revenue and expense transactions presented here have been for cash. There are many business transactions that will not initially or directly affect cash, such as performing a service for a customer where cash is not received immediately, or incurring an expense where cash is not paid until a later date. These types of transactions will be covered in detail in a later chapter.

## PROPRIETOR'S DRAWING ACCOUNT

Many owners devote most of their time and effort to their businesses. They may have sources of outside income such as stock, rental property, or interest on savings, but their principal livelihood is the business profits. An owner may have a profitable business yet not know until the end of the accounting period exactly how much profit has been made. In the meantime, the owner may need money to pay daily living expenses. Withdrawals of certain amounts of cash from the business may be made at regular intervals to pay these personal expenses. The amounts withdrawn during the period reduce the owner's equity and, when combined with the net income or net loss for the period, help determine the end-of-period capital balance.

These withdrawals of assets reduce the owner's equity and could be shown as a direct reduction in the owner's capital account. However, it is desirable to set up a separate, temporary capital account called a *drawing account* in which these withdrawals can be recorded.

*Drawings* are the owner's withdrawals of assets from the business in anticipation of profits. In addition to cash, merchandise, supplies, or other assets are sometimes withdrawn. The drawing account should not include withdrawals that are intended as permanent changes in the invested capital. Such permanent changes should be recorded directly in the owner's capital account.

Drawing is a temporary account which represents a subdivision of the owner's capital account. At the end of the period after the financial statements have been prepared, the balance of the drawing account is transferred to the owner's capital account.

Drawing should not in any way be confused with an expense. An expense is the cost of goods or services used in the process of producing revenue, whereas drawing is the withdrawal of business assets by the owner in anticipation of profits.

Since drawing is a reduction in owner's capital, the drawing account has a normal debit balance and is increased by debits to the account and decreased by credits as illustrated below.

**OWNER'S CAPITAL**

| Debit | Credit |
|---|---|
| **Decreases** | **Increases** |

**DRAWING ACCOUNT**

| Dr. | Cr. |
|---|---|
| (+) | (−) |

If a cash withdrawal from the business is made by the owner, the transaction is recorded by a debit to Drawing and a credit to Cash. If the owner withdraws assets other than cash for personal use, supplies for example, Drawing would be debited for the cost of the supplies and the supplies account would be credited.

The drawing account is shown on the capital statement as a deduction from net income in arriving at the net increase or decrease in capital for the period.

Transaction: July 31. Penny withdrew $1,000 from the business to pay personal expenses.

**CASH**

| | | | |
|---|---|---|---|
| July 1 Bal. | 1,940 | July 29 | 5,000 |
| 3 | 8,000 | 31 | 500 |
| | | 31 | 1,000 |

**BILL PENNY, DRAWING**

| | | | |
|---|---|---|---|
| July 31 | 1,000 | | |

**Analysis:** This transaction is recorded as a debit to Bill Penny, Drawing and a credit to Cash for $1,000. After this transaction has been completed, the ledger accounts in T-account form appear as shown below. (The accounts are arranged to show their relationship to the basic accounting equation.)

**ASSETS = LIABILITIES + OWNER'S EQUITY**

**ASSETS**

**CASH**

| | Debit | | Credit |
|---|---|---|---|
| July 1 Bal. | 1,940 | July 29 | 5,000 |
| 3 | 8,000 | 31 | 500 |
| | | 31 | 1,000 |

**PRINTING SUPPLIES**

| | Debit | | Credit |
|---|---|---|---|
| July 1 Bal. | 900 | | |

**PRINTING EQUIPMENT**

| | Debit | | Credit |
|---|---|---|---|
| July 1 Bal. | 16,000 | | |

**LIABILITIES**

**ACCOUNTS PAYABLE — DOW PAPER CO.**

| | Debit | | Credit |
|---|---|---|---|
| | | July 1 Bal. | 1,000 |

**OWNER'S EQUITY**

**BILL PENNY, CAPITAL**

| | Debit | | Credit |
|---|---|---|---|
| | | July 1 Bal. | 17,840 |

**BILL PENNY, DRAWING**

| | Debit | | Credit |
|---|---|---|---|
| July 31 | 1,000 | | |

**REVENUE FROM PRINTING**

| | Debit | | Credit |
|---|---|---|---|
| | | July 3 | 8,000 |

**ADVERTISING EXPENSE**

| | Debit | | Credit |
|---|---|---|---|
| July 31 | 500 | | |

**SALARY EXPENSE**

| | Debit | | Credit |
|---|---|---|---|
| July 29 | 5,000 | | |

The general ledger of Bill Penny appears below and on page 31 followed by the trial balance prepared from the ledger.

ACCOUNT *Cash* ACCOUNT NO.

| DATE | | ITEM | POST. REF. | DEBIT | DATE | | ITEM | POST. REF. | CREDIT |
|---|---|---|---|---|---|---|---|---|---|
| 1982 July | 1 | Balance | | 1940 00 | 1982 July | 29 | | | 5000 00 |
| | 3 | | | 8000 00 | | 31 | | | 500 00 |
| | | 3,440.00 | | 9940 00 | | 31 | | | 1000 00 |
| | | | | | | | | | 6500 00 |

ACCOUNT *Printing Supplies* ACCOUNT NO.

| DATE | | ITEM | POST. REF. | DEBIT | DATE | | ITEM | POST. REF. | CREDIT |
|---|---|---|---|---|---|---|---|---|---|
| 1982 July | 1 | Balance | | 900 00 | | | | | |

ACCOUNT *Printing Equipment* ACCOUNT NO.

| DATE | | ITEM | POST. REF. | DEBIT | DATE | | ITEM | POST. REF. | CREDIT |
|---|---|---|---|---|---|---|---|---|---|
| 1982 July | 1 | Balance | | 16000 00 | | | | | |

ACCOUNT *Accounts Payable – Dow Paper Co.* ACCOUNT NO.

| DATE | | ITEM | POST. REF. | DEBIT | DATE | | ITEM | POST. REF. | CREDIT |
|---|---|---|---|---|---|---|---|---|---|
| | | | | | 1982 July | 1 | Balance | | 1000 00 |

*General Ledger – Bill Penny, Printer*

ACCOUNT *Bill Penny, Capital* ACCOUNT NO.

| DATE | | ITEM | POST. REF. | DEBIT | DATE | | ITEM | POST. REF. | CREDIT |
|---|---|---|---|---|---|---|---|---|---|
| | | | | | 1982 July | 1 | Balance | | 17840 00 |

ACCOUNT *Bill Penny, Drawing* ACCOUNT NO.

| DATE | | ITEM | POST. REF. | DEBIT | DATE | | ITEM | POST. REF. | CREDIT |
|---|---|---|---|---|---|---|---|---|---|
| 1982 July | 31 | | | 1000 00 | | | | | |

ACCOUNT *Revenue from Printing* ACCOUNT NO.

| DATE | | ITEM | POST. REF. | DEBIT | DATE | | ITEM | POST. REF. | CREDIT |
|---|---|---|---|---|---|---|---|---|---|
| | | | | | 1982 July | 3 | | | 8000 00 |

ACCOUNT *Advertising Expense* ACCOUNT NO.

| DATE | | ITEM | POST. REF. | DEBIT | DATE | | ITEM | POST. REF. | CREDIT |
|---|---|---|---|---|---|---|---|---|---|
| 1982 July | 31 | | | 500 00 | | | | | |

ACCOUNT *Salary Expense* ACCOUNT NO.

| DATE | | ITEM | POST. REF. | DEBIT | DATE | | ITEM | POST. REF. | CREDIT |
|---|---|---|---|---|---|---|---|---|---|
| 1982 July | 29 | | | 5000 00 | | | | | |

***General Ledger – Bill Penny, Printer (concluded)***

*Bill Penny, Printer*
*Trial Balance*
*July 31, 1982*

| | | |
|---|---|---|
| Cash | 3440 00 | |
| Printing Supplies | 900 00 | |
| Printing Equipment | 16000 00 | |
| Accounts Payable – Dow Paper Co. | | 1000 00 |
| Bill Penny, Capital | | 17840 00 |
| Bill Penny, Drawing | 1000 00 | |
| Revenue from Printing | | 8000 00 |
| Advertising Expense | 500 00 | |
| Salary Expense | 5000 00 | |
| | 26840 00 | 26840 00 |

***Trial Balance – Bill Penny, Printer***

The trial balance provides the information necessary to prepare the financial statements. The financial statements for Penny at the end of July can be prepared from the trial balance above and would appear as shown on page 32.

| Bill Penny, Printer<br>Income Statement<br>For Month Ended July 31, 1982 | | |
|---|---|---|
| Revenue from printing | | 800000 |
| | | |
| Expenses: | | |
| Salary expense | 500000 | |
| Advertising expense | 50000 | |
| Total expenses | | 550000 |
| Net income | | 250000 |

Income Statement – Bill Penny, Printer

| Bill Penny, Printer<br>Capital Statement<br>For Month Ended July 31, 1982 | | |
|---|---|---|
| Capital, July 1, 1982 | | 1784000 |
| Net income for the month | 250000 | |
| Less withdrawals | 100000 | |
| Increase in capital | | 150000 |
| Capital, July 31, 1982 | | 1934000 |

Capital Statement – Bill Penny, Printer

| Bill Penny, Printer<br>Balance Sheet<br>July 31, 1982 | | |
|---|---|---|
| Assets | | |
| Cash | 344000 | |
| Printing supplies | 90000 | |
| Printing equipment | 1600000 | |
| Total assets | | 2034000 |
| | | |
| Liabilities | | |
| Accounts payable: | | |
| Dow Paper Co. | | 100000 |
| | | |
| Owner's Equity | | |
| Bill Penny, capital | | 1934000 |
| Total liabilities and owner's equity | | 2034000 |

Balance Sheet – Bill Penny, Printer

The drawing account does *not* affect the income statement or the net income for the period. Withdrawals are shown only on the capital statement as a reduction from net income to determine the increase or decrease in capital for the period.

## ARRANGEMENT OF ACCOUNTS IN THE LEDGER

The accounts are normally arranged in the ledger with balance sheet accounts appearing first, then capital statement accounts, and lastly income statement accounts. The balance sheet accounts are shown in the order in which they appear on the balance sheet: assets, liabilities, then owner's equity. The drawing account from the capital statement appears next. The income statement accounts are shown in the order in which they appear on the income statement: first revenues, then expenses. This arrangement of accounts is usually considered desirable as it aids in the preparation of financial reports for the manager or owner. Each account in the ledger is a separate sheet or card, and any new accounts needed as a result of later transactions can easily be inserted in the proper order. As was previously mentioned, the expense accounts are often listed on the income statement in descending order by amount. Since it is impossible to determine in advance of operations which accounts will have the largest amounts, the expense accounts may be listed in the ledger alphabetically or in some other predetermined format.

### QUESTIONS FOR DISCUSSION

1. Why are revenue and expense accounts called temporary accounts?
2. What is the purpose of the proprietor's drawing account?
3. Donna Wee, a local business person, had capital of $11,200 at the beginning of the year. At the end of the year, Wee's capital was $26,000. She made no additional investments or withdrawals during the period. She therefore knew that her profit for the year was $14,800, and felt that she did not need to keep a detailed record of transactions or prepare an income statement. Do you agree with Wee's reasoning? Explain the advantages of keeping a detailed record of revenue and expense transactions and preparing an income statement.
4. How are the accounts usually arranged in the ledger?

## EXERCISES

1. Ron Duval, an electrician, completed the transactions listed below. Using the following headings, record the account debited, the account credited, and the amount for each transaction.

| TRANSACTION | ACCOUNT DEBITED | ACCOUNT CREDITED | AMOUNT |
|---|---|---|---|

(a) Invested cash in the business, $2,000.
(b) Paid cash for equipment, $600.
(c) Paid rent for the month, $250.
(d) Received revenue for services rendered, $730.
(e) Bought electrical supplies on account from Kester's Supplies, $75.
(f) Withdrew cash, $120.

2. Plum Company had a capital balance of $40,000 on March 1. During the month of March, the company had a net income of $8,400, and Celeste Plum withdrew $3,000 for personal use. Prepare a capital statement for Plum Company for the month of March.

3. Lawrence Stevens is a tailor. During the month of November, he had the following revenue and expenses: Revenue, $1,670; Rent Expense, $225; Utilities Expense, $80; Supplies Expense, $35; Miscellaneous Expense, $30. Prepare an income statement for Stevens' Custom Tailoring for the month of November.

4. List the following accounts in the order in which they should appear in the ledger of David Sanchez, attorney-at-law:

(1) David Sanchez, Drawing
(2) Accounts Payable
(3) Office Supplies
(4) David Sanchez, Capital
(5) Utilities Expense
(6) Cash
(7) Rent Expense
(8) Fees Earned
(9) Office Equipment
(10) Salary Expense

## ASSIGNMENT 2-B

**Tear out pages 341–348 and complete Assignment 2-B. After completing the assignment, you may proceed with the textbook discussion in Chapter 3 until the next assignment is required.**

Chapter **3**

# THE ACCOUNTING CYCLE

In the previous chapter, transactions were analyzed to determine their effect on account balances. All debit and credit amounts were entered directly in the accounts. That procedure was used to help the student understand the effect of transactions on the accounts. The ability to analyze transactions in this way is essential to the understanding of the double-entry system of accounting. The analysis of transactions in terms of accounts to be debited and credited is the basic purpose of this chapter also, but the method of recording the transactions will be more practical. The use of a special bookkeeping device designed for recording transactions will be illustrated.

## PART A *THE JOURNAL*

The ultimate objective of double-entry accounting, as illustrated in the preceding chapter, is to record correct amounts in the proper ledger accounts. For practical reasons, however, there is a very important accounting function that precedes the recording of debits and credits in the ledger accounts. The transactions are first entered in a preliminary record called a *journal*, commonly known as a *book of original entry*. The process of recording the transactions in the journal is called *journalizing*. After the amounts are journalized, they are then *posted* (transferred) to the appropriate ledger accounts. Some of the reasons for using a journal are:

1. It provides a chronological record of all transactions.
2. It fulfills the need for recording in one place all of the debits and credits of each transaction.
3. It provides more information, such as a detailed explanation of a transaction, than can conveniently be recorded in the individual ledger accounts.

The reasons for using a journal will become more evident as the student of accounting becomes more familiar with the types and volume of transactions recorded by most businesses. Also, the desirability of having techniques that assure maximum accuracy in recording transactions and that facilitate the location and correction of any errors is an important reason for using the journalizing techniques explained in this chapter.

The original sources of information concerning most transactions are sales tickets, purchase invoices, contracts, cash register tapes, checks, and various other types of business papers. Such papers are called *source documents*. Information obtained from the source documents often helps in analyzing transactions to determine which accounts should be debited and which accounts should be credited. The source documents also provide valuable evidence to support the accuracy of the accounts and financial statements.

The purpose of the journal is to provide a chronological record of all transactions completed. It includes the date of each transaction, the titles of the accounts to be debited and credited, and the amounts of the debits and credits. The journal contains all the information necessary to record debit and credit amounts in the ledger accounts. The flow of information of business transactions into the accounting records can be diagrammed as follows:

| *SOURCE DOCUMENTS* → | *JOURNAL* → | *LEDGER* → | *FINANCIAL STATEMENTS* |
|---|---|---|---|
| provide the data concerning business transactions. | provides a complete chronological record of transactions data by recording in one place all the elements of an individual transaction. | summarizes data into individual accounts. | show the results of operations for the period and the financial position at the end of the period. |

## THE JOURNAL FORMAT

As shown in the diagram above, the source documents provide the basic information concerning the transactions of the business, but the journal represents the first point where the data are formally entered in the accounting records. This is why the journal is known as the book of original entry. Various types of journals may be used, depending on the size of the firm and the nature of its operations. The simplest form is a two-column journal, called the *general journal*. It has two amount columns, one for recording debits and one for recording credits. The basic form of the general journal is illustrated below. The columns have been numbered to identify them with the following discussion.

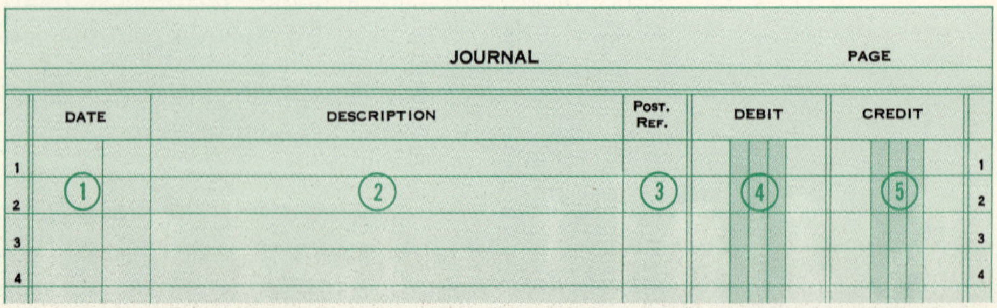


*Two-Column General Journal*

(1) **Date Column.** The date of the transaction is entered in the Date column. The left side of this column is for the year and month and this information is shown only once on each page unless an entry

for a new month or year is made later on the page. The year is written in small figures at the top of the left column and the month is written on the first line. It may be necessary to abbreviate the name of the month. The right side of the column is for the day. The day is entered on the first line of each transaction.

(2) **Description Column.** The Description column is used to record the titles of the accounts involved in the transaction as well as an explanation of the transaction. Each transaction involves two or more accounts and each account affected must be recorded. The accounts to be debited are recorded first, beginning at the left margin of the column. The accounts to be credited are written below the debits and are indented one-half inch (approximately 1.3 centimeters) to be easily distinguishable. A separate line is used to record each account. A short explanation or description of the transaction is written on the line or lines following the last credit of the entry and is indented about one inch (approximately 2.5 centimeters) from the left margin.

(3) **Posting Reference Column.** The Posting Reference column (Post. Ref.) is used when information is transferred from the journal to the ledger. Posting references are discussed in detail later in the chapter.

(4) **Debit Column.** The Debit column is used to record the dollar amount of each account debited in the transaction. The debit column is the *left* amount column.

(5) **Credit Column.** The Credit column is used to record the dollar amount of each account credited in the transaction. The credit column is the *right* amount column.

## RECORDING TRANSACTIONS IN THE JOURNAL

To illustrate the recording of a transaction in the journal, assume that on October 1, 1982, Krista Mosley invested $800 cash to begin her own business, a dance studio. This transaction increases Cash by a debit of $800 and Krista Mosley, Capital by a credit for the same amount. The transaction is recorded on the first page of the general journal as follows:

JOURNAL — PAGE 1

| | DATE | | DESCRIPTION | POST. REF. | DEBIT | CREDIT | |
|---|---|---|---|---|---|---|---|
| | 1982 | | | | | | |
| 1 | Oct. | 1 | Cash | | 800 00 | | 1 |
| 2 | | | Krista Mosley, Capital | | | 800 00 | 2 |
| 3 | | | Invested cash in dance studio | | | | 3 |
| 4 | | | | | | | 4 |
| 5 | | | | | | | 5 |
| 6 | | | | | | | 6 |
| 7 | | | | | | | 7 |
| 8 | | | | | | | 8 |
| 9 | | | | | | | 9 |

The following items should be noted in the recording of the preceding entry:

1. Because this is the first entry on the page, the year is written at the top of the Date column. The month and day are written on the first line of the Date column.
2. The name of the account debited, Cash, is written on the first line of the Description column at the left margin of the column. The amount of the debit, $800, is written on the same line in the Debit column.
3. The name of the account credited, Krista Mosley, Capital, is written on the second line and is indented one-half inch from the left margin of the Description column. The amount of the credit, $800, is written on the same line in the Credit column.
4. The explanation of the transaction is written on the next line and is indented one inch from the left margin.
5. Nothing will be recorded in the Posting Reference column until the entry is posted to the ledger accounts.

The recording of the entire entry, including an explanation, in the journal provides a summary of each transaction, which is a valuable reference if there is some future question about the transaction.

The transactions recorded in the journal are entered as debits and credits to specific accounts. Since these debits and credits will be posted to the ledger, it is necessary that the account titles used in the journal be exactly the same as those found in the ledger.

## The Journalizing Procedure Expanded

The following additional transactions were completed by Mosley during October.

**Transaction:** October 2. Purchased studio equipment on account from Tune Equipment Co. for $2,000.

| | | | | | | |
|---|---|---|---|---|---|---|
| 4 | | 2 | Studio Equipment | | 2000 00 | | 4 |
| 5 | | | Accounts Pay.–Tune Equip. Co. | | | 2000 00 | 5 |
| 6 | | | Purchased equip. on acct. | | | | 6 |
| 7 | | | | | | | 7 |

**Analysis:** This transaction increases the asset account, Studio Equipment, and is recorded as a debit. The liability account, Accounts Payable — Tune Equipment Co., is also increased and therefore is credited.

**Transaction:** October 4. Purchased studio supplies for cash, $180.

| | | | | | | | |
|---|---|---|---|---|---|---|---|
| 7 | | 4 | Studio Supplies | | 180 00 | | 7 |
| 8 | | | Cash | | | 180 00 | 8 |
| 9 | | | Purchased studio supplies. | | | | 9 |
| 10 | | | | | | | 10 |
| 11 | | | | | | | 11 |

**Analysis:** This transaction increases the asset studio supplies, (debit) and decreases the asset, cash (credit). There is no effect on liabilities or owner's equity.

**Transaction:** October 15. Recorded $650 cash for revenue received during the period October 1–15. Normally revenue would be recorded each day as it is received. This transaction is presented in summary form to simplify the illustration.

| Date | Account Title and Explanation | Debit | Credit |
|---|---|---|---|
| 15 | Cash | 650 00 | |
| | Revenue from Lessons | | 650 00 |
| | Revenue received Oct. 1-15. | | |

**Analysis:** When the customers pay for their lessons, an entry is made to increase Cash (debit) and to record the revenue earned in the revenue account (credit).

**Transaction:** October 16. Paid for advertising in a local newspaper, $75.

| Date | Account Title and Explanation | Debit | Credit |
|---|---|---|---|
| 16 | Advertising Expense | 75 00 | |
| | Cash | | 75 00 |
| | Paid for newspaper ad. | | |

**Analysis:** This transaction increases the advertising expense account (debit) and decreases the cash account (credit).

**Transaction:** October 19. Paid rent on the dance studio for the month of October, $200.

| Date | Account Title and Explanation | Debit | Credit |
|---|---|---|---|
| 19 | Rent Expense | 200 00 | |
| | Cash | | 200 00 |
| | Paid October rent. | | |

**Analysis:** The rent payment is recorded as a debit to the expense account, Rent Expense, and as a credit to the asset account, Cash.

**Transaction:** October 20. Purchased studio supplies from B-J Suppliers on account, $150.

| Date | Account Title and Explanation | Debit | Credit |
|---|---|---|---|
| 20 | Studio Supplies | 150 00 | |
| | Accounts Pay.-B-J Suppliers | | 150 00 |
| | Purchased supplies on acct. | | |

**Analysis:** The assets of the firm are increased by a debit to the studio supplies account and its liabilities are increased by a credit to Accounts Payable — B-J Suppliers.

**Transaction:** October 25. Paid Tune Equipment Co. $300 of the amount owed.

| Date | Account Title and Explanation | Debit | Credit |
|---|---|---|---|
| 25 | Accounts Payable—Tune Equip. Co. | 300 00 | |
| | Cash | | 300 00 |
| | Paid on account owed. | | |
| | | | |

**Analysis:** This transaction reduced the liability to Tune Equipment Co. by debiting the accounts payable account. The assets are reduced by a credit to Cash.

**Transaction:** October 27. Paid heat, light, and water bill (Utilities Expense) for the month, $158.

| Date | Account Title and Explanation | Debit | Credit |
|---|---|---|---|
| 27 | Utilities Expense | 158 00 | |
| | Cash | | 158 00 |
| | Paid utilities for Oct. | | |
| | | | |

**Analysis:** The expenses are increased by a debit to the utilities expense account. The cash account is reduced by the credit.

**Transaction:** October 29. Paid assistant's monthly salary, $250.

| Date | Account Title and Explanation | Debit | Credit |
|---|---|---|---|
| 29 | Salary Expense | 250 00 | |
| | Cash | | 250 00 |
| | Paid assistant's salary | | |
| | for October. | | |

**Analysis:** Salary Expense is debited to reflect the expense for the period and the cash account is credited for the amount paid.

**Transaction:** October 30. Recorded revenue for the period October 16–30, $610.

| Date | Account Title and Explanation | Debit | Credit |
|---|---|---|---|
| 30 | Cash | 610 00 | |
| | Revenue from Lessons | | 610 00 |
| | Revenue received Oct. 16-30. | | |
| | | | |

**Analysis:** Assets are increased by the debit to Cash for the money received, $610, and the revenue account, Revenue from Lessons, is increased by a credit for the same amount.

**Transaction:** October 30. Mosley withdrew $300 for personal living expenses.

| Date | Account Title and Explanation | Debit | Credit |
|---|---|---|---|
| 30 | Krista Mosley, Drawing | 300 00 | |
| | Cash | | 300 00 |
| | Personal withdrawal. | | |
| | | | |

**Analysis:** Mosley has taken cash from the business for personal use. This represents withdrawal in anticipation of a profit and should be recorded as a debit to Krista Mosley, Drawing. The cash account is reduced by a credit.

**Transaction:** October 31. Record revenue of $125 earned by providing dance lessons to Jane Powers on account. During the month of November, Powers will pay for the lessons received in October.

| Date | Description | Post. Ref. | Debit | Credit |
|---|---|---|---|---|
| 31 | Accounts Receivable—Jane Powers | | 125 00 | |
| | Revenue from Lessons | | | 125 00 |
| | Lessons given on account. | | | |
| | | | | |

**Analysis:** Assets are increased by the debit to Accounts Receivable for the claim against the customer, $125. The revenue account, Revenue from Lessons, is increased by a credit for the same amount.

The complete journal containing all of the above transactions for Mosley's Dance Studio is illustrated below and on page 42.

JOURNAL PAGE 1

| Date | | Description | Post. Ref. | Debit | Credit |
|---|---|---|---|---|---|
| 1982 Oct. | 1 | Cash | | 800 00 | |
| | | Krista Mosley, Capital | | | 800 00 |
| | | Invested cash in dance studio | | | |
| | 2 | Studio Equipment | | 2,000 00 | |
| | | Accounts Pay.—June Equip. Co. | | | 2,000 00 |
| | | Purchased equip. on acct. | | | |
| | 4 | Studio Supplies | | 180 00 | |
| | | Cash | | | 180 00 |
| | | Purchased studio supplies. | | | |
| | 15 | Cash | | 650 00 | |
| | | Revenue from Lessons | | | 650 00 |
| | | Revenue received Oct. 1–15. | | | |
| | 16 | Advertising Expense | | 75 00 | |
| | | Cash | | | 75 00 |
| | | Paid for newspaper ad. | | | |
| | 19 | Rent Expense | | 200 00 | |
| | | Cash | | | 200 00 |
| | | Paid October rent. | | | |
| | 20 | Studio Supplies | | 150 00 | |
| | | Accounts Pay.—B-J Suppliers | | | 150 00 |
| | | Purchased supplies on acct. | | | |
| | 25 | Accounts Payable—June Equip. Co. | | 300 00 | |
| | | Cash | | | 300 00 |
| | | Paid on account owed. | | | |
| | 27 | Utilities Expense | | 158 00 | |
| | | Cash | | | 158 00 |
| | | Paid utilities for Oct. | | | |
| | 29 | Salary Expense | | 250 00 | |
| | | Cash | | | 250 00 |
| | | Paid assistant's salary | | | |
| | | for October. | | | |
| | 30 | Cash | | 610 00 | |
| | | Revenue from Lessons | | | 610 00 |
| | | Revenue received Oct. 16-30. | | | |

***General Journal Entries — Mosley's Dance Studio***

| | Date | | Description | Post. Ref. | Debit | Credit | |
|---|---|---|---|---|---|---|---|
| 35 | | 30 | Krista Mosley, Drawing | | 300 00 | | 35 |
| 36 | | | Cash | | | 300 00 | 36 |
| 37 | | | Personal withdrawal. | | | | 37 |
| 38 | | 31 | Accounts Receivable-Jane Powers | | 125 00 | | 38 |
| 39 | | | Revenue from Lessons | | | 125 00 | 39 |
| 40 | | | Lessons given on account. | | | | 40 |
| 41 | | | | | | | 41 |
| 42 | | | | | | | 42 |

*General Journal Entries — Mosley's Dance Studio (concluded)*

## Compound Journal Entries

In each transaction recorded above there was only one debit and one credit. Many business transactions require the use of more than one debit or credit. Any entry in the general journal requiring more than one debit or credit is called a *compound journal entry*. In recording a compound journal entry the total dollar amount debited and credited in each entry must always be equal. To illustrate the recording of compound entries in a general journal, assume the following transactions were made by Mosley during October.

**Transaction:** October 1. Mosley invested $800 cash and $60 of studio supplies in the business. This compound entry is:

JOURNAL — PAGE 1

| | Date | | Description | Post. Ref. | Debit | Credit | |
|---|---|---|---|---|---|---|---|
| 1 | 1982 Oct. | 1 | Cash | | 800 00 | | 1 |
| 2 | | | Studio Supplies | | 60 00 | | 2 |
| 3 | | | Krista Mosley, Capital | | | 860 00 | 3 |
| 4 | | | Invested cash and | | | | 4 |
| 5 | | | studio supplies. | | | | 5 |

**Analysis:** The entry requires two debits, to Cash and to Studio Supplies, but only one credit to Krista Mosley, Capital. It should be noted that the total debits of $860 ($800 + $60) are equal to the one credit of $860.

**Transaction:** October 2. Mosley purchased studio equipment from Tune Equipment Co. for $2,000, paying $500 in cash and agreeing to pay the balance on account. The following compound entry is required:

| | Date | | Description | Post. Ref. | Debit | Credit | |
|---|---|---|---|---|---|---|---|
| 6 | | 2 | Studio Equipment | | 2000 00 | | 6 |
| 7 | | | Cash | | | 500 00 | 7 |
| 8 | | | Accounts Payable-Tune Equip. Co. | | | 1500 00 | 8 |
| 9 | | | Purchased equip. on acct. | | | | 9 |

**Analysis:** The debit to the studio equipment account of $2,000 is equal to the combined credits to Cash and Accounts Payable — Tune Equipment Co., of $2,000 (500 + $1,500). The ledger remains in balance.

## QUESTIONS FOR DISCUSSION

1. Why is the journal referred to as a book of original entry?
2. Name three reasons for using a journal.
3. What information about each transaction is given (a) in both the journal and the ledger and (b) in the journal but not in the ledger?
4. Buck Waters plans to save the time that was required in making journal entries by making entries directly to the ledger. He expects to avoid any difficulty in locating a mistake by writing an explanation of each transaction in each account. What are the objections to this plan?
5. In the journal form below, the column headings have been omitted and each column has been numbered. Give the heading for each column and explain what information would be recorded in each.

## EXERCISES

1. Explain the flow of information regarding the transactions of a business through its accounting system, using the letters given in the chart below:

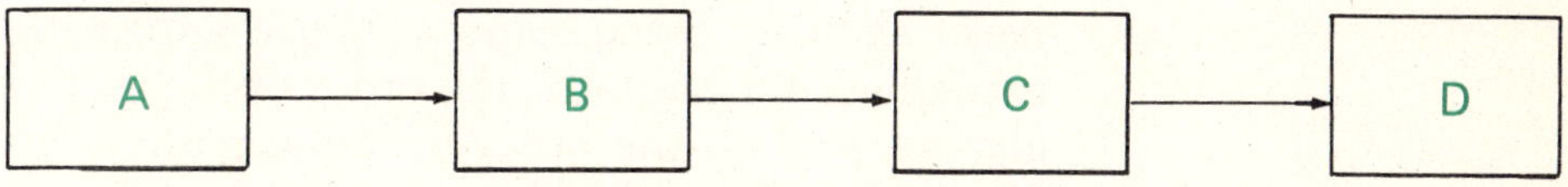


2. In a general journal, record the following transactions for Brenda Company.

   Jan. 2. Helen Brenda invested $1,200 cash in the business.
   4. Purchased office supplies from Kibler Supplies on account, $120.
   8. Purchased office equipment from Robb Equipment Company on account, $1,600.
   10. Paid advertising expense, $40.
   14. Received service revenues, $420.
   18. Paid Kibler Supplies on account, $120.

3. In a general journal, record the following compound journal entries for Vaughan Pearson.

   Sept. 1. Pearson invested in the business $1,850 cash and store supplies of $180.
   4. Purchased land $15,000, and building, $40,000, issuing a note payable for the full amount, $55,000.
   8. Purchased store supplies, $85, and store equipment, $700, from South Equipment Company. Paid $200 cash with the balance on account.

## ASSIGNMENT 3-A

**Tear out pages 349–354 and complete Assignment 3-A. Submit your papers for approval. After completion, continue with the chapter discussion until the next assignment is required.**

# PART B THE CHART OF ACCOUNTS AND POSTING

This section explains procedures which facilitate the transfer of information from the journal to the individual ledger accounts. It also shows how cross-referencing between the journal and the ledger is provided to enable checking of previously recorded transactions.

## THE CHART OF ACCOUNTS

The number of accounts to be kept for a particular business depends upon the size and nature of its operations. Mosley's Dance Studio requires relatively few accounts compared to a large manufacturing enterprise which would have to keep a great number of accounts to insure the availability of the necessary financial information. For example, a large company may maintain separate accounts for electricity expense, water expense, and telephone and telegraph expense, while a small business may combine all of these expenses into a utilities expense account.

The account titles used on the balance sheet and the income statement should be the same as those appearing in the ledger. As was explained in Chapter 2, the order of the accounts in the ledger should also agree with the order of the account titles as they appear on the financial statements. This requires the following sequence of account classes: assets, liabilities, owner's equity, revenue, and expenses. Normally a summary of the accounts that are to be used is prepared. This summary is called a *chart of accounts*.

The accounts are numbered to facilitate identification, filing, handling, and for use as a posting reference in the journal. The numbering of the accounts should follow a uniform pattern which becomes a code. A common system using a two-digit code is to have all asset accounts begin with a 1, liability accounts with a 2, owner's equity accounts with a 3, revenue accounts with a 4, and expense accounts with a 5. The first digit indicates the major division of the ledger where an account has been placed while the second digit refers to the position of the account within its division. This type of numbering system also has the advantage of allowing for the addition of new accounts when needed without disturbing the other account numbers. For example, in the chart of accounts on page 45, Mosley's Dance Studio has two accounts payable, Accounts Payable — B-J Suppliers (No. 21) and Accounts Payable — Tune Equipment Co. (No. 22). If necessary, a new account could easily be added, for example, Accounts Payable — Sams Company, and assigned account number 23 without affecting any existing account numbers.

As the business grows and the number of accounts increases, the numbering system for the accounts may need to be expanded to three digits or more. In larger businesses, the ledger is kept on a computer and account numbers of seven or more digits are not uncommon.

The chart of accounts for Mosley's Dance Studio, using a two-digit code, is shown below.

**MOSLEY'S DANCE STUDIO**
**Chart of Accounts**

**Assets**
11 Cash
12 Accounts Receivable — Jane Powers
13 Studio Supplies
14 Studio Equipment

**Liabilities**
21 Accounts Payable — B-J Suppliers
22 Accounts Payable — Tune Equipment Co.

**Owner's Equity**
31 Krista Mosley, Capital
32 Krista Mosley, Drawing

**Revenue**
41 Revenue from Lessons

**Expenses**
51 Advertising Expense
52 Rent Expense
53 Salary Expense
54 Utilities Expense

## POSTING

The process by which the debits and credits recorded in the journal are transferred to accounts in the ledger is called *posting*. It consists of transferring each amount in the debit column of the journal to the debit column of the appropriate account in the ledger, and transferring each amount in the credit column of the journal to the credit column of the appropriate account in the ledger. The entries may be posted in sequence as they appear in the journal, posting the debit of the transaction and then the credit. If there is a considerable amount of posting to be done, it is usually more convenient to post all the debits first, and then all the credits. This procedure reduces the likelihood of posting items to the wrong side of the accounts.

In most businesses, the posting is done by accounting machines. The conversion of the bookkeeping process and the accounting records to a computerized operation has become very common among businesses. When the posting is done manually, the steps for posting each debit and credit are performed as illustrated on page 46. The steps involved in posting from the journal to the ledger are explained below:

1. The date of the transaction as recorded in the journal is also entered in the ledger account.
2. The letter "J" to indicate "journal" and the number of the journal page on which the transaction is recorded are written in the Posting Reference column of the ledger account.
3. The amounts recorded in the journal entry are transferred to the appropriate account in the ledger. A debit in the journal is posted to the debit side of the appropriate ledger account, and a credit in the journal is posted to the credit side of that account.
4. The ledger account number to which the item is posted is written in the Posting Reference column of the journal. This procedure serves two purposes: (a) it provides a cross-reference of the transaction between the journal and the ledger, and (b) the Posting Reference column in the journal enables the bookkeeper to readily determine which items have been posted and which ones have not. The bookkeeper then knows exactly where to resume posting after an interruption and is less likely to omit or duplicate a posting.

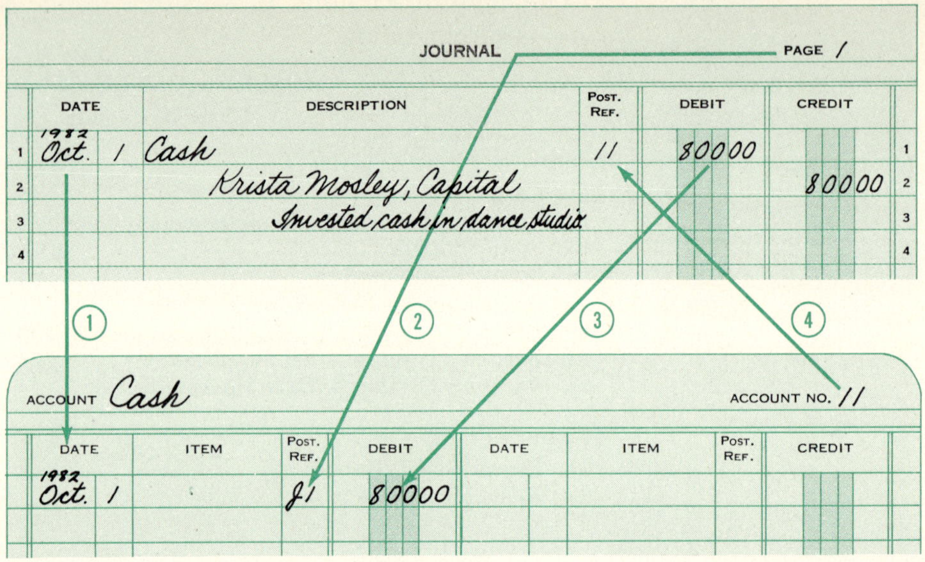


***Posting the Debit***

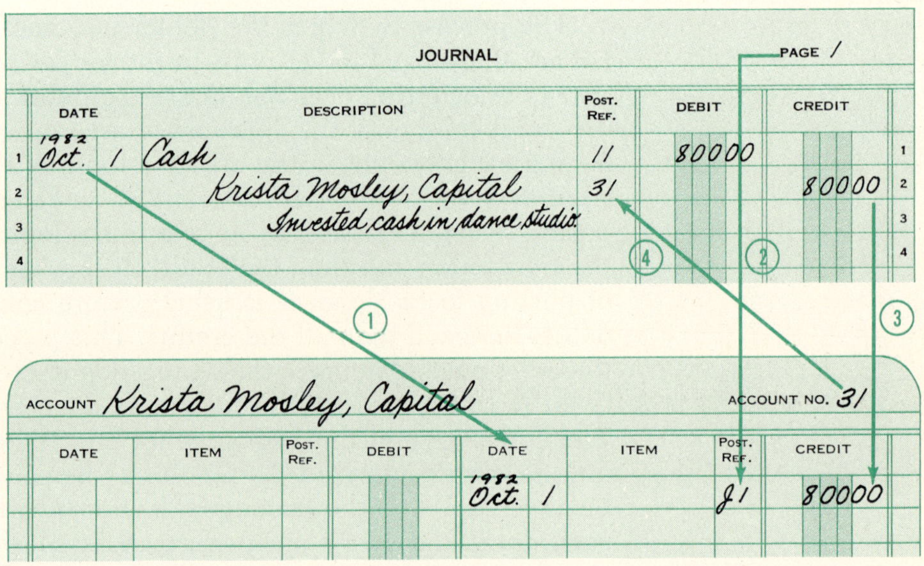


***Posting the Credit***

The general ledger for Mosley's Dance Studio after posting the transactions from the journal on pages 41 and 42 is presented on the following pages. The steps in the posting, explained on page 45, were followed for each transaction.

Once the postings have been completed, the information recorded in the journal will appear in summary form in the ledger. The posting reference columns provide a cross-reference between the journal and the ledger, making it possible to trace a transaction by account number from the journal to the ledger or by page number from the ledger to the journal.

In the posting process, care should be taken to make sure that debits in the journal are entered as debits in the ledger and that credits in the journal are entered as credits in the ledger. And, be certain that the date recorded in the ledger account is the date that the transaction occurred, even if the posting is not done until a later date.

**ACCOUNT** *Cash* **ACCOUNT NO.** *11*

| DATE | ITEM | POST. REF. | DEBIT | DATE | ITEM | POST. REF. | CREDIT |
|---|---|---|---|---|---|---|---|
| 1982 Oct. 1 | | J1 | 800 00 | 1982 Oct. 4 | | J1 | 180 00 |
| 15 | | J1 | 650 00 | 16 | | J1 | 75 00 |
| 30 | | J1 | 610 00 | 19 | | J1 | 200 00 |
| | 597.00 | | 2060 00 | 25 | | J1 | 300 00 |
| | | | | 27 | | J1 | 158 00 |
| | | | | 29 | | J1 | 250 00 |
| | | | | 30 | | J1 | 300 00 |
| | | | | | | | 1463 00 |

**ACCOUNT** *Accounts Receivable—Jane Powers* **ACCOUNT NO.** *12*

| DATE | ITEM | POST. REF. | DEBIT | DATE | ITEM | POST. REF. | CREDIT |
|---|---|---|---|---|---|---|---|
| 1982 Oct. 31 | | J1 | 125 00 | | | | |

**ACCOUNT** *Studio Supplies* **ACCOUNT NO.** *13*

| DATE | ITEM | POST. REF. | DEBIT | DATE | ITEM | POST. REF. | CREDIT |
|---|---|---|---|---|---|---|---|
| 1982 Oct. 4 | | J1 | 180 00 | | | | |
| 20 | | J1 | 150 00 | | | | |
| | | | 330 00 | | | | |

**ACCOUNT** *Studio Equipment* **ACCOUNT NO.** *14*

| DATE | ITEM | POST. REF. | DEBIT | DATE | ITEM | POST. REF. | CREDIT |
|---|---|---|---|---|---|---|---|
| 1982 Oct. 2 | | J1 | 2000 00 | | | | |

**ACCOUNT** *Accounts Payable—B-J Suppliers* **ACCOUNT NO.** *21*

| DATE | ITEM | POST. REF. | DEBIT | DATE | ITEM | POST. REF. | CREDIT |
|---|---|---|---|---|---|---|---|
| | | | | 1982 Oct. 20 | | J1 | 150 00 |

**ACCOUNT** *Accounts Payable—June Equipment Co.* **ACCOUNT NO.** *22*

| DATE | ITEM | POST. REF. | DEBIT | DATE | ITEM | POST. REF. | CREDIT |
|---|---|---|---|---|---|---|---|
| 1982 Oct. 25 | | J1 | 300 00 | 1982 Oct. 2 | 1,700.00 | J1 | 2000 00 |

**ACCOUNT** *Krista Mosley, Capital* **ACCOUNT NO.** *31*

| DATE | ITEM | POST. REF. | DEBIT | DATE | ITEM | POST. REF. | CREDIT |
|---|---|---|---|---|---|---|---|
| | | | | 1982 Oct. 1 | | J1 | 800 00 |

***General Ledger — Mosley's Dance Studio***

ACCOUNT *Krista Mosley, Drawing* — ACCOUNT NO. 32

| DATE | | ITEM | POST. REF. | DEBIT | DATE | | ITEM | POST. REF. | CREDIT |
|---|---|---|---|---|---|---|---|---|---|
| 1982 Oct. | 30 | | J1 | 300 00 | | | | | |

ACCOUNT *Revenue from Lessons* — ACCOUNT NO. 41

| DATE | | ITEM | POST. REF. | DEBIT | DATE | | ITEM | POST. REF. | CREDIT |
|---|---|---|---|---|---|---|---|---|---|
| | | | | | 1982 Oct. | 15 | | J1 | 650 00 |
| | | | | | | 30 | | J1 | 610 00 |
| | | | | | | 31 | | J1 | 125 00 |
| | | | | | | | | | 1385 00 |

ACCOUNT *Advertising Expense* — ACCOUNT NO. 51

| DATE | | ITEM | POST. REF. | DEBIT | DATE | | ITEM | POST. REF. | CREDIT |
|---|---|---|---|---|---|---|---|---|---|
| 1982 Oct. | 16 | | J1 | 75 00 | | | | | |

ACCOUNT *Rent Expense* — ACCOUNT NO. 52

| DATE | | ITEM | POST. REF. | DEBIT | DATE | | ITEM | POST. REF. | CREDIT |
|---|---|---|---|---|---|---|---|---|---|
| 1982 Oct. | 19 | | J1 | 200 00 | | | | | |

ACCOUNT *Salary Expense* — ACCOUNT NO. 53

| DATE | | ITEM | POST. REF. | DEBIT | DATE | | ITEM | POST. REF. | CREDIT |
|---|---|---|---|---|---|---|---|---|---|
| 1982 Oct. | 29 | | J1 | 250 00 | | | | | |

ACCOUNT *Utilities Expense* — ACCOUNT NO. 54

| DATE | | ITEM | POST. REF. | DEBIT | DATE | | ITEM | POST. REF. | CREDIT |
|---|---|---|---|---|---|---|---|---|---|
| 1982 Oct. | 27 | | J1 | 158 00 | | | | | |

***General Ledger — Mosley's Dance Studio (concluded)***

## PREPARING THE TRIAL BALANCE AND FINANCIAL STATEMENTS

After the posting has been completed, the ledger accounts are footed to determine the current balances. A trial balance as of October 31, 1982, can then be prepared.

The trial balance, page 49, insures that the ledger accounts are in balance, that is, total debits equal total credits. It also provides all the information necessary to prepare the financial statements for Mosley's Dance Studio at the end of business on October 31, 1982. Mosley's income statement, capital statement, and balance sheet are illustrated on pages 49 and 50.

| Mosley's Dance Studio<br>Trial Balance<br>October 31, 1982 | | |
|---|---|---|
| Cash | 597 00 | |
| Accounts Receivable — Jane Powers | 125 00 | |
| Studio Supplies | 330 00 | |
| Studio Equipment | 2000 00 | |
| Accounts Payable — B-J Suppliers | | 150 00 |
| Accounts Payable — June Equipment Co. | | 1700 00 |
| Krista Mosley, Capital | | 800 00 |
| Krista Mosley, Drawing | 300 00 | |
| Revenue from Lessons | | 1385 00 |
| Advertising Expense | 75 00 | |
| Rent Expense | 200 00 | |
| Salary Expense | 250 00 | |
| Utilities Expense | 158 00 | |
| | 4035 00 | 4035 00 |

Trial Balance — Mosley's Dance Studio

| Mosley's Dance Studio<br>Income Statement<br>For Month Ended October 31, 1982 | | |
|---|---|---|
| Revenue from lessons | | 1385 00 |
| Expenses: | | |
| Salary expense | 250 00 | |
| Rent expense | 200 00 | |
| Utilities expense | 158 00 | |
| Advertising expense | 75 00 | |
| Total expenses | | 683 00 |
| Net income | | 702 00 |

Income Statement — Mosley's Dance Studio

| Mosley's Dance Studio<br>Capital Statement<br>For Month Ended October 31, 1982 | | |
|---|---|---|
| Capital, October 1, 1982 | | 800 00 |
| Net income for the month | 702 00 | |
| Less withdrawals | 300 00 | |
| Increase in capital | | 402 00 |
| Capital, October 31, 1982 | | 1202 00 |

Capital Statement — Mosley's Dance Studio

| Mosley's Dance Studio<br>Balance Sheet<br>October 31, 1982 | | |
|---|---|---|
| Assets | | |
| Cash | 597 00 | |
| Accounts receivable — Jane Powers | 125 00 | |
| Studio supplies | 330 00 | |
| Studio equipment | 2000 00 | |
| Total assets | | 3052 00 |
| Liabilities | | |
| Accounts payable | | |
| B-J Suppliers | 150 00 | |
| June Equipment Co. | 1700 00 | |
| Total liabilities | | 1850 00 |
| Owner's Equity | | |
| Krista Mosley, capital | | 1202 00 |
| Total liabilities and owner's equity | | 3052 00 |

Balance Sheet — Mosley's Dance Studio

When the changes in owner's equity for the period are limited to net income and personal withdrawals, as was the case for Mosley, it may be desirable to record the information contained in the capital statement directly in the owner's equity section of the balance sheet. This would eliminate the need for a separate capital statement. The information from the capital statement, page 49, could be included in the owner's equity section of the balance sheet as shown below.

| Owner's Equity | | | |
|---|---|---|---|
| Krista Mosley, capital: | | | |
| Capital, October 1, 1982 | | 800 00 | |
| Net income for the month | 702.00 | | |
| Less withdrawals | 300.00 | | |
| Increase in capital | | 402 00 | |
| Capital, October 31, 1982 | | | 1202 00 |
| Total liabilities and owner's equity | | | 3052 00 |

Owner's Equity Section of the Balance Sheet — Mosley's Dance Studio

## QUESTIONS FOR DISCUSSION

1. Why are the ledger accounts numbered?
2. Explain the basic number coding that is used in a chart of accounts.
3. Describe the step-by-step procedure of posting an item from the journal to a ledger account.
4. State two purposes that the posting reference serves.
5. How does the Posting Reference column provide a cross-reference between the journal and the ledger?
6. (a) Explain two ways the data from the journal can be posted to the ledger. (b) Which method would be more convenient if there are a large number of transactions to post? Why?

7. Larry Boaz wishes to know the reason for a posting to one of the ledger accounts. Explain exactly how he may obtain this information.

## EXERCISES

1. Below is an alphabetical listing of the account balances for Duchemin Company as of May 31:

| | | | |
|---|---|---|---|
| Accounts Payable — Green Co. | 450 | Rent Expense | 200 |
| Accounts Payable — Starr Supplies | 280 | Salary Expense | 400 |
| Advertising Expense | 50 | Service Revenue | 1,360 |
| Cash | 625 | Store Equipment | 4,000 |
| Dan Duchemin, Capital | 7,480 | Store Supplies | 230 |
| Dan Duchemin, Drawing | 175 | Truck | 3,800 |
| Delivery Expense | 90 | | |

**Required:** Prepare a chart of accounts for Duchemin Company, using a two-digit code. Prepare a trial balance for Duchemin Company as of May 31 of the current year.

2. Following are four general journal entries of the Thames Company that were recorded during March.

JOURNAL — PAGE 4

| DATE | | DESCRIPTION | POST. REF. | DEBIT | CREDIT |
|---|---|---|---|---|---|
| 19-- | | | | | |
| Mar. | 3 | Cash | | 700 00 | |
| | | Revenue | | | 700 00 |
| | | Revenue received March 1–3. | | | |
| | 7 | Advertising Expense | | 30 00 | |
| | | Cash | | | 30 00 |
| | | Paid for advertisement. | | | |
| | 12 | Accounts Payable — Stanley Co. | | 300 00 | |
| | | Cash | | | 300 00 |
| | | Paid on account. | | | |
| | 15 | Joan Thames, Capital | | 500 00 | |
| | | Cash | | | 500 00 |
| | | Personal withdrawal. | | | |

**Required:** Set up a ledger account for Cash with a balance as of March 1 of $840. Post the four journal entries above to this cash account. Foot the account and determine its balance after posting. (Note: Students are required to post only half of each entry — that portion related to the cash account.)

**ASSIGNMENT 3-B**

**Tear out pages 355–374 and complete Assignment 3-B. Submit your papers to the instructor for approval. After completion, continue with the chapter reading until the next assignment is required.**

# PART C LOCATING AND CORRECTING ERRORS

If the total of the debit amount column of the trial balance does not equal the total of the credit amount column, the cause of this inequality must be located and corrected. Furthermore, the fact that a trial balance is in balance does not prove the accuracy of the accounting records. This section examines errors that could be caused by incorrect journalizing, posting, footing, and trial balance preparation.

## TYPES OF ERRORS

If the total debits and total credits of the trial balance are not equal, the trial balance is said to be out of balance. This discrepancy can be caused by one or more of the following types of errors:

1. Posting the transaction from the journal to the ledger:
   (a) Failing to post an amount.
   (b) Posting a debit amount to the credit side of a ledger account, or vice versa.
   (c) Posting an incorrect amount.
   (d) Posting the same amount twice.
2. Computing the ledger account balance.
   (a) Adding one or both sides of the account incorrectly.
   (b) Incorrectly computing the balance of the account when subtracting the debit total from the credit total, or vice versa.
3. Preparing the trial balance.
   (a) Recording a debit balance as a credit on the trial balance, or vice versa.
   (b) Transferring the wrong amount from an account to the trial balance.

There are also many types of errors which will not cause the trial balance to be out of balance. Common examples of these errors are:

1. Failure to record an entire transaction in the journal.
2. Failure to post an entire transaction to the ledger.
3. Recording or posting the same transaction twice.
4. Posting the debit (or credit) part of a transaction to the wrong account but to the correct side. For example, a $200 debit to Office Supplies posted as a $200 debit to Office Equipment.
5. Recording the same wrong amount for both the debit and credit parts of a transaction.

## LOCATING THE ERROR

When the trial balance is out of balance, first determine the amount of the discrepancy. Knowing the amount of the difference will be helpful in locating the following common errors:

1. *Omission of an amount*. For example, if the amount of the difference in the trial balance totals is $360, it is possible that an account with that balance was not shown on the trial balance or that a posting of that amount was omitted. The trial balance and the transactions should be examined to see if a $360 amount can be located.
2. *Amount recorded on wrong side of an account*. If the amount of the discrepancy is evenly divisible by 2, there is a possibility that a debit amount has been erroneously posted as a credit, or vice versa. If, for example, $180 had been paid on accounts payable, the entry in the journal should have been recorded as a debit to Accounts Payable and a credit to Cash. If, however, both Accounts Payable and Cash were posted as debits, this would reflect $360 ($180 + $180) in debits in the ledger and no credits, causing the accounts to be out of balance by $360.
3. *Transpositions*. A transposition is an error caused by reversing the digits of a number, such as writing $840 as $480 or $260 as $620. If the

transposition error involves only two digits, the amount of the error, $360 in both cases, will always be evenly divisible by 9. Therefore, a discrepancy should be divided by nine to see if the possibility of a transposition error exists.

4. *Sliding error*. A sliding error occurs when the decimal point is in the wrong place. This type of error is called a "slide" because the decimal point is, in effect, moved one or more places to the left or right of its proper position. For example, if $275.00 is written as $2,750.00 this would cause a discrepancy of $2,475.00. A sliding error is also evenly divisible by 9.

If more than one error has occurred, the discrepancy in the trial balance totals will not give any indication of the nature of the error. In order to find the error as quickly as possible, the usual procedure is to check the records and the trial balance in the reverse order in which they were prepared. The detailed procedure is as follows:

1. The trial balance is retotaled.
2. The account titles and balances in the trial balance are checked against the titles and balances in the ledger, making certain that all accounts have been included in the trial balance and their balances shown in the proper column (debit or credit).
3. The pencil footings and the ledger account balances are rechecked.
4. The journal entries are reviewed to see that the debits in each entry equal the credits.
5. The posting of the individual debits and credits from the journal to the ledger accounts is checked. As each posting is verified, a check mark (√) is placed at the left of the amount in the ledger account and at the left of the corresponding amount in the journal. An item may have been omitted, posted twice, entered on the wrong side of the account, or copied incorrectly.

## CORRECTING THE ERROR

If the posting of an entry has been omitted, the amount is immediately posted to the proper account. In cases where an item has been posted twice, a line is drawn through the second posting in the account. If an item has been posted to the wrong account or posted at the wrong amount, a line is drawn through the incorrect item in the account and then the correct amount is posted. To illustrate these corrections, assume that the journal entry of Mosley's Dance Studio on October 19 for the payment of rent expense in the amount of $200 was posted twice to the ledger account, Rent Expense. The following shows the journal entry and the corrected posting.

| | | | | | | |
|---|---|---|---|---|---|---|
| 16 | 19 | Rent Expense | 52 | 200 00 | | 16 |
| 17 | | Cash | 11 | | 200 00 | 17 |
| 18 | | Paid October rent. | | | | 18 |

ACCOUNT Rent Expense ACCOUNT NO. 52

| DATE | | ITEM | POST. REF. | DEBIT | DATE | ITEM | POST. REF. | CREDIT |
|---|---|---|---|---|---|---|---|---|
| 1982 Oct. | 19 | | J1 | 200 00 | | | | |
| | ~~19~~ | ~~ ~~ | ~~J1~~ | ~~200 00~~ | | | | |

**Entry Posted Twice**

If the $200 debit to Rent Expense had been posted to the utilities expense account, a line would be drawn through the debit to Utilities Expense and the correct amount would be debited to Rent Expense as shown below.

ACCOUNT *Utilities Expense* ACCOUNT NO. *54*

| DATE | | ITEM | POST. REF. | DEBIT | DATE | ITEM | POST. REF. | CREDIT |
|---|---|---|---|---|---|---|---|---|
| *1982* ~~*Oct.*~~ | ~~*19*~~ | | ~~*J1*~~ | ~~*200 00*~~ | | | | |

***Entry Posted to Wrong Account***

ACCOUNT *Rent Expense* ACCOUNT NO. *52*

| DATE | | ITEM | POST. REF. | DEBIT | DATE | ITEM | POST. REF. | CREDIT |
|---|---|---|---|---|---|---|---|---|
| *1982* *Oct.* | *19* | | *J1* | *200 00* | | | | |

If the $200 had been erroneously recorded in the rent expense account as $20 (a sliding error) the correction would be made by drawing a line through the $20 posting and inserting the correct amount of $200 as shown below.

***Entry Posted at Wrong Amount***

ACCOUNT *Rent Expense* ACCOUNT NO. *52*

| DATE | | ITEM | POST. REF. | DEBIT | DATE | ITEM | POST. REF. | CREDIT |
|---|---|---|---|---|---|---|---|---|
| *1982* *Oct.* | *19* | | *J1* | *200 00* ~~*20 00*~~ | | | | |

If a wrong account title or amount is recorded in the journal and discovered before it has been posted, the correction is made by drawing a line through the error and writing the correct account title or amount immediately above. For example, if Mosley's payment of $158 for utilities on October 27 had been erroneously recorded in the journal as a debit to Advertising Expense but was discovered before it was posted, the correction would be made as follows:

***Entry Recorded to Wrong Account***

| | | | | | | |
|---|---|---|---|---|---|---|
| 25 | *27* | *Utilities Expense* ~~*Advertising Expense*~~ | | *158 00* | | 25 |
| 26 | | *Cash* | | | *158 00* | 26 |
| 27 | | *Paid utilities for Oct.* | | | | 27 |

When an erroneous entry has been made in the journal and posted to the ledger before being discovered, it should be corrected by means of another entry known as a *correcting entry*. For example, if the above payment of $158 for utilities had been recorded in the journal and posted to the ledger as a $158 debit to Advertising Expense, a correcting entry should be made.

In preparing correcting entries, the following procedure is recommended: **(1)** analyze the erroneous entry as it was actually recorded, **(2)** determine the entry as it should have been recorded, and **(3)** prepare the correcting entry. This procedure is followed in the example shown on the following page.

*Incorrect Entry Recorded*

| Date | Description | Post. Ref. | Debit | Credit |
|---|---|---|---|---|
| 27 | Advertising Expense | 51 | 158 00 | |
| | Cash | 11 | | 158 00 |
| | Paid utilities for Oct. | | | |

*Entry Which Should Have Been Recorded*

| Date | Description | Post. Ref. | Debit | Credit |
|---|---|---|---|---|
| 27 | Utilities Expense | 54 | 158 00 | |
| | Cash | 11 | | 158 00 |
| | Paid utilities for Oct. | | | |

Comparison of the two entries shows that the credit to Cash is correct but that the debit to Advertising Expense should be corrected by a $158 credit to the account and Utilities Expense should be debited for the same amount as follows:

*Correcting Entry*

| Date | Description | Post. Ref. | Debit | Credit |
|---|---|---|---|---|
| 30 | Utilities Expense | 54 | 158 00 | |
| | Advertising Expense | 51 | | 158 00 |
| | To correct erroneous | | | |
| | debit to Advertising | | | |
| | Expense on October 27. | | | |

The fact that correcting entries were made in the journal and posted to the accounts in the preceding illustrations is very important. Under no circumstances should an erasure be made in any of the accounting records. Erasures have often caused or been related to errors that could never be located or explained because data had been erased. Further, an erasure obviously indicates some type of error was made; if there is no explanation of the original error, the erasure, or the current entry in the account, an auditor may have cause to doubt whether the balances in the accounts are genuine or accurate.

## QUESTIONS FOR DISCUSSION

1. What are some of the common mistakes that can be made in posting from the journal to the ledger?
2. Name three types of errors that will not cause a trial balance to be out of balance.
3. What procedure is used to discover a transposition error or a sliding error?
4. Discuss the procedure to be used in finding the error when the trial balance does not balance.
5. What procedure is recommended for preparing correcting entries?

## EXERCISES

1. At the end of March, the Bing Company prepared a trial balance. The totals for the trial balance are: debit, $16,560; credit, $15,940. If it is determined that the difference was caused by a single error in recording the transactions, give two possible reasons and the amount of the transaction in each case.

2. Indicate which of the following entries would cause the trial balance to be out of balance and by what amount.
   (a) Revenue of $550 from a customer was not recorded because the cash had not been received.
   (b) Equipment purchased on account for $320 was recorded as a debit to Equipment of $320 and a credit to Accounts Payable of $230.
   (c) Supplies purchased for cash, $200, were recorded as a debit to Supplies of $300 and a credit to Cash of $300.
   (d) A payment of $250 on accounts payable was recorded as a credit of $250 to Accounts Payable and a credit to Cash, $250.

3. The bookkeeper for the Seattle Company made the following errors in journalizing and posting transactions during the month of November:
   (1) The $250 payment for rent expense for the month was recorded and posted as a debit to Repairs Expense and a credit to Cash.
   (2) The monthly utility bill was $98. The check was written for $89 and recorded and posted as a debit to Utilities Expense and a credit to Cash for $89.
   (3) Equipment was purchased from the ABC Company for cash, $400. The entry was recorded and posted as a debit to Equipment and a credit to Accounts Payable — ABC Company for $400.

   **Instructions:** Prepare the entries necessary to correct these errors on November 30.

## ASSIGNMENT 3-C

**Tear out pages 375–378 and complete Assignment 3-C. Submit your papers for approval. After completion proceed with the study of Chapter 4 until the next assignment is required.**

Chapter **4**

# COMPLETION OF THE ACCOUNTING CYCLE FOR A SERVICE ENTERPRISE

The first three chapters discussed accounting procedures for a service enterprise *during* the accounting period. There are also certain other accounting activities which must be performed at the *end* of an accounting period so that accurate financial statements can be prepared and the accounting records can be made ready to receive entries relating to the new accounting period. This chapter examines these end-of-period accounting activities for a service enterprise.

## PART A ADJUSTING ENTRIES

The ledger accounts normally provide a continuous record of the transactions entered into by the business. As each transaction occurs, it is analyzed, journalized, and the appropriate accounts are debited and credited to reflect the effect of the transaction on the financial condition and operating results of the business.

Immediate recording of every event that has some effect on the financial condition or operating results is not practical, however. For example, office supplies are used constantly, but to prepare a journal entry to record the use of each sheet of stationery, each pencil, or each typewriter ribbon would be very impractical. As another example, insurance premiums are often paid a year or more in advance and the cost is recorded in the asset account, Prepaid Insurance. Each day, or even each minute to carry it to an extreme, a portion of the prepaid insurance is used and becomes a form of expense. To prepare an entry each day to reduce the asset and increase the expense account would be very time consuming and expensive.

The preceding examples illustrate that there are many events or changes in the business that do affect the financial condition and results of operations but for which it is not practical or desirable to prepare a journal entry each day. Such events and changes must be summarized and journalized at the end of the accounting period, however, in order to ensure that all revenues and all expenses, as well as all balances in asset and liability accounts, are properly reported in the financial statements.

## JOURNALIZING AND POSTING ADJUSTING ENTRIES

The accounts are brought up to date at the end of the accounting period by journal entries which are called *adjusting entries*. To illustrate the process of journalizing and posting adjusting entries, consider the following information for the Hull Delivery Service.

### Office Supplies

When office supplies are purchased, the transactions are normally recorded by debits to the asset account, Office Supplies. No attempt is made to record the use of such items as paper, paper clips, or pencils on a daily basis, but at the end of the accounting period an inventory is taken of the office supplies still on hand. The difference between the balance in the office supplies account and the amount of supplies still on hand indicates the amount of supplies used during the period.

To illustrate, assume that the office supplies on hand at the beginning of the period are $120 and that this amount was properly recorded as an asset in the office supplies account. If during the period an additional $50 of supplies are purchased, the asset account, Office Supplies, is increased and its balance is now $170. If a count of the supplies on hand at the end of the period reveals an inventory of office supplies of only $110, it is apparent that $60 ($170–$110) of office supplies have been used during the period, and this amount should be reported on the income statement as an expense for the period.

Increases in expense accounts are recorded as debits and decreases in assets are recorded as credits; therefore, the following adjusting journal entry would be made:

**JOURNAL** — PAGE 1

| DATE | DESCRIPTION | POST. REF. | DEBIT | CREDIT |
|---|---|---|---|---|
| 31 | Office Supplies Expense | | 60 00 | |
| | Office Supplies | | | 60 00 |
| | To record supplies used. | | | |
| | | | | |

After this entry has been posted, the asset account, Office Supplies, will correctly reflect the amount of supplies on hand at the end of the period, $110; the expense account, Office Supplies Expense, will correctly reflect the amount of office supplies used during the period, $60.

**OFFICE SUPPLIES (12)**

| | | | |
|---|---|---|---|
| Dec. 1 | 120 | Dec. 31 | 60 |
| 14 | 50 | | |
| *110* | *170* | | |

**OFFICE SUPPLIES EXPENSE (53)**

| | | | |
|---|---|---|---|
| Dec. 31 | 60 | | |

### Insurance

If the company pays in advance an insurance premium of $420 on its property for one year, this amount should be debited to an asset account, Prepaid Insurance, which represents the cost of insurance coverage acquired. With the passage of time the asset prepaid insurance becomes a form of expense, insurance expense.

If the $420 premium was paid on December 1 of the current year to provide coverage on the business property for the next 12 months, the entry on December 1 to record the transaction would be a debit to Prepaid Insurance for $420 and a credit to Cash for $420.

As was mentioned earlier, the insurance coverage expires with the passage of time and could be measured in hours or days. However, such a degree of exactness is not necessary, and adjustments to the prepaid insurance account will be required only at the end of the accounting period prior to the preparation of the financial statements.

Assuming that the accounting period ends on December 31, an adjusting entry on that date would be required to transfer one month of the insurance premium from an asset account, Prepaid Insurance, to an expense account, Insurance Expense. Since the insurance was paid for twelve months, the adjustment will be for one twelfth of the premium or $35 (1/12 × $420).

| | | | | Debit | Credit |
|---|---|---|---|---|---|
| | 31 | Insurance Expense | | 35 00 | |
| | | Prepaid Insurance | | | 35 00 |
| | | To record insurance expired. | | | |
| | | | | | |

The prepaid insurance account now has a balance of $385 ($420 − $35) which is an asset representing the unexpired portion of the insurance premium. The insurance expense account has a balance of $35, representing the cost of insurance coverage for the period, which is reported on the income statement as an expense.

After the adjusting entry is posted, the two accounts would appear as follows:

| PREPAID INSURANCE | | | (13) |
|---|---|---|---|
| Dec. 1 385 | 420 | Dec. 31 | 35 |

| INSURANCE EXPENSE | | | (52) |
|---|---|---|---|
| Dec. 31 | 35 | | |

This same procedure is used for all other prepayments.

## Plant Assets

Assets that will be used for a number of years in the operations of the business are called *plant assets* or *fixed assets*. All plant assets except land will wear out or become useless with the passage of time. For example, a building may be useful for fifty years or longer, whereas a delivery truck may be useful for only three or four years. An effort should be made to estimate the portion of the asset's cost which has been used up (*expired*) during the accounting period. This amount should be recorded as an expense of the period. The expired portion of the asset's cost is called *depreciation*.

The expense account used to record the expired cost of a plant asset is called Depreciation Expense. The adjusting entry to record depreciation requires a transfer of the expired cost from an asset account to an expense account. However, due to the uncertainties that exist as to the length of usefulness of various assets, the amount of depreciation must be estimated. Because of this estimating procedure and the desirability of presenting both the original cost of the asset and its depreciated amount to date on the balance sheet, the reduction of the asset is credited to a *contra asset account* entitled Accumulated Depreciation rather than credited directly to the asset account.

A *contra* account is an account which is used to partially or fully offset another account. For example, a credit to an accumulated depreciation account offsets the normal debit balance in a plant asset account. The various methods of estimating depreciation will be discussed in a later chapter.

Assuming that the estimated amount of depreciation on an $8,400 truck for the month of December is $175, the adjusting entry to record the depreciation expense of the truck would be as follows:

| | Date | Account | P.R. | Debit | Credit |
|---|---|---|---|---|---|
| | 31 | **Depreciation Expense — Truck........** | | **175 00** | |
| | | **Accumulated Deprec. — Truck .....** | | | **175 00** |
| | | **To record deprec. for Dec.** | | | |
| | | | | | |

The ledger accounts would appear as follows after the above entry is posted.

**TRUCK (14)**

| Debit | | Credit | |
|---|---|---|---|
| Dec. 1 Bal. | 8,400 | | |

**DEPRECIATION EXPENSE — TRUCK (51)**

| Debit | | Credit | |
|---|---|---|---|
| Dec. 31 | 175 | | |

**ACCUMULATED DEPRECIATION — TRUCK (14.1)**

| Debit | | Credit | |
|---|---|---|---|
| | | Dec. 31 | 175 |

Since the accumulated depreciation account is a contra asset account, the effect of the credit to that account is to reduce the balance of the asset. Consequently, the basic rules of debit and credit, as first represented in Chapter Two, are being applied.

The account number of Accumulated Depreciation — Truck, No. 14.1, indicates that on the balance sheet its balance is subtracted from the balance in account No. 14, Truck. The use of decimals signifies contra accounts whose balances are subtracted from the related account with the same whole number. Accumulated Depreciation has a normal credit balance and is increased by a credit and decreased by a debit. This account appears in the asset section of the balance sheet as a reduction from the truck account as shown below.

| | | |
|---|---|---|
| Truck | $8,400 | |
| Less accumulated depreciation | 175 | $8,225 |

The difference between the cost of a depreciable asset and the accumulated depreciation to date represents the unexpired cost of the asset and is called *book value*. It is also known as *undepreciated cost*. The book value of the above truck is $8,225 at the end of its first month of use. At the end of its second month in operation its accumulated depreciation would be $350 ($175 + $175) and its book value would be $8,050.

## Salaries

As previously discussed, some goods and services are paid for at the time they are used while others, such as prepaid insurance or prepaid rent, are paid in advance of their use. There are also expenses which are not paid until some time after their use. A common example of such an expense is salaries owed to employees. Salaries are earned on an hourly or daily basis but are usually paid in periods of a week or longer. It frequently happens that the last day of the accounting period is not the same as the last day of the payroll period. An adjusting entry is required to record the salary expense that has accumulated from the last payroll period to the end of the accounting period. An adjusting entry for salaries owed is necessary to record both the salary expense which has been incurred but not paid and the liability of the employer.

To illustrate, assume that Hull Delivery Service pays its employees every Wednesday and that December 31, the last day of the accounting period, is on Friday. The salaries earned by employees between Wednesday and Friday, but not yet paid, require an adjusting entry to properly state both the expense for the period and the liability as of December 31, the date on which the financial statements are prepared.

If the company had paid salaries to its employees from December 1 through the last Wednesday of the month, December 29, amounting to $720, the salary expense account prior to adjustment would show a $720 debit. Assuming the salaries due to employees for the incomplete payroll period of Thursday the 30th and Friday the 31st amounted to $85, the adjusting entry would be:

| | | | | |
|---|---|---|---|---|
| 31 | **Salary Expense** | | 85 00 | |
| | **Salaries Payable** | | | 85 00 |
| | **To record unpaid salaries.** | | | |

After posting the entry, the accounts would appear as follows:

**SALARIES PAYABLE (23)**

| | | | |
|---|---|---|---|
| | | Dec. 31 | 85 |

**SALARY EXPENSE (56)**

| | | | |
|---|---|---|---|
| Dec. 1 | 70 | | |
| 8 | 135 | | |
| 15 | 180 | | |
| 22 | 165 | | |
| 29 | 170 | | |
| 31 | 85 | | |
| | *805* | | |

The salary expense for the month is now $805, which is the actual amount earned by the employees, and the liability for salaries payable is $85, which is the amount still owed to employees.

For illustration purposes, a written explanation was included with each of the adjusting entries presented in this part of the chapter. Normally, explanations are not used for adjusting entries. The reason being that these entries are presented as a group in the journal with a heading indicating that they are adjusting entries. The four adjustments previously presented would properly be recorded in the journal as shown on page 62.

| DATE | | DESCRIPTION | POST. REF. | DEBIT | CREDIT |
|---|---|---|---|---|---|
| **JOURNAL** | | | | | **PAGE 3** |
| 1982 | | **Adjusting Entries** | | | |
| Dec. | 31 | Office Supplies Expense | | 60 00 | |
| | | Office Supplies | | | 60 00 |
| | 31 | Insurance Expense | | 35 00 | |
| | | Prepaid Insurance | | | 35 00 |
| | 31 | Depreciation Expense — Truck | | 175 00 | |
| | | Accumulated Deprec. — Truck | | | 175 00 |
| | 31 | Salary Expense | | 85 00 | |
| | | Salaries Payable | | | 85 00 |

*Adjusting Entries — Hull Delivery Service*

## ELIMINATING THE NEED FOR ADJUSTMENTS

In the first two adjustments shown above, a product or service that was purchased in advance of its use was properly debited to an asset account. The asset was reduced and an expense was debited as the supply or service was used. However, when it is definitely known at the time of purchase that the entire amount of an item will be consumed during the period and that no part of it will remain as an asset at the end of the fiscal period, the amount paid for the item is normally debited to an expense account instead of an asset account. This procedure avoids the necessity of an adjusting entry at the end of the period.

Thus, if $240 rent had been paid on December 1 for the month of December, the entry would be recorded by a debit of $240 to Rent Expense rather than to the asset account, Prepaid Rent.

| DATE | | DESCRIPTION | POST. REF. | DEBIT | CREDIT |
|---|---|---|---|---|---|
| 1982 | | | | | |
| Dec. | 1 | Rent Expense | | 240 00 | |
| | | Cash | | | 240 00 |
| | | Paid rent for Dec. | | | |

This treatment eliminates the need for an adjustment at the end of the period, because the $240 rent used during the period has already been recorded as an expense.

### QUESTIONS FOR DISCUSSION

1. What is the purpose of adjusting entries?
2. Give three examples of accounts that will normally have to be adjusted, and explain why each adjustment is necessary.
3. On the first day of May, Ruth Booker paid $600 rent on her shop for the months of May through July and debited the amount to Prepaid Rent. If the books were adjusted at the end of each month, what adjusting entry for rent would be required on May 31?
4. If the $600 paid by Booker in 3. above had been the rent for the month of May only, what account should have been debited on May 1 for the payment? Why?
5. (a) What is depreciation? (b) How is it recorded in the accounts? (c) When the depreciation expense on equipment is recorded at the end of the period, what account will be credited? Why?

## EXERCISES

1. The following is the ledger account, Cleaning Supplies, for the month of September.

ACCOUNT **Cleaning Supplies** ACCOUNT NO. **13**

| DATE | | ITEM | POST. REF. | DEBIT | DATE | | ITEM | POST. REF. | CREDIT |
|---|---|---|---|---|---|---|---|---|---|
| 19-- Sept. | 1 | | | 135 00 | | | | | |

A count of cleaning supplies on hand on September 30 totaled $80. Prepare the journal entry necessary to adjust the cleaning supplies account at the end of the month.

2. The Shep Company had a balance of $600 in the prepaid advertising account as of December 31. Prepare the necessary adjusting entry as of December 31 in each of the following situations: (a) The advertising used during the period was $225; (b) The prepaid advertising applicable to future periods is $410.

3. The Syble Company purchased equipment on January 2 for $5,600 cash. The depreciation on the equipment for the year ended December 31 was $700. Required: (a) Prepare the entries to record the purchase of the equipment on January 2 and to record the adjustment for depreciation on December 31. (b) Show how the accounts relating to the equipment will be shown on the balance sheet of Syble Company on December 31.

4. At the end of a fiscal period the trial balance of Richard Hildebrand, contractor, is as follows:

**RICHARD HILDEBRAND, CONTRACTOR**
**Trial Balance**
**December 31, 19--**

| | | |
|---|---|---|
| Cash | 1,900 | |
| Supplies | 100 | |
| Prepaid Insurance | 240 | |
| Equipment | 6,200 | |
| Accumulated Depreciation — Equipment | | 1,400 |
| Accounts Payable — Wilburn Enterprises | | 1,600 |
| Richard Hildebrand, Capital | | 4,480 |
| Richard Hildebrand, Drawing | 300 | |
| Revenue | | 2,100 |
| Salary Expense | 700 | |
| Utilities Expense | 140 | |
| | 9,580 | 9,580 |

**Instructions:** (1) Which of the accounts in the trial balance would be most likely to require an adjustment? (2) How will the amount of the adjustment be determined for each account?

## ASSIGNMENT 4-A

**Tear out pages 379–386 and complete Assignment 4-A. After completing the assignment, continue with the following discussion until the next assignment is required.**

# PART B THE WORK SHEET AND FINANCIAL STATEMENTS

At the end of the fiscal period a form called a *work sheet* is prepared by the bookkeeping department prior to recording the adjusting entries and posting them to the ledger accounts. It summarizes all the information necessary to complete the end-of-period financial reports. The work sheet reduces the chance of omitting an adjustment, provides a check on the equality of the debit and credit balances, and lists the ledger accounts in a format which facilitates preparation of the financial statements. This discussion explains the preparation of a work sheet and the financial statements which can be obtained from the work sheet information.

## THE WORK SHEET

A standard form of work sheet is illustrated for Hull Delivery Service on page 65. The heading of the work sheet is consistent with that of other financial reports and includes the name of the company, the name of the statement (Work Sheet), and the period covered by the statement.

The work sheet of Hull Delivery Service has eight amount columns and is therefore called an *eight-column work sheet*. The eight-column work sheet has four sets of amount columns. In each set, the left column is for the debits and the right column is for the credits. The headings of the four sets of amount columns are:

**Trial Balance** **Adjustments** **Income Statement** **Balance Sheet**

### Trial Balance Columns

The end-of-period summary is begun by preparing a trial balance of the ledger accounts to ensure that the debit and credit totals are equal. This trial balance is normally prepared in the first two columns of the work sheet. The trial balance for Hull Delivery Service is taken from the ledger account balances before adjustments as shown on pages 76 to 78.

### Adjustments Columns

As discussed earlier, some of the accounts required adjustment at the end of the period. These adjustments must be made to insure that each account has the proper balance prior to the preparation of the financial statements. To facilitate this process, the second set of columns on the work sheet is used to record the adjusting entries. The adjustments are recorded on the work sheet in the same manner as they are recorded in the journal; that is, the debit is recorded on the left side of the Adjustments columns and the credit is entered on the right side. Since the debit and credit parts of an adjusting entry may be widely separated on the work sheet, it is desirable to cross-reference each adjustment by placing a small letter at the left of each entry.

Inasmuch as the trial balance usually includes only the accounts in the ledger which have a balance at the time of preparation, some of the accounts requiring adjustments will not appear in the trial balance. Certain expense accounts, such as Depreciation Expense, may have been used in previous periods but have not had any entries during the current period. Some liabilities, Salaries Payable for example, may have been accumulated in a prior period and paid in the current period and will therefore have a zero balance before adjustment. In these instances, the account titles are inserted below the trial balance accounts as they are required.

At the beginning of this chapter general journal entries were prepared to illustrate month-end adjustments to the accounts. In actual practice the adjusting entries are normally first entered directly on the work sheet, and after the work sheet and financial statements have been completed, they are then entered in the journal and posted to the ledger. The adjustments shown on the work sheet below are listed on page 66.

Hull Delivery Service
Work Sheet
For Month Ended December 31, 1982

| ACCOUNT TITLE | TRIAL BALANCE | | ADJUSTMENTS | | INCOME STATEMENT | | BALANCE SHEET | |
|---|---|---|---|---|---|---|---|---|
| | DEBIT (1) | CREDIT (2) | DEBIT (3) | CREDIT (4) | DEBIT (5) | CREDIT (6) | DEBIT (7) | CREDIT (8) |
| Cash | 400 00 | | | | | | 400 00 | |
| Office Supplies | 170 00 | | | (a) 60 00 | | | 110 00 | |
| Prepaid Insurance | 420 00 | | | (b) 35 00 | | | 385 00 | |
| Truck | 8400 00 | | | | | | 8400 00 | |
| Accts. Pay.-Arnold Sup. Co. | | 300 00 | | | | | | 300 00 |
| Accts. Pay.-Horn Equip. Co. | | 1200 00 | | | | | | 1200 00 |
| Charles Hull, Capital | | 6490 00 | | | | | | 6490 00 |
| Charles Hull, Drawing | 200 00 | | | | | | 200 00 | |
| Delivery Revenue | | 2700 00 | | | | 2700 00 | | |
| Rent Expense | 240 00 | | | | 240 00 | | | |
| Repairs Expense | 60 00 | | | | 60 00 | | | |
| Salary Expense | 720 00 | | (d) 85 00 | | 805 00 | | | |
| Utilities Expense | 80 00 | | | | 80 00 | | | |
| | 10690 00 | 10690 00 | | | | | | |
| Office Supplies Expense | | | (a) 60 00 | | 60 00 | | | |
| Insurance Expense | | | (b) 35 00 | | 35 00 | | | |
| Depreciation Exp.-Truck | | | (c) 175 00 | | 175 00 | | | |
| Accum. Depreciation-Truck | | | | (c) 175 00 | | | | 175 00 |
| Salaries Payable | | | | (d) 85 00 | | | | 85 00 |
| | | | 355 00 | 355 00 | 1455 00 | 2700 00 | 9495 00 | 8250 00 |
| Net Income | | | | | 1245 00 | | | 1245 00 |
| | | | | | 2700 00 | 2700 00 | 9495 00 | 9495 00 |

*Work Sheet — Hull Delivery Service*

**(a) Office Supplies.** The office supplies account has a debit balance of $170 on the trial balance. The inventory of office supplies on hand at the end of the month is $110. Therefore, the office supplies expense for December is $60 ($170 − $110). This adjustment is recorded by entering (1) Office Supplies Expense in the Account Title column, (2) $60 in the Adjustments Debit column on the same line, and (3) $60 in the Adjustments Credit column on the Office Supplies line.

**(b) Insurance.** Prepaid Insurance has a balance of $420 on the trial balance representing the insurance premiums for twelve months beginning December 1. The insurance expense for December is one twelfth of the $420 annual premium, or $35. This adjustment is recorded by entering (1) Insurance Expense in the Account Title column, (2) $35 in the Adjustments Debit column on the same line, and (3) $35 in the Adjustments Credit column on the Prepaid Insurance line.

**(c) Depreciation.** The depreciation of the truck for the month is estimated at $175. This adjustment is recorded by entering (1) Depreciation Expense — Truck in the Account Title column, (2) $175 in the Adjustments Debit column on the same line, (3) Accumulated Depreciation — Truck in the Account Title column, and (4) $175 in the Adjustments Credit column on the same line.

**(d) Salaries.** The salaries owed but not paid at the end of December totaled $85. The adjustment is recorded by entering (1) $85 in the Adjustments Debit column on the Salary Expense line, (2) Salaries Payable in the Account Title column, and (3) $85 in the Adjustments Credit column on the same line.

After all the adjustments have been recorded in the Adjustments columns, the debit and credit columns are totaled to make sure they are equal. The columns are then ruled with a double line.

## Income Statement and Balance Sheet Columns

To assist in the preparation of the financial statements directly from the work sheet, the balances of the asset, liability, capital, and drawing accounts are extended to the Balance Sheet columns, and the revenue and expense account balances are extended to the Income Statement columns. The capital and drawing accounts are extended to the Balance Sheet columns although they will appear on the capital statement when the financial statements are prepared. There is no separate set of columns on the work sheet for the capital statement.

The account balances are extended line by line to the appropriate set of columns starting with the account at the top line of the Account Title column. Account balances which require no adjusting entries may be extended directly from the Trial Balance columns to either the Income Statement or Balance Sheet columns. For example, Cash on Line 1 of the work sheet has a $400 debit balance in the Trial Balance column. Since there is no entry in the Adjustments columns for Cash, the $400 is extended to the Balance Sheet Debit column as an asset. The account balances on Lines 4, 5, 6, 7, 8, 9, 10, 11, and 13 of the work sheet are extended in a similar manner.

For accounts which were adjusted, the amount in the Trial Balance columns must be combined with the amount in the Adjustments columns and the resulting balance is then extended to the appropriate set of columns. For example, Office Supplies on Line 2 of the work sheet had a $170 debit balance in the Trial Balance columns and a $60 credit in the Adjustments columns. The amount extended to the Balance Sheet Debit column for Office Supplies is $110 ($170 debit − $60 credit). The account balance on Line 3 of the work sheet is extended in a similar manner. When the amount in the Trial Balance column and the amount in the Adjustments column are both debits (or both credits) they are added and the sum is extended. For example, Salary Expense, Line 12, had a $720 debit balance in the Trial Balance column and an $85 debit in the Adjustments columns. The amount extended to the Income Statement Debit column for Salary Expense is $805 ($720 debit + $85 debit).

Accounts listed below the Trial Balance column totals did not have a balance before the adjusting entries were made. Therefore, the amount of the adjustments to these accounts will also be the amount which is extended to either the Income Statement or Balance Sheet columns. For example, on Line 15 of the work sheet, Office Supplies Expense was debited in the Adjustments column for the $60 of supplies used during the period. This $60 expense was extended to the Income Statement Debit column. The account balances on Lines 16, 17, 18, and 19 are extended in a similar manner.

After all of the account balances are extended, the Income Statement columns and the Balance Sheet columns are totaled. If the credit side of the Income Statement columns is larger than the debit side, revenue is greater than expenses. This results in a net income for the period in the amount of the difference between the column totals. For example, in the work sheet on page 65 the computation of net income is as follows:

| | |
|---|---:|
| Total of credit column (revenue) | $2,700 |
| Total of debit column (expenses) | 1,455 |
| **Net income (excess of revenue over expenses)** | **$1,245** |

The amount of net income, $1,245, is then added to the Income Statement Debit column to indicate that the expenses plus net income are equal to the revenue. The $1,245 is then added to the credit side of the Balance Sheet columns because the net income represents an increase in owner's equity. If the work sheet has been prepared correctly, the total of the Balance Sheet Credit column after the net income has been added should equal the total of the Balance Sheet Debit column, thus proving that the increase in equity is equal to the increase in the net assets.

The totals for the four columns under the headings Income Statement and Balance Sheet are brought down to the same line, and the columns are ruled with double lines. Since the work sheet is normally used only by the accountant involved in summarizing the end-of-period information, it is customarily prepared in pencil and without dollar signs.

If the debit side of the Income Statement columns had been larger than the credit side, expenses would have been greater than revenue. This would have resulted in a net loss for the period. The amount of the net loss for the period would have been entered on the credit side of the Income Statement columns and transferred to the debit side of the Balance Sheet columns, representing a decrease in owner's equity.

## FINANCIAL STATEMENTS FROM THE WORK SHEET

The completed work sheet contains all of the information necessary to prepare the income statement and the balance sheet. In preparing the capital statement, it is also necessary to refer to the capital account in the ledger to determine the beginning balance and additional investments, if any, made during the period. The preparation of financial statements for Hull Delivery Service is discussed below.

### Income Statement

All of the information needed to prepare the income statement for Hull Delivery Service is found in the Income Statement columns of the work sheet on page 65. The Credit column contains the revenue for the month, Delivery Revenue $2,700. The Debit column lists the individual expenses for the period totaling $1,455. The income statement for Hull Delivery Service is presented below. The net income on the income statement, $1,245, is the same amount as that shown for net income on the work sheet.

**Hull Delivery Service**
**Income Statement**
**For Month Ended December 31, 1982**

| | | |
|---|---|---|
| Delivery revenue | | 2 700 00 |
| Expenses: | | |
| Salary expense | 805 00 | |
| Rent expense | 240 00 | |
| Depreciation expense — truck | 175 00 | |
| Utilities expense | 80 00 | |
| Office supplies expense | 60 00 | |
| Repairs expense | 60 00 | |
| Insurance expense | 35 00 | |
| Total expenses | | 1 455 00 |
| Net income | | 1 245 00 |

*Income Statement — Hull Delivery Service*

## Capital Statement

The second statement to be prepared is the capital statement. The capital statement includes the amount of net income reported on the Income Statement columns of the work sheet and the balances for Charles Hull, Capital and Charles Hull, Drawing from the Balance Sheet columns. It is also necessary to refer to the ledger account, Charles Hull, Capital (page 77) to determine if any additional investments were made during the period. Hull's capital account remained unchanged during the month of December; therefore, no additional investments were made.

The capital statement is prepared by listing the beginning capital balance of $6,490, adding the net income of $1,245 for the month, and subtracting withdrawals for the month, $200. The formal capital statement is presented below.

**Hull Delivery Service**
**Capital Statement**
**For Month Ended December 31, 1982**

| | | |
|---|---|---|
| Capital, December 1, 1982 | | 6 490 00 |
| Net income for the month | 1 245 00 | |
| Less withdrawals | 200 00 | |
| Increase in capital | | 1 045 00 |
| Capital, December 31, 1982 | | 7 535 00 |

*Capital Statement — Hull Delivery Service*

## Balance Sheet

The information necessary to prepare the balance sheet for Hull Delivery Service is found in the Balance Sheet columns of the work sheet. The ending capital balance of $7,535 on December 31, as shown in the capital statement, is also needed. The Balance Sheet Debit column in the work sheet contains the four assets to be included on the balance sheet. It also contains a $200 debit to Charles Hull, Drawing which has already been included in the capital statement. The Balance Sheet Credit column provides the liabilities of the company on December 31: Accounts Payable — Arnold Supply Co., $300; Accounts Payable — Horn Equipment Co., $1,200; and Salaries Payable, $85. The credit side also contains a credit to Accumulated Depreciation — Truck for $175, which is a contra asset account to be subtracted from the truck account in the asset section of the balance sheet, and a credit to Charles Hull, Capital, which has already been included in the capital statement.

The balance sheet for Hull Delivery Service at December 31 is presented at the top of page 70.

**Hull Delivery Service**
**Balance Sheet**
**December 31, 1982**

| | | |
|---|---|---|
| **Assets** | | |
| Cash | | 400 00 |
| Office supplies | | 110 00 |
| Prepaid insurance | | 385 00 |
| Truck | 8 400 00 | |
| Less accumulated depreciation | 175 00 | 8 225 00 |
| Total assets | | 9 120 00 |
| **Liabilities** | | |
| Accounts payable: | | |
| Arnold Supply Co. | 300 00 | |
| Horn Equipment Co. | 1 200 00 | 1 500 00 |
| Salaries payable | | 85 00 |
| Total liabilities | | 1 585 00 |
| **Owner's Equity** | | |
| Charles Hull, capital | | 7 535 00 |
| Total liabilities and owner's equity | | 9 120 00 |

*Balance Sheet — Hull Delivery Service*

After the financial statements have been prepared, the adjustments shown on the work sheet are recorded in the accounts to bring the ledger amounts into agreement with the financial statements. As is true with all entries, the adjusting entries must first be recorded in the journal and then posted to the ledger. The entries are recorded directly from the Adjustments columns of the work sheet to the next available space in the journal. The adjusting entries for Hull Delivery Service appear on page 62.

## QUESTIONS FOR DISCUSSION

1. What is the purpose of a work sheet?
2. Identify the column headings labeled A, B, C, and D in the eight-column work sheet below and describe the information which would be shown in each.

| A | | B | | C | | D | | |
|---|---|---|---|---|---|---|---|---|
| DEBIT | CREDIT | DEBIT | CREDIT | DEBIT | CREDIT | DEBIT | CREDIT | |
| | | | | | | | | 1 |
| | | | | | | | | 2 |
| | | | | | | | | 3 |
| | | | | | | | | 4 |

3. On the work sheet of Ned Schwartz, the debit side of the Income Statement columns is larger than the credit side. Explain what this means. How will the amount be shown in the Balance Sheet columns? Why?

4. Can the capital statement always be prepared directly from the work sheet? Explain.

5. Accumulated Depreciation in the Balance Sheet columns of the work sheet is $350 larger than in the Trial Balance columns of the work sheet. Explain how this is possible.

6. Some accounts appear in the Income Statement and Balance Sheet columns of the work sheet which do not appear in the Trial Balance columns. Explain the cause of this and give two examples of such accounts.

## EXERCISES

1. Below are given selected account balances in the Trial Balance columns (before adjustment) and the balances in the Balance Sheet columns of the Sahara Company work sheet prepared December 31.

| | Trial Balance | | Balance Sheet | |
|---|---|---|---|---|
| | Dr. | Cr. | Dr. | Cr. |
| Store Supplies | 275 | | 130 | |
| Prepaid Rent | 375 | | 250 | |
| Accumulated Depreciation — Furniture | | 900 | | 1,100 |
| Salaries Payable | — | — | | 235 |

By analyzing the changes in the account balances shown, prepare the adjusting entries that were made for Sahara Company at the end of the current year.

2. The totals for the Income Statement columns and the Balance Sheet columns of the work sheet for the Tonya Company as of June 30 are as follows:

| Income Statement | | Balance Sheet | |
|---|---|---|---|
| Dr. | Cr. | Dr. | Cr. |
| 17,430 | 21,670 | 56,290 | 52,050 |

On a separate sheet of paper, balance and total the columns and label any significant amount.

3. If the Balance Sheet columns for Tonya Company in Exercise 2 also showed a debit balance for Tonya Dean, Drawing of $600 and a credit balance for Tonya Dean, Capital of $31,090, prepare a capital statement for Tonya Company for the six months ended June 30, assuming that there were no additional investments during the period.

## ASSIGNMENT 4-B

**Tear out pages 387–394 and complete Assignment 4-B. After completion, continue with the study of the following discussion until Assignment 4-C is required.**

# PART C CLOSING ENTRIES, POST-CLOSING TRIAL BALANCE, AND SUMMARY OF ACCOUNTING CYCLE

As was explained in Chapter 2, to obtain the maximum benefit from the accounting records, the proprietor must maintain separate ledger accounts to show the detailed causes of the change in owner's equity during the period. To provide the necessary information, individual revenue and expense accounts and a drawing account are maintained. At the end of the fiscal period, after the revenue and expense accounts have been used to prepare the income statement, the balances in these temporary capital accounts should be reduced to zero so that they may be used to record the revenue and expenses for the next period. It is also necessary for the net effect of these accounts, including drawing, to be transferred to the capital account so that its balance may properly reflect the amount of owner's equity at the end of the accounting period.

## THE CLOSING PROCESS

Both of these objectives, reducing the temporary account balances to zero and transferring this information in summary form to the capital account, are accomplished by a process called the *closing process*. The entries made are called *closing entries*. This section explains and illustrates the closing process, includes the preparation of a trial balance after the closing entries have been made, and summarizes all of the steps in the accounting cycle.

Rather than transfer each revenue and expense account balance directly to the capital account, thereby creating an undesirable amount of detail in the capital account, a summary account is used to facilitate the closing process. This summary account is titled Income Summary. The income summary account is used only at the end of the accounting period and is opened and closed during the closing process. This account is sometimes called Revenue and Expense Summary or Profit and Loss Summary.

The procedure to close the temporary accounts consists of the following four steps:

1. Close each revenue account to Income Summary.
2. Close each expense account to Income Summary.
3. Close Income Summary to the capital account.
4. Close the drawing account to the capital account.

The closing procedure for Hull Delivery Service as of December 31, 1982, is illustrated below and through page 75.

(1) Close the revenue account to Income Summary. Since Delivery Revenue has a credit balance, a debit to this account is required to obtain a zero balance. Income Summary is credited.

| Date | Description | Post. Ref. | Debit | Credit |
|---|---|---|---|---|
| 31 | Delivery Revenue | | 2,700 00 | |
| | Income Summary | | | 2,700 00 |
| | To close revenue account. | | | |

This entry transfers the credit balance in Delivery Revenue to the credit side of Income Summary:

| INCOME SUMMARY | | | (33) |
|---|---|---|---|
| | | Dec. 31 | 2,700 |

| DELIVERY REVENUE | | | (41) |
|---|---|---|---|
| Dec. 31 | 2,700 | Dec. 1 | 600 |
| | | 10 | 600 |
| | | 20 | 700 |
| | | 30 | 800 |
| | | | *2,700* |

(2) Close all expense accounts to Income Summary. Since the expense accounts all have debit balances, they have to be credited to obtain zero balances. The Income Summary account is debited for the total of all the credits to the expense accounts.

| Date | Description | Post. Ref. | Debit | Credit |
|---|---|---|---|---|
| 31 | Income Summary | | 1,455 00 | |
| | Depreciation Expense — Truck | | | 175 00 |
| | Insurance Expense | | | 35 00 |
| | Office Supplies Expense | | | 60 00 |
| | Rent Expense | | | 240 00 |
| | Repairs Expense | | | 60 00 |
| | Salary Expense | | | 805 00 |
| | Utilities Expense | | | 80 00 |
| | To close expense accounts. | | | |

This entry transfers the debit balances in the expense accounts to the debit side of Income Summary as shown in the illustration below:

| DEPRECIATION EXPENSE — TRUCK | | | (51) |
|---|---|---|---|
| Dec. 31 | 175 | Dec. 31 | 175 |

| INSURANCE EXPENSE | | | (52) |
|---|---|---|---|
| Dec. 31 | 35 | Dec. 31 | 35 |

| OFFICE SUPPLIES EXPENSE | | | (53) |
|---|---|---|---|
| Dec. 31 | 60 | Dec. 31 | 60 |

| RENT EXPENSE | | | (54) |
|---|---|---|---|
| Dec. 1 | 240 | Dec. 31 | 240 |

| REPAIRS EXPENSE | | | (55) |
|---|---|---|---|
| Dec. 11 | 60 | Dec. 31 | 60 |

| SALARY EXPENSE | | | (56) |
|---|---|---|---|
| Dec. 1 | 70 | Dec. 31 | 805 |
| 8 | 135 | | |
| 15 | 180 | | |
| 22 | 165 | | |
| 29 | 170 | | |
| 31 | 85 | | |
| | *805* | | |

| UTILITIES EXPENSE | | | (57) |
|---|---|---|---|
| Dec. 17 | 80 | Dec. 31 | 80 |

| INCOME SUMMARY | | | (33) |
|---|---|---|---|
| Dec. 31 | 1,455 | Dec. 31 | 2,700 |
| | | Balance *1,245* | |

After the revenue and expenses have been closed to the income summary account, its balance represents the net income or the net loss (if expenses exceed revenue) for the period. The T-account below shows the relationship between the amounts appearing in the income summary account.

| INCOME SUMMARY | | | (33) |
|---|---|---|---|
| **Expenses** | **1,455** | **Revenue** | **2,700** |
| | | **Net Income** *1,245* | |

(3) Close Income Summary to the owner's capital account. The only purpose of the income summary account is to facilitate the closing of revenue and expenses to the capital account. By summarizing this information in one account and then closing its balance to the capital account, the net income or net loss for the period is represented. Once the revenue and expenses have been closed to Income Summary, this account has served its purpose and can be closed to the capital account as shown by the following journal entry and the posting to the ledger accounts.

| Date | Account | Debit | Credit |
|---|---|---|---|
| 31 | **Income Summary** | **1 245 00** | |
| | **Charles Hull, Capital** | | **1 245 00** |
| | **To close summary account.** | | |

| CHARLES HULL, CAPITAL | | | (31) |
|---|---|---|---|
| | | Dec. 1 Bal. | 6,490 |
| | | 31 | **1,245** |

| INCOME SUMMARY | | | (33) |
|---|---|---|---|
| Dec. 31 | 1,455 | Dec. 31 | 2,700 |
| 31 | **1,245** | | |

(4) Close the drawing account to the capital account. The drawing account is a temporary proprietorship account, but it is neither a revenue nor an expense account. Therefore, this account is closed directly to the capital account by a separate entry. The entry to close Hull's drawing account is as follows:

| Date | Account | Debit | Credit |
|---|---|---|---|
| 31 | **Charles Hull, Capital** | **200 00** | |
| | **Charles Hull, Drawing** | | **200 00** |
| | **To close drawing account.** | | |

This entry completes the closing process of transferring all the temporary account balances to the capital account. The net income for the period, represented by the balance in Income Summary, increases capital, and the drawing account balance decreases capital. When these changes are applied to the beginning capital balance, plus any additional investments that may have been made during this period, the capital account reflects the balance as of the end of the period. Hull's capital account is now in agreement with the ending capital balance of $7,535 as shown on the balance sheet on page 70.

| CHARLES HULL, DRAWING | | | (32) |
|---|---|---|---|
| Dec. 18 | 200 | Dec. 31 | **200** |

| CHARLES HULL, CAPITAL | | | (31) |
|---|---|---|---|
| Dec. 31 | **200** | Dec. 1 Bal. | 6,490 |
| | | 31 | 1,245 |
| | | *7,535* | *7,735* |

The information needed to prepare the closing entries may be obtained from the work sheet, the income statement, and the capital statement, or directly from the ledger accounts. An advantage of using the work sheet as the source of this information is that all of the needed data appear in one place. The amounts shown in the Income Statement columns reflect the balances of the revenue and expense accounts and may be used in preparing the first two closing entries. The amount of net income or net loss appears at the bottom of the Income Statement and Balance Sheet columns and is used for the entry to close Income Summary. The drawing account balance is shown in the Balance Sheet Debit column and may be used in recording the last closing entry.

The closing entries for Hull Delivery Service as they would appear in a general journal are shown below. As was the case for adjusting entries, no individual explanation is needed for each closing entry when they are journalized as a group. The heading "Closing Entries" is sufficient explanation. The accounts to which these closing entries are posted are shown in the ledger of Hull Delivery Service on pages 76 to 78. For illustration purposes, all adjusting and closing entries are identified in the Item column of the accounts. This procedure is not necessary in actual practice.

**JOURNAL** PAGE 4

| DATE | | DESCRIPTION | POST. REF. | DEBIT | | CREDIT | |
|---|---|---|---|---|---|---|---|
| 1982 | | **Closing Entries** | | | | | |
| Dec. | 31 | Delivery Revenue | 41 | 2 700 | 00 | | |
| | | Income Summary | 33 | | | 2 700 | 00 |
| | 31 | Income Summary | 33 | 1 455 | 00 | | |
| | | Depreciation Expense — Truck | 51 | | | 175 | 00 |
| | | Insurance Expense | 52 | | | 35 | 00 |
| | | Office Supplies Expense | 53 | | | 60 | 00 |
| | | Rent Expense | 54 | | | 240 | 00 |
| | | Repairs Expense | 55 | | | 60 | 00 |
| | | Salary Expense | 56 | | | 805 | 00 |
| | | Utilities Expense | 57 | | | 80 | 00 |
| | 31 | Income Summary | 33 | 1 245 | 00 | | |
| | | Charles Hull, Capital | 31 | | | 1 245 | 00 |
| | 31 | Charles Hull, Capital | 31 | 200 | 00 | | |
| | | Charles Hull, Drawing | 32 | | | 200 | 00 |

*Closing Entries — Hull Delivery Service*

## Four-Column Account Form

The four-column ledger account form is utilized in the general ledger of Hull Delivery Service. The T-account form presented earlier in the text emphasizes the contrast between debit and credit entries. This is the major reason why the T-account form was used as an introduction to the concept of debits and credits in the ledger.

The four-column form is widely used in businesses today. The main advantage of the four-column form is that it clearly displays the amount and the debit-credit nature of account balances. This feature also reduces possible confusion and errors in determining account balances.

ACCOUNT **Cash** ACCOUNT NO. **11**

| DATE | | ITEM | POST. REF. | DEBIT | CREDIT | BALANCE DEBIT | BALANCE CREDIT |
|---|---|---|---|---|---|---|---|
| 1982 | | | | | | | |
| Dec. | 1 | Balance | √ | | | 420 00 | |
| | 1 | | J2 | 600 00 | | 1 020 00 | |
| | 1 | | J2 | | 420 00 | 600 00 | |
| | 1 | | J2 | | 240 00 | 360 00 | |
| | 1 | | J2 | | 70 00 | 290 00 | |
| | 8 | | J2 | | 135 00 | 155 00 | |
| | 10 | | J2 | 600 00 | | 755 00 | |
| | 11 | | J2 | | 60 00 | 695 00 | |
| | 15 | | J2 | | 180 00 | 515 00 | |
| | 17 | | J2 | | 80 00 | 435 00 | |
| | 20 | | J2 | 700 00 | | 1 135 00 | |
| | 22 | | J2 | | 165 00 | 970 00 | |
| | 29 | | J2 | | 170 00 | 800 00 | |
| | 30 | | J2 | 800 00 | | 1 600 00 | |
| | 30 | | J2 | | 1 000 00 | 600 00 | |
| | 30 | | J2 | | 200 00 | 400 00 | |

ACCOUNT **Office Supplies** ACCOUNT NO. **12**

| DATE | | ITEM | POST. REF. | DEBIT | CREDIT | BALANCE DEBIT | BALANCE CREDIT |
|---|---|---|---|---|---|---|---|
| 1982 | | | | | | | |
| Dec. | 1 | Balance | √ | | | 120 00 | |
| | 14 | | J2 | 50 00 | | 170 00 | |
| | 31 | Adjusting | J3 | | 60 00 | 110 00 | |

ACCOUNT **Prepaid Insurance** ACCOUNT NO. **13**

| DATE | | ITEM | POST. REF. | DEBIT | CREDIT | BALANCE DEBIT | BALANCE CREDIT |
|---|---|---|---|---|---|---|---|
| 1982 | | | | | | | |
| Dec. | 1 | | J2 | 420 00 | | 420 00 | |
| | 31 | Adjusting | J3 | | 35 00 | 385 00 | |

ACCOUNT **Truck** ACCOUNT NO. **14**

| DATE | | ITEM | POST. REF. | DEBIT | CREDIT | BALANCE DEBIT | BALANCE CREDIT |
|---|---|---|---|---|---|---|---|
| 1982 | | | | | | | |
| Dec. | 1 | Balance | √ | | | 8 400 00 | |

ACCOUNT **Accumulated Depreciation — Truck** ACCOUNT NO. **14.1**

| DATE | | ITEM | POST. REF. | DEBIT | CREDIT | BALANCE DEBIT | BALANCE CREDIT |
|---|---|---|---|---|---|---|---|
| 1982 | | | | | | | |
| Dec. | 31 | Adjusting | J3 | | 175 00 | | 175 00 |

***Four-Column General Ledger — Hull Delivery Service***

**ACCOUNT** Accounts Payable — Arnold Supply Co. **ACCOUNT NO.** 21

| DATE | | ITEM | POST. REF. | DEBIT | CREDIT | BALANCE | |
|---|---|---|---|---|---|---|---|
| | | | | | | DEBIT | CREDIT |
| 1982 | | | | | | | |
| Dec. | 1 | Balance | √ | | | | 250 00 |
| | 14 | | J2 | | 50 00 | | 300 00 |

**ACCOUNT** Accounts Payable — Horn Equipment Co. **ACCOUNT NO.** 22

| DATE | | ITEM | POST. REF. | DEBIT | CREDIT | BALANCE | |
|---|---|---|---|---|---|---|---|
| | | | | | | DEBIT | CREDIT |
| 1982 | | | | | | | |
| Dec. | 1 | Balance | √ | | | | 2 200 00 |
| | 30 | | J2 | 1 000 00 | | | 1 200 00 |

**ACCOUNT** Salaries Payable **ACCOUNT NO.** 23

| DATE | | ITEM | POST. REF. | DEBIT | CREDIT | BALANCE | |
|---|---|---|---|---|---|---|---|
| | | | | | | DEBIT | CREDIT |
| 1982 | | | | | | | |
| Dec. | 31 | Adjusting | J3 | | 85 00 | | 85 00 |

**ACCOUNT** Charles Hull, Capital **ACCOUNT NO.** 31

| DATE | | ITEM | POST. REF. | DEBIT | CREDIT | BALANCE | |
|---|---|---|---|---|---|---|---|
| | | | | | | DEBIT | CREDIT |
| 1982 | | | | | | | |
| Dec. | 1 | Balance | √ | | | | 6 490 00 |
| | 31 | Closing | J4 | | 1 245 00 | | 7 735 00 |
| | 31 | Closing | J4 | 200 00 | | | 7 535 00 |

**ACCOUNT** Charles Hull, Drawing **ACCOUNT NO.** 32

| DATE | | ITEM | POST. REF. | DEBIT | CREDIT | BALANCE | |
|---|---|---|---|---|---|---|---|
| | | | | | | DEBIT | CREDIT |
| 1982 | | | | | | | |
| Dec. | 30 | | J2 | 200 00 | | 200 00 | |
| | 31 | Closing | J4 | | 200 00 | — | — |

**ACCOUNT** Income Summary **ACCOUNT NO.** 33

| DATE | | ITEM | POST. REF. | DEBIT | CREDIT | BALANCE | |
|---|---|---|---|---|---|---|---|
| | | | | | | DEBIT | CREDIT |
| 1982 | | | | | | | |
| Dec. | 31 | Closing | J4 | | 2 700 00 | | 2 700 00 |
| | 31 | Closing | J4 | 1 455 00 | | | 1 245 00 |
| | 31 | Closing | J4 | 1 245 00 | | — | — |

**ACCOUNT** Delivery Revenue **ACCOUNT NO.** 41

| DATE | | ITEM | POST. REF. | DEBIT | CREDIT | BALANCE | |
|---|---|---|---|---|---|---|---|
| | | | | | | DEBIT | CREDIT |
| 1982 | | | | | | | |
| Dec. | 1 | | J2 | | 600 00 | | 600 00 |
| | 10 | | J2 | | 600 00 | | 1 200 00 |
| | 20 | | J2 | | 700 00 | | 1 900 00 |
| | 30 | | J2 | | 800 00 | | 2 700 00 |
| | 31 | Closing | J4 | 2 700 00 | | — | — |

*Four-Column General Ledger —Hull Delivery Service (continued)*

ACCOUNT **Depreciation Expense — Truck** ACCOUNT NO. **51**

| DATE | | ITEM | POST. REF. | DEBIT | CREDIT | BALANCE DEBIT | BALANCE CREDIT |
|---|---|---|---|---|---|---|---|
| 1982 | | | | | | | |
| Dec. | 31 | Adjusting | J3 | 175 00 | | 175 00 | |
| | 31 | Closing | J4 | | 175 00 | — | — |

ACCOUNT **Insurance Expense** ACCOUNT NO. **52**

| DATE | | ITEM | POST. REF. | DEBIT | CREDIT | BALANCE DEBIT | BALANCE CREDIT |
|---|---|---|---|---|---|---|---|
| 1982 | | | | | | | |
| Dec. | 31 | Adjusting | J3 | 35 00 | | 35 00 | |
| | 31 | Closing | J4 | | 35 00 | — | — |

ACCOUNT **Office Supplies Expense** ACCOUNT NO. **53**

| DATE | | ITEM | POST. REF. | DEBIT | CREDIT | BALANCE DEBIT | BALANCE CREDIT |
|---|---|---|---|---|---|---|---|
| 1982 | | | | | | | |
| Dec. | 31 | Adjusting | J3 | 60 00 | | 60 00 | |
| | 31 | Closing | J4 | | 60 00 | — | — |

ACCOUNT **Rent Expense** ACCOUNT NO. **54**

| DATE | | ITEM | POST. REF. | DEBIT | CREDIT | BALANCE DEBIT | BALANCE CREDIT |
|---|---|---|---|---|---|---|---|
| 1982 | | | | | | | |
| Dec. | 1 | | J2 | 240 00 | | 240 00 | |
| | 31 | Closing | J4 | | 240 00 | — | — |

ACCOUNT **Repairs Expense** ACCOUNT NO. **55**

| DATE | | ITEM | POST. REF. | DEBIT | CREDIT | BALANCE DEBIT | BALANCE CREDIT |
|---|---|---|---|---|---|---|---|
| 1982 | | | | | | | |
| Dec. | 11 | | J2 | 60 00 | | 60 00 | |
| | 31 | Closing | J4 | | 60 00 | — | — |

ACCOUNT **Salary Expense** ACCOUNT NO. **56**

| DATE | | ITEM | POST. REF. | DEBIT | CREDIT | BALANCE DEBIT | BALANCE CREDIT |
|---|---|---|---|---|---|---|---|
| 1982 | | | | | | | |
| Dec. | 1 | | J2 | 70 00 | | 70 00 | |
| | 8 | | J2 | 135 00 | | 205 00 | |
| | 15 | | J2 | 180 00 | | 385 00 | |
| | 22 | | J2 | 165 00 | | 550 00 | |
| | 29 | | J2 | 170 00 | | 720 00 | |
| | 31 | Adjusting | J3 | 85 00 | | 805 00 | |
| | 31 | Closing | J4 | | 805 00 | — | — |

ACCOUNT **Utilities Expense** ACCOUNT NO. **57**

| DATE | | ITEM | POST. REF. | DEBIT | CREDIT | BALANCE DEBIT | BALANCE CREDIT |
|---|---|---|---|---|---|---|---|
| 1982 | | | | | | | |
| Dec. | 17 | | J2 | 80 00 | | 80 00 | |
| | 31 | Closing | J4 | | 80 00 | — | — |

***Four-Column General Ledger — Hull Delivery Service (concluded)***

## POST-CLOSING TRIAL BALANCE

The final step in the accounting cycle is the preparation of a *post-closing trial balance*. The purpose of a post-closing trial balance is to insure that the debits and credits in the ledger are still in balance after the adjusting and closing procedures have been completed. The accounts and amounts shown on the post-closing trial balance are the same as those shown on the balance sheet. The post-closing trial balance on December 31 for Hull Delivery Service is shown below.

**Hull Delivery Service**
**Post-Closing Trial Balance**
**December 31, 1982**

| Account | Debit | Credit |
|---|---|---|
| Cash | 400 00 | |
| Office Supplies | 110 00 | |
| Prepaid Insurance | 385 00 | |
| Truck | 8 400 00 | |
| Accumulated Depreciation — Truck | | 175 00 |
| Accounts Payable — Arnold Supply Co. | | 300 00 |
| Accounts Payable — Horn Equipment Co. | | 1 200 00 |
| Salaries Payable | | 85 00 |
| Charles Hull, Capital | | 7 535 00 |
| | 9 295 00 | 9 295 00 |

***Post-Closing Trial Balance — Hull Delivery Service***

## SUMMARY OF THE ACCOUNTING CYCLE

The sequence of accounting procedures for a business enterprise is essentially the same from period to period. This sequence of performing the accounting procedures on a repetitive basis is called the *accounting cycle*. The sequence of the procedures involved in the accounting cycle is as follows:

1. Journalize the transactions.
2. Post to the ledger accounts.
3. Prepare a trial balance.
4. Accumulate the information necessary to adjust the accounts.
5. Complete the work sheet.
6. Prepare the financial statements.
7. Journalize and post the adjusting entries.
8. Journalize and post the closing entries.
9. Prepare a post-closing trial balance.

It is important to realize that Steps 3 through 9 of the accounting cycle are assumed to be performed as of the last day of the accounting period. The accountant may not actually be able to perform these steps at that time. It may take several days following the close of the accounting period to assemble the information necessary to complete the accounting cycle. Even so, the work sheet, financial statements, and adjusting and closing entries are dated as of the last day of the accounting period. The transactions for the new period are recorded in the journal in the usual manner. However, none of these entries will be posted to the ledger until the accounting cycle for the period just ended has been completed.

## QUESTIONS FOR DISCUSSION

1. What are the reasons for preparing closing entries at the end of the period?
2. What three types of accounts are closed at the end of the period?
3. Name the four steps in the closing process.
4. Where will the income summary account be shown in the financial statements? Explain.
5. What is the purpose of the post-closing trial balance?
6. (a) Name the steps involved in the accounting cycle. (b) When are most of these steps performed?

## EXERCISES

1. The following are the Income Statement columns of the work sheet for Spain Company for the month ended September 30.

| | Income Statement Dr. | Income Statement Cr. |
|---|---|---|
| Service Revenue | | 1,830 |
| Salary Expense | 960 | |
| Rent Expense | 180 | |
| Depreciation Expense | 75 | |
| Advertising Expense | 60 | |
| Office Supplies Expense | 45 | |
| Miscellaneous Expense | 20 | |
| | 1,340 | 1,830 |
| | 490 | |
| | 1,830 | 1,830 |

The work sheet also reflects the following balances: Sally Spain, Drawing, $150; Sally Spain, Capital, $3,880. Prepare the necessary closing entries for Spain Company at September 30.

2. Using the information in Exercise 1, prepare a capital statement for Spain Company for the month ended September 30, assuming no additional investments were made by Spain during the month.

3. Using the format illustrated below, indicate which of the following accounts will normally appear in a post-closing trial balance.

| | Yes | No |
|---|---|---|
| a. Cleaning Supplies | | |
| b. Miscellaneous Expense | | |
| c. John Grubbs, Drawing | | |
| d. Cleaning Equipment | | |
| e. Cleaning Revenue | | |
| f. Accounts Payable | | |
| g. John Grubbs, Capital | | |
| h. Income Summary | | |
| i. Salaries Payable | | |
| j. Accumulated Depreciation — Cleaning Equipment | | |

## ASSIGNMENT 4-C

**Tear out pages 395–402 and complete Assignment 4-C. If you have any difficulty completing this assignment, a review of the material in this chapter is necessary. After completion, proceed to the textbook discussion in Chapter 5.**

Chapter **5**

# ACCOUNTING FOR CASH

The first four chapters contained a presentation of the basic elements of the accounting cycle. Beginning with this chapter, a more detailed discussion of accounting for some of the specific asset, liability, and owner's equity items will be presented. This chapter contains a discussion of control and accounting procedures for the asset cash.

*Cash* includes bank deposits, currency and coin, checks, money orders, and traveler's checks. These represent monetary items that are available to meet current obligations of the business. A single cash account often includes both cash on hand and cash in banks. Sometimes separate accounts are maintained: Cash on Hand and Cash in Bank. The cash account or accounts appear as assets on the balance sheet.

For most businesses there are many transactions that involve receiving or paying cash, so there is a strong possibility of making an error in recording these transactions. Also, the desirability of cash creates a need for adequate protection against mishandling. Consequently, there is a need for a system of control to assure that all cash transactions are properly accounted for and that cash is adequately protected.

Although control over cash is normally only a small portion of an overall *system of internal control* for a business, the discussion in this chapter is limited to cash. There are four basic elements in a good system of internal control of cash:

1. Separation of custody and accounting functions.
2. Deposit on a daily basis of all cash received.
3. A system of authorization for all disbursements of cash.
4. An internal audit function.

If good accounting control is established over all cash at the time it first enters the business, the separation of handling of and accounting for cash is simplified. When one individual has custodial responsibility for the cash and another individual has accounting responsibility, the possibility of error in recording transactions and the opportunity for undetected misappropriations are greatly reduced.

When all cash receipts are deposited in a bank, the bank's record of deposits may be compared with the business accounting records, thus providing two separate sets of accounts for the same transactions. If the system provides proper control and accountability for all cash and if all cash is deposited in the bank, then adequate protection can be established to assure that cash is disbursed only with proper approval for necessary business purposes. Usually such control is achieved by requiring that all payments be made by check. Checks are signed only by designated individuals who are responsible for determining that the disbursements were properly approved in advance.

The internal audit function may include, but is not limited to, activities such as surprise counts of cash on hand, examination of cash-related transactions, checking of documents supporting cash disbursements, and comparing of bank records with the business records. These activities are discussed in more detail in this chapter.

## PART A RECORDING CASH

In most businesses the number of transactions involving cash are very large in relation to other types of transactions. All transactions previously discussed, including those for cash, have been recorded in a two-column general journal. In businesses where the number of cash transactions is small, a general journal may be all that is needed. However, in businesses where the number of cash transactions is large, the numerous postings of debits and credits to the cash account would be time-consuming and would increase the probability of errors. To eliminate these problems, many companies use a 4-column general journal.

### FOUR-COLUMN GENERAL JOURNAL

The four-column general journal is designed to summarize the cash transactions by providing two additional columns to be used exclusively for cash debits and cash credits. An illustration of this form is shown below.

**JOURNAL**

| | CASH | | DATE | DESCRIPTION | POST. REF. | GENERAL | | |
|---|---|---|---|---|---|---|---|---|
| | DEBIT | CREDIT | | | | DEBIT | CREDIT | |
| 1 | | | | | | | | 1 |
| 2 | | | | | | | | 2 |
| 3 | | | | | | | | 3 |
| 4 | | | | | | | | 4 |
| 5 | | | | | | | | 5 |

*Four-Column Journal*

This journal is similar to the two-column journal except that two additional amount columns have been added to the left side of the page to be used only for recording debits and credits to Cash. The two General amount columns on the right side of the page are to be used for all amounts to be posted to other accounts. The transactions of Hull Delivery Service are recorded in the four-column journal on page 83.

| JOURNAL | | | | | PAGE 2 | |
|---|---|---|---|---|---|---|
| CASH | | DATE | DESCRIPTION | POST. REF. | GENERAL | |
| DEBIT | CREDIT | | | | DEBIT | CREDIT |
| 600 00 | | 1982 Dec. 1 | Delivery Revenue | 41 | | 600 00 |
| | 420 00 | 1 | Prepaid Insurance | 13 | 420 00 | |
| | 240 00 | 1 | Rent Expense | 54 | 240 00 | |
| | 70 00 | 1 | Salary Expense | 56 | 70 00 | |
| | 135 00 | 8 | Salary Expense | 56 | 135 00 | |
| 600 00 | | 10 | Delivery Revenue | 41 | | 600 00 |
| | 60 00 | 11 | Repairs Expense | 55 | 60 00 | |
| | | 14 | Office Supplies | 12 | 50 00 | |
| | | | Accts. Pay.—Arnold Supply Co. | 21 | | 50 00 |
| | 180 00 | 15 | Salary Expense | 56 | 180 00 | |
| | 80 00 | 17 | Utilities Expense | 57 | 80 00 | |
| 700 00 | | 20 | Delivery Revenue | 41 | | 700 00 |
| | 165 00 | 22 | Salary Expense | 56 | 165 00 | |
| | 170 00 | 29 | Salary Expense | 56 | 170 00 | |
| 800 00 | | 30 | Delivery Revenue | 41 | | 800 00 |
| | 1 000 00 | 30 | Accounts Payable—Horn Equip. Co. | 22 | 1 000 00 | |
| | 200 00 | 30 | Charles Hull, Drawing | 32 | 200 00 | |
| 2 700 00 | 2 720 00 | | | | 2 770 00 | 2 750 00 |
| 2 700 00 | 2 720 00 | | | | 2 770 00 | 2 750 00 |
| (11) | (11) | | | | (✓) | (✓) |

*Four-Column Journal — Hull Delivery Service*

## Cash Columns

In each transaction that involves the cash account (either a debit or a credit), the name of the account to receive the related debit or credit is written at the left margin of the Description column. Only one line is used and no indentation is made. When Cash is debited in the Cash columns, the related account listed in the Description column is credited in the General columns, and vice versa.

## General Columns

Transactions that do not involve cash are recorded in the same manner as they are in a two-column journal. The account debited is written at the left margin of the Description column and the amount is recorded in the General Debit column. The account credited is indented 1.2 cm in the Description column and the amount is recorded in the General Credit column. For example, see the entry for the purchase of office supplies on December 14.

Explanations are not given immediately below each entry because most transactions are self-explanatory. For example, the second entry on December 1 is obviously the payment of insurance premiums. Additional information about the transaction could easily be obtained by referring to the insurance policy. If an explanation is needed, it may be shown on the line immediately below the transaction in the same manner as in a two-column journal. If the explanation is brief, it may be shown parenthetically on the same line. For example, it might be desirable to indicate that the insurance policy is for two years by using the notation (two-year policy).

## Posting Reference Column

As will be explained later, the Posting Reference column is completed at the time the accounts are posted to the ledger, not during the journalizing process.

## Proving the Four-Column Journal

```
2,700·00+
2,770·00+
5,470·00*

2,720·00+
2,750·00+
5,470·00*
```

***Adding Machine Tape — Proof of Journal Footings***

Because there is more than one column each for debits and for credits, the equality of debits and credits in the journal must be proved at the end of the month before any postings to the ledger are made. The journal on page 83 would be *proved* by first totaling each amount column and recording these totals in small pencil figures immediately below the last entry. These small pencil figures are commonly called *footings*. Then the equality of debits and credits would be determined by comparing the sum of the Debit columns to the sum of the Credit columns. If these sums are not equal, the journal entries must be reviewed and the errors corrected.

The adding machine tape illustrated at the left was prepared to prove the equality of the Debit and Credit columns for the four-column journal of Hull Delivery Service. Note that the Debit columns ($2,700 + $2,770) equal $5,470 and the Credit columns ($2,720 + $2,750) also equal $5,470.

## Ruling the Four-Column Journal

The four-column journal should be footed, proved, and ruled at the end of each month. After having been proved, the totals should be recorded in ink on the same horizontal line immediately below the pencil footings. A single line should be drawn across all amount columns immediately above the totals, and double lines should be drawn below all amount columns.

If more than one journal page is required during the month, no entry should be made on the last line of each completed page. This line is used to record the column totals. "Balances Carried Forward" is written in the Description column. The column totals are entered in pencil until the footings have been proved, after which the totals are written in ink. The column totals are then entered on the first line of the new page and "Balances Carried Forward" is written in the Description column. A check mark (√) should be placed in the Posting Reference column to indicate that no posting is required.

## Posting the Four-Column Journal

The purpose of the four-column journal is to provide special columns for debits and credits to Cash. Therefore, the only amounts appearing in the Cash Debit column are increases in cash and the only amounts appearing in the Cash Credit column are decreases in cash. Because these special columns include only one type of transaction, it is not necessary to post each individual debit or credit to Cash. The posting from these columns is *by totals*, at daily, weekly, or monthly intervals. For example, instead of posting individually the four debits to Cash, page 83, the amounts are totaled and posted as one debit to the Debit column of the cash account in the ledger. The eleven credits to Cash are also totaled and posted as one credit to the Credit column of the cash account. There could be hundreds of debits and credits to Cash for the month, and they still would be totaled in the four-column journal and posted as only one debit and one credit to the cash account in the ledger. When the totals of the Cash columns are posted, the ledger account number for Cash, (11), is shown in parentheses as a posting reference immediately below the column totals. The cash account for Hull Delivery Service would appear as follows after posting the four-column journal on page 83.

ACCOUNT **Cash** ACCOUNT NO. **11**

| DATE | | ITEM | POST. REF. | DEBIT | CREDIT | BALANCE DEBIT | BALANCE CREDIT |
|---|---|---|---|---|---|---|---|
| 1982 Dec. | 1 | Balance | √ | 420 00 | | 420 00 | |
| | 31 | | J2 | 2 700 00 | | 3 120 00 | |
| | 31 | | J2 | | 2 720 00 | 400 00 | |

The procedure for posting the items in the General Debit and General Credit columns is the same as for the two-column journal. The items are posted individually to the appropriate ledger accounts. The posting of these individual accounts may be done as often as is convenient, but the date of the transaction is always the date recorded in the ledger account. When the posting is made from these General columns, the ledger account number to which the amount is posted should be entered in the Posting Reference column. A check mark (√) is shown in parentheses below the General Debit and General Credit columns to indicate that these columns are not posted in total.

The adjusting and closing entries would be recorded in the four-column journal below the column totals which have been ruled and posted. Since neither the adjusting nor the closing entries affect cash, they would be recorded in the General Debit and General Credit columns in exactly the same manner as they would appear in a two-column journal. After the adjusting and closing entries have been posted to the individual accounts, the journal would once again be totaled and proved to insure the equality of debits and credits. All amount columns would be ruled with double lines to prepare the journal for the new period.

## COMBINED CASH JOURNAL

The *combined cash journal* is an expanded four-column journal which includes special columns for other frequently used accounts in addition to Cash. For example, the transactions for the Hull Delivery Service during the month of December included five entries involving Salary Expense. Similarly, the delivery revenue account was utilized four times during the month. In some instances, revenue may even be recorded on a daily basis. Special columns for such frequently used accounts may be desirable. An illustration of the combined cash journal for Hull Delivery Service with special columns for Delivery Revenue and Salary Expense, in addition to the Cash Debit, Cash Credit, and two General columns is shown below.

The combined cash journal has all of the basic characteristics of any book of original entry: (1) Debit and Credit columns to record the amount of each transaction; (2) a Check Number column to record the number of each check issued since all payments recorded in the combined cash journal were made by check (this number is helpful if the accountant wishes to trace the transaction to the check stub and the canceled check); (3) a Day column to show the date of the transaction; (4) a Description column to record the titles of the accounts affected and an explanation if necessary (a check mark signifies there is a special column for the account; therefore the account title need not be written); and (5) a Posting Reference column to indicate the ledger account to which each item was posted.

PAGE 1 — COMBINED CASH JOURNAL

| CASH DEBIT 11 | CASH CREDIT 11 | CK. NO. | DAY | DESCRIPTION | POST. REF. |
|---|---|---|---|---|---|
| 600 00 | | | 1 | ✓ | ✓ |
| | 420 00 | 125 | 1 | Prepaid Insurance | 13 |
| | 240 00 | 126 | 1 | Rent Expense | 54 |
| | 70 00 | 127 | 1 | ✓ | ✓ |
| | 135 00 | 128 | 8 | ✓ | ✓ |
| 600 00 | | | 10 | ✓ | ✓ |
| | 60 00 | 129 | 11 | Repairs Expense | 55 |
| | | | 14 | Office Supplies | 12 |
| | | | | Accounts Pay.—Arnold Supply Co. | 21 |
| | 180 00 | 130 | 15 | ✓ | ✓ |
| | 80 00 | 131 | 17 | Utilities Expense | 57 |
| 700 00 | | | 20 | ✓ | ✓ |
| | 165 00 | 132 | 22 | ✓ | ✓ |
| | 170 00 | 133 | 29 | ✓ | ✓ |
| 800 00 | | | 30 | ✓ | ✓ |
| | 1000 00 | 134 | 30 | Accounts Payable—Horn Equip. Co. | 22 |
| | 200 00 | 135 | 30 | Charles Hull, Drawing | 32 |
| 2700 00<br>2700 00 | 2720 00<br>2720 00 | | | | |
| (11) | (11) | | | | |
| | | | | | |
| | | | | | |
| | | | | | |

***Combined Cash Journal — Hull Delivery Service (Left Page)***

## Proving the Combined Cash Journal

As in the four-column journal, the equality of the debit and credit amount columns must be proved before posting the column totals to the ledger accounts. An adding machine tape of the combined cash journal column totals appears at the bottom of the page.

## Ruling the Combined Cash Journal

The columns in the combined cash journal are footed, proved, and ruled in the same manner as in the four-column journal. The totals should be recorded in ink on the same horizontal line immediately below the pencil footings. A single-ruled line should be drawn across all amount columns immediately above the totals. A double-ruled line is then drawn below all amount columns.

## Posting the Combined Cash Journal

The purpose of special columns in any journal is to simplify the recording and posting process. A special column in the combined cash journal is totaled and posted as one amount in exactly the same manner as the Cash Debit and Cash Credit columns are posted in the four-column journal.

FOR MONTH OF *December* 19 *82* PAGE *1*

| | GENERAL | | DELIVERY REVENUE 41 CR. | SALARY EXPENSE 56 DR. | |
|---|---|---|---|---|---|
| | DEBIT | CREDIT | | | |
| 1 | | | 600 00 | | 1 |
| 2 | 420 00 | | | | 2 |
| 3 | 240 00 | | | | 3 |
| 4 | | | | 70 00 | 4 |
| 5 | | | | 135 00 | 5 |
| 6 | | | 600 00 | | 6 |
| 7 | 60 00 | | | | 7 |
| 8 | 50 00 | | | | 8 |
| 9 | | 50 00 | | | 9 |
| 10 | | | | 180 00 | 10 |
| 11 | 80 00 | | | | 11 |
| 12 | | | 700 00 | | 12 |
| 13 | | | | 165 00 | 13 |
| 14 | | | | 170 00 | 14 |
| 15 | | | 800 00 | | 15 |
| 16 | 1000 00 | | | | 16 |
| 17 | 200 00 | | | | 17 |
| | 2050 00 | 50 00 | 2700 00 | 720 00 | |
| 18 | 2050 00 | 50 00 | 2700 00 | 720 00 | 18 |
| 19 | (✓) | (✓) | (41) | (56) | 19 |
| 20 | | | | | 20 |
| 21 | | | | | 21 |
| 22 | | | | | 22 |

*Combined Cash Journal — Hull Delivery Service (Right Page)*

| |
|---|
| 2,700·00+ |
| 2,050·00+ |
| 720·00+ |
| 5,470·00* |
| |
| 2,720·00+ |
| 50·00+ |
| 2,700·00+ |
| 5,470·00* |

*Adding Machine Tape — Proof of Combined Cash Journal Footings*

In the combined cash journal on pages 86 and 87, the Salary Expense Dr. column would be posted as one debit to the ledger account for the total of $720. At the time this posting is completed, the ledger account number of Salary Expense (56) is recorded in parentheses just below the column total. The charges to Salary Expense made during the month on December 1, 8, 15, 22, and 29 are not posted individually. A check mark (√) is placed in the Posting Reference column on these dates to indicate that these entries are not posted individually. The same procedure is followed for posting the Delivery Revenue Cr., the Cash Debit, and the Cash Credit columns.

There is no limit to the number of special columns a journal may have. The number and types of columns will vary depending on the needs of the particular business. Regardless of the number of special columns, there will always be a need for General Debit and General Credit columns to record unusual or infrequent transactions. Adjusting and closing entries are also recorded in the General columns. The entries to the General columns in the combined cash journal are posted individually during the month in the same manner as was done in the four-column journal. Other types of special journals are discussed in later chapters.

## PETTY CASH

As is fully explained later in this chapter, one of the advantages of having a checking account with a bank is that it allows excellent control over cash if all receipts are deposited and all disbursements are made by check. The business then would need to keep only a minimum amount of cash on hand to make change and to pay miscellaneous items. An office fund is often established to eliminate the necessity of writing numerous checks for small amounts. For example, if postage due on a package is $1.80, it would be unreasonably costly and time consuming to write a check for this amount. It is more convenient to have a small amount of cash in the office fund to pay the postage. This fund is commonly referred to as a *petty cash fund* — "petty" meaning small.

### Establishing the Petty Cash Fund

To establish the petty cash fund, a check is made payable to the account, Petty Cash, for the estimated amount of the petty cash disbursements for a certain period of time. The check is recorded in the journal by debiting Petty Cash and crediting Cash. The check is then converted into currency which is placed in a drawer or a box used for the petty cash fund.

### Operating the Petty Cash Fund

All petty cash disbursements are made from this fund and are recorded in a *petty cash book* rather than in a journal. A page from a petty cash book is illustrated on pages 90 and 91.

The disbursing of the money and recording of the payments may be performed by the bookkeeper or by someone else designated as the petty cashier. The person responsible for the petty cash fund should be able to account for the amount of the fund at any time.

In order to maintain proper control over the petty cash fund, disbursements from the fund should be evidenced by a voucher or a receipt. A *petty cash voucher*, which represents authority to pay the expense and also serves as a receipt, is shown below.

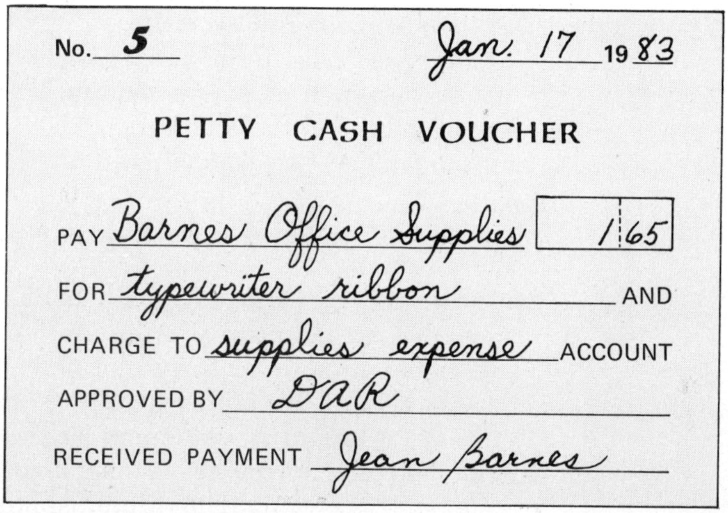

No. 5 Jan. 17 1983

PETTY CASH VOUCHER

PAY Barnes Office Supplies 1.65

FOR typewriter ribbon AND

CHARGE TO supplies expense ACCOUNT

APPROVED BY DAR

RECEIVED PAYMENT Jean Barnes

***Petty Cash Voucher***

Petty cash vouchers are numbered consecutively to prevent the same voucher from being used more than once in support of cash payments. When signed by the proper official of the company, the voucher becomes the petty cashier's authority to pay the amount stated. Upon making the payment, the cashier should require the person to whom the voucher is issued to sign the voucher, providing proof that the authorized payment was made. If a separate receipt for the payment is obtained, it should be attached to the voucher as a supporting document.

## Replenishing the Petty Cash Fund

The petty cash fund should be replenished at the end of the month or even sooner if the fund is depleted. To replenish the fund, a check is drawn for the amount of petty cash disbursements made to date and an entry for this transaction is recorded in the journal. The expense accounts listed in the petty cash book are debited. Cash is credited for the amount of the check. It should be emphasized that Petty Cash is not debited for the amount of the check. If the petty cash account were debited in this entry, it would increase the amount shown in the fund. The purpose of this entry is to replenish the fund for the expenses paid from it, not to increase the fund beyond its original balance.

The petty cash fund is a continuous fund and does not change in amount unless a decision is made to increase or decrease the fund. The amount of cash actually in the fund plus the total of the petty cash vouchers paid should always equal the amount originally put into the petty cash fund.

## Petty Cash Book

The petty cash book below shows that a check was issued January 3 to establish the fund. The $45 amount for which the fund was established is recorded in the Description column of the petty cash book. The transaction is also recorded in the combined cash journal on pages 92 and 93 by debiting Petty Cash and crediting Cash.

When payments are made from the petty cash fund, they are recorded in the Total Amount column. The amounts are then extended to the special columns at the right, which represent the various types of expenses paid from petty cash. When a charge is made to an account for which no special columns have been provided, the name of the account and the amount are recorded in the Account and Amount columns. The two special columns in this example are for Miscellaneous Expense and Supplies Expense. The Account and Amount columns are used to record debits to any other account for which a payment is made.

The design of a petty cash book, such as that illustrated below, may provide additional columns for any other accounts which are subject to numerous charges for petty cash payments.

At the end of January, only $7.85 remained in the petty cash drawer. A summary statement of the disbursements and supporting vouchers was prepared. A check for $37.15, the exact total of the vouchers, was issued to replenish the fund to its original amount. This amount was recorded as a credit to Cash in the combined cash journal. The totals for Miscellaneous Expense and Supplies Expense were recorded in the General Debit column of the combined cash journal. The individual amounts for Salary Expense and Truck Expense from the Account and Amount columns were also recorded. After this entry had been made, the accounts show the correct debit balances just as they would had the payments been recorded in a combined cash journal at the time they were made. The entry to record these transactions in a combined cash journal is shown on pages 92 and 93.

PAGE 1 — PETTY CASH DISBURSEMENTS

| DAY | DESCRIPTION | | VOU. NO. | TOTAL AMOUNT | SUP. EXP. | MISC. EXP. |
|---|---|---|---|---|---|---|
| 3 | Established fund | 45.00 | ✓ | | | |
| 3 | Telegram | | 1 | 4.30 | | 4.30 |
| 5 | Stamps and postage | | 2 | 2.25 | | 2.25 |
| 10 | Ink and carbon paper | | 3 | 4.60 | 4.60 | |
| 15 | Part-time help | | 4 | 15.00 | | |
| 17 | Typewriter ribbon | | 5 | 1.65 | 1.65 | |
| 19 | Washing company truck | | 6 | 3.00 | | |
| 24 | Broom for office | | 7 | 4.75 | 4.75 | |
| 31 | Telegram | | 8 | 1.60 | | 1.60 |
| | | | | 37.15 | 11.00 | 8.15 |
| 31 | Balance | 7.85 | | | | |
| 31 | Replenish fund | 37.15 | | | | |
| | Total | 45.00 | | | | |

***Petty Cash Book — (Left Page)***

The petty cash book was then footed, proved, and ruled, and the amount of the check to replenish the fund was entered in the Description column. The check was cashed and the money was placed in the petty cash drawer. The amount of cash in the petty cash drawer is again equal to the original amount of the fund, $45.

## Summary of the Petty Cash System

The following features of a petty cash system should be reviewed.

1. The fund should always be replenished for the exact total of the petty cash disbursements made.
2. The balance in the petty cash ledger account never changes unless the size of the fund is permanently increased or decreased.
3. The petty cash book is a memorandum record and not part of the books of original entry.
4. The expense accounts affected by payments from petty cash are recorded in the journal whenever the fund is replenished.
5. In addition to replenishing the fund when the cash balance becomes low, it should always be replenished at the end of the accounting period to bring the ledger accounts up to date prior to preparation of the financial statements.

# CASH SHORT AND OVER

In a business such as a grocery store or restaurant where many transactions involving cash are conducted each day, it is difficult to avoid occasional errors in making change. These errors cause the cash on hand to vary from the cash records. A discrepancy in the cash account may also be due to any one of several other causes such as failure to record a cash item, an error in counting the cash, recording a cash item at the wrong amount, or cash lost or mislaid. There is always the possibility of a cash shortage due to dishonesty, but most discrepancies are the result of honest mistakes.

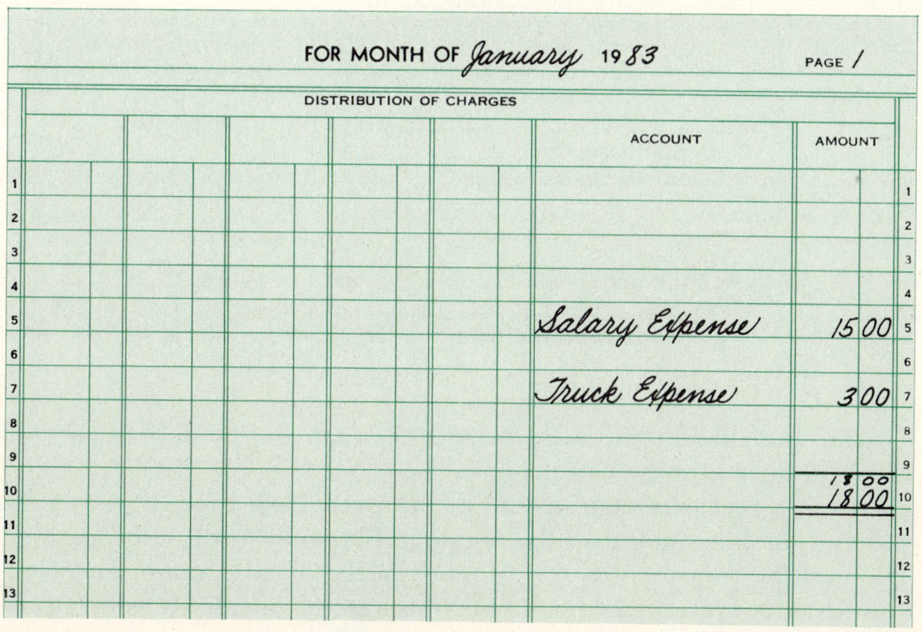

FOR MONTH OF *January* 19*83* PAGE *1*

DISTRIBUTION OF CHARGES

| | Account | Amount | |
|---|---|---|---|
| 1 | | | 1 |
| 2 | | | 2 |
| 3 | | | 3 |
| 4 | | | 4 |
| 5 | *Salary Expense* | 15 00 | 5 |
| 6 | | | 6 |
| 7 | *Truck Expense* | 3 00 | 7 |
| 8 | | | 8 |
| 9 | | | 9 |
| 10 | | 18 00<br>18 00 | 10 |
| 11 | | | 11 |
| 12 | | | 12 |
| 13 | | | 13 |

***Petty Cash Book — (Right Page)***

*Combined Cash Journal Entries for Petty Cash — (Left Page)*

PAGE 2 — COMBINED CASH JOURNAL

| CASH DEBIT 11 | CASH CREDIT 11 | CK. NO. | DAY | DESCRIPTION | POST. REF. |
|---|---|---|---|---|---|
| | 45 00 | 136 | 3 | Petty Cash | 10 |
| | 37 15 | 159 | 31 | Miscellaneous Expense | 59 |
| | | | 31 | Supplies Expense | 55 |
| | | | 31 | Salary Expense | 53 |
| | | | 31 | Truck Expense | 56 |

Once the discrepancy is evident, an effort should be made to determine the reason for it. The cash should be recounted. The cash receipts and cash payments recorded since the last time cash was proved should be thoroughly checked. Unfortunately, if the discrepancy is due to an error in making change or to lost or mislaid currency, no amount of checking will reveal the cause of the cash overage or shortage.

If the source of the discrepancy cannot be found, an entry in the journal debiting or crediting the ledger account, Cash Short and Over, should be made to bring the cash account into agreement with the cash actually on hand. At the end of the fiscal period, a debit or a credit balance remaining in the cash short and over account will be treated as an expense or revenue and closed to Income Summary.

To illustrate the use of a cash short and over account, assume that there was a cash overage of $4.70 on December 9, and a cash shortage of $9.60 on December 16. The journal entries below would be required to record the discrepancies.

JOURNAL — PAGE 12

| DATE | | DESCRIPTION | POST. REF. | DEBIT | CREDIT |
|---|---|---|---|---|---|
| 1982 | | | | | |
| Dec. | 9 | Cash | 11 | 4 70 | |
| | | Cash Short and Over | 64 | | 4 70 |
| | | To record cash overage. | | | |
| | 16 | Cash Short and Over | 64 | 9 60 | |
| | | Cash | 11 | | 9 60 |
| | | To record cash shortage. | | | |

After the above entries are posted, the cash short and over account would appear as shown on page 93.

When a cash shortage occurs in the petty cash fund, a petty cash voucher for the amount of the shortage is issued to the fund cashier. The cashier then records the voucher in the Total Amount and General Account and Amount columns of the petty cash book to bring the

FOR MONTH OF January 19 83 PAGE 2

| | GENERAL | | DELIVERY REVENUE 41 CR. | SALARY EXPENSE 56 DR. | |
|---|---|---|---|---|---|
| | DEBIT | CREDIT | | | |
| 1 | 45 00 | | | | 1 |
| 2 | | | | | 2 |
| 21 | 8 15 | | | | 21 |
| 22 | 11 00 | | | | 22 |
| 23 | | | | 15 00 | 23 |
| 24 | 3 00 | | | | 24 |
| 25 | | | | | 25 |
| 26 | | | | | 26 |
| 27 | | | | | 27 |
| 28 | | | | | 28 |
| 29 | | | | | 29 |
| 30 | | | | | 30 |
| 31 | | | | | 31 |
| 32 | | | | | 32 |
| 33 | | | | | 33 |

*Combined Cash Journal Entries for Petty Cash — (Right Page)*

petty cash book balance into agreement with the actual amount of currency in the petty cash drawer. If there is an overage in the petty cash fund, currency equal to the amount of the overage is taken from the petty cash drawer and merged with the day's cash receipts. An entry debiting Cash and crediting Cash Short and Over is made in the journal.

ACCOUNT **Cash Short and Over** ACCOUNT NO. **64**

| DATE | | ITEM | POST. REF. | DEBIT | CREDIT | BALANCE | |
|---|---|---|---|---|---|---|---|
| | | | | | | DEBIT | CREDIT |
| 1982 Dec. | 9 | | J12 | | 4 70 | | 4 70 |
| | 16 | | J12 | 9 60 | | 4 90 | |

Assuming no other shortages or overages during the month, the debit balance of $4.90 in the cash short and over account would be closed to Income Summary at the end of December. It would be shown on the December income statement as a miscellaneous expense. If there was a credit balance in the cash short and over account at the end of the period, this cash overage would be shown as miscellaneous revenue on the income statement.

## QUESTIONS FOR DISCUSSION

1. What are the basic elements in a good system of internal control of cash?
2. (a) What is the purpose of a four-column journal? (b) Explain how the four-column journal is proved at the end of the period. (c) Explain in detail how postings would be made to the ledger from each column of the four-column journal.
3. What is the difference between a combined cash journal and a four-column journal?
4. How is it possible at any time to prove the accuracy of the balance in the petty cash fund?

5. Discuss the operation of the petty cash fund, emphasizing the following points: (a) establishing the fund, (b) precautions to be observed by the cashier when making payments, and (c) replenishing the fund.

6. In making a daily cash count, the cash register tape indicated a balance of $127.20 in the cash drawer, but the amount of cash determined by count was only $125.70. If the cause of the discrepancy cannot be found, how should this difference be recorded?

## EXERCISES

1. Using the format shown below, indicate on a separate sheet of paper which of the following items would be cash in an accounting sense:

| | Yes | No |
|---|---|---|
| a. Checking account in bank | | |
| b. Money orders received | | |
| c. Postage stamps | | |
| d. Currency | | |
| e. Personal checks from customers | | |
| f. Note receivable from customer | | |
| g. Traveler's checks received | | |
| h. Trading stamps | | |
| i. Government savings bond | | |
| j. Change in cash drawer | | |

2. Record the following entries in a two-column journal for the Marx Company during July:

July 1 — Issued a check to establish a petty cash fund, $50.
July 26 — Issued a check for $42.80 to replenish the petty cash fund for the following: office supplies expense,$12.75; store supplies expense, $9.80; repairs expense, $17.60; miscellaneous expense, $2.65.
July 26 — Issued a check to increase the petty cash fund to $75.

3. The Koslow Company had the following discrepancies in its cash account during April: April 6, cash overage of $3.60; April 17, cash shortage of $6.10. Prepare the necessary entries in a two-column journal.

## ASSIGNMENT 5-A

**Tear out pages 403–414 and complete Assignment 5-A. Submit your papers to your instructor for approval, then proceed to the following discussion until the next assignment is required.**

# PART B BANKING PROCEDURES

A *bank* is a financial institution offering a wide variety of services and facilities to its customers. One of the best devices available to both businesses and individuals for controlling cash is a bank checking account. Through a bank checking account the depositor issues a written order directing the bank to pay cash from the account. This written order is called a *check*. The person writing the check is the *drawer*. The one to whom the bank is directed to pay cash is the *payee*. The bank to whom the order is directed is the *drawee*.

Some of the conveniences and safeguards provided by bank checking accounts are:

1. A dual record of cash receipts and disbursements.
2. Control over cash receipts by making deposits.
3. Control over cash payments by writing checks.
4. Determination of cash balances by preparing monthly bank reconciliations.

## DUAL RECORD OF RECEIPTS AND DISBURSEMENTS

Businesses that deposit all cash receipts and make all payments by check have a dual record of cash receipts and disbursements: (1) the bank's record, which is reported to the business on a monthly bank statement, and (2) the business' record, which is kept in the combined cash journal and the checkbook. It is a distinct advantage for the business to have a separate record kept by the bank. The bank's record simplifies the work of checking the cash records and provides the business with a means of verifying the checkbook and combined cash journal balances at the end of the month.

When all the cash receipts are deposited in the bank, the Cash Debit column of the combined cash journal becomes a record of bank deposits as well as a record of cash receipts. There are three records of cash receipts which must be in agreement: the entries made in the combined cash journal, the record of deposits made on the checkbook stubs, and the bank's record of deposits which is reported to the depositor on the monthly bank statement. Each of these records provides verification of the other. It is possible to trace the cash receipts deposited in the bank by checking the entries on the monthly bank statement against the receipts entered in the combined cash journal and on checkbook stubs. Full accountability for all cash receipts is thereby assured.

If all cash disbursements are made by check, the Cash Credit column of the combined cash journal becomes a record of withdrawals from the bank as well as a record of cash disbursements. Three separate records of the disbursements are provided: the entries made in the combined cash journal, the record of checks written made on the checkbook stubs, and the bank's record of withdrawals included on the monthly bank statement. Each of these records may be used as a check against the others for the purpose of detecting errors and omissions committed by either the business or the bank.

## BANK DEPOSITS

One very important feature of depositing all cash receipts is that, as mentioned above, it provides a cross check on these receipts by comparing the cash received as entered in the business records with the deposits recorded on the bank's books. It is desirable to make deposits each day to minimize the amount of cash on hand at any time.

Another service available to depositors is the use of the night deposit safe at the bank. The night deposit drop (opening) is usually located outside the bank in a place easily accessible by car. The bank will supply the customer with a depositor's safety bag which can be locked. Once the deposit has been placed in the night deposit drop, it moves to a vault within the bank and must be claimed inside the bank during banking hours. These facilities are particularly valuable for depositors without a safe who daily collect large sums of cash which cannot be deposited during banking hours.

## Deposit Slip

The bank provides depositors with a form called a *deposit slip* or *deposit ticket* to use for a detailed listing of items being deposited. A completed deposit slip is illustrated below.

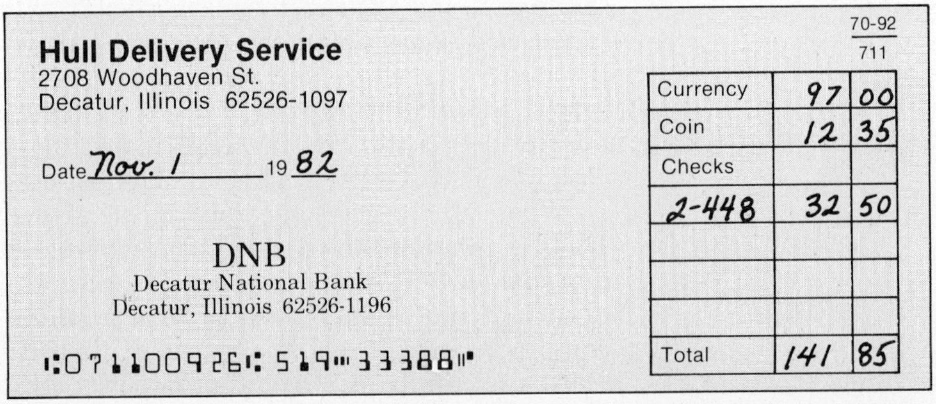
70-92
711

**Hull Delivery Service**
2708 Woodhaven St.
Decatur, Illinois 62526-1097

Date Nov. 1 19 82

DNB
Decatur National Bank
Decatur, Illinois 62526-1196

⑆071100926⑆ 519⑈33388⑈

| | | |
|---|---|---|
| Currency | 97 | 00 |
| Coin | 12 | 35 |
| Checks | | |
| 2-448 | 32 | 50 |
| | | |
| | | |
| | | |
| Total | 141 | 85 |

***Deposit Slip***

The name and address of the account are preprinted on the deposit slip and the date is written in the space provided. The amount of cash, including both currency and coin, should be entered on the appropriate lines in the amount column. All checks to be deposited should be listed on separate lines as shown in the illustration and should be identified by the number of the bank on which the check has been drawn.

The numbers used to designate specific banks are assigned by the American Bankers Association and are referred to as *ABA numbers*. They appear on deposit slips and checks at the top right corner. On the deposit slip above, the ABA number for the Decatur National Bank is $\frac{70\text{-}92}{711}$, which is coded as follows:

1. The number **70** in the numerator is assigned to banks in the Decatur, Illinois area.
2. The number **92** in the numerator is assigned to the Decatur National Bank in particular.
3. The denominator of the fraction, **711**, is the routing symbol used by the Federal Reserve System to bring about faster sorting and greater efficiency in collecting checks. This number is not used when listing checks on deposit slips. The numbers at the bottom left side of the deposit slip are known as *MICR (magnetic ink character recognition)* numbers and will be explained on page 98.

## Endorsements

Checks received by the business (the payee) have to be signed by the owner or another authorized individual before they can be deposited. This signature, known as an *endorsement*, transfers title of the check to the bank. The endorsement is also the endorser's guarantee that if the check is not paid by its drawer, the bank can look to the payee for collection. The check is endorsed by signing it on the back using exactly the same name as appears on the face of the check. All checks received by the business should use a restrictive endorsement to prevent the unauthorized cashing of checks payable to the business. A *restrictive endorsement* is one that specifies to whom the check is to be paid, normally the bank, and should include the statement "For deposit only." This makes it impossible for anyone other than the bank to cash the check. An excellent procedure for handling checks received by the business is to record the restrictive endorsement with a rubber stamp on the back of the check at the time it is received. A check that has been stamped with the endorsement "For deposit only" is shown below.

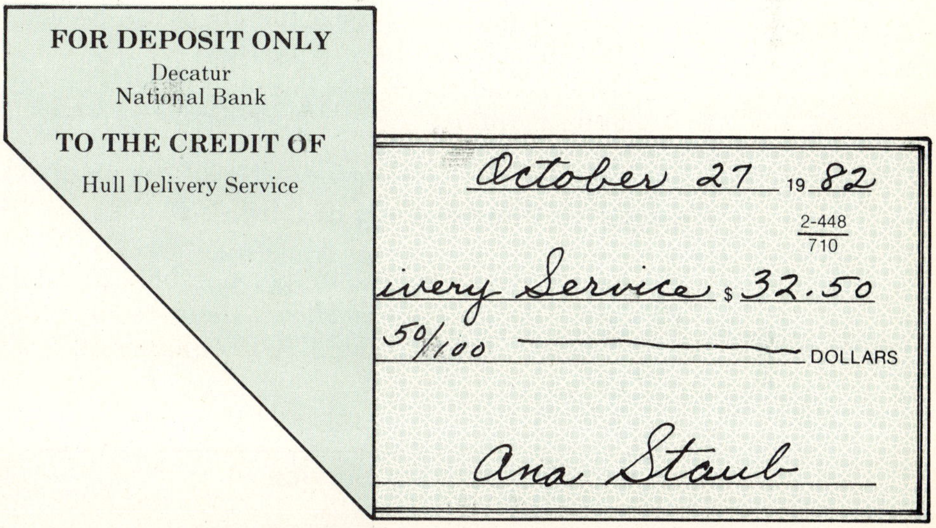


***Endorsed Check***

The above check, payable to the Hull Delivery Service was included in the deposit made on November 1. Note that the numerator of the ABA number, 2-448, and the amount of the check, $32.50, appear on the Hull Delivery Service's deposit slip shown on page 96.

# PAYMENTS BY CHECK

If a business establishes the policy of making all payments by check, this practice will provide excellent security in a very vulnerable area of business operations. A check provides the business with a duplicate record of all cash payments. The first record is the canceled check which is returned to the drawer after it has been paid by its bank and subtracted from its account balance. The second record is kept by the bank which records all checks cleared on checking accounts. The business also has a record of the checks in its checkbook stubs and in the combined cash journal. The practice of paying all bills by check allows the business to keep only a minimum amount of cash on hand for making change and for disbursing incidental items through its petty cash fund.

When opening a checking account with a bank, all persons authorized to write checks on the account must sign a *signature card* which is kept on file by the bank. This card provides the bank with a verification of the depositor's signature as it appears on issued checks.

## The Checkbook

Another control feature offered by a checking account is the checkbook. The bank provides the business with a preprinted checkbook. The printing of the checks and check stubs includes consecutive numbering of the checks. The check and its stub should have the same number. The numbering of all checks is essential for control of checks written. Prenumbered checks are also a valuable aid in reconciling the checkbook with the bank's record of the checking account. If a check is prepared incorrectly and cannot be used, it should be invalidated by writing VOID across the check and its stub. This practice enables even unusable checks to be accounted for. A page from the checkbook of the Hull Delivery Service is presented on page 99. The second check was improperly prepared and had to be invalidated and rewritten.

## Computer Processing of Checks

Checks have a series of numbers printed along their lower left-hand margin which allows them to be processed by magnetic ink character recognition (MICR) equipment.

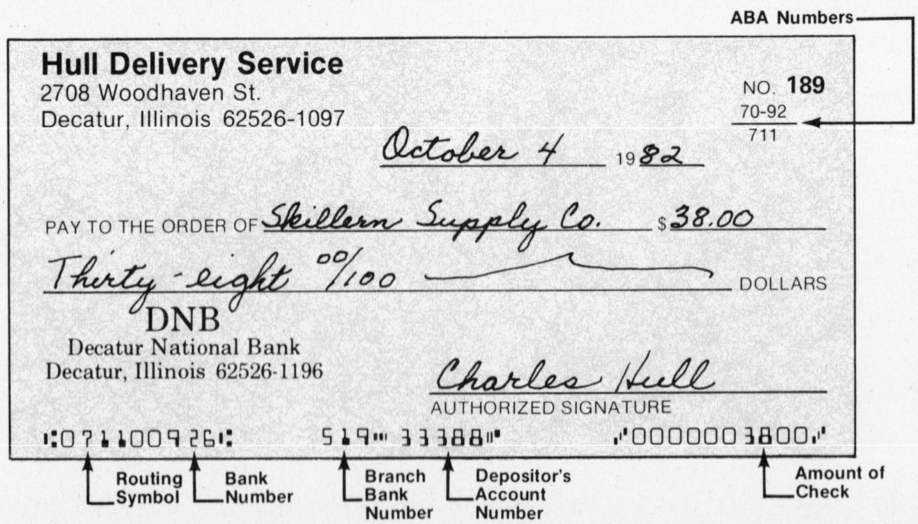


***Check Illustrating ABA Numbers and Magnetic Ink Characters***

In the check illustrated above the numbers are coded as follows:

1. 0711 indicates the Federal Reserve district in which the bank is located and is known as the routing symbol.
2. 0092 indicates the specific bank.

3. The digit following the bank number, "6" in this example, is a check digit that is used in combination with the eight preceding digits for the purpose of verifying their accuracy in computer processing.
4. 519 is the branch of the Decatur National Bank in which the account is located.
5. 33388 is the account number of the depositor.
6. To further aid in processing the check, the first bank that handles it will print the dollar amount of the check in magnetic ink characters directly below the signature line on the lower right-hand side of the check.

Another cash control device used in some businesses is the *checkwriter*, a small machine which prepares checks mechanically. The checkwriter is used to write and perforate the amount of a check in figures and in words, making it impossible to change the dollar amount for which the check is written.

***Page from a Checkbook***

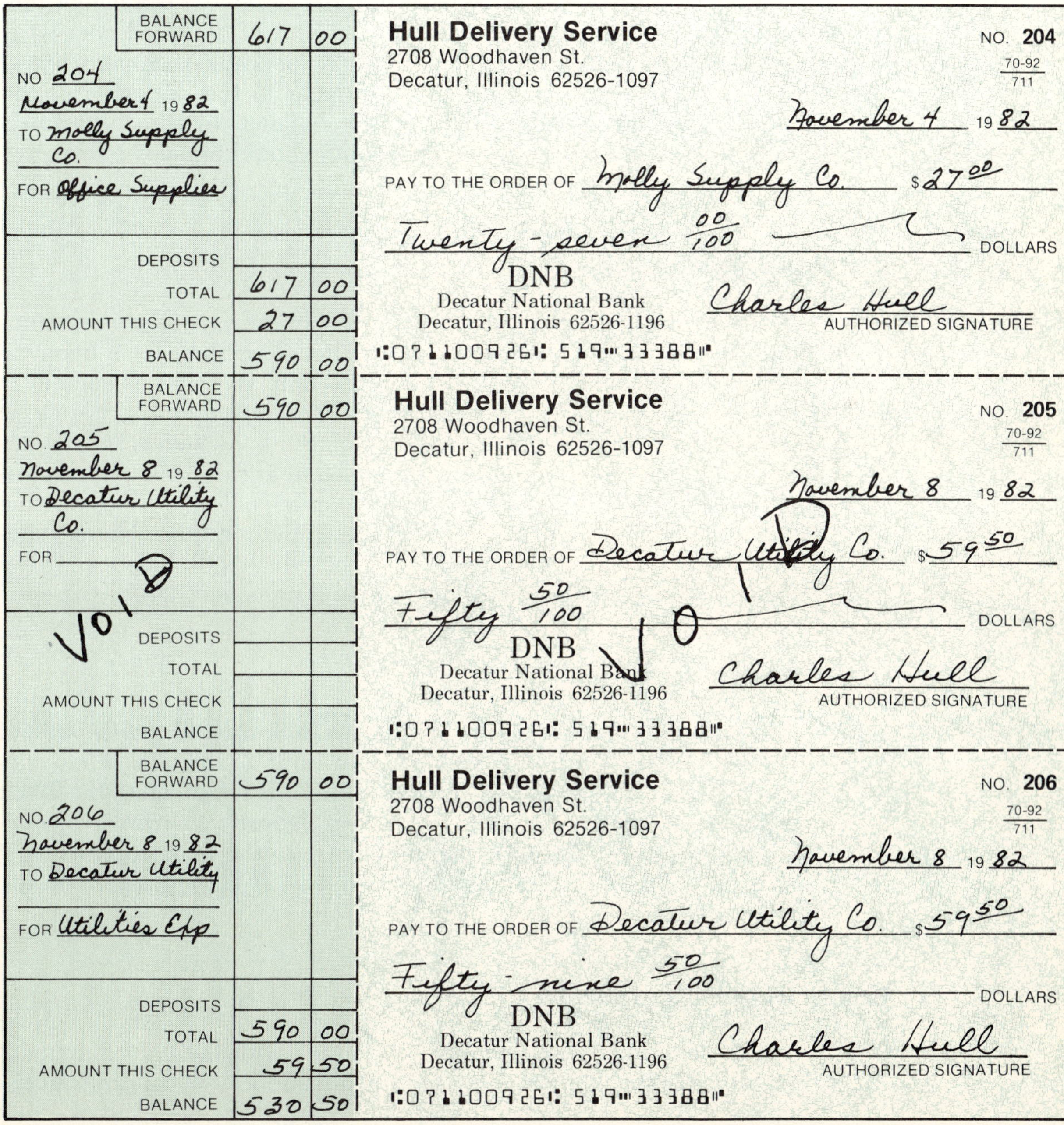

| | | |
|---|---|---|
| BALANCE FORWARD | 617 | 00 |
| NO 204 November 4 1982 TO Molly Supply Co. FOR Office Supplies | | |
| DEPOSITS | | |
| TOTAL | 617 | 00 |
| AMOUNT THIS CHECK | 27 | 00 |
| BALANCE | 590 | 00 |

**Hull Delivery Service** NO. **204**
2708 Woodhaven St. 70-92/711
Decatur, Illinois 62526-1097
November 4 1982
PAY TO THE ORDER OF Molly Supply Co. $27.00
Twenty-seven 00/100 DOLLARS
DNB
Decatur National Bank
Decatur, Illinois 62526-1196
Charles Hull
AUTHORIZED SIGNATURE
⑆071100926⑆ 519⑈33388⑈

| | | |
|---|---|---|
| BALANCE FORWARD | 590 | 00 |
| NO. 205 November 8 1982 TO Decatur Utility Co. FOR | | |
| VOID | | |
| DEPOSITS | | |
| TOTAL | | |
| AMOUNT THIS CHECK | | |
| BALANCE | | |

**Hull Delivery Service** NO. **205**
2708 Woodhaven St. 70-92/711
Decatur, Illinois 62526-1097
November 8 1982
PAY TO THE ORDER OF Decatur Utility Co. $59.50
Fifty 50/100 DOLLARS
VOID
DNB
Decatur National Bank
Decatur, Illinois 62526-1196
Charles Hull
AUTHORIZED SIGNATURE
⑆071100926⑆ 519⑈33388⑈

| | | |
|---|---|---|
| BALANCE FORWARD | 590 | 00 |
| NO. 206 November 8 1982 TO Decatur Utility FOR Utilities Exp | | |
| DEPOSITS | | |
| TOTAL | 590 | 00 |
| AMOUNT THIS CHECK | 59 | 50 |
| BALANCE | 530 | 50 |

**Hull Delivery Service** NO. **206**
2708 Woodhaven St. 70-92/711
Decatur, Illinois 62526-1097
November 8 1982
PAY TO THE ORDER OF Decatur Utility Co. $59.50
Fifty-nine 50/100 DOLLARS
DNB
Decatur National Bank
Decatur, Illinois 62526-1196
Charles Hull
AUTHORIZED SIGNATURE
⑆071100926⑆ 519⑈33388⑈

## THE BANK STATEMENT AS A MEANS OF CONTROL

The checkbook contains a record of bank deposits and withdrawals. If it contains no errors or omissions, the checkbook balance represents the correct amount of the depositor's cash. At the end of each month the checkbook balance is proved by comparing it with the amount of cash in the bank account as shown on the monthly bank statement.

The *bank statement* is a copy of the bank's record of the depositor's account. It shows the balance of the account at the beginning of the month, the deposits and withdrawals made during the month, and the balance at the end of the month. Enclosed with the statement are the depositor's canceled checks which the bank has paid and charged to (subtracted from) the account during the period. If the bank's record of deposits and withdrawals (in the form of canceled checks) is complete, the final balance appearing on the bank statement represents the amount of cash actually available to the depositor at the bank. Under these circumstances, the balance in the depositor's checkbook as of the last day of the month should equal the final balance on the monthly bank statement.

### Outstanding Checks

The bank's record of the depositor's withdrawals is seldom complete. Usually a few of the depositor's checks will not have been received and processed by the bank at the time the bank statement is prepared. These *outstanding checks* will not appear among the items deducted from the depositor's balance on the bank statement. To determine the correct amount of cash available at the bank, the depositor must adjust the reported bank statement balance by deducting from it the total of these outstanding checks. This adjusted bank statement balance is then compared with the checkbook balance. If the two amounts agree, the checkbook record is considered to be correct.

### Deposits in Transit

Certain deposits, such as mailed deposits or night deposits, are not credited to the depositor's bank account until a later day. These deposits, which are added to the depositor's account after the bank statement has been prepared, are called *deposits in transit* or *outstanding deposits*. The true amount of cash in the bank account must be determined by adding the deposits in transit to the balance on the bank statement.

### Errors in the Checkbook

If the checkbook balance does not agree with the bank statement balance after the adjustments have been made for outstanding checks and deposits in transit, the discrepancy is probably the result of errors or omissions in the checkbook. Some of the more common errors and omissions in the checkbook are:

1. Errors in adding, deducting, or carrying forward amounts on the check stubs.
2. The amount of a check is entered incorrectly on the check stub.
3. Additions made to the depositor's account by the bank have not been recorded in the checkbook. This type of omission will frequently occur when a note has been collected by the bank for the depositor and credited (added) to the account.
4. Charges (deductions) made directly to the depositor's account by the bank have not yet been recorded in the checkbook. The monthly *bank service charge*, which is the amount that the bank charges the depositor for handling the account, is the most common example.

The items listed above fall into two classes: (1) those that cause the checkbook balance to be less than the correct amount, and (2) those that cause the checkbook balance to be greater than the correct amount. The total of the first group is added to the checkbook balance, and the total of the second group is subtracted from the checkbook balance. The net result should provide a checkbook balance that is in agreement with the adjusted balance of the bank statement.

There are two common items requiring further explanation which often appear on the bank's books but are not known by the depositor until the bank statement is received. The two items are dishonored checks and notes collected by the bank.

## Dishonored Checks

*Dishonored checks* are customers' checks which have been deposited, but the bank, for reasons which are usually stated, has refused to pay them. The most common reason for a bank refusing to pay a check is that the drawer of the check does not have sufficient funds on deposit to cover the amount of the check. This situation is indicated on the bank statement as "NSF" (not sufficient funds). Since the depositor guarantees all items deposited, any customer checks that are dishonored will be charged back against the depositor's bank account, thereby reducing the balance. The bank must deduct the amount of these checks from the depositor's balance because they were assumed by the bank to be good and were added to the account when the deposit was initially made.

To bring the checkbook balance into agreement with the bank statement, the depositor should deduct all dishonored checks from the checkbook balance and prepare a journal entry debiting Accounts Receivable, representing a claim against the customer for the amount of the check, and crediting Cash as shown below.

| | Date | Account | | Debit | Credit |
|---|---|---|---|---|---|
| | 29 | Accounts Receivable — Al Trull | | 41 00 | |
| | | Cash | | | 41 00 |
| | | Amount reinstated for NSF check. | | | |

## Notes Collected by the Bank

A customer's note payable to the depositor may be collected by the bank. As a convenience to both the depositor and the customer, arrangements are often made to have the note paid at the bank and the amount of the note credited to the depositor's account. The collection of the note (and the interest on the note, if any) by the bank will appear on the bank statement as an increase in the depositor's balance. This amount will be revealed when the bank statement is received and should be added to the checkbook balance to bring it into agreement with the bank balance. The entry to adjust the books is a debit to the cash account and a credit to Notes Receivable. If interest has been earned on the note, Cash is debited for the full amount collected, Notes Receivable is credited for the face value of the note, and Interest Income is credited for the interest earned. For example, Claudia Wright owed Dan Dohanich $200 on a note, and Wright paid the note plus $14 interest at Dohanich's bank. Dohanich made the following entry to account for the collection of the note.

| | Date | Account Title | Post. Ref. | Debit | Credit |
|---|---|---|---|---|---|
| | 30 | Cash | | 214 00 | |
| | | Notes Receiv. — Claudia Wright | | | 200 00 |
| | | Interest Income | | | 14 00 |
| | | Note collected from C. Wright. | | | |
| | | | | | |
| | | | | | |

A detailed discussion of notes and interest is presented in a later chapter.

# RECONCILING THE BANK STATEMENT

The process of bringing the checkbook and bank statement balances into agreement is called *reconciling the bank statement*. The reconciliation should be made when the monthly bank statement is received.

The first step in making the reconciliation is to determine the total of the outstanding checks as follows:

1. Arrange the canceled checks received with the bank statement in numerical order.
2. Check each canceled check against the corresponding stub in the checkbook and place a check mark on each stub for which a canceled check has been returned.
3. Make a list of the number and the amount of each check not returned by the bank. Each check stub that doesn't contain a check mark represents an outstanding check.
4. Determine the total amount of outstanding checks.

Next, a review should be made of the deposits during the period to determine the amount, if any, of the deposits in transit. Then subtract the total of the outstanding checks from, and add the deposits in transit to, the balance shown on the bank statement. The amount of the monthly bank service charge, and of any dishonored checks, which will appear as deductions on the bank statement, should be subtracted from the checkbook balance. The amount of any notes collected by the bank should be added to the checkbook balance. If the amount resulting from these computations does not agree with the checkbook balance, the following steps should be taken to discover the causes of the discrepancy:

1. Compare the entries on the check stubs with the record of deposits and withdrawals appearing on the bank statement.
2. Check the mathematical accuracy of additions, subtractions, and amounts carried forward on the stubs completed since the preceding bank reconciliation.
3. Check the mathematical accuracy of the bank statement.
4. If there are any items on the bank statement which cannot be accounted for, the bank should be notified at once.

After the causes of the discrepancy have been discovered, the final reconciliation step is to adjust the checkbook and bank statement balances as illustrated beginning below through page 105.

A permanent record of the reconciliation should be filed for future reference. When the next bank statement and canceled checks are received, the depositor can refer to the preceding reconciliation to determine whether the checks that were previously outstanding have been presented for payment.

## Bank Reconciliation Illustrated

A standard form of bank statement is shown below for the Hull Delivery Service for the month of December. The following information is shown on the bank statement: (1) checks processed and paid from the depositor's account during the period, (2) deposits made

DNB
Decatur National Bank
Decatur, Illinois 62526-1196

ACCOUNT NUMBER: 519-33388

STATEMENT OF ACCOUNT

HULL DELIVERY SERVICE
2708 WOODHAVEN ST.
DECATUR, IL 62526-1097

12/31/82
DATE OF STATEMENT

| BALANCE FROM PREVIOUS STATEMENT | NUMBER OF DEBITS | AMOUNT OF CHECKS AND DEBITS | NUMBER OF CREDITS | AMOUNT OF DEPOSITS AND CREDITS | SERVICE CHARGE | STATEMENT BALANCE |
|---|---|---|---|---|---|---|
| 420.00 | 9 | 1,520.00 | 3 | 1,900.00 | 4.00 | 796.00 |

| DATE | CHECKS DEBITS | CHECKS DEBITS | DEPOSITS CREDITS | BALANCE |
|---|---|---|---|---|
| 12/02 | | | 600.00 | 1,020.00 |
| 12/03 | 420.00 | 70.00 | | 530.00 |
| 12/06 | 240.00 | | | 290.00 |
| 12/09 | 135.00 | | | 155.00 |
| 12/11 | | | 600.00 | 755.00 |
| 12/15 | 60.00 | | | 695.00 |
| 12/16 | 180.00 | | | 515.00 |
| 12/20 | 80.00 | | | 435.00 |
| 12/23 | 165.00 | | 700.00 | 970.00 |
| 12/30 | 170.00 | | | 800.00 |
| 12/31 | 4.00SC | | | 796.00 |

PLEASE EXAMINE AT ONCE. IF NO ERROR IS REPORTED WITHIN 10 DAYS THE ACCOUNT WILL BE CONSIDERED CORRECT AND VOUCHERS GENUINE. REFER ANY DISCREPANCY OR ERROR TO OUR BOOKKEEPING DEPT.

EC — ERROR CORRECTION MS — MISCELLANEOUS SC — SERVICE CHARGE
NSF — NOT SUFFICIENT FUNDS OD — OVERDRAFT

***Bank Statement***

during the period, (3) a running balance of the checking account throughout the month, and (4) any other charges or credits to the account for the period (i.e., $4 service charge).

For this illustration it is assumed that Hull Delivery Service makes all cash payments by check. Therefore, the checks written for the month are represented by the credits to Cash in the combined cash journal on pages 86 and 87. The checkbook stubs reflect the following checks written during the month of December.

| *Check No.* | *Amount* | *Check No.* | *Amount* |
|---|---|---|---|
| 125 | $420 | | |
| 126 | 240 | 131 | $ 80 |
| 127 | 70 | 132 | 165 |
| 128 | 135 | 133 | 170 |
| 129 | 60 | 134 | 1,000 |
| 130 | 180 | 135 | 200 |

The checkbook also shows four deposits for the month — December 1, $600; December 10, $600; December 20, $700; December 30, $800 — and a balance as of December 31 of $400.

The reconciliation of the bank account with the checkbook balance is accomplished by the following steps:

1. Determine the outstanding checks by comparing the checkbook stubs with the canceled checks received with the bank statement. This comparison reveals that two checks written during December have not cleared the bank and are therefore outstanding. These outstanding checks should be subtracted from the bank balance. The checks outstanding are:

| | |
|---|---|
| #134 — Horn Equipment Co. | $1,000 |
| #135 — Charles Hull, Drawing | 200 |
| Total outstanding checks | $1,200 |

2. Determine whether any deposits made during the month were not recorded on the bank statement. The bank statement includes three deposits for the month, $600, $600, and $700; therefore the deposit made on December 30 for $800 is a deposit in transit and should be added to the bank balance.
3. Check to see if any items have been recorded by the bank that are not entered in the checkbook. The only item on the December bank statement which has not been recorded in the checkbook is the bank service charge (SC) of $4, which is shown as a deduction from the bank balance on December 31. This service charge should be deducted from the checkbook balance in the reconciliation process.

A common form for a bank reconciliation is shown at the top of page 105.

## Correcting the Cash Records

The checkbook adjustments that appear on the reconciliation statement should be entered in the checkbook to reflect the correct balance of cash in the bank. The checkbook and the cash account of Hull Delivery Service have a balance on December 31 of $400. The bank service charge for the month of December has been deducted from the bank account but has not been recorded in the checkbook or

**Hull Delivery Service**
**Bank Reconciliation**
**December 31, 1982**

| | | |
|---|---|---|
| Balance per bank statement, December 31 | | 796 00 |
| Add deposit in transit, December 31 | | 800 00 |
| | | 1 596 00 |
| Deduct outstanding checks: | | |
| No. 134 | 1 000 00 | |
| No. 135 | 200 00 | 1 200 00 |
| Adjusted bank balance, December 31 | | 396 00 |
| | | |
| Checkbook balance, December 31 | | 400 00 |
| Deduct bank service charge | | 4 00 |
| Adjusted checkbook balance, December 31 | | 396 00 |

*Bank Reconciliation*

cash account. This service charge of $4 should be shown on the check stub as a deduction from the checkbook balance. This subtraction adjusts the checkbook balance to the correct amount of $396.

The cash account and the checkbook records should always be in agreement. A journal entry is required to record the service charge (miscellaneous expense) and to reduce cash. The entry required for the above reconciliation is:

| Date | Account | Debit | Credit |
|---|---|---|---|
| 31 | Miscellaneous Expense | 4 00 | |
| | Cash | | 4 00 |
| | Bank service charge for Dec. | | |

After the entry has been posted to the ledger accounts, the balance in the cash account will agree with the checkbook balance.

## Cycle Billing

Most banks now use *cycle billing* for handling their depositors' statements. They process and mail the bank statements in cycles during the month rather than handle all accounts at the end of the month. For example, the bank might process and mail one third of the statements on the tenth of the month, one third on the twentieth, and one third on the thirtieth. This billing procedure spreads the bank's work load over the entire month.

From the depositor's standpoint, cycle billing will not affect the reconciliation procedure, except that the period being reconciled should be that covered by the bank statement. For example, if a business receives its bank statement for the period ending on the sixteenth day of the month, it would reconcile its checking account balance as of that date.

## QUESTIONS FOR DISCUSSION

1. Name some of the important features of a plan for controlling and protecting cash.
2. How does a business maintain a dual record of its cash?
3. What are the chief advantages of such practices as depositing all cash receipts, issuing checks for all disbursements recorded in the combined cash journal, and using a petty cash fund to meet small cash expenditures?
4. (a) How does the practice of depositing all cash receipts provide a check on the accuracy of the cash receipts record of a business? (b) How does the practice of making payments by check provide a check on the accuracy of the cash payments record of a business?
5. The cashier of the Derby Roller Rink receives cash and makes payments authorized by the manager. Small claims are paid from cash on hand and the remainder of the cash is deposited in the bank. (a) What are the weaknesses of this system? (b) Describe a better system of handling cash for this business.
6. In most checking accounts, the balance of the account shown by the bank statement is usually greater than the depositor's checkbook balance. What is the major cause of this situation?
7. How are outstanding checks identified when preparing a bank reconciliation?

## EXERCISES

1. On June 8, Kathy Everest received a check from Barry Brown, a customer, in the amount of $53, and deposited the check on that date. On June 11, the bank notified Everest that Brown's check was being returned due to insufficient funds and the $53 was being deducted from her bank balance. Prepare the journal entry necessary on Everest's books to record the returned check.
2. In reconciling his bank statement at the end of March, Ross Wang discovered that a $150 note receivable from Joe Bacsik had been collected by the bank plus $5 interest. The $155 was added to Wang's account during March. Prepare the journal entry on Wang's books to record the collection of the note and interest.
3. Reconcile the bank account of the Murphy Magic Shop for February of the current year, using the following information:

| | |
|---|---|
| Balance per checkbook, February 28 | $549 |
| Bank service charge | 6 |
| Checks outstanding, February 28 | 184 |
| Balance per bank statement, February 28 | 612 |
| Deposit in transit, February 28 | 115 |

## ASSIGNMENT 5-B

**Tear out pages 415–420 and complete Assignment 5-B. After submitting your papers for approval, begin reading Chapter 6 until the next assignment is required.**

Chapter **6**

# ACCOUNTING FOR THE SALE OF MERCHANDISE

The previous chapters contained accounting procedures for a service enterprise. This chapter is concerned with the accounting procedures for a merchandising enterprise.

A *merchandising enterprise* is a business that buys and sells goods. *Merchandise* consists of goods held for resale purposes and is commonly called *merchandise inventory* or simply *inventory*. Inventory includes only the items that are held for sale in the normal course of business operations. For example, typewriters are inventory for an office machines enterprise, but typewriters are office equipment for most other businesses; automobiles are inventory for a car dealer but are equipment for others.

Merchandising activities may be conducted at either the wholesale or retail level. Many of the accounting procedures discussed for a service enterprise are also applicable to a mercantile enterprise. The major differences are found in the transactions related to buying and selling the merchandise. The procedures involved in accounting for the sale of merchandise are discussed in this chapter, and accounting for the buying of merchandise is explained in the following chapter.

## PART A SALES AND ACCOUNTS RECEIVABLE

Merchandise may be sold for cash or on credit with an agreement that the account will be paid at a later date. This latter type of transaction is commonly called a *sale on account*. When merchandise is sold, a revenue account, Sales, is credited for the selling price of the goods. For example, assuming a sale of merchandise is made on March 12 for $200 cash, the entry would be:

**JOURNAL** PAGE 2

| | DATE | | DESCRIPTION | POST. REF. | DEBIT | CREDIT | |
|---|---|---|---|---|---|---|---|
| | 1982 | | | | | | |
| 1 | Mar. | 12 | Cash | | 200 00 | | 1 |
| 2 | | | Sales | | | 200 00 | 2 |
| 3 | | | Sold merchandise for cash. | | | | 3 |

Some businesses, such as supermarkets, sell goods only for cash. Appliance dealers and furniture stores sell mostly on credit. Many firms have a large number of both types of transactions.

If the preceding transaction had been made on account to R. C. Bradley, the entry would be:

JOURNAL PAGE 2

| DATE | | DESCRIPTION | POST. REF. | DEBIT | CREDIT |
|---|---|---|---|---|---|
| 1982 Mar. | 12 | Accounts Receiv. — R. C. Bradley ... | | 200 00 | |
| | | Sales ........................................ | | | 200 00 |
| | | Sold merchandise on account. | | | |

The above entry is necessary because the customer will normally receive the merchandise at the time the sale is made. This transaction constitutes a legal contract, and for accounting purposes the revenue earned from the sale should properly be reported at the time the sale is made. Also, the amount receivable from the customer should be recorded in the asset account, Accounts Receivable, until it has been collected. When the account receivable is collected, the entry would be:

| DATE | | DESCRIPTION | POST. REF. | DEBIT | CREDIT |
|---|---|---|---|---|---|
| | 27 | Cash ........................................ | | 200 00 | |
| | | Accounts Receiv. — R. C. Bradley | | | 200 00 |
| | | Received cash for balance due. | | | |

This entry reflects the increase of one asset and the reduction of another. No entry is required in the sales account because the revenue was recorded at the time of sale.

## THE SALES TICKET

A *sales ticket* is a business document used by a retail business to record information pertaining to a sale. A sales ticket normally includes the following data: ticket number, date of sale, name and address of the seller, name and address of the customer (if charge sale), amount, type, unit price, and total price of the goods sold, and the name, initials, or code number of the person making the sale. In a manufacturing or wholesale business the document used as proof of the sale is called a *sales invoice*.

The format used for the sales ticket will vary depending upon the needs of the individual business. For example, a department store would probably require that the name or number of the department making the sale be recorded on each ticket. A sales ticket is shown at the top of the next page.

In most stores, salespeople have their own sales books with the tickets prenumbered for control purposes. Frequently, each salesperson also has a separate cash register drawer. The sales tickets are normally prepared in duplicate. The original is placed in the salesperson's cash register drawer to be used later by the bookkeeper as the source document for recording the sales information in the account-

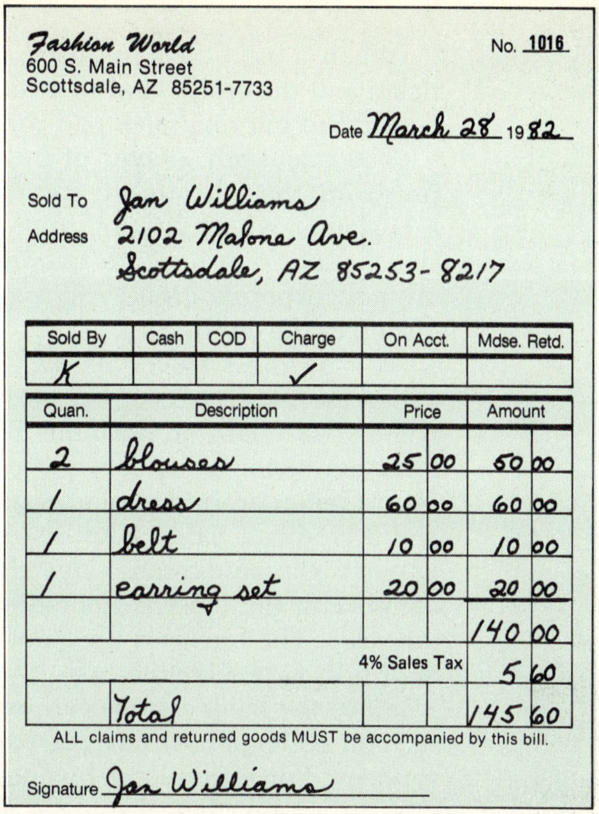

*Fashion World* No. 1016
600 S. Main Street
Scottsdale, AZ 85251-7733

Date March 28 1982

Sold To Jan Williams
Address 2102 Malone Ave.
Scottsdale, AZ 85253-8217

| Sold By | Cash | COD | Charge | On Acct. | Mdse. Retd. |
|---|---|---|---|---|---|
| K | | | ✓ | | |

| Quan. | Description | Price | Amount |
|---|---|---|---|
| 2 | blouses | 25 00 | 50 00 |
| 1 | dress | 60 00 | 60 00 |
| 1 | belt | 10 00 | 10 00 |
| 1 | earring set | 20 00 | 20 00 |
| | | | 140 00 |
| | | 4% Sales Tax | 5 60 |
| | Total | | 145 60 |

ALL claims and returned goods MUST be accompanied by this bill.

Signature Jan Williams

***Sales Ticket***

ing records. A copy of the sales ticket is given to the customer as a receipt.

If it is a charge sale, the customer is normally required to sign the ticket to verify receipt of the goods.

## CREDIT CARDS

One convenient method used extensively in retailing for identifying an approved charge customer is the credit card. Among the best known credit cards are Visa, Diners' Club, MasterCard, American Express and those issued by major oil companies. Retail stores sometimes issue their own credit cards to customers. This method of credit buying has increased rapidly and is now a common means of buying almost all goods and services offered for sale. Most credit cards are plastic plates embossed with the customer's name, account number, and expiration date on the face of the card. The customer's signature also appears on the card for verification when making purchases. A credit card issued by Visa® is illustrated below.

***Credit Card***

When a credit card is used, the salesperson will place the sales ticket and the credit card in a small machine. This machine prints the credit card information on all copies of the sales ticket.

The major advantages of the credit card are that it saves time in preparing the sales ticket, and it provides immediate identification of a customer who has been approved for credit. As a means of additional protection for both the customer and the business, some firms are now experimenting with requiring a recent photo of the customer affixed to the credit card.

If a business issues its own credit cards, the sale to a customer using the card is recorded in the usual manner for a charge sale, namely, as a debit to Accounts Receivable and a credit to Sales. If the business honors a bank credit card, such as MasterCard or Visa, the sale is recorded in the same way as a cash sale, ie., by a debit to Cash and a credit to Sales. The reason for this is that when the business deposits the credit card sales slips with the bank, the business's account with the bank is immediately credited for the total amount of the sales. The business does not have to wait until the customers pay their bills to receive the cash.

Since the bank assumes all expenses related to credit granting and account collection, it charges participating merchants a fee for these services. For example, a business submitting $10,000 of credit card slips to a bank that charges a 3% fee would be charged $300. The amount of the service charge would be deducted on the monthly bank statement. The entry to record the service charge would appear on the company's books as follows:

| | Debit | Credit |
|---|---|---|
| **Credit Card Fee Expense** | **300** | |
| **Cash** | | **300** |
| **Bank credit card fee for March.** | | |

## RECORDING ACCOUNTS RECEIVABLE

It is not unusual for businesses to make charge sales to a large number of customers. An accurate record of both the sales and the payments made by each customer is needed. If these individual records are not maintained, a firm may fail to collect the full amount when due. A record of accounts receivable is maintained by keeping a separate account for each customer. For example, Tom Rose, a wholesale grocer, made the following sales on account during the first part of June, 1982.

June 5 — Sales Invoice No. 530 to Coda's Quik Stop, $285.
7 — Sales Invoice No. 531 to Chung Supermarket, $555.
9 — Sales Invoice No. 532 to Giese Grocery, $410.
10 — Sales Invoice No. 533 to Morris Co., $650.
10 — Sales Invoice No. 534 to Cruz Restaurant, $380.

For each transaction the asset is recorded by a debit to Accounts Receivable in the general ledger and the customer's account, and the revenue is recorded by a credit to Sales. These transactions would be recorded in a general journal as shown on the following page.

**JOURNAL** PAGE 1

| DATE | | DESCRIPTION | POST. REF. | DEBIT | CREDIT |
|---|---|---|---|---|---|
| 1982 | | | | | |
| June | 5 | Accts. Rec.—Coda's Quik Stop......... | | 285 00 | |
| | | Sales................................................ | | | 285 00 |
| | | Sales Invoice No. 530. | | | |
| | 7 | Accts. Rec.—Chung Supermarket.... | | 555 00 | |
| | | Sales................................................ | | | 555 00 |
| | | Sales Invoice No. 531. | | | |
| | 9 | Accts. Rec.—Giese Grocery............. | | 410 00 | |
| | | Sales................................................ | | | 410 00 |
| | | Sales Invoice No. 532. | | | |
| | 10 | Accts. Rec.—Morris Co..................... | | 650 00 | |
| | | Sales................................................ | | | 650 00 |
| | | Sales Invoice No. 533. | | | |
| | 10 | Accts. Rec.—Cruz Restaurant .......... | | 380 00 | |
| | | Sales................................................ | | | 380 00 |
| | | Sales Invoice No. 534. | | | |

*General Journal Entries – Rose Wholesale Co.*

When the above entries have been posted to the ledger, the accounts will appear in T-account form as follows:

General Ledger

**ACCOUNTS RECEIVABLE — CODA'S QUIK STOP (14)**

| | | | |
|---|---|---|---|
| June 5 | 285 | | |

**ACCOUNTS RECEIVABLE — MORRIS CO. (17)**

| | | | |
|---|---|---|---|
| June 10 | 650 | | |

**ACCOUNTS RECEIVABLE — CHUNG SUPERMARKET (15)**

| | | | |
|---|---|---|---|
| June 7 | 555 | | |

**ACCOUNTS RECEIVABLE — CRUZ RESTAURANT (18)**

| | | | |
|---|---|---|---|
| June 10 | 380 | | |

**ACCOUNTS RECEIVABLE — GIESE GROCERY (16)**

| | | | |
|---|---|---|---|
| June 9 | 410 | | |

**SALES (41)**

| | | | |
|---|---|---|---|
| | | June 5 | 285 |
| | | 7 | 555 |
| | | 9 | 410 |
| | | 10 | 650 |
| | | 10 | 380 |

## Accounts Receivable Subsidiary Ledger

The ledger of the Rose Wholesale Co. includes five accounts receivable accounts, one for each customer. A business which has many charge customers will find the procedure of maintaining a separate general ledger account for each charge customer impractical; it would make the preparation of the trial balance and work sheet a burdensome task. The balance sheet itself would be several pages long. This practice would also make errors more difficult to find.

The process of recording and reporting accounts receivable can be simplified by having only one accounts receivable account in the general ledger showing the total amount of accounts receivable from all customers. An account in the general ledger that summarizes a number of individual accounts is called a *control account*. If a single accounts receivable control account is maintained in the general ledger, it is necessary to set up a separate ledger for the individual customers' accounts so that the balance due from each customer is known at all times. This separate customers' ledger is called a *subsidiary ledger*. The subsidiary ledger of customers' accounts is often called an *accounts receivable ledger*.

If Rose, in the preceding illustration, had maintained a separate subsidiary ledger for accounts receivable, the posting of the journal entries on page 111 would be reflected in the following T-accounts.

**General Ledger**

| ACCOUNTS RECEIVABLE | | | (12) |
|---|---|---|---|
| June 5 | 285 | | |
| 7 | 555 | | |
| 9 | 410 | | |
| 10 | 650 | | |
| 10 | 380 | | |

| SALES | | | (41) |
|---|---|---|---|
| | | June 5 | 285 |
| | | 7 | 555 |
| | | 9 | 410 |
| | | 10 | 650 |
| | | 10 | 380 |

**Accounts Receivable Ledger**

| CHUNG SUPERMARKET | | | |
|---|---|---|---|
| June 7 | 555 | | |

| CODA'S QUIK STOP | | | |
|---|---|---|---|
| June 5 | 285 | | |

| CRUZ RESTAURANT | | | |
|---|---|---|---|
| June 10 | 380 | | |

| GIESE GROCERY | | | |
|---|---|---|---|
| June 9 | 410 | | |

| MORRIS CO. | | | |
|---|---|---|---|
| June 10 | 650 | | |

The accounts receivable account in the general ledger shows the total amount to be collected from all charge customers. Therefore, the Accounts Receivable balance should always be equal to the total of the individual accounts in the accounts receivable ledger. Any increase in one of the customer's accounts would be recorded as an increase in the accounts receivable account in the general ledger. Any decrease in one of the customer's accounts would be recorded as a decrease in the accounts receivable account.

To continue the above illustration, assume that Chung Supermarket pays its account in full on June 19. The following entry would be made to record the transaction:

| | | | | | |
|---|---|---|---|---|---|
| | 19 | Cash | 11 | 555 00 | |
| | | Accts. Rec.—Chung Supermarket | 12/√ | | 555 00 |
| | | Received $555 on acct. owed. | | | |

This entry would be posted to the cash account as a debit for $555, and the credit would be posted to both Accounts Receivable in the general ledger and Chung Supermarket in the accounts receivable ledger. To facilitate the posting of the credit amount to both the control account in the general ledger and to the customer's account in the subsidiary ledger, a diagonal line should be placed in the journal's Posting Reference column when the entry is recorded. When the posting is made to the control account, the account number for Accounts Receivable is placed on the left side of the diagonal line. A check mark is entered on the right side when the amount is posted to the customer's account.

After the posting of the journal entry, page 112, has been completed, the control account in the general ledger and the customer's account in the subsidiary ledger would appear as follows:

**General Ledger**

ACCOUNTS RECEIVABLE (11)

| Date | Debit | Date | Credit |
|---|---|---|---|
| June 5 | 285 | June 19 | 555 |
| 7 | 555 | | |
| 9 | 410 | | |
| 10 | 650 | | |
| 10 | 380 | | |

**Accounts Receivable Ledger**

CHUNG SUPERMARKET

| Date | Debit | Date | Credit |
|---|---|---|---|
| June 7 | 555 | June 19 | 555 |

Because the $555 credit was recorded in both the general ledger and the accounts receivable ledger, the balance of the accounts receivable account in the general ledger is still equal to the sum of the individual customers' accounts in the subsidiary ledger.

The customers' accounts in the accounts receivable ledger are arranged alphabetically and do not have a ledger account number assigned to them in the chart of accounts. In previous chapters, each customer's account was given a separate account number in the general ledger. By maintaining a subsidiary ledger for customers' accounts, the account numbers that were assigned to Rose's customers in the general ledger (Nos. 14–18) may now be assigned to other asset accounts.

## SALES JOURNAL

In merchandising firms, numerous sales transactions are recorded. In each of the five sales transactions recorded in the preceding illustration, the same journal entry was made: a debit to Accounts Receivable and a credit to Sales. The only difference in the recording of these transactions was in the customers' accounts in the subsidiary ledger.

Any merchandising enterprise which grants credit to its customers would have a large number of transactions involving the sale of goods on account. To facilitate the recording and posting of this type of transaction, it would be possible to add an Accounts Receivable Dr. column and a Sales Cr. column to the combined cash journal discussed in the preceding chapter. This procedure would be satisfactory in a business that has a limited number of sales on account.

Most businesses have a sufficient number of transactions to justify a separate *sales journal* to be used exclusively for recording the sale of merchandise on account. The sales journal is a book of original entry, and transactions recorded in it are posted directly to the general ledger and the accounts receivable ledger.

Since the only transactions which appear in the sales journal are sales of merchandise on account, the entry will always be a debit to Accounts Receivable and a credit to Sales for the same amount. Therefore, only one amount column is required.

## Sales Journal Illustrated

The following transactions relate to the sales for Rose Wholesale Co. for the month of June, 1982. They are presented to provide a detailed illustration of the recording of such transactions in the sales journal and the postings from the journal to the ledger accounts.

June 5. Sold $285 of merchandise on account to Coda's Quik Stop, Sales Invoice No. 530.
7. Sold $555 of merchandise on account to Chung Supermarket, Sales Invoice No. 531.
9. Sold $410 of merchandise on account to Giese Grocery, Sales Invoice No. 532.
10. Sold $650 of merchandise on account to Morris Co., Sales Invoice No. 533.
10. Sold $380 of merchandise on account to Cruz Restaurant, Sales Invoice No. 534.
12. Sold $950 of merchandise on account to Giese Grocery, Sales Invoice No. 535.
21. Sold $500 of merchandise on account to Coda's Quik Stop, Sales Invoice No. 536.
28. Sold $445 of merchandise on account to Chung Supermarket, Sales Invoice No. 537.
28. Sold $800 of merchandise on account to Coda's Quik Stop, Sales Invoice No. 538.

After the preceding entries have been recorded, the sales journal for the company would appear as shown below.

SALES JOURNAL PAGE 1

| | DATE | | ACCOUNT DEBITED | SALE NO. | POST. REF. | ACCTS. REC. DR. SALES CR. | |
|---|---|---|---|---|---|---|---|
| 1 | 1982 June | 5 | Coda's Quik Stop | 530 | ✓ | 285 00 | 1 |
| 2 | | 7 | Chung Supermarket | 531 | ✓ | 555 00 | 2 |
| 3 | | 9 | Giese Grocery | 532 | ✓ | 410 00 | 3 |
| 4 | | 10 | Morris Co. | 533 | ✓ | 650 00 | 4 |
| 5 | | 10 | Cruz Restaurant | 534 | ✓ | 380 00 | 5 |
| 6 | | 12 | Giese Grocery | 535 | ✓ | 950 00 | 6 |
| 7 | | 21 | Coda's Quik Stop | 536 | ✓ | 500 00 | 7 |
| 8 | | 28 | Chung Supermarket | 537 | ✓ | 445 00 | 8 |
| 9 | | 28 | Coda's Quik Stop | 538 | ✓ | 800 00 | 9 |
| 10 | | 30 | Total | | | 4 975 00 | 10 |
| 11 | | | | | | (12) (41) | 11 |
| 12 | | | | | | | 12 |

Sales Journal – Rose Wholesale Co.

Columns are provided in the sales journal to record the date of the sale, the name of the customer's account to be debited in the subsidiary ledger, the sales invoice number, the posting reference, and the amount of the sale. Each sale of merchandise on account is entered on a separate line in the journal. The sales invoice number is entered in the Sale No. column to provide a reference to the sales invoice should the need arise.

A major advantage of having a separate sales journal is that it permits division of labor within the accounting department. An employee can be recording transactions in the general journal while another employee is recording in the sales journal.

## Posting the Sales Journal

Each entry in the sales journal is posted individually as a debit to the customer's account in the accounts receivable ledger. Posting to the customers' accounts should be made daily if possible, so that the status of their accounts is kept current. This is especially important in a wholesale business where customers purchase large quantities of merchandise on account at one time. Whether the authorized individual, usually the credit manager, would grant further credit depends largely upon the amount owed by the customer and the promptness of the payments. Only an up-to-date customer's ledger account could provide this information.

The posting to the accounts receivable ledger is indicated by a check mark in the Posting Reference column of the sales journal. The letter "S," indicating the sales journal, and the journal page number are recorded in the Posting Reference column of the subsidiary account.

In a manual accounting system the subsidiary ledger of customers' accounts is normally kept in a loose-leaf binder or on individual cards in a file drawer or box. The accounts should be arranged alphabetically, with new accounts being inserted in the proper place. In many merchandising businesses the accounts receivable ledger is kept on a computer, making the assignment of account numbers essential. In these instances, the accounts should be kept by number and all transactions affecting these accounts will require the customer's account number.

The posting of the transactions from the sales journal to the customers' accounts is shown below and on the following page.

NAME Chung Supermarket
ADDRESS 510 N. Main Street, Oklahoma City, OK 73102-6351 TERMS:

| DATE | | ITEM | POST. REF. | DEBIT | CREDIT | BALANCE |
|---|---|---|---|---|---|---|
| 1982 June | 7 | | S1 | 555 00 | | 555 00 |
| | 28 | | S1 | 445 00 | | 445 00 |

***Accounts Receivable Ledger After Posting from Sales Journal***

NAME **Coda's Quik Stop**
ADDRESS **2701 Emelyn Avenue, Norman, OK 73069-7478** TERMS:

| DATE | | ITEM | POST. REF. | DEBIT | CREDIT | BALANCE |
|---|---|---|---|---|---|---|
| 1982 June | 5 | | S1 | 285 00 | | 285 00 |
| | 21 | | S1 | 500 00 | | 500 00 |
| | 28 | | S1 | 800 00 | | 1 300 00 |

NAME **Cruz Restaurant**
ADDRESS **601 E. Cottonwood Road, Norman, OK 73071-6871** TERMS:

| DATE | | ITEM | POST. REF. | DEBIT | CREDIT | BALANCE |
|---|---|---|---|---|---|---|
| 1982 June | 10 | | S1 | 380 00 | | 380 00 |

NAME **Giese Grocery**
ADDRESS **1602 Park Road, W., Oklahoma City, OK 73129-5943** TERMS:

| DATE | | ITEM | POST. REF. | DEBIT | CREDIT | BALANCE |
|---|---|---|---|---|---|---|
| 1982 June | 9 | | S1 | 410 00 | | 410 00 |
| | 12 | | S1 | 950 00 | | 1 360 00 |

NAME **Morris Co.**
ADDRESS **309 Ridgecrest Road, Shawnee, OK 74801-1114** TERMS:

| DATE | | ITEM | POST. REF. | DEBIT | CREDIT | BALANCE |
|---|---|---|---|---|---|---|
| 1982 June | 10 | | S1 | 650 00 | | 650 00 |

***Accounts Receivable Ledger After Posting from Sales Journal (Concluded)***

Because the normal balance in the accounts receivable subsidiary ledger accounts is a debit, a three-column ledger account is used instead of the four-column account form. This form is also designed to show the balance in the account after each transaction.

One of the major advantages of special columns in either a general journal or special journals is that they allow the summarizing of transactions affecting the same account and permit postings to be made by totals rather than individually. Since the sales journal is used to record only the sale of merchandise on account, the total of the amount column can be posted at intervals, usually monthly, as a debit to Accounts Receivable and a credit to Sales. In the preceding illustration, there were nine entries in the sales journal which, if posted separately, would have required nine debits to Accounts Receivable and nine credits to Sales. By posting the total monthly, only one debit and one credit posting to these general ledger accounts is required regardless of the number of transactions in the sales journal. The transactions must still be posted frequently, usually daily, to the customers' accounts in the accounts receivable ledger to keep their account balances current.

When the postings of the totals have been completed, the ledger account numbers of Accounts Receivable (12) and Sales (41) will be inserted below the double-ruled lines in the amount column of the sales journal to indicate that these postings have been made. The two general ledger accounts after posting are shown below:

*General Ledger Accounts After Posting from Sales Journal*

ACCOUNT **Accounts Receivable** ACCOUNT NO. **12**

| DATE | | ITEM | POST. REF. | DEBIT | CREDIT | BALANCE DEBIT | BALANCE CREDIT |
|---|---|---|---|---|---|---|---|
| 1982 June | 30 | | S1 | 4,975.00 | | 4,975.00 | |

ACCOUNT **Sales** ACCOUNT NO. **41**

| DATE | | ITEM | POST. REF. | DEBIT | CREDIT | BALANCE DEBIT | BALANCE CREDIT |
|---|---|---|---|---|---|---|---|
| 1982 June | 30 | | S1 | | 4,975.00 | | 4,975.00 |

## Posting from Sales Tickets

In businesses with many sales on account, the postings to Sales and Accounts Receivable are often made directly from the sales tickets. This practice eliminates the need for a sales journal. The postings to the customers' accounts can be made from these tickets on a daily basis. At the end of the month, the sales tickets are then totaled on an adding machine to determine the amount of sales on account for the period. This total is used to make the entry in the general journal debiting Accounts Receivable and crediting Sales. The sales tickets and the adding machine tape are then filed for future reference.

By eliminating the recording of each transaction in the sales journal, substantial savings in time and expense are realized. The possibility of error is also reduced because amounts are recorded and transferred less often.

## QUESTIONS FOR DISCUSSION

1. From an accounting standpoint, what is the major difference between a service enterprise and a merchandising enterprise?
2. Define the term *merchandise* as used in accounting.
3. Explain how a chair can be classified as inventory in one business and as office equipment in another.
4. (a) What advantage does a firm receive by issuing credit cards to its customers? (b) When does the use of a customer account number become necessary in a business?
5. (a) What type of entry is recorded in the sales journal? (b) Why is it necessary for the sales journal to have only one amount column?
6. Explain the posting of the sales journal to (a) the general ledger and (b) the subsidiary ledger.
7. Green's Shoe Store, a retail store, has about 200 charge sales each month. If a sales journal is used, how much work would be saved in (a) recording and (b) posting these transactions each month as opposed to recording the transactions in a two-column journal?

## EXERCISES

1. In each case listed, name one type of business that would *not* consider the item as inventory and state how the account would be classified in the financial statements using the following form:

| Item | Business *not* considered inventory | How account classified |
|---|---|---|
| a. Stove and oven | *Restaurant* | *Cooking equipment* |
| b. Typewriter | | |
| c. Automobile | | |
| d. Desk | | |
| e. Bed | | |
| f. Stationery | | |

2. Record the following transactions for Russell's Department Store in a two-column general journal:

   Nov. 4. Sold merchandise to Doris Kane on account, $75.
   10. Sold merchandise to Ben Chalk for cash, $105.
   12. Received check from Doris Kane for sale on November 4, $75.
   15. Sold merchandise to Eva Torres on account, $60.

3. Gervin's Men's Shop uses sales tickets as a sales journal. There were 970 sales tickets for charge sales in the month of May. An adding machine tape of these tickets totaled $21,400.

   **Instructions:**
   (1) Prepare the entry in a two-column journal to record this information.
   (2) Explain the procedure for posting to the individual accounts in the subsidiary ledger.
   (3) What are the advantages of using this procedure to record sales on account?

4. Carol's Boutique honors the City Bank Charge Card. During the month of November, charge card sales totaled $8,240. The charge card slips are deposited in City Bank throughout the month, and a 4% fee is deducted for the service on the monthly bank statement.

   **Required:** (a) Prepare a journal entry to record the total charge card sales for November for Carol's Boutique. (b) Prepare the journal entry to record the service charge on November sales. (c) Suppose that Carol's Boutique offered its own credit card. What would be the journal entry to record November's sales?

## ASSIGNMENT 6-A

**Tear out pages 421–424 and complete Assignment 6-A. Submit your papers to your instructor for approval. After completion, continue with the textbook discussion until Assignment 6-B is required.**

# PART B CASH RECEIPTS

The two most common sources of cash receipts in merchandising businesses are cash sales and collections from customers on account.

As described in Chapter 5, the large number of cash transactions in most businesses makes it necessary to provide either special columns in the general journal or a separate cash journal to record these entries. The combined cash journal, which was illustrated in Chapter 5, is frequently used by small businesses to record cash transactions. However, as the business grows and the number of transactions increases, it is desirable to separate the recording of cash receipts from cash payments. This can be accomplished by establishing a special journal for recording all cash received, and a special journal for recording all cash paid out. (The cash payments journal is discussed in the following chapter.)

## CASH RECEIPTS JOURNAL

The *cash receipts journal* is a special journal designed to record all cash received by the business. Since all transactions recorded in the cash receipts journal involve the receipt of cash, there will always be a special column for debits to cash. Because the two most frequent sources of cash receipts are cash sales and collections from customers on account, a Sales Cr. column and an Accounts Receivable Cr. column are also provided. There may be infrequent receipts of cash from other sources necessitating a General Accounts Cr. column. A standard form of cash receipts journal is shown below.

CASH RECEIPTS JOURNAL — PAGE

| | DATE | | ACCOUNT CREDITED | POST. REF. | GENERAL ACCOUNTS CR. | SALES CR. | ACCOUNTS REC. CR. | CASH DR. | |
|---|---|---|---|---|---|---|---|---|---|
| 1 | | | | | | | | | 1 |
| 2 | | | | | | | | | 2 |
| 3 | | | | | | | | | 3 |
| 4 | | | | | | | | | 4 |
| 5 | | | | | | | | | 5 |
| 6 | | | | | | | | | 6 |

***Cash Receipts Journal***

### Cash Receipts Journal Illustrated

The following transactions relate to the cash receipts for Rose Wholesale Co. for the month of June, 1982. They are presented to provide a detailed illustration of the recording of such transactions in the cash receipts journal and the postings from the journal to the ledger accounts.

June 1. Rose invested $20,000 cash in the business.
7. Recorded cash sales for the week, $3,200.
14. Recorded cash sales for the week, $3,800.
16. Received a check from Coda's Quik Stop in payment of Sales Invoice No. 530.
19. Chung Supermarket paid their account in full, $555.
21. Recorded cash sales for the week, $3,640.
24. Received check from Giese Grocery for $1,360 in payment of Sales Invoice Nos. 532 and 535.
28. Recorded cash sales for the week, $3,225.

**CASH RECEIPTS JOURNAL** PAGE 1

| | DATE | | ACCOUNT CREDITED | POST. REF. | GENERAL ACCOUNTS CR. | SALES CR. | ACCOUNTS REC. CR. | CASH DR. | |
|---|---|---|---|---|---|---|---|---|---|
| 1 | 1982 June | 1 | Tom Rose, Capital | 31 | 20000 00 | | | 20000 00 | 1 |
| 2 | | 7 | ✓ | ✓ | | 3200 00 | | 3200 00 | 2 |
| 3 | | 14 | ✓ | ✓ | | 3800 00 | | 3800 00 | 3 |
| 4 | | 16 | Coda's Quik Stop | ✓ | | | 285 00 | 285 00 | 4 |
| 5 | | 19 | Chung Supermarket | ✓ | | | 555 00 | 555 00 | 5 |
| 6 | | 21 | ✓ | ✓ | | 3640 00 | | 3640 00 | 6 |
| 7 | | 24 | Giese Grocery | ✓ | | | 1360 00 | 1360 00 | 7 |
| 8 | | 28 | ✓ | ✓ | | 3225 00 | | 3225 00 | 8 |
| | | | | | 20000 00 | 13865 00 | 2200 00 | 36065 00 | |
| 9 | | 30 | Totals | | 20000 00 | 13865 00 | 2200 00 | 36065 00 | 9 |
| 10 | | | | | (✓) | (41) | (12) | (11) | 10 |

*Cash Receipts Journal – Rose Wholesale Co.*

## Posting the Cash Receipts Journal

The posting from the cash receipts journal follows the same rules as posting from any special journal. All special columns are posted by total at the end of the month. All entries in the General Accounts Cr. column are posted individually; the total for this column is not posted. All subsidiary customers' accounts are posted individually at regular intervals, usually daily.

At the end of the month, prior to posting the column totals, the cash receipts journal amount columns should be pencil footed; the equality of the debits and credits should be proved; the column totals should be entered in ink; and the journal columns should be ruled. The cash receipts journal would be proved by adding machine tape or by a schedule as shown below.

| Debit Column | | Credit Columns | |
|---|---|---|---|
| Cash | $36,065 | Sales | $13,865 |
| | | Accounts Receivable | 2,200 |
| | | General Accounts | 20,000 |
| | $36,065 | | $36,065 |

The posting from each column would be accomplished as follows:

**General Accounts Cr.** The purpose of this column is to record all credits in the cash receipts journal which do not belong in a special column. Since this is a general column where many accounts are recorded, these accounts must be posted individually during the month. The column will be totaled and ruled; however, the column total will not be posted. A check mark is placed below the column total to indicate that the total is not posted. When an individual account is posted, the account number is entered in the Posting Reference column of the journal. The initials *CR*, indicating cash receipts journal, and the journal page number where the transaction was recorded are entered in the Posting Reference column of the ledger account.

**Sales Cr.** The individual cash sales are tallied in the cash register and the accumulated total is recorded in the cash receipts journal when the register is checked and cleared. This would normally be accomplished daily, but in small businesses it might be done at less frequent intervals such as weekly. In the preceding illustration, the cash sales were recorded weekly. All cash sales of merchandise are recorded in the Sales Cr. column of the cash receipts journal. Remember, only sales on account are recorded in the sales journal.

When cash sales are recorded in the cash receipts journal, a check mark is placed in the Account Credited column and the amount is recorded in the Sales Cr. and Cash Dr. columns. For example, the transaction on June 7 represents the recording of weekly cash sales. Since the Sales Cr. column will be posted as a total at the end of the month, a check mark is inserted in the Posting Reference column to indicate that the individual amount is not posted. When the Sales Cr. column is posted in total, the ledger account number for Sales (41) is written below the double-ruled total.

**Accounts Receivable Cr.** Cash received from customers in payment of their accounts is recorded in the Accounts Receivable Cr. column and the Cash Dr. column. Note the transaction for Coda's Quik Stop on June 16. The name of the customer's account is written in the Account Credited column. The posting to the customer's subsidiary ledger account should be made daily to keep the account balance current. When the posting is made to the customer's account in the subsidiary ledger, a check mark is placed in the Posting Reference column.

At the end of the month, the total of the Accounts Receivable Cr. column is posted to Accounts Receivable in the general ledger. When this posting is completed, the ledger account number for Accounts Receivable (12) is written below the ruled column total.

**Cash Dr.** The purpose of the cash receipts journal is to record all transactions involving the receipt of cash. Therefore the Cash Dr. column will have an entry for every transaction recorded in this journal. This column is posted to the cash account in the general ledger as a total at the end of the period, and the account number for Cash (11) is recorded below the ruled column total.

After posting the transactions from both the sales and cash receipts journals, the general ledger accounts would appear as shown below and on the following page.

ACCOUNT **Cash** ACCOUNT NO. **11**

| DATE | | ITEM | POST. REF. | DEBIT | CREDIT | BALANCE DEBIT | BALANCE CREDIT |
|---|---|---|---|---|---|---|---|
| 1982 June | 30 | | CR1 | 36 065 00 | | 36 065 00 | |

ACCOUNT **Accounts Receivable** ACCOUNT NO. **12**

| DATE | | ITEM | POST. REF. | DEBIT | CREDIT | BALANCE DEBIT | BALANCE CREDIT |
|---|---|---|---|---|---|---|---|
| 1982 June | 30 | | S1 | 4 975 00 | | 4 975 00 | |
| | 30 | | CR1 | | 2 200 00 | 2 775 00 | |

*General Ledger Accounts After Posting from Sales Journal and Cash Receipts Journal*

| ACCOUNT Tom Rose, Capital | | | | | ACCOUNT NO. 31 | |
|---|---|---|---|---|---|---|
| DATE | ITEM | POST. REF. | DEBIT | CREDIT | BALANCE | |
| | | | | | DEBIT | CREDIT |
| 1982 June 1 | | CR1 | | 20 000 00 | | 20 000 00 |

| ACCOUNT Sales | | | | | ACCOUNT NO. 41 | |
|---|---|---|---|---|---|---|
| DATE | ITEM | POST. REF. | DEBIT | CREDIT | BALANCE | |
| | | | | | DEBIT | CREDIT |
| 1982 June 30 | | S1 | | 4 975 00 | | 4 975 00 |
| 30 | | CR1 | | 13 865 00 | | 18 840 00 |

*General Ledger Accounts After Posting from Sales Journal and Cash Receipts Journal (concluded)*

## SCHEDULE OF ACCOUNTS RECEIVABLE

After Rose's sales journal and cash receipts journal have been posted for the month of June, the accounts receivable account shown on page 121 has a debit balance of $2,775. This consists of the $4,975 debit from the sales journal and the $2,200 credit from the cash receipts journal.

Since Accounts Receivable is the control account for the customers' subsidiary ledger, the balance in the accounts receivable account should be the same as the total of the balances in the customers' accounts. A schedule of the balances in the accounts receivable ledger should be prepared at the end of the month to insure that the sum of the customers' account balances is equal to the balance in the accounts receivable control account. If the total of the subsidiary ledger and the general ledger controlling account are not in agreement, the discrepancy must be found and corrected. However, the fact that the two totals are in agreement does not guarantee correctness. For example, a posting of the correct amount to the wrong customer's account would not be revealed by this comparison.

A schedule of accounts receivable prepared from the subsidiary ledger on page 123 is shown below. The Giese Grocery account was omitted from the schedule because it had a zero balance at the end of the month.

**Rose Wholesale Co.**
**Schedule of Accounts Receivable**
**June 30, 1982**

| | | |
|---|---|---|
| Chung Supermarket | | 445 00 |
| Coda's Quik Stop | | 1 300 00 |
| Cruz Restaurant | | 380 00 |
| Morris Co. | | 650 00 |
| Total accounts receivable | | 2 775 00 |

*Schedule of Accounts Receivable*

The total of the above schedule, $2,775, agrees with the balance in Accounts Receivable in the general ledger. It is also possible to summarize the accounts receivable ledger by merely preparing an adding machine tape of the account balances. The total of the customers' account balances is then compared to the balance in the general ledger control account.

NAME Chung Supermarket

ADDRESS 510 N. Main Street, Oklahoma City, OK 73102-6351 TERMS:

| DATE | | ITEM | POST. REF. | DEBIT | CREDIT | BALANCE |
|---|---|---|---|---|---|---|
| 1982 | | | | | | |
| June | 7 | | S1 | 555 00 | | 555 00 |
| | 19 | | CR1 | | 555 00 | — |
| | 28 | | S1 | 445 00 | | 445 00 |

NAME Coda's Quik Stop

ADDRESS 2701 Emelyn Avenue, Norman, OK 73069-7478 TERMS:

| DATE | | ITEM | POST. REF. | DEBIT | CREDIT | BALANCE |
|---|---|---|---|---|---|---|
| 1982 | | | | | | |
| June | 5 | | S1 | 285 00 | | 285 00 |
| | 16 | | CR1 | | 285 00 | — |
| | 21 | | S1 | 500 00 | | 500 00 |
| | 28 | | S1 | 800 00 | | 1 300 00 |

NAME Cruz Restaurant

ADDRESS 601 E. Cottonwood Road, Norman, OK 73071-6871 TERMS:

| DATE | | ITEM | POST. REF. | DEBIT | CREDIT | BALANCE |
|---|---|---|---|---|---|---|
| 1982 | | | | | | |
| June | 10 | | S1 | 380 00 | | 380 00 |

NAME Giese Grocery

ADDRESS 1602 Park Road, W., Oklahoma City, OK 73129-5943 TERMS:

| DATE | | ITEM | POST. REF. | DEBIT | CREDIT | BALANCE |
|---|---|---|---|---|---|---|
| 1982 | | | | | | |
| June | 9 | | S1 | 410 00 | | 410 00 |
| | 12 | | S1 | 950 00 | | 1 360 00 |
| | 24 | | CR1 | | 1 360 00 | — |

NAME Morris Co.

ADDRESS 309 Ridgecrest Road, Shawnee, OK 74801-1114 TERMS:

| DATE | | ITEM | POST. REF. | DEBIT | CREDIT | BALANCE |
|---|---|---|---|---|---|---|
| 1982 | | | | | | |
| June | 10 | | S1 | 650 00 | | 650 00 |

*Accounts Receivable Ledger After Posting from Sales Journal and Cash Receipts Journal*

## SALES TAXES

Most states and many cities impose a sales tax. A *sales tax* is a fixed percentage tax based on retail sales of goods and services. In many areas both state and local sales taxes are assessed.

Sales tax is usually imposed on the consumer, but the seller must collect the tax, file a sales tax return, and remit the amount due at specified intervals. In some states the tax is levied directly upon the seller.

Certain types of commodities are often exempt from sales taxes. These include the sale of food for consumption off the premises of the seller and such items as gasoline and cigarettes which are subject to special state taxes. Also sales made to state agencies and other public institutions, such as state police, the national guard, and schools, are frequently exempt from sales tax.

### Recording the Sales Tax on Charge Sales

If the law imposes the sales tax on the consumer but requires the retailer to collect and remit the tax, the amount of the sales tax must be added to each sale. The tax is added at the time of the sale, regardless of when the cash is to be collected. Therefore, the liability for the tax should be recorded at the time of the sale.

To illustrate, assume that Van Horn Pharmacy in Mobile, Alabama, must collect a 5% sales tax on all merchandise sold. If Van Horn sells merchandise to Kyle Ellis for $100 plus the 5% sales tax, the entry, in general journal form, would be:

**JOURNAL** PAGE 2

| | DATE | | DESCRIPTION | POST. REF. | DEBIT | CREDIT | |
|---|---|---|---|---|---|---|---|
| | 1982 | | | | | | |
| 1 | June | 12 | Accounts Receivable — Kyle Ellis ... | | 105 00 | | 1 |
| 2 | | | Sales........ | | | 100 00 | 2 |
| 3 | | | Sales Tax Payable........ | | | 5 00 | 3 |
| 4 | | | Sales Invoice No. 217. | | | | 4 |
| 5 | | | | | | | 5 |

Sales Tax Payable represents the amount owed to the state for the sales tax collected and is shown on the balance sheet as a liability until paid.

If a business operates in a state or city where a sales tax is imposed on most sales, it is desirable to provide a column in the sales journal for Sales Tax Payable Cr., as illustrated below.

**SALES JOURNAL** PAGE 2

| | DATE | | INV. NO. | ACCOUNT DEBITED | POST. REF. | ACCOUNTS RECEIVABLE DR. | SALES TAX PAYABLE CR. | SALES CR. | |
|---|---|---|---|---|---|---|---|---|---|
| 1 | 1982 June | 12 | 217 | Kyle Ellis | | 105 00 | 5 00 | 100 00 | 1 |
| 2 | | | | | | | | | 2 |
| 3 | | | | | | | | | 3 |
| 4 | | | | | | | | | 4 |
| 5 | | | | | | | | | 5 |

*Three-Column Sales Journal*

At the end of the period, this three-column sales journal is totaled and checked for accuracy by adding the Sales Tax Payable Cr. and the Sales Cr. column totals to insure that they are equal to the Accounts Receivable Dr. column total.

When the invoice is paid, the entry is a debit to Cash and a credit to Accounts Receivable, as shown in the cash receipts journal below.

**CASH RECEIPTS JOURNAL** PAGE 2

| DATE | | ACCOUNT CREDITED | POST. REF. | GENERAL ACCOUNTS CR. | SALES CR. | ACCOUNTS RECEIVABLE CR. | CASH DR. |
|---|---|---|---|---|---|---|---|
| 1982 July | 8 | Kyle Ellis | | | | 105 00 | 105 00 |

## Recording the Sales Tax on Cash Sales

If the above sale had been for cash, the entry would have been a debit to Cash and a credit to Sales and to Sales Tax Payable:

**JOURNAL** PAGE 2

| DATE | | DESCRIPTION | POST. REF. | DEBIT | CREDIT |
|---|---|---|---|---|---|
| 1982 June | 12 | Cash | | 105 00 | |
| | | Sales | | | 100 00 |
| | | Sales Tax Payable | | | 5 00 |
| | | To record cash sale. | | | |

If special journals are being used by Van Horn Pharmacy, the above transaction would be recorded in the cash receipts journal. If Van Horn Pharmacy has frequent cash sales involving sales taxes, it is desirable to include a special column for Sales Tax Payable Cr. in the cash receipts journal. The preceding entry would be recorded in the cash receipts journal as follows:

**CASH RECEIPTS JOURNAL** PAGE 2

| DATE | | ACCOUNT CREDITED | POST. REF. | GENERAL ACCOUNTS CR. | SALES CR. | ACCOUNTS REC. CR. | SALES TAX PAYABLE CR. | CASH DR. |
|---|---|---|---|---|---|---|---|---|
| 1982 June | 12 | ✓ | ✓ | | 100 00 | | 5 00 | 105 00 |

*Cash Receipts Journal with Sales Tax Column*

## Paying Sales Taxes

The sales tax collected by the retailer must be paid to the proper governmental unit. When and how sales tax is paid depends on the regulations of the taxing authority. In many states the sales tax is paid quarterly (every three months), while other states require sales tax to be paid monthly.

When the tax is paid, an entry is made debiting the liability Sales Tax Payable and crediting Cash. To illustrate, assume that Van Horn Pharmacy owed sales tax of $410.60 for the first quarter of the year. The entry, in general journal form, to record the payment would be as shown below.

**JOURNAL** PAGE 1

| DATE | | DESCRIPTION | POST. REF. | DEBIT | CREDIT |
|---|---|---|---|---|---|
| 1982 | | | | | |
| April | 2 | Sales Tax Payable.................................... | | 410 60 | |
| | | Cash .................................................... | | | 410 60 |
| | | Payment of quarterly sales tax. | | | |
| | | | | | |

## QUESTIONS FOR DISCUSSION

1. (a) Name the two most common sources of cash receipts in a merchandising business. (b) How are these sources of cash recorded in the cash receipts journal?
2. If the bookkeeper makes an error in adding the Sales Cr. column in the cash receipts journal, how will this error be detected?
3. A $400 sale of merchandise on account to Jake Waller was erroneously posted as a $400 debit to the account of Jack Wallis in the accounts receivable subsidiary ledger. Would this error be discovered when a schedule of accounts receivable was prepared and checked against the accounts receivable account in the general ledger? Explain.
4. (a) How often should the accounts in the accounts receivable subsidiary ledger be posted from the sales journal and cash receipts journal? (b) Why is this posting done more frequently than the posting to the accounts in the general ledger?
5. (a) At what level (wholesale or retail) are most sales taxes levied? (b) What type of organizations are frequently exempt from sales taxes?
6. Where will the account Sales Tax Payable be shown on the balance sheet?

## EXERCISES

1. Below you are given the totals for the cash receipts journal of Holly Company at the end of August.

**CASH RECEIPTS JOURNAL** PAGE 3

| DATE | | ACCOUNT CREDITED | POST. REF. | GENERAL ACCOUNTS CR. | SALES CR. | ACCOUNTS RECEIVABLE CR. | CASH DR. |
|---|---|---|---|---|---|---|---|
| 19-- | | | | | | | |
| Aug. | | | | | | | |
| | 31 | | | 300 00 | 865 00 | 275 00 | 1 440 00 |

**Required:**

(a) Prepare a schedule to prove the totals in the cash receipts journal.

(b) What will be the total credit amount posted to the accounts receivable subsidiary ledger from the cash receipts journal. Why?

2. You have the following account in your accounts receivable subsidiary ledger:

NAME **Marvin Berkeley**

ADDRESS **13958 Hughes Lane, Ft. Wayne, IN 40805-1492** TERMS:

| DATE | | ITEM | POST. REF. | DEBIT | CREDIT | BALANCE |
|---|---|---|---|---|---|---|
| 19-- | | | | | | |
| Mar. | 3 | | S6 | 214 00 | | 214 00 |
| | 22 | | S7 | 205 00 | | 419 00 |
| | 29 | | CR4 | | 214 00 | 205 00 |
| Apr. | 5 | | S8 | 190 00 | | 395 00 |
| | 16 | | CR5 | | 205 00 | 190 00 |

**Required:** From the information given, record in a general journal the entries reflected in Berkeley's account. Indicate the special journal in which each entry would have been properly recorded.

3. On November 7, a retailer sells $220 of merchandise to Jane Quigley on account and adds to the sales ticket 4% state sales tax. (a) Present the general journal entry to record the transaction. (b) Present the general journal entry to record receipt of payment on November 30 for the invoice in the transaction in (a).

## ASSIGNMENT 6-B

**Tear out pages 425–436 and complete Assignment 6-B. Submit your papers for approval. After completion, proceed to the study of Chapter 7 until the next assignment is required.**

Chapter 7

# ACCOUNTING FOR THE PURCHASE OF MERCHANDISE

The procedures involved in accounting for the sale of merchandise and the receipt of cash were discussed in Chapter 6. This chapter examines accounting procedures related to the purchase of merchandise and the disbursement of cash.

## PART A *PURCHASES AND ACCOUNTS PAYABLE*

The account that shows the cost of merchandise bought for resale to customers is titled Purchases. The use of the purchases account is limited specifically to merchandise transactions, as was the sales account in Chapter 6. These accounts are used to identify goods which the business acquires for the expressed purpose of resale.

Other items such as supplies and equipment that are purchased for use in the business rather than for resale are debited to individual asset accounts rather than the purchases account.

The purchases and sales accounts are temporary accounts. They are shown on the income statement at the end of the accounting period and are closed to Income Summary along with the other income statement accounts. The merchandise acquired during the period is charged to Purchases but any goods on hand at the end of the period will be shown on the balance sheet as an asset, merchandise inventory. The end-of-period procedures for closing the sales and purchases accounts to the income summary account and for adjusting the merchandise inventory account are discussed in Chapter 9.

### RECORDING PURCHASES

When merchandise is acquired either for cash or on account, the purchases account is debited for the cost of the goods. For example, if merchandise was purchased on May 5 for $200 cash, the entry in general journal form would be:

**JOURNAL** — PAGE 4

| DATE | | DESCRIPTION | POST. REF. | DEBIT | CREDIT |
|---|---|---|---|---|---|
| 1982 | | | | | |
| May | 5 | Purchases | | 200 00 | |
| | | Cash | | | 200 00 |
| | | Purchased merch. for cash. | | | |

Most businesses find it more convenient to buy merchandise on account. Buying on account often gives the merchant time to sell the goods and collect the revenue from customers before paying the creditors. This allows a large volume of business activity without requiring additional invested capital.

When a merchant purchases merchandise and promises to pay for it in the future, Purchases and Accounts Payable are increased. For example, if the $200 of merchandise had been purchased on account from the FBC Co., the entry would be:

| DATE | | DESCRIPTION | POST. REF. | DEBIT | CREDIT |
|---|---|---|---|---|---|
| | 15 | Purchases | | 200 00 | |
| | | Accounts Payable — FBC Co. | | | 200 00 |
| | | Purchased merchandise on account. | | | |

This entry reflects the receipt of the goods. It also indicates a legal debt of the business to the company from whom the goods were acquired. This liability would be shown on the balance sheet until it is paid. When the liability is paid, the entry is:

| DATE | | DESCRIPTION | POST. REF. | DEBIT | CREDIT |
|---|---|---|---|---|---|
| | 20 | Accounts Payable — FBC Co. | | 200 00 | |
| | | Cash | | | 200 00 |
| | | Paid account in full. | | | |

This entry reduces both the liability accounts payable and the asset cash. No entry is required in the purchases account because the merchandise was recorded at the time of purchase.

## PURCHASE INVOICE

An *invoice* is a business document showing the names and addresses of the buyer and the seller, the date and terms of the sale, the description, quantity, unit price, and total price of the goods purchased, and the mode of transportation to be used. The seller calls this document a *sales invoice* whereas it is known as a *purchase invoice* to the buyer. A copy of the invoice is usually mailed by the seller to the buyer when the goods are shipped.

The purchase invoice provides the buyer with the information necessary to record the purchase. An invoice received by Rose Wholesale Co. for goods shipped by the Warren Gum Company is shown below. The arrangement of the information on the invoice varies depending upon the needs of the seller. Note the *purchase invoice number* (41) in the upper right corner of the invoice. This should not be confused with the *sales invoice number* (J5-207) of the seller. The purchase invoice number is assigned by the buyer when the invoice is received. The consecutive numbering of the invoices as they are received enables the buyer to easily account for every purchase.

PHONE 214:271-1188

No. **41**

**Warren Gum Company**

RECEIVED June 15, 1982

TERMS 2/10, n/30

5107 Akard Street
Dallas, TX 75215-1330

SOLD TO
ROSE WHOLESALE CO.
208 SCOTT ST.
OKLAHOMA CITY, OK 73115-2357

| INVOICE NO. | INVOICE DATE | DATE SHIPPED | SHIPPED VIA |
|---|---|---|---|
| J5-207 | June 9, 1982 | June 10, 1982 | Freight |

| QUANTITY | DESCRIPTION | UNIT PRICE | TOTAL |
|---|---|---|---|
| 30 boxes | Spearmint | 7.00 | 210.00 |
| 40 boxes | Sugarless | 7.50 | 300.00 |
| 70 boxes | Bubble gum | 2.00 | 140.00 |
| 10 boxes | Peppermint | 7.50 | 75.00 |
| | | | 725.00 |

***Purchase Invoice***

The invoice usually arrives before the goods. The items, terms, quantities, and prices on the invoice should be compared to the data on the purchase order. The *purchase order* is the original request by the buyer to have the goods shipped. When the merchandise is received, it should be inspected and counted. The following verifications are made: **(1)** that the items received were in good condition, **(2)** that the items received were those ordered as to quantity and description, **(3)** that the unit prices were those originally quoted by the seller, and **(4)** that the extensions and invoice total are correct. The *extensions* are the individual totals arrived at by multiplying the quantity of each item received by its unit price. After the invoice has been checked, the purchase is recorded and the invoice is filed for payment at the appropriate time.

## RECORDING ACCOUNTS PAYABLE

The purchase of merchandise on account is recorded as a debit to Purchases and a credit to Accounts Payable. An account is opened for each creditor so that the proper amounts may be paid when due. The use of individual accounts also enables the total amount owed to a creditor to be readily determined at any time. As with Accounts Receivable, recording in the general ledger the details of the individual account with each creditor is neither necessary nor desirable. The total of the accounts payable to all creditors is shown in the general ledger by use of the control account, Accounts Payable. A separate subsidiary ledger containing the details of each creditor's account is also maintained. This subsidiary ledger is often called the *accounts payable ledger* or the *creditors ledger*.

To illustrate the accounting for purchases of merchandise on account, the June transactions of Rose Wholesale Co. are presented below. Purchases for other items that are not considered merchandise were also made during the month of June; however these items are not illustrated. Therefore, in the example, the purchase invoice numbers will not appear in consecutive order. June is the first month of business operations.

June 2. Purchased merchandise on account from Checker Sugar Co., $1,185. Purchase Invoice No. 39.
9. Purchased merchandise on account from Warren Gum Company, $725. Purchase Invoice No. 41.
12. Purchased merchandise on account from Sweet Candy Co., $2,135. Purchase Invoice No. 42.
17. Purchased merchandise on account from Davis Pickles, $1,196. Purchase Invoice No. 44.

After the purchases are recorded and posted, the general journal, general ledger, and accounts payable subsidiary ledger, appear as follows:

**JOURNAL** PAGE 2

| DATE | | DESCRIPTION | POST. REF. | DEBIT | CREDIT |
|---|---|---|---|---|---|
| | 2 | Purchases | 51 | 1 185 00 | |
| | | Accts. Pay.—Checker Sugar Co. | 21/√ | | 1 185 00 |
| | | Purchase Invoice No. 39. | | | |
| | 9 | Purchases | 51 | 725 00 | |
| | | Accts. Pay.—Warren Gum Co. | 21/√ | | 725 00 |
| | | Purchase Invoice No. 41. | | | |
| | 12 | Purchases | 51 | 2 135 00 | |
| | | Accts. Pay.—Sweet Candy Co. | 21/√ | | 2 135 00 |
| | | Purchase Invoice No. 42. | | | |
| | 17 | Purchases | 51 | 1 196 00 | |
| | | Accts. Pay.—Davis Pickles | 21/√ | | 1 196 00 |
| | | Purchase Invoice No. 44. | | | |

*General Journal Entries – Rose Wholesale Co.*

ACCOUNT **Accounts Payable** ACCOUNT NO. **21**

| DATE | | ITEM | POST. REF. | DEBIT | CREDIT | BALANCE DEBIT | BALANCE CREDIT |
|---|---|---|---|---|---|---|---|
| 1982 June | 2 | | J2 | | 1 185 00 | | 1 185 00 |
| | 9 | | J2 | | 725 00 | | 2 241 00 |
| | 12 | | J2 | | 2 135 00 | | 4 376 00 |
| | 17 | | J2 | | 1 196 00 | | 8 814 00 |

ACCOUNT **Purchases** ACCOUNT NO. **51**

| DATE | | ITEM | POST. REF. | DEBIT | CREDIT | BALANCE DEBIT | BALANCE CREDIT |
|---|---|---|---|---|---|---|---|
| 1982 June | 2 | | J2 | 1 185 00 | | 1 185 00 | |
| | 9 | | J2 | 725 00 | | 11 110 00 | |
| | 12 | | J2 | 2 135 00 | | 13 245 00 | |
| | 17 | | J2 | 1 196 00 | | 14 441 00 | |

*General Ledger Accounts – Rose Wholesale Co.*

NAME **Checker Sugar Co.**
ADDRESS **2107 Georgia Ave., N.E., St. Louis, MO 63135-1097** TERMS:

| DATE | | ITEM | POST. REF. | DEBIT | CREDIT | BALANCE |
|---|---|---|---|---|---|---|
| 1982 June | 2 | | J2 | | 1 185 00 | 1 185 00 |

NAME **Davis Pickles**
ADDRESS **17401 Sunset Drive, Tulsa, OK 74114-3283** TERMS:

| DATE | | ITEM | POST. REF. | DEBIT | CREDIT | BALANCE |
|---|---|---|---|---|---|---|
| 1982 June | 17 | | J2 | | 1 196 00 | 1 196 00 |

NAME **Sweet Candy Co.**
ADDRESS **900 S. Fairmont Ave., Oklahoma City, OK 73129-5155** TERMS:

| DATE | | ITEM | POST. REF. | DEBIT | CREDIT | BALANCE |
|---|---|---|---|---|---|---|
| 1982 June | 12 | | J2 | | 2 135 00 | 2 135 00 |

NAME **Warren Gum Company**
ADDRESS **5107 Akard Street, Dallas, TX 75215-1330** TERMS:

| DATE | | ITEM | POST. REF. | DEBIT | CREDIT | BALANCE |
|---|---|---|---|---|---|---|
| 1982 June | 9 | | J2 | | 725 00 | 725 00 |

*Accounts Payable Ledger – Rose Wholesale Co.*

Because the normal balance in the accounts payable subsidiary ledger accounts is a credit, a three-column ledger account is used instead of the four-column account form. This form indicates the balance owed to the creditor after each transaction. The address of each creditor is entered on the subsidiary ledger account to avoid confusing accounts with similar names. Ready access to the address also facilitates payment.

The accounts payable account in the general ledger is a control account representing the total of all the individual creditors' accounts in the accounts payable ledger. The balance in the accounts payable account, after all postings have been made, should equal the total of the balances of the subsidiary accounts.

When an entry is made in the journal involving both a control account and a subsidiary account, a diagonal line is placed in the Posting Reference column to facilitate the posting to both accounts. For example, see the first transaction dated June 2 on page 131. When the posting is made to the control account, Accounts Payable, the account number (21) is placed on the left side of the diagonal line. When the amount is posted to the creditor's account, Checker Sugar Co., a check mark is entered on the right side of the diagonal line.

## PURCHASES JOURNAL

Although a business usually makes fewer purchases than sales, purchases nevertheless occur frequently. If these purchases are recorded in a two-column journal as on page 131, it is necessary to show the account to be debited on one line and the account to be credited on another line. Furthermore, each transaction requires three postings: one each to Purchases, Accounts Payable, and the creditor's account in the subsidiary ledger. Since each of Rose's four transactions were purchases of merchandise on account, it is evident that a less laborious method of recording purchases is desirable. These transactions may be recorded in a separate book of original entry called a *purchases journal*.

### Single-Column Purchases Journal

In a business where the volume of purchases on account is large, a single-column purchases journal may be used. The transactions for Rose, recorded in a single-column purchases journal, are shown below.

PURCHASES JOURNAL — PAGE 1

| | DATE | | ACCOUNT CREDITED | PURCH. NO. | POST. REF. | PURCHASES. DR. ACCTS. PAY. CR. | |
|---|---|---|---|---|---|---|---|
| | 1982 | | | | | | |
| 1 | June | 2 | Checker Sugar Co. | 39 | ✓ | 1 185 00 | 1 |
| 2 | | 9 | Warren Gum Company | 41 | ✓ | 725 00 | 2 |
| 3 | | 12 | Sweet Candy Co. | 42 | ✓ | 2 135 00 | 3 |
| 4 | | 17 | Davis Pickles | 44 | ✓ | 1 196 00 | 4 |
| 5 | | | | | | | 5 |
| 6 | | | | | | | 6 |

**Single-Column Purchases Journal – Rose Wholesale Co.**

The single-column purchases journal is similar to the sales journal shown on page 114. With only one amount column, the purchases journal is restricted to purchases of merchandise on account. The posting of the amount column total would be accomplished monthly, or more often if necessary, with a debit to Purchases and a credit to Accounts Payable in the general ledger. The individual creditors' accounts would be posted daily to the subsidiary ledger. When each posting is made, a check mark (√) is written in the Posting Reference column of the purchases journal. The letter "P," indicating the origin of the entry as the purchases journal and the page number where the entry appears are written in the Posting Reference column of both the general ledger accounts and the subsidiary ledger accounts. The subsidiary ledger accounts would appear exactly the same as shown earlier on page 132 except that the posting reference would be P1.

## Multicolumn Purchases Journal Illustrated

The format for the purchases journal varies widely among businesses and depends upon such factors as the size and nature of the business and the amount of information desired by the owner. In most businesses, assets in addition to merchandise are purchased on account. The most common assets regularly purchased on account by a mercantile enterprise are: (1) merchandise inventory to be sold to customers, (2) supplies, and (3) equipment. Since goods are normally ordered in large quantities, thus limiting the number of purchases of merchandise in any one period, and because a variety of other assets are bought on account, the purchases journal is often expanded to accommodate the recording of all purchases on account. This expanded form of purchases journal is called a *multicolumn purchases journal*. A multicolumn purchases journal for Rose Wholesale Co. is illustrated on page 135 by expanding the June transactions as follows:

June 2. Purchased merchandise on account from Checker Sugar Co., $1,185. Purchase Invoice No. 39.
- 7. Purchased the following from Queen Supply Co. on account: store supplies, $156; office supplies, $175. Purchase Invoice No. 40.
- 9. Purchased merchandise on account from Warren Gum Company, $725. Purchase Invoice No. 41.
- 12. Purchased merchandise on account from Sweet Candy Co., $2,135. Purchase Invoice No. 42.
- 16. Purchased store equipment, $3,100, and store supplies, $142, on account from Omni Equipment Co. Purchase Invoice No. 43.
- 17. Purchased merchandise on account from Davis Pickles, $1,196. Purchase Invoice No. 44.
- 21. Purchased office equipment on account from Omni Equipment Co., $850. Purchase Invoice No. 45.
- 23. Purchased the following on account from Queen Supply Co.: store supplies, $170; office supplies, $120. Purchase Invoice No. 46.
- 26. Purchased merchandise on account from Davis Pickles, $920. Purchase Invoice No. 47.
- 28. Purchased merchandise on account from Checker Sugar Co., $1,220. Purchase Invoice No. 48.

Since the purpose of the multicolumn purchases journal is to record all purchases on account, each transaction recorded in this journal requires a credit to Accounts Payable. Therefore, as a matter of convenience, the Accounts Payable Cr. column is usually the first amount column listed. This is normally the only credit column in the journal.

PURCHASES JOURNAL — PAGE 1

| DATE | | ACCOUNT CREDITED | POST. REF. | ACCOUNTS PAYABLE CR. | PURCHASES DR. | STORE SUPPLIES DR. | GENERAL ACCOUNTS DR. ACCOUNT | POST. REF. | AMOUNT |
|---|---|---|---|---|---|---|---|---|---|
| 1982 June | 2 | Checker Sugar Co. | ✓ | 1185 00 | 1185 00 | | | | |
| | 7 | Queen Supply Co. | ✓ | 331 00 | | 156 00 | Office Supplies | 15 | 175 00 |
| | 9 | Warren Gum Company | ✓ | 725 00 | 725 00 | | | | |
| | 12 | Sweet Candy Co. | ✓ | 2135 00 | 2135 00 | | | | |
| | 16 | Omni Equipment Co. | ✓ | 3242 00 | | 142 00 | Store Equipment | 17 | 3100 00 |
| | 17 | Davis Pickles | ✓ | 1196 00 | 1196 00 | | | | |
| | 21 | Omni Equipment Co. | ✓ | 850 00 | | | Office Equipment | 18 | 850 00 |
| | 23 | Queen Supply Co. | ✓ | 290 00 | | 170 00 | Office Supplies | 15 | 120 00 |
| | 26 | Davis Pickles | ✓ | 920 00 | 920 00 | | | | |
| | 28 | Checker Sugar Co. | ✓ | 1220 00 | 1220 00 | | | | |
| | | | | 12094 00 | 7381 00 | 468 00 | | | 4245 00 |
| | 30 | Totals | | 12094 00 | 7381 00 | 468 00 | | | 4245 00 |
| | | | | (21) | (51) | (14) | | | (✓) |

***Multicolumn Purchases Journal – Rose Wholesale Co.***

The other special columns are used to record debits to individual accounts with frequent purchases. The Purchases Dr. column is used to record merchandise purchased for resale. The use of special columns such as the Store Supplies Dr. column above is based on the assumption that purchases of this type of asset will occur frequently.

The last set of columns, under the heading of General Accounts Dr., is used to record assets purchased on account which do not occur with enough frequency to merit individual columns.

**Posting the Multicolumn Purchases Journal.** The individual amounts in the Accounts Payable Cr. column of the purchases journal are posted daily to the creditors' accounts in the accounts payable subsidiary ledger following the same procedure as posting from a single-column purchases journal.

The subsidiary ledger of accounts payable, after the postings from the purchases journal have been completed for the month of June, is shown below and on the following page.

***Accounts Payable Ledger After Posting from Multicolumn Purchases Journal***

NAME **Checker Sugar Co.**
ADDRESS **2107 Georgia Ave., N.E., St. Louis, MO 63135-1097** TERMS:

| DATE | | ITEM | POST. REF. | DEBIT | CREDIT | BALANCE |
|---|---|---|---|---|---|---|
| 1982 June | 2 | | P1 | | 1 185 00 | 1 185 00 |
| | 28 | | P1 | | 1 220 00 | 1 220 00 |

*Accounts Payable Ledger After Posting from Multicolumn Purchases Journal (concluded)*

**NAME** Davis Pickles
**ADDRESS** 17401 Sunset Drive, Tulsa, OK 74114-3283 **TERMS:**

| DATE | | ITEM | POST. REF. | DEBIT | CREDIT | BALANCE |
|---|---|---|---|---|---|---|
| 1982 | | | | | | |
| June | 17 | | P1 | | 1 196 00 | 1 196 00 |
| | 26 | | P1 | | 920 00 | 2 116 00 |

**NAME** Omni Equipment Co.
**ADDRESS** 512 College Ave., W., Oklahoma City, OK 73106-3592 **TERMS:**

| DATE | | ITEM | POST. REF. | DEBIT | CREDIT | BALANCE |
|---|---|---|---|---|---|---|
| 1982 | | | | | | |
| June | 16 | | P1 | | 3 242 00 | 3 242 00 |
| | 21 | | P1 | | 850 00 | 4 092 00 |

**NAME** Queen Supply Co.
**ADDRESS** 1743 S. Chisholm Rd., Oklahoma City, OK 73127-6718 **TERMS:**

| DATE | | ITEM | POST. REF. | DEBIT | CREDIT | BALANCE |
|---|---|---|---|---|---|---|
| 1982 | | | | | | |
| June | 7 | | P1 | | 331 00 | 331 00 |
| | 23 | | P1 | | 290 00 | 621 00 |

**NAME** Sweet Candy Co.
**ADDRESS** 900 S. Fairmont Ave., Oklahoma City, OK 73129-5155 **TERMS:**

| DATE | | ITEM | POST. REF. | DEBIT | CREDIT | BALANCE |
|---|---|---|---|---|---|---|
| 1982 | | | | | | |
| June | 12 | | P1 | | 2 135 00 | 2 135 00 |

**NAME** Warren Gum Company
**ADDRESS** 5107 Akard Street, Dallas, TX 75215-1330 **TERMS:**

| DATE | | ITEM | POST. REF. | DEBIT | CREDIT | BALANCE |
|---|---|---|---|---|---|---|
| 1982 | | | | | | |
| June | 9 | | P1 | | 725 00 | 725 00 |

The subsidiary ledger should be arranged alphabetically to simplify the handling of these accounts. It is usually in the form of a loose-leaf binder or file drawer. Each account is kept on a separate page to allow for the insertion of new accounts, the discarding of inactive accounts, and the withdrawal of pages as they are filled.

At the end of the month, the individual amount columns in the purchases journal should be pencil-footed; the equality of the debits and credits should be proved; the amount column totals should be entered in ink; and the journal columns should be ruled. The equality of the debits and credits may be proved by running an adding machine tape of the column footings or by preparing a schedule as shown below:

| Debit Columns | | Credit Column | |
|---|---|---|---|
| Purchases | $ 7,381 | Accounts Payable | $12,094 |
| Store Supplies | 468 | | |
| General Accounts | 4,245 | | |
| | $12,094 | | $12,094 |

The posting from each column would be accomplished as follows:

*Accounts Payable Cr.* The total of this column is posted as a credit to the accounts payable control account in the general ledger. After posting, the ledger account number of Accounts Payable (21) is written below the double-ruled column total. The source of the credit in the accounts payable account in the ledger is indicated by P1 (page 1 of the purchases journal) in the Posting Reference column.

*Purchases Dr.* The total of the Purchases Dr. column is posted to the purchases account in the general ledger. The account number for Purchases (51) is written below the double-ruled column total in the journal. The Posting Reference column in the purchases account would contain P1 (page 1 of the purchases journal).

*Store Supplies Dr.* In the purchases journal, a special column was maintained for debits to Store Supplies on the assumption that Rose's business would purchase this type of asset often enough to justify the use of a special column. Other than Accounts Payable Cr. and Purchases Dr., the special columns used in the purchases journal depend upon the needs of the individual company.

Because the asset store supplies has a special column in the purchases journal illustrated on page 135, it is posted by column total. After posting, the ledger account number for Store Supplies (14) is entered below the double-ruled column total. Again, the posting reference P1 will be entered in the Posting Reference column of this ledger account.

*General Accounts Dr.* The General Accounts Dr. section is used to record debits to individual accounts which are used infrequently. This section of the purchases journal provides space for recording the account to be debited, the posting reference, and the amount. Each amount in the General Accounts Dr. column is posted individually to the appropriate account during the month. The ledger account number is entered in the Posting Reference column, for example, the account number for Store Equipment (17). Because the amounts are posted individually from this column, a check mark is placed below the column total to indicate that no posting of the total is required. The journal posting reference P1 is entered in the Posting Reference column of the appropriate ledger accounts.

The general ledger accounts affected by the postings from the purchases journal are presented below and on page 138.

ACCOUNT **Store Supplies** ACCOUNT NO. **14**

| DATE | | ITEM | POST. REF. | DEBIT | CREDIT | BALANCE DEBIT | BALANCE CREDIT |
|---|---|---|---|---|---|---|---|
| 1982 June | 30 | | P1 | 468 00 | | 468 00 | |

ACCOUNT **Office Supplies** ACCOUNT NO. **15**

| DATE | | ITEM | POST. REF. | DEBIT | CREDIT | BALANCE DEBIT | BALANCE CREDIT |
|---|---|---|---|---|---|---|---|
| 1982 June | 7 | | P1 | 175 00 | | 175 00 | |
| | 23 | | P1 | 120 00 | | 370 00 | |

***General Ledger Accounts After Posting from Multicolumn Purchases Journal***

**ACCOUNT** Store Equipment **ACCOUNT NO.** 17

| DATE | | ITEM | POST. REF. | DEBIT | CREDIT | BALANCE DEBIT | BALANCE CREDIT |
|---|---|---|---|---|---|---|---|
| 1982 June | 16 | | P1 | 3 100 00 | | 3 100 00 | |

**ACCOUNT** Office Equipment **ACCOUNT NO.** 18

| DATE | | ITEM | POST. REF. | DEBIT | CREDIT | BALANCE DEBIT | BALANCE CREDIT |
|---|---|---|---|---|---|---|---|
| 1982 June | 21 | | P1 | 850 00 | | 850 00 | |

**ACCOUNT** Accounts Payable **ACCOUNT NO.** 21

| DATE | | ITEM | POST. REF. | DEBIT | CREDIT | BALANCE DEBIT | BALANCE CREDIT |
|---|---|---|---|---|---|---|---|
| 1982 June | 30 | | P1 | | 12 094 00 | | 12 094 00 |

**ACCOUNT** Purchases **ACCOUNT NO.** 51

| DATE | | ITEM | POST. REF. | DEBIT | CREDIT | BALANCE DEBIT | BALANCE CREDIT |
|---|---|---|---|---|---|---|---|
| | 30 | | P1 | 7 381 00 | | 16 581 00 | |

***General Ledger Accounts After Posting from Multicolumn Purchases Journal (concluded)***

## POSTING FROM THE PURCHASE INVOICES

Some businesses do not keep a purchases journal, but instead make all of their daily postings directly from the purchase invoices to the creditors' subsidiary accounts. At the end of the month, the invoices are first separated by the type of assets purchased and are then totaled. An entry is made in the general journal debiting Purchases and the other assets acquired during the period and crediting Accounts Payable. To illustrate, assume Rose used this procedure for recording the June purchases. The journal entry at the end of the month prepared from the adding machine totals for each type of invoice would be:

| | | | | |
|---|---|---|---|---|
| 30 | Store Supplies | 14 | 468 00 | |
| | Office Supplies | 15 | 295 00 | |
| | Store Equipment | 17 | 3 100 00 | |
| | Office Equipment | 18 | 850 00 | |
| | Purchases | 51 | 7 381 00 | |
| | Accounts Payable | 21 | | 12 094 00 |
| | Purchased assets on account. | | | |

## QUESTIONS FOR DISCUSSION

1. A retail merchant averages four purchases on account each day. He records these purchases in a general journal. If he adopts a single-column purchases journal, how much labor will he save in (a) recording purchases and (b) posting purchases?

2. (a) What two special columns will a multicolumn purchases journal always have? (b) Name three other accounts that might require special columns in this journal.

3. The receiving department of the KZ Co. is provided with a carbon copy of a purchase order which does not show the quantities of the goods ordered. The receiving department is required to insert this information on the invoice when the goods are received. What is the purpose of this procedure?

4. (a) What information is normally shown on a purchase invoice? (b) What verifications should be made when the ordered items arrive? (c) What is meant by verifying the extensions on an invoice?

5. Retail stores that sell only for cash usually purchase merchandise on account. Explain the advantage to the retailer using this practice.

6. Hiram Friedsom purchases office supplies from the Massie Co. for $180 on account. Explain how this transaction would be recorded in the purchases journal and posted (a) if a special column is provided for office supplies and (b) if no special column is provided for office supplies.

7. A purchase of merchandise of $750 on account from Morris Co. was erroneously posted from the purchases journal to the subsidiary account of the Morrison Co. in the creditors ledger. Would the preparation of the schedule of accounts payable reveal this error? If not, how would this error be found?

## EXERCISES

1. Record the following transactions for Anne's Fabric Shop in a two-column general journal.

   Dec. 2. Purchased merchandise on account from Georgia Mills, $800.
   7. Purchased store supplies on account from Kee Stationery, $130.
   10. Purchased merchandise on account from Holly Fabric Company, $640.
   12. Purchased store equipment on account from Banjo Equipment Co., $1,000.
   15. Paid Georgia Mills for purchase of December 2, $800.

2. On January 31, the totals of the columns used in the purchases journal of the Chavez Company were: Accounts Payable Cr., $6,120; Purchases Dr., $3,610; Office Supplies Dr., $270; General Accounts, Dr., $2,240 (consisting of Store Equipment, $2,000, and Store Supplies, $240). (a) Prepare a schedule to prove that the journal is in balance. (b) Explain the posting procedure for each column in the purchases journal to (1) the general ledger, and (2) the subsidiary ledger.

3. Mulkey Hardware does not use a purchases journal but makes all postings to the subsidiary ledger and general ledger from the purchase invoices. At the end of July, Mulkey separated the purchase invoices and determined the following totals: merchandise, $1,935; office equipment, $400; office supplies, $67; store supplies, $76.

   **Required:** Prepare the entry in a two-column journal to record this information for the month of July.

## ASSIGNMENT 7-A

**Tear out pages 437–444 and complete Assignment 7-A. Submit your papers to your instructor for approval. After completion, continue with the following discussion until Assignment 7-B is required.**

# PART B CASH PAYMENTS

The most common sources of cash payments in a merchandising business are to creditors for merchandise and supplies bought on account and for the payment of operating expenses such as rent, salaries, and utilities when they become due. The remainder of this chapter explains procedures involved in accounting for these cash payments.

## CASH PAYMENTS JOURNAL

The desirability of having special journals for cash receipts and cash payments was discussed in Chapter 6. The cash receipts journal was explained and illustrated in that chapter.

The *cash payments journal* is a special journal used to record all cash paid by the business. An illustration of a typical cash payments journal is presented below.

CASH PAYMENTS JOURNAL

| | DATE | CK. NO. | ACCOUNT DEBITED | POST. REF. | GENERAL ACCOUNTS DR. | ACCOUNTS PAYABLE DR. | CASH CR. | |
|---|---|---|---|---|---|---|---|---|
| 1 | | | | | | | | 1 |
| 2 | | | | | | | | 2 |
| 3 | | | | | | | | 3 |

*Cash Payments Journal*

The special columns to be used in the cash payments journal are determined in the same manner as the selection of columns for the other special journals. Those accounts which are used frequently enough to justify posting by totals at the end of the month merit individual columns.

Since the cash payments journal includes all payments of cash by the business, there will always be a Cash Cr. column. In a mercantile enterprise the most frequent payment of cash is to creditors, thus requiring an Accounts Payable Dr. column. In the cash payments journal illustrated, no other special columns were provided. If frequent payments are made for one or more operating expenses, such as salaries, special columns for these accounts can easily be included.

The General Accounts Dr. column is used to record debits for all other items which require the payment of cash.

## Cash Payments Journal Illustrated

The following transactions relating to cash payments for Rose Wholesale Co. for the month of June are presented to provide a detailed illustration of the recording of such transactions in the cash payments journal and the postings from this journal.

June 1. Paid one year insurance policy in advance, $288; Check No. 821.
2. Paid rent expense for June, $920; Check No. 822.
4. Purchased merchandise for cash, $9,200; Check No. 823.
7. Paid for advertising expense, $350; Check No. 824.
15. Paid salaries for the first half of the month: sales salaries, $870; office salaries, $740. Check No. 825.
16. Paid cash for office supplies, $75. Check No. 826.
18. Paid on account to Checker Sugar Co., $1,185. Check No. 827.
25. Paid on account to Queen Supply Co., $331. Check No. 828.
26. Paid on account to Warren Gum Co., $500. Check No. 829.
26. Withdrew cash for personal use, $1,000. Check No. 830.
28. Paid utilities for the month, $385. Check No. 831.
28. Paid on account to Omni Equipment Co., $3,242. Check No. 832.
30. Paid salaries for the second half of the month: sales salaries, $820; office salaries, $790. Check No. 833.

After these entries have been recorded, the cash payments journal appears as shown below.

CASH PAYMENTS JOURNAL — PAGE 1

| DATE | | CK. NO. | ACCOUNT DEBITED | POST. REF. | GENERAL ACCOUNTS DR. | ACCOUNTS PAYABLE DR. | CASH CR. |
|---|---|---|---|---|---|---|---|
| 1982 | | | | | | | |
| June | 1 | 821 | Prepaid Insurance | 16 | 288 00 | | 288 00 |
| | 2 | 822 | Rent Expense | 75 | 920 00 | | 920 00 |
| | 4 | 823 | Purchases | 51 | 9 200 00 | | 9 200 00 |
| | 7 | 824 | Advertising Expense | 61 | 350 00 | | 350 00 |
| | 15 | 825 | Sales Salary Expense | 63 | 870 00 | | 1 610 00 |
| | | | Office Salary Expense | 73 | 740 00 | | |
| | 16 | 826 | Office Supplies | 15 | 75 00 | | 75 00 |
| | 18 | 827 | Checker Sugar Co. | √ | | 1 185 00 | 1 185 00 |
| | 25 | 828 | Queen Supply Co. | √ | | 331 00 | 331 00 |
| | 26 | 829 | Warren Gum Co. | √ | | 500 00 | 500 00 |
| | 26 | 830 | Tom Rose, Drawing | 32 | 1 000 00 | | 1 000 00 |
| | 28 | 831 | Utilities Expense | 76 | 385 00 | | 385 00 |
| | 28 | 832 | Omni Equipment Co. | √ | | 3 242 00 | 3 242 00 |
| | 30 | 833 | Sales Salary Expense | 63 | 820 00 | | 1 610 00 |
| | | | Office Salary Expense | 73 | 790 00 | | |
| | | | | | *15 438 00* | *5 258 00* | *20 696 00* |
| | 30 | | Totals | | 15 438 00 | 5 258 00 | 20 696 00 |
| | | | | | (√) | (21) | (11) |

***Cash Payments Journal — Rose Wholesale Co.***

## Posting the Cash Payments Journal

The posting of the cash payments journal, as is the case with all special journals, is accomplished by posting all special columns by total at the end of the month. All transactions in the General Accounts Dr. column are posted individually; the total is not posted. All creditors' subsidiary accounts are posted daily.

At the end of the month, before the column totals are posted, the cash payments journal is footed, proved, and ruled. The equality of the debits and credits should be checked to insure the accuracy of the footings. The cash payments journal is proved as follows:

| Debit Columns | | Credit Column | |
|---|---|---|---|
| General Accounts .................. | $15,438.00 | Cash........................................ | $20,696.00 |
| Accounts Payable .................. | 5,258.00 | | |
| | $20,696.00 | | $20,696.00 |

The posting from each column would be accomplished as follows:

**General Accounts Dr.** The purpose of this column is to record all debits in the cash payments journal which are not recorded in a special column. The various accounts recorded in this column are posted individually during the month. A check mark is placed below the column total to indicate that posting by total is unnecessary.

As the individual account is posted, its ledger account number is entered in the Posting Reference column of the cash payments journal. For example, the transaction on June 4 is a purchase of merchandise for cash. This purchase is not recorded in the purchases journal because it was made for cash rather than on account. Since no special column has been provided for cash purchases, this transaction is recorded in the General Accounts Dr. column and posted individually. When posted, the ledger account number for Purchases (51) is entered in the Posting Reference column of the cash payments journal and the journal source CP1 (cash payments journal, page 1) is entered in the Posting Reference column of the purchases account in the general ledger.

**Accounts Payable Dr.** Cash paid to creditors on account is recorded in the Accounts Payable Dr. and Cash Cr. columns. The name of the creditor's account in the subsidiary ledger, for example Checker Sugar Co. in the entry on June 18, is written in the Account Debited column. When the daily posting is made to the customer's account in the accounts payable subsidiary ledger, a check mark is placed in the Posting Reference column of the cash payments journal to indicate that the amount has been posted individually to the subsidiary ledger.

The total of the Accounts Payable Dr. column is posted to Accounts Payable in the general ledger at the end of the month. When this total is posted, the ledger account number for Accounts Payable (21) is written at the bottom of the double-ruled column.

**Cash Cr.** Since the purpose of the cash payments journal is to record all cash paid by the business, the Cash Cr. column has an entry for each transaction in the journal. This column total is posted at the end of the period as a credit to Cash in the general ledger and the ledger account number for Cash (11) is recorded below the column total.

One of the methods of safeguarding cash, discussed in Chapter 5, is to make all payments by check. Since Rose follows this practice of internal control over assets, a check number (Ck. No.) column is provided in the cash payments journal to record the number of the check used in making each payment.

The general ledger accounts of Rose Wholesale Co. affected by postings from the purchases journal and cash payments journal, are presented below. The debit entry in the cash account was discussed in Chapter 6, on page 121.

**ACCOUNT** Cash **ACCOUNT NO.** 11

| DATE | | ITEM | POST. REF. | DEBIT | CREDIT | BALANCE DEBIT | BALANCE CREDIT |
|---|---|---|---|---|---|---|---|
| 1982 | | | | | | | |
| June | 30 | | CR1 | 36 065 00 | | 36 065 00 | |
| | 30 | | CP1 | | 20 696 00 | 15 369 00 | |

**ACCOUNT** Store Supplies **ACCOUNT NO.** 14

| DATE | | ITEM | POST. REF. | DEBIT | CREDIT | BALANCE DEBIT | BALANCE CREDIT |
|---|---|---|---|---|---|---|---|
| 1982 | | | | | | | |
| June | 30 | | P1 | 468 00 | | 468 00 | |

**ACCOUNT** Office Supplies **ACCOUNT NO.** 15

| DATE | | ITEM | POST. REF. | DEBIT | CREDIT | BALANCE DEBIT | BALANCE CREDIT |
|---|---|---|---|---|---|---|---|
| 1982 | | | | | | | |
| June | 7 | | P1 | 175 00 | | 175 00 | |
| | 16 | | CP1 | 75 00 | | 250 00 | |
| | 23 | | P1 | 120 00 | | 370 00 | |

**ACCOUNT** Prepaid Insurance **ACCOUNT NO.** 16

| DATE | | ITEM | POST. REF. | DEBIT | CREDIT | BALANCE DEBIT | BALANCE CREDIT |
|---|---|---|---|---|---|---|---|
| 1982 | | | | | | | |
| June | 1 | | CP1 | 288 00 | | 288 00 | |

**ACCOUNT** Store Equipment **ACCOUNT NO.** 17

| DATE | | ITEM | POST. REF. | DEBIT | CREDIT | BALANCE DEBIT | BALANCE CREDIT |
|---|---|---|---|---|---|---|---|
| 1982 | | | | | | | |
| June | 16 | | P1 | 3 100 00 | | 3 100 00 | |

**ACCOUNT** Office Equipment **ACCOUNT NO.** 18

| DATE | | ITEM | POST. REF. | DEBIT | CREDIT | BALANCE DEBIT | BALANCE CREDIT |
|---|---|---|---|---|---|---|---|
| 1982 | | | | | | | |
| June | 21 | | P1 | 850 00 | | 850 00 | |

**ACCOUNT** Accounts Payable **ACCOUNT NO.** 21

| DATE | | ITEM | POST. REF. | DEBIT | CREDIT | BALANCE DEBIT | BALANCE CREDIT |
|---|---|---|---|---|---|---|---|
| 1982 | | | | | | | |
| June | 30 | | P1 | | 12 094 00 | | 12 094 00 |
| | 30 | | CP1 | 5 258 00 | | | 6 836 00 |

*General Ledger Accounts After Posting from Purchases Journal and Cash Payments Journal*

ACCOUNT **Tom Rose, Drawing** ACCOUNT NO. 32

| DATE | | ITEM | POST. REF. | DEBIT | CREDIT | BALANCE DEBIT | BALANCE CREDIT |
|---|---|---|---|---|---|---|---|
| 1982 | | | | | | | |
| June | 26 | | CP1 | 1 000 00 | | 1 000 00 | |

ACCOUNT **Purchases** ACCOUNT NO. 51

| DATE | | ITEM | POST. REF. | DEBIT | CREDIT | BALANCE DEBIT | BALANCE CREDIT |
|---|---|---|---|---|---|---|---|
| 1982 | | | | | | | |
| June | 4 | | CP1 | 9 200 00 | | 9 200 00 | |
| | 30 | | P1 | 7 381 00 | | 16 581 00 | |

ACCOUNT **Advertising Expense** ACCOUNT NO. 61

| DATE | | ITEM | POST. REF. | DEBIT | CREDIT | BALANCE DEBIT | BALANCE CREDIT |
|---|---|---|---|---|---|---|---|
| 1982 | | | | | | | |
| June | 7 | | CP1 | 350 00 | | 350 00 | |

ACCOUNT **Sales Salary Expense** ACCOUNT NO. 63

| DATE | | ITEM | POST. REF. | DEBIT | CREDIT | BALANCE DEBIT | BALANCE CREDIT |
|---|---|---|---|---|---|---|---|
| 1982 | | | | | | | |
| June | 15 | | CP1 | 870 00 | | 870 00 | |
| | 30 | | CP1 | 820 00 | | 1 690 00 | |

ACCOUNT **Office Salary Expense** ACCOUNT NO. 73

| DATE | | ITEM | POST. REF. | DEBIT | CREDIT | BALANCE DEBIT | BALANCE CREDIT |
|---|---|---|---|---|---|---|---|
| 1982 | | | | | | | |
| June | 15 | | CP1 | 740 00 | | 740 00 | |
| | 30 | | CP1 | 790 00 | | 1 530 00 | |

ACCOUNT **Rent Expense** ACCOUNT NO. 75

| DATE | | ITEM | POST. REF. | DEBIT | CREDIT | BALANCE DEBIT | BALANCE CREDIT |
|---|---|---|---|---|---|---|---|
| 1982 | | | | | | | |
| June | 2 | | CP1 | 920 00 | | 920 00 | |

ACCOUNT **Utilities Expense** ACCOUNT NO. 76

| DATE | | ITEM | POST. REF. | DEBIT | CREDIT | BALANCE DEBIT | BALANCE CREDIT |
|---|---|---|---|---|---|---|---|
| 1982 | | | | | | | |
| June | 28 | | CP1 | 385 00 | | 385 00 | |

*General Ledger Accounts After Posting from Purchases Journal and Cash Payments Journal — (concluded)*

## SEQUENCE OF POSTING THE JOURNALS

The entries in the general ledger accounts indicate the sequence of posting from the purchases journal and cash payments journal. For example, the purchases account contains a posting from the cash payments journal during the month and a posting from the purchases journal at the end of the month. This is as it should be because this account was recorded in the General Accounts Dr. column in the cash payments journal rather than as a column total at the end of the month. Purchases of merchandise on account occurred frequently enough to merit a special column in the purchases journal. Consequently, purchases would be posted in total from the purchases journal at the end of the month.

## SCHEDULE OF ACCOUNTS PAYABLE

After the purchases and cash payments journals have been posted for the month of June, Accounts Payable on page 143 has a credit balance of $6,836. This consists of the $12,094 credit from the purchases journal and the $5,258 debit from the cash payments journal.

The accounts payable account is the control account for the creditors' subsidiary ledger. The balance in Accounts Payable at the end of June should be the same as the total of the balances in the creditors' accounts. The accounts payable subsidiary ledger for Rose Wholesale Co. at the end of June after all postings have been completed is shown below and on page 146.

**NAME** Checker Sugar Co.
**ADDRESS** 2107 Georgia Ave., N.E., St. Louis, MO 63135-1097 **TERMS:**

| DATE | | ITEM | POST. REF. | DEBIT | CREDIT | BALANCE |
|---|---|---|---|---|---|---|
| 1982 | | | | | | |
| June | 2 | | P1 | | 1 185 00 | 1 185 00 |
| | 18 | | CP1 | 1 185 00 | | — |
| | 28 | | P1 | | 1 220 00 | 1 220 00 |

**NAME** Davis Pickles
**ADDRESS** 17401 Sunset Drive, Tulsa, OK 74114-3283 **TERMS:**

| DATE | | ITEM | POST. REF. | DEBIT | CREDIT | BALANCE |
|---|---|---|---|---|---|---|
| 1982 | | | | | | |
| June | 17 | | P1 | | 1 196 00 | 1 196 00 |
| | 26 | | P1 | | 920 00 | 2 116 00 |

**NAME** Omni Equipment Co.
**ADDRESS** 512 College Ave., W., Oklahoma City, OK 73106-3592 **TERMS:**

| DATE | | ITEM | POST. REF. | DEBIT | CREDIT | BALANCE |
|---|---|---|---|---|---|---|
| 1982 | | | | | | |
| June | 16 | | P1 | | 3 242 00 | 3 242 00 |
| | 21 | | P1 | | 850 00 | 4 092 00 |
| | 28 | | CP1 | 3 242 00 | | 850 00 |

*Accounts Payable Ledger After Posting from Purchases Journal and Cash Payments Journal*

NAME Queen Supply Co.
ADDRESS 1743 S. Chisholm Rd., Oklahoma City, OK 73127-6718 TERMS:

| DATE | | ITEM | POST. REF. | DEBIT | CREDIT | BALANCE |
|---|---|---|---|---|---|---|
| 1982 | | | | | | |
| June | 7 | | P1 | | 331 00 | 331 00 |
| | 23 | | P1 | | 290 00 | 621 00 |
| | 25 | | CP1 | 331 00 | | 290 00 |

NAME Sweet Candy Co.
ADDRESS 900 S. Fairmont Ave., Oklahoma City, OK 73129-5155 TERMS:

| DATE | | ITEM | POST. REF. | DEBIT | CREDIT | BALANCE |
|---|---|---|---|---|---|---|
| 1982 | | | | | | |
| June | 12 | | P1 | | 2 135 00 | 2 135 00 |

NAME Warren Gum Company
ADDRESS 5107 Akard Street, Dallas, TX 75215-1330 TERMS:

| DATE | | ITEM | POST. REF. | DEBIT | CREDIT | BALANCE |
|---|---|---|---|---|---|---|
| 1982 | | | | | | |
| June | 9 | | P1 | | 725 00 | 725 00 |
| | 26 | | CP1 | 500 00 | | 225 00 |

*Accounts Payable Ledger After Posting from Purchases Journal and Cash Payments Journal (concluded)*

A schedule of the balances in the accounts payable ledger should be prepared at the end of the month to determine if the sum of the balances of the creditors' accounts equals the balance in the accounts payable control account. If the total of the schedule of accounts payable does not agree with the balance in the control account, the discrepancy must be found and corrected.

A schedule of accounts payable prepared from the subsidiary ledger is shown below:

**Rose Wholesale Co.**
**Schedule of Accounts Payable**
**June 30, 1982**

| | | |
|---|---|---|
| Checker Sugar Co. | | 1 220 00 |
| Davis Pickles | | 2 116 00 |
| Omni Equipment Co. | | 850 00 |
| Queen Supply Co. | | 290 00 |
| Sweet Candy Co. | | 2 135 00 |
| Warren Gum Company | | 225 00 |
| Total accounts payable | | 6 836 00 |

*Schedule of Accounts Payable*

The total of the above schedule, $6,836, agrees with the balance in the accounts payable control account in the general ledger. If there are several accounts in the subsidiary ledger, it may be simpler to run an adding machine tape of the balances of the individual creditors' accounts and compare the total with the balance in the control account.

## QUESTIONS FOR DISCUSSION

1. On December 31, the totals of the columns of the cash payments journal of Apache Co. were: General Accounts Dr., $1,030 (consisting of: Advertising Expense, $70; Salary Expense, $285; Office Supplies, $225; and Purchases, $450); Accounts Payable Dr., $1,205; Cash Cr., $2,235. Explain the posting procedure from the cash payments journal to the general ledger.
2. Explain the posting procedure from the cash payments journal to the subsidiary ledger in Question 1.
3. Purchases of merchandise for cash are not recorded in a purchases journal. Why not? Where are they recorded?
4. (a) At the end of the month, the Accounts Payable Dr. column in the cash payments journal was added incorrectly, resulting in a total of $100 too much. If no other errors have been made in recording or posting, how will this error be found? (b) If the Cash Cr. column had also been $100 too much, how would the error in (a) have been found?
5. Name three accounts (other than Accounts Payable) that might require special columns in the cash payments journal.

## EXERCISES

1. The following subsidiary ledger account was found on the floor of the accounting department of the Gidry Company. Should it be filed in the accounts receivable or accounts payable subsidiary ledger? Why?

NAME **Cavendar Company**
ADDRESS **1220 Wayne Road, Cranston, RI 02910-4315** TERMS:

| DATE | | ITEM | POST. REF. | DEBIT | CREDIT | BALANCE |
|---|---|---|---|---|---|---|
| 19-- | | | | | | |
| April | 10 | | P21 | | 600 00 | 600 00 |
| | 27 | | CP19 | 600 00 | | —— |

2. Prepare the entries in general journal form to record the Gidry Company's transactions with the Cavendar Company as evidenced by the subsidiary ledger account in Exercise 1 above.
3. On October 2, Lugo Retailers purchased $1,700 of merchandise from Sahara Wholesalers. Lugo paid the invoice on October 30th. Record the two transactions in general journal form and name the special journal in which each transaction would properly be recorded for (a) Lugo Retailers and (b) Sahara Wholesalers.

## ASSIGNMENT 7-B

**Tear out pages 445–458 and complete Assignment 7-B. Submit your papers for approval. After completion, proceed to the study of Chapter 8 until the next assignment is required.**

Chapter **8**

# ADDITIONAL MERCHANDISING TRANSACTIONS

In Chapters 6 and 7, accounting for the sale and purchase of merchandise was presented. In this chapter, additional accounting topics related to the sale and purchase of merchandise are examined. These topics include returns, allowances, discounts granted on sales and purchases transactions, and transportation costs.

## PART A *RETURNS AND ALLOWANCES*

In a mercantile business, it is common for merchandise to be returned by the customer for a variety of reasons. The wrong quantity, size, or color may have been shipped. The customer may decide that the goods do not satisfy the need for which they were intended. Items purchased as gifts are often returned for exchange or refund. If the goods prove to be defective or damaged, the customer may be granted an allowance that reduces the original sales price.

On occasion it may be necessary for a business to return merchandise to the supplier from whom it was bought. If the merchandise received is damaged or is not of the quality ordered, the firm may agree to keep the goods if given an allowance which reduces the original purchase price.

Businesses have various policies pertaining to the return of merchandise. Some firms have a definite no-return policy. Others allow merchandise to be returned and exchanged for other merchandise but will not grant cash refunds. Most businesses, however, exercise great care in satisfying customers by allowing them to exchange merchandise, by granting them credit on their accounts for returned goods, or by refunding their money on cash sales. For control purposes, businesses frequently require that all returns or allowances be approved by the owner or department manager. In large businesses a separate department may be established to handle returns of merchandise.

## SALES RETURNS AND ALLOWANCES

The effect of sales returns or allowances is a reduction in sales. The revenue account, Sales, has a normal credit balance. A reduction in sales could be recorded as a debit to the sales account. If the sales account were to be debited directly, the balance in the account at the end of the period would represent net sales which is total sales less returns, allowances, and discounts. However, there would be no separate disclosure of the amount of sales returns and allowances for the period. It is important that management be aware of the amount of sales returns and allowances for the accounting period. An unusually large number of returns could indicate that the quality of the merchandise being sold is not up to normal standards or that selling procedures may need to be reviewed. An excessive number of allowances may indicate that defective goods are being sold to customers or that these goods are damaged while being transported to the customer. Because of the loss of revenue resulting from returns and allowances and the additional expenses involved in transporting, repairing, handling, and packing returned goods, it is essential to have this information separated from the sales account. This segregation for control purposes is accomplished by debiting returns and allowances to a contra account called Sales Returns and Allowances.

### Sales Returns and Allowances for Cash

If the customer is given a cash refund for a sales return or allowance, a *sales return slip* or *cash payment ticket* may be prepared showing the date, the name of the customer, the nature of the merchandise returned, and the reason for the return or allowance. This ticket should be approved by the proper person and signed by the customer as evidence of the receipt of the amount stated. When this transaction is made, an entry should be recorded in the cash payments journal, debiting Sales Returns and Allowances and crediting Cash.

The balance in the sales returns and allowances account is treated as a reduction in revenue rather than as an expense. This account has a normal debit balance (the opposite of Sales). Sales returns and allowances are shown on the income statement as a subtraction from sales. The sales returns and allowances account is a temporary account and is closed at the end of the fiscal period, along with all revenue and expense accounts, to the income summary account.

### Sales Returns and Allowances for Credit

When goods sold on account are returned by the customer or when an allowance on the original selling price is granted, the seller will normally issue a *credit memorandum* to the customer showing the amount of the credit and the reason for it. The customer's account receivable has a normal debit balance on the books of the company, and when the goods are returned, the customer's account is reduced by a credit, thus the term "credit memorandum." A standard form of credit memorandum is shown on the following page.

Credit Memorandum **CREDIT** No. 16

**ROSE WHOLESALE CO.**
208 Scott Street Oklahoma City, OK 73115-2357

To CHUNG SUPERMARKET
510 N. MAIN STREET
OKLAHOMA CITY, OK 73102-6351

Date JULY 2, 1982

we credit your account as follows:

| Quantity | Description | Unit Price | Amount |
|---|---|---|---|
| 5 boxes | Spearmint gum | 8.00 | 40.00 |

***Credit Memorandum***

The return of merchandise indicated by the credit memorandum is recorded in the general journal as shown below:

| | | | | | | |
|---|---|---|---|---|---|---|
| 21 | 2 | Sales Returns and Allowances . . . . . | 41.1 | 40 00 | | 21 |
| 22 | | Accts. Rec.—Chung Supermarket | 12/√ | | 40 00 | 22 |
| 23 | | Credit Memo No. 16. | | | | 23 |
| 24 | | | | | | 24 |

The credit in this entry is posted to both the accounts receivable control account in the general ledger and the customer's account in the subsidiary ledger. To indicate that this dual posting is necessary, a diagonal line is drawn in the Posting Reference column when the journal entry is made. This diagonal line signifies that the amount must be posted to both the general ledger (Accounts Receivable) and the subsidiary ledger account of Chung Supermarket. When the amount is posted to the customer's account, a check mark is placed on the right side of the diagonal line, and when the transaction is posted to Accounts Receivable in the general ledger, the account number (12) is entered on the left side of the line. Note that the account number for Sales Returns and Allowances is 41.1, indicating that its balance is subtracted on the financial statements from the balance in account No. 41, Sales.

## Sales Returns and Allowances Journal

All transactions may be entered originally in the general journal; however, when a transaction of one type is repeated frequently, a special book of original entry should be provided for it. Sales returns and allowances for credit often occur with sufficient frequency to make it advisable to use a special journal. A standard form of the sales returns and allowances journal is illustrated on page 151. This sales returns and allowances journal represents a continuation of the illustration of Rose Wholesale Co. used in Chapters 6 and 7. The July transactions shown on the following page are for the returns on June sales (Chapter 6). The illustration is concluded in Chapter 9.

| | SALES RETURNS AND ALLOWANCES JOURNAL | | | | PAGE 2 |
|---|---|---|---|---|---|
| DATE | | CR. MEMO NO. | ACCOUNT CREDITED | POST. REF. | SALES RET. & ALLOW. DR. ACCTS. REC. CR. |
| 1982 July | 1 | 15 | Cruz Restaurant | ✓ | 20 00 |
| | 2 | 16 | Chung Supermarket | ✓ | 40 00 |
| | 3 | 17 | Coda's Quik Stop | ✓ | 100 00 |
| | 31 | | Total | | 442 00 |
| | | | | | (41.1) (12) |

*Sales Returns and Allowances Journal – Rose Wholesale Co.*

The above entries in the sales returns and allowances journal may be explained as follows:

July 1 — Issued Credit Memorandum No. 15 to Cruz Restaurant for an allowance of $20 off the sales price of the goods sold on June 10 (see page 114) because certain items were damaged in transit.

July 2 — Issued Credit Memorandum No. 16 for $40 to Chung Supermarket for the return of damaged merchandise cause by faulty packing. The original sale occurred on June 28 (see page 114).

July 3 — Issued Credit Memorandum No. 17 to Coda's Quik Stop for an allowance of $100 off the sale price of the goods sold on June 28 (see page 114) because the quantity sent was less than the quantity ordered.

The only transactions which appear in the sales returns and allowances journal are those involving the return or allowance of merchandise sold on account for which the customers are given credit on their accounts. Therefore, this journal will require only one amount column because all transactions represent a debit to Sales Returns and Allowances and a credit to Accounts Receivable.

The postings from the sales returns and allowances journal to the customers' subsidiary ledger should be made daily. When a posting is completed, a check mark is placed in the Posting Reference column of the journal and the code "SR" (indicating the sales returns and allowances journal) and the journal page number are entered in the Posting Reference column of the customer's account.

The subsidiary ledger account of Chung Supermarket, after the posting from the sales returns and allowances journal has been completed, is presented below.

NAME **Chung Supermarket**
ADDRESS **510 N. Main Street, Oklahoma City, OK 73102-6351** TERMS:

| DATE | | ITEM | POST. REF. | DEBIT | CREDIT | BALANCE |
|---|---|---|---|---|---|---|
| 1982 | | | | | | |
| June | 7 | | S1 | 555 00 | | 555 00 |
| | 19 | | CR1 | | 555 00 | ——— |
| | 28 | | S1 | 445 00 | | 445 00 |
| July | 2 | | SR2 | | 40 00 | 405 00 |

At the end of the month, the total of the amount column in the sales returns and allowances journal is posted as a debit to the sales returns and allowances account and as a credit to the accounts receivable account. By posting this total monthly, only one debit to Sales Returns and Allowances and one credit to Accounts Receivable is required to transfer the information from the journal to the general ledger.

After the postings of the total are completed, the account numbers of Sales Returns and Allowances (41.1) and Accounts Receivable (12) are inserted below the double-ruled column total in the journal. The accounts receivable account and the sales returns and allowances account in the general ledger now appear as follows:

ACCOUNT **Accounts Receivable** ACCOUNT NO. 12

| DATE | | ITEM | POST. REF. | DEBIT | CREDIT | BALANCE DEBIT | BALANCE CREDIT |
|---|---|---|---|---|---|---|---|
| 1982 July | 1 | Balance | √ | | | 2 775 00 | |
| | 31 | | SR2 | | 442 00 | 3 118 00 | |

ACCOUNT **Sales Returns and Allowances** ACCOUNT NO. 41.1

| DATE | | ITEM | POST. REF. | DEBIT | CREDIT | BALANCE DEBIT | BALANCE CREDIT |
|---|---|---|---|---|---|---|---|
| 1982 July | 31 | | SR2 | 442 00 | | 442 00 | |

# PURCHASES RETURNS AND ALLOWANCES

The effect of a purchase return or allowance is a reduction in purchases. It is desirable for management to know both the total amount of purchases and the total amount of purchases returns and allowances. If the purchases returns are unusually high in any period, it is necessary to find out if the suppliers are sending incorrect quantities, inferior quality goods, or sizes and colors which do not conform to the purchase orders. By maintaining a contra account for purchases returns and allowances, the firm is able to exercise better control over this very important phase of the business operation.

## Purchases Returns and Allowances for Cash

If a purchase is returned for a cash refund, the entry is recorded in the cash receipts journal as a debit to Cash and a credit to Purchases Returns and Allowances.

Purchases returns and allowances are viewed as a reduction in the cost of the goods purchased rather than as a revenue. They are shown on the income statement as a subtraction from purchases. The normal balance for the purchases returns and allowances account is a credit (the opposite of Purchases). The purchases returns and allowances account is a temporary account which is closed to Income Summary at the end of the fiscal period.

## Purchases Returns and Allowances for Credit

When merchandise purchased on account is returned or an allowance is requested, the buyer will frequently notify the seller by use of a *debit memorandum*. The seller's account on the books of the buyer is an account payable which has a normal credit balance. When the buyer returns goods, permission is being requested to debit the seller's account, thus the term "debit memorandum." A debit memorandum shows the names of the buyer and the seller, the amount of the return or allowance, the seller's invoice number, and the reason for the return. A debit memorandum is illustrated below.

Debit Memorandum **DEBIT** No. 6

**ROSE WHOLESALE CO.**
208 Scott Street Oklahoma City, OK 73115-2357

To DAVIS PICKLES
17401 SUNSET DRIVE
TULSA, OK 74114-3283

Date JULY 3, 1982

we debit your account as follows:

| Quantity | Description | Unit Price | Amount |
|---|---|---|---|
| 2 cases | Pickles — wrong size<br>Ordered 32 oz.,<br>received 16 oz.<br><br>Invoice No. K-792 | 13.50 | 27.00 |

***Debit Memorandum***

After the buyer issues the debit memorandum, the supplier then issues a credit memorandum. Either a copy of the buyer's debit memorandum or the supplier's credit memorandum may be used as the source document to record the following entry in the general journal of the buyer.

| Date | Account | Post. Ref. | Debit | Credit |
|---|---|---|---|---|
| 3 | Accounts Payable — Davis Pickles | 21/✓ | 27 00 | |
| | Purchases Returns and Allow. . . . | 51.1 | | 27 00 |
| | Debit Memo No. 6. | | | |

Note that the account number for Purchases Returns and Allowances is 51.1, indicating that its balance is subtracted on the financial statements from the balance in account No. 51, Purchases.

## Purchases Returns and Allowances Journal

If frequent returns or allowances are required for merchandise purchased on account, it is desirable to maintain a special journal. A standard form of the purchases returns and allowances journal is illustrated below. Consistent with the sales returns and allowances journal, the transactions in the purchases returns and allowances journal shown here are July returns and allowances on June purchases (Chapter 7), representing a continuation of the illustration for Rose Wholesale Co. The illustration is concluded in Chapter 9.

**Purchases Returns and Allowances Journal – Rose Wholesale Co.**

PURCHASES RETURNS AND ALLOWANCES JOURNAL — PAGE 2

| | DATE | | DEBIT MEMO. NO. | ACCOUNT DEBITED | POST. REF. | ACCTS. PAY. DR. PURCH. RET. & ALLOW. CR. | |
|---|---|---|---|---|---|---|---|
| | 1982 | | | | | | |
| 1 | July | 3 | 6 | Davis Pickles | ✓ | 27 00 | 1 |
| 2 | | 5 | 7 | Checker Sugar Co. | ✓ | 120 00 | 2 |
| 5 | | 31 | | Total | | 398 00 | 5 |
| 6 | | | | | | (511)(21) | 6 |

The entries in the purchases returns and allowances journal shown above are explained as follows:

July 3 — Issued Debit Memorandum No. 6 to Davis Pickles for the return of goods which were not the size ordered. The pickles purchased on June 17 (see page 135) were ordered in quart sizes, but pint jars were sent. The two cases amounting to $27 were returned for credit.

July 5 — Issued Debit Memorandum No. 7 to Checker Sugar Co. for an allowance of $120 off the purchase price of the goods bought on June 28 (see page 135) because certain items were found to be defective.

The transactions recorded in the purchases returns and allowances journal are limited to the return of merchandise purchased on credit. Merchandise returned for cash is recorded in the cash receipts journal. Only one amount column is required because all transactions in this journal represent a debit to Accounts Payable and a credit to Purchases Returns and Allowances.

The posting from the purchases returns and allowances journal to the creditors' subsidiary ledger should be made daily. After posting, a check mark is placed in the Posting Reference column of the journal and the designation "PR" (for purchases returns and allowances journal) and the journal page number are entered in the Posting Reference column of the creditor's account.

The subsidiary ledger account of Davis Pickles is shown below after the posting from the purchases returns and allowances journal has been completed.

NAME **Davis Pickles**
ADDRESS **17401 Sunset Drive, Tulsa, OK 74114-3283** TERMS:

| DATE | | ITEM | POST. REF. | DEBIT | CREDIT | BALANCE |
|---|---|---|---|---|---|---|
| 1982 | | | | | | |
| June | 17 | | P1 | | 1 196 00 | 1 196 00 |
| | 26 | | P1 | | 920 00 | 2 116 00 |
| July | 3 | | PR2 | 27 00 | | 2 089 00 |

At the end of the month, the total of the amount column in the purchases returns and allowances journal is posted as a debit to Accounts Payable and a credit to Purchases Returns and Allowances in the general ledger. Again, by posting the monthly total of the journal, only one debit and one credit posting to the general ledger is required.

As the postings of the total are completed, the account numbers of Accounts Payable (21) and Purchases Returns and Allowances (51.1) are entered below the double-ruled column total in the journal. These two ledger accounts would then appear as follows:

ACCOUNT **Accounts Payable** ACCOUNT NO. **21**

| DATE | | ITEM | POST. REF. | DEBIT | CREDIT | BALANCE DEBIT | BALANCE CREDIT |
|---|---|---|---|---|---|---|---|
| 1982 July | 1 | Balance | √ | | | | 6 836 00 |
| | 31 | | PR2 | 398 00 | | | 7 230 00 |

ACCOUNT **Purchases Returns and Allowances** ACCOUNT NO. **51.1**

| DATE | | ITEM | POST. REF. | DEBIT | CREDIT | BALANCE DEBIT | BALANCE CREDIT |
|---|---|---|---|---|---|---|---|
| 1982 July | 31 | | PR2 | | 398 00 | | 398 00 |

## Returns Other Than Merchandise

When assets other than merchandise are returned to the creditor or an allowance is granted on such assets, the debit is made to Accounts Payable and the credit is recorded directly to the asset being returned. For example, if $18 of office supplies are returned by Rose on July 10 to Queen Supply Co. for credit, the following entry is made in the general journal.

JOURNAL PAGE 2

| | DATE | | DESCRIPTION | POST. REF. | DEBIT | CREDIT | |
|---|---|---|---|---|---|---|---|
| | 1982 | | | | | | |
| 1 | July | 10 | Accts. Pay. — Queen Supply Co. | 21/√ | 18 00 | | 1 |
| 2 | | | Office Supplies | 15 | | 18 00 | 2 |
| 3 | | | Returned office supplies | | | | 3 |
| 4 | | | Debit Memo No. 8. | | | | 4 |
| 5 | | | | | | | 5 |
| 6 | | | | | | | 6 |

The number of returns of nonmerchandise items is normally so small that no value is derived from establishing separate return accounts for these items. These transactions are infrequent enough that special journals or special journal columns are not required.

## QUESTIONS FOR DISCUSSION

1. Give three reasons why a customer might return merchandise to a men's clothier.
2. Why might an appliance store return merchandise to a manufacturer?
3. What control procedures should a business have to handle a sales return for cash?
4. Why do most businesses use a sales returns and allowances account rather than debiting the sales account directly?
5. (a) What is the purpose of the sales returns and allowances journal? (b) Explain in detail the posting procedure from this journal.
6. What information will normally be shown in a debit memorandum?

## EXERCISES

1. Record the following transactions in a two-column general journal for the Barnett Company.
   (a) Sale of merchandise to Bob Bond on account, $135.
   (b) Issued Credit Memorandum No. 41 to Danny Amos on account for merchandise returned due to defect in packaging, $25.
   (c) Sold merchandise to Jana Wooten for cash, $75.
   (d) Issued Credit Memorandum No. 42 to Philip Reeder for merchandise returned due to wrong model number, $20.
   (e) Issued a check to Gladys Johnson for merchandise returned, $27.
2. On a separate sheet of paper, indicate the normal balance (debit or credit) for each of the following accounts:
   (a) Accounts Receivable
   (b) Purchases
   (c) Accounts Payable
   (d) Sales Returns and Allowances
   (e) Sales
   (f) Purchases Returns and Allowances
3. The account for Curano Sales Company in the accounts payable subsidiary ledger of Ajax Laundry Company is presented below.

NAME **Curano Sales Company**
ADDRESS **57 Winnipeg Road, Ogden, MT 84403-6442** TERMS:

| DATE | | ITEM | POST. REF. | DEBIT | CREDIT | BALANCE |
|---|---|---|---|---|---|---|
| 19-- Mar. | 5 | | P17 | | 218 00 | 218 00 |
| | 9 | | PR6 | 35 00 | | 183 00 |
| | 20 | | CP15 | 183 00 | | —— |

   (a) Based on the postings to the Curano account, record the entries in a two-column general journal to represent Ajax's transactions with Curano for March.
   (b) Indicate the special journal in which each transaction was recorded.

## ASSIGNMENT 8-A

Tear out pages 459–472 and complete Assignment 8-A. Submit your papers for approval. After completion, continue with the chapter discussion until Assignment 8-B is required.

# PART B DISCOUNTS AND TRANSPORTATION COSTS

This section of the chapter examines the accounting procedures employed to record various kinds of discounts offered on the sale of goods. The accounting entries required of both buyers and sellers of goods are illustrated. Transportation costs incurred on goods sold is another special area relating to the accounting for merchandise transactions. Accounting for these costs is examined from the point of view of both buyer and seller.

## CREDIT TERMS

In all transactions, there should be a definite understanding between the buyer and the seller concerning when the payment is to be made. This agreement is known as the *credit terms* of the sale. Many businesses require payment at the time of the sale, stating the credit terms as "cash" or "net cash." When the purchaser is allowed a period of time in which to pay, this time is known as the *credit period*.

Credit periods vary widely depending upon the nature of the business and management's policy. Retailers, for example, often stipulate that all purchases in any given month must be paid by the tenth of the following month. Many retailers and major credit card issuers have *revolving credit plans* which allow customers to pay a certain percentage of their bills plus a finance charge each month.

In wholesale and manufacturing operations it is customary for the credit period to begin on the date of the invoice. Credit terms are usually stated as a specific number of days from the invoice date. If, for example, the credit terms are expressed as "net 30 days," this means that payment is due 30 days from the invoice date, and is shown on the invoice as "n/30." The term "net end of month" is frequently used in business and means that payment of the invoice is due by the end of the month in which the transaction was made. This would be expressed on the invoice as "n/EOM."

## CASH DISCOUNTS

It is the practice of many businesses to offer a deduction from the invoice price for prompt payment. For example, on July 2, Rose sells $275 worth of merchandise to Giese Grocery with the agreement that payment may be delayed for 30 days but that 2% will be deducted from the invoice price if payment is made within 10 days. If Giese pays Rose $269.50 within 10 days, the obligation is satisfied. The $5.50 ($275 × 2%) reduction from the invoice price allowed for prompt payment is called a *cash discount*.

The rate of discount available is usually shown on the invoice in abbreviated form. For example, on the invoice illustrated on page 130, it is shown as 2/10, n/30. This means that a discount of 2% will be allowed for payment within 10 days, but if the discount is not taken, the total amount is still due within 30 days of the invoice date.

Some industries have very liberal credit terms, allowing a cash discount if the invoice is paid either by the end of the month or by a certain number of days after the end of the month. For example, the terms 4/10 EOM, n/60 would indicate a 4% cash discount is allowed if paid within 10 days after the end of the month. If the discount is not taken, the invoice price is still due 60 days from the invoice date.

Many firms receive discounts on purchases and grant them on sales. The discount received on purchases is called a *purchases discount*, and the discount allowed on sales is known as a *sales discount*. When cash discounts are offered by the seller, the goods, in effect, are being offered for sale at the invoice price less the discount. It is expected that the buyer will take advantage of the discount offered. Therefore, the seller should consider cash discounts as a deduction from sales and the buyer should consider them as a reduction in the invoice price of the goods purchased.

## Recording Sales Discounts

When goods are sold with the agreement that a discount will be allowed for prompt payment, the sale is recorded at the invoice price. If the invoice is paid within the discount period, Cash is debited for the amount actually received, a sales discount account is debited for the amount of the discount, and Accounts Receivable and the customer's subsidiary account are credited for the full invoice price. The payment received, which is less than the invoice price by the amount of the discount, represents full settlement of the account.

For example, the entry in journal form to record the sale to Giese Grocery would be:

| | Date | Description | Post. Ref. | Debit | Credit |
|---|---|---|---|---|---|
| | 2 | Accts. Rec. — Giese Grocery........... | | 275 00 | |
| | | Sales................................................ | | | 275 00 |
| | | Sales Invoice No. 539. | | | |

If Giese pays the invoice on July 9, which would be within the 10-day discount period, the remittance would be only $269.50, the invoice price less 2% . The entry on Rose's books to record receipt of the payment would be:

| | Date | Description | Post. Ref. | Debit | Credit |
|---|---|---|---|---|---|
| | 9 | Cash.................................................... | | 269 50 | |
| | | Sales Discount.................................. | | 5 50 | |
| | | Accts. Rec. — Giese Grocery........ | | | 275 00 |
| | | Received payment on account owed. | | | |

If Rose were using special journals, such as those discussed in Chapters 6 and 7, the entry on July 2 would be recorded in the sales journal as shown on the following page.

**SALES JOURNAL** PAGE 2

| DATE | | ACCOUNT DEBITED | SALE NO. | POST. REF. | ACCOUNTS REC. DR. SALES CR. |
|---|---|---|---|---|---|
| 1982 July | 2 | Giese Grocery | 539 | ✓ | 275 00 |
| | | | | | |

The receipt of payment on July 9 would be recorded in the cash receipts journal as shown below.

**CASH RECEIPTS JOURNAL** PAGE 2

| DATE | ACCOUNT CREDITED | POST. REF. | GENERAL ACCOUNTS CR. | SALES CR. | ACCOUNTS RECEIVABLE CR. | SALES DISCOUNT DR. | CASH DR. |
|---|---|---|---|---|---|---|---|
| 9 | Giese Grocery | | | | 275 00 | 5 50 | 269 50 |
| | | | 4 000 00 | 15 033 00 | 3 905 00 | 25 70 | 22 912 30 |
| 31 | Totals | | 4 000 00 | 15 033 00 | 3 905 00 | 25 70 | 22 912 30 |
| | | | (✓) | (41) | (12) | (41.2) | (11) |

Note that a special column for Sales Discount Dr. is provided in the cash receipts journal. This special column is essential to any firm that grants cash discounts to its customers. The total of the Sales Discount Dr. column in the cash receipts journal is posted at the end of the month to the sales discount account in the general ledger:

ACCOUNT **Sales Discount** ACCOUNT NO. **41.2**

| DATE | | ITEM | POST. REF. | DEBIT | CREDIT | BALANCE DEBIT | BALANCE CREDIT |
|---|---|---|---|---|---|---|---|
| 1982 July | 31 | | CR2 | 25 70 | | 25 70 | |

Sales Discount is a contra account representing a reduction in sales and having a normal debit balance. It is assigned the decimal account number 41.2, just as Sales Returns and Allowances was numbered 41.1 to indicate that its balance is subtracted on the financial statements from the balance in account No. 41, Sales. Sales Discount is a temporary account and is closed to Income Summary at the end of the period.

The subsidiary account for Giese Grocery in the accounts receivable ledger after the two entries have been posted would appear as follows:

NAME **Giese Grocery**
ADDRESS **1602 Park Road, W., Oklahoma City, OK 73129-5943** TERMS: **2/10, n/30**

| DATE | | ITEM | POST. REF. | DEBIT | CREDIT | BALANCE |
|---|---|---|---|---|---|---|
| 1982 June | 9 | | S1 | 410 00 | | 410 00 |
| | 12 | | S1 | 950 00 | | 1 360 00 |
| | 24 | | CR1 | | 1 360 00 | ——— |
| July | 2 | | S2 | 275 00 | | 275 00 |
| | 9 | | CR2 | | 275 00 | ——— |

## Recording Purchases Discounts

When goods are purchased on account with the agreement that a discount will be allowed for prompt payment, the purchase is recorded at the invoice price. If the invoice is paid within the discount period, Accounts Payable in the general ledger and the creditor's account in the subsidiary ledger are debited for the full amount of the invoice, Cash is credited for the amount actually paid, and a purchases discount account is credited for the amount of the discount.

For example, if Rose purchased merchandise on June 28 from Checker Sugar Co. for $1,220, terms 3/10, n/30, the entry in journal form to record the purchase would be:

| Date | Account | Post. Ref. | Debit | Credit |
|---|---|---|---|---|
| 28 | Purchases | | 1 220 00 | |
| | Accts. Pay. — Checker Sugar Co. | | | 1 220 00 |
| | Purchased merch. on account. | | | |
| | Purchase Invoice No. 48. | | | |

Also assume that on July 5, Rose was granted an allowance of $120 off the purchase price for defective goods. The entry in journal form to record the allowance would be:

| Date | Account | Post. Ref. | Debit | Credit |
|---|---|---|---|---|
| 5 | Accts. Pay. — Checker Sugar Co. | | 120 00 | |
| | Purchases Returns and Allow. | | | 120 00 |
| | To record allowance. | | | |
| | Debit Memo No. 7. | | | |

If Rose pays the invoice within the discount period on July 8, the amount required to settle the account would be $1,067 [$1,100 − $33 ($1,100 × 3%)]. The $1,100 represents the invoice price of $1,220 less the allowance of $120. Discounts are not granted on the dollar amount of merchandise returns or allowances. That is why the $120 allowance had to be deducted before the discount was computed. The journal entry to record the payment would be:

| Date | Account | Post. Ref. | Debit | Credit |
|---|---|---|---|---|
| 8 | Accts. Pay. — Checker Sugar Co. | | 1 100 00 | |
| | Cash | | | 1 067 00 |
| | Purchases Discount | | | 33 00 |
| | Paid on account owed. | | | |

If Rose were using special journals, the entry to record the purchase on June 28 would be recorded in the purchases journal as follows:

**PURCHASES JOURNAL** PAGE 1

| Date | Account Credited | Post. Ref. | Accounts Payable Cr. | Purchases Dr. | Store Supplies Dr. | General Accounts Dr. — Account | Post. Ref. | Amount |
|---|---|---|---|---|---|---|---|---|
| 28 | Checker Sugar Co. | √ | 1 220 00 | 1 220 00 | | | | |

The allowance granted on July 5 would be recorded in the purchases returns and allowances journal as shown on the following page.

**PURCHASES RETURNS AND ALLOWANCES JOURNAL** PAGE 2

| DATE | | DR. MEMO NO. | ACCOUNT DEBITED | POST. REF. | ACCTS. PAY. DR. PURCH. RET. & ALLOW. CR. |
|---|---|---|---|---|---|
| | 5 | 7 | Checker Sugar Co. | √ | 120 00 |

The payment of the invoice on July 8 would be recorded in the cash payments journal as follows:

**CASH PAYMENTS JOURNAL** PAGE 2

| DATE | | CK. NO. | ACCOUNT DEBITED | POST. REF. | GENERAL ACCOUNTS DR. | ACCOUNTS PAYABLE DR. | PURCHASES DISCOUNT CR. | CASH CR. |
|---|---|---|---|---|---|---|---|---|
| | 8 | 838 | Checker Sugar Co. | | | 1 100 00 | 33 00 | 1 067 00 |
| | | | | | 12 674 00 | 7 702 00 | 65 80 | 20 310 20 |
| | 31 | | Totals | | 12 674 00 | 7 702 00 | 65 80 | 20 310 20 |
| | | | | | (√) | (21) | (51.2) | (11) |

A special column for Purchases Discount Cr. is needed in the cash payments journal of any firm which is allowed cash discounts by its creditors. The total of the Purchases Discount Cr. column in the cash payments journal is posted at the end of the month to the purchases discount account in the general ledger as follows:

ACCOUNT **Purchases Discount** ACCOUNT NO. **51.2**

| DATE | | ITEM | POST. REF. | DEBIT | CREDIT | BALANCE DEBIT | BALANCE CREDIT |
|---|---|---|---|---|---|---|---|
| 1982 July | 31 | | CP2 | | 65 80 | | 65 80 |

Purchases Discount is a contra account representing a reduction in purchases and having a normal credit balance. It is assigned the decimal number 51.2, just as Purchases Returns and Allowances was numbered 51.1, to indicate that its balance is subtracted on the financial statements from the balance in account No. 51, Purchases. Purchases Discount is a temporary account and is closed to Income Summary at the end of the period.

The subsidiary account for Checker Sugar Co. in the accounts payable ledger after the three entries have been posted would appear as follows:

NAME **Checker Sugar Co.**
ADDRESS **2107 Georgia Ave., N.E., St. Louis, MO 63135-1097** TERMS: **3/10, n/30**

| DATE | | ITEM | POST. REF. | DEBIT | CREDIT | BALANCE |
|---|---|---|---|---|---|---|
| 1982 June | 2 | | P1 | | 1 185 00 | 1 185 00 |
| | 18 | | CP1 | 1 185 00 | | —— |
| | 28 | | P1 | | 1 220 00 | 1 220 00 |
| July | 5 | | PR2 | 120 00 | | 1 100 00 |
| | 8 | | CP2 | 1 100 00 | | —— |

## Importance of Taking Purchases Discounts

It is extremely important for a business to take steps to insure that all invoices are paid on time. If a firm does not pay its bills on time, this negligence may cause unfavorable relations with creditors, damage its credit rating, and may lead to its being able to purchase goods only on a *COD (cash on delivery)* basis.

In almost every instance, businesses should take advantage of cash discounts offered, even if they have to borrow the money to do it. To illustrate, consider a May purchase of merchandise which Rose makes from Sweet Candy Co. for $300 with terms of 3/15, n/30. If Rose pays this invoice within 15 days, only $291 will be required to be paid, which is a savings of $9 for paying 15 days early. If Rose borrowed the $291 from a bank for the remaining 15 days of the credit period and paid a 12% interest rate, the interest expense for the 15-day period would only be $1.46. Rose would save $7.54, which is the difference between the $9.00 discount and the $1.46 interest expense.

There are many procedures which can be used to insure payment of the invoice either within the discount period or on the due date. One of the simplest but most effective methods is to set up a file consisting of a group of folders numbered from 1 to 31, the numbers representing the days of the month. The unpaid invoices are filed by the due date or the date when the purchaser wishes to make payments if a discount is involved. For example, if the invoice from the Sweet Candy Co. is dated May 6 with credit terms of 3/15, n/30, the invoice should be filed in the folder number "21." On May 21, this folder would be pulled from the file and all the enclosed invoices would be paid. If for some reason Rose decided not to take advantage of the discount, the invoice from Sweet Candy Co. would be refiled in the folder labeled "5" representing June 5, which would be the last day of the 30-day credit period.

## Trade Discounts

In many manufacturing and wholesaling operations, catalogs are published showing the product lines at retail prices, commonly called *list prices*. Large discounts from these list prices are offered to various dealers and institutions as well as to large volume buyers. These discounts from catalog prices, often as large as 40% to 50%, are called *trade discounts*. The manufacturer will often publish expensive catalogs and the cost of republishing them for every price change would be too costly. The trade discounts, which are published as a separate list, allow for the changing of prices without printing a new catalog.

Trade discounts are also used when different prices are offered to various classes of customers. A pharmaceutical distributor may sell certain items to a hospital at one price and to a drug store at a different price.

Trade discounts are not recorded in the accounting records. They are used only to determine the selling price. This selling price, which is list price minus trade discount, is used for accounting purposes. For example, an item listed at $150 with a trade discount of 40%

($60), would be recorded by both the buyer and seller at $90. Any cash discount quoted would be applied to the net price of $90. If the terms of the invoice were 2/10, n/30, and payment was made within the discount period, there would be a $1.80 cash discount, ($90 × 2%). The entries in general journal form on the books of the buyer, Mr. B, and the seller, Mr. S, for these transactions would be:

| Buyer's Books — Mr. B | | | Seller's Books — Mr. S | | |
|---|---|---|---|---|---|
| Purchases | 90.00 | | Accounts Receivable — B ....... | 90.00 | |
| Accounts Payable — S.......... | | 90.00 | Sales .................................... | | 90.00 |
| Record purchase. | | | Record sale. | | |
| Accounts Payable — S ............ | 90.00 | | Cash ........................................ | 88.20 | |
| Cash...................................... | | 88.20 | Sales Discount......................... | 1.80 | |
| Purchases Discount............. | | 1.80 | Accounts Receivable — B.... | | 90.00 |
| Paid invoice within the discount period. | | | Received payment within the discount period. | | |

## TRANSPORTATION COSTS OF MERCHANDISE SOLD

The sales agreement should always state the provisions concerning the cost of transporting the goods to the buyer. If the terms are *FOB (free on board) destination*, the seller is responsible for the cost of the delivery. If the goods are *FOB shipping point*, the buyer must pay the transportation costs.

When the seller is responsible for paying the transportation costs, the amount paid to a trucking company, airline, railroad, or other common carrier is debited to an expense account, Delivery Expense. Sometimes the account title Freight Out is used.

When the purchaser is responsible for paying the transportation charges, the amounts paid for freight, postage, express, or other delivery costs are debited to an account titled Freight In or Transportation In. The amount of shipping costs paid in buying merchandise is properly considered an additional cost of the goods. Freight In is therefore shown as an addition to purchases in determining the cost of goods sold to be reported on the income statement.

Sometimes the seller prepays the transportation charges on merchandise even when the terms are FOB shipping point. This may be done for the convenience of the purchaser or it may be required by the transporter of the goods. When this situation occurs, the transportation costs should be listed separately on the sales invoice and the total of the selling price plus the transportation charges should be debited to the customer's account.

The cash discount allowed on an invoice does not apply to prepaid freight charges. For example, if a company buys merchandise from the ZIP Co. on November 1 for $800, with credit terms of 2/10, n/30, and must reimburse the seller for prepaid freight charges of $50, the purchaser would remit $834 if payment was made on November 9 (within the discount period). The $834 represents the $800 invoice price of the merchandise less 2% discount of $16, plus the freight in charges of $50 ($800 − $16 + $50 = $834). The entries to record the purchase and payment on the books of the purchaser would be as shown on the following page.

JOURNAL PAGE 19

| DATE | | DESCRIPTION | POST. REF. | DEBIT | CREDIT |
|---|---|---|---|---|---|
| 1982 | | | | | |
| Nov. | 1 | Purchases | | 800 00 | |
| | | Freight In | | 50 00 | |
| | | Accounts Payable — ZIP Co. | | | 850 00 |
| | | Purchased merch. on account. | | | |
| | 9 | Accounts Payable — ZIP Co. | | 850 00 | |
| | | Cash | | | 834 00 |
| | | Purchases Discount | | | 16 00 |
| | | Paid for merch. purchased. | | | |

## SUMMARY OF SPECIAL JOURNALS

In this and the two preceding chapters, six special journals have been discussed. A summary discussion of each of these special journals is presented below. The posting reference abbreviation for each journal is shown in parentheses.

### Sales Journal (S)

The purpose of the sales journal is to record the sale of merchandise on account. Since the sale of merchandise on account is the only type of transaction recorded in this journal, the entry is always a debit to Accounts Receivable (including a debit to the customer's subsidiary account) and a credit to Sales. Consequently, only one amount column is required for the sales journal.

Cash sales are not recorded in the sales journal. They are recorded in the cash receipts journal.

### Sales Returns and Allowances Journal (SR)

The purpose of the sales returns and allowances journal is to record the return of merchandise which was sold on account. The entry in this journal will always be a debit to Sales Returns and Allowances and a credit to Accounts Receivable, including a credit to the individual customer's account. This journal also requires only one amount column.

### Purchases Journal (P)

Since all purchases on account are recorded in the purchases journal, there will always be an Accounts Payable Cr. column and a Purchases Dr. column for recording purchases of merchandise on account. There may also be special columns for other assets frequently purchased on account such as office supplies, store supplies, and office equipment. The purchases journal also includes a General Accounts Dr. column for recording the purchase of assets for which no special column is provided.

Cash purchases are not recorded in the purchases journal. They are recorded in the cash payments journal.

## Purchases Returns and Allowances Journal (PR)

The purpose of the purchases returns and allowances journal is to record the returns or allowances of merchandise which was purchased on account. This journal is restricted to the returns of merchandise because returns and allowances on other assets do not normally occur frequently enough to justify special columns. The entry in this journal is always a debit to Accounts Payable, including the creditor's subsidiary account, and a credit to Purchases Returns and Allowances. Therefore, this journal only requires one amount column.

## Cash Receipts Journal (CR)

All cash received by the business is recorded in the cash receipts journal. Since there are many sources of cash receipts, this journal normally has several columns. The two most common sources of cash receipts are cash sales and collections from customers on their accounts. Therefore, special columns for Sales Cr. and Accounts Receivable Cr. are necessary. A General Accounts Cr. column is also included. Other special credit columns may be included, if necessary. There is always a Cash Dr. column because all transactions recorded in this journal represent the receipt of cash. If the business allows its customers a cash discount for prompt payment, a Sales Discount Dr. column is also included.

## Cash Payments Journal (CP)

All cash paid out by the business is recorded in the cash payments journal. Most businesses buy their merchandise on account and the entry to record the subsequent payment requires a debit to Accounts Payable and a credit to Cash. Therefore, an Accounts Payable Dr. column is needed in the cash payments journal. Other special debit columns are included if particular transactions occur often enough to justify them. For example, frequent cash purchases of merchandise would merit inclusion of a Purchases Dr. column. There is also a General Accounts Dr. column to record the payment of items not covered by the special columns. Since the disbursement of cash is a prerequisite for inclusion in the cash payments journal, a Cash Cr. column is always required. If the creditors of the firm allow cash discounts for prompt payment, a Purchases Discount Cr. column should be included.

The posting procedures for the above special journals have been discussed in previous chapters. The columns should be totaled at the end of the month and those journals with more than one amount column should be checked to insure the equality of the debit and credit totals. All special columns are posted by totals at the end of the month or more frequently, if necessary. The entries in the General Accounts column are posted individually during the month and the total of this column is not posted. The postings to the accounts receivable and accounts payable subsidiary ledgers should be made at frequent intervals during the month, preferably daily.

## General Journal (J or G)

All of the special journals explained on pages 164–166 may be used in a firm's record keeping system. The special journals used and the columns included in these journals depend upon the needs of the particular business enterprise. Most businesses that have sales on account use a sales journal. Almost all businesses require a cash receipts journal and a cash payments journal, although in smaller firms a combined cash journal such as the one illustrated on pages 86 and 87, may be sufficient. Only the larger companies would have enough transactions to justify a sales returns and allowances journal or a purchases returns and allowances journal.

Even if a business uses all of the special journals discussed, it still needs a general journal to record those transactions which are not recorded in the special journals. The most common items recorded in a general journal are correcting entries and adjusting and closing entries made at the end of the period.

## QUESTIONS FOR DISCUSSION

1. Explain the meaning of the following credit terms:
   (a) n/30
   (b) n/EOM
   (c) 2/10, n/30
2. Differentiate between a purchases discount and a sales discount.
3. (a) What is a trade discount? (b) How are trade discounts shown in the accounting records?
4. Julie Miller, owner of Julie's Boutique, owes $1,000 for merchandise purchased. She can deduct a discount of 2% if payment is made within 10 days. The net amount of the invoice must be paid in 30 days. At the end of the 10-day period, Miller does not have sufficient cash to pay the invoice, so she borrows $1,000 from the bank, giving a 20-day note payable with an interest rate of 9%. The interest expense on this note for 20 days is $5. (a) How much does Miller save by borrowing the money and paying the invoice within the discount period? (b) Explain how a savings is possible if Miller pays interest of 9% to take advantage of a 2% discount.
5. Zisk Teen Shop has the option of buying five dozen jackets from the Krum Co. for $175 per dozen, terms FOB destination, 3/10, n/30. Zisk can buy the same quality jackets from the Horn Co. for $160 per dozen, terms FOB shipping point, n/30. The cost of freight on the merchandise will amount to $80 in both cases. From which company would you recommend that Zisk buy the merchandise? Explain your answer.

## EXERCISES

**1.** (a) Prepare a list showing the last date each of the following invoices would have to be paid in order to receive the discount. (b) List the net amount to be paid for each invoice if paid within the discount period.

| *Invoice No.* | *Invoice Date* | *Invoice Price* | *Terms* |
|---|---|---|---|
| D402 | July 23 | $120 | 3/10, n/30 |
| D407 | August 4 | 250 | 4/20, n/60 |
| D410 | August 15 | 180 | 3/10 EOM, n/60 |

**2.** On January 6, Ying Company purchases merchandise with a list price of $700 and a 40% trade discount from LeBaron Wholesalers on account. The terms of the sale are 3/10, n/30. (a) Prepare the entries to record the purchase of the merchandise on Ying's books. (b) Prepare the entry to record the payment of the invoice by Ying on January 15.

**3.** Prepare the entries on January 6 and 15 on LeBaron's books for the transactions with Ying in Exercise 2 above.

**4.** Assuming that the Hacienda Company maintains all of the following journals, name the possible journal sources of debits and credits for each account listed below using the abbreviations for the following journals:

(a) Sales Journal (S)
(b) Multicolumn Purchases Journal (P)
(c) Sales Returns and Allowances Journal (SR)
(d) Purchases Returns and Allowances Journal (PR)
(e) Cash Receipts Journal (CR)
(f) Cash Payments Journal (CP)
(g) General Journal (J)

| *Accounts* | *Debits* | *Credits* |
|---|---|---|
| 0. Cash (example)................ | CR | CP |
| 1. Sales................................ | ______ | ______ |
| 2. Accounts Payable............ | ______ | ______ |
| 3. Purchases Returns and Allowances................... | ______ | ______ |
| 4. Store Supplies................. | ______ | ______ |
| 5. Purchases......................... | ______ | ______ |
| 6. Accounts Receivable ....... | ______ | ______ |

## ASSIGNMENT 8-B

**Tear out pages 473–482 and complete Assignment 8-B. Submit your papers for approval. After completion, study the discussion in Chapter 9 until the next assignment is required.**

Chapter 9

# COMPLETION OF THE ACCOUNTING CYCLE FOR A MERCHANDISING ENTERPRISE

The basic steps in the accounting cycle for a service enterprise were presented in Chapter 4. The additional materials studied since that time which alter some of the steps and procedures in the accounting cycle are: **(1)** the use of special journals in the recording process; **(2)** the use of subsidiary ledgers for accounts receivable and accounts payable; and **(3)** the inclusion of a merchandising enterprise, whose business consists of buying and selling merchandise. This chapter examines the end-of-period accounting activities for a merchandising enterprise.

## PART A ACCOUNTING CYCLE FOR A MERCHANDISING ENTERPRISE

The accounting cycle for a merchandising business includes the following steps:

1. Journalize the transactions in the proper journal.
2. Post from the journals to the general and subsidiary ledgers. The General Accounts columns are posted individually and the special columns are posted by totals at the end of the period. The subsidiary accounts are posted individually, preferably daily.
3. Prepare a trial balance of the general ledger.
4. Prepare a schedule of each subsidiary ledger and determine that it is in agreement with the related control account in the general ledger.
5. Accumulate the information necessary to adjust the accounts.
6. Complete the work sheet.
7. Prepare the financial statements from the data on the work sheet.
8. Journalize and post the adjusting entries.
9. Journalize and post the closing entries.
10. Prepare a post-closing trial balance.

Steps 1 through 4 above have been explained in Chapters 6–8. Step 5, the preparation of adjusting entries, has been discussed for a service business. However, the preparation of adjusting entries for a merchandising business also includes two additional adjustments of the merchandise inventory account. These adjustments must be explained before an illustration of the completed accounting cycle, including Steps 6 through 10, can be understood.

## ADJUSTMENTS FOR MERCHANDISE INVENTORY

The need for adjusting entries at the end of the accounting period for a service enterprise was discussed in Chapter 4. The only additional adjustments required for a merchandising enterprise are those which adjust the merchandise inventory account.

The balance in Merchandise Inventory at the beginning of the accounting period represents the amount of inventory on hand at the end of the preceding period. This balance was determined by taking a physical count of the inventory. Normally no entries are made to the merchandise inventory account during the period. The only exception is when errors made in the account in preceding periods are discovered during the current period. As merchandise is purchased during the period, the transactions are recorded by a debit to Purchases and a credit to Cash or Accounts Payable. Since there is an assumption that the items in the beginning inventory have been sold, an entry should be made to transfer the beginning balance out of the inventory account. The ending balance (again determined by counting the goods on hand) will then be recorded in the inventory account.

The above objectives are accomplished with two adjusting entries for merchandise inventory. To illustrate, assume that Rose Wholesale Co.'s inventory on hand at the beginning of the month was $6,111, and a physical count at the end of the month totaled $6,800. First, the beginning inventory is transferred to the income summary account with the following entry:

**JOURNAL** PAGE 3

| DATE | | DESCRIPTION | POST. REF. | DEBIT | CREDIT |
|---|---|---|---|---|---|
| 1982 | | Adjusting Entries | | | |
| July | 31 | Income Summary | 33 | 6 111 00 | |
| | | Merchandise Inventory | 13 | | 6 111 00 |
| | | Transfer beginning inventory | | | |
| | | to Income Summary. | | | |

The second adjusting entry is made to record the amount of the ending inventory in Merchandise Inventory. Income Summary is credited when the new inventory balance is recorded.

| | | | | | |
|---|---|---|---|---|---|
| | 31 | Merchandise Inventory | 13 | 6 800 00 | |
| | | Income Summary | 33 | | 6 800 00 |
| | | Record ending inventory. | | | |

After the above entries have been posted, the merchandise inventory account will appear as follows:

ACCOUNT **Merchandise Inventory** ACCOUNT NO. 13

| DATE | | ITEM | POST. REF. | DEBIT | CREDIT | BALANCE DEBIT | BALANCE CREDIT |
|---|---|---|---|---|---|---|---|
| 1982 | | | | | | | |
| July | 1 | Balance | ✓ | | | 6 111 00 | |
| | 31 | Adjusting | J3 | | 6 111 00 | — | — |
| | 31 | Adjusting | J3 | 6 800 00 | | 6 800 00 | |

The balance in the merchandise inventory account after the two entries are posted is a debit of $6,800, which is the amount of the inventory on hand at the end of the month as determined by the physical count. This account will be shown on the balance sheet as an asset.

## COMPLETION OF THE ACCOUNTING CYCLE ILLUSTRATED

To illustrate the procedures for completion of the accounting cycle at the end of the period, the data for Rose Wholesale Co. for the month of July are used. The chart of accounts is as follows:

**ROSE WHOLESALE CO.**
**Chart of Accounts**

**Assets**

11 Cash
12 Accounts Receivable
13 Merchandise Inventory
14 Store Supplies
15 Office Supplies
16 Prepaid Insurance
17 Store Equipment
17.1 Accumulated Depreciation — Store Equipment
18 Office Equipment
18.1 Accumulated Depreciation — Office Equipment

**Liabilities**

21 Accounts Payable
22 Salaries Payable
23 Mortgage Note Payable

**Owner's Equity**

31 Tom Rose, Capital
32 Tom Rose, Drawing
33 Income Summary

**Revenue**

41 Sales
41.1 Sales Returns and Allowances
41.2 Sales Discount

**Cost of Goods Sold**

51 Purchases
51.1 Purchases Returns and Allowances
51.2 Purchases Discount

**Expenses**

Selling Expenses:

61 Advertising Expense
62 Depreciation Expense — Store Equipment
63 Sales Salary Expense
64 Store Supplies Expense
65 Miscellaneous Selling Expense

General Expenses:

71 Depreciation Expense — Office Equipment
72 Insurance Expense
73 Office Salary Expense
74 Office Supplies Expense
75 Rent Expense
76 Utilities Expense
77 Miscellaneous General Expense

The post-closing trial balance and schedules of accounts receivable and accounts payable as of June 30 are presented on page 171.

The total of the schedule of accounts receivable is $2,775 which is the same as the balance of Accounts Receivable on the post-closing trial balance at June 30. The total of the schedule of accounts payable, $6,836, also matches the accounts payable account balance on the June post-closing trial balance. If all postings are up to date, the total of the subsidiary accounts should always equal the balance of the control account in the general ledger. If these two items are not in agreement, steps should be taken to determine the cause of the discrepancy.

Rose Wholesale Co.
Post-Closing Trial Balance
June 30, 1982

| Account | Debit | Credit |
|---|---|---|
| Cash | 15 369 00 | |
| Accounts Receivable | 2 775 00 | |
| Merchandise Inventory | 6 111 00 | |
| Store Supplies | 468 00 | |
| Office Supplies | 370 00 | |
| Prepaid Insurance | 264 00 | |
| Store Equipment | 3 100 00 | |
| Accumulated Depreciation — Store Equipment | | 125 00 |
| Office Equipment | 850 00 | |
| Accumulated Depreciation — Office Equipment | | 50 00 |
| Accounts Payable | | 6 836 00 |
| Tom Rose, Capital | | 22 296 00 |
| | 29 307 00 | 29 307 00 |

*Post-Closing Trial Balance – Rose Wholesale Co.*

Rose Wholesale Co.
Schedule of Accounts Receivable
June 30, 1982

| | | |
|---|---|---|
| Chung Supermarket | | 445 00 |
| Coda's Quik Stop | | 1 300 00 |
| Cruz Restaurant | | 380 00 |
| Morris Co. | | 650 00 |
| Total accounts receivable | | 2 775 00 |

*Schedule of Accounts Receivable – Rose Wholesale Co.*

Rose Wholesale Co.
Schedule of Accounts Payable
June 30, 1982

| | | |
|---|---|---|
| Checker Sugar Co. | | 1 220 00 |
| Davis Pickles | | 2 116 00 |
| Omni Equipment Co. | | 850 00 |
| Queen Supply Co. | | 290 00 |
| Sweet Candy Co. | | 2 135 00 |
| Warren Gum Co. | | 225 00 |
| Total accounts payable | | 6 836 00 |

*Schedule of Accounts Payable – Rose Wholesale Co.*

## The Journals

The journals after all the July transactions have been recorded are presented on pages 172 through 174. The special journals have been totaled and checked for accuracy. Only two transactions were recorded in the general journal as explained below:

July 10. Returned office supplies to Queen Supply Co. for credit on account, $18. The entry is not recorded in the purchases returns and allowances journal because merchandise is not being returned.

30. Purchased store equipment giving a three-year mortgage note payable.

*General Journal – Rose Wholesale Co.*

## JOURNAL

PAGE 2

| DATE | | DESCRIPTION | POST. REF. | DEBIT | CREDIT |
|---|---|---|---|---|---|
| 1982 | | | | | |
| July | 10 | Accts. Pay. — Queen Supply Co. | 21/√ | 18 00 | |
| | | Office Supplies | 15 | | 18 00 |
| | | Returned office supplies | | | |
| | | Debit Memo No. 8. | | | |
| | 30 | Store Equipment | 17 | 1 500 00 | |
| | | Mortgage Note Payable | 23 | | 1 500 00 |
| | | Bought store equipment giving | | | |
| | | a $1,500, 3-year note. | | | |

*Sales Journal – Rose Wholesale Co.*

## SALES JOURNAL

PAGE 2

| DATE | | ACCOUNT DEBITED | SALE NO. | POST. REF. | ACCOUNTS REC. DR. SALES CR. |
|---|---|---|---|---|---|
| 1982 | | | | | |
| July | 2 | Giese Grocery | 539 | √ | 275 00 |
| | 6 | Morris Co. | 540 | √ | 205 00 |
| | 8 | Chung Supermarket | 541 | √ | 410 00 |
| | 10 | Coda's Quik Stop | 542 | √ | 175 00 |
| | 14 | Cruz Restaurant | 543 | √ | 250 00 |
| | 22 | Giese Grocery | 544 | √ | 1 160 00 |
| | 28 | Chung Supermarket | 545 | √ | 1 225 00 |
| | 30 | Cruz Restaurant | 546 | √ | 990 00 |
| | | | | | 4 690 00 |
| | 31 | Total | | | 4 690 00 |
| | | | | | (12) (41) |

*Sales Returns and Allowances Journal – Rose Wholesale Co.*

## SALES RETURNS AND ALLOWANCES JOURNAL

PAGE 2

| DATE | | CR. MEMO NO. | ACCOUNT CREDITED | POST. REF. | SALES RET. & ALLOW. DR. ACCTS. REC. CR. |
|---|---|---|---|---|---|
| 1982 | | | | | |
| July | 1 | 15 | Cruz Restaurant | √ | 20 00 |
| | 2 | 16 | Chung Supermarket | √ | 40 00 |
| | 3 | 17 | Coda's Quik Stop | √ | 100 00 |
| | 15 | 18 | Morris Co. | √ | 25 00 |
| | 26 | 19 | Giese Grocery | √ | 257 00 |
| | 31 | | Total | | 442 00 |
| | | | | | (41.1) (12) |

## CASH RECEIPTS JOURNAL

PAGE 2

| DATE | | ACCOUNT CREDITED | POST. REF. | GENERAL ACCOUNTS CR. | SALES CR. | ACCOUNTS RECEIVABLE CR. | SALES DISCOUNT DR. | CASH DR. |
|---|---|---|---|---|---|---|---|---|
| 1982 | | | | | | | | |
| July | 2 | Cruz Restaurant .......... | √ | | | 360 00 | | 360 00 |
| | 3 | Morris Co. .................... | √ | | | 650 00 | | 650 00 |
| | 5 | √ .................................... | √ | | 3 127 00 | | | 3 127 00 |
| | 6 | Tom Rose, Capital ....... | 31 | 4 000 00 | | | | 4 000 00 |
| | 7 | Chung Supermarket.... | √ | | | 405 00 | 8 10 | 396 90 |
| | 9 | Giese Grocery............. | √ | | | 275 00 | 5 50 | 269 50 |
| | 12 | √ .................................... | √ | | 4 000 00 | | | 4 000 00 |
| | 13 | Coda's Quik Stop......... | √ | | | 1 200 00 | | 1 200 00 |
| | 16 | Morris Co. .................... | √ | | | 180 00 | 3 60 | 176 40 |
| | 19 | √ .................................... | √ | | 4 200 00 | | | 4 200 00 |
| | 19 | Chung Supermarket.... | √ | | | 410 00 | | 410 00 |
| | 19 | Coda's Quik Stop......... | √ | | | 175 00 | 3 50 | 171 50 |
| | 24 | Cruz Restaurant .......... | √ | | | 250 00 | 5 00 | 245 00 |
| | 26 | √ .................................... | √ | | 3 706 00 | | | 3 706 00 |
| | | | | 4 000 00 | 15 033 00 | 3 905 00 | 25 70 | 22 912 30 |
| | 31 | Totals ........................... | | 4 000 00 | 15 033 00 | 3 905 00 | 25 70 | 22 912 30 |
| | | | | (√) | (41) | (12) | (41.2) | (11) |

*Cash Receipts Journal – Rose Wholesale Co.*

## PURCHASES JOURNAL

PAGE 2

| DATE | | ACCOUNT CREDITED | POST. REF. | ACCOUNTS PAYABLE CR. | PURCHASES DR. | STORE SUPPLIES DR. | GENERAL ACCOUNTS DR. ACCOUNT | POST. REF. | AMOUNT |
|---|---|---|---|---|---|---|---|---|---|
| 1982 | | | | | | | | | |
| July | 2 | Queen Supply Company . | √ | 360 00 | | 220 00 | Office Supplies ...... | 15 | 140 00 |
| | 8 | Checker Sugar Co. .......... | √ | 480 00 | 480 00 | | | | |
| | 10 | Omni Equipment Co......... | √ | 3 370 00 | | | Store Equipment ... | 17 | 2 000 00 |
| | | | | | | | Office Equipment .. | 18 | 1 370 00 |
| | 12 | Sweet Candy Co. ............. | √ | 285 00 | 285 00 | | | | |
| | 16 | Davis Pickles ................... | √ | 157 00 | 157 00 | | | | |
| | 19 | Checker Sugar Co. .......... | √ | 280 00 | 280 00 | | | | |
| | 21 | Queen Supply Co. ........... | √ | 105 00 | | 105 00 | | | |
| | 26 | Warren Gum Company .... | √ | 1 200 00 | 1 200 00 | | | | |
| | 29 | Sweet Candy Co. ............. | √ | 2 275 00 | 2 275 00 | | | | |
| | | | | 8 512 00 | 4 677 00 | 325 00 | | | 3 510 00 |
| | 31 | Totals ............................. | | 8 512 00 | 4 677 00 | 325 00 | | | 3 510 00 |
| | | | | (21) | (51) | (14) | | | (√) |

*Purchases Journal – Rose Wholesale Co.*

## PURCHASES RETURNS AND ALLOWANCES JOURNAL

PAGE 2

| DATE | | DR. MEMO NO. | ACCOUNT DEBITED | POST. REF. | ACCTS. PAY. DR. PURCH. RET. & ALLOW. CR. |
|---|---|---|---|---|---|
| 1982 | | | | | |
| July | 3 | 6 | Davis Pickles ........................................................... | √ | 27 00 |
| | 5 | 7 | Checker Sugar Co. ..................................................... | √ | 120 00 |
| | 19 | 9 | Sweet Candy Co. ....................................................... | √ | 212 00 |
| | 26 | 10 | Davis Pickles ........................................................... | √ | 39 00 |
| | 31 | | Total ........................................................................ | | 398 00 |
| | | | | | (51.1) (21) |

*Purchases Returns and Allowances Journal – Rose Wholesale Co.*

## CASH PAYMENTS JOURNAL

PAGE 2

| DATE | | CK. NO. | ACCOUNT DEBITED | POST. REF. | GENERAL ACCOUNTS DR. | ACCOUNTS PAYABLE DR. | PURCHASES DISCOUNT CR. | CASH CR. |
|---|---|---|---|---|---|---|---|---|
| 1982 | | | | | | | | |
| July | 1 | 834 | Queen Supply Co. | √ | | 290 00 | | 290 00 |
| | 1 | 835 | Rent Expense | 75 | 920 00 | | | 920 00 |
| | 3 | 836 | Warren Gum Company | √ | | 225 00 | | 225 00 |
| | 5 | 837 | Davis Pickles | √ | | 2 089 00 | 18 40 | 2 070 60 |
| | 8 | 838 | Checker Sugar Co. | √ | | 1 100 00 | 33 00 | 1 067 00 |
| | 9 | 839 | Omni Equipment Co. | √ | | 850 00 | | 850 00 |
| | 10 | 840 | Purchases | 51 | 7 300 00 | | | 7 300 00 |
| | 15 | 841 | Sales Salary Expense | 63 | 850 00 | | | 1 570 00 |
| | | | Office Salary Expense | 73 | 720 00 | | | |
| | 16 | 842 | Queen Supply Co. | √ | | 342 00 | | 342 00 |
| | 17 | 843 | Checker Sugar Co. | √ | | 480 00 | 14 40 | 465 60 |
| | 20 | 844 | Sweet Candy Co. | √ | | 2 135 00 | | 2 135 00 |
| | 22 | 845 | Miscellaneous Selling Expense | 65 | 68 00 | | | 68 00 |
| | 22 | 846 | Miscellaneous General Expense | 77 | 31 00 | | | 31 00 |
| | 23 | 847 | Advertising Expense | 61 | 342 00 | | | 342 00 |
| | 28 | 848 | Sweet Candy Co. | √ | | 73 00 | | 73 00 |
| | 28 | 849 | Tom Rose, Drawing | 32 | 400 00 | | | 400 00 |
| | 29 | 850 | Utilities Expense | 76 | 413 00 | | | 413 00 |
| | 30 | 851 | Sales Salary Expense | 63 | 840 00 | | | 1 630 00 |
| | | | Office Salary Expense | 73 | 790 00 | | | |
| | 31 | 852 | Davis Pickles | √ | | 118 00 | | 118 00 |
| | | | | | 12 674 00 | 7 702 00 | 65 80 | 20 310 20 |
| | 31 | | Totals | | 12 674 00 | 7 702 00 | 65 80 | 20 310 20 |
| | | | | | (√) | (21) | (51.2) | (11) |

***Cash Payments Journal – Rose Wholesale Co.***

In the cash receipts journal, a 2% cash discount was granted to customers for invoices paid within 10 days. Four payments were not received within the discount period: Cruz Restaurant on July 2, Morris Co. on July 3, Coda's Quik Stop on July 13, and Chung Supermarket on July 19.

In the cash payments journal, credit terms made available by creditors varied. Omni Equipment Co. and Queen Supply Company did not allow any discount. The invoices paid to Warren Gum Company on July 3, Sweet Candy Co. on July 20 and 28, and Davis Pickles on July 31 were not within the respective discount periods.

The postings from the journals to the subsidiary ledger were recorded on a daily basis allowing customers' and creditors' account balances to be current at all times. The order of posting the column totals of the journals to the general ledger accounts at the end of the month should follow the sequence of the transactions. For example, sales transactions would first involve the sale, then any sales returns and allowances, and lastly cash receipts. For purchases, the order of recording transactions would be purchases, purchases returns and allowances, and cash payments.

When special journals are used, there are relatively few transactions recorded during the month in the general journal. When this is the case, it is most convenient to post first from the general journal and then from the special journals.

## Preparing the Trial Balance

After the journals have been posted and the ledger account balances have been determined, a trial balance should be taken of the general ledger to insure that the accounts are in balance. It is convenient to prepare the trial balance directly in the first two columns of the work sheet. If the trial balance is not in balance, steps should be taken to determine the cause of the discrepancy. The sum of the balances of the accounts in the accounts receivable ledger and the accounts payable ledger should also be determined and compared with the balances of their controlling accounts in the general ledger. The schedules of accounts receivable and accounts payable as of July 31 are presented below.

***Schedule of Accounts Receivable – Rose Wholesale Co.***

**Rose Wholesale Co.**
**Schedule of Accounts Receivable**
**July 31, 1982**

| | | |
|---|---|---|
| Chung Supermarket | | 1 225 00 |
| Cruz Restaurant | | 990 00 |
| Giese Grocery | | 903 00 |
| Total accounts receivable | | 3 118 00 |

***Schedule of Accounts Payable – Rose Wholesale Co.***

**Rose Wholesale Co.**
**Schedule of Accounts Payable**
**July 31, 1982**

| | | |
|---|---|---|
| Checker Sugar Co. | | 280 00 |
| Omni Equipment Co. | | 3 370 00 |
| Queen Supply Co. | | 105 00 |
| Sweet Candy Co. | | 2 275 00 |
| Warren Gum Company | | 1 200 00 |
| Total accounts payable | | 7 230 00 |

## Completing the Work Sheet

The next step in the accounting cycle is the completion of the work sheet. After the trial balance is proven, the data for adjustments are assembled and the adjustments are entered in the Adjustments column of the work sheet. The ten-column work sheet for Rose Wholesale Co. is presented on page 176.

Rose Wholesale Co.
Work Sheet
For Month Ended July 31, 1982

| ACCOUNT TITLE | TRIAL BALANCE | | ADJUSTMENTS | | ADJUSTED TRIAL BALANCE | | INCOME STATEMENT | | BALANCE SHEET | |
|---|---|---|---|---|---|---|---|---|---|---|
| | DEBIT | CREDIT | DEBIT | CREDIT | DEBIT | CREDIT | DEBIT | CREDIT | DEBIT | CREDIT |
| Cash | 17,971.10 | | | | 17,971.10 | | | | 17,971.10 | |
| Accounts Receivable | 3,118.00 | | | | 3,118.00 | | | | 3,118.00 | |
| Merchandise Inventory | 6,111.00 | | (b) 6,800.00 | (a) 6,111.00 | 6,800.00 | | | | 6,800.00 | |
| Store Supplies | 793.00 | | | (g) 610.00 | 183.00 | | | | 183.00 | |
| Office Supplies | 492.00 | | | (h) 232.00 | 260.00 | | | | 260.00 | |
| Prepaid Insurance | 264.00 | | | (d) 24.00 | 240.00 | | | | 240.00 | |
| Store Equipment | 6,600.00 | | | | 6,600.00 | | | | 6,600.00 | |
| Accum. Depr. — Store Equipment | | 125.00 | | (e) 125.00 | | 250.00 | | | | 250.00 |
| Office Equipment | 2,220.00 | | | | 2,220.00 | | | | 2,220.00 | |
| Accum. Depr. — Office Equipment | | 50.00 | | (f) 50.00 | | 100.00 | | | | 100.00 |
| Accounts Payable | | 7,230.00 | | | | 7,230.00 | | | | 7,230.00 |
| Mortgage Note Payable | | 1,500.00 | | | | 1,500.00 | | | | 1,500.00 |
| Tom Rose, Capital | | 26,296.00 | | | | 26,296.00 | | | | 26,296.00 |
| Tom Rose, Drawing | 400.00 | | | | 400.00 | | | | 400.00 | |
| Sales | | 19,723.00 | | | | 19,723.00 | | 19,723.00 | | |
| Sales Returns and Allowances | 442.00 | | | | 442.00 | | 442.00 | | | |
| Sales Discount | 25.70 | | | | 25.70 | | 25.70 | | | |
| Purchases | 11,977.00 | | | | 11,977.00 | | 11,977.00 | | | |
| Purchases Returns and Allowances | | 398.00 | | | | 398.00 | | 398.00 | | |
| Purchases Discount | | 65.80 | | | | 65.80 | | 65.80 | | |
| Advertising Expense | 342.00 | | | | 342.00 | | 342.00 | | | |
| Sales Salary Expense | 1,690.00 | | (c) 80.00 | | 1,770.00 | | 1,770.00 | | | |
| Miscellaneous Selling Expense | 68.00 | | | | 68.00 | | 68.00 | | | |
| Office Salary Expense | 1,510.00 | | (c) 75.00 | | 1,585.00 | | 1,585.00 | | | |
| Rent Expense | 920.00 | | | | 920.00 | | 920.00 | | | |
| Utilities Expense | 413.00 | | | | 413.00 | | 413.00 | | | |
| Miscellaneous General Expense | 31.00 | | | | 31.00 | | 31.00 | | | |
| | 55,387.80 | 55,387.80 | | | | | | | | |
| Income Summary | | | (a) 6,111.00 | (b) 6,800.00 | 6,111.00 | 6,800.00 | 6,111.00 | 6,800.00 | | |
| Salaries Payable | | | | (c) 155.00 | | 155.00 | | | | 155.00 |
| Insurance Expense | | | (d) 24.00 | | 24.00 | | 24.00 | | | |
| Depr. Exp. — Store Equipment | | | (e) 125.00 | | 125.00 | | 125.00 | | | |
| Depr. Exp. — Office Equipment | | | (f) 50.00 | | 50.00 | | 50.00 | | | |
| Store Supplies Expense | | | (g) 610.00 | | 610.00 | | 610.00 | | | |
| Office Supplies Expense | | | (h) 232.00 | | 232.00 | | 232.00 | | | |
| | | | 14,107.00 | 14,107.00 | 62,517.80 | 62,517.80 | 24,725.70 | 26,986.80 | 37,792.10 | 35,531.00 |
| Net Income | | | | | | | 2,261.10 | | | 2,261.10 |
| | | | | | | | 26,986.80 | 26,986.80 | 37,792.10 | 37,792.10 |

**Adjusting Data.** In preparing the work sheet for Rose, the following data concerning the required adjustments were considered:

(a) and (b) Merchandise inventory, July 31, $6,800.
(c) Sales salaries unpaid on July 31, $80; office salaries unpaid, $75.
(d) Insurance expired during July, $24.
(e) Depreciation expense on store equipment for the month, $125.
(f) Depreciation expense on office equipment for the month, $50.
(g) Store supplies on hand on July 31, $183.
(h) Office supplies on hand on July 31, $260.

The major difference between the procedures for recording the adjustments presented in Chapter 4 and those in this chapter is the inclusion of the two adjusting entries for merchandise inventory. The adjustments shown on the work sheet on page 176 are briefly described below.

*(a) and (b) Merchandise Inventory.* The $6,111 balance of merchandise inventory shown on the trial balance represents the inventory at the beginning of the period. This beginning inventory is transferred out of the account by a debit to Income Summary and a credit to Merchandise Inventory.

The amount of the inventory on hand at the end of the period, as determined by a physical count, is $6,800. This represents a current asset and must be debited to Merchandise Inventory. The credit is to Income Summary.

*(c) Unpaid Sales Salaries and Office Salaries.* The sales and office salaries owed but not yet paid at the end of the period are $80 and $75, respectively. Since these salaries were incurred during July, they should be recorded as an expense of that month. The adjusting entry is a debit to Sales Salary Expense for $80, a debit to Office Salary Expense for $75, and a credit to Salaries Payable for $155.

*(d) Expired Insurance.* The prepaid insurance account represents the premiums paid in advance for insurance coverage. During the month of July, $24 of the insurance premiums expired and should be debited to an expense account. It is also necessary to reduce the asset account, Prepaid Insurance. The adjusting entry is a debit to Insurance Expense and a credit to Prepaid Insurance for $24.

*(e) and (f) Depreciation Expense.* The expired cost of a plant asset is recorded by a debit to a depreciation expense account and a credit to the corresponding accumulated depreciation account. Separate accounts for the expense and for the accumulated depreciation are maintained for each plant asset. Adjustment (e) is the entry for store equipment and includes a debit to Depreciation Expense — Store Equipment and a credit to Accumulated Depreciation — Store Equipment for $125. Entry (f) is for office equipment and requires a debit to Depreciation Expense — Office Equipment and a credit to Accumulated Depreciation — Office Equipment for $50.

*(g) and (h) Supplies.* The $793 balance in Store Supplies on the trial balance represents the sum of the supplies on hand at the beginning of the month, $468, plus the purchases of store supplies during the month, $325. The inventory of store supplies on hand at the end of the period, as determined by a physical count, is $183. The difference of $610 ($793 − $183) represents the amount of store supplies

used during the month. The accounts are adjusted by debiting Store Supplies Expense and crediting Store Supplies for $610.

The adjustment for office supplies is determined in the same manner. The balance in the trial balance is $492, representing the office supplies on hand at the beginning of the month, $370, plus the office supplies purchased during the month, $140, less those returned on July 10, $18. The inventory of office supplies at the end of the month is $260. Therefore, the adjusting entry debiting Office Supplies Expense and crediting Office Supplies is for $232 ($492 – $260).

After the adjusting entries have been made on the work sheet, the Adjustments columns are totaled to insure that the debits and credits are equal.

**Adjusted Trial Balance Columns.** As the work sheet becomes longer and more detailed, it may be desirable to include two additional columns for an adjusted trial balance. The amounts in the Trial Balance columns are combined with the amounts in the Adjustments columns and the account totals are extended to the proper columns of the Adjusted Trial Balance section. The combining procedure is exactly the same as was explained in Chapter 4 for the eight-column work sheet. Unlike the eight-column work sheet, the total for each account is first extended to the Adjusted Trial Balance columns rather than directly to the Income Statement and Balance Sheet columns.

When all accounts have been extended, the arithmetical accuracy of the debits and credits is checked by totaling the Adjusted Trial Balance columns. The main advantage of including an adjusted trial balance is that it reduces the possibility of error when combining and extending the account balances on the work sheet. This procedure insures that the accounts are still in balance after the adjustments have been entered in the Adjustments columns.

**Income Statement and Balance Sheet Columns.** After the Adjusted Trial Balance columns have been totaled, the account balances are extended to the Income Statement and Balance Sheet columns. The best way to extend the account balances to these columns is to begin at the top of the work sheet and extend each item in order.

Both adjustments to Income Summary for merchandise inventory are entered in the Income Statement columns of the work sheet. The $6,111 debit adjustment for the beginning inventory is extended to the debit column of the Income Statement section and the $6,800 credit adjustment for the ending inventory is extended to the credit column. It would be possible to extend only the difference in the two adjustments, in this case $689 ($6,800 – $6,111), as a credit to Income Summary without affecting the computation of net income at the bottom of the columns. However, this method is not used because it is desirable to have *both* inventory amounts extended, thereby providing all the information necessary to prepare the income statement from the Income Statement columns of the work sheet.

After all of the accounts have been extended to either the Income Statement or Balance Sheet columns, these columns are totaled and the net income or loss for the period is determined. In the work sheet for Rose Wholesale Co., the credit total exceeds the debit total in the

Income Statement columns by $2,261.10. This signifies a net income for the period. The debit total of the Balance Sheet columns exceeds the credit total by the same $2,261.10, representing the increase in owner's equity by the amount of net income for the period.

## INCOME STATEMENT FOR A MERCHANDISING ENTERPRISE

The major sections of an income statement prepared for a mercantile business are as follows:

Net sales
Less cost of goods sold
Gross profit on sales
Less operating expenses
  Selling expenses
  General expenses
Net income

In the preceding chapters, no attempt was made to determine the net income for a merchandising enterprise, the reason being that the first step in the determination of the net income or loss for the period is the computation of the *gross profit on sales*, also called *gross margin*. This computation requires an understanding of the terminology and transactions related to a merchandising operation. Gross profit is equal to net sales minus cost of goods sold.

### Net Sales

The *net sales* for the period are defined as gross (total) sales less sales returns and allowances and sales discounts. As was stated in Chapter 8, both the sales returns and allowances and sales discount accounts are to be shown as reductions in sales on the income statement.

In the work sheet on page 176, the sales for the period were $19,723.00 with sales returns and allowances of $442.00 and sales discounts of $25.70. The computation of net sales is as follows:

| | | | |
|---|---|---|---|
| Revenue: | | | |
| Sales | | $19,723.00 | |
| Less: Sales returns and allowances | $442.00 | | |
| Sales discount | 25.70 | 467.70 | |
| Net sales | | | $19,255.30 |

### Cost of Goods Sold

In recording the sale of merchandise, the entry is a debit to Accounts Receivable or Cash and a credit to Sales. The credit to Sales represents revenue to the business and, if analyzed, could be thought of as two distinct elements: (1) the cost of the merchandise sold, and (2) the gross profit on the sale. For example, if a jacket which cost $90 is sold by a department store for $125, the effect of the transaction is a decrease in the merchandise in stock by $90 and an increase in gross profit of $35 ($125 − $90). In most businesses, particularly smaller ones, it is not practical to attempt to make this computation and record these two elements at the time of the sale. The normal procedure is to ignore this distinction at the time of the sale and to record the entire amount in the sales account. The cost of the goods sold is then determined at the end of the period and is subtracted from the net sales for the period to determine the gross profit.

The cost of goods sold for the period is determined by first adding the cost of the merchandise inventory on hand at the beginning of the period to the purchases of merchandise that were recorded in the purchases account during the period to determine the cost of the total amount of merchandise available for sale. The cost of the merchandise inventory on hand at the end of the period is determined by a physical count of the goods. This procedure is called "taking the inventory." The cost of the inventory on hand at the end of the period is then subtracted from the cost of all the merchandise available for sale during the period to determine the cost of the goods sold. For example, if the cost of the inventory on hand at the beginning of the period was $6,111.00, and merchandise has been purchased during the period at a net cost of $11,513.20, then the total goods available for sale during the period was $17,624.20. If the inventory taken at the end of the period has a cost of $6,800.00, then the cost of the goods sold during the period is $10,824.20 ($17,624.20 − $6,800.00). This information is presented in the cost of goods sold section of the income statement as follows:

| | | |
|---|---|---|
| Cost of goods sold: | | |
| Merchandise inventory, July 1, 1982 | $ 6,111.00 | |
| Net purchases | 11,513.20 | |
| Merchandise available for sale | $17,624.20 | |
| Less merchandise inventory, July 31, 1982 | 6,800.00 | |
| Cost of goods sold | | $10,824.20 |

## Net Purchases

In the above computation of the cost of goods sold, the net purchases for the period were listed as $11,513.20. For the sake of simplicity, purchases returns and allowances and purchases discounts were not illustrated. However, as was indicated in Chapter 8, purchases are first recorded at the gross amount. When a business has purchases returns and allowances or purchases discounts, they are subtracted from gross purchases to determine the net purchases for the period. This information is presented in the income statement as follows:

| | | | | |
|---|---|---|---|---|
| Cost of goods sold: | | | | |
| Merchandise inventory, July 1, 1982 | | | $ 6,111.00 | |
| Purchases | | $11,977.00 | | |
| Less: Purchases returns and allowances | $398.00 | | | |
| Purchases discount | 65.80 | 463.80 | | |
| Net purchases | | | 11,513.20 | |
| Merchandise available for sale | | | $17,624.20 | |
| Less merchandise inventory, July 31, 1982 | | | 6,800.00 | |
| Cost of goods sold | | | | $10,824.20 |

## Gross Profit on Sales

The gross profit on sales for the period is determined by subtracting the cost of goods sold from the net sales. This information appears on the income statement as shown below.

**Rose Wholesale Co.**
**Income Statement**
**For Month Ended July 31, 1982**

| | | | | | | |
|---|---|---|---|---|---|---|
| Revenue: | | | | | | |
| Sales | | | 19 723 | 00 | | |
| Less: Sales returns and allowances | 442 | 00 | | | | |
| Sales discount | 25 | 70 | 467 | 70 | | |
| Net sales | | | | | 19 255 | 30 |
| Cost of goods sold: | | | | | | |
| Merchandise inventory, July 1 | | | 6 111 | 00 | | |
| Purchases | 11 977 | 00 | | | | |
| Less: Purchases ret. & allow. .... 398.00 | | | | | | |
| Purchases discount ........ 65.80 | 463 | 80 | | | | |
| Net purchases | | | 11 513 | 20 | | |
| Merchandise available for sale | | | 17 624 | 20 | | |
| Less: Merchandise inventory, July 31 | | | 6 800 | 00 | | |
| Cost of goods sold | | | | | 10 824 | 20 |
| Gross profit on sales | | | | | 8 431 | 10 |

*Gross Profit on Sales Shown on Income Statement*

## Operating Expenses

The operating expenses section of the income statement is the only section which has not yet been discussed. The operating expenses of a firm may be classified into a variety of groups. Large businesses with diverse and complex activities may use many expense classifications for control and analysis of their operations. In a smaller business such as Rose's, it is usually sufficient to classify operating expenses into two categories, selling expenses and general expenses, as is done on the income statement on page 184.

**Selling Expenses.** Selling expenses are those expenses which are directly related to the sale of merchandise. Salaries and commissions paid to sales clerks, store supplies used, advertising expense, delivery expense, and depreciation of store equipment and delivery equipment are common examples.

The account Miscellaneous Selling Expense may be used to record other minor and infrequent expenses. However, the use of this account should be kept to a minimum.

**General Expenses.** General expenses are those expenses relating to the general operations of the business. Office salaries, office supplies used, rent expense, insurance expense, property taxes, and depreciation of office equipment are normally classified in this group. Some of the expenses listed in this category, such as rent, insurance, and property taxes on the sales area of the store, may apply to selling expenses as well. In small businesses, this differentiation is normally not necessary. In addition to the accounts listed on page 181, Miscellaneous General Expense may be used to report small, infrequent general expenses.

The order in which operating expenses are presented on the income statement, within the two categories listed, varies from one firm to another. One widely used procedure is to list the expenses in the order of their amount, with the larger amounts listed first. The miscellaneous expense account, selling or general, is normally shown last, regardless of its amount.

## QUESTIONS FOR DISCUSSION

1. Name the steps involved in the accounting cycle for a merchandising business.
2. (a) How is the dollar amount of merchandise inventory on hand at the end of the period determined? (b) How is the amount of the beginning inventory determined?
3. It may be said that every sale a business makes consists of two elements: (1) the cost of the goods sold and (2) the gross profit. If this is true, why is no attempt made to record the information in this manner when the sale is made?
4. During the fiscal period, the Waters Company had a gross profit of $7,300 and operating expenses of $9,100. How much net income or net loss would be shown on the income statement?
5. In the Income Statement columns of the work sheet, the income summary account has a debit of $6,300 and a credit of $5,600. (a) What does each of these amounts represent? (b) Why are both of these amounts extended to the Income Statement columns?

## EXERCISES

1. Below are given the major sections of an income statement for a mercantile business. Rearrange the sections into the proper form for an income statement.

   | | |
   |---|---|
   | General expenses | Cost of goods sold |
   | Net income | Selling expenses |
   | Net sales | Gross profit on sales |
   | Operating expenses | |

2. The Hodo Carpet Company had merchandise inventory on August 1 of $27,430,and a physical count of the merchandise on August 31 totaled $30,123. Prepare the adjusting entries for merchandise inventory on August 31.

3. The following account balances were taken from the Adjusted Trial Balance columns of the Weber Company prepared December 31.

| | |
|---|---|
| Purchases Returns and Allowances | $ 381 |
| Sales Returns and Allowances | 407 |
| Purchases | 7,120 |
| Purchases Discount | 146 |
| Sales Discount | 273 |
| Sales | 11,400 |

(a) Compute the net sales for the month, showing your computations as they would appear on the income statement. (b) Compute the net purchases for the month in income statement format.

**ASSIGNMENT 9-A**

**Tear out pages 483–488 and complete Assignment 9-A. Submit your papers for approval. After completion, proceed with the chapter discussion until the next assignment is required.**

# PART B FINANCIAL STATEMENTS AND COMPLETION OF THE ACCOUNTING CYCLE

The sequence and nature of the end-of-period activities for a merchandising enterprise are similar to those of a service enterprise. The financial statements for a merchandising enterprise are prepared after the completion of the work sheet. After the financial statements have been prepared, the adjusting and closing entries are recorded in the journal and posted to the ledger. The final step in the accounting cycle is the preparation of the post-closing trial balance.

## CLASSIFIED INCOME STATEMENT

A *classified income statement* for Rose Wholesale Co., showing the various sections discussed earlier in this chapter, is presented on the following page. Carefully observe the rulings, captions, indentations, and subtotals used in the statement. They are valuable aids in assisting statement readers to understand the information being presented.

### Income Statement Analysis

One important use of the income statement is to compare the results of operations for the current period with those of previous periods. For example, Rose may wish to compare the income statement prepared for July with those prepared in May and June of the same year or with the July income statement of the preceding year.

Another important analysis of income data is to determine the major items on the income statement as a percent of net sales and to compare these percentages with those of preceding periods. In income statement analysis, net sales is normally considered the base, representing 100%. For example, Rose's gross profit on sales for July is 43.8% of net sales ($8,431.10 ÷ $19,255.30); the operating expenses are 32% of net sales ($6,170.00 ÷ $19,255.30); and the net income is 11.7% of net sales ($2,261.10 ÷ $19,255.30). Each of these percentages should be compared to those of preceding periods to determine any significant trends.

**Rose Wholesale Co.**
**Income Statement**
**For Month Ended July 31, 1982**

| | | | | |
|---|---|---|---|---|
| **Revenue:** | | | | |
| Sales | | | 19 723 00 | |
| Less: Sales returns and allowances | | 442 00 | | |
| Sales discount | | 25 70 | 467 70 | |
| Net sales | | | | 19 255 30 |
| **Cost of goods sold:** | | | | |
| Merchandise inventory, July 1 | | | 6 111 00 | |
| Purchases | | 11 977 00 | | |
| Less: Purchases ret. & allow. | 398.00 | | | |
| Purchases discount | 65.80 | 463 80 | | |
| Net purchases | | | 11 513 20 | |
| Merchandise available for sale | | | 17 624 20 | |
| Less: Merchandise inventory, July 31 | | | 6 800 00 | |
| Cost of goods sold | | | | 10 824 20 |
| Gross profit on sales | | | | 8 431 10 |
| **Operating expenses:** | | | | |
| Selling expenses: | | | | |
| Sales salary expense | | 1 770 00 | | |
| Store supplies expense | | 610 00 | | |
| Advertising expense | | 342 00 | | |
| Depreciation expense — store equip. | | 125 00 | | |
| Miscellaneous selling expense | | 68 00 | | |
| Total selling expense | | | 2 915 00 | |
| General expenses: | | | | |
| Office salary expense | | 1 585 00 | | |
| Rent expense | | 920 00 | | |
| Utilities expense | | 413 00 | | |
| Office supplies expense | | 232 00 | | |
| Depreciation expense — office equip. | | 50 00 | | |
| Insurance expense | | 24 00 | | |
| Miscellaneous general expense | | 31 00 | | |
| Total general expense | | | 3 255 00 | |
| Total operating expenses | | | | 6 170 00 |
| Net income | | | | 2 261 10 |

*Classified Income Statement – Rose Wholesale Co.*

## CLASSIFIED BALANCE SHEET

In the previous chapters, the balance sheets have contained only a few items which were classified simply as assets, liabilities, or owner's equity. The major purpose of the balance sheet is to present to the statement readers as much information as possible concerning the financial condition of the business. This purpose is best accomplished by further classification of the items on the balance sheet.

### Assets

When a business has a number of assets, it is customary to group similar assets together. The basis for the grouping is: (**1**) the purpose or use of the asset in the business, and (**2**) the availability of the asset for the payment of debts. For balance sheet purposes, it has become standard practice to classify assets as either *current assets* or *plant assets*.

*Current assets* include cash and other assets that may reasonably be expected to be converted into cash or consumed in normal business operations usually within a period of not more than one year.

In addition to cash, the current assets in a merchandising business normally include accounts receivable, notes receivable, merchandise inventory, supplies, and prepaid expenses. The presentation of current assets on the balance sheet is normally in the order listed above, which is the order of their expected conversion into cash. Supplies and prepaid expenses, such as unexpired insurance or prepaid rent, are not expected to be converted into cash, but they are included as current assets because they will normally be used in business operations during the accounting period.

*Plant assets*, also called *fixed assets*, include those tangible assets that are expected to be used in the business for a number of years and which will not be sold as long as they serve the needs of the business.

Assets frequently included in this section of the balance sheet are store equipment, delivery equipment, office equipment, furniture and fixtures, buildings, and land. Land is the only one of these assets which is really permanent. However, all of the assets in this group are expected to be used in the business for more than one accounting period.

Since all of the plant assets except land will eventually wear out, it is necessary to recognize the portion of the asset's cost which has been used up during the accounting period. As was explained in Chapter 4, this decrease in usefulness of a plant asset is known as *depreciation*. For example, if it is expected that a delivery truck will wear out in five years, one fifth of its cost may be charged to depreciation expense each year.

The order of presentation of plant assets on the balance sheet varies among companies. Some accountants prefer to list the shortest-lived assets first, while others list the most permanent items first. This text presents the shortest-lived assets first.

## Liabilities

There are normally fewer liability accounts than asset accounts appearing on a balance sheet. However, there are usually enough liability accounts to justify classification. The standard balance sheet classifications of liabilities are *current liabilities* and *long-term liabilities.*

*Current liabilities* are those debts which will become due within a short time (usually not more than one year) and which will be paid from current assets. The current liabilities of a business normally include accounts payable, notes payable, salaries payable, rent payable, taxes payable, and interest payable.

*Long-term liabilities* are those obligations which would not require the use of current assets because they will not become due until more than one year hence. These liabilities are usually incurred for the purchase of plant assets. If a long-term debt is to be paid in installments, that portion of the liability which becomes due within a year should be classified as a current liability. The long-term liabilities of a company may include long-term notes payable, mortgage notes payable, and bonds payable. *Long-term notes payable* are promissory notes which are not due within the next year. A *mortgage note payable* is a promissory note that is accompanied by a claim to specific business assets in the form of a mortgage; it gives the creditor the right to claim these assets if the debt is not paid. *Bonds payable* are formal certificates of indebtedness representing long-term obligations. A *bond* is a general credit obligation which is secured by the overall assets of the corporation or by specific business assets.

## Owner's Equity

In earlier chapters, the owner's equity was usually reported on the balance sheet as one amount, with the changes being shown on the capital statement. In some instances, however, it may be desirable to show all of the changes in owner's equity on the balance sheet itself. When this procedure is followed, no separate capital statement is necessary.

The classified balance sheet for Rose Wholesale Co., is illustrated on the following page.

## Balance Sheet Analysis

Two of the most often used analyses from balance sheet information involve the *current ratio* and *working capital*, both of which are used to indicate the ability of a firm to pay its current liabilities as they become due.

The *current ratio* is determined by dividing current assets by current liabilities and expresses the relationship of current assets to current liabilities. For example, the current ratio computed from the July balance sheet of Rose Wholesale Co. is 3.87 to 1 ($28,572.10 ÷ $7,385.00.) There is no agreed-upon standard as to what constitutes a satisfactory current ratio. The standards vary widely depending upon

**Rose Wholesale Co.**
**Balance Sheet**
**July 31, 1982**

| | | | | |
|---|---|---|---|---|
| **Assets** | | | | |
| Current assets: | | | | |
| Cash | | | 17 971 10 | |
| Accounts receivable | | | 3 118 00 | |
| Merchandise inventory | | | 6 800 00 | |
| Store supplies | | | 183 00 | |
| Office supplies | | | 260 00 | |
| Prepaid insurance | | | 240 00 | |
| Total current assets | | | | 28 572 10 |
| Plant assets: | | | | |
| Store equipment | 6 600 00 | | | |
| Less accum. depr.—store equipment | 250 00 | | 6 350 00 | |
| Office equipment | 2 220 00 | | | |
| Less accum. depr.—office equipment | 100 00 | | 2 120 00 | |
| Total plant assets | | | | 8 470 00 |
| Total assets | | | | 37 042 10 |
| **Liabilities** | | | | |
| Current liabilities: | | | | |
| Accounts payable | | | 7 230 00 | |
| Salaries payable | | | 155 00 | |
| Total current liabilities | | | | 7 385 00 |
| Long-term liabilities: | | | | |
| Mortgage note payable | | | | 1 500 00 |
| Total liabilities | | | | 8 885 00 |
| **Owner's Equity** | | | | |
| Tom Rose, capital: | | | | |
| Capital, July 1, 1982 | | | 22 296 00 | |
| Additional investment | | | 4 000 00 | |
| Total | | | 26 296 00 | |
| Net income for month | 2 261 10 | | | |
| Less withdrawals | 400 00 | | | |
| Increase in capital | | | 1 861 10 | |
| Capital, July 31, 1982 | | | | 28 157 10 |
| Total liabilities and owner's equity | | | | 37 042 10 |

*Classified Balance Sheet - Rose Wholesale Co.*

the size and nature of the business. An often-used standard to approximate a firm's ability to meet its current obligations as they become due is that the dollar amount of current assets should be twice the dollar amount of current liabilities (2:1).

Another indication of a firm's ability to meet its current obligations is the dollar excess of current assets over current liabilities, which is known as *working capital*. Working capital indicates the amount of current assets that would be available for operations if all of the current liabilities were to be paid. Rose's working capital on July 31, is \$21,187.10 (current assets, \$28,572.10, minus current liabilities, \$7,385.00).

Most of the individual items appearing on the balance sheet are of little importance when viewed alone. Even groups of items such as current assets are of limited value when considered by themselves. An accurate picture of the balance sheet data can best be formed by comparing single items to groups of items as they relate to an individual balance sheet, or by comparing the same items on various balance sheets. For example, Rose's cash balance on the July balance sheet was $17,971.10 which is 63% of total current assets ($17,971.10 ÷ $28,572.10) and 49% of total assets ($17,971.10 ÷ $37,042.10). These percentages can be compared to those on earlier balance sheets to determine any significant trends.

## CAPITAL STATEMENT

In the balance sheet prepared for Rose, all of the details of changes in capital have been included in the owner's equity section, eliminating the need for a separate capital statement. If a separate capital statement had been prepared, it would appear as shown below.

If a separate capital statement had been prepared, the owner's equity section of the balance sheet would have consisted of only one line:

Tom Rose, Capital...................... $28,157.10

**Rose Wholesale Co.**
**Capital Statement**
**For Month Ended July 31, 1982**

| | | |
|---|---|---|
| Capital, July 1, 1982 | | 22 296 00 |
| Additional investment | | 4 000 00 |
| Total | | 26 296 00 |
| Net income for the month | 2 261 10 | |
| Less withdrawals | 400 00 | |
| Increase in capital | | 1 861 10 |
| Capital, July 31, 1982 | | 28 157 10 |

*Capital Statement – Rose Wholesale Co.*

In preparing the capital statement or owner's equity section of the balance sheet, it is necessary to refer to the capital account in the general ledger to determine whether there have been any additional investments during the period. In the above illustration, Rose invested an additional $4,000 on July 6.

## ADJUSTING ENTRIES

After the financial statements have been prepared, the adjusting entries are recorded in the journal and posted to the ledger. The adjusting entries can be taken directly from the Adjustments columns of the work sheet. The adjusting entries for Rose are presented at the top of page 189.

JOURNAL PAGE 3

| DATE | | DESCRIPTION | POST. REF. | DEBIT | CREDIT |
|---|---|---|---|---|---|
| 1982 | | Adjusting Entries | | | |
| July | 31 | Income Summary | 33 | 6 111 00 | |
| | | Merchandise Inventory | 13 | | 6 111 00 |
| | 31 | Merchandise Inventory | 13 | 6 800 00 | |
| | | Income Summary | 33 | | 6 800 00 |
| | 31 | Sales Salary Expense | 63 | 80 00 | |
| | | Office Salary Expense | 73 | 75 00 | |
| | | Salaries Payable | 22 | | 155 00 |
| | 31 | Insurance Expense | 72 | 24 00 | |
| | | Prepaid Insurance | 16 | | 24 00 |
| | 31 | Depr. Expense — Store Equip. | 62 | 125 00 | |
| | | Accum. Depr. — Store Equip. | 17.1 | | 125 00 |
| | 31 | Depr. Expense — Office Equip. | 71 | 50 00 | |
| | | Accum. Depr. — Office Equip. | 18.1 | | 50 00 |
| | 31 | Store Supplies Expense | 64 | 610 00 | |
| | | Store Supplies | 14 | | 610 00 |
| | 31 | Office Supplies Expense | 74 | 232 00 | |
| | | Office Supplies | 15 | | 232 00 |

*Adjusting Entries – Rose Wholesale Co.*

The posting of these adjusting entries appears in the general ledger accounts presented on pages 193 to 197. After the adjusting entries are posted, the ledger account balances will be the same as the corresponding amounts shown on the financial statements.

## CLOSING ENTRIES

As was discussed in Chapter 4, there are two reasons for closing the revenue, expense, and drawing accounts at the end of the accounting period:

1. After the income statement has been prepared, the balances in these temporary proprietorship accounts should be reduced to zero so that they may be used to record the revenue, expenses, and drawings for the following period.
2. It is also necessary for these accounts to be transferred to the capital account so that its balance reflects the amount of owner's equity at the end of the period. This balance should agree with the amount of owner's capital shown in the financial statements.

The four-step procedure that was given in Chapter 4 for closing the books is expanded here to include the accounts used in a merchandising enterprise, Sales, Sales Returns and Allowances, Sales Discount, Purchases, Purchases Returns and Allowances, and Purchases Discount.

1. Close all revenue accounts and all other income statement accounts with a credit balance (Purchases Returns and Allowances and Purchases Discount) to Income Summary.
2. Close all expense accounts and all other income statement accounts with a debit balance (Sales Returns and Allowances and Sales Discount) to Income Summary.

3. Close the balance in Income Summary to the capital account. This balance should be the amount of the net income or net loss for the period.
4. Close the drawing account to the capital account.

The closing entries are journalized below. These closing entries are posted to the general ledger accounts appearing on pages 195 to 197.

**JOURNAL** PAGE 4

| DATE | | DESCRIPTION | POST. REF. | DEBIT | CREDIT |
|---|---|---|---|---|---|
| 1982 | | Closing Entries | | | |
| July | 31 | Sales | 41 | 19 723 00 | |
| | | Purchases Returns and Allow. | 51.1 | 398 00 | |
| | | Purchases Discount | 51.2 | 65 80 | |
| | | Income Summary | 33 | | 20 186 80 |
| | 31 | Income Summary | 33 | 18 614 70 | |
| | | Sales Returns and Allowances | 41.1 | | 442 00 |
| | | Sales Discount | 41.2 | | 25 70 |
| | | Purchases | 51 | | 11 977 00 |
| | | Advertising Expense | 61 | | 342 00 |
| | | Depr. Expense — Store Equip. | 62 | | 125 00 |
| | | Sales Salary Expense | 63 | | 1 770 00 |
| | | Store Supplies Expense | 64 | | 610 00 |
| | | Miscellaneous Selling Expense | 65 | | 68 00 |
| | | Depr. Expense — Office Equip. | 71 | | 50 00 |
| | | Insurance Expense | 72 | | 24 00 |
| | | Office Salary Expense | 73 | | 1 585 00 |
| | | Office Supplies Expense | 74 | | 232 00 |
| | | Rent Expense | 75 | | 920 00 |
| | | Utilities Expense | 76 | | 413 00 |
| | | Miscellaneous General Expense | 77 | | 31 00 |
| | 31 | Income Summary | 33 | 2 261 10 | |
| | | Tom Rose, Capital | 31 | | 2 261 10 |
| | 31 | Tom Rose, Capital | 31 | 400 00 | |
| | | Tom Rose, Drawing | 32 | | 400 00 |

*Closing Entries – Rose Wholesale Co.*

## Analysis of Closing Entries In Income Summary

If, in addition to the two adjusting entries for inventories, the effect of the entries closing Purchases, Purchases Returns and Allowances, and Purchases Discount to the income summary account are considered, it becomes apparent that the flow of the adjusting and closing entries into Income Summary is consistent with the computation of the cost of goods sold.

To illustrate, consider separately the adjustment to transfer the beginning inventory to Income Summary and the closing entries for the purchase accounts mentioned above. These entries, for purposes of explanation only, are recorded as shown on page 191.

JOURNAL — PAGE 5

| DATE | | DESCRIPTION | POST. REF. | DEBIT | CREDIT |
|---|---|---|---|---|---|
| 1982 | | | | | |
| July | 31 | Income Summary | 33 | 6 111 00 | |
| | | Merchandise Inventory | 13 | | 6 111 00 |
| | | Transfer beginning inventory | | | |
| | | to Income Summary. | | | |
| | 31 | Income Summary | 33 | 11 513 20 | |
| | | Purchases Returns and Allow. | 51.1 | 398 00 | |
| | | Purchases Discount | 51.2 | 65 80 | |
| | | Purchases | 51 | | 11 977 00 |
| | | Close purchases accounts. | | | |

ACCOUNT Income Summary — ACCOUNT NO. 33

| DATE | | ITEM | POST. REF. | DEBIT | CREDIT | BALANCE DEBIT | BALANCE CREDIT |
|---|---|---|---|---|---|---|---|
| 1982 | | | | | | | |
| July | 31 | Adjusting | J5 | 6 111 00 | | 6 111 00 | |
| | 31 | Closing | J5 | 11 513 20 | | 17 624 20 | |

If the entries are posted to the income summary account, the balance will represent the cost of the merchandise available for sale $17,624.20 (the beginning inventory, $6,111.00, plus net purchases, $11,513.20.

If the second adjusting entry for merchandise, recording the ending inventory on the books, is now journalized and posted, the balance in the income summary account will reflect the cost of goods sold $10,824.20 (cost of merchandise available for sale, $17,624.20 debit, minus ending inventory, $6,800.00 credit).

| DATE | | DESCRIPTION | POST. REF. | DEBIT | CREDIT |
|---|---|---|---|---|---|
| | 31 | Merchandise Inventory | 13 | 6 800 00 | |
| | | Income Summary | 33 | | 6 800 00 |
| | | Record ending inventory. | | | |

ACCOUNT Income Summary — ACCOUNT NO. 33

| DATE | | ITEM | POST. REF. | DEBIT | CREDIT | BALANCE DEBIT | BALANCE CREDIT |
|---|---|---|---|---|---|---|---|
| 1982 | | | | | | | |
| July | 31 | Adjusting | J5 | 6 111 00 | | 6 111 00 | |
| | 31 | Closing | J5 | 11 513 20 | | 17 624 20 | |
| | 31 | Adjusting | J5 | | 6 800 00 | 10 824 20 | |

With the cost of goods sold isolated in the income summary account, the illustration can be developed one step further by closing all the sales accounts to Income Summary as follows:

| DATE | | DESCRIPTION | POST. REF. | DEBIT | CREDIT |
|---|---|---|---|---|---|
| | 31 | Sales | 41 | 19 723 00 | |
| | | Sales Returns and Allowances | 41.1 | | 442 00 |
| | | Sales Discount | 41.2 | | 25 70 |
| | | Income Summary | 33 | | 19 255 30 |
| | | Close sales accounts. | | | |

After this entry is posted, the balance in the income summary account represents the gross profit on sales, $8,431.10 (net sales, $19,255.30 credit minus cost of goods sold, $10,824.20 debit).

**ACCOUNT** Income Summary **ACCOUNT NO.** 33

| DATE | | ITEM | POST. REF. | DEBIT | CREDIT | BALANCE DEBIT | BALANCE CREDIT |
|---|---|---|---|---|---|---|---|
| 1982 | | | | | | | |
| July | 31 | Adjusting | J5 | 6 111 00 | | 6 111 00 | |
| | 31 | Closing | J5 | 11 513 20 | | 17 624 20 | |
| | 31 | Adjusting | J5 | | 6 800 00 | 10 824 20 | |
| | 31 | Closing | J5 | | 19 255 30 | | 8 431 10 |

The final closing entry would be to close the operating expenses to Income Summary. This entry would be recorded as follows:

| | | | | |
|---|---|---|---|---|
| 31 | Income Summary | 33 | 6 170 00 | |
| | Advertising Expense | 61 | | 342 00 |
| | Depr. Expense — Store Equip. | 62 | | 125 00 |
| | Sales Salary Expense | 63 | | 1 770 00 |
| | Store Supplies Expense | 64 | | 610 00 |
| | Miscellaneous Selling Expense | 65 | | 68 00 |
| | Depr. Expense — Office Equip. | 71 | | 50 00 |
| | Insurance Expense | 72 | | 24 00 |
| | Office Salary Expense | 73 | | 1 585 00 |
| | Office Supplies Expense | 74 | | 232 00 |
| | Rent Expense | 75 | | 920 00 |
| | Utilities Expense | 76 | | 413 00 |
| | Miscellaneous General Expense | 77 | | 31 00 |
| | Close expense accounts. | | | |

After this entry is posted, the balance in Income Summary is the net income for the period, $2,261.10 (gross profit on sales, $8,431.10 credit minus operating expenses, $6,170.00 debit).

**ACCOUNT** Income Summary **ACCOUNT NO.** 33

| DATE | | ITEM | POST. REF. | DEBIT | CREDIT | BALANCE DEBIT | BALANCE CREDIT |
|---|---|---|---|---|---|---|---|
| 1982 | | | | | | | |
| July | 31 | Adjusting | J5 | 6 111 00 | | 6 111 00 | |
| | 31 | Closing | J5 | 11 513 20 | | 17 624 20 | |
| | 31 | Adjusting | J5 | | 6 800 00 | 10 824 20 | |
| | 31 | Closing | J5 | | 19 255 30 | | 8 431 10 |
| | 31 | Closing | J5 | 6 170 00 | | | 2 261 10 |

It must be emphasized that the above sequence is not presented to show *how* the adjustment of merchandise and the closing entries are made to Income Summary, because these entries are *not* made in the order or format shown here. The illustration is to show *why* the entries are made and to emphasize the effect these entries have in the accounts and how they conform to the information presented on the income statement.

# GENERAL AND SUBSIDIARY LEDGERS ILLUSTRATED

After the closing entries have been posted, the accounts in the general ledger are in proper form to record the transactions for the next period. Only the asset, liability, and capital accounts remain open. The balances in these accounts are those shown on the balance sheet at the end of the period.

The general ledger and the accounts receivable and accounts payable ledgers are shown on pages 193 through 200 after all July postings have been completed.

ACCOUNT Cash — ACCOUNT NO. 11

| DATE | | ITEM | POST. REF. | DEBIT | CREDIT | BALANCE DEBIT | BALANCE CREDIT |
|---|---|---|---|---|---|---|---|
| 1982 | | | | | | | |
| July | 1 | Balance | √ | | | 15 369 00 | |
| | 31 | | CR2 | 22 912 30 | | 38 281 30 | |
| | 31 | | CP2 | | 20 310 20 | 17 971 10 | |

ACCOUNT Accounts Receivable — ACCOUNT NO. 12

| DATE | | ITEM | POST. REF. | DEBIT | CREDIT | BALANCE DEBIT | BALANCE CREDIT |
|---|---|---|---|---|---|---|---|
| 1982 | | | | | | | |
| July | 1 | Balance | √ | | | 2 775 00 | |
| | 31 | | S2 | 4 690 00 | | 7 465 00 | |
| | 31 | | CR2 | | 3 905 00 | 3 560 00 | |
| | 31 | | SR2 | | 442 00 | 3 118 00 | |

ACCOUNT Merchandise Inventory — ACCOUNT NO. 13

| DATE | | ITEM | POST. REF. | DEBIT | CREDIT | BALANCE DEBIT | BALANCE CREDIT |
|---|---|---|---|---|---|---|---|
| 1982 | | | | | | | |
| July | 1 | Balance | √ | | | 6 111 00 | |
| | 31 | Adjusting | J3 | | 6 111 00 | — | — |
| | 31 | Adjusting | J3 | 6 800 00 | | 6 800 00 | |

ACCOUNT Store Supplies — ACCOUNT NO. 14

| DATE | | ITEM | POST. REF. | DEBIT | CREDIT | BALANCE DEBIT | BALANCE CREDIT |
|---|---|---|---|---|---|---|---|
| 1982 | | | | | | | |
| July | 1 | Balance | √ | | | 468 00 | |
| | 31 | | P2 | 325 00 | | 793 00 | |
| | 31 | Adjusting | J3 | | 610 00 | 183 00 | |

ACCOUNT Office Supplies — ACCOUNT NO. 15

| DATE | | ITEM | POST. REF. | DEBIT | CREDIT | BALANCE DEBIT | BALANCE CREDIT |
|---|---|---|---|---|---|---|---|
| 1982 | | | | | | | |
| July | 1 | Balance | √ | | | 370 00 | |
| | 2 | | P2 | 140 00 | | 510 00 | |
| | 10 | | J2 | | 18 00 | 492 00 | |
| | 31 | Adjusting | J3 | | 232 00 | 260 00 | |

*General Ledger – Rose Wholesale Co.*

ACCOUNT **Prepaid Insurance** ACCOUNT NO. 16

| DATE | | ITEM | POST. REF. | DEBIT | CREDIT | BALANCE DEBIT | BALANCE CREDIT |
|---|---|---|---|---|---|---|---|
| 1982 | | | | | | | |
| July | 1 | Balance | √ | | | 264 00 | |
| | 31 | Adjusting | J3 | | 24 00 | 240 00 | |

ACCOUNT **Store Equipment** ACCOUNT NO. 17

| DATE | | ITEM | POST. REF. | DEBIT | CREDIT | BALANCE DEBIT | BALANCE CREDIT |
|---|---|---|---|---|---|---|---|
| 1982 | | | | | | | |
| July | 1 | Balance | √ | | | 3 100 00 | |
| | 10 | | P2 | 2 000 00 | | 5 100 00 | |
| | 30 | | J2 | 1 500 00 | | 6 600 00 | |

ACCOUNT **Accumulated Depreciation — Store Equipment** ACCOUNT NO. 17.1

| DATE | | ITEM | POST. REF. | DEBIT | CREDIT | BALANCE DEBIT | BALANCE CREDIT |
|---|---|---|---|---|---|---|---|
| 1982 | | | | | | | |
| July | 1 | Balance | √ | | | | 125 00 |
| | 31 | Adjusting | J3 | | 125 00 | | 250 00 |

ACCOUNT **Office Equipment** ACCOUNT NO. 18

| DATE | | ITEM | POST. REF. | DEBIT | CREDIT | BALANCE DEBIT | BALANCE CREDIT |
|---|---|---|---|---|---|---|---|
| 1982 | | | | | | | |
| July | 1 | Balance | √ | | | 850 00 | |
| | 10 | | P2 | 1 370 00 | | 2 220 00 | |

ACCOUNT **Accumulated Depreciation — Office Equipment** ACCOUNT NO. 18.1

| DATE | | ITEM | POST. REF. | DEBIT | CREDIT | BALANCE DEBIT | BALANCE CREDIT |
|---|---|---|---|---|---|---|---|
| 1982 | | | | | | | |
| July | 1 | Balance | √ | | | | 50 00 |
| | 31 | Adjusting | J3 | | 50 00 | | 100 00 |

ACCOUNT **Accounts Payable** ACCOUNT NO. 21

| DATE | | ITEM | POST. REF. | DEBIT | CREDIT | BALANCE DEBIT | BALANCE CREDIT |
|---|---|---|---|---|---|---|---|
| 1982 | | | | | | | |
| July | 1 | Balance | √ | | | | 6 836 00 |
| | 10 | | J2 | 18 00 | | | 6 818 00 |
| | 31 | | P2 | | 8 512 00 | | 15 330 00 |
| | 31 | | CP2 | 7 702 00 | | | 7 628 00 |
| | 31 | | PR2 | 398 00 | | | 7 230 00 |

ACCOUNT **Salaries Payable** ACCOUNT NO. 22

| DATE | | ITEM | POST. REF. | DEBIT | CREDIT | BALANCE DEBIT | BALANCE CREDIT |
|---|---|---|---|---|---|---|---|
| 1982 | | | | | | | |
| July | 31 | Adjusting | J3 | | 155 00 | | 155 00 |

*General Ledger – Rose Wholesale Co. (continued)*

**ACCOUNT** Mortgage Note Payable **ACCOUNT NO.** 23

| DATE | | ITEM | POST. REF. | DEBIT | CREDIT | BALANCE DEBIT | BALANCE CREDIT |
|---|---|---|---|---|---|---|---|
| 1982 | | | | | | | |
| July | 30 | | J2 | | 1 500 00 | | 1 500 00 |

**ACCOUNT** Tom Rose, Capital **ACCOUNT NO.** 31

| DATE | | ITEM | POST. REF. | DEBIT | CREDIT | BALANCE DEBIT | BALANCE CREDIT |
|---|---|---|---|---|---|---|---|
| 1982 | | | | | | | |
| July | 1 | Balance | √ | | | | 22 296 00 |
| | 6 | | CR2 | | 4 000 00 | | 26 296 00 |
| | 31 | Closing | J4 | | 2 261 10 | | 28 557 10 |
| | 31 | Closing | J4 | 400 00 | | | 28 157 10 |

**ACCOUNT** Tom Rose, Drawing **ACCOUNT NO.** 32

| DATE | | ITEM | POST. REF. | DEBIT | CREDIT | BALANCE DEBIT | BALANCE CREDIT |
|---|---|---|---|---|---|---|---|
| 1982 | | | | | | | |
| July | 28 | | CP2 | 400 00 | | 400 00 | |
| | 31 | Closing | J4 | | 400 00 | — | — |

**ACCOUNT** Income Summary **ACCOUNT NO.** 33

| DATE | | ITEM | POST. REF. | DEBIT | CREDIT | BALANCE DEBIT | BALANCE CREDIT |
|---|---|---|---|---|---|---|---|
| 1982 | | | | | | | |
| July | 31 | Adjusting | J3 | 6 111 00 | | 6 111 00 | |
| | 31 | Adjusting | J3 | | 6 800 00 | | 689 00 |
| | 31 | Closing | J4 | | 20 186 80 | | 20 875 80 |
| | 31 | Closing | J4 | 18 614 70 | | | 2 261 10 |
| | 31 | Closing | J4 | 2 261 10 | | — | — |

**ACCOUNT** Sales **ACCOUNT NO.** 41

| DATE | | ITEM | POST. REF. | DEBIT | CREDIT | BALANCE DEBIT | BALANCE CREDIT |
|---|---|---|---|---|---|---|---|
| 1982 | | | | | | | |
| July | 31 | | CR2 | | 15 033 00 | | 15 033 00 |
| | 31 | | S2 | | 4 690 00 | | 19 723 00 |
| | 31 | Closing | J4 | 19 723 00 | | — | — |

**ACCOUNT** Sales Returns and Allowances **ACCOUNT NO.** 41.1

| DATE | | ITEM | POST. REF. | DEBIT | CREDIT | BALANCE DEBIT | BALANCE CREDIT |
|---|---|---|---|---|---|---|---|
| 1982 | | | | | | | |
| July | 31 | | SR2 | 442 00 | | 442 00 | |
| | 31 | Closing | J4 | | 442 00 | — | — |

**ACCOUNT** Sales Discount **ACCOUNT NO.** 41.2

| DATE | | ITEM | POST. REF. | DEBIT | CREDIT | BALANCE DEBIT | BALANCE CREDIT |
|---|---|---|---|---|---|---|---|
| 1982 | | | | | | | |
| July | 31 | | CR2 | 25 70 | | 25 70 | |
| | 31 | Closing | J4 | | 25 70 | — | — |

*General Ledger – Rose Wholesale Co. (continued)*

ACCOUNT **Purchases** ACCOUNT NO. 51

| DATE | | ITEM | POST. REF. | DEBIT | CREDIT | BALANCE DEBIT | BALANCE CREDIT |
|---|---|---|---|---|---|---|---|
| 1982 | | | | | | | |
| July | 10 | | CP2 | 7 300 00 | | 7 300 00 | |
| | 31 | | P2 | 4 677 00 | | 11 977 00 | |
| | 31 | Closing | J4 | | 11 977 00 | — | — |

ACCOUNT **Purchases Returns and Allowances** ACCOUNT NO. 51.1

| DATE | | ITEM | POST. REF. | DEBIT | CREDIT | BALANCE DEBIT | BALANCE CREDIT |
|---|---|---|---|---|---|---|---|
| 1982 | | | | | | | |
| July | 31 | | PR2 | | 398 00 | | 398 00 |
| | 31 | Closing | J4 | 398 00 | | — | — |

ACCOUNT **Purchases Discount** ACCOUNT NO. 51.2

| DATE | | ITEM | POST. REF. | DEBIT | CREDIT | BALANCE DEBIT | BALANCE CREDIT |
|---|---|---|---|---|---|---|---|
| 1982 | | | | | | | |
| July | 31 | | CP2 | | 65 80 | | 65 80 |
| | 31 | Closing | J4 | 65 80 | | — | — |

ACCOUNT **Advertising Expense** ACCOUNT NO. 61

| DATE | | ITEM | POST. REF. | DEBIT | CREDIT | BALANCE DEBIT | BALANCE CREDIT |
|---|---|---|---|---|---|---|---|
| 1982 | | | | | | | |
| July | 23 | | CP2 | 342 00 | | 342 00 | |
| | 31 | Closing | J4 | | 342 00 | — | — |

ACCOUNT **Depreciation Expense — Store Equipment** ACCOUNT NO. 62

| DATE | | ITEM | POST. REF. | DEBIT | CREDIT | BALANCE DEBIT | BALANCE CREDIT |
|---|---|---|---|---|---|---|---|
| 1982 | | | | | | | |
| July | 31 | Adjusting | J3 | 125 00 | | 125 00 | |
| | 31 | Closing | J4 | | 125 00 | — | — |

ACCOUNT **Sales Salary Expense** ACCOUNT NO. 63

| DATE | | ITEM | POST. REF. | DEBIT | CREDIT | BALANCE DEBIT | BALANCE CREDIT |
|---|---|---|---|---|---|---|---|
| 1982 | | | | | | | |
| July | 15 | | CP2 | 850 00 | | 850 00 | |
| | 30 | | CP2 | 840 00 | | 1 690 00 | |
| | 31 | Adjusting | J3 | 80 00 | | 1 770 00 | |
| | 31 | Closing | J4 | | 1 770 00 | — | — |

ACCOUNT **Store Supplies Expense** ACCOUNT NO. 64

| DATE | | ITEM | POST. REF. | DEBIT | CREDIT | BALANCE DEBIT | BALANCE CREDIT |
|---|---|---|---|---|---|---|---|
| 1982 | | | | | | | |
| July | 31 | Adjusting | J3 | 610 00 | | 610 00 | |
| | 31 | Closing | J4 | | 610 00 | — | — |

*General Ledger – Rose Wholesale Co. (continued)*

ACCOUNT **Miscellaneous Selling Expense** ACCOUNT NO. 65

| DATE | | ITEM | POST. REF. | DEBIT | CREDIT | BALANCE DEBIT | BALANCE CREDIT |
|---|---|---|---|---|---|---|---|
| 1982 | | | | | | | |
| July | 22 | | CP2 | 68 00 | | 68 00 | |
| | 31 | Closing | J4 | | 68 00 | — | — |

ACCOUNT **Depreciation Expense — Office Equipment** ACCOUNT NO. 71

| DATE | | ITEM | POST. REF. | DEBIT | CREDIT | BALANCE DEBIT | BALANCE CREDIT |
|---|---|---|---|---|---|---|---|
| 1982 | | | | | | | |
| July | 31 | Adjusting | J3 | 50 00 | | 50 00 | |
| | 31 | Closing | J4 | | 50 00 | — | — |

ACCOUNT **Insurance Expense** ACCOUNT NO. 72

| DATE | | ITEM | POST. REF. | DEBIT | CREDIT | BALANCE DEBIT | BALANCE CREDIT |
|---|---|---|---|---|---|---|---|
| 1982 | | | | | | | |
| July | 31 | Adjusting | J3 | 24 00 | | 24 00 | |
| | 31 | Closing | J4 | | 24 00 | — | — |

ACCOUNT **Office Salary Expense** ACCOUNT NO. 73

| DATE | | ITEM | POST. REF. | DEBIT | CREDIT | BALANCE DEBIT | BALANCE CREDIT |
|---|---|---|---|---|---|---|---|
| 1982 | | | | | | | |
| July | 15 | | CP2 | 720 00 | | 720 00 | |
| | 30 | | CP2 | 790 00 | | 1 510 00 | |
| | 31 | Adjusting | J3 | 75 00 | | 1 585 00 | |
| | 31 | Closing | J4 | | 1 585 00 | — | — |

ACCOUNT **Office Supplies Expense** ACCOUNT NO. 74

| DATE | | ITEM | POST. REF. | DEBIT | CREDIT | BALANCE DEBIT | BALANCE CREDIT |
|---|---|---|---|---|---|---|---|
| 1982 | | | | | | | |
| July | 31 | Adjusting | J3 | 232 00 | | 232 00 | |
| | 31 | Closing | J4 | | 232 00 | — | — |

ACCOUNT **Rent Expense** ACCOUNT NO. 75

| DATE | | ITEM | POST. REF. | DEBIT | CREDIT | BALANCE DEBIT | BALANCE CREDIT |
|---|---|---|---|---|---|---|---|
| 1982 | | | | | | | |
| July | 1 | | CP2 | 920 00 | | 920 00 | |
| | 31 | Closing | J4 | | 920 00 | — | — |

ACCOUNT **Utilities Expense** ACCOUNT NO. 76

| DATE | | ITEM | POST. REF. | DEBIT | CREDIT | BALANCE DEBIT | BALANCE CREDIT |
|---|---|---|---|---|---|---|---|
| 1982 | | | | | | | |
| July | 29 | | CP2 | 413 00 | | 413 00 | |
| | 31 | Closing | J4 | | 413 00 | — | — |

ACCOUNT **Miscellaneous General Expense** ACCOUNT NO. 77

| DATE | | ITEM | POST. REF. | DEBIT | CREDIT | BALANCE DEBIT | BALANCE CREDIT |
|---|---|---|---|---|---|---|---|
| 1982 | | | | | | | |
| July | 22 | | CP2 | 31 00 | | 31 00 | |
| | 31 | Closing | J4 | | 31 00 | — | — |

*General Ledger – Rose Wholesale Co. (concluded)*

# ACCOUNTS RECEIVABLE LEDGER

NAME Chung Supermarket
ADDRESS 510 N. Main Street, Oklahoma City, OK 73102-6351 TERMS: 2/10, n/30

| DATE | | ITEM | POST. REF. | DEBIT | CREDIT | BALANCE |
|---|---|---|---|---|---|---|
| 1982 | | | | | | |
| June | 7 | | S1 | 555 00 | | 555 00 |
| | 19 | | CR1 | | 555 00 | — |
| | 28 | | S1 | 445 00 | | 445 00 |
| July | 2 | | SR2 | | 40 00 | 405 00 |
| | 7 | | CR2 | | 405 00 | — |
| | 8 | | S2 | 410 00 | | 410 00 |
| | 19 | | CR2 | | 410 00 | — |
| | 28 | | S2 | 1 225 00 | | 1 225 00 |

NAME Coda's Quik Stop
ADDRESS 2701 Emelyn Avenue, Norman, OK 73069-7478 TERMS: 2/10, n/30

| DATE | | ITEM | POST. REF. | DEBIT | CREDIT | BALANCE |
|---|---|---|---|---|---|---|
| 1982 | | | | | | |
| June | 5 | | S1 | 285 00 | | 285 00 |
| | 16 | | CR1 | | 285 00 | — |
| | 21 | | S1 | 500 00 | | 500 00 |
| | 28 | | S1 | 800 00 | | 1 300 00 |
| July | 3 | | SR2 | | 100 00 | 1 200 00 |
| | 10 | | S2 | 175 00 | | 1 375 00 |
| | 13 | | CR2 | | 1 200 00 | 175 00 |
| | 19 | | CR2 | | 175 00 | — |

NAME Cruz Restaurant
ADDRESS 601 E. Cottonwood Road, Norman, OK 73071-6871 TERMS: 2/10, n/30

| DATE | | ITEM | POST. REF. | DEBIT | CREDIT | BALANCE |
|---|---|---|---|---|---|---|
| 1982 | | | | | | |
| June | 10 | | S1 | 380 00 | | 380 00 |
| July | 1 | | SR2 | | 20 00 | 360 00 |
| | 2 | | CR2 | | 360 00 | — |
| | 14 | | S2 | 250 00 | | 250 00 |
| | 24 | | CR2 | | 250 00 | — |
| | 30 | | S2 | 990 00 | | 990 00 |

NAME Giese Grocery
ADDRESS 1602 Park Road, W., Oklahoma City, OK 73129-5943 TERMS: 2/10, n/30

| DATE | | ITEM | POST. REF. | DEBIT | CREDIT | BALANCE |
|---|---|---|---|---|---|---|
| 1982 | | | | | | |
| June | 9 | | S1 | 410 00 | | 410 00 |
| | 12 | | S1 | 950 00 | | 1 360 00 |
| | 24 | | CR1 | | 1 360 00 | — |
| July | 2 | | S2 | 275 00 | | 275 00 |
| | 9 | | CR2 | | 275 00 | — |
| | 22 | | S2 | 1 160 00 | | 1 160 00 |
| | 26 | | SR2 | | 257 00 | 903 00 |

*Accounts Receivable Ledger – Rose Wholesale Co.*

NAME Morris Co.

ADDRESS 309 Ridgecrest Road, Shawnee, OK 74801-1114 TERMS: 2/10, n/30

| DATE | | ITEM | POST. REF. | DEBIT | CREDIT | BALANCE |
|---|---|---|---|---|---|---|
| 1982 | | | | | | |
| June | 10 | | S1 | 650 00 | | 650 00 |
| July | 3 | | CR2 | | 650 00 | ——— |
| | 6 | | S2 | 205 00 | | 205 00 |
| | 15 | | SR2 | | 25 00 | 180 00 |
| | 16 | | CR2 | | 180 00 | ——— |

*Accounts Receivable Ledger – Rose Wholesale Co. (concluded)*

## ACCOUNTS PAYABLE LEDGER

NAME Checker Sugar Co.

ADDRESS 2107 Georgia Ave., N.E., St. Louis, MO 63135-1097 TERMS: 3/10, n/30

| DATE | | ITEM | POST. REF. | DEBIT | CREDIT | BALANCE |
|---|---|---|---|---|---|---|
| 1982 | | | | | | |
| June | 2 | | P1 | | 1 185 00 | 1 185 00 |
| | 18 | | CP1 | 1 185 00 | | ——— |
| | 28 | | P1 | | 1 220 00 | 1 220 00 |
| July | 5 | | PR2 | 120 00 | | 1 100 00 |
| | 8 | | CP2 | 1 100 00 | | ——— |
| | 8 | | P2 | | 480 00 | 480 00 |
| | 17 | | CP2 | 480 00 | | ——— |
| | 19 | | P2 | | 280 00 | 280 00 |

NAME Davis Pickles

ADDRESS 17401 Sunset Drive, Tulsa, OK 74114-3283 TERMS: 2/10, n/30

| DATE | | ITEM | POST. REF. | DEBIT | CREDIT | BALANCE |
|---|---|---|---|---|---|---|
| 1982 | | | | | | |
| June | 17 | | P1 | | 1 196 00 | 1 196 00 |
| | 26 | | P1 | | 920 00 | 2 116 00 |
| July | 3 | | PR2 | 27 00 | | 2 089 00 |
| | 5 | | CP2 | 2 089 00 | | ——— |
| | 16 | | P2 | | 157 00 | 157 00 |
| | 26 | | PR2 | 39 00 | | 118 00 |
| | 31 | | CP2 | 118 00 | | ——— |

NAME Omni Equipment Co.

ADDRESS 512 College Ave., W., Oklahoma City, OK 73106-3592 TERMS: n/30

| DATE | | ITEM | POST. REF. | DEBIT | CREDIT | BALANCE |
|---|---|---|---|---|---|---|
| 1982 | | | | | | |
| June | 16 | | P1 | | 3 242 00 | 3 242 00 |
| | 21 | | P1 | | 850 00 | 4 092 00 |
| | 28 | | CP1 | 3 242 00 | | 850 00 |
| July | 9 | | CP2 | 850 00 | | ——— |
| | 10 | | P2 | | 3 370 00 | 3 370 00 |

*Accounts Payable Ledger – Rose Wholesale Co.*

NAME Queen Supply Co.

ADDRESS 1743 S. Chisholm Rd., Oklahoma City, OK 73127-6718 TERMS: n/30

| DATE | | ITEM | POST. REF. | DEBIT | CREDIT | BALANCE |
|---|---|---|---|---|---|---|
| 1982 | | | | | | |
| June | 7 | | P1 | | 331 00 | 331 00 |
| | 23 | | P1 | | 290 00 | 621 00 |
| | 25 | | CP1 | 331 00 | | 290 00 |
| July | 1 | | CP2 | 290 00 | | — |
| | 2 | | P2 | | 360 00 | 360 00 |
| | 10 | | J2 | 18 00 | | 342 00 |
| | 16 | | CP2 | 342 00 | | — |
| | 21 | | P2 | | 105 00 | 105 00 |

NAME Sweet Candy Co.

ADDRESS 900 S. Fairmont Ave., Oklahoma City, OK 73129-5155 TERMS: 3/15, n/30

| DATE | | ITEM | POST. REF. | DEBIT | CREDIT | BALANCE |
|---|---|---|---|---|---|---|
| 1982 | | | | | | |
| June | 12 | | P1 | | 2 135 00 | 2 135 00 |
| July | 12 | | P2 | | 285 00 | 2 420 00 |
| | 19 | | PR2 | 212 00 | | 2 208 00 |
| | 20 | | CP2 | 2 135 00 | | 73 00 |
| | 28 | | CP2 | 73 00 | | — |
| | 29 | | P2 | | 2 275 00 | 2 275 00 |

NAME Warren Gum Company

ADDRESS 5107 Akard Street, Dallas, TX 75215-1330 TERMS: 2/10, n/30

| DATE | | ITEM | POST. REF. | DEBIT | CREDIT | BALANCE |
|---|---|---|---|---|---|---|
| 1982 | | | | | | |
| June | 9 | | P1 | | 725 00 | 725 00 |
| | 26 | | CP1 | 500 00 | | 225 00 |
| July | 3 | | CP2 | 225 00 | | — |
| | 26 | | P2 | | 1 200 00 | 1 200 00 |

*Accounts Payable Ledger – Rose Wholesale Co. (concluded)*

## POST-CLOSING TRIAL BALANCE

The final step in the accounting cycle is the preparation of the post-closing trial balance. The purpose of the post-closing trial balance is to check the equality of the debits and credits in the ledger after the adjusting and closing entries have been recorded. The account balances shown on the post-closing trial balance will be the same as those appearing on the balance sheet. The post-closing trial balance may be taken by simply running an adding machine tape of the debit balances in the ledger and another of the credit balances, or it may be presented in schedule form as shown on page 201.

**Rose Wholesale Co.**
**Post-Closing Trial Balance**
**July 31, 1982**

| Account | Debit | Credit |
|---|---|---|
| Cash | 17 971 10 | |
| Accounts Receivable | 3 118 00 | |
| Merchandise Inventory | 6 800 00 | |
| Store Supplies | 183 00 | |
| Office Supplies | 260 00 | |
| Prepaid Insurance | 240 00 | |
| Store Equipment | 6 600 00 | |
| Accumulated Depreciation — Store Equipment | | 250 00 |
| Office Equipment | 2 220 00 | |
| Accumulated Depreciation — Office Equipment | | 100 00 |
| Accounts Payable | | 7 230 00 |
| Salaries Payable | | 155 00 |
| Mortgage Note Payable | | 1 500 00 |
| Tom Rose, Capital | | 28 157 10 |
| | 37 392 10 | 37 392 10 |

*Post-Closing Trial Balance – Rose Wholesale Co.*

## QUESTIONS FOR DISCUSSION

1. Give three examples of long-term liabilities.
2. On December 31, 1983, the Eva Co. owed the First City Bank $9,000 on a long-term mortgage payable. The mortgage is payable in annual installments of $1,000 on January 10 of each year. How will the Eva Co. show the mortgage payable on its balance sheet as of December 31, 1983?
3. What is the difference between adjusting entries and closing entries?
4. The bookkeeper for the Ripple Ice Cream Company prepares a work sheet at the end of a fiscal period. He then decides that he will not prepare a balance sheet and income statement since all of the information that would be shown on these reports appears on the work sheet. Do you consider it advisable for him to omit the preparation of these financial statements?
5. The bookkeeper for Trippe Dental Supply Company feels that the accuracy of her work has been proved by her post-closing trial balance. Do you agree with her?

## EXERCISES

**1.** Indicate which of the following accounts (a) will normally require an adjusting entry at the end of the period, and (b) will require a closing entry at the end of the period.

| Account | Account |
|---|---|
| 1. Prepaid Insurance | 6. Office Supplies |
| 2. Accounts Payable | 7. Salary Expense |
| 3. Merchandise Inventory | 8. Salaries Payable |
| 4. Sales Discount | 9. Depreciation Expense |
| 5. Owner's Drawing | 10. Owner's Capital |

**2.** In Column I below you are given selected account balances from the trial balance of the Blum Company as of December 31, the end of the current fiscal period. Column II contains the account balances after the adjustments were recorded:

| | **Column I Trial Balance** | | **Column II Adjusted Trial Balance** | |
|---|---|---|---|---|
| | *Dr.* | *Cr.* | *Dr.* | *Cr.* |
| Merchandise Inventory | 15,300 | .......... | 14,700 | .......... |
| Office Supplies | 465 | .......... | 390 | .......... |
| Prepaid Insurance | 900 | .......... | 800 | .......... |
| Accumulated Depreciation — Equipment | .......... | 2,700 | .......... | 3,000 |
| Salary Expense | 1,120 | .......... | 1,260 | .......... |
| Income Summary | .......... | .......... | 15,300 | 14,700 |
| Office Supplies Expense | .......... | .......... | 75 | .......... |
| Insurance Expense | .......... | .......... | 100 | .......... |
| Depreciation Expense — Equipment | .......... | .......... | 300 | .......... |
| Salaries Payable | .......... | .......... | .......... | 140 |

Prepare the adjusting entries that were made for the Blum Company at the end of the current period. None of the accounts had more than one debit or credit as part of the adjusting entry.

**3.** The capital, drawing, income summary, revenue, and expense accounts for Barret Print Shop on December 31, after all adjustments have been made and posted, are presented below. Prepare the journal entries to close the books for Barret.

| | *Dr.* | *Cr.* |
|---|---|---|
| Richard Barret, Capital | .......... | 12,700 |
| Richard Barret, Drawing | 350 | .......... |
| Income Summary (after Merchandise Inventory adjustments) | 2,650 | 2,400 |
| Sales | .......... | 8,200 |
| Sales Returns and Allowances | 260 | .......... |
| Purchases | 5,060 | .......... |
| Purchases Discount | .......... | 405 |
| Salary Expense | 1,200 | .......... |
| Rent Expense | 400 | .......... |
| Depreciation Expense | 310 | .......... |
| Utilities Expense | 130 | .......... |

## ASSIGNMENT 9-B

**Tear out pages 489–498 and complete Assignment 9-B. Submit your papers for approval. If you have any difficulty doing the assignment, review the material in the chapter.**

Chapter **10**

# PAYROLL ACCOUNTING AND THE VOUCHER SYSTEM

As a business entity grows in size, maintaining adequate control over its activities becomes more difficult. The accounting system must be designed to assure that the increased number of business transactions are recorded and summarized efficiently and accurately.

One area of the accounting system that requires special attention is the accounting for salaries and wages paid to employees. Part A of this chapter provides an introduction to accounting for payroll. Part B includes a discussion of payroll taxes and payroll records. Part C deals with the problems of internal control and the use of a voucher system in providing adequate internal control.

## PART A COMPUTING AND RECORDING THE PAYROLL

The importance of an adequate payroll system cannot be overemphasized. It is one of the most critical areas of record keeping in a business enterprise. Businesses are required by law to collect certain taxes levied against the earnings of their employees. These taxes are collected by deducting them from the employees' pay. Most employers are also subject to federal and state taxes levied on their payrolls. All employee withholding taxes and employer payroll taxes must be properly accounted for and paid at prescribed intervals. Payroll records are also useful to management in analyzing and controlling operations and in negotiating labor contracts.

### EMPLOYEES DEFINED

An individual who performs services subject to the will and control of an employer, both as to what shall be done and how it shall be done, is an *employee*. This does not mean that every person who performs services for a business is an employee. For example, architects, lawyers, and certified public accountants sell their services to a business but do not become its employees. They are told what to do but not how to do it and are therefore considered independent contractors. The compensation they are paid for their services is called a *fee*.

The difference between an employee and an independent contractor is legally significant. Fees paid to independent contractors are not subject to payroll taxes and should not be included as part of the company payroll. Also, the responsibilities and obligations of a contractor and a client to each other and to third parties are quite different from the legal relationship of an employer and employee.

## TYPES OF COMPENSATION

Compensation paid to an employee for managerial, administrative, or similar services is commonly referred to as a *salary*. A salary is usually expressed in terms of a weekly, monthly, or yearly amount. Remuneration stated on an hourly or piecework basis, for either skilled or unskilled labor, is normally referred to as a *wage*. In actual practice, the terms salary and wage are often used interchangeably. Salaries and wages are usually paid in money, and they are frequently supplemented by bonuses, commissions, profit-sharing plans, and other benefits. Compensation may also be in other forms, such as meals, lodging, shares of stock, or other property.

## COMPUTATION OF GROSS EARNINGS

Most employees' earnings are based on the number of hours worked during the pay period. Other bases used for determining earnings include units of output (piecework) or sales volume (bonus or commission).

If earnings are based on time, a record of the hours worked by each employee is required. If the number of employees is small, a record of hours worked may be kept in a memorandum book. When there are a large number of workers, time clocks may be used to record the time worked by each employee. Under this system a time card is provided for each employee and a time clock is used to record the daily arrival and departure times on the time cards. The payroll clerk uses the time cards to determine the total time worked by each employee during the pay period. The employee's pay for the period is computed by multiplying the number of hours worked, as determined from the time card, by the hourly wage rate.

### Overtime and Premium Rates

If the business is engaged in interstate commerce, the wage rates paid must conform to the requirements of the Fair Labor Standards Act, commonly referred to as the Federal Wage and Hour Law. This act provides that all employees covered by the statute must be paid a minimum of 1½ times the regular rate for all hours worked in excess of 40 hours per week. Certain supervisory positions are not covered by this provision of the law.

The practice of paying premium rates for overtime and for less desirable work hours, such as night shifts, has been extended considerably in certain industries through union contract agreements. Certain overtime hours, such as Sundays and holidays, may be paid at double the regular rate and are frequently considered as overtime regardless of the total hours worked during the week.

### Computation of Gross Earnings Illustrated

To illustrate the computation of gross earnings, assume that Bob E. Hall, a press operator for a newspaper, earns $6.00 per hour for the first 40 hours worked each week, 1½ times the regular rate for all hours worked in excess of 40 per week, and double the regular rate for all hours worked on Sundays and holidays. During the week ended April 30, Hall worked 8 hours per day Monday through Saturday and 5 hours on Sunday. Hall's gross earnings for the week would be computed as follows:

| | |
|---|---|
| 40 hours at regular rate (Monday–Friday)......40 × $ 6.00 = | $240.00 |
| 8 hours at time and a half (Saturday) ........... 8 × $ 9.00 = | 72.00 |
| 5 hours at double time (Sunday) .................. 5 × $12.00 = | 60.00 |
| Gross earnings for the week ............................................. | $372.00 |

## PAYROLL DEDUCTIONS

In almost all businesses, employers are required to withhold certain deductions from employees' gross earnings. The most common deductions are for federal income tax and FICA tax. FICA tax is required by the Federal Insurance Contributions Act and is often referred to as social security tax. Some states and cities also require income tax to be deducted from employees' earnings. In addition to deductions required by law, various other deductions may be made at the employees' requests.

### Employee Income Taxes Withheld

Generally, employers are required to withhold federal income tax from wages paid to employees. This is referred to as the *pay-as-you-go system* of paying income tax. The amount to be withheld is determined by the (1) gross earnings of the employee, (2) length of the payroll period, (3) marital status of the employee, and (4) number of withholding allowances claimed. The amount to be withheld for federal income tax is computed on gross earnings before any deductions are made for such items as retirement pension, FICA tax, health or life insurance, and union dues.

The amount of income tax to be withheld can be computed by either the "percentage" method or the "wage-bracket" method. The *percentage method* requires determining the taxable earnings and then multiplying by the appropriate tax rate. The *wage-bracket method* uses tables based on wage ranges to determine the income tax to be withheld. Tables are provided for weekly, biweekly, semimonthly, monthly, and daily or miscellaneous payroll periods for both married and single individuals. Most businesses use the wage-bracket method because of its simplicity. A section of a wage-bracket withholding table for married persons with a weekly payroll period is shown below.

**WEEKLY Payroll Period—Employee MARRIED**

| And the wages are- | | And the number of withholding allowances claimed is— | | | | | | | | | | |
|---|---|---|---|---|---|---|---|---|---|---|---|---|
| At least | But less than | 0 | 1 | 2 | 3 | 4 | 5 | 6 | 7 | 8 | 9 | 10 or more |
| | | The amount of income tax to be withheld shall be— | | | | | | | | | | |
| $300 | $310 | $47.50 | $43.00 | $39.00 | $34.90 | $30.90 | $26.90 | $23.40 | $19.90 | $16.50 | $13.00 | $10.00 |
| 310 | 320 | 49.90 | 45.30 | 41.10 | 37.00 | 33.00 | 28.90 | 25.20 | 21.70 | 18.30 | 14.80 | 11.50 |
| 320 | 330 | 52.30 | 47.70 | 43.20 | 39.10 | 35.10 | 31.00 | 27.00 | 23.50 | 20.10 | 16.60 | 13.20 |
| 330 | 340 | 54.70 | 50.10 | 45.50 | 41.20 | 37.20 | 33.10 | 29.10 | 25.30 | 21.90 | 18.40 | 15.00 |
| 340 | 350 | 57.10 | 52.50 | 47.90 | 43.30 | 39.30 | 35.20 | 31.20 | 27.20 | 23.70 | 20.20 | 16.80 |
| 350 | 360 | 59.50 | 54.90 | 50.30 | 45.70 | 41.40 | 37.30 | 33.30 | 29.30 | 25.50 | 22.00 | 18.60 |
| 360 | 370 | 61.90 | 57.30 | 52.70 | 48.10 | 43.50 | 39.40 | 35.40 | 31.40 | 27.30 | 23.80 | 20.40 |
| 370 | 380 | 64.60 | 59.70 | 55.10 | 50.50 | 45.90 | 41.50 | 37.50 | 33.50 | 29.40 | 25.60 | 22.20 |
| 380 | 390 | 67.40 | 62.10 | 57.50 | 52.90 | 48.30 | 43.70 | 39.60 | 35.60 | 31.50 | 27.50 | 24.00 |
| 390 | 400 | 70.20 | 64.80 | 59.90 | 55.30 | 50.70 | 46.10 | 41.70 | 37.70 | 33.60 | 29.60 | 25.80 |
| 400 | 410 | 73.00 | 67.60 | 62.30 | 57.70 | 53.10 | 48.50 | 43.80 | 39.80 | 35.70 | 31.70 | 27.60 |
| 410 | 420 | 75.80 | 70.40 | 65.00 | 60.10 | 55.50 | 50.90 | 46.20 | 41.90 | 37.80 | 33.80 | 29.70 |
| 420 | 430 | 78.60 | 73.20 | 67.80 | 62.50 | 57.90 | 53.30 | 48.60 | 44.00 | 39.90 | 35.90 | 31.80 |
| 430 | 440 | 81.40 | 76.00 | 70.60 | 65.20 | 60.30 | 55.70 | 51.00 | 46.40 | 42.00 | 38.00 | 33.90 |
| 440 | 450 | 84.20 | 78.80 | 73.40 | 68.00 | 62.70 | 58.10 | 53.40 | 48.80 | 44.20 | 40.10 | 36.00 |
| 650 | 660 | 156.00 | 148.90 | 141.70 | 134.60 | 127.50 | 120.40 | 114.10 | 107.90 | 101.80 | 95.60 | 89.50 |
| 660 | 670 | 159.70 | 152.60 | 145.40 | 138.30 | 131.20 | 124.10 | 117.30 | 111.10 | 105.00 | 98.80 | 92.70 |
| 670 | 680 | 163.40 | 156.30 | 149.10 | 142.00 | 134.90 | 127.80 | 120.70 | 114.30 | 108.20 | 102.00 | 95.90 |
| 680 | 690 | 167.10 | 160.00 | 152.80 | 145.70 | 138.60 | 131.50 | 124.40 | 117.50 | 111.40 | 105.20 | 99.10 |
| 690 | 700 | 170.80 | 163.70 | 156.50 | 149.40 | 142.30 | 135.20 | 128.10 | 121.00 | 114.60 | 108.40 | 102.30 |
| 700 | 710 | 174.50 | 167.40 | 160.20 | 153.10 | 146.00 | 138.90 | 131.80 | 124.70 | 117.80 | 111.60 | 105.50 |
| 710 | 720 | 178.20 | 171.10 | 163.90 | 156.80 | 149.70 | 142.60 | 135.50 | 128.40 | 121.20 | 114.80 | 108.70 |
| 720 | 730 | 181.90 | 174.80 | 167.60 | 160.50 | 153.40 | 146.30 | 139.20 | 132.10 | 124.90 | 118.00 | 111.90 |
| 730 | 740 | 185.60 | 178.50 | 171.30 | 164.20 | 157.10 | 150.00 | 142.90 | 135.80 | 128.60 | 121.50 | 115.10 |
| 740 | 750 | 189.30 | 182.20 | 175.00 | 167.90 | 160.80 | 153.70 | 146.60 | 139.50 | 132.30 | 125.20 | 118.30 |
| 750 | 760 | 193.00 | 185.90 | 178.70 | 171.60 | 164.50 | 157.40 | 150.30 | 143.20 | 136.00 | 128.90 | 121.80 |
| 760 | 770 | 196.70 | 189.60 | 182.40 | 175.30 | 168.20 | 161.10 | 154.00 | 146.90 | 139.70 | 132.60 | 125.50 |
| 770 | 780 | 200.40 | 193.30 | 186.10 | 179.00 | 171.90 | 164.80 | 157.70 | 150.60 | 143.40 | 136.30 | 129.20 |
| 780 | 790 | 204.10 | 197.00 | 189.80 | 182.70 | 175.60 | 168.50 | 161.40 | 154.30 | 147.10 | 140.00 | 132.90 |
| 790 | 800 | 207.80 | 200.70 | 193.50 | 186.40 | 179.30 | 172.20 | 165.10 | 158.00 | 150.80 | 143.70 | 136.60 |
| | | 37 percent of the excess over $850 plus— | | | | | | | | | | |
| $850 and over | | 228.10 | 221.00 | 213.90 | 206.80 | 199.70 | 192.50 | 185.40 | 178.30 | 171.20 | 164.10 | 157.00 |

***Withholding Table***

To illustrate the use of the wage-bracket withholding table, refer to the gross earnings of $372 presented earlier for Bob E. Hall. Assuming Hall is married and claimed a total of three withholding allowances, his withholding can be determined by finding in the first two columns (the amount of wages) the "At least $370, But less than $380" line and following across to the withholding allowances claimed under the column for three allowances. The amount of income tax to be withheld is shown as $50.50.

It should be emphasized that the methods used to determine the amount of income tax to be withheld from an employee's earnings are only approximations. An employee's actual income tax is determined only at the end of the year when an income tax return is filed. The difference between the actual income tax for the year and the amount withheld from earnings during the year is relatively small in most cases. If not enough was withheld from earnings, payment for the difference should be included with the tax return. If the amount deducted was too large, a refund may be claimed when the tax return is filed.

Many states also impose a state income tax. Some states provide income tax withholding tables similar to the federal tables, while others determine the amount of state withholding by merely applying a percentage to the federal withholding.

## FICA (Social Security) Tax

The Federal Insurance Contributions Act (FICA) provides for a federal program of old age, disability, hospital, and survivors' benefits to be financed through FICA tax. This program is commonly referred to as the *social security system*. Employers are required to withhold FICA tax from employees' wages at a specified rate up to a specified amount paid in a calendar year.[1]

The FICA tax rate and the maximum earnings subject to the tax are often changed by Congress. Because of these frequent changes, a 7% rate applied to earnings up to $25,000, or a maximum annual tax of $1,750, will be used in this text to allow for ease in computation in problems and illustrations.

Based on the above, the FICA tax to be withheld from Hall's wages for the week of April 30 is $26.04 ($372 × 7%).

## Other Deductions from Earnings

Some states require an amount to be withheld from employees' wages for unemployment compensation or disability benefits. State and city income taxes may also be required to be withheld from employees' pay.

All of the payroll deductions mentioned are required by law. In addition to these deductions, however, there may be other deductions authorized by the employees, either individually or as a group. Some of the more common examples of these payroll deductions are:

1. Insurance premiums for life, accident, or medical insurance.
2. Contributions to pension funds, retirement programs, or profit sharing funds.
3. Employees' union dues.
4. Purchase of United States savings bonds.
5. Contributions to charitable groups, such as the United Fund.
6. Repayment of loans to the company or to the company credit union.

Regardless of the nature of the deduction, the employer must keep an accurate record of the amounts deducted, and the amounts withheld must be disposed of as authorized. Most of the deductions from employees' earnings are shown as current liabilities of the employer until they are paid.

## Computation of Net Pay

The *net pay* is gross earnings less payroll deductions. This is the amount of money actually received on payday and is often referred to as "take-home-pay."

[1]Effective January 1, 1982, the FICA tax rate was set at 6.70% on maximum earnings of $32,100. The maximum FICA tax paid by an employee is $2,150.70 ($32,100 × 6.70%).

The payroll data presented earlier for Bob E. Hall are used to illustrate the computation of net pay. Hall earned $372 and has three withholding allowances. Prior to this week, his total earnings for the year were $5,208. Hall's withholding for federal income tax is $50.50 and his FICA tax deduction is $26.04 as determined in previous illustrations. He has also authorized his employer to deduct $8.50 per week for a group health insurance plan and $5.00 per week for union dues.

The various weekly deductions and net pay for Hall are shown below:

| | | |
|---|---|---|
| Gross earnings for the week | | $372.00 |
| Deductions: | | |
| Federal income tax | $50.50 | |
| FICA tax | 26.04 | |
| Health insurance plan | 8.50 | |
| Union dues | 5.00 | |
| Total deductions | | 90.04 |
| Net pay | | $281.96 |

The employer normally furnishes a statement of earnings and deductions to each employee with each wage payment. One widely used system is the use of payroll checks with detachable stubs. The check stub indicates pay period, gross earnings, deductions, and net pay. It is detached by the employee before the check is cashed.

An example of a payroll check with a detachable stub is presented below:

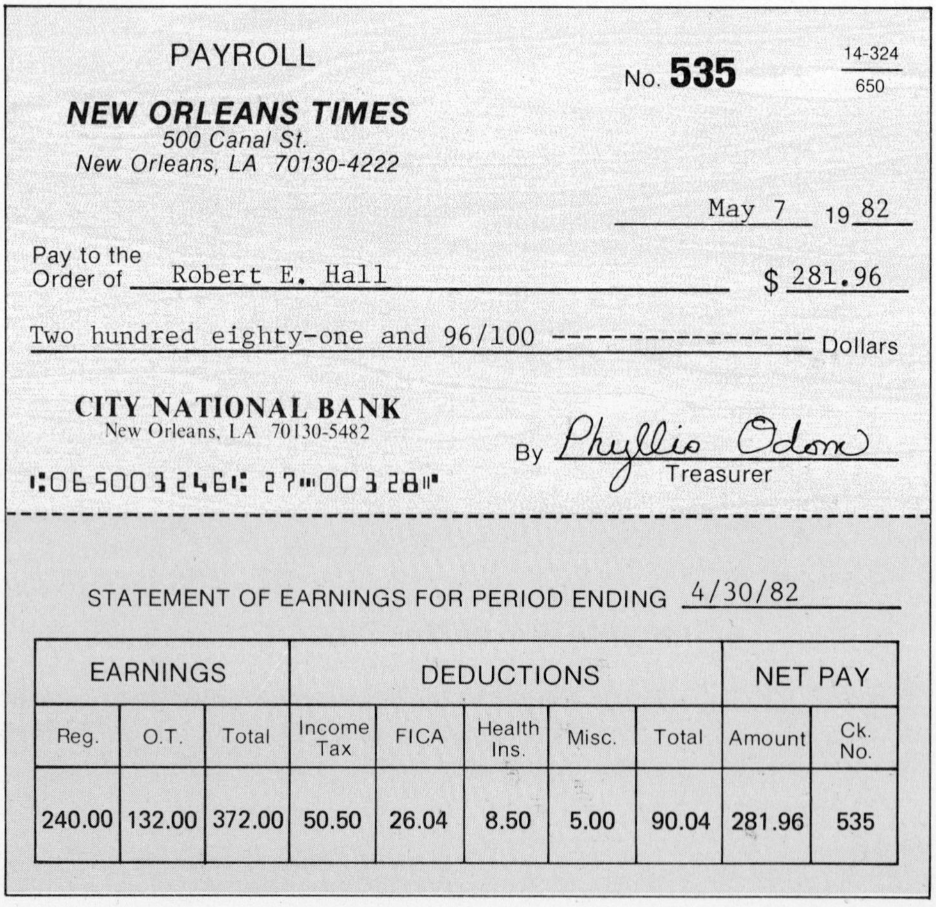
PAYROLL

No. 535

14-324
650

**NEW ORLEANS TIMES**
500 Canal St.
New Orleans, LA 70130-4222

May 7 19 82

Pay to the Order of Robert E. Hall $ 281.96

Two hundred eighty-one and 96/100 ---------------- Dollars

**CITY NATIONAL BANK**
New Orleans, LA 70130-5482

By Phyllis Odom
Treasurer

⑆0650032461⑆ 27⑈00328⑈

STATEMENT OF EARNINGS FOR PERIOD ENDING 4/30/82

| EARNINGS | | | DEDUCTIONS | | | | | NET PAY | |
|---|---|---|---|---|---|---|---|---|---|
| Reg. | O.T. | Total | Income Tax | FICA | Health Ins. | Misc. | Total | Amount | Ck. No. |
| 240.00 | 132.00 | 372.00 | 50.50 | 26.04 | 8.50 | 5.00 | 90.04 | 281.96 | 535 |

*Payroll Check*

## THE PAYROLL REGISTER

A list of employees, showing their earnings for a specific pay period together with other relevant information concerning their pay, is called a *payroll*. The payroll data for each pay period are recorded in a *payroll register*. A payroll register is normally used as the basic document for journalizing payroll information for each pay period. Its design varies widely, depending upon the specific payroll data to be recorded by a business. As an example, the payroll register for Ganzer Dairy for the week ended November 26 is shown on pages 210 and 211.

Several items in the payroll register should be noted: The payroll period should be shown at the top of the payroll register. The payroll period for Ganzer Dairy is the week ended November 26, 1982. The company has five employees whose year-to-date earnings as of the end of the previous week are shown in the Earnings to Date column (1). This information is needed, since Ganzer must deduct FICA tax from the individual wages until the employee has earned $25,000. In the illustration, David Osborne has earnings to date of $25,061 which exceeds the $25,000 limit; therefore his pay is no longer subject to FICA tax during the current year.

The employer is required to match the employees' FICA contribution and to pay unemployment taxes on the first $6,000 earned by each employee, thus the need for an individual listing of taxable earnings (Columns 11 and 12). Employer payroll taxes are discussed in Part B of this chapter.

The No. of Allowances column (2) is used for income tax withholding purposes. The payroll clerk will also need to know if the employee is single or married to determine the proper table for computing the income tax to be deducted for the period (Column 3). In the payroll register shown below, all employees are married except Jane Beasley.

The hours worked each day are shown in the Daily Hours column (4). This information is available from employee time cards or a time memorandum book. The Hourly Rate column (5) shows the amount of the employee's regular hourly wage rate. In the illustration, all hours worked in excess of 40 per week are paid at 1½ times the regular rate. For example, Amy Williams worked 50 hours (Columns 6 and 7) and is paid at a regular rate of $6 per hour. Her overtime pay is $9 per hour, which is 1½ times her regular pay. Her weekly earnings are computed as follows:

| | | |
|---|---|---|
| Regular earnings ................................ | 40 hours × $6.00 = $240 | (Column 8) |
| Overtime earnings ................................ | 10 hours × 9.00 = 90 | (Column 9) |
| Total earnings for the week ................................ | $330 | (Column 10) |

The total of $330 represents Williams' gross earnings for the week. The $330 is also the amount of salary expense to Ganzer Dairy.

The federal income tax to be withheld from Williams is based on her gross earnings of $330. Williams is married and has three withholding allowances. Since the payroll period is weekly and Williams is married, the withholding table on page 206 is used to determine

**PAYROLL FOR WEEK ENDING**

| | (1) | (2) | (3) | (4) | | | | | | (5) | (6) | (7) | (8) | (9) | (10) |
|---|---|---|---|---|---|---|---|---|---|---|---|---|---|---|---|
| EMPLOYEE | EARNINGS TO DATE | NO. OF ALLOWANCES | MARITAL STATUS | DAILY HOURS | | | | | | HOURLY RATE | REGULAR HOURS | OVERTIME HOURS | EARNINGS | | |
| | | | | M | T | W | Th | F | S | | | | REGULAR | OVERTIME | TOTAL |
| Beasley, Jane | 3,340.00 | 1 | S | 8 | 8 | 8 | 8 | 8 | 4 | 4.50 | 40 | 4 | 180.00 | 27.00 | 207.00 |
| Gandee, Scott | 2,830.00 | 4 | M | 12 | 10 | 10 | 12 | 10 | | 5.50 | 40 | 14 | 220.00 | 115.50 | 335.50 |
| Osborne, David | 25,061.00 | 4 | M | 8 | 8 | 8 | 8 | 9 | 6 | 13.00 | 40 | 7 | 520.00 | 136.50 | 656.50 |
| Roberts, Gary | 24,750.00 | 6 | M | 10 | 10 | 10 | 10 | 8 | 8 | 12.00 | 40 | 16 | 480.00 | 288.00 | 768.00 |
| Williams, Amy | 12,190.00 | 3 | M | 8 | 9 | 9 | 8 | 8 | 8 | 6.00 | 40 | 10 | 240.00 | 90.00 | 330.00 |
| | | | | | | | | | | | | | 1,640.00 | 657.00 | 2,297.00 |

*Payroll Register – (Left Page)*

the amount of federal income tax to be withheld. In the first two columns in the withholding table, read down to the "At least $330, But less than $340" line. Since Williams claims three withholding allowances, read across to the "3 withholding allowances" column and locate the amount to be withheld, $41.20 (Column 13 of the payroll register).

The FICA tax to be withheld from Williams' pay is also based on the gross earnings of $330. Her cumulative earnings prior to this week's payroll were $12,190; therefore her pay is still subject to the 7% FICA tax because she has not yet reached the $25,000 limit. The FICA tax would be $330 × 7% = $23.10 (Column 14).

In the pay period that an employee reaches the $25,000 limit, only a portion of the weekly earnings will be subject to the FICA tax. For example, Gary Roberts had cumulative earnings of $24,750 prior to the current payroll, and his pay for the current period totaled $768. Only $250 ($25,000 − $24,750) of this week's pay would be subject to the FICA tax.

All of Ganzer's employees are participating in a group health insurance plan and have authorized deductions for their portion of the premiums (Column 15). A $5 per week deduction for union dues has also been authorized by all employees (Column 16). Column 17 contains the total of all deductions for each employee. For example, Amy Williams' total deductions can be computed as follows:

| | |
|---|---|
| Federal income tax withheld | $41.20 |
| FICA tax | 23.10 |
| Health insurance premiums | 5.00 |
| Union dues | 5.00 |
| Total deductions | $74.30 |

The net pay for Williams is her gross earnings of $330 less total deductions of $74.30, or $255.70 (Column 18). Check Number 803 (Column 19) is written to Williams for $255.70. Each employee's net pay is computed in this manner, and the information is recorded in the payroll register in the proper columns. The columns are totaled

NOVEMBER 26, 1982

| (11) | (12) | (13) | (14) | (15) | (16) | (17) | (18) | (19) | (20) |
|---|---|---|---|---|---|---|---|---|---|
| TAXABLE EARNINGS | | DEDUCTIONS | | | | | NET PAID | | SALARY EXPENSE DR. |
| FICA | UNEMPLOY-MENT COMP. | FEDERAL INCOME TAX | FICA | HEALTH INSUR. | UNION DUES | TOTAL | AMOUNT | CK. NO. | |
| 207.00 | 207.00 | 29.10 | 14.49 | 3.00 | 5.00 | 51.59 | 155.41 | 799 | 207.00 |
| 335.50 | 335.50 | 37.20 | 23.49 | 5.00 | 5.00 | 70.69 | 264.81 | 800 | 335.50 |
| ——— | ——— | 127.50 | ——— | 5.00 | 5.00 | 137.50 | 519.00 | 801 | 656.50 |
| 250.00 | ——— | 154.00 | 17.50 | 5.00 | 5.00 | 181.50 | 586.50 | 802 | 768.00 |
| 330.00 | ——— | 41.20 | 23.10 | 5.00 | 5.00 | 74.30 | 255.70 | 803 | 330.00 |
| 1,122.50 | 542.50 | 389.00 | 78.58 | 23.00 | 25.00 | 515.58 | 1,781.42 | | 2,297.00 |

***Payroll Register – (Right Page)***

and the totals are verified before the payroll is recorded in the journal or the checks are issued. The computations to verify the accuracy of the payroll register for the week of November 26 are as follows:

| | | | |
|---|---|---|---|
| Earnings: | | | |
| Regular | $1,640.00 | | |
| Overtime | 657.00 | | |
| Total earnings | | | $2,297.00 |
| Less deductions: | | | |
| Federal income tax | | $389.00 | |
| FICA tax | | 78.58 | |
| Health insurance | | 23.00 | |
| Union dues | | 25.00 | |
| Total deductions | | | 515.58 |
| Net pay | | | $1,781.42 |

## RECORDING THE PAYROLL

The general journal entry to record the payroll for Ganzer Dairy for the week ending November 26 is as follows:

| | | | | |
|---|---|---|---|---|
| Nov. | 26 | Salary Expense | 2,297.00 | |
| | | Employees' Income Tax Payable | | 389.00 |
| | | FICA Tax Payable | | 78.58 |
| | | Health Insurance Payable | | 23.00 |
| | | Union Dues Payable | | 25.00 |
| | | Salaries Payable | | 1,781.42 |
| | | Payroll for week ended November 26. | | |

The debit to Salary Expense is for the gross amount of the payroll, $2,297, because this is the amount of wages expense incurred by the company for the week. All of the deductions withheld from employee earnings must ultimately be paid to the appropriate agencies: the federal government, the union, and the insurance company. These withholdings are properly recorded as employer liabilities until paid.

The payroll entry would be posted to the proper accounts as illustrated in T-account form as follows:

**SALARY EXPENSE**

| Debit | | Credit | |
|---|---|---|---|
| Nov. 26 | 2,297.00 | | |

**HEALTH INSURANCE PAYABLE**

| Debit | | Credit | |
|---|---|---|---|
| | | Nov. 26 | 23.00 |

**EMPLOYEES' INCOME TAX PAYABLE**

| Debit | | Credit | |
|---|---|---|---|
| | | Nov. 26 | 389.00 |

**UNION DUES PAYABLE**

| Debit | | Credit | |
|---|---|---|---|
| | | Nov. 26 | 25.00 |

**FICA TAX PAYABLE**

| Debit | | Credit | |
|---|---|---|---|
| | | Nov. 26 | 78.58 |

**SALARIES PAYABLE**

| Debit | | Credit | |
|---|---|---|---|
| | | Nov. 26 | 1,781.42 |

## PAYING THE PAYROLL

Employees may be paid in cash or by check. They are sometimes paid in cash when the pay period is weekly or when check cashing facilities are not readily available. If the payroll is paid in cash, it is desirable to use pay envelopes for inserting both the money and the employee's earnings statement. The front of the envelope may be printed in a manner which allows recording the payroll information on it. Many businesses that pay their payroll in cash, write one check payable to Payroll for the total amount to be disbursed. The check is then cashed at the bank and the cash is inserted in the individual pay envelopes. Although paying the payroll in cash is often more convenient for the employees, it usually is not good business practice because of the greater risk of error or theft.

A business that pays its payroll by check, especially one with a large number of employees, will frequently use a special payroll bank account and draw all payroll checks against the account. When this procedure is followed, one check for the net amount of the payroll is written against the regular bank account and deposited in the separate payroll account. The individual checks for each employee are then written against the payroll account. The advantage of this procedure is that the payroll account receives the exact amount needed to cover the amount of payroll checks written, thus reducing the possibility of error and simplifying the reconciliation of the payroll bank account. The use of a payroll bank account also simplifies the reconciliation of the regular bank account by eliminating the inclusion of the payroll checks.

The entry, in general journal form, to record the payment of Ganzer's November 26 payroll would be as shown below.

| Date | | Account | Debit | Credit |
|---|---|---|---|---|
| Nov. | 26 | Salaries Payable | 1,781.42 | |
| | | Cash | | 1,781.42 |

When the employer pays the liability for a payroll deduction, the entry is a debit to the liability account and a credit to Cash. For example, assuming the union dues deducted from the wages of Ganzer's employees are paid to the union on November 30, the entry would be:

| Date | | Account | Debit | Credit |
|---|---|---|---|---|
| Nov. | 30 | Union Dues Payable | 25.00 | |
| | | Cash | | 25.00 |

If special journals are used, both of the preceding entries would be recorded in a cash payments journal. After the entries are posted, the liability accounts for union dues and salaries will have a zero balance as shown below:

| UNION DUES PAYABLE | | | |
|---|---|---|---|
| Nov. 30 | 25.00 | Nov. 26 | 25.00 |

| SALARIES PAYABLE | | | |
|---|---|---|---|
| Nov. 26 | 1,781.42 | Nov. 26 | 1,781.42 |

## QUESTIONS FOR DISCUSSION

1. Why is it important that a company maintain adequate payroll records?
2. Differentiate between the following terms:
   (a) "employee" and "independent contractor."
   (b) "salary" and "wage."
3. What does "FICA" stand for? What is a common term used for this tax?
4. Name three payroll deductions that are *not* required by law.
5. What is "take-home-pay"?
6. (a) What is a payroll register?
   (b) What column headings would normally be included in this register?
7. In the journal entry to record the payroll, the debit to Salary Expense and the credit to Salaries Payable will not be for the same amount. Explain.
8. (a) Why would a business pay its payroll in cash rather than by check?
   (b) Explain what procedures should be followed if the payroll is to be paid in cash.
9. What are the advantages of using a payroll bank account for paying the payroll?

## EXERCISES

1. Compute the gross earnings for each of the following employees of the Harris County Memorial Hospital for the week ended August 27. Employees are paid 1½ times their hourly rate for all hours worked over 40 each week.

| Employee | Hourly Rate | Number of Hours | Withholding Allowances |
|---|---|---|---|
| Debbi Smith | $5.80 | 51 | 2 |
| Tony Pizon | 6.10 | 50 | 4 |
| Jerry Young | 5.40 | 56 | 5 |

2. Assuming that all employees in Exercise 1 are married, determine the federal income tax to be withheld from each of their paychecks for the week ended August 27, using the withholding table on page 206.

3. Determine the FICA tax to be withheld from each of the following employees (use 7% rate on $25,000):

| Employee | Earnings Prior to This Week | Earnings This Week |
|---|---|---|
| A | $26,400 | $2,370 |
| B | 8,200 | 910 |
| C | 24,600 | 1,460 |
| D | 17,370 | 1,150 |

4. Crissy Hellums is employed by the University Book Store at the rate of $5.80 per hour, with 1½ times the regular rate for all hours worked over

40 each week. Information to be considered for Hellum's pay for the week ended September 17 of the current year is as follows:

hours worked, 51;
federal income tax to be withheld, $39.10;
earnings this year prior to this week, $4,730;
deduction for health insurance, $9.00.

(a) For the week ended September 17 compute (1) Hellum's gross earnings, (2) FICA tax to be withheld from her pay (use 7% rate on $25,000) and (3) Hellum's net earnings.
(b) Prepare the general journal entry to record Hellum's pay on the books of her employer.

**ASSIGNMENT 10-A**

**Tear out pages 499–504 and complete Assignment 10-A. After submitting your papers for approval, proceed with the following discussion until the next assignment is required.**

# PART B EMPLOYER'S PAYROLL TAXES AND PAYROLL RECORDS

The payroll deductions discussed in Part A were all deducted from the employees' gross pay. The income tax and FICA tax withheld are in effect paid by the employees and do not result in an additional expense to the business. This part of the chapter discusses the payroll taxes imposed on the employer and how these taxes are recorded and paid. The various payroll records kept for each employee are also presented.

## EMPLOYER'S PAYROLL TAXES

In addition to the taxes that must be paid by the employees and withheld from their pay, there are certain payroll taxes imposed on the employer. These taxes are the employer's share of the FICA tax, the federal unemployment tax, and the state unemployment tax.

### FICA Tax

The Federal Insurance Contributions Act requires payment of social security tax by both the employer and the employee. The law requires the employer to pay FICA tax at the same rate and on the same earnings base as is used in computing the employee portions of the tax. For illustration purposes in this text, the employer is required to pay 7% on the first $25,000 earned by each employee. Any wages paid to an employee during the year in excess of $25,000 are exempt from this tax. The FICA tax paid by the employer is an expense of the business and is properly recorded in the books as a payroll tax expense.

## Federal Unemployment Compensation Tax

The Federal Unemployment Tax Act provides unemployment insurance for those persons who become unemployed and are covered by the act. Federal unemployment tax must be paid by an employer who (a) paid wages of $1,500 or more in any calendar quarter, or (b) had one or more employees at any time in each of 20 or more calendar weeks.

The federal unemployment tax rate is 3.4% on the first $6,000 of wages paid to each employee during the calendar year. A credit of up to 2.7% on the first $6,000 may be taken for timely contributions paid by employers into state unemployment funds. Since all states participate in the unemployment program, the effective rate of the federal unemployment tax is only .7%. This money is used by the federal government to administer the state programs. No employee benefits are paid from federal funds.

The federal unemployment tax is imposed only on employers. It represents a business expense to the employer and is recorded in the payroll tax expense accounts.

## State Unemployment Compensation Tax

All fifty states and the District of Columbia have adopted unemployment compensation laws providing for cash payments to qualified unemployed workers. The money paid to unemployed persons comes from the state unemployment tax. In most states, the plan is financed entirely by taxes levied against the employers. However, in a few states the employees are also required to contribute to the plan, and in these states the employee's share of the tax is obtained through payroll deductions.

There is some variation in the state laws concerning coverage, tax rates, tax bases, and benefits available to qualified workers. Many states have *merit ratings* which provide tax-saving incentives by reducing the rate charged to companies that maintain steady employment and experience low employee turnover.

## Recording Payroll Taxes

All payroll taxes levied against the employer under federal and state laws are business expenses of the company. As indicated above, one expense account, Payroll Taxes Expense, is normally debited for all of these taxes.

The employer's payroll taxes are usually recorded at the end of each payroll period. This procedure is desirable so that the employer's expense and the liability for such taxes are recorded in the same period as the payroll on which the taxes are based.

The basic data needed to determine the employer's payroll taxes are provided by the payroll register. The payroll register appearing on pages 210 and 211 shows that the earnings subject to FICA tax are $1,122.50 (Column 11) and those subject to unemployment taxes are $542.50 (Column 12). If the company is subject to a state unemployment tax rate of 2.7%, the employer's payroll taxes for the week are computed as follows:

| | |
|---|---:|
| FICA tax — 7% of $1,122.50 | $78.58 |
| Federal unemployment tax — .7% of $542.50 | 3.80 |
| State unemployment tax — 2.7% of $542.50 | 14.65 |
| Total payroll taxes | $97.03 |

The journal entry to record the employer's payroll taxes expense and the related liabilities for the various taxes is shown below.

| Date | Account | Debit | Credit |
|---|---|---:|---:|
| 26 | **Payroll Taxes Expense** | **97 03** | |
| | **FICA Tax Payable** | | **78 58** |
| | **Federal Unemployment Tax Pay...** | | **3 80** |
| | **State Unemployment Tax Pay.** | | **14 65** |
| | **Payroll taxes for week ended November 26.** | | |

After the preceding entry has been posted, the accounts affected by the payroll transactions in this chapter appear in T-account form as follows:

**SALARY EXPENSE**

| Debit | | Credit | |
|---|---:|---|---:|
| Nov. 26 | 2,297.00 | | |

**UNION DUES PAYABLE**

| Debit | | Credit | |
|---|---:|---|---:|
| Nov. 30 | 25.00 | Nov. 26 | 25.00 |

**PAYROLL TAXES EXPENSE**

| Debit | | Credit | |
|---|---:|---|---:|
| Nov. 26 | 97.03 | | |

**FEDERAL UNEMPLOYMENT TAX PAYABLE**

| Debit | | Credit | |
|---|---:|---|---:|
| | | Nov. 26 | 3.80 |

**EMPLOYEES' INCOME TAX PAYABLE**

| Debit | | Credit | |
|---|---:|---|---:|
| | | Nov. 26 | 389.00 |

**STATE UNEMPLOYMENT TAX PAYABLE**

| Debit | | Credit | |
|---|---:|---|---:|
| | | Nov. 26 | 14.65 |

**FICA TAX PAYABLE**

| Debit | | Credit | |
|---|---:|---|---:|
| | | Nov. 26 | 78.58 |
| | | 26 | 78.58 |
| | | | *157.16* |

**SALARIES PAYABLE**

| Debit | | Credit | |
|---|---:|---|---:|
| Nov. 30 | 1,781.42 | Nov. 26 | 1,781.42 |

**HEALTH INSURANCE PAYABLE**

| Debit | | Credit | |
|---|---:|---|---:|
| | | Nov. 26 | 23.00 |

Note that the liability for FICA tax payable totals $157.16, which represents both the amount deducted from the employees' earnings ($78.58) and the employer's expense ($78.58).

## PAYING WITHHOLDING TAXES AND PAYROLL TAXES

The income tax and FICA tax withheld from the employees' wages, as well as the employer's share of FICA tax, and state and federal unemployment taxes, are recorded on the books of the employer as current liabilities until they are paid. The regulations concerning the payment of each of these taxes to the proper authorities are discussed in the following sections.

### Employees' Income Tax and FICA Tax

The employees' federal income tax and FICA tax withheld *plus* the employer's share of FICA tax are payable quarterly by the last day of the month following the end of the calendar quarter. However, if the combined amount of these taxes exceeds $500 at the end of any month of the quarter, this total must be paid by depositing the amount by the 15th of the following month in the District Federal Reserve Bank or any commercial bank qualified as a depository for federal taxes. More frequent payments are due when the combined amount of these taxes exceeds $3,000 during any month.

To illustrate the procedures involved in the payment of these taxes, assume that Ganzer's payroll for the week of November 26 was the only payroll paid during the month; therefore, the figures shown in the T-accounts above would represent the totals for the month. A check would be written for $546.16 ($389.00 employees' income tax plus $157.16 FICA tax) and deposited by December 15 in a depository or Federal Reserve bank. The entry, in general journal form, to record this transaction is:

| | | | | |
|---|---|---|---|---|
| Dec. | 15 | Employees' Income Tax Payable | 389.00 | |
| | | FICA Tax Payable | 157.16 | |
| | | Cash | | 546.16 |

The Employer's Quarterly Federal Tax Return (Form 941) for employees' federal income tax withheld and FICA tax must be filed by employers by the last day of the month following the end of a calendar quarter.

### State Unemployment Tax

Although requirements for reporting and paying state unemployment tax vary from state to state, as a general rule employers are required to pay these taxes on or before the last day of the month following each calendar quarter. Assuming that the Ganzer Dairy has a liability for state unemployment tax of $138.64 for the October to December quarter, the entry, in general journal form, to record payment of the liability is:

| | | | | |
|---|---|---|---|---|
| Jan. | 31 | State Unemployment Tax Payable | 138.64 | |
| | | Cash | | 138.64 |

## Federal Unemployment Tax

Federal unemployment tax is paid annually by January 31 of the following year if the annual total is less than $100. The payment must be accompanied by an unemployment tax return (Form 940). If the liability is $100 or more, it is paid quarterly or after the calendar quarter in which it reaches $100. Like the other federal taxes discussed, the federal unemployment tax is paid by depositing the amount with an authorized depository or Federal Reserve bank.

If Ganzer Dairy had a federal unemployment tax of $91.40 for the calendar year, the entry in general journal form to record payment of the liability by January 31 of the following year would be:

| | | | | |
|---|---|---|---|---|
| Jan. | 31 | Federal Unemployment Tax Payable.................... | 91.40 | |
| | | Cash ..................................................................... | | 91.40 |

# PAYROLL RECORDS

Every business subject to any of the employment taxes described in this chapter is required to keep all records pertinent to these taxes available for inspection by the Internal Revenue Service and other federal and state agencies. These payroll records also provide valuable data to management for internal decisions and employee evaluation. No specific form is required for such records, but they should include: the amounts and dates of all wage payments subject to these taxes; the names, addresses, and social security numbers of employees receiving these wages; the periods of employment; wage rates; sick pay received; income tax withholding allowance certificates; the employer's identification number; copies of returns filed; and receipts of deposits made.

The records are required to be kept for a period of at least four years after the date the taxes to which they relate become due, or the date the taxes are paid, whichever is later.

## Employee's Earnings Record

A separate record should be kept of each employee's earnings to facilitate the preparation of the various federal, state, and local reports required of employers, and also to provide the employee with earnings and withholding information at the end of the year. The employee's earnings record may also be used to provide information concerning sick leave, accrued vacation, bonuses, and pensions. The payroll register, discussed earlier in this chapter, is a record of the earnings and deductions of all employees of the business for each payroll period, whereas the earnings record is a summary of the annual earnings of each employee.

Forms used for the employee's earnings record vary, but all show essentially the same information. An example of an earnings record for David Osborne, an employee of Ganzer Dairy, is shown at the top of page 219.

The form presented is essentially self-explanatory. The top section is used to record personal data about the employee such as name,

**EMPLOYEE'S EARNINGS RECORD**

NAME David Osborne | SOC. SEC. NO. 433-72-1879

ADDRESS 1571 Bradford Lane, Madison, WI 53714-3284 | DATE OF BIRTH Dec. 7, 1951

PHONE 262-7685 | RATE 13.00 | NO. OF ALLOWANCES 4

| PAY PERIOD ENDING | HOURS WORKED | | EARNINGS | | | | DEDUCTIONS | | | | | NET PAY |
|---|---|---|---|---|---|---|---|---|---|---|---|---|
| | REGULAR | OVERTIME | REGULAR | OVERTIME | TOTAL | TOTAL YEAR-TO-DATE | FICA | FED. INCOME TAX | HEALTH INS. | UNION DUES | TOTAL | |
| Oct. 1 | 40 | 6 | 520.00 | 117.00 | 637.00 | 20,407.00 | 44.59 | 120.10 | 5.00 | 5.00 | 174.69 | 462.31 |
| 8 | 40 | 9 | 520.00 | 175.50 | 695.50 | 21,102.50 | 48.69 | 142.30 | 5.00 | 5.00 | 200.99 | 494.51 |
| 15 | 40 | 8 | 520.00 | 156.00 | 676.00 | 21,778.50 | 47.32 | 134.90 | 5.00 | 5.00 | 192.22 | 483.78 |
| 22 | 40 | 7 | 520.00 | 136.50 | 656.50 | 22,435.00 | 45.96 | 127.50 | 5.00 | 5.00 | 183.46 | 473.04 |
| 29 | 40 | 5 | 520.00 | 97.50 | 617.50 | 23,052.50 | 43.23 | 113.60 | 5.00 | 5.00 | 166.83 | 450.67 |
| Nov. 5 | 40 | 9 | 520.00 | 175.50 | 695.50 | 23,748.00 | 48.69 | 142.30 | 5.00 | 5.00 | 200.99 | 494.51 |
| 12 | 40 | 8 | 520.00 | 156.00 | 676.00 | 24,424.00 | 47.32 | 134.90 | 5.00 | 5.00 | 192.22 | 483.78 |
| 19 | 40 | 6 | 520.00 | 117.00 | 637.00 | 25,061.00 | 40.32 | 120.10 | 5.00 | 5.00 | 170.42 | 466.58 |
| 26 | 40 | 7 | 520.00 | 136.50 | 656.50 | 25,717.50 | — | 127.50 | 5.00 | 5.00 | 137.50 | 519.00 |
| 4th QUARTER TOTALS | | | 7,280.00 | 2,086.50 | 9,366.50 | — | 366.12 | 1,852.50 | 70.00 | 70.00 | 2,358.62 | 7,007.88 |

***Employee's Earnings Record***

address, social security number, and number of withholding allowances. The bottom section of the form provides space for details relating to each payroll period (in this case each week), quarterly totals, and total earnings to date. The column headings are very similar to those on the payroll register.

It should be noted that during the week of November 19, Osborne's cumulative earnings went over the $25,000 FICA maximum. His cumulative earnings for the week ended November 12 were $24,424; therefore, he lacked only $576 to reach the $25,000 limit. Osborne's FICA tax for the week of November 19 was $40.32 (7% of $576.00), and his earnings for the remainder of the year will not be subject to FICA tax. The $25,061 total earnings at November 19, is the amount shown on the November 26 payroll register (pages 210 and 211) in the Earnings to Date column.

## Wage and Tax Statement (Form W-2)

Businesses must provide each employee with a statement of total earnings and total income and FICA tax deductions for the year. This statement is made on a Form W-2, Wage and Tax Statement, and must be given to the employee on or before January 31, of the following year. In the case of an employee leaving the service of an employer before the end of the year, the Form W-2 must be furnished to the employee within 30 days after the last wages are paid if the employee so requests.

The Form W-2 is prepared in four copies, with the original (Copy A) being sent to the Social Security Administration; Copies B and C are given to the employee, and Copy D is retained by the employer.

Copy B of Form W-2 must be submitted with the employee's income tax return. A completed Form W-2 for David Osborne for the year ending December 31, 1982, is shown below. The Form W-2 is prepared from the information on the employee earnings record.

| | | |
|---|---|---|
| 1 Control number: 22222 | For Official Use Only | |
| 2 Employer's name, address, and ZIP code<br>GANZER DAIRY<br>22 ALPINE ROAD<br>MADISON, WI 53714-4576 | 3 Employer's identification number<br>00-0000000 | 4 Employer's State number |
| | 5 Stat. employee ☐ Deceased ☐ Pension plan ☐ Legal rep. ☐ 942 emp. ☐ Subtotal ☐ Correction ☐ Void ☐ | |
| | 6 • | 7 Advance EIC payment |
| 8 Employee's social security number: 433-72-1879<br>9 Federal income tax withheld: $5,086.20 | 10 Wages, tips, other compensation<br>$29,136.00 | 11 FICA tax withheld<br>$1,750.00 |
| 12 Employee's name (first, middle, last) | 13 FICA wages<br>$25,000.00 | 14 FICA tips |
| DAVID OSBORNE<br>1571 BRADFORD LANE<br>MADISON, WI 53714-3284 | 16 Employer's use | |
| | 17 State income tax / 18 State wages, tips, etc. | 19 Name of State |
| 15 Employee's address and ZIP code | 20 Local income tax / 21 Local wages, tips, etc. | 22 Name of locality |

Form **W-2 Wage and Tax Statement 19--** Copy A For Social Security Administration • See Instructions for Forms W-2 and W-2P Department of the Treasury Internal Revenue Service

***Wage and Tax Statement (Form W-2)***

## QUESTIONS FOR DISCUSSION

1. What three payroll taxes are imposed on the employer?
2. What is the wage base that is used for computing the Federal Unemployment Compensation Tax?
3. Explain how and when FICA taxes are paid.
4. What information should be recorded in the payroll records of a company?
5. (a) What is an employee's earnings record?
   (b) What information should be recorded in this record?
6. (a) What is a Form W-2?
   (b) What information is provided on this statement?
   (c) When is this statement given to the employee?

## EXERCISES

1. Harold Okura is a computer programmer employed at an hourly rate of $9.20, with time and one-half for all hours over 40 each week. Okura worked 44 hours during the week ended February 27 and had cumulative earnings prior to that week of $2,625. Okura has deductions of $7.20 for medical insurance and $10 for a savings plan with the company credit union. Tax rates for federal and state unemployment and FICA are .7%, 2.7%, and 7%, respectively. Okura is married and claims 4 withholding allowances. Prepare the general journal entry to record Okura's payroll on the books of his employer for the week ended February 27.

2. Using the information in Exercise 1, prepare the general journal entry to record the payroll taxes expense for Harold Okura on the books of his employer for the week ended February 27.

3. You are given the following payroll information for the Northwest Logging Company for the week ended September 20:

| Earnings subject to: | | Earnings: | | Deductions: | |
|---|---|---|---|---|---|
| FICA | $9,666.00 | Regular rate | $7,160.00 | Income tax | $1,256.00 |
| Unemployment | 1,950.00 | Overtime | 2,506.00 | FICA | 676.62 |
| | | Total | $9,666.00 | Insurance | 140.00 |

(a) Prepare the entry to record the payroll for the Northwest Logging Company for the week ended September 20. (b) Prepare the entry to record Northwest Logging's payroll taxes expense for the week, assuming a federal unemployment tax rate of .7% and a state unemployment tax rate of 2.7%.

**ASSIGNMENT 10-B**

**Tear out pages 505–510 and complete Assignment 10-B. Submit your papers to your instructor for approval and continue with Part C until the next assignment is required.**

# PART C INTERNAL CONTROL; THE VOUCHER SYSTEM

The organization plan and the procedures used to control business operations are referred to as a *system of internal control*. A main component that is used when attempting to obtain good internal control is a voucher system. A *voucher system* consists of the records and procedures involved in approving expenditures, verifying liabilities, and issuing checks for their payment. The records used in a voucher system include the vouchers, a voucher register, an unpaid voucher file, a paid voucher file, and a check register. Part C of this chapter is devoted to an explanation of the basic principles of internal control and the basic features of a voucher system, with emphasis on recording vouchers in a voucher register.

An effective system of internal control establishes operating procedures within a firm to:

1. Protect the assets of the firm.
2. Provide accurate accounting information.
3. Promote efficient operations.
4. Require adherence to established company policies.

Every business requires the use of internal control procedures. One common example is the use of a checking account. A checking account provides a dual record of cash receipts and disbursements, assures control over cash receipts and cash payments by making deposits and by writing checks, respectively, and allows a monthly reconciliation of the cash account to be made. Cash registers, sales invoices, checkwriters, and petty cash funds are other examples of basic devices included in a system of internal control.

## Basic Principles of Internal Control

Although the details of a system of internal control must be flexible enough to meet the needs of the individual business, every system should adhere to the following basic principles:

**Clearly Defined Responsibility.** For maximum efficiency, each employee's responsibilities should be clearly defined. For example, in handling cash receipts within a given department, all sales clerks should have their own sales books and separate drawers in the cash register, allowing a daily proof of cash for each employee. In addition, the system should insure that there are no duplications of effort or undefined areas of responsibility.

**Division of Responsibilities for a Sequence of Operations.** One of the most important principles of an effective system of internal control is the division of duties among different employees for a sequence of related operations. No one employee should be allowed to receive cash, balance the cash at the end of the day, post to the accounts receivable ledger, make the bank deposit, and reconcile the bank statement. If one person is responsible for this sequence of events, it would be very easy for that person to cover cash shortages and discrepancies, at least on a temporary basis. Likewise, no one employee should be allowed to order merchandise, verify the receipt of the goods, and pay the invoices. The separation of the duties encourages each employee to be more careful in the performance of these duties and reduces the temptation of a dishonest act.

For example, if an employee has the responsibility of ordering merchandise but will not receive the goods or pay the invoices, that person would not consider preparing orders from fictitious companies or listing goods as received unless they were actually on hand. Frequently, a purchase order is sent to the receiving department with the quantities omitted. This requires the employee receiving and counting the goods to do a thorough job of checking the goods received and entering the quantities on a receiving report. The accounting department then compares the purchase order with the receiving report to ensure that the quantities agree.

**Division of Responsibilities for Operations and Accounting.** The responsibility for the safekeeping of assets should not be assigned to the same persons responsible for keeping the accounting records. Separation of responsibility allows the accounting records to provide an independent verification of operations. For example, an employee who receives payments from customers on account should not have the responsibility of posting to the accounts receivable subsidiary ledger.

**Trained Personnel.** The success of any accounting system depends largely on the capabilities of the personnel operating it. It is imperative, therefore, that employees be properly trained and supervised in the duties they are expected to perform. A job description and checklist of duties for each employee is also highly desirable.

**Rotation of Jobs.** Whenever possible, the employees involved in the bookkeeping and office duties should be rotated from job to job for a short period of time. Knowing that someone else will perform their duties at a later date encourages employees to follow prescribed procedures. Rotation also provides valuable cross-training of employees which enhances flexibility of job assignments in case of sickness or sudden termination.

**Adequate Security Precautions.** Proper security procedures should be required to protect the assets of the business and provide reliable accounting information. Many of the techniques and procedures that should be used have been discussed in earlier chapters. Examples include daily deposits of cash on hand, use of checks for all cash payments, and storage of valuable contracts and other documents in a safe or bank safety-deposit box. The use of various types of mechanical equipment, such as cash registers, checkwriters, ticket machines in theatres, and automatic counters in athletic stadiums, also provides excellent control features.

**Periodic Evaluation of the Effectiveness of the System.** As a check on the effectiveness of the system of internal control, a periodic review should be conducted by someone not involved in the day-to-day operations. In large organizations, a staff of internal auditors is normally used. In small firms, the owner or the appropriate company officer may perform this task. Certified public accountants can also be employed to evaluate the effectiveness of a company's system of internal control.

## THE VOUCHER SYSTEM

One basic feature of a good internal control system is the payment of all invoices by check. In small businesses, the owner is usually responsible for the purchasing of all goods and services and, therefore, has personal knowledge that the terms of all contracts have been complied with and that the amounts shown on the invoices are correct. In larger businesses, the responsibilities for placing orders, checking goods received, and verifying and extending invoice amounts are normally divided among several employees or departments. An effective system of record keeping designed to coordinate these related activities and to maximize internal control over cash disbursements is the voucher system.

## Preparing the Voucher

A *voucher* is a form used to record specific information about a purchase and the approval of its payment. The completed voucher normally represents written authorization to make a payment. A voucher form is illustrated below and on page 225.

The front of the voucher provides space for recording the date it is prepared, the voucher number, the name and address of the creditor (payee), and the details of the liability, such as the invoice number, date, amount, and credit terms. The back of the voucher often contains spaces for the account distribution and the voucher and payment summaries.

The voucher is usually prepared by the accounting department after the following verifications have been made:

1. The invoice is in agreement with the purchase order as to quantities, prices, and terms.
2. The invoice is in agreement with the receiving report.
3. The extensions and total of the invoice have been verified.

When the above verifications have been completed, the invoice is attached to the voucher and presented for final approval and subsequent payment.

Voucher
***WARDLOW HARDWARE***
*101 Main Street*
*Denver, CO 80204-6337*

Date: May 14, 1982 Voucher No.: 221

Payee: FAIRFAX DISTRIBUTING CO.
1512 FAIRFAX AVENUE
DENVER, CO 80222-1479
Terms: 2/10, n/30

| DATE | DETAILS | AMOUNT |
|---|---|---|
| May 10, 1982 | Invoice No. 649-0 | 205.00 |

Attach Supporting Documents

***Voucher – Front***

| ACCOUNT DISTRIBUTION | | |
|---|---|---|
| **Debit** | **Amount** | |
| Purchases | 205 | 00 |
| Office Supplies | | |
| Store Supplies | | |
| Advertising Expenses | | |
| Misc. Selling Expenses | | |
| Misc. General Expenses | | |
| | | |
| | | |
| | | |
| Credit Accounts Payable | 205 | 00 |
| Distribution Approved *James Allen* | | |

**VOUCHER**

Date 5/14/82 No. 221
Due 5/20/82

FAIRFAX DISTRIBUTING CO.
1512 FAIRFAX AVENUE
DENVER, CO 80222-1479

| Voucher Summary | | |
|---|---|---|
| Amount | 205 | 00 |
| Discount | 4 | 10 |
| Net | 200 | 90 |

Approved *Joseph Wardlow*
Recorded *MB*

**Payment Summary**

Date 5/20/82
Amount 200.90 Ck. No. 460
Approved *D. S. Strietmann*
Recorded *LR*

***Voucher – Back***

# THE VOUCHER REGISTER

When the voucher has been approved, it is recorded in a special journal called a *voucher register*. The voucher register accomplishes many of the same purposes as the purchases journal described in Chapter 7. When a voucher register is used, it replaces a purchases journal as one of the books of original entry. A common form of voucher register is illustrated on pages 226 and 227.

**Entries in the Voucher Register.** Vouchers are recorded in the voucher register in numerical order. Since the purpose of issuing a voucher is to authorize the payment of a bill, the credit entry in the voucher register will always be to Accounts Payable, also called Vouchers Payable. Consequently, the only credit column required in the voucher register is Accounts Payable Cr. For ease of recording, this is usually the first column in a voucher register. The debit entries in the voucher register are made to the account or accounts charged with the expenditure. Special debit columns are provided for those accounts used often enough to justify them. For example, any business that purchases merchandise will have a special column for Purchases Dr. The headings of the other debit columns depend on the specific needs of the business. In the illustration on pages 226 and 227, special columns are provided for Purchases Dr., Store Supplies Dr., and Office Supplies Dr.

**Proving the Voucher Register Columns.** As in all journals, the special columns in the voucher register are provided to facilitate the recording and posting process and to reduce the possibility of errors. Prior to posting, the columns in the voucher register are footed and

| DATE | | VOU. NO. | PAYEE | PAID DATE | | PAID CK. NO. | ACCOUNTS PAYABLE CR. |
|---|---|---|---|---|---|---|---|
| 1982 | | | | | | | |
| May | 3 | 218 | Adelman Supplies | May | 17 | 457 | 60 00 |
| | 4 | 219 | Lee Company | May | 18 | 458 | 110 00 |
| | 10 | 220 | Daily Globe | May | 20 | 459 | 30 00 |
| | 14 | 221 | Fairfax Distributing Co. | May | 20 | 460 | 205 00 |
| | 18 | 222 | Parker Store Supplies | May | 24 | 461 | 60 00 |
| | 20 | 223 | Brockman Co. | May | 27 | 462 | 35 00 |
| | 24 | 224 | P. R. Wholesalers | | | | 80 00 |
| | 25 | 225 | Parker Store Supplies | May | 30 | 463 | 75 00 |
| | 27 | 226 | Fairfax Distributing Co. | | | | 100 00 |
| | 31 | 227 | Adelman Supplies | | | | 45 00 |
| | | | | | | | 800 00 |
| | 31 | | | | | | 800 00 |
| | | | | | | | (22) |

*Voucher Register – Wardlow Hardware (Left Page)*

these totals are then proved. The sum of all the debit column totals must equal the total of the Accounts Payable Cr. column. A schedule to prove the column totals of the voucher register above is prepared as follows:

| Debit Columns | | Credit Column | |
|---|---|---|---|
| Purchases | $530 | Accounts Payable | $800 |
| Store Supplies | 135 | | |
| Office Supplies | 105 | | |
| General Accounts | 30 | | |
| | $800 | | $800 |

After the voucher register is totaled and ruled, each of the special columns is posted to the general ledger by total. The number of the account to which each special column is posted is written in parentheses below the column total. The items in the General Accounts Dr. column are posted individually; therefore, the column total is not posted. A check mark is placed below this column total to indicate that it is not posted.

When a voucher is paid, the date of payment and number of the check issued in payment are entered in the appropriate columns in the register. This procedure allows the determination at any time of the number and amount of unpaid vouchers. For example, a schedule of unpaid vouchers at May 31 for Wardlow Hardware, prepared from the illustration above and on page 227, is as follows:

Wardlow Hardware
Schedule of Unpaid Vouchers
May 31, 1982

| Voucher No. | Payee | Amount |
|---|---|---|
| 224 | P.R. Wholesalers | $ 80 |
| 226 | Fairfax Distributing Co. | 100 |
| 227 | Adelman Supplies | 45 |
| | | $225 |

REGISTER PAGE 6

| | PURCHASES DR. | STORE SUPPLIES DR. | OFFICE SUPPLIES DR. | GENERAL ACCOUNTS DR. ACCOUNT | POST. REF. | AMOUNT | |
|---|---|---|---|---|---|---|---|
| 1 | | | 60 00 | | | | 1 |
| 2 | 110 00 | | | | | | 2 |
| 3 | | | | Advertising Expense | 63 | 30 00 | 3 |
| 4 | 205 00 | | | | | | 4 |
| 5 | | 60 00 | | | | | 5 |
| 6 | 35 00 | | | | | | 6 |
| 7 | 80 00 | | | | | | 7 |
| 8 | | 75 00 | | | | | 8 |
| 9 | 100 00 | | | | | | 9 |
| 10 | | | 45 00 | | | | 10 |
| 11 | 530 00 | 135 00 | 105 00 | | | 30 00 | 11 |
| 12 | 530 00 | 135 00 | 105 00 | | | 30 00 | 12 |
| 13 | (51) | (14) | (15) | | | (√) | 13 |
| 14 | | | | | | | 14 |
| 15 | | | | | | | 15 |
| 16 | | | | | | | 16 |
| 17 | | | | | | | 17 |
| 18 | | | | | | | 18 |

*Voucher Register – Wardlow Hardware (Right Page)*

## FILING UNPAID VOUCHERS

When a voucher system is used, a voucher must be prepared for each expenditure, and checks are issued only in payment of properly approved vouchers. Some vouchers will be paid immediately and the payment of others will be delayed, depending upon the credit terms of the invoice.

If a voucher is not to be paid immediately, it is filed in an unpaid voucher file until its due date. Each unpaid voucher represents a credit to accounts payable, and the individual vouchers represent an accounts payable subsidiary record. Consequently, a separate subsidiary ledger for accounts payable is not necessary when the voucher system is used. The total of the unpaid vouchers should always equal the balance in the accounts payable control account.

The accounts payable account for Wardlow Hardware as of May 31 would appear as follows after all vouchers and payments have been posted.

ACCOUNT **Accounts Payable** ACCOUNT NO. **22**

| DATE | | ITEM | POST. REF. | DEBIT | CREDIT | BALANCE DEBIT | BALANCE CREDIT |
|---|---|---|---|---|---|---|---|
| 1982 | | | | | | | |
| May | 31 | | VR6 | | 800 00 | | 800 00 |
| | 31 | | CP8 | 575 00 | | | 225 00 |

Every voucher system should provide for the payment of all vouchers within the discount period. The unpaid vouchers may be filed using a folder file. The folders are numbered from 1 to 31, representing the days of the month, and the unpaid vouchers are filed according to the due date (last day of discount period, if applicable). When a voucher becomes due, it is removed from the unpaid voucher file and a check is prepared for its payment. The date, number, and the amount of the check are recorded on the back of the voucher. These notations on the voucher plus stamping "PAID" on the supporting documents prevent accidental or intentional reuse.

The account balance, $225, agrees with the total in the schedule of unpaid vouchers shown on page 226. The debit entry to the account represents the vouchers paid during the month.

## FILING PAID VOUCHERS

After payment, vouchers should be filed numerically in a paid voucher file. This method provides a convenient reference to specific information concerning expenditures. In larger firms, vouchers are often prepared in duplicate and the second copy of the paid voucher is then filed alphabetically in a creditor file.

## CHECK REGISTER

The voucher system provides a business with control over ordering, approving, and recording purchases and other expenditures. To complete the system of control over the expenditures and liabilities of a business, all payments of approved vouchers are made by check. These payments are recorded in a special journal called the *check register*.

The check register is a complete record of all checks issued by the business. It is similar to, and takes the place of, the cash payments journal.

A standard form of check register is presented below.

**CHECK REGISTER** PAGE 8

| | DATE | | CK. NO. | PAYEE | VOU. NO. | ACCOUNTS PAYABLE DR. | PURCHASES DISCOUNT CR. | CASH CR. | |
|---|---|---|---|---|---|---|---|---|---|
| | 1982 | | | | | | | | |
| 1 | May | 17 | 457 | Adelman Supplies | 218 | 60 00 | | 60 00 | 1 |
| 2 | | 18 | 458 | Lee Supplies | 219 | 110 00 | | 110 00 | 2 |
| 3 | | 20 | 459 | Daily Globe | 220 | 30 00 | | 30 00 | 3 |
| 4 | | 20 | 460 | Fairfax Distributing Co. | 221 | 205 00 | 4 10 | 200 90 | 4 |
| 5 | | 24 | 461 | Parker Store Supplies | 222 | 60 00 | | 60 00 | 5 |
| 6 | | 27 | 462 | Brockman Co. | 223 | 35 00 | | 35 00 | 6 |
| 7 | | 30 | 463 | Parker Store Supplies | 225 | 75 00 | | 75 00 | 7 |
| 8 | | | | | | 575 00 | 4 10 | 570 90 | 8 |
| 9 | | 31 | | | | 575 00 | 4 10 | 570 90 | 9 |
| 10 | | | | | | (22) | (51.1) | (11) | 10 |
| 11 | | | | | | | | | 11 |
| 12 | | | | | | | | | 12 |
| 13 | | | | | | | | | 13 |
| 14 | | | | | | | | | 14 |
| 15 | | | | | | | | | 15 |
| 16 | | | | | | | | | 16 |

***Check Register – Wardlow Hardware***

Every check issued is in payment of a voucher that has been recorded in the voucher register. All vouchers in the voucher register are recorded as credits to Accounts Payable; therefore, each entry in the check register represents a debit to Accounts Payable and a credit to Cash. When discounts are allowed on purchases, a Purchases Discount Cr. column is also provided in the check register.

## VOUCHER REGISTER AND CHECK REGISTER ILLUSTRATED

The following information relating to the voucher system of Wardlow Hardware for the month of June, is presented to provide a detailed illustration of the recording of transactions in the voucher register and the check register and the postings from these registers.

The cash and accounts payable accounts in the general ledger as of June 1 are as follows:

ACCOUNT **Cash** ACCOUNT NO. **11**

| DATE | | ITEM | POST. REF. | DEBIT | CREDIT | BALANCE DEBIT | BALANCE CREDIT |
|---|---|---|---|---|---|---|---|
| 1982 June | 1 | Balance | √ | | | 485 00 | |

ACCOUNT **Accounts Payable** ACCOUNT NO. **22**

| DATE | | ITEM | POST. REF. | DEBIT | CREDIT | BALANCE DEBIT | BALANCE CREDIT |
|---|---|---|---|---|---|---|---|
| 1982 June | 1 | Balance | √ | | | | 225 00 |

The schedule of unpaid vouchers for Wardlow Hardware on May 31 was shown on page 226.

The unpaid vouchers total $225, which agrees with the Accounts Payable balance in the general ledger. These unpaid vouchers represent the subsidiary accounts for accounts payable; therefore, a separate subsidiary ledger is unnecessary.

The following selected transactions relating to purchases, expenses, and payments were completed by Wardlow Hardware during the month of June.

June 1. Issued Check No. 464 to P.R. Wholesalers for Voucher No. 224, $80 less a 2% discount.
2. Recorded Voucher No. 228 payable to Harvey Realty for monthly rent, $125.
2. Issued Check No. 465 in payment of Voucher No. 228.
3. Recorded Voucher No. 229 payable to Lee Company for merchandise purchased, $140.
5. Issued Check No. 466 to Fairfax Distributing Co. in payment of Voucher No. 226, $100 less a 2% discount.
9. Recorded Voucher No. 230 payable to Parker Store Supplies for store supplies purchased, $35.
9. Issued Check No. 467 to Lee Company in payment of Voucher No. 229, $140.
10. Issued Check No. 468 to Adelman Supplies in payment of Voucher No. 227, $45.
11. Recorded Voucher No. 231 payable to Adelman Supplies for office supplies purchased, $47.
14. Issued Check No. 469 to Parker Store Supplies in payment of Voucher No. 230, $35.
18. Recorded Voucher No. 232 to Parker Store Supplies for store supplies purchased, $55.
19. Issued Check No. 470 to Adelman Supplies in payment of Voucher No. 231, $47.

PAGE 7 VOUCHER

| DATE | | VOU. NO. | PAYEE | PAID DATE | | PAID CK. NO. | ACCOUNTS PAYABLE CR. |
|---|---|---|---|---|---|---|---|
| 1982 | | | | | | | |
| June | 2 | 228 | Harvey Realty | June | 2 | 465 | 125 00 |
| | 3 | 229 | Lee Company | June | 9 | 467 | 140 00 |
| | 9 | 230 | Parker Store Supplies | June | 14 | 469 | 35 00 |
| | 11 | 231 | Adelman Supplies | June | 19 | 470 | 47 00 |
| | 18 | 232 | Parker Store Supplies | | | | 55 00 |
| | 21 | 233 | Daily Globe | June | 21 | 471 | 30 00 |
| | 22 | 234 | Fairfax Distributing Co. | June | 30 | 472 | 220 00 |
| | 24 | 235 | Adelman Supplies | | | | 33 00 |
| | 28 | 236 | P. R. Wholesalers | | | | 95 00 |
| | | | | | | | 780 00 |
| | 30 | | | | | | 780 00 |
| | | | | | | | (22) |

*Voucher Register – Wardlow Hardware (Left Page)*

21. Recorded Voucher No. 233 to Daily Globe for advertising, $30.
21. Issued Check No. 471 in payment of Voucher No. 233, $30.
22. Recorded Voucher No. 234 to Fairfax Distributing Co. for merchandise purchased, $220.
24. Recorded Voucher No. 235 to Adelman Supplies for office supplies purchased, $33.
28. Recorded Voucher No. 236 to P.R. Wholesalers for merchandise purchased, $95.
30. Issued Check No. 472 to Fairfax Distributing Co. in payment of Voucher No. 234, $220 less a 2% discount.

The voucher register and check register of Wardlow Hardware, after these transactions have been recorded, would appear as shown on this page and page 231.

CHECK REGISTER PAGE 9

| DATE | | CK. NO. | PAYEE | VOU. NO. | ACCOUNTS PAYABLE DR. | PURCHASES DISCOUNT CR. | CASH CR. |
|---|---|---|---|---|---|---|---|
| 1982 | | | | | | | |
| June | 1 | 464 | P. R. Wholesalers | 224 | 80 00 | 1 60 | 78 40 |
| | 2 | 465 | Harvey Realty | 228 | 125 00 | | 125 00 |
| | 5 | 466 | Fairfax Distributing Co. | 226 | 100 00 | 2 00 | 98 00 |
| | 9 | 467 | Lee Company | 229 | 140 00 | | 140 00 |
| | 10 | 468 | Adelman Supplies | 227 | 45 00 | | 45 00 |
| | 14 | 469 | Parker Store Supplies | 230 | 35 00 | | 35 00 |
| | 19 | 470 | Adelman Supplies | 231 | 47 00 | | 47 00 |
| | 21 | 471 | Daily Globe | 233 | 30 00 | | 30 00 |
| | 30 | 472 | Fairfax Distributing Co. | 234 | 220 00 | 4 40 | 215 60 |
| | | | | | 822 00 | 8 00 | 814 00 |
| | 30 | | | | 822 00 | 8 00 | 814 00 |
| | | | | | (22) | (51.1) | (11) |

*Check Register – Wardlow Hardware*

**Proving the Column Totals.** Prior to posting the voucher register and check register, all columns are footed and these totals are then proved. The check register columns are verified as follows:

| Debit Column | | Credit Columns | |
|---|---|---|---|
| Accounts Payable .............. | $822 | Cash .......................... | $814 |
| | | Purchases Discount ............ | 8 |
| | $822 | | $822 |

**REGISTER** PAGE 7

| Purchases Dr. | Store Supplies Dr. | Office Supplies Dr. | General Accounts Dr. Account | Post. Ref. | Amount |
|---|---|---|---|---|---|
| | | | Rent Expense | 62 | 125 00 |
| 140 00 | | | | | |
| | 35 00 | | | | |
| | | 47 00 | | | |
| | 55 00 | | | | |
| | | | Advertising Expense | 63 | 30 00 |
| 220 00 | | | | | |
| | | 33 00 | | | |
| 95 00 | | | | | |
| 455 00 | 90 00 | 80 00 | | | 155 00 |
| 455 00 | 90 00 | 80 00 | | | 155 00 |
| (51) | (14) | (15) | | | (√) |

***Voucher Register – Wardlow Hardware (Right Page)***

The voucher register columns are verified as follows:

| Debit Columns | | Credit Column | |
|---|---|---|---|
| Purchases | $455 | Accounts Payable | $780 |
| Store Supplies | 90 | | |
| Office Supplies | 80 | | |
| General Accounts | 155 | | |
| | $780 | | $780 |

## Posting to the General Ledger

After all columns have been totaled and ruled, the special columns are posted to the general ledger by totals. The number of the account to which each special column is posted is written in parentheses below the column total. The items in the General Accounts Dr. column in the voucher register are posted individually; therefore, the column total is not posted. A check is placed below the column total to indicate that it is not posted.

After all postings have been completed at the end of June, the cash and accounts payable accounts would appear as shown below.

ACCOUNT **Cash** ACCOUNT NO. **11**

| Date | | Item | Post. Ref. | Debit | Credit | Balance Debit | Balance Credit |
|---|---|---|---|---|---|---|---|
| 1982 | | | | | | | |
| June | 1 | Balance | √ | | | 485 00 | |
| | 30 | | CR11 | 960 00 | | 1 445 00 | |
| | 30 | | CP9 | | 814 00 | 631 00 | |

ACCOUNT **Accounts Payable** ACCOUNT NO. **22**

| Date | | Item | Post. Ref. | Debit | Credit | Balance Debit | Balance Credit |
|---|---|---|---|---|---|---|---|
| 1982 | | | | | | | |
| June | 1 | Balance | √ | | | | 225 00 |
| | 30 | | VR7 | | 780 00 | | 1 005 00 |
| | 30 | | CP9 | 822 00 | | | 183 00 |

The cash account also includes deposits of $960 made during June that were posted from the cash receipts journal. Some companies maintain a special column in the check register for deposits.

The other ledger accounts are not shown here; they would be posted in the same manner as illustrated in earlier chapters. Note that the posting reference used for the Check Register is "CP," the same as was used for the cash payments journal. The reference "CR" cannot be used because it is the abbreviation used for the cash receipts journal.

## Schedule of Unpaid Vouchers

The $183 credit balance in the accounts payable account as of June 30 represents the total of the unpaid vouchers. A schedule of unpaid vouchers should be prepared as of June 30 and compared to the total in the control account.

Wardlow Hardware
Schedule of Unpaid Vouchers
June 30, 1982

| Voucher No. | Payee | Amount |
|---|---|---|
| 232 | Parker Store Supplies | $ 55 |
| 235 | Adelman Supplies | 33 |
| 236 | P.R. Wholesalers | 95 |
| | | $183 |

## Voided Voucher or Check

From time to time a voucher or check is prepared incorrectly and has to be voided. In such instances the voucher or check should be canceled and the word "VOID" written across the face of the document. The number of the voucher or check should be entered in the appropriate register in numerical order and the word "VOIDED" written in the payee column.

## Advantages of a Voucher System

In large and medium-size companies, a voucher system can be a valuable addition to the internal control of liabilities and cash payments. It also provides other advantages for effective business management. For example, the voucher system provides information essential in planning future cash requirements. It helps assure that all available cash discounts are taken and that invoices not involving a discount are paid on time, thus minimizing costs and insuring a high credit rating for the business.

## QUESTIONS FOR DISCUSSION

1. (a) What is meant by a system of internal control?
   (b) What are the objectives of a system of internal control?
2. Name the basic principles of an internal control system.

3. Frequently a purchase order will be sent to the receiving department with the quantities omitted. (a) How does this procedure assist in internal control? (b) What basic principle of internal control is involved in this procedure?

4. (a) What is a voucher system?
   (b) What records are used in a voucher system?

5. What verifications are normally made by the accounting department prior to the preparation of a voucher?

6. Explain why the only credit column required in the voucher register is Accounts Payable Cr.

7. (a) How are unpaid vouchers filed?
   (b) What is the advantage of this system of filing unpaid vouchers?
   (c) How are paid vouchers filed?

8. (a) What is a check register?
   (b) What special journal does the check register replace?

9. Explain why the Accounts Payable Dr. column is the only debit column in the check register.

10. What are the two credit columns in a check register?

11. Explain why a separate subsidiary ledger of accounts payable (vouchers payable) is not necessary when the voucher system is used.

## EXERCISES

1. Explain the importance of each of the following items in a good system of internal control, and give an example of each.
   (a) Division of responsibilities for a sequence of operations.
   (b) Separation of responsibilities for safeguarding assets and keeping the accounting records.
   (c) Rotation of jobs for a short period of time.
   (d) Use of mechanical equipment for control of information.
   (e) Evaluation of accounting system and internal control procedures by someone not involved in the day-to-day operations.

2. You are given the schedule of unpaid vouchers for the Nettleton Furniture Company at April 30.

| Voucher No. | Date | Payee | Terms | Amount |
|---|---|---|---|---|
| 177 | Mar. 14 | Padgett Co. | 2/20, n/40 | $ 400 |
| 180 | Apr. 12 | Baker Bedding | n/30 | 600 |
| 183 | Apr. 18 | Spicer Mfg. | 2/20, n/60 | 1,000 |
| 184 | Apr. 22 | Godwin Co. | 4/10, n/30 | 800 |

   (a) What is the balance in the Accounts Payable account of Nettleton Furniture Company at April 30?
   (b) Prepare the following entries in general journal form:
      (1) Apr. 22 — Issued Voucher No. 184 for merchandise purchased.
      (2) May 6 — Issued check in payment of Voucher No. 183.
      (3) May 10 — Issued check in payment of Voucher No. 180.

## ASSIGNMENT 10-C

**Tear out pages 511–522 and complete Assignment 10-C. After submitting your papers for approval, proceed with the study of Chapter 11 until the next assignment is required.**

Chapter 11

# ACCRUALS AND DEFERRALS

In recording accounting transactions, the importance of the timing of when revenue is recognized or when an expense is incurred cannot be overemphasized. The basis of accounting that recognizes all revenue in the period it is earned and all expenses in the period they are incurred is known as the *accrual basis*. The basis of accounting that recognizes revenue in the period the cash is received and expenses in the period the cash payment is made is called the *cash basis*.

In the determination of net income for an accounting period, emphasis is placed on recording the revenue earned during the period and offsetting against this revenue the expenses incurred in generating it. This process of offsetting the expenses against the revenue for a specific period is called the *matching concept*.

In this chapter and those that follow, emphasis is placed on accounting procedures involved in income determination for a business enterprise. An understanding of accrual accounting and the matching concept is necessary in this study.

## PART A ACCRUED EXPENSES AND REVENUE

Some expenses are incurred in one fiscal period and the payment is made in a later period. Some revenues are earned in one fiscal period and collection is made in a later period. Expenses or revenues which have been incurred or earned but not recorded at the end of the period are called *accruals*.

Accrual accounting requires that expenses and revenues be recorded in the period in which they are incurred or earned, regardless of when they are paid or received.

### ACCRUED EXPENSES

Expenses which have been incurred but not yet recorded at the end of the period require an adjusting entry to recognize both the expense for the period on the income statement and the liability on the balance sheet as of the end of the period. Such items are commonly called *accrued expenses* or *accrued liabilities*.

## Accrued Expenses Illustrated

One of the most common examples of an accrued expense is salaries. Employees earn wages on an hourly or a daily basis, but payment is normally made weekly or monthly. If the last day of the fiscal period is not the same as the last day of the pay period, an adjusting entry is necessary to recognize the amount of salaries accrued from the date of the last payroll to the end of the fiscal period. This adjusting entry requires a debit to Salary Expense and a credit to Salaries Payable.

To illustrate, assume that a business pays its employees every Friday for the normal work week Monday through Friday. If the last day of the fiscal period is a Wednesday, an adjusting entry is required for the salaries earned by the employees from Monday through Wednesday.

If the business had paid salaries of $26,240 to its employees as of the last full payroll period, the salary expense ledger account below would contain a debit balance of $26,240 before adjustments. If the salaries due to employees for the incomplete payroll period from Monday through Wednesday totaled $325, the adjusting entry for accrued salaries would be:

| | | | | | |
|---|---|---|---|---|---|
| 1982 | | | | | |
| Dec. | 31 | Salary Expense | 62 | 325 00 | |
| | | Salaries Payable | 22 | | 325 00 |
| | | Accrued salaries Dec. 29–31. | | | |

As a result of this entry, the total salary expense for the period and the liability for salaries owed as of the end of the fiscal period are properly stated.

When the adjusting entry is posted, the ledger accounts for Salary Expense and Salaries Payable appear as follows:

ACCOUNT **Salaries Payable** ACCOUNT NO. 22

| DATE | | ITEM | POST. REF. | DEBIT | CREDIT | BALANCE DEBIT | BALANCE CREDIT |
|---|---|---|---|---|---|---|---|
| 1982 | | | | | | | |
| | 31 | Adjusting | J17 | | 325 00 | | 325 00 |

ACCOUNT **Salary Expense** ACCOUNT NO. 62

| DATE | | ITEM | POST. REF. | DEBIT | CREDIT | BALANCE DEBIT | BALANCE CREDIT |
|---|---|---|---|---|---|---|---|
| 1982 | | | | | | | |
| | 26 | | CP16 | 580 00 | | 26 240 00 | |
| | 31 | Adjusting | J17 | 325 00 | | 26 565 00 | |

After the adjusting entry has been posted, Salary Expense for the year will have a balance of $26,565. This amount is shown on the income statement as an operating expense. There is also an outstanding liability of $325 for salaries owed to employees as of the end of the year. Salaries Payable is shown on the balance sheet as a current liability.

Based on the information above, the entry to record payment of the weekly payroll on Friday, January 2, assuming total salaries for the week to be $530, is:

| | | | | |
|---|---|---|---|---|
| Jan. 2 | Salaries Payable | 22 | 325 | |
| | Salaries Expense | 62 | 205 | |
| | Cash | 11 | | 530 |

Notice that the entry above is shown without vertical rules or an explanation. This is done to distinguish this type of entry from those normally made in the general journal, such as the Dec. 31 entry shown on page 235. In practice, the Jan. 2 entry would be recorded in a special journal (cash payments) rather than in the general journal. Because of its greater simplicity and clarity, the general journal format will continue to be used to illustrate entries throughout this module. Ledger accounts will continue to show the posting reference from the appropriate special journal.

In the entry on January 2, the total debits for the weekly salary, $530, must be allocated between those salaries accrued at the end of the last period (December 29–31), $325, and the salaries earned during the current period (January 1 and 2), $205. The ledger accounts for Salaries Payable and Salary Expense after the above entry is posted are shown below:

ACCOUNT **Salaries Payable** ACCOUNT NO. **22**

| DATE | | ITEM | POST. REF. | DEBIT | CREDIT | BALANCE DEBIT | BALANCE CREDIT |
|---|---|---|---|---|---|---|---|
| 1982 | | | | | | | |
| | 31 | Adjusting | J17 | | 325 00 | | 325 00 |
| 1983 Jan. | 2 | | CP17 | 325 00 | | — | — |

ACCOUNT **Salary Expense** ACCOUNT NO. **62**

| DATE | | ITEM | POST. REF. | DEBIT | CREDIT | BALANCE DEBIT | BALANCE CREDIT |
|---|---|---|---|---|---|---|---|
| 1982 | | | | | | | |
| | 26 | | CP16 | 580 00 | | 26 240 00 | |
| | 31 | Adjusting | J17 | 325 00 | | 26 565 00 | |
| | 31 | Closing | J18 | | 26 565 00 | — | — |
| 1983 Jan. | 2 | | CP17 | 205 00 | | 205 00 | |

Note that the salary expense account was closed to Income Summary on December 31, resulting in a zero balance at the beginning of the new period. The $205 balance in the account as of January 2 represents the salaries earned by the employees for the first two days of the new period.

## Reversing Entries for Accrued Expenses

The recording of the preceding transactions can be simplified by the use of reversing entries. A *reversing entry* is an entry made at the beginning of the new year which is the direct opposite of an adjusting entry made at the end of the preceding year. The reversing entry process is a technique designed to simplify the recording of entries in the current period for items which have been affected by adjusting entries at the end of the preceding period.

Reversing entries are recorded on the first day of the new period after all adjusting and closing entries for the preceding period have been posted. To illustrate this procedure, assume the same adjusting entry for salaries as shown on page 235:

| | | | | | |
|---|---|---|---|---|---|
| 1982 | | | | | |
| Dec. | 31 | Salary Expense | 62 | 325 00 | |
| | | Salaries Payable | 22 | | 325 00 |
| | | Accrued salaries Dec. 29–31. | | | |

After posting this entry, the ledger accounts appear as follows:

ACCOUNT **Salaries Payable** ACCOUNT NO. **22**

| DATE | | ITEM | POST. REF. | DEBIT | CREDIT | BALANCE DEBIT | BALANCE CREDIT |
|---|---|---|---|---|---|---|---|
| 1982 | | | | | | | |
| | 31 | Adjusting | J17 | | 325 00 | | 325 00 |

ACCOUNT **Salary Expense** ACCOUNT NO. **62**

| DATE | | ITEM | POST. REF. | DEBIT | CREDIT | BALANCE DEBIT | BALANCE CREDIT |
|---|---|---|---|---|---|---|---|
| 1982 | | | | | | | |
| | 26 | | CP16 | 580 00 | | 26 240 00 | |
| | 31 | Adjusting | J17 | 325 00 | | 26 565 00 | |

Next, the salary expense account is closed to Income Summary. This is done as part of the closing process at the end of the period. After closing, Salary Expense has a zero balance, and the account appears as follows:

ACCOUNT **Salary Expense** ACCOUNT NO. **62**

| DATE | | ITEM | POST. REF. | DEBIT | CREDIT | BALANCE DEBIT | BALANCE CREDIT |
|---|---|---|---|---|---|---|---|
| 1982 | | | | | | | |
| | 26 | | CP16 | 580 00 | | 26 240 00 | |
| | 31 | Adjusting | J17 | 325 00 | | 26 565 00 | |
| | 31 | Closing | J18 | | 26 565 00 | — | — |

The salaries payable account is not closed. It is shown on the balance sheet at December 31, as a current liability of $325.

On the first day of the new period the adjustment for accrued salaries is reversed by the following entry:

| Date | | Account | Post. Ref. | Debit | Credit |
|---|---|---|---|---|---|
| 1983 | | | | | |
| Jan. | 1 | Salaries Payable | 22 | 325 00 | |
| | | Salary Expense | 62 | | 325 00 |
| | | Reversing entry. | | | |

This entry is the opposite of the adjustment made on December 31. Salary Expense now has a credit balance which is, of course, unusual for an expense account. Salaries Payable now has a zero balance. The ledger accounts after the reversing entry is posted are as follows:

ACCOUNT **Salaries Payable** ACCOUNT NO. 22

| DATE | | ITEM | POST. REF. | DEBIT | CREDIT | BALANCE DEBIT | BALANCE CREDIT |
|---|---|---|---|---|---|---|---|
| 1982 | | | | | | | |
| | 31 | Adjusting | J17 | | 325 00 | | 325 00 |
| 1983 | | | | | | | |
| Jan. | 1 | Reversing | J19 | 325 00 | | —— | —— |

ACCOUNT **Salary Expense** ACCOUNT NO. 62

| DATE | | ITEM | POST. REF. | DEBIT | CREDIT | BALANCE DEBIT | BALANCE CREDIT |
|---|---|---|---|---|---|---|---|
| 1982 | | | | | | | |
| | 26 | | CP16 | 580 00 | | 26 240 00 | |
| | 31 | Adjusting | J17 | 325 00 | | 26 565 00 | |
| | 31 | Closing | J18 | | 26 565 00 | —— | —— |
| 1983 | | | | | | | |
| Jan. | 1 | Reversing | J19 | | 325 00 | | 325 00 |

When the payroll for the week of January 2 is paid, an entry is made debiting Salary Expense and crediting Cash for $530, the full amount of the weekly payroll.

| | | | | Debit | Credit |
|---|---|---|---|---|---|
| Jan. | 2 | Salary Expense | 62 | 530 | |
| | | Cash | 11 | | 530 |

After posting, the salary expense account appears as shown on page 239.

Salary Expense now has a debit balance of $205, which is the amount of salaries earned by employees for the first two days in the new accounting period.

The purpose of reversing entries is to allow the accountant to make a normal entry in the current period for items which have been affected by adjusting entries at the end of the preceding period. The necessity of referring to the adjusting entry and allocating the debit between two accounts when recording the payment of the first payroll of the new period is thus eliminated. Reversing entries can be used advantageously for all accrued expense and revenue items.

**ACCOUNT** Salary Expense **ACCOUNT NO.** 62

| DATE | | ITEM | POST. REF. | DEBIT | CREDIT | BALANCE DEBIT | BALANCE CREDIT |
|---|---|---|---|---|---|---|---|
| 1982 | | | | | | | |
| | 26 | | CP16 | 580 00 | | 26 240 00 | |
| | 31 | Adjusting | J17 | 325 00 | | 26 565 00 | |
| | 31 | Closing | J18 | | 26 565 00 | — | — |
| 1983 | | | | | | | |
| Jan. | 1 | Reversing | J19 | | 325 00 | | 325 00 |
| | 2 | | CP17 | 530 00 | | 205 00 | |

## ACCRUED REVENUE

Although some revenue items, such as rent income and interest income, accrue daily, it is customary not to record these revenues until payment is received. Accrual accounting requires that all revenue earned during a fiscal period be reported in that period whether or not payment has yet been received. Items accrued but not received at the end of the fiscal period represent both a revenue and an asset and require adjusting entries. These accruals are referred to as *accrued income, accrued receivables*, or *accrued assets*.

A good example of accrued revenue is rent. Assume that on December 1, 1982, a landlord rents office space to a tenant for $500 per month, payable at the end of a three-month period. Since the collection of the rent does not coincide with the fiscal period ending December 31, an adjusting entry is required on the landlord's books to record the amount of rent earned for the month of December, $500. The adjusting entry is a debit to Accrued Rent Receivable and a credit to Rent Income, as shown below.

| | | | | | |
|---|---|---|---|---|---|
| | 31 | Accrued Rent Receivable.................. | 16 | 500 00 | |
| | | Rent Income.................................... | 54 | | 500 00 |
| | | Accrued rent for December. | | | |

When the adjusting entry is posted, the ledger accounts for Accrued Rent Receivable and Rent Income appear as follows:

**ACCOUNT** Accrued Rent Receivable **ACCOUNT NO.** 16

| DATE | | ITEM | POST. REF. | DEBIT | CREDIT | BALANCE DEBIT | BALANCE CREDIT |
|---|---|---|---|---|---|---|---|
| 1982 | | | | | | | |
| Dec. | 31 | Adjusting | J35 | 500 00 | | 500 00 | |

**ACCOUNT** Rent Income **ACCOUNT NO.** 54

| DATE | | ITEM | POST. REF. | DEBIT | CREDIT | BALANCE DEBIT | BALANCE CREDIT |
|---|---|---|---|---|---|---|---|
| 1982 | | | | | | | |
| Dec. | 31 | Adjusting | J35 | | 500 00 | | 500 00 |

Accrued Rent Receivable will be shown on the balance sheet as a current asset and Rent Income will be shown as revenue on the income statement.

The rent is due on March 1. If collection is made on that date, the following entry is recorded:

| | | | | | |
|---|---|---|---|---|---|
| Mar. | 1 | Cash | 11 | 1,500 | |
| | | Accrued Rent Receivable | 16 | | 500 |
| | | Rent Income | 54 | | 1,000 |

The total credits for rent, $1,500, must be allocated between the rent accrued as of December 31, $500, and the rent earned during January and February of the current period, $1,000. The ledger accounts for Accrued Rent Receivable and Rent Income after the above entry is posted are shown below.

ACCOUNT **Accrued Rent Receivable** ACCOUNT NO. **16**

| DATE | | ITEM | POST. REF. | DEBIT | CREDIT | BALANCE DEBIT | BALANCE CREDIT |
|---|---|---|---|---|---|---|---|
| 1982 | | | | | | | |
| Dec. | 31 | Adjusting | J35 | 500 00 | | 500 00 | |
| 1983 | | | | | | | |
| Mar. | 1 | | CR20 | | 500 00 | — | — |

ACCOUNT **Rent Income** ACCOUNT NO. **54**

| DATE | | ITEM | POST. REF. | DEBIT | CREDIT | BALANCE DEBIT | BALANCE CREDIT |
|---|---|---|---|---|---|---|---|
| 1982 | | | | | | | |
| Dec. | 31 | Adjusting | J35 | | 500 00 | | 500 00 |
| | 31 | Closing | J35 | 500 00 | | — | — |
| 1983 | | | | | | | |
| Mar. | 1 | | CR20 | | 1 000 00 | | 1 000 00 |

Note that Rent Income was closed to Income Summary on December 31, resulting in a zero balance at the beginning of the new period. The $1,000 balance in the account on March 1 represents the rent earned for January and February of the current period.

## Reversing Entries for Accrued Revenue

Reversing entries can also be used for accrued revenues. Using the preceding example, a reversing entry would allow the entire amount of rent to be credited to Rent Income when the rent is collected without regard to the amount accrued in the prior period.

If the reversing entry technique is used, the following sequence of entries is required:

| | | | | | |
|---|---|---|---|---|---|
| | | **Adjusting entry** | | | |
| 1982 | | | | | |
| Dec. | 31 | Accrued Rent Receivable | 16 | 500 00 | |
| | | Rent Income | 54 | | 500 00 |
| | | **Closing entry** | | | |
| | 31 | Rent Income | 54 | 500 00 | |
| | | Income Summary | 33 | | 500 00 |
| | | **Reversing entry** | | | |
| 1983 | | | | | |
| Jan. | 1 | Rent Income | 54 | 500 00 | |
| | | Accrued Rent Receivable | 16 | | 500 00 |

The ledger accounts for Accrued Rent Receivable and Rent Income, after the above entries have been posted, are shown below. After the reversing entry is posted, Accrued Rent Receivable has a zero balance and Rent Income has a debit balance.

ACCOUNT **Accrued Rent Receivable** ACCOUNT NO. 16

| DATE | | ITEM | POST. REF. | DEBIT | CREDIT | BALANCE DEBIT | BALANCE CREDIT |
|---|---|---|---|---|---|---|---|
| 1982 | | | | | | | |
| Dec. | 31 | Adjusting | J35 | 500 00 | | 500 00 | |
| 1983 | | | | | | | |
| Jan. | 1 | Reversing | J36 | | 500 00 | — | — |

ACCOUNT **Rent Income** ACCOUNT NO. 54

| DATE | | ITEM | POST. REF. | DEBIT | CREDIT | BALANCE DEBIT | BALANCE CREDIT |
|---|---|---|---|---|---|---|---|
| 1982 | | | | | | | |
| Dec. | 31 | Adjusting | J35 | | 500 00 | | 500 00 |
| | 31 | Closing | J35 | 500 00 | | — | — |
| 1983 | | | | | | | |
| Jan. | 1 | Reversing | J36 | 500 00 | | 500 00 | |

The entry to record collection of the rent can now be prepared without regard to the adjustment made at the end of 1982. The collection entry on March 1 would appear as follows:

| | | | | | |
|---|---|---|---|---|---|
| Mar. | 1 | Cash | 11 | 1,500 | |
| | | Rent Income | 54 | | 1,500 |

After this entry is posted, Rent Income will have a credit balance of $1,000, representing the rent earned during January and February of the current year.

**ACCOUNT Rent Income** **ACCOUNT NO. 54**

| DATE | | ITEM | POST. REF. | DEBIT | CREDIT | BALANCE | |
|---|---|---|---|---|---|---|---|
| | | | | | | DEBIT | CREDIT |
| 1982 | | | | | | | |
| Dec. | 31 | Adjusting | J35 | | 500 00 | | 500 00 |
| | 31 | Closing | J35 | 500 00 | | — | — |
| 1983 | | | | | | | |
| Jan. | 1 | Reversing | J36 | 500 00 | | 500 00 | |
| Mar. | 1 | | CR20 | | 1 500 00 | | 1 000 00 |

## QUESTIONS FOR DISCUSSION

1. Explain the following statement: Accrual accounting requires the recording of all accrued expenses and revenue at the end of the fiscal period.
2. How do reversing entries simplify accounting for accrued expenses?
3. Do adjusting entries for accrued revenue affect both the income statement and the balance sheet? Explain.
4. On January 17, a new accounting clerk discovered that the rent income account had a debit balance of $150. Inasmuch as revenue accounts have a normal credit balance, explain to the clerk the probable cause of this situation.
5. The Eagle Company had $360 in accrued salaries at the end of the fiscal year. (a) After the closing entries have been posted, what will be the balance in Salaries Payable? (b) If the salaries paid by Eagle Company for the year had been $16,230 (prior to the accrual above), what would be the balance in Salary Expense after the books have been closed?
6. If Eagle Company reversed the adjusting entry for salaries (5. above) at the beginning of the new fiscal period: (a) What would be the balance in Salaries Payable after the reversing entry is posted? (b) What would be the balance in Salary Expense after the reversing entry is posted?

## EXERCISES

1. The Norfolk Company had $540 in accrued salaries on December 31, the end of the fiscal year.

   **Required:**

   (a) Prepare the adjusting entry for salaries at December 31.

   (b) Prepare the entry, in general journal form, to pay the salaries for the week ended January 2, of $1,980. (Norfolk did not prepare a reversing entry.)

2. Below is presented the salary expense account for the Matson Company. The entries in the account identified by letters are related to the end of period summary and the first payroll in January. Record the necessary entries in general journal form and indicate whether they are adjusting, closing, or reversing.

**ACCOUNT** **Salary Expense** **ACCOUNT NO. 62**

| DATE | | ITEM | POST. REF. | DEBIT | CREDIT | BALANCE DEBIT | BALANCE CREDIT |
|---|---|---|---|---|---|---|---|
| 1982 | | | | | | | |
| Dec. | 29 | Balance | ✓ | | | 31 260 00 | |
| | 31 | (a) | | 660 00 | | 31 920 00 | |
| | 31 | (b) | | | 31 920 00 | — | — |
| 1983 | | | | | | | |
| Jan. | 1 | (c) | | | 660 00 | | 660 00 |
| | 5 | (d) | | 1 380 00 | | 720 00 | |

3. On December 1, Action Magazine accepted an order for two monthly ads from a small chain of men's clothing stores. The ads are to run in December and January at a monthly cost of $400 per ad.

**Required:** Prepare the entries in general journal form on Action's books to record the following transactions:

(a) December 31 — Adjustment for the advertising accrual of income for December.

(b) December 31 — Close Advertising Income for December.

(c) January 20 — Receipt of $800 for the two monthly ads.

**ASSIGNMENT 11-A**

**Tear out pages 523–528 and complete Assignment 11-A. After submitting your papers for approval, continue with the following textbook discussion until the next assignment is required.**

## PART B DEFERRED EXPENSES AND REVENUE

In addition to accruals there may be some expense items for which payment has been made in advance, or payment may have been received for goods or services to be delivered in future periods. These prepayments of expenses or advanced receipt of revenues are called deferrals. Accounting for deferrals not only concerns the revenue and expense account balances for the period, but also the assets and liabilities reported on the balance sheet at the end of the period.

## DEFERRED EXPENSES

A *deferred expense* represents a cash expenditure made in the current period, which is not charged to an expense until it is used in a future period. Deferred expenses are commonly called *prepaid expenses* or *deferred charges*. Prepaid expenses are normally for a short period of time and are listed on the balance sheet as current assets. If the deferral is for more than one year, it should be presented in a separate balance sheet category entitled "Deferred charges."

### Prepaid Expenses

Prepaid expenses represent payments for goods and services which have not been used at the time of payment. The amount of goods or services used should be recorded as an expense for the period. The amount of any unused goods and services at the end of the period should be shown on the balance sheet as a current asset. This prepaid amount will become an expense when used in the following period. Common examples of prepaid expenses are insurance, store supplies, office supplies, rent, and interest.

There are two methods of accounting for prepaid expenses. The expenditure may be recorded initially as an asset by debiting a prepaid expense account, or it may be recorded as an expense by debiting an expense account. The method used in recording the initial payment affects the adjustments made at the end of the year.

**Prepaid Expenses Recorded as Assets.** One expenditure that is commonly charged to an asset account at the time of prepayment is rent. Although the amount of rent applicable to the current period is known at the time the payment is made, the recording of the amount of the expense is deferred until the end of the period.

For example, assume that the annual office rent of $2,400 is paid in advance on September 1, the date that a company begins its operations. If this payment is recorded initially as an asset, the entry is:

| | | | | | |
|---|---|---|---|---|---|
| Sept. | 1 | Prepaid Rent | 18 | 2,400 | |
| | | Cash | 11 | | 2,400 |

Assuming that the company's fiscal year ends December 31, an adjusting entry is required to transfer $800 (4 months at $200 per month) of the prepaid rent to an expense account.

| | | | | | | | |
|---|---|---|---|---|---|---|---|
| 1982 | | | | | | | |
| Dec. | 31 | Rent Expense | 65 | 800 | 00 | | |
| | | Prepaid Rent | 18 | | | 800 | 00 |
| | | Four months' rental. | | | | | |

After the above entry is posted, the prepaid rent and rent expense accounts appear as shown at the top of page 245.

Prepaid rent of $1,600, representing the rent paid in advance for the next eight months, would be shown on the balance sheet as a current asset. This amount will become an expense in the following period. Rent expense of $800, representing the expense for the four months, September through December, of the current year would be

ACCOUNT **Prepaid Rent** ACCOUNT NO. **18**

| DATE | | ITEM | POST. REF. | DEBIT | CREDIT | BALANCE DEBIT | BALANCE CREDIT |
|---|---|---|---|---|---|---|---|
| 1982 | | | | | | | |
| Sept. | 1 | | CP12 | 2 400 00 | | 2 400 00 | |
| Dec. | 31 | Adjusting | J53 | | 800 00 | 1 600 00 | |

ACCOUNT **Rent Expense** ACCOUNT NO. **65**

| DATE | | ITEM | POST. REF. | DEBIT | CREDIT | BALANCE DEBIT | BALANCE CREDIT |
|---|---|---|---|---|---|---|---|
| 1982 | | | | | | | |
| Dec. | 31 | Adjusting | J53 | 800 00 | | 800 00 | |

shown on the income statement as an operating expense. When prepaid expenses are recorded initially as assets, no reversing entry is required at the beginning of the following period.

**Prepaid Expenses Recorded as Expenses.** The second method of recording prepaid expenses is to debit the expense account at the time the payment is initially made. This method requires an adjusting entry at the end of the year to transfer the unused amount from an expense account to an asset account.

Assume that in the preceding example the $2,400 rent payment on September 1 was debited to Rent Expense. The entries to record the initial payment and the year-end adjustment are:

| | | | | | |
|---|---|---|---|---|---|
| Sept. | 1 | Rent Expense ........................................ | 65 | 2,400 | |
| | | Cash ........................................ | 11 | | 2,400 |

| | | | | | |
|---|---|---|---|---|---|
| 1982 | | | | | |
| Dec. | 31 | Prepaid Rent ........................................ | 18 | 1 600 00 | |
| | | Rent Expense ........................................ | 65 | | 1 600 00 |
| | | Eight months' rent prepaid. | | | |

After these entries have been posted, the ledger accounts appear as follows:

ACCOUNT **Prepaid Rent** ACCOUNT NO. **18**

| DATE | | ITEM | POST. REF. | DEBIT | CREDIT | BALANCE DEBIT | BALANCE CREDIT |
|---|---|---|---|---|---|---|---|
| 1982 | | | | | | | |
| Dec. | 31 | Adjusting | J53 | 1 600 00 | | 1 600 00 | |

ACCOUNT **Rent Expense** ACCOUNT NO. **65**

| DATE | | ITEM | POST. REF. | DEBIT | CREDIT | BALANCE DEBIT | BALANCE CREDIT |
|---|---|---|---|---|---|---|---|
| 1982 | | | | | | | |
| Sept. | 1 | | CP12 | 2 400 00 | | 2 400 00 | |
| Dec. | 31 | Adjusting | J53 | | 1 600 00 | 800 00 | |

The balance in Rent Expense, $800, is the amount of rent expense for the current period. This amount would be shown on the income statement as an operating expense. The $1,600 balance in Prepaid Rent represents the unused rent at the end of the period and is reported on the balance sheet as a current asset.

By use of this method, the company chose to initially record rental payments in an expense account. It is therefore necessary to make a reversing entry of the above adjustment to transfer the $1,600 of prepaid rent back to the expense account at the beginning of the next period. The reversing entry would be:

| Date | | Account | Post. Ref. | Debit | Credit |
|---|---|---|---|---|---|
| 1983 | | | | | |
| Jan. | 1 | Rent Expense | 65 | 1 600 00 | |
| | | Prepaid Rent | 18 | | 1 600 00 |
| | | Reversing entry. | | | |

After the reversing entry has been posted, the ledger accounts appear as follows:

ACCOUNT Prepaid Rent — ACCOUNT NO. 18

| DATE | | ITEM | POST. REF. | DEBIT | CREDIT | BALANCE DEBIT | BALANCE CREDIT |
|---|---|---|---|---|---|---|---|
| 1982 | | | | | | | |
| Dec. | 31 | Adjusting | J53 | 1 600 00 | | 1 600 00 | |
| 1983 | | | | | | | |
| Jan. | 1 | Reversing | J54 | | 1 600 00 | ——— | ——— |

ACCOUNT Rent Expense — ACCOUNT NO. 65

| DATE | | ITEM | POST. REF. | DEBIT | CREDIT | BALANCE DEBIT | BALANCE CREDIT |
|---|---|---|---|---|---|---|---|
| 1982 | | | | | | | |
| Sept. | 1 | | CP12 | 2 400 00 | | 2 400 00 | |
| Dec. | 31 | Adjusting | J53 | | 1 600 00 | 800 00 | |
| | 31 | Closing | J53 | | 800 00 | ——— | ——— |
| 1983 | | | | | | | |
| Jan. | 1 | Reversing | J54 | 1 600 00 | | 1 600 00 | |

The remaining prepaid rent of $1,600 has been returned to the rent expense account. No adjusting entry will be required at the end of the second period for the $1,600 since the reversing entry has returned it to the rent expense account.

**Comparison of the Two Methods for Recording Prepaid Expenses.** The two methods of recording prepaid expenses, including payment, adjusting, closing, and reversing entries, are compared on page 247.

## PREPAID EXPENSES

| Entry | Recorded initially in *asset* account. | Recorded initially in *expense* account. |
|---|---|---|
| Entry When Paid<br><br>**Sept. 1** | Payment debited to prepaid expense.<br>**Prepaid Rent .............. 2,400**<br>**Cash ........................ 2,400**<br>PREPAID RENT: Dr. 2,400 \| Cr. —<br>RENT EXPENSE: Dr. — \| Cr. — | Payment debited to expense account.<br>**Rent Expense ............. 2,400**<br>**Cash ........................ 2,400**<br>PREPAID RENT: Dr. — \| Cr. —<br>RENT EXPENSE: Dr. 2,400 \| Cr. — |
| Adjusting Entry<br><br>**Dec. 31** | Transfer amount used during the period to expense.<br>**Rent Expense ............. 800**<br>**Prepaid Rent ........... 800**<br>PREPAID RENT: Dr. 2,400 (Bal. 1,600) \| Cr. 800<br>RENT EXPENSE: Dr. 800 \| Cr. — | Transfer amount not used to asset account.<br>**Prepaid Rent .............. 1,600**<br>**Rent Expense ......... 1,600**<br>PREPAID RENT: Dr. 1,600 \| Cr. —<br>RENT EXPENSE: Dr. 2,400 (Bal. 800) \| Cr. 1,600 |
| | (Note: Balances in the accounts are the same for both methods after adjustment.) | |
| Closing Entry<br><br>**Dec. 31** | Close balance in expense account to Income Summary.<br>**Income Summary ....... 800**<br>**Rent Expense ......... 800**<br>PREPAID RENT: Dr. 1,600 \| Cr. —<br>RENT EXPENSE: Dr. 800 \| Cr. 800 | Close balance in expense account to Income Summary.<br>**Income Summary ....... 800**<br>**Rent Expense ......... 800**<br>PREPAID RENT: Dr. 1,600 \| Cr. —<br>RENT EXPENSE: Dr. 800 \| Cr. 800 |
| | (Note: Same closing entry for both methods.) | |
| Reversing Entry<br><br>**Jan. 1** | Not required. Balance of prepayment at the beginning of the year is properly shown in asset account.<br>No entry<br>PREPAID RENT: Dr. 1,600 \| Cr. —<br>RENT EXPENSE: Dr. — \| Cr. — | Reversing entry is required to be consistent with policy of carrying prepayments in expense account. Entry results in transfer of balance from asset account to expense account.<br>**Rent Expense ............. 1,600**<br>**Prepaid Rent ........... 1,600**<br>PREPAID RENT: Dr. 1,600 \| Cr. 1,600<br>RENT EXPENSE: Dr. 1,600 \| Cr. — |

In comparing the two methods of recording prepaid expenses, the following points should be noted:

1. After the adjusting entry is posted, the balance in the asset account Prepaid Rent is the same for both methods, $1,600. The reason is that

regardless of the method used to record the initial payment, the amount prepaid at December 31 is for the first eight months of the next period at $200 per month. This amount is reported as an asset at the end of the current period.

2. The balance in the expense account at December 31, after adjustment, is also the same for both methods. The amount of expense for the current year is four-months' rent, September through December, at $200 per month, or $800.
3. Since the amount of expense reported for the year is the same for both methods, the entry to close Rent Expense will also be the same.
4. The method used for recording a particular expense should be followed consistently from period to period; however, different methods may be used for different expenses. For example, the asset method is normally used for prepayments of one year or longer, such as two- or three-year insurance premiums. The expense method is normally used for short prepayments of one year or less, such as advertising expense.

The advantage of the expense method is that if the asset is entirely used up by the end of the accounting period no adjusting entry will be required.

## DEFERRED REVENUE

*Deferred revenue* is revenue which is received in the current period but not fully earned until later periods. Deferred revenue is often referred to as *unearned revenue* or *deferred credits*. Unearned revenue is normally for a short period of time and is listed on the balance sheet as a current liability. If the deferral is for more than one year, it should be presented in a separate balance sheet category entitled "Deferred credits."

### Unearned Revenue

*Unearned revenue* represents payment received for goods to be delivered or services to be performed in future periods. At the end of the accounting period, the unearned portion of a payment received in advance is a liability to the business.

Examples of revenue received in advance include premiums on insurance policies, subscriptions received by newspapers or magazines, season tickets to cultural activities or athletic events, and unearned rent or interest.

As with prepaid expenses, there are two acceptable methods of accounting for unearned revenue. Receipts may be recorded initially as liabilities by crediting an unearned revenue account, or they may be recorded by crediting a revenue account.

**Unearned Revenue Recorded as a Liability.** An example of a revenue received in advance that may be initially credited to a liability account at the time of receipt is rent income. Assume that on April 1, First National Bank rents four parking spaces to the Zellner Company for a 12-month period and that the rent for the entire period, $1,800, is collected in advance. If the payment received by First

National Bank is initially credited to a liability account, the following entry is made:

| | | | | |
|---|---|---|---|---|
| Apr. 1 | Cash | 11 | 1,800 | |
| | Unearned Rent | 28 | | 1,800 |

On December 31, the end of the fiscal year, an adjusting entry is required to record the rent earned for 9 months, April through December, at $150 per month. The entry is a debit to Unearned Rent and a credit to Rent Income for $1,350.

| Date | | Account | Post. Ref. | Debit | Credit |
|---|---|---|---|---|---|
| 1982 | | | | | |
| Dec. | 31 | Unearned Rent | 28 | 1 350 00 | |
| | | Rent Income | 72 | | 1 350 00 |
| | | Rent earned for 9 months at $150 per month. | | | |

The adjusting entry reduces the liability for unearned rent to $450 which is the amount of the three-months' rent still unearned at the end of the year. After the adjusting entry is posted, the unearned rent and rent income accounts appear as follows:

ACCOUNT Unearned Rent — ACCOUNT NO. 28

| DATE | | ITEM | POST. REF. | DEBIT | CREDIT | BALANCE DEBIT | BALANCE CREDIT |
|---|---|---|---|---|---|---|---|
| 1982 | | | | | | | |
| Apr. | 1 | | CR11 | | 1 800 00 | | 1 800 00 |
| Dec. | 31 | Adjusting | J46 | 1 350 00 | | | 450 00 |

ACCOUNT Rent Income — ACCOUNT NO. 72

| DATE | | ITEM | POST. REF. | DEBIT | CREDIT | BALANCE DEBIT | BALANCE CREDIT |
|---|---|---|---|---|---|---|---|
| 1982 | | | | | | | |
| Dec. | 31 | Adjusting | J46 | | 1 350 00 | | 1 350 00 |

The unearned rent of $450 is shown on the year-end balance sheet as a current liability. It represents a service to be rendered by the First National Bank during the next period. Rent income of $1,350, assuming that there was no other rent income for the year, is reported on the income statement. When the unearned revenue is recorded initially as a liability, no reversing entry is required.

**Unearned Revenue Recorded as Revenue.** The preceding transaction for renting the parking spaces could have been recorded initially on the books of First National Bank by crediting the proceeds of the rental contract to Rent Income. If this method had been used and all of the income received had not been earned by the end of the fiscal year, an adjusting entry would have been required to reduce the amount credited to rent income and transfer the unearned portion to the liability account Unearned Rent. The entry to record the receipt of payment and the adjusting entry would be as follows:

| | | | | |
|---|---|---|---|---|
| Apr. 1 | Cash | 11 | 1,800 | |
| | Rent Income | 72 | | 1,800 |

| | | | | | |
|---|---|---|---|---|---|
| 1982 | | | | | |
| Dec. | 31 | Rent Income | 72 | 450 00 | |
| | | Unearned Rent | 28 | | 450 00 |
| | | To recognize unearned rent for 3 months. | | | |

After these entries have been posted, the unearned rent and rent income accounts would appear as follows:

ACCOUNT **Unearned Rent** ACCOUNT NO. **28**

| DATE | | ITEM | POST. REF. | DEBIT | CREDIT | BALANCE DEBIT | BALANCE CREDIT |
|---|---|---|---|---|---|---|---|
| 1982 | | | | | | | |
| Dec. | 31 | Adjusting | J46 | | 450 00 | | 450 00 |

ACCOUNT **Rent Income** ACCOUNT NO. **72**

| DATE | | ITEM | POST. REF. | DEBIT | CREDIT | BALANCE DEBIT | BALANCE CREDIT |
|---|---|---|---|---|---|---|---|
| 1982 | | | | | | | |
| Apr. | 1 | | CR11 | | 1 800 00 | | 1 800 00 |
| Dec. | 31 | Adjusting | J46 | 450 00 | | | 1 350 00 |

To be consistent with the company's policy of recording the rent received in advance to a revenue account, the balance in Unearned Rent should be returned to Rent Income at the beginning of the new period by means of a reversing entry.

| | | | | | |
|---|---|---|---|---|---|
| 1983 | | | | | |
| Jan. | 1 | Unearned Rent | 28 | 450 00 | |
| | | Rent Income | 72 | | 450 00 |
| | | Reversing entry. | | | |

After the closing and reversing entries are posted, the accounts appear as follows:

ACCOUNT **Unearned Rent** ACCOUNT NO. **28**

| DATE | | ITEM | POST. REF. | DEBIT | CREDIT | BALANCE DEBIT | BALANCE CREDIT |
|---|---|---|---|---|---|---|---|
| 1982 | | | | | | | |
| Dec. | 31 | Adjusting | J46 | | 450 00 | | 450 00 |
| 1983 | | | | | | | |
| Jan. | 1 | Reversing | J47 | 450 00 | | — | — |

ACCOUNT **Rent Income** ACCOUNT NO. **72**

| DATE | | ITEM | POST. REF. | DEBIT | CREDIT | BALANCE DEBIT | BALANCE CREDIT |
|---|---|---|---|---|---|---|---|
| 1982 | | | | | | | |
| Apr. | 1 | | CR11 | | 1 800 00 | | 1 800 00 |
| Dec. | 31 | Adjusting | J46 | 450 00 | | | 1 350 00 |
| | 31 | Closing | J46 | 1 350 00 | | — | — |
| 1983 | | | | | | | |
| Jan. | 1 | Reversing | J47 | | 450 00 | | 450 00 |

**Comparison of the Two Methods for Recording Unearned Revenue.** The two methods of recording unearned revenue, including adjusting, closing, and reversing entries, are compared below.

UNEARNED REVENUE

<table>
<tr><th>Entry</th><th>Recorded initially in liability account.</th><th>Recorded initially in revenue account.</th></tr>
<tr><td>Entry When Received<br><br>Apr. 1</td><td>Collection credited to unearned revenue.<br><br>Cash ........ 1,800<br>  Unearned Rent ....... 1,800<br><br>UNEARNED RENT — Dr.: ; Cr.: 1,800<br>RENT INCOME — Dr.: ; Cr.: </td><td>Collection credited to revenue account.<br><br>Cash ........ 1,800<br>  Rent Income ........... 1,800<br><br>UNEARNED RENT — Dr.: ; Cr.: <br>RENT INCOME — Dr.: ; Cr.: 1,800</td></tr>
<tr><td>Adjusting Entry<br><br>Dec. 31</td><td>Transfer amount earned during period to a revenue account.<br><br>Unearned Rent ........... 1,350<br>  Rent Income ........... 1,350<br><br>UNEARNED RENT — Dr.: 1,350; Cr.: 1,800 (Bal. 450)<br>RENT INCOME — Dr.: ; Cr.: 1,350</td><td>Transfer amount still unearned at end of period to a liability account.<br><br>Rent Income ............... 450<br>  Unearned Rent ....... 450<br><br>UNEARNED RENT — Dr.: ; Cr.: 450<br>RENT INCOME — Dr.: 450; Cr.: 1,800 (Bal. 1,350)</td></tr>
<tr><td></td><td colspan="2">(Note: Balances in accounts are the same for both methods after adjustment.)</td></tr>
<tr><td>Closing Entry<br><br>Dec. 31</td><td>Close balance in revenue account to Income Summary.<br><br>Rent Income ............... 1,350<br>  Income Summary... 1,350<br><br>UNEARNED RENT — Dr.: ; Cr.: 450<br>RENT INCOME — Dr.: 1,350; Cr.: 1,350</td><td>Close balance in revenue account to Income Summary.<br><br>Rent Income ............... 1,350<br>  Income Summary... 1,350<br><br>UNEARNED RENT — Dr.: ; Cr.: 450<br>RENT INCOME — Dr.: 1,350; Cr.: 1,350</td></tr>
<tr><td></td><td colspan="2">(Note: Same closing entry for both methods.)</td></tr>
<tr><td>Reversing Entry<br><br>Jan. 1</td><td>Not required. Balance of unearned revenue at the beginning of the year is properly shown in the liability account.<br><br>No entry<br><br>UNEARNED RENT — Dr.: ; Cr.: 450<br>RENT INCOME — Dr.: ; Cr.: </td><td>Reversing entry is required to be consistent with policy of returning balance in unearned revenue account to revenue account.<br><br>Unearned Rent........... 450<br>  Rent Income ........... 450<br><br>UNEARNED RENT — Dr.: 450; Cr.: 450<br>RENT INCOME — Dr.: ; Cr.: 450</td></tr>
</table>

In comparing the two methods of recording unearned revenues the following points should be noted:

1. After the adjusting entry is posted, the balance in the liability account Unearned Rent is the same for both methods, $450. The reason is that regardless of the method used to record the initial receipt of payment, the amount unearned at December 31 is for the first three months of the next period at $150 per month. This amount is reported as a liability at the end of the current period.
2. The balance in the revenue account at December 31, after adjustment, is also the same for both methods. The revenue earned during the current period is for nine months, April through December, at $150 per month, or $1,350.
3. Since the amount of revenue reported will be the same for both methods, the entry to close Rent Income will also be the same.
4. Different methods may be used for different revenues; however, the method used for recording each specific unearned revenue should be followed consistently from period to period.

## ACCOUNTING FOR PROPERTY TAXES

Legally all property is divided into two classes, real and personal. *Real property* includes land and anything permanently attached to the land, such as buildings, trees, sidewalks, fences, water lines, and sewers.

*Personal property* includes all property other than real property. *Personal property* includes such items as equipment, furniture, vehicles, and merchandise inventory.

A tax which is assessed on real or personal property is commonly called a *property tax*. A property tax is assessed on the basis of the value of the property. This type of tax is known as an *ad valorem* tax, which translated from the Latin means "according to value." Property taxes are levied mostly by local government units such as cities, counties, and school districts. The property tax normally represents a major source of revenue for these units.

### Recording Property Taxes

Property taxes are presented here because, by their nature, they represent a combination of deferral and accrual accounting. A property tax may be paid in advance, and thus be accounted for as a prepaid expense (deferral). On the other hand, property taxes may not be paid for several months after the tax period begins and thus require accrual accounting. Taxes, real or personal, paid on business properties are operating expenses. Property taxes do not legally accrue during the period but are levied against the property as of a particular date. For example, taxes may be levied as of January 1, the first day of the governmental unit's fiscal year.

If the business prepares its income statement once a year, the expense for property taxes will be the amount of taxes levied for that year. For example, if a company received on January 15 its statement for property taxes of $1,800 for the current year, payable without penalty by March 31, the entry to record the payment of these taxes on March 31 is as follows:

| | | | | |
|---|---|---|---|---|
| Mar. 31 | Property Tax Expense | 66 | 1,800 | |
| | Cash | 11 | | 1,800 |

## Accrual of Property Taxes

As indicated previously, the liability for property taxes does not legally accrue on a daily basis as does rent, salaries, or interest. Rather, the charge for property taxes relates to the ownership of the property as of the date the property is valued for tax purposes. This date is known as the *assessment date*. However, from an economic standpoint, the property taxes are paid for the privilege of using the property during the entire year. Therefore, if a business reports its operations on a monthly basis, the property tax expense should be prorated and charged against revenue over the fiscal year of the taxing authority. In the preceding example, this would require the accrual of property tax expense in January and February to be recorded as follows:

| | | | | | |
|---|---|---|---|---|---|
| 1982 | | | | | |
| Jan. | 31 | Property Tax Expense | 66 | 150 00 | |
| | | Property Tax Payable | 27 | | 150 00 |
| | | To record 1/12 of property taxes (January). | | | |

| | | | | | |
|---|---|---|---|---|---|
| 1982 | | | | | |
| Feb. | 28 | Property Tax Expense | 66 | 150 00 | |
| | | Property Tax Payable | 27 | | 150 00 |
| | | To record 1/12 of property taxes (February). | | | |

When the payment is made in March, the accrued liability for the first two months would be eliminated, the expense for March would be recorded, and property taxes for the remaining nine months would be shown as Prepaid Property Tax.

| | | | | |
|---|---|---|---|---|
| Mar. 31 | Property Tax Payable | 27 | 300 | |
| | Property Tax Expense | 66 | 150 | |
| | Prepaid Property Tax | 17 | 1,350 | |
| | Cash | 11 | | 1,800 |

After the above entries have been posted to the ledger, Prepaid Property Tax, Property Tax Payable, and Property Tax Expense would appear as shown below and on the following page.

ACCOUNT **Prepaid Property Tax** ACCOUNT NO. **17**

| DATE | | ITEM | POST. REF. | DEBIT | CREDIT | BALANCE | |
|---|---|---|---|---|---|---|---|
| | | | | | | DEBIT | CREDIT |
| 1982 | | | | | | | |
| Mar. | 31 | | CP7 | 1 350 00 | | 1 350 00 | |

**ACCOUNT** Property Tax Payable **ACCOUNT NO.** 27

| DATE | | ITEM | POST. REF. | DEBIT | CREDIT | BALANCE DEBIT | BALANCE CREDIT |
|---|---|---|---|---|---|---|---|
| 1982 | | | | | | | |
| Jan. | 31 | | J10 | | 150 00 | | 150 00 |
| Feb. | 28 | | J11 | | 150 00 | | 300 00 |
| Mar. | 31 | | CP7 | 300 00 | | — | — |

**ACCOUNT** Property Tax Expense **ACCOUNT NO.** 66

| DATE | | ITEM | POST. REF. | DEBIT | CREDIT | BALANCE DEBIT | BALANCE CREDIT |
|---|---|---|---|---|---|---|---|
| 1982 | | | | | | | |
| Jan. | 31 | | J10 | 150 00 | | 150 00 | |
| Feb. | 28 | | J11 | 150 00 | | 300 00 | |
| Mar. | 31 | | CP7 | 150 00 | | 450 00 | |

## Adjustment for Prepaid Property Tax

As of March 31, property taxes for the remainder of the year are prepaid. Each month an adjusting entry is prepared transferring $150 from Prepaid Property Tax to Property Tax Expense. The April adjustment would be:

| | | | | | |
|---|---|---|---|---|---|
| 1982 | | | | | |
| Apr. | 30 | Property Tax Expense ........................ | 66 | 150 00 | |
| | | Prepaid Property Tax ...................... | 17 | | 150 00 |
| | | To record April tax expense. | | | |

After the April adjustment is posted, the ledger accounts for Prepaid Property Tax and Property Tax Expense appear as follows:

**ACCOUNT** Prepaid Property Tax **ACCOUNT NO.** 17

| DATE | | ITEM | POST. REF. | DEBIT | CREDIT | BALANCE DEBIT | BALANCE CREDIT |
|---|---|---|---|---|---|---|---|
| 1982 | | | | | | | |
| Mar. | 31 | | CP7 | 1 350 00 | | 1 350 00 | |
| Apr. | 30 | | J13 | | 150 00 | 1 200 00 | |

**ACCOUNT** Property Tax Expense **ACCOUNT NO.** 66

| DATE | | ITEM | POST. REF. | DEBIT | CREDIT | BALANCE DEBIT | BALANCE CREDIT |
|---|---|---|---|---|---|---|---|
| 1982 | | | | | | | |
| Jan. | 31 | | J10 | 150 00 | | 150 00 | |
| Feb. | 28 | | J11 | 150 00 | | 300 00 | |
| Mar. | 31 | | CP7 | 150 00 | | 450 00 | |
| Apr. | 30 | | J13 | 150 00 | | 600 00 | |

The adjustment made each month reduces Prepaid Property Tax and increases Property Tax Expense. After the adjustment on December 31, Prepaid Property Tax would have a zero balance, and Property Tax Expense would contain an $1,800 debit balance, the total amount of the expense for the year.

## Property Taxes on Property Purchased

In some instances, property that is purchased will be subject to delinquent taxes and penalties. For example, an investor bought a small parcel of land for $16,000 and agreed to pay $700 of delinquent taxes and penalties assessed against the property. These expenditures are an additional cost of the land rather than expenses, because they constitute part of the total consideration the buyer was willing to give to acquire the asset. If cash is paid for the land, the entry to record the transaction is:

| | | | | | |
|---|---|---|---|---|---|
| May | 7 | Land | 14 | 16,700 | |
| | | Cash | 11 | | 16,700 |

The only taxes or penalties that would be added to the cost of an asset purchased are those that are delinquent at the time of acquisition. All current and future taxes would be recorded as expenses in the period incurred.

### QUESTIONS FOR DISCUSSION

1. (a) What are the two acceptable methods of recording prepaid expenses?
   (b) Will a reversing entry be required for each method? Explain.
2. (a) What two methods of recording unearned revenue may be used?
   (b) Will the amount of revenue reported on the income statement differ under each method? Explain.
3. Explain the difference between prepaid rent and unearned rent.
4. Explain the difference between prepaid interest and accrued interest receivable.
5. Distinguish between real property and personal property.
6. What is an "ad valorem" tax?
7. On January 1, Terry Telfer purchased land for $4,000 which had delinquent property taxes and penalties of $420 assessed against it. The property taxes on this land for the current year are $315. What is the cost of the land to Telfer? Explain your answer.

### EXERCISES

1. During the year, the Bando Company purchased store supplies for $570. At the end of the year the supplies on hand totaled $180. Prepare the adjusting entry required:
   (a) if the purchase had originally been debited to Store Supplies Expense.
   (b) if the purchase had originally been debited to Store Supplies.
2. On November 1, the *Daily Planet*, a local newspaper, received $660 for advertising from Chic Department Stores for the months of November, December, and January. Assuming the *Daily Planet* initially credits the $660 to Unearned Advertising, prepare the entries required on:
   (a) November 1, to record receipt of payment for the advertising.
   (b) December 31, adjusting entry at the end of the period.
   (c) December 31, closing entry for Advertising Income.
   (d) January 1, reversing entry (if required).

3. Prepare the entries for the *Daily Planet* in #2, page 255, if the $660 had been credited initially to Advertising Income.

4. Indicate whether each of the following accounts would be classified as current asset, current liability, revenue, or expense.

| | |
|---|---|
| (a) Prepaid Insurance | (f) Salary Expense |
| (b) Salaries Payable | (g) Unearned Commission Income |
| (c) Accrued Rent Receivable | (h) Prepaid Property Tax |
| (d) Interest Expense | (i) Interest Receivable |
| (e) Insurance Expense | (j) Property Tax Payable |

5. On January 10, Mayo Motor Company receives a statement for property taxes of $2,700 for the current year, payable without penalty by February 28.

   **Required:** Assuming Mayo reports its operations on a monthly basis:

   (a) Prepare the entry required for the accrual of property taxes on January 31.

   (b) Prepare the entry on February 28 to record the payment of property taxes for the year.

## ASSIGNMENT 11-B

**Tear out pages 529–538 and complete Assignment 11-B. After completion, submit your papers to your instructor and proceed to the study of Chapter 12 until the next assignment is required.**

Chapter **12**

# ACCOUNTS RECEIVABLE, NOTES RECEIVABLE AND PAYABLE

Most business transactions involve the granting of credit. Credit means that payment for goods and services is delayed until some time after the goods and services have been delivered. This chapter provides an introduction to accounting for credit transactions. Accounts receivable and some of the special problems of accounting for uncollectible accounts are discussed in Part A. Part B includes accounting for notes receivable, notes payable, interest income, and interest expense.

## PART A ACCOUNTS RECEIVABLE AND UNCOLLECTIBLE ACCOUNTS

Payment of cash for goods and services at the time of acquisition has become the exception rather than the rule in the U.S. economy. Credit cards, revolving charge accounts, and deferred payment plans are examples of ways that credit is commonly used in today's society. Customers can charge items such as gasoline, clothing, furniture, airline tickets, motel lodging, car rentals, and medical and dental services. Credit transactions are obviously a very important part of our economic system, and it is essential for business people to understand the accounting required to maintain timely and accurate records of these transactions.

### RECORDING REVENUE REALIZED FROM CREDIT TRANSACTIONS

As was previously stated, when the accrual basis of accounting is used, revenue should be recognized at the time it is earned rather than waiting until the cash is collected. The sections that follow explain how the most common types of credit transactions are recorded in the accounts.

## Merchandise Sold on Account

When merchandise is sold with an agreement that it will be paid for at a later date, the transaction is referred to as a *sale on account*. The entry recorded at the time the sale is made includes a debit to the asset account, Accounts Receivable, and a credit to the revenue account, Sales. For example, if a business sold $140 of merchandise on account to Nancy Moses, the sale could be recorded in general journal form as follows:

| | | | | |
|---|---|---|---|---|
| Jan. | 16 | Accounts Receivable — Nancy Moses | 140 | |
| | | Sales | | 140 |

In many businesses, the entry to record the sale of merchandise would be entered in a sales journal. The procedures for using sales journals are illustrated in Chapter 6. The general journal format, rather than the special journals, will be used to illustrate the entries in this chapter because of its simplicity and clarity for instructional purposes.

When the receivable is collected, Cash is debited for the amount received and Accounts Receivable is credited. If Moses pays her account in full, the following entry is required:

| | | | | |
|---|---|---|---|---|
| Feb. | 4 | Cash | 140 | |
| | | Accounts Receivable — Nancy Moses | | 140 |

This entry has no effect on the sales account. The revenue was recognized when the sale was made in January.

## Services Performed on Account

When a service is performed on account, the transaction is recorded by debiting Accounts Receivable and crediting a revenue account. For example, assume that on May 10 an exterminating company sprayed and treated the building of Hoe Co. for a fee of $350. If Hoe Co. is to pay at a later date, the following entry would be recorded on the books of the exterminating company:

| | | | | |
|---|---|---|---|---|
| May | 10 | Accounts Receivable — Hoe Co. | 350 | |
| | | Fees Earned | | 350 |

If Hoe Co. pays its account in full, the entry would be:

| | | | | |
|---|---|---|---|---|
| June | 3 | Cash | 350 | |
| | | Accounts Receivable — Hoe Co. | | 350 |

## Accounts Receivable Subsidiary Ledger

As explained in Chapter 6, the process of recording and reporting accounts receivable is simplified by having one control account, Accounts Receivable, in the general ledger. The balance in this control account is the total amount of accounts receivable from all customers.

The use of a control account in the general ledger requires a separate detailed ledger for the individual customers' accounts. This separate ledger of customers' accounts is called a *subsidiary ledger* and contains an account for each customer. Because the individual customers' accounts contain information which is necessary for making sound credit decisions, it is important that these accounts be kept current by posting all charges and payments on a daily basis to determine current balances.

## RECORDING BAD DEBTS

Experience has consistently shown that no matter how much care is exercised in approving customers for credit, some will be unable or unwilling to pay their accounts. When a customer fails to pay the amount owed, the account is referred to as a *bad debt* or an *uncollectible account*. An expense account entitled Bad Debts Expense or Uncollectible Accounts Expense, should be debited to record bad debts. There are two methods commonly used to record bad debts. One is called the *direct write-off method* and the other is the *allowance method*.

Using the *direct write-off method*, the bad debts expense is recorded at the time the customer's account is determined to be uncollectible. Under the *allowance method* an adjusting entry is made at the end of the year to record the estimated amount of bad debts expense related to the sales for that year. Both methods are acceptable for accounting and for federal income tax purposes. However, the allowance method is usually preferred, because it conforms to the matching concept of recording the expense for bad debts in the same period that the related revenue from sales is recognized.

### Direct Write-Off Method

Since the direct write-off method recognizes the expense for bad debts only when a specific customer's account is determined to be uncollectible, the expense will frequently not be recorded in the same period in which the sale was recognized. Recording the bad debts expense in a later period is undesirable from the standpoint of matching revenue with the related expenses for a period. However, it is an acceptable practice in certain situations. For instance, a firm making most of its sales on a cash basis and having a very small number of acounts receivable could use the direct write-off method without seriously distorting its net income for the period. Also, a company might use this method if it sells merchandise in large orders to a few companies, all of which have excellent credit records. Probably the major advantage of the direct write-off method is that it is easy to use.

**Recording Bad Debts Expense Under the Direct Write-Off Method.** To illustrate the procedure to write off an account using the direct write-off method, assume that Ron Ashby's account balance of $60 is considered uncollectible. The entry to record the expense and write off the account receivable would be:

| | | | | | |
|---|---|---|---|---|---|
| Nov. | 11 | Bad Debts Expense........................... | 66 | 60 00 | |
| | | Accounts Receiv. — Ron Ashby ... | 12/√ | | 60 00 |
| | | To write off uncollectible account. | | | |

The classification of Bad Debts Expense on the income statement depends on the type of business organization and on who has the responsibility for granting credit and making collections. Usually the general office staff has the responsibility for credit and collections, and bad debts should be classified as a general expense. In this text, Bad Debts Expense will be classified on the income statement as a general expense.

**Recovery of Accounts Written Off in the Same Period.** Occasionally an account that has been written off will be recovered at a later date. Under the direct write-off method, the timing of the recovery is significant. If the recovery is in the same accounting period as the write-off, the amount of the bad debts expense is still on the books. An entry should be made to reverse the original entry made to write off the account:

| | | | | | |
|---|---|---|---|---|---|
| Dec. | 15 | Accounts Receiv. — Ron Ashby | 12/√ | 60 00 | |
| | | Bad Debts Expense | 66 | | 60 00 |
| | | To reinstate account written off. | | | |

A separate entry is needed to record the receipt of cash:

| | | | | |
|---|---|---|---|---|
| Dec. | 15 | Cash | 60 | |
| | | Accounts Receivable — Ron Ashby | | 60 |

One entry, debiting Cash and crediting Bad Debts Expense, could have been made to record the above information. However, it is preferable to show separately the entry reinstating the account receivable, so that this information can then be posted to the customer's account in the subsidiary ledger for future credit reference. If a single entry had been made, the customer's account would not indicate that payment was made. Ashby's account in the subsidiary ledger, after posting all entries, would appear as follows:

NAME Ron Ashby
ADDRESS 9816 Pine Drive, Shreveport, LA 71106-4858 TERMS:

| DATE | | ITEM | POST. REF. | DEBIT | CREDIT | BALANCE |
|---|---|---|---|---|---|---|
| 1982 | | | | | | |
| May | 7 | (To record sale) | S4 | 60 00 | | 60 00 |
| Nov. | 11 | Account written off | J2 | | 60 00 | ——— |
| Dec. | 15 | Reinstate account | J3 | 60 00 | | 60 00 |
| | 15 | (Collection of account) | CR6 | | 60 00 | ——— |

The entries to record the sale on May 7 and the collection on December 15 would ordinarily not require an explanation in the ledger, because they are normal entries to the account. The entries for the write-off on November 11 and the reinstatement on December 15 should be explained, however, because they are unusual. The explanation would also be of value to the person responsible for making decisions about granting future credit to this customer.

**Recovery of Accounts in a Subsequent Period.** If the recovery of an account is made in a subsequent accounting period, the reinstatement procedure just described may be followed. However, since

Bad Debts Expense would have been closed to Income Summary at the end of the period in which the write-off was made, an alternative entry for the reinstatement can be made with a credit to a special account such as Recovery of Bad Debts. The entry to record the receipt of cash would be the same as previously shown. If the bad debt of Ron Ashby, recorded on November 11, is recovered on January 15 of the following year, the entries would be:

| | | | | | |
|---|---|---|---|---|---|
| Jan. | 15 | Accounts Receiv. — Ron Ashby ....... | | 60 00 | |
| | | Recovery of Bad Debts ................. | | | 60 00 |
| | | To reinstate account written off. | | | |

| | | | | |
|---|---|---|---|---|
| Jan. | 15 | Cash ................................ | 60.00 | |
| | | Accounts Receivable — Ron Ashby ................. | | 60.00 |

Ashby's account in the accounts receivable ledger would appear exactly the same as shown on page 260 except for the different dates for recovery. The recovery of bad debts account has a credit balance and may be reported on the income statement as a deduction from bad debts expense, or only the net amount of the expense may be reported.

## Allowance Method

When the allowance method of recording bad debts is used, an estimate is made of the probable future losses arising from bad debts. This procedure has two distinct advantages: (1) it is consistent with the matching concept because the expense for bad debts is charged to the same period in which the revenue is recognized, and (2) accounts receivable on the balance sheet reflects the amount actually expected to be collected, since the estimate of bad debts is shown as a deduction from accounts receivable.

**Recording Bad Debts Expense Under the Allowance Method.** When the allowance method is used, the bad debts expense is recorded by an adjusting entry at the end of the period. To illustrate, assume that the Foust Company had accounts receivable of $163,000 at the end of its first year of business. Although management cannot determine at this time which accounts will become uncollectible, the experience of similar businesses indicates that approximately 1%, or $1,630, of these receivables will eventually prove to be worthless. Based on this information the adjusting entry would be made as shown below:

| | | | | | |
|---|---|---|---|---|---|
| Dec. | 31 | Bad Debts Expense ............................ | 66 | 1 630 00 | |
| | | Allowance for Bad Debts ............... | 12.1 | | 1 630 00 |
| | | Adjusting entry for bad debts. | | | |

The adjusting entry shows a debit to Bad Debts Expense of $1,630, recognizing as an expense the estimated amount of uncollectibles for the current period.

**Allowance for Bad Debts Account.** Because the preceding adjustment is based on an estimate, none of the customers' account balances would be reduced at this time. Since the accounts receivable account in the general ledger represents a total of the individual customers' account balances, it would only be increased or decreased when changes occur in the customers' accounts. Thus, the credit in the above entry cannot be made directly to Accounts Receivable as this would cause its balance to differ from the balance in the customers' ledger. A contra account called Allowance for Bad Debts should be credited. The allowance for bad debts account will normally have a credit balance, the opposite of Accounts Receivable.

After the adjusting entry for bad debts has been posted, the general ledger accounts would appear as follows:

ACCOUNT **Accounts Receivable** ACCOUNT NO. **12**

| DATE | | ITEM | POST. REF. | DEBIT | CREDIT | BALANCE DEBIT | BALANCE CREDIT |
|---|---|---|---|---|---|---|---|
| 1982 | | | | | | | |
| Dec. | 31 | | S20 | 13 000 00 | | 163 000 00 | |

ACCOUNT **Allowance for Bad Debts** ACCOUNT NO. **12.1**

| DATE | | ITEM | POST. REF. | DEBIT | CREDIT | BALANCE DEBIT | BALANCE CREDIT |
|---|---|---|---|---|---|---|---|
| 1982 | | | | | | | |
| Dec. | 31 | Adjusting | J6 | | 1 630 00 | | 1 630 00 |

ACCOUNT **Bad Debts Expense** ACCOUNT NO. **66**

| DATE | | ITEM | POST. REF. | DEBIT | CREDIT | BALANCE DEBIT | BALANCE CREDIT |
|---|---|---|---|---|---|---|---|
| 1982 | | | | | | | |
| Dec. | 31 | Adjusting | J6 | 1 630 00 | | 1 630 00 | |

Bad Debts Expense is a temporary account and is closed to Income Summary at the end of the period. The balance in Accounts Receivable represents the total claims against customers on account. This balance is equal to the sum of the balances in the customers' accounts in the subsidiary ledger. The credit balance in the allowance for bad debts account represents the estimated uncollectible accounts as of the end of the accounting period.

**Allowance for Bad Debts on the Balance Sheet.** Accounts receivable are shown on the balance sheet as a current asset. Allowance for Bad Debts is a contra asset account which is subtracted from accounts receivable on the balance sheet. The result will be the net amount of receivables expected to be collected. This amount, $161,370, in the illustration on page 263, is called the *net realizable value* of the accounts receivable.

Foust Company
Balance Sheet
December 31, 1982

| | | |
|---|---|---|
| Current assets: | | |
| Cash | | $ xxx |
| Accounts receivable | $163,000 | |
| Less Allowance for bad debts | 1,630 | 161,370 |

**Writing Off Bad Debts to the Allowance Account.** The individual customer's account should be written off when it proves to be uncollectible. Some companies have a policy of writing off an account after it has been past due for a specified period of time. Bankruptcy, death, or disappearance of the debtor may also cause an account to be considered worthless.

The entry made to write off the account is a debit to Allowance for Bad Debts and a credit to Accounts Receivable. Assume that the Foust Company, from the previous example, is now in its second year of operations. If the company determines that the $250 account of Dan McKee has become uncollectible, the following entry would be made:

| | | | | | |
|---|---|---|---|---|---|
| Apr. | 12 | Allowance for Bad Debts | 12.1 | 250 00 | |
| | | Accounts Receiv. — Dan McKee | 12/√ | | 250 00 |
| | | To write off uncollectible account. | | | |

Bad Debts Expense is not debited for the write-off because the expense was recorded in the adjusting entry at the end of the first year of operations. Allowance for Bad Debts was originally credited in that adjusting entry. Now that a specific customer's account has been identified as being uncollectible, Allowance for Bad Debts is debited and Accounts Receivable, as well as Dan McKee's subsidiary account, is credited. The entry to write off the account does not change the net realizable value of the accounts receivable. Allowance for Bad Debts merely serves as a "valuation" account until the individual customers' accounts which will become uncollectible can be identified. When an uncollectible account has been identified, an entry like the one above causes a reduction in Accounts Receivable and an equal reduction in Allowance for Bad Debts. Since the balance of the valuation account, Allowance for Bad Debts, is subtracted from Accounts Receivable, this equal reduction does not change the net realizable value.

**Recording Collection of Account Written Off.** When an account that has been written off under the allowance method is later collected, two entries are required. The first entry reinstates the account receivable by reversing the entry made at the time the account was written off. For example, the entry to reinstate the account receivable of Dan McKee would be as follows:

| | | | | | |
|---|---|---|---|---|---|
| May | 24 | Accounts Receiv. — Dan McKee | 12/√ | 250 00 | |
| | | Allowance for Bad Debts | 12.1 | | 250 00 |
| | | To reinstate account written off. | | | |

The second entry is made to record the receipt of cash in the usual manner:

| | | | | |
|---|---|---|---|---|
| May 24 | Cash | 11 | 250 | |
| | Accounts Receivable — Dan McKee | 12/√ | | 250 |

The reinstatement and collection of an account under the allowance method does not involve an expense or revenue account. The estimated bad debts expense was recorded as an adjusting entry in the year in which the sale was made. When McKee's account was determined to be uncollectible, it was written off to Allowance for Bad Debts. When the account proved to be collectible, the entry for the write-off was reversed and an entry to record the collection was made. This subsequent collectibility of McKee's account does not prove the estimate to be incorrect. It merely means that accounts other than McKee's comprise the group of uncollectibles which were previously estimated. McKee's account in the accounts receivable subsidiary ledger would appear as follows after the above transactions have been posted:

NAME Dan McKee
ADDRESS 1212 Ridgeway, Shreveport, LA 71107-3023 TERMS:

| DATE | | ITEM | POST. REF. | DEBIT | CREDIT | BALANCE |
|---|---|---|---|---|---|---|
| 1982 | | | | | | |
| Dec. | 5 | | S9 | 250 00 | | 250 00 |
| 1983 | | | | | | |
| Apr. | 12 | Account written off | J14 | | 250 00 | — |
| May | 24 | Reinstate account | J15 | 250 00 | | 250 00 |
| | 24 | | CR8 | | 250 00 | — |

## METHODS OF ESTIMATING BAD DEBTS

The allowance method of recording bad debts requires an estimate to be made at the end of the accounting period as to the probable future losses on customers' accounts. This estimate is based on the past experience of the individual firm and on averages for similar types of businesses. Current and future economic conditions, the type of merchandise or service sold, the kind of customer the business attracts, the care taken in granting credit, and the extent of collection efforts must all be considered.

There are two widely recognized methods of estimating losses from uncollectible accounts: (1) the *percentage-of-sales* method, and (2) the *analysis-of-accounts-receivable* method.

### Percentage-of-Sales Method

Sales on account are the origin of all accounts receivable. The estimate of bad debts for the period may therefore be based on the ratio of actual losses to *net* sales made on account during the past years. If a business does not maintain a record of charge sales separately from cash sales, then the percentage of estimated loss would have to be based on *total* sales. This method is usually satisfactory provided the ratio of cash sales to charge sales remains approximately the same from year to year.

**Estimate Based on Charge Sales.** Assume that the Rico Company can determine from past experience that approximately 2% of net sales on account will become uncollectible and that net charge sales for the current year totaled $180,000. The estimated loss from bad debts for the year would be $3,600 ($180,000 × .02) and the adjusting entry at the end of the period would be:

| | | | | |
|---|---|---|---|---|
| Dec. | 31 | Bad Debts Expense | 3,600.00 | |
| | | Allowance for Bad Debts | | 3,600.00 |
| | | Adjusting entry for bad debts. | | |

**Estimate Based on Total Sales.** Now assume that the Rico Company does not maintain a separate record of charge sales. It had net sales for the year of $240,000 and used a percentage of 1½% of net sales as an estimate of uncollectible accounts. The adjusting entry required to record the estimated loss from bad debts would be identical to the one above, $3,600 ($240,000 × .015).

In the following period, as individual accounts become uncollectible, Allowance for Bad Debts will be debited and Accounts Receivable will be credited. Since the adjustment for bad debts at the end of the period is based on an estimate, the actual write-offs in the following period will not usually equal the amount provided for in the allowance account. If the amount provided for in the allowance account differs only slightly from the actual amounts written off, the percentage being used to estimate bad debts is acceptable.

If, however, over several years, the amount of write-offs is consistently larger or smaller than the allowance provided for in the adjusting entry, the reasons for the variance must be determined and the percentage being applied to sales may have to be changed. For example, if Allowance for Bad Debts has a debit balance of $400 and the allowance for the year had been estimated at $2,100, this indicates that $2,500 of accounts actually became uncollectible during the year. Therefore, bad debts were underestimated by $400. Although this single instance of incorrect estimation would not indicate the need for a change in the estimating procedure, a recurring difference of this type would indicate the need to change the percentage applied to sales.

## Analysis-of-Accounts-Receivable Method

The second method of estimating losses from uncollectible accounts involves analyzing accounts receivable at the end of the period as to amount and length of time owed. This analysis helps determine the amount of receivables that will probably not be collected. This method is known as *aging the accounts receivable.*

**Procedure for Aging the Accounts.** When accounts receivable are aged, the individual accounts in the subsidiary ledger are classified according to the length of time they have been outstanding. For example, the categories might be as follows: current accounts; 1–30 days past due; 31–60 days past due; 61–90 days past due; 3–6 months past due; and over 6 months past due. A percentage of estimated losses based on past experience is applied to each category. A successively higher percentage of estimated losses is applied to the age groups of accounts which are past due the longest.

In aging accounts receivable, it is necessary to determine the percentage of estimated losses to be applied to each age group. After the percentage is determined, it is multiplied by the total amount of receivables in the appropriate age group to determine the probable loss from uncollectible accounts within that group. The probable losses for each age group are added together to determine the total amount of uncollectible accounts. This total represents the balance which should appear in Allowance for Bad Debts after the adjusting entry has been made.

The Cable Company ages its accounts receivable in determining estimated bad debts. An analysis by age of its accounts receivable ledger is shown below.

This schedule indicates that the longer an account is outstanding, the higher the probability of loss. For example, only 1% of current accounts is estimated to be uncollectible, whereas 4% of those 1–30 days past due, and 7% of those 31–60 days past due are considered worthless. Of the accounts over 6 months past due, 50% are probably not collectible.

*Schedule of Aging Accounts Receivable*

| AGE INTERVAL | AMOUNT OF RECEIVABLES | PERCENT UNCOLLECTIBLE | ALLOWANCE FOR BAD DEBTS |
|---|---|---|---|
| Current accounts (not yet due) | $14,300 | 1% | $ 143 |
| 1–30 days past due | 8,400 | 4 | 336 |
| 31–60 days past due | 3,200 | 7 | 224 |
| 61–90 days past due | 1,640 | 10 | 164 |
| 3–6 months past due | 1,160 | 20 | 232 |
| Over 6 months past due | 1,290 | 50 | 645 |
| Total | $29,990 | | $1,744 |

The above schedule shows that $1,744 of the $29,990 of outstanding receivables will probably not be collected. The result will be the $28,246 net realizable value of accounts receivable appearing on the balance sheet as shown below:

Cable Company
Balance Sheet
December 31, 19--

| | | |
|---|---|---|
| Current assets: | | |
| Cash | | $ xxx |
| Accounts receivable | $29,990 | |
| Less Allowance for bad debts | 1,744 | 28,246 |

**Effect of Allowance Account Balance on Adjusting Entry.** The aging method of estimating bad debts emphasizes the net realizable value of all outstanding accounts receivable. With this method, the computation for the adjusting entry is determined from the balance required in Allowance for Bad Debts. For this reason, it is necessary to consider any previous balance remaining in the allowance account prior to making the adjusting entry. To illustrate, assume the allowance for bad debts account has a $260 credit balance before the adjusting entry is made. This balance exists because actual uncollectible accounts were $260 less than the amount estimated to be uncollectible.

The aging schedule on the previous page indicates that a total of $1,744 of outstanding accounts receivable are estimated to be uncollectible. An adjusting entry for bad debts in the amount of $1,484 is required to bring the allowance account to the proper balance. The $1,484 adjustment is determined by subtracting the present credit balance in the allowance account of $260 from the total desired balance of $1,744 appearing on the aging schedule. The adjusting entry to bring the allowance account up to the desired balance, and the allowance for bad debts and bad debts expense ledger accounts after posting appear as follows:

| | | | | | |
|---|---|---|---|---|---|
| Dec. | 31 | Bad Debts Expense.......................... | 66 | 1 484 00 | |
| | | Allowance for Bad Debts.............. | 12.1 | | 1 484 00 |
| | | Adjusting entry for bad debts. | | | |

**ACCOUNT** Allowance for Bad Debts **ACCOUNT NO.** 12.1

| DATE | | ITEM | POST. REF. | DEBIT | CREDIT | BALANCE DEBIT | BALANCE CREDIT |
|---|---|---|---|---|---|---|---|
| 1982 | | | | | | | |
| Dec. | 31 | | J5 | 100 00 | | | 260 00 |
| | 31 | Adjusting | J6 | | 1 484 00 | | 1 744 00 |

**ACCOUNT** Bad Debts Expense **ACCOUNT NO.** 66

| DATE | | ITEM | POST. REF. | DEBIT | CREDIT | BALANCE DEBIT | BALANCE CREDIT |
|---|---|---|---|---|---|---|---|
| 1982 | | | | | | | |
| Dec. | 31 | Adjusting | J6 | 1 484 00 | | 1 484 00 | |

The bad debts expense for the period is merely the amount determined to be added to the allowance account. In the preceding illustration, the bad debts expense for the year is $1,484, the same amount required to be added to the allowance account. This amount will be shown as an expense on the income statement and transferred to Income Summary by a closing entry.

Assume that in the preceding illustration the balance in Allowance for Bad Debts before adjustment had been a $310 debit. This indicates that the amount of accounts which were written off during the period exceeded the estimated uncollectibles by $310. An adjusting entry for $2,054 would have to be made. This amount would offset the $310 debit balance in the allowance for bad debts account and result in the desired credit balance of $1,744, as determined from the aging schedule on page 266.

The adjusting entry and the ledger accounts after adjustment would appear as follows:

| | | | | | |
|---|---|---|---|---|---|
| Dec. | 31 | Bad Debts Expense | 66 | 2 054 00 | |
| | | Allowance for Bad Debts | 12.1 | | 2 054 00 |
| | | Adjusting entry for bad debts. | | | |

ACCOUNT **Allowance for Bad Debts** ACCOUNT NO. **12.1**

| DATE | | ITEM | POST. REF. | DEBIT | CREDIT | BALANCE DEBIT | BALANCE CREDIT |
|---|---|---|---|---|---|---|---|
| 1982 | | | | | | | |
| Dec. | 31 | | J5 | 100 00 | | 310 00 | |
| | 31 | Adjusting | J6 | | 2 054 00 | | 1 744 00 |

ACCOUNT **Bad Debts Expense** ACCOUNT NO. **66**

| DATE | | ITEM | POST. REF. | DEBIT | CREDIT | BALANCE DEBIT | BALANCE CREDIT |
|---|---|---|---|---|---|---|---|
| 1982 | | | | | | | |
| Dec. | 31 | Adjusting | J6 | 2 054 00 | | 2 054 00 | |

In this example, a bad debts expense of $2,054 would be shown on the income statement for the period. As in the previous example, the bad debts expense for the period is equal to the amount added to the allowance account. In both examples, Accounts Receivable and Allowance for Bad Debts would be presented on the year-end balance sheet as shown on page 266. Although the adjusting entries in each of these examples differed because of the remaining balance in the allowance for bad debts account, the account after posting the adjustment contains a $1,744 credit balance in each example.

## PERCENTAGE-OF-SALES METHOD VERSUS ANALYSIS-OF-ACCOUNTS-RECEIVABLE METHOD

Now that the two methods of estimating bad debts have been discussed, several points should be noted as to their similarities and differences.

The percentage-of-sales method emphasizes the amount of bad debts expense to be recorded for the period based directly on the amount of sales made during the same period. This practice is consistent with the matching concept of recording expenses in the same period as the revenues to which they relate. The current balance in the allowance for bad debts account is not considered in making the end-of-period adjustment. This method is often referred to as the "income statement approach" to bad debts because the emphasis is on the bad debts expense account, which is an income statement item.

When the analysis-of-accounts-receivable method is used, the emphasis is placed on determining the balance needed in Allowance for Bad Debts so that this account will reflect the total amount of uncollectible accounts as determined from the aging schedule. The amount of bad debts expense to appear on the income statement is the amount required to establish the desired balance in the allowance account. The aging method is often referred to as the "balance sheet approach" to bad debts, because the emphasis is on Allowance for Bad Debts which is a contra asset account on the balance sheet.

It should be emphasized that for either method of estimating bad debts, the only entries to Bad Debts Expense will be the end-of-period adjusting and closing entries. Under either method, when an account is written off, the debit is to Allowance for Bad Debts and the credit is to Accounts Receivable because the estimated loss has become a reality. The bad debts expense account was debited in the adjusting entry at the end of the previous period and the fact that certain of the estimated uncollectible accounts can now be identified does not change the amount of the expense.

## QUESTIONS FOR DISCUSSION

1. A customer purchased merchandise on December 11, 1982, and paid the account in full on February 2, 1983. If the accrual basis is used, in what year should the revenue be realized? Explain.
2. Explain what is meant by the matching concept.
3. What advantages are there to estimating bad debts at the end of a period?
4. When an account that has been written off is subsequently collected, the normal procedure is to make two entries, one to reinstate the account and a second to record the cash received. What is the purpose of this procedure?
5. What effect will the balance in Allowance for Bad Debts have on the adjusting entry for bad debts if (a) the percentage-of-sales method is used? (b) the analysis-of-accounts-receivable method is used?
6. The Doke Company uses the percentage-of-sales method of estimating bad debts. An analysis of the allowance for bad debts account shows the following balances prior to adjustments:

   | | |
   |---|---|
   | Year 1 — $270 credit | Year 3 — $ 720 credit |
   | Year 2 — $460 credit | Year 4 — $1,010 credit |

   What action, if any, would you recommend regarding the percentage being used to determine the estimate? Explain.
7. The Leo Company had accounts receivable of $16,870 and an allowance for bad debts of $1,245 on November 30. On this date the company decided to write off the account of Florence Day as uncollectible in the amount of $140. (a) Explain the effect, if any, this entry will have on the current assets of the Leo Company. (b) What effect will it have on the net income for the period?
8. Explain the procedure for aging accounts receivable.

## EXERCISES

**1.** At the end of the first year of operations, Vegas Glass and Mirror Company has accounts receivable of $8,440. Of this amount, it is estimated $337 will ultimately prove to be uncollectible.

**Required:**

(a) Prepare the adjusting entry to record the bad debts expense at the end of the first year.

(b) Show how accounts receivable of Vegas would be presented on the balance sheet at the end of the first year.

**2.** The Brian Company uses the direct write-off method of recording bad debts. On July 17 of the current year, the credit manager determines the account of Pam Fuller, in the amount of $125, is uncollectible.

**Required:**

(a) Using the direct write-off method, prepare the journal entry to write off the account of Pam Fuller on July 17.

(b) If Fuller paid her account in full on November 4 of the same year, prepare the entries required to record the collection on Brian's books.

(c) Assuming instead that Fuller paid her account on January 11 of the following year, prepare the entries required to record the collection on Brian's books.

**3.** If the Brian Company in 2 above used the *allowance method* of recording bad debts, prepare the following entries related to the account of Pam Fuller:

(a) July 17 — Write off Fuller's account in the amount of $125.
(b) November 4 — Record payment of $125 from Fuller for her account written off July 17.

**4.** Selected account balances, prior to the adjustment for bad debts, for the Farr Furniture Company are given below:

| | |
|---|---|
| Accounts Receivable | $21,200 |
| Allowance for Bad Debts | 140 cr. |
| Sales | 84,600 |
| Sales Returns and Allowances | 1,600 |

**Required:** Prepare the adjusting entry for bad debts at the end of the year assuming:

(a) the percentage-of-sales method is used. (Losses are estimated at 3 percent of net sales.)

(b) the analysis of accounts receivable method is used. An aging schedule shows that $1,960 of the present accounts receivable will probably be uncollectible.

(c) What will be the net realizable value of accounts receivable for Farr Furniture in (b) above?

**5.** The following transactions are for the Threlkeld Company:

1982

Dec. 31. Net sales for the period were $140,000. Threlkeld uses the percentage-of-sales method of estimating bad debts. Bad debt losses are estimated at 1½% of net sales.

1983

Feb. 12. The account receivable of Paul Hawks was determined to be uncollectible and written off, $95.

Apr. 6. Notice was received that Jill Marsh, a customer, was bankrupt. Final settlement of $75 was accepted as full payment for this account of $250.

June 12. Paul Hawks paid on his account which had been written off February 12, $95.

**Required:** Prepare the entries, in general journal form, to record each of the above transactions.

**ASSIGNMENT 12-A**

**Tear out pages 539–550 and complete Assignment 12-A. Submit your papers for approval and proceed to the study of Part B until the next assignment is required.**

# PART B NOTES RECEIVABLE AND NOTES PAYABLE

In the discussions of buying on credit in Part A, the transactions involved the sale or purchase of goods or services on *open account*. This means the accounts receivable or accounts payable were open for settlement at some time within the near future. In this part, a more formal type of business credit is discussed, namely the promissory note.

A *promissory note* is a written promise to pay a specified sum of money on demand or at some definite future date. A note is a legal instrument. It is signed by the *maker* and is made payable to the *payee*. In the promissory note illustrated below, Henry Burge is the maker and Mary Rumsey is the payee.

$ 300.00 WEST PLAINS, MO. March 2 19 82

Sixty days AFTER DATE I PROMISE TO PAY TO

THE ORDER OF Mary Rumsey

Three hundred 00/100 DOLLARS

PAYABLE AT Second National Bank

WITH INTEREST AT 15%

NO. 14 DUE May 1, 1982 Henry Burge

*Promissory Note*

The following definitions of terms used in discussing a promissory note are keyed to the illustration above.

| Term | Definition | Burge's Note |
|---|---|---|
| **1.** Principal or face value | The amount the borrower (maker) promises to pay. | $300 |
| **2.** Maker | The person who signs the note and promises to make payment. | Henry Burge |
| **3.** Payee | The party to whom the note is payable. | Mary Rumsey |
| **4.** Date | The date the note is issued. | March 2, 1982 |
| **5.** Time | The amount of time from the date the note is issued until it is to be paid. | 60 days |
| **6.** Maturity date | The date the note is due to be paid. | May 1, 1982 |
| **7.** Annual interest rate | The percentage of face value paid for borrowing the money. | 15% |

The individual or business receiving the note, Mary Rumsey in the preceding illustration, records it at its face amount in the account, Notes Receivable. A note receivable is an asset similar to an account receivable. A note receivable is frequently given for a period of one year or less and is therefore classified as a current asset. When the term of a note is longer than one year, it is not a current asset. Usually, notes for a period in excess of one year are shown under the caption "Investments" on the balance sheet. The investments section is shown immediately below the current assets section.

## NOTE RECEIVED TO REPLACE ACCOUNT RECEIVABLE

Most small business entities receive very few notes. Occasionally a note may be given by a customer who cannot pay an account on time and wishes an extension of the payment period. For example, if Henry Burge could not pay his account when it was due, he might have given Mary Rumsey a written promise to pay in 60 days with interest at 15%. The note receivable would be recorded on Rumsey's books as follows:

| | | | | | |
|---|---|---|---|---|---|
| Mar. | 2 | Notes Receivable.............................. | 13 | 300 00 | |
| | | Accounts Receiv. — Henry Burge | 12/√ | | 300 00 |
| | | Received 60-day, 15% note to replace account receivable. | | | |

The above entry transfers the claim against Burge on Rumsey's books from Accounts Receivable to Notes Receivable. Assuming that the Accounts Receivable balance prior to receiving the note is $3,682, after the above entry is posted, the ledger accounts are as follows:

ACCOUNT Accounts Receivable ACCOUNT NO. 12

| DATE | | ITEM | POST. REF. | DEBIT | CREDIT | BALANCE DEBIT | BALANCE CREDIT |
|---|---|---|---|---|---|---|---|
| 1982 Mar. | 1 | Balance | √ | | | 3 682 00 | |
| | 2 | | J57 | | 300 00 | 3 382 00 | |

ACCOUNT Notes Receivable ACCOUNT NO. 13

| DATE | | ITEM | POST. REF. | DEBIT | CREDIT | BALANCE DEBIT | BALANCE CREDIT |
|---|---|---|---|---|---|---|---|
| 1982 Mar. | 2 | | J57 | 300 00 | | 300 00 | |

NAME Henry Burge
ADDRESS 2978 Horn Ave., West Plains, MO 65775-8311 TERMS:

| DATE | | ITEM | POST. REF. | DEBIT | CREDIT | BALANCE |
|---|---|---|---|---|---|---|
| 1982 Mar. | 1 | Balance | √ | | | 300 00 |
| | 2 | | J57 | | 300 00 | —— |

It is not necessary to maintain a subsidiary ledger for notes receivable. Each note provides all the necessary information. If several notes are received, however, a notes receivable register summarizing the details of all notes receivable may be useful as a quick reference.

## NOTE RECEIVED FOR MERCHANDISE

If a customer buys merchandise and desires an extended payment arrangement, a note may be given at the time of sale.

If the note illustrated on page 271 had been received by Rumsey at the time of sale, the following entry would have been made:

| | | | | | | | |
|---|---|---|---|---|---|---|---|
| Mar. | 2 | Notes Receivable | | 300 | 00 | | |
| | | Sales | | | | 300 | 00 |
| | | Received 60-day, 15% note from Henry Burge. | | | | | |

The above entry normally would be recorded in the general journal. It should not be recorded in a single-column sales journal, because that journal is designed to record only sales on open account (accounts receivable).

## NOTE RECEIVED FOR CASH

Under certain conditions, a business may, as a favor or convenience, lend cash to a customer, employee, or other individual. If a promissory note is received in such a transaction, it would be recorded as follows:

| | | | | |
|---|---|---|---|---|
| Mar. | 2 | Notes Receivable | 300.00 | |
| | | Cash | | 300.00 |

## COLLECTION OF NOTES RECEIVABLE

If Burge pays the note plus interest when due, the following entry would be made in Rumsey's books:

| | | | | |
|---|---|---|---|---|
| May | 1 | Cash | 307.50 | |
| | | Notes Receivable | | 300.00 |
| | | Interest Income | | 7.50 |
| | | Collected note plus interest. | | |

The debit to Cash represents the total amount received from Burge, the face amount of the note, $300, plus the $7.50 interest earned over the 60-day period at the rate of 15%. The credit to Notes Receivable is for the specified sum of $300, the amount debited when the note was received. Notes are always recorded at their *principal* or *face value*.

## INTEREST ON NOTES

The amount paid for the use of money is called *interest*. One major advantage of receiving a note from a customer is that notes receivable normally earn interest. A note requiring interest to be paid for the period of the note, from date of issuance to due date, is called an *interest-bearing* note. If the note does not require interest to be paid, it is called a *non-interest-bearing* note. Interest received by a business on a note receivable is called *interest income*. The interest paid on a note payable is called *interest expense*.

### Computation of Interest

Interest rates are normally quoted on a yearly basis unless otherwise stated. Thus the annual interest on a $300, 1-year, 15% note would be $45 ($300 × 15/100). An interest rate of 15% on a $300 note for six months would be $22.50 ($45 ÷ 2). The note on page 271 calls for interest at 15% for 60 days, approximately 1/6 of a year, which would be $7.50 ($300 × 15/100 × 1/6).

The above examples illustrate the use of the basic formula for computing interest:

**Principal (P) × Rate (R) × Time (T) = Interest (I)**

$300.00 × 15/100 × 60/360 = $7.50

*Principal* is the face value of the note, that is, the amount being borrowed. *Rate* is the amount of interest expressed as an annual percentage. *Time* is the number of days, or fraction of a year, for which the note is issued. In the computation of interest, a business year is normally considered to be 360 days. Therefore, 360 days is used as the denominator in the fraction. As in the example above, interest on a 60-day note will be computed as 60/360 which is 1/6 of a year.

Assuming a $500, 90-day, 12% note, the interest would be computed as follows:

P × R × T = I

$500 × 12/100 × 90/360 = $15

Notes issued for a period of longer than one year will usually provide for interest payments at regular intervals, such as semiannually or annually. Most notes issued in business transactions are for less than a year and the interest is payable when the note matures.

## DETERMINING THE DUE DATE OF A NOTE

The determination of the due date of a note depends on whether the time of the note is expressed in days or months. If the term of a note is expressed in days, the due date is the exact number of days from the date the note is issued.

The computation of the due date when the terms of a note are expressed in days is made as follows:

1. Determine the number of days the note will be outstanding in the month it is issued.
2. Add the number of days in each full month without exceeding the number of days in the note.
3. Add the number of days in 1. and 2. Subtract the total of 1. and 2. from the total days in the note.

This procedure applied to a 90-day note dated July 11, would be:

| | | |
|---|---|---|
| Time of the note (days) | | 90 |
| 1. Days in July | 31 | |
| Date note is issued | 11 | |
| Days outstanding | 20 | |
| 2. August | 31 | |
| September | 30 | |
| Total | | 81 |
| 3. Date due, October | | 9 |

When the time of the note is expressed in months, the due date is found by counting the number of months from the date the note was issued. If the note dated July 11 is a 3-month note, the due date would be October 11. A 6-month note dated December 14 would be due on June 14. If a 3-month note is dated March 31, it would be due on June 30, since there is no date in the month of maturity that corresponds to the issue date.

## NOTES PAYABLE

All of the procedures discussed for notes receivable are valid in the study of notes payable. For example, the procedures for computing interest and due dates are exactly the same.

Most businesses issue only a few notes payable, and the notes are usually recorded in one general ledger account. There is normally no advantage to maintaining a subsidiary ledger for notes payable, because the file containing a copy of each note would provide all the necessary information.

Notes payable represent a liability to the business. They are shown on the balance sheet as a current liability if payment is due within one year of the balance sheet date. Notes that are not due within one year are shown in the long-term liabilities section of the balance sheet.

## NOTE ISSUED TO REPLACE ACCOUNTS PAYABLE

Occasionally, a business person will need additional time to pay a creditor the amount owed. One method of extending the time of payment is to give a promissory note. The entry on the books of the maker of the note includes a debit to Accounts Payable and to the subsidiary ledger account and a credit to Notes Payable. On page 271, Henry Burge issued a 60-day, 15% note to Mary Rumsey for $300. If this note is in payment of his account, Burge will make the following entry:

| | | | | | |
|---|---|---|---|---|---|
| Mar. | 2 | Accounts Payable — Mary Rumsey. | | 300 00 | |
| | | Notes Payable................................ | | | 300 00 |
| | | Issued 60-day, 15% note to replace account payable. | | | |

The above entry transfers the liability on Burge's books by reducing the amount of accounts payable and establishing the new liability account, Notes Payable.

## NOTE ISSUED FOR MERCHANDISE

If a firm buys merchandise and desires an extended credit arrangement, a note payable may be issued at the time the purchase is made. If Burge gives Rumsey the $300 note for merchandise received, the following entry is required:

| | | | | | |
|---|---|---|---|---|---|
| Mar. | 2 | Purchases | | 300 00 | |
| | | Notes Payable | | | 300 00 |
| | | Issued 60-day, 15% note to Mary Rumsey. | | | |

Both of the preceding entries were recorded in the general journal. If a large number of notes payable are issued by a business, it may be desirable to maintain a notes payable register for summarizing the details of all notes issued.

## NOTE ISSUED FOR CASH

A majority of notes issued by businesses are short-term notes issued to banks or other financial institutions to borrow cash. If Burge had given a $300 note to the Second National Bank for cash, he would make the following entry:

| | | | | |
|---|---|---|---|---|
| Mar. | 2 | Cash | 300.00 | |
| | | Notes Payable | | 300.00 |

## PAYMENT OF NOTES PAYABLE

The note issued by Burge in each example was a $300, 60-day, 15% note. When the note matures on May 1, Burge is obligated to pay both the principal of the note, $300, plus the accrued interest of $7.50 ($300 × 15/100 × 60/360). The entry to record the payment of the note plus interest would be made as follows:

| | | | | |
|---|---|---|---|---|
| May | 1 | Notes Payable | 300.00 | |
| | | Interest Expense | 7.50 | |
| | | Cash | | 307.50 |

Notes Payable is debited for the face value of the note, $300. Interest Expense is debited for the interest charge during the period, $7.50. Cash is credited for the total amount paid, $307.50.

## DISCOUNTING NOTES

When banks make loans to their customers, it is not unusual for them to collect interest in advance. They deduct the interest charge from the face of the note and give the customer the remainder. This procedure of deducting the interest in advance is called *discounting*. The rate used in determining the interest to be deducted is known as the *discount rate*. The interest deducted in advance is called the *discount*, and the difference between the face of the note and the discount is known as the *proceeds*.

The computation of the discount on a note is exactly the same as the computation of the interest paid when a note becomes due except that the discount rate is always computed on the maturity value of the note. The *maturity value* of a note is the amount due when the note matures, which is principal plus interest. The maturity value of a non-interest-bearing note is the same as its face value. The only difference in the terms "interest" and "discount" is that discount represents interest deducted in advance. The formula for computing discount is:

Maturity Value (MV) × Discount Rate (R) × Time (T) = Discount (D)

## Discounting Note Payable

If a firm wishes to borrow money from the bank by discounting its own note, the simplest procedure is to give the bank a non-interest-bearing note so that the maturity value and the face value will be the same. Assume that Lee Mahle issues an $800, 60-day, non-interest-bearing note to the Second National Bank on June 11, and the bank charges a discount rate of 18%. The discount is computed on the maturity value of the note, $800, which in this example is the same as the face value because it is a non-interest-bearing note. The discount is computed as follows:

$$MV \times R \times T = D$$
$$\$800 \times 18/100 \times 60/360 = \$24.00$$

The proceeds of the note will be $776 ($800 MV − $24.00 D). The entry is recorded in Mahle's journal as shown below:

| | | | |
|---|---|---|---|
| June 11 | Cash | 776.00 | |
| | Interest Expense | 24.00 | |
| | Notes Payable | | 800.00 |

When Mahle pays the note on August 10, he will pay the bank $800, the maturity value of the note. There will be no additional interest at date of payment, since the interest was recorded at the time the note was issued. The entry to record the payment is as follows:

| | | | |
|---|---|---|---|
| Aug. 10 | Notes Payable | 800.00 | |
| | Cash | | 800.00 |

## Discounting a Customer's Note Receivable

One advantage of receiving a note from a customer is that if money is needed before the note is due, the business may discount the customer's note at a bank instead of issuing its own note payable. The period from the date the note is discounted until the day the note is due is called the *discount period.* The bank will charge interest for the discount period.

**Discounting a Non-Interest-Bearing Note.** When the customer's note is non-interest-bearing, the maturity value and the face value are the same. Assume that on March 5, Barbara Wilson received a $450,

90-day, non-interest-bearing note from Lara Lopez, a customer, to replace her outstanding account receivable. Wilson would record this transaction in the general journal as follows:

| | | | | |
|---|---|---|---|---|
| Mar. | 5 | Notes Receivable ................ | 450 00 | |
| | | Accounts Receiv. — Lara Lopez.. | | 450 00 |
| | | Received 90-day, non-interest-bearing note. | | |

If on May 4, sixty days later, Wilson needs additional cash, she can discount Lopez's note at the bank. Assuming the bank agrees to discount the note at 18% for the remaining thirty days, the bank will deduct \$6.75 for interest (\$450 × 18/100 × 30/360 = \$6.75) and give Wilson the proceeds of \$443.25 (\$450.00 − \$6.75). This transaction may be recorded in Wilson's journal as follows:

| | | | | |
|---|---|---|---|---|
| May | 4 | Cash ........................................ | 443.25 | |
| | | Interest Expense .............................. | 6.75 | |
| | | Notes Receivable .......................... | | 450.00 |

**Discounting an Interest-Bearing Note.** When a customer's interest-bearing note receivable is discounted, the maturity value of the note will be greater than face value and will have to be computed before the amount of the discount can be determined. For example, assume the \$450, 90-day note received on March 5 by Wilson from Lopez was interest-bearing at the rate of 15%. Wilson would record the receipt of the note on March 5 as shown below:

| | | | | |
|---|---|---|---|---|
| Mar. | 5 | Notes Receivable............................ | 450 00 | |
| | | Accounts Receiv. — Lara Lopez... | | 450 00 |
| | | Received 90-day, 15% note. | | |

If Wilson discounts the note at the bank on May 4 at a discount rate of 18%, the amount of the discount and the proceeds of the note are computed in the following sequence:

**Step 1:** Determine the maturity value of the note:

$$\textbf{P} + \textbf{I} = \textbf{MV}$$
$$\$450.00 + \$16.88 = \$466.88$$

The interest of \$16.88 was computed as follows:

$$P \times R \times T = I$$
$$\$450.00 \times 15/100 \times 90/360 = \$16.88$$

**Step 2:** Compute the amount of the discount at 18% for 30 days, based on the maturity value of \$466.88:

$$MV \times R \times T = D$$
$$\$466.88 \times 18/100 \times 30/360 = \$7.00$$

**Step 3:** Compute the proceeds:

$$MV - D = Amt.$$
$$\$466.88 - \$7.00 = \$459.88$$

By discounting the note on May 4, thirty days prior to maturity, Wilson receives $459.88, representing $450.00 principal plus $9.88, which is the difference between the interest income of $16.88 when held to maturity and the bank discount of $7.00.

The entry in Wilson's journal to record the discounting of the note is as follows:

| | | | | |
|---|---|---|---|---|
| May | 4 | Cash | 459.88 | |
| | | Notes Receivable | | 450.00 |
| | | Interest Income | | 9.88 |

In this example, Wilson has interest income from the note when she discounts. In some instances, an interest-bearing note being discounted will result in an interest expense to the payee. This situation would occur when the proceeds from discounting a note receivable are less than the face value of the note.

### Contingent Liability on Notes Receivable Discounted

When the payee discounts a customer's note, the note must be endorsed. By endorsing the note, the payee is guaranteeing payment, and if the maker of the note fails to pay the bank when the note comes due, the payee will have to pay the bank. This possible future liability arising from discounting a customer's note is called a *contingent liability*.

In preparing a balance sheet at the end of the period it is necessary to disclose the contingent liability for notes receivable which have been discounted but have not yet matured. A common method of disclosing the contingent liability on the balance sheet is by means of a footnote such as the following:

"Contingent liability on notes receivable discounted, $600."

## DISHONORED NOTES

When a note is not paid at maturity, it is said to be *dishonored*. When a note is dishonored, it loses its legal status as a note and is no longer negotiable. The amount due should therefore be transferred to the accounts receivable account on the payee's books. To illustrate, assume that a 60-day, 9% note for $500 was received by Barbara Wilson from Sarah Johnson on August 19 and was dishonored. The general journal entry to write off the note and to charge the debt, including interest, back to the customer's account would be as follows:

| | | | | | |
|---|---|---|---|---|---|
| Oct. | 18 | Accts. Receiv. — Sarah Johnson | | 507 50 | |
| | | Notes Receivable | | | 500 00 |
| | | Interest Income | | | 7 50 |
| | | Dishonored note. | | | |

If the claim against Johnson is collected at a later date, an entry would be made debiting Cash and crediting Accounts Receivable for $507.50. If the debt of Johnson proves to be uncollectible, the $507.50 will be written off as a bad debt.

If a customer's note that has been discounted at the bank is dishonored, the bank will notify and request payment from the endorser. The endorser will then have to pay the note plus interest and any service charges assessed by the bank. Assume that the bank notifies Wilson on June 5 that Lara Lopez has dishonored her $450 90-day, 15% note dated March 5 and discounted at the bank on May 4 (see page 278). The note was due June 3 and the bank requests payment of the maturity value of the note, $466.88, plus a $5 service charge. Wilson will make the following journal entry:

| | | | | |
|---|---|---|---|---|
| June | 3 | Accounts Receivable — Lara Lopez | 471.88 | |
| | | Cash | | 471.88 |

The entire amount paid by Wilson is charged to Lopez, the maker of the note. If Lopez subsequently pays Wilson, Wilson will debit Cash and credit Accounts Receivable for $471.88. If Lopez does not pay, the $471.88 will be written off as a bad debt.

## INTEREST INCOME AND INTEREST EXPENSE ON THE INCOME STATEMENT

Unless the business is a financial institution, such as a bank or loan company, interest income and interest expense are not considered part of the ordinary operations of the firm. These items do affect the net income or loss of the enterprise, but they are considered separately from the *income from operations* — gross profit minus operating expenses. Interest income is normally reported as *other income* (nonoperating income) on the income statement, and interest expense is shown as *other expense* (nonoperating expense). These items would be presented on the income statement following "Income from operations," as shown below:

| | | |
|---|---|---|
| Income from operations | | $7,760 |
| Other income: | | |
| Interest income | $79 | |
| Other expense: | | |
| Interest expense | 56 | 23 |
| Income before taxes | | $7,783 |

If the total "Other expense" exceeds "Other income," the difference is shown as a deduction from "Income from operations" on the income statement.

**QUESTIONS FOR DISCUSSION**

1. Why would a business prefer a note receivable rather than an account receivable if a customer asked for an extension of time to pay?
2. Why is it not necessary to maintain a subsidiary ledger for notes receivable?
3. What is the formula for computing interest?

4. (a) Distinguish between the following terms as they relate to a promissory note: (1) face value; (2) principal; and (3) maturity value. (b) Under what circumstances will the face value and the maturity value be the same?

5. Tom Alvarez discounted a customer's $500 note at the bank on December 1. The note does not mature until February 1. How will Alvarez show this note on his year-end balance sheet on December 31?

6. (a) How should interest income be shown on the income statement of a pharmacy? (b) How should interest expense be shown on the income statement of a pharmacy?

## EXERCISES

1. Prepare in general journal form the entry required to record receipt of the following notes receivable:
   (a) Received note from Scott Manson for $250 in payment of account.
   (b) Received note from Ruth Booker in payment of merchandise, $175.
   (c) Accepted Gordon Manoa's $500 non-interest-bearing note in exchange for cash.

2. Ray Pittman receives $624 from Peggy Duval in payment of her $600 note plus interest. Prepare the entry in general journal form to record the transaction:
   (a) on Pittman's books.
   (b) on Duval's books.

3. Compute the interest on each of the following notes.
   (a) 90-day, 8 percent with a face value of $400.
   (b) 60-day, 12 percent with a face value of $1,000.
   (c) 120-day, 9 percent with a face value of $800.
   (d) 60-day, 15 percent with a face value of $600.

4. On July 31, Bill Orr discounted a customer's $500, 90-day, non-interest-bearing note at First State Bank. The discount rate charged by the bank was 12 percent. The note was dated June 1 and matures August 30.
   (a) Prepare the entry, in general journal form, to record the discounting of the note on Orr's books.
   (b) Prepare the entry to record the discounting of the note on Orr's books assuming the note was interest-bearing at 10 percent and the discount rate was 12 percent.

## ASSIGNMENT 12-B

**Tear out pages 551–558 and complete Assignment 12-B. After completing the assignment, continue with the textbook discussion in Chapter 13 until the next assignment is required.**

Chapter 13

# MERCHANDISE INVENTORY

In a mercantile enterprise, the principal business activity is the buying and selling of merchandise. *Merchandise* consists of those goods purchased by a business specifically for the purpose of resale. Usually there are many transactions involving merchandise and a large investment is required to maintain a sufficient inventory. Merchandise inventory is frequently the largest current asset in the business. The cost of merchandise sold is normally the greatest single expense on the income statement. It is very important, therefore, to keep timely and accurate records of all merchandise transactions.

The basic record keeping procedures involved in buying, selling, and adjusting merchandise inventory, and the computations of cost of goods sold and gross profit were presented in previous chapters. This chapter is devoted to some of the procedures involved in accounting for inventories. These procedures are **(1)** accounting for inventories by the *periodic method* and the *perpetual method,* **(2)** determining the quantities, unit cost, and value of the inventory on hand at the end of the period, and **(3)** estimating the amount of inventory on hand.

## PART A RECORDING AND COSTING INVENTORIES

The *periodic method* of inventory accounting is a system whereby the amount of merchandise inventory on hand is determined by a physical count at specified times. Normally, the inventory is determined at the end of the accounting period. In accounting for the sale of merchandise, the usual procedure is to record the revenue from sales at the time the transaction is completed, but no entry is made to record the cost of the sale or the reduction in inventory. The entry for the sale is a debit to Accounts Receivable or Cash and a credit to Sales. The entry to record the acquisition of merchandise is a debit to Purchases and a credit to Accounts Payable or Cash. This entry does not reflect an increase in the account, Merchandise Inventory. The end-of-period adjustments to Merchandise Inventory and the computation of cost of goods sold, as presented in earlier chapters, were based on the periodic inventory system. The perpetual method of inventory accounting requires a knowledge of inventory costing methods discussed in the following pages; therefore, discussion of the perpetual method will be postponed until Part B of this chapter.

## RECORDING THE INVENTORY

When the periodic inventory system is used, the amount of merchandise available for sale is determined by adding the amount of the purchases made during the period to the amount of the merchandise on hand at the beginning of the period, referred to as the *beginning inventory*. In order to compute the cost of goods sold for the period, it is necessary to determine how much of the merchandise is still on hand at the end of the period, called the *ending inventory*. The amount of the ending inventory is then deducted from the merchandise available for sale during the period to determine the cost of goods sold.

The first step in determining the ending inventory is to take a physical count of the merchandise on hand at the end of the period. This counting of the merchandise on hand is referred to as "taking the inventory."

The time and effort involved in taking a physical inventory can be substantial. This is a major task in a business such as a wholesale automobile parts store or a pharmacy whose inventories consist of a large number and variety of items. Some businesses are able to count the inventory during regular business hours, others find it more convenient to count their inventory at night after the store is closed, and still others close to take the inventory. Taking inventory is such a major job for some businesses that they hire service companies which specialize in taking inventory.

Many retailers take their inventory shortly after the Christmas rush, and companies engaged in seasonal business operations usually take inventory during the period of least activity. The job of taking the inventory is less difficult if the inventory is taken at a time when the amount of stock on hand is at a minimum level.

### The Inventory Sheet

The procedures used in counting and recording the inventory vary. Care must always be taken to ensure that every item in stock is counted and that no item is counted more than once. A good way to count the inventory is in two-person teams; one person counts the goods and the other records the information on a form known as an *inventory sheet*. One common form of inventory sheet used in retail apparel stores is shown on page 284.

The inventory sheet includes columns to show the stock number of each item, the description of the goods, unit cost, unit of measure, quantity on hand, and the extension. The first four columns of the sheet would normally be filled in before the counting is begun. The quantity is entered as the goods are counted, and the extensions are made after the count is completed. The extensions are computed by multiplying unit cost by quantity. Each page of the inventory is totaled and the sheets are arranged by departments.

| INVENTORY | | | | | |
|---|---|---|---|---|---|
| Department | Boys | | Sheet No. | 4 | |
| Counted by | H.E.B. | | Date of Inventory | Dec. 31, 1982 | |
| Entered by | C.M. | | Extended by | J.P.N. | |

| Stock No. | Description | Unit Cost | Unit | Quantity | Extension |
|---|---|---|---|---|---|
| B15 | Jackets | 36.60 | ea. | 14 | 512.40 |
| B19 | Top coats | 59.50 | ea. | 16 | 952.00 |
| B24 | Dress shirts | 288.00 | doz. | 2½ doz. | 720.00 |
| B50 | Belts | 8.10 | ea. | 21 | 170.10 |
| | Total | | | | 2,354.50 |

*Inventory Sheet*

Some firms make a carbon copy of each inventory sheet and have the original copy extended and totaled by one person and the carbon copy extended and totaled by another person. The accuracy of the computations can be determined by checking the page totals of the original copy with those of the carbon copy. The extensions and totals can be recomputed on those pages where differences occur.

In counting the inventory, care must be taken to ensure that only the goods that belong to the business are included. For example, merchandise that has been sold but not yet shipped should be excluded from the inventory count. It is equally important to include all merchandise that is owned by the firm on the inventory date. Goods received but not unloaded from trucks or freight cars is an example of merchandise that may be overlooked in counting the ending inventory.

A special situation in determining the inventory of a business is presented by consigned goods. *Merchandise on consignment* is merchandise delivered to a merchant with the agreement that he is not obligated to pay for the goods unless he sells them. Title to the goods is retained by the supplier until they are sold. If a firm has goods out on consignment, they must be included in its ending inventory. The business holding goods received on consignment should not include them in its ending inventory.

## COSTING THE INVENTORY

Another major task in the inventory process is determining the cost to be assigned to the units on hand at the end of the year. Identical units of merchandise may have been acquired at different costs during the period. If all purchases of an item were made at the same unit cost, there is no problem in determining the cost to be used for the inventory. However, if the unit cost for an item varies during the period, it must be determined which costs should be assigned to the units sold during the period and which costs should be assigned to the units on hand at the end of the period.

To illustrate the procedure of assigning unit costs to items in the ending inventory and to items sold during the period, assume that during the month, 55 identical units of inventory are available for sale. The units available for sale and the unit cost of each are shown below.

| | | |
|---|---|---|
| Beginning inventory, December 1 | 10 units @ $18 = | $ 180 |
| Purchased on December 5 | 15 units @ 20 = | 300 |
| Purchased on December 13 | 10 units @ 23 = | 230 |
| Purchased on December 27 | 20 units @ 25 = | 500 |
| Merchandise available for sale | 55 | $1,210 |

During the month, 30 of the units were sold and 25 units are in the inventory at month's end. If the cost of the units on hand at the end of the month can be specifically identified, there is no problem in computing the cost of the inventory.

Frequently it will be impossible to know which units have been sold and which units are still on hand. In addition, specific identification of unit costs is impractical and costly for certain types of goods. For example, the specific cost of canned goods on a grocery shelf or nails in a hardware bin would be almost impossible to determine. To avoid this problem, an assumption as to the flow of inventory costs has to be made. The three most common methods of determining the flow of inventory costs are (1) first-in, first-out, (2) last-in, first-out, and (3) weighted average.

## First-In, First-Out Method

The *first-in, first-out (fifo)* method of costing inventory assumes that the first goods purchased are the first goods sold. Therefore, with the fifo method, the unit costs of merchandise are charged to cost of goods sold in the same order as the units were acquired. Consequently, the units on hand at the end of the period are those received last.

To illustrate the application of the fifo method, assume that a physical count showed that 25 of the units in the schedule above are on hand at the end of the period. Since the first-in, first-out method assumes that the inventory is composed of the latest purchases, the cost of the 25 units would be determined as follows:

| | | |
|---|---|---|
| December 27 purchases | 20 units @ $25 = | $500 |
| December 13 purchases | 5 units @ 23 = | 115 |
| Ending inventory, December 31 | 25 | $615 |

The cost of the units sold can now be determined as follows:

| | |
|---|---|
| Merchandise available for sale | $1,210 |
| Less ending inventory (fifo) | 615 |
| **Cost of goods sold** | **$ 595** |

The fifo method of determining inventory costs is normally consistent with the actual flow of the goods, because most businesses make an effort to rotate their stock by selling the goods in the order of their acquisition. This is particularly true of perishable or stylish goods.

## Last-In, First-Out Method

The *last-in, first-out (lifo)* method of costing inventory assumes that the last goods purchased are the first goods sold. Therefore, under the lifo method, the most recent unit costs of merchandise are charged to cost of goods sold. The unit cost of goods on hand at the end of the period is composed of those units acquired first.

Using the data in the schedule at the top of page 285, the cost of the 25 units on hand at the end of the month would be determined by the lifo method as follows:

| | | |
|---|---|---|
| Beginning inventory, December 1 | 10 units @ $18 = | $180 |
| December 5 purchases | 15 units @ 20 = | 300 |
| Ending inventory, December 31 | 25 | $480 |

The cost of goods sold, using lifo, would be computed as follows:

| | |
|---|---|
| Merchandise available for sale | $1,210 |
| Less ending inventory (lifo) | 480 |
| Cost of goods sold | $ 730 |

A strong argument for the use of the lifo method is that it matches the cost of the most recent purchases against the current revenue from sales. Under this method, the cost of goods sold as shown on the income statement is approximately the current cost to replace the goods sold. A weakness of the lifo method is that the inventory account reflects the oldest costs which are usually lower. This means that, in time, the amount of the inventory as reported on the balance sheet will be greatly understated if prices have increased significantly since the items were first included in inventory.

## Weighted Average Method

The third method of allocating the cost of goods between the units sold and those in inventory is the weighted average method. This method is called *weighted average* because both the number of units and the unit cost are considered. From the data in the schedule on page 285 the total cost of the 55 units available for sale was $1,210. The weighted average cost per unit is $22 ($1,210 ÷ 55). Using the weighted average method, the ending inventory would be computed as follows:

| | |
|---|---|
| Ending inventory, December 31 | 25 units @ $22 = $550 |

The cost of goods sold under the weighted average method can now be determined as follows:

| | |
|---|---|
| Merchandise available for sale | $1,210 |
| Less ending inventory (weighted average) | 550 |
| Cost of goods sold | $ 660 |

The weighted average method combines the unit cost of every purchase as well as the beginning inventory. This method assigns the same unit cost to both ending inventory and cost of goods sold. The weighted average method is particularly appropriate for businesses that have inventories of identical units that are mingled, such as grain stored in silos or oil in tanks. In these situations the weighted average method often approximates the actual physical flow of goods.

## Comparison of Methods of Costing Inventory

In a period of rising or falling prices, the weighted average method of costing the inventory yields an inventory cost that is between fifo and lifo. This can be illustrated by summarizing the computations for each of the three methods.

| | *Fifo* | *Weighted Average* | *Lifo* |
|---|---|---|---|
| Merchandise available for sale | $1,210 | $1,210 | $1,210 |
| Less ending inventory | 615 | 550 | 480 |
| **Cost of goods sold** | **$ 595** | **$ 660** | **$ 730** |

The inventory method being used has no effect on the amount of revenue from sales or the amount of operating expenses reported. The amount of cost of goods sold, which is affected by the choice of the inventory costing method, affects the amount of gross profit and the net income.

To illustrate this point, assume that sales of 30 units for the period totaled $1,350 and that operating expenses for the period were $475. The summary comparing the three methods of costing the inventory can now be expanded to include the computation of gross profit and net income.

| | *Fifo* | | *Weighted Average* | | *Lifo* |
|---|---|---|---|---|---|
| Sales | $1,350 | | $1,350 | | $1,350 |
| Cost of goods sold | 595 | | 660 | | 730 |
| Gross profit | $ 755 | | $ 690 | | $ 620 |
| Operating expenses | 475 | | 475 | | 475 |
| Net income | $ 280 | | $ 215 | | $ 145 |
| **Differences** | | **$65** | | **$70** | |
| Cost of ending inventory | **$ 615** | | **$ 550** | | **$ 480** |
| **Differences** | | **$65** | | **$70** | |

It is apparent from the above schedule that the higher the ending inventory, the lower the cost of goods sold and thus the higher the net income. Consequently, the difference in the cost of the ending inventory under each method is equal to the difference in the net income reported under each method.

The above illustration is based on an assumption of a period of rising prices. Under these circumstances, the fifo method will yield the highest net income, because it has the highest prices included in its ending inventory and the lowest prices in its cost of goods sold.

A major advantage of using the lifo method during a period of rising prices is that the latest costs, which are the highest, are assigned to the cost of goods sold. This results in a lower taxable income and consequently a smaller income tax liability. In the examples above, the inventory costed at fifo was assigned a value of $615 and the amount of cost of goods sold was $595. The lifo method resulted in an inventory cost of only $480 and a cost of goods sold of $730. Cost of goods sold was $135 more when using lifo than when using fifo. Therefore, the lifo method resulted in a net income of $135 less than the fifo method. When unit cost is decreasing, the use of the lifo method will result in reported income being higher than for the fifo method.

## QUESTIONS FOR DISCUSSION

1. What is a periodic inventory system?
2. (a) Explain some of the difficulties associated with taking a physical inventory. (b) Why do so many retail businesses take their inventory shortly after Christmas?
3. Frank Keel recently purchased a small grocery store and is concerned about taking inventory for the first time. Explain the procedures to be followed in taking a physical inventory for a small grocery store.
4. Spring River Grocery Company takes an annual inventory and uses inventory sheets numbered by departments. After the inventory is counted and recorded, the accountant makes all extensions and totals the pages. A clerk then rechecks each inventory sheet for extensions and page totals. Can you suggest an easier procedure for checking the inventory computations?
5. After Spring River Grocery Company (Question 4 above) had taken inventory, it was discovered that seven cases of coffee that had not been unloaded from one of the trucks were mistakenly omitted from the inventory count. The total cost of the coffee on the truck was $310. (a) What effect did this error have on the ending inventory? (b) What was the effect of the error on cost of goods sold? (c) What was the effect of the error on net income reported for the period?
6. Explain the terms fifo and lifo as they apply to inventory costing.
7. The unit cost of three purchases of product A made during the period were $40, $42, and $44 respectively. Assuming there was no beginning inventory, will the unit cost of the goods on hand at the end of the period be $42 if the weighted average method of inventory costing is used? Explain.

## EXERCISES

1. The beginning inventory and the purchases of commodity VIP for the month are presented below:

   COMMODITY VIP

   | | |
   |---|---|
   | Beginning inventory | 20 units @ $16 |
   | Purchase February 2 | 50 units @ $18 |
   | Purchase February 12 | 60 units @ $20 |
   | Purchase February 19 | 40 units @ $22 |

   There were 50 units of VIP on hand at the end of the month.

   **Required:**

   (a) Determine the cost of goods (VIP) available for sale during the month.

   (b) Compute the cost of VIP in ending inventory by the *fifo* method.

   (c) Compute the cost of VIP sold during the month by the *fifo* method.

2. (a) Compute the cost of VIP in the ending inventory in (1) above by the *lifo* method. (b) Compute the cost of VIP sold for the month by the *lifo* method.
3. There were 30 units of Item H on hand at the beginning of the month with a unit cost of $36. During the month there were three purchases of H as follows: 45 units @ $40; 30 units @ $46; and 60 units @ $50. One

hundred forty units of Item H were sold during the month. Determine the following, showing your computations in good form.

a. Merchandise (Item H) available for sale during the month.
b. Cost of ending inventory of Item H using weighted average method.
c. Cost of Item H sold during the month.

**4.** The merchandise available for sale for the Benji Pet Food Company for the period was $162,000. The ending inventory determined by the fifo method was $16,140 and by the lifo method was $14,800. Present computations to show the effect that the choice of inventory method will have on cost of goods sold and net income for the period.

## ASSIGNMENT 13-A

**Tear out pages 559–566 and complete Assignment 13-A. Submit your papers to your instructor for approval. After completion, continue with the textbook discussion until Assignment 13-B is required.**

# PART B SPECIAL PROCEDURES IN INVENTORY VALUATION

The primary basis of accounting for inventories is cost. Under certain circumstances, it may be necessary to record the inventory below cost. In some situations it will be desirable or necessary to estimate the inventory on hand. The procedures involved in accounting for inventories in these situations are discussed in this part of the chapter. Part B concludes with a discussion of the perpetual inventory system.

## LOWER OF COST OR MARKET

In some instances it is necessary to record the ending inventory at less than its cost. For example, when the cost to replace the goods is less than the original cost, the inventory may be recorded at replacement cost. This is an extension of the procedure for computing the cost of the inventory and is known as valuing the inventory at the *lower of cost or market*. This procedure should be used only when the replacement cost has declined below original cost by a substantial amount and the decline is considered permanent.

*Market*, as used in the concept of "lower of cost or market," is the cost of replacing the goods at the inventory date. The concept of lower of cost or market is based on the assumption that a decline in the market price will normally be accompanied by a reduction in the selling price, and thus the value of the inventory on hand is decreased. The decline in the value of the inventory on hand is recognized by charging the loss to cost of goods sold in the period in which the decline occurred. To illustrate, assume that the cost of the inventory, determined by the first-in, first-out method, is $11,500, and due to a decline in the market price, the inventory could be replaced at a cost of $10,700. If the inventory is valued at this lower market price, the $800 decline is transferred to the cost of goods sold for the period and the net income for the period will be $800 less. The schedule below illustrates the direct effect the value of the ending inventory has on net income.

| | *Cost* | | *Market* | |
|---|---|---|---|---|
| Sales | | $55,000 | | $55,000 |
| Cost of goods sold: | | | | |
| Merchandise inventory, January 1 | $13,200 | | $13,200 | |
| Purchases | 28,400 | | 28,400 | |
| Merchandise available for sale | $41,600 | | $41,600 | |
| Less ending inventory, December 31 | | | | |
| At cost (fifo) | 11,500 | | | |
| At market | | | 10,700 | |
| Cost of goods sold | | 30,100 | | 30,900 |
| Gross profit | | $24,900 | | $24,100 |
| Operating expenses | | 16,300 | | 16,300 |
| Net income | | $ 8,600 | | $ 7,800 |

In applying the "lower of cost or market" rule, the "cost" of the inventory must first be determined and then compared to "market" (replacement cost). For example, the cost of the inventory on hand could be computed by specifically identifying the cost of each unit or by using first-in, first-out, or the weighted average method.

If the last-in, first-out basis of determining inventory cost is used, the lower of cost or market rule cannot be applied. Tax laws specifically disallow "lower of cost or market" when inventory is valued on a lifo basis. It further requires that when lifo is used for income tax purposes, it must also be used for financial reporting. Tax laws also specify that when the lower of cost or market procedure is used, it must be followed consistently from year to year.

The lower of cost or market rule may be used for (1) each item in the inventory, (2) departments or lines of goods, or (3) the inventory in total. A comparison of the three methods is presented on page 291.

| Description | Quantity | Unit Cost | Unit Market | Total | | Lower of Cost or Market | | |
|---|---|---|---|---|---|---|---|---|
| | | | | Cost | Market | By Item | By Dept. | By Total |
| Dept. AD | | | | | | | | |
| Item 102 | 50 | $3.10 | $3.00 | $ 155 | $ 150 | $ 150 | | |
| Item 103 | 100 | 2.10 | 2.12 | 210 | 212 | 210 | | |
| Item 106 | 40 | 1.60 | 1.65 | 64 | 66 | 64 | | |
| Dept. total | | | | $ 429 | $ 428 | | $ 428 | |
| Dept. BK | | | | | | | | |
| Item 211 | 200 | 2.40 | 2.50 | $ 480 | $ 500 | 480 | | |
| Item 214 | 600 | .30 | .35 | 180 | 210 | 180 | | |
| Item 215 | 340 | 1.05 | .95 | 357 | 323 | 323 | | |
| Dept. total | | | | $1,017 | $1,033 | | 1,017 | |
| Total inventory | | | | $1,446 | $1,461 | | | $1,446 |
| Total valuation | | | | | | $1,407 | $1,445 | $1,446 |

***Comparison of Lower of Cost or Market Methods***

As shown in the comparison, the lower of cost or market rule applied to each item will always yield the smallest inventory value.

## MERCHANDISE INVENTORY ON THE BALANCE SHEET

Merchandise inventory is a current asset and is shown immediately below receivables on the balance sheet, as illustrated below.

**Xavier Company**
**Balance Sheet**
**December 31, 1982**

| Assets | | |
|---|---|---|
| **Current assets:** | | |
| **Cash** | | **4 250 00** |
| **Accounts receivable** | **6 680 00** | |
| **Less Allowance for bad debts** | **300 00** | **6 380 00** |
| **Merchandise inventory — at lower of cost (fifo) or market** | | **10 700 00** |

If a company is valuing its inventory at lower of cost or market, this should be shown on the balance sheet by a parenthetical note or as a footnote. The method used to determine the cost of the inventory, lifo, fifo, or weighted average, should also be disclosed.

## ESTIMATING INVENTORIES

Many businesses, because of the time and expenses involved, take a physical inventory only once a year. These businesses may, however, prepare financial statements for interim periods such as monthly or quarterly. The financial statements prepared for these periods are referred to as *interim statements*. If the income statement and balance sheet are to be prepared on a monthly or quarterly basis and no physical inventory is taken, the amount of inventory on hand at the end of the interim period has to be estimated. Other circumstances may also make it necessary to estimate the amount of inventory on hand. For example, if goods are destroyed in a fire, an estimate has to be made of the goods lost. The two methods of estimating inventories are the gross profit method and the retail method.

## Gross Profit Method

Under the *gross profit method*, the inventory value is determined by use of the estimated percentage of gross profit to sales for the period. The gross profit percentage estimate is based on past experience adjusted for any current changes in business conditions.

Assume that the following information is obtained from the business records for the month of January:

| | |
|---|---|
| Inventory, January 1 | $1,480 |
| Net purchases for January | 4,360 |
| Net sales for January | 6,600 |
| Estimated gross profit rate | 40% |

The January 31 inventory, using the gross profit method, would be determined as outlined below:

The first step in the gross profit method is the computation of the cost of the merchandise available for sale. The amount of merchandise available for sale can be computed from the information in the accounting records. In its simplest form this computation involves adding the net purchases during the period to the inventory on hand at the beginning of the period.

| | |
|---|---|
| Inventory, January 1 | $1,480 |
| Net purchases for January | 4,360 |
| Merchandise available for sale | $5,840 |

The second step is the determination of the estimated cost of goods sold for the period. The accounting records provide the amount of sales for the period. The gross profit earned on these sales is then estimated and is deducted from the amount of sales to determine the cost of goods sold.

Continuing the illustration, net sales for the month of January totaled $6,600 and the gross profit rate for the business is estimated at 40% of sales. The cost of goods sold can be determined as follows:

| | |
|---|---|
| Net sales for January at retail | $6,600 |
| Less estimated gross profit ($6,600 × 40%) | 2,640 |
| Estimated cost of goods sold | $3,960 |

The third and final step is to subtract the estimated cost of goods sold for the period from the merchandise available for sale to determine the January 31 inventory on hand. The estimated inventory, $1,880, is determined as follows:

| | |
|---|---|
| Merchandise available for sale | $5,840 |
| Less estimated cost of goods sold | 3,960 |
| Estimated inventory on hand, January 31 | $1,880 |

Normally all of the above steps would be completed in one schedule as shown at the top of the following page:

| | | |
|---|---|---|
| Inventory, January 1 | | $1,480 |
| Net purchases | | 4,360 |
| Merchandise available for sale | | $5,840 |
| Net sales for the period, at retail | $6,600 | |
| Less estimated gross profit ($6,600 × 40%) | 2,640 | |
| Estimated cost of goods sold | | 3,960 |
| Estimated inventory on hand, January 31 | | $1,880 |

## Retail Method

A second method of estimating the cost of the inventory is the retail method. The *retail method* of valuing inventory requires maintaining records for purchases and inventories at both cost and retail prices.

Assume that the following information is determined from the business records for the month of March:

| | |
|---|---|
| Inventory, March 1 at cost | $2,750 |
| Inventory, March 1 at retail | 4,500 |
| Net purchases in March at cost | 4,400 |
| Net purchases in March at retail | 8,500 |
| Net sales in March | 6,700 |

The computation of the March 31 inventory, using the retail method, would be as follows:

Step One requires the computation of merchandise available for sale during the period at both cost and retail prices. This is done by adding the beginning inventory to the purchases for the period as follows:

| | *Cost* | *Retail* |
|---|---|---|
| Inventory, March 1 | $2,750 | $ 4,500 |
| Net purchases in March | 4,400 | 8,500 |
| Merchandise available for sale | $7,150 | $13,000 |

Step Two is the computation of the percentage of cost to retail. By comparing the amounts of merchandise available for sale at cost and at retail, the relationship of cost to retail for the period can be determined. This relationship is called the *cost ratio* or *percentage of cost to retail*. The calculation of the percentage of cost to retail is as follows:

Percentage of cost to retail .......... $\frac{\$\ 7{,}150}{\$13{,}000} = 55\%$

Step Three is the computation of the ending inventory at retail. The ending inventory at retail is determined by subtracting the net sales for the period from the retail value of merchandise available for sale:

| | |
|---|---|
| Merchandise available for sale, at retail | $13,000 |
| Less net sales for March | 6,700 |
| Inventory, March 31, at retail | $ 6,300 |

Step Four is the computation of the ending inventory at cost. In Step Two the percentage of cost to retail was computed as 55%. In Step Three the value of the ending inventory at retail was determined to be $6,300. The cost of the ending inventory can now be computed by multiplying the ending inventory at retail by the percentage of cost to retail as follows:

| | |
|---|---|
| Inventory, March 31, at retail | $6,300 |
| Percentage of cost to retail | × .55 |
| Estimated inventory, March 31, at cost | $3,465 |

The steps in calculating the estimated cost of the ending inventory by the retail method can be consolidated into one schedule as shown below:

| | Cost | Retail |
|---|---|---|
| Inventory, March 1 | $2,750 | $ 4,500 |
| Net purchases in March | 4,400 | 8,500 |
| Merchandise available for sale | $7,150 | $13,000 |
| Percentage of cost to retail $\frac{\$\ 7,150}{\$13,000} = 55\%$ | | |
| Less net sales for March | | 6,700 |
| Inventory, March 31, at retail | | $ 6,300 |
| Estimated inventory, March 31, at cost ($6,300 × 55%) | | $ 3,465 |

The retail method is widely used in retail businesses. This method assumes that the percentage of cost to retail computed from the merchandise available for sale for the period is a representative average of the relationship of cost to selling price for the goods in the ending inventory. It is highly unlikely that all items in the inventory will have the same cost percentage. For example, the 55% of cost to retail in the illustration above, represents an average for all the items in the inventory. Some items will perhaps have a cost percentage of 50% and others 60%. The assumption made in the retail method is that the "mix" of these goods in the ending inventory, in terms of their cost percentage to retail, is approximately the same as that for all merchandise available for sale during the period.

## PERPETUAL INVENTORY SYSTEM

Certain types of businesses may find it necessary to maintain a day-to-day record of the inventory they have on hand. For example, an automobile parts department needs to know at all times what parts they have in stock and if a reorder is necessary. A retail shoe store needs inventory information by size, color, and style for all shoes on hand. An up-to-date inventory which provides the needed information is called a *perpetual inventory system.*

### Purchases and Sales Using Perpetual Inventories

The basic feature of a perpetual inventory is the immediate recording of all increases and decreases directly to the merchandise inventory account. Under this system, there will not be a purchases account. When merchandise is purchased, the merchandise inventory account is debited. For example, assume that an appliance dealer buys a washing machine on July 22 at a cost of $240 from the Western Company on account. The following entry is required:

| | | | | | | | |
|---|---|---|---|---|---|---|---|
| July | 22 | Merchandise Inventory.................... | | 240 | 00 | | |
| | | Accounts Payable — Western Co. | | | | 240 | 00 |
| | | Purchased merchandise on account. | | | | | |

When merchandise is sold, two entries are required. The first entry is to record the sale at the retail price. The second entry is to record the cost of the goods sold and to reduce the merchandise inventory account for the cost. Therefore, under the perpetual inventory system, the merchandise inventory account always reflects the amount of inventory actually on hand.

To illustrate the entries to be made when merchandise is sold under the perpetual system, assume that the appliance dealer above sells the washing machine on August 9 to Carmen Evans for $400 on account. The following entries are required:

| | | | | |
|---|---|---|---|---|
| Aug. | 9 | Accounts Receivable — Carmen Evans............... | 400 | |
| | | Sales.................................................................. | | 400 |

| | | | | | | | |
|---|---|---|---|---|---|---|---|
| Aug. | 9 | Cost of Goods Sold .......................... | | 240 | 00 | | |
| | | Merchandise Inventory................. | | | | 240 | 00 |
| | | To record cost of washer and to reduce inventory. | | | | | |

When a perpetual inventory system is used, a detailed subsidiary record for each type of merchandise should be maintained. The merchandise inventory account in the general ledger is a control account. As the merchandise is sold, the cost of the goods may be assigned on a fifo, lifo, or weighted average basis.

## Inventory Stock Record Card

A perpetual inventory system stock record card with costs assigned on a fifo basis is illustrated on the following page.

The heading of the card shows the description of the inventory item, the stock number, the department where the inventory is located, the maximum and minimum inventory levels and how long it takes to receive additional units ordered.

The body of the card shows the information concerning the units of inventory and is divided into four parts (1) DATE, for recording the dates on which the various transactions occur; (2) RECEIVED, showing the purchase order number, the quantity of units purchased, and the unit cost price; (3) ISSUED, showing the sales ticket number, the quantity of units sold, and the unit cost price; (4) BALANCE, showing the quantity of units in stock, the unit cost price, and the total cost of units on hand.

A major advantage of maintaining perpetual inventory records is the control provided. For example, the inventory card on page 296 shows a maximum stock of 20 tires. This limit will prevent overstocking. The inventory card also indicates a minimum stock level of six tires and that it takes four days to receive additional tires ordered.

| INVENTORY STOCK RECORD CARD | | | | | | | | | |
|---|---|---|---|---|---|---|---|---|---|
| Description: Tires H78 × 14 Whitewall | | | | | | Stock No.: T247 | | | |
| Inventory Level: Maximum 20 | | | | | | Minimum 6 | | | |
| Department: Automotive | | | | | | Reorder Time: 4 days | | | |
| DATE | RECEIVED | | | ISSUED | | | BALANCE | | |
| | Pur. Order | Quantity | Unit Price | Sales Ticket No. | Quantity | Unit Price | Quantity | Unit Price | Total |
| *1-1* | | | | | | | *6* | *21.00* | *126.00* |
| *2-4* | *2107* | *10* | *21.40* | | | | *6*<br>*10* | *21.00*<br>*21.40* | *126.00*<br>*214.00* |
| *2-11* | | | | *5607* | *4* | *21.00* | *2*<br>*10* | *21.00*<br>*21.40* | *42.00*<br>*214.00* |
| *3-2* | | | | *5934* | *4* | *2 @ 21.00*<br>*2 @ 21.40* | *8* | *21.40* | *171.20* |
| | | | | | | | | | |

***Inventory Stock Record Card***

A sale of four tires was made on February 11, sales ticket Number 5607, to Vern Horner at a retail price of $45 per tire. The entries to account for the sale could be recorded as follows:

| | | | | |
|---|---|---|---|---|
| **Feb.** | **11** | **Accounts Receivable — Vern Horner** | **180** | |
| | | **Sales** | | **180** |

| | | | | | |
|---|---|---|---|---|---|
| **Feb.** | **11** | **Cost of Goods Sold** | | **84 00** | |
| | | **Merchandise Inventory** | | | **84 00** |
| | | **Four T247 @ $21.** | | | |

Although perpetual inventories are maintained, a physical count of the inventory would still be required at least once each year to detect shortages and correct any errors.

## Maintaining Perpetual Inventory Records by Electronic Data Processing

Many businesses maintain their inventory records on a perpetual basis by utilizing electronic data processing equipment. One such system requires that each item in the inventory have a prepunched ticket attached to it with the size, color, cost, and stock number encoded. When the item is sold, this ticket is torn off and filed. At the end of the day these tickets are sent to the computer center where they are processed and the inventory records are updated.

Another system is to use a cash register equipped with punched paper tape. When the sale is made, it is recorded in the cash register. At the same time the inventory code (stock number, size, color, and cost) can also be recorded on the punched paper tape inside the cash register. At the end of the day the punched paper tape is sent to the computer center and the perpetual inventory record is updated.

Cash registers can also be designed to connect directly to an electronic computer. When the sale is recorded, the inventory data are transferred directly to the computer. Thus, the inventory records are updated immediately.

Regardless of the system used, once the information on units sold has been fed into the computer, an up-to-date inventory report can be printed out upon request. Some stores have an inventory status report printed for their department buyers on a regular basis: daily, weekly, or monthly. These reports assist in purchasing new stock, help discover shortages, and provide information for determining the cost of the inventory on hand for use in interim statements.

## QUESTIONS FOR DISCUSSION

1. Define the term "market" as used in the term "lower of cost or market."
2. What disclosure should be made on the balance sheet for the merchandise inventory when it is being valued at "lower of cost or market"?
3. In addition to the preparation of interim financial statements, what other circumstances would make it necessary for a business to be able to estimate the amount of merchandise inventory on hand?
4. Explain the procedure involved in estimating inventory by the gross profit method.
5. How is the percentage of cost to retail determined when the retail method of valuing inventory is used?
6. When the retail method is used, what assumption is made regarding the "mix" of the goods in the ending inventory?
7. When goods are sold on account under a perpetual inventory system, what two entries are required to record the sale?
8. How have electronic computers facilitated the keeping of inventories on a perpetual basis?

## EXERCISES

1. The Red Star Sales Company had the following items in its ending inventory at June 30.

| Item | Quantity | Unit Cost | Unit Market |
|---|---|---|---|
| K127 | 430 | $ 4.10 | $ 4.30 |
| J208 | 380 | 5.00 | 4.95 |
| R511 | 375 | 6.20 | 6.40 |
| X300 | 200 | 10.50 | 10.00 |

Determine the value of the inventory using "cost or market, whichever is lower" applied to (a) each individual item, and (b) the inventory as a whole.

2. From the records of the Apache Pharmacy, the following information for the month of January is determined: Inventory, January 1, $21,000; net purchases, $64,000; net sales $94,000; estimated rate of gross profit on sales, 40%.

   **Required:** Compute the estimated cost of the inventory on January 31 for Apache Pharmacy using the gross profit method.

3. Leola Davenport owns and operates Leola's Millinery Shop. Davenport has maintained a retail inventory system for several years and prepares interim financial statements quarterly. The following information is available from the accounting records as of March 31: merchandise, January 1 at retail, $36,000, at cost, $24,000; net purchases for the first quarter at retail, $160,000, at cost, $113,200; net sales for the period $105,000. Determine the estimated cost of the inventory on March 31, using the retail inventory method.

4. Roger Cody owns Sound City, a complete stereo, record, and music equipment retail store. Cody maintains a perpetual inventory system. Record the following transactions in general journal form utilizing a perpetual inventory system:

   May 7. Purchased stereo model A117 from Ace Distributors, $700 on account.

   15. Sold stereo model A117 above to Joe Cooley on account, $1,050.

## ASSIGNMENT 13-B

**Tear out pages 567–572 and complete Assignment 13-B. Submit your papers for approval. After completion, proceed to the study of Chapter 14 until the next assignment is required.**

Chapter **14**

# ACCOUNTING FOR PLANT ASSETS

Land, buildings, equipment, office machines, and furniture and fixtures are examples of assets that are used by most businesses. These assets are shown on the balance sheet under a major caption entitled "Plant assets." Plant assets, which usually have a life of several years, are also sometimes referred to as *fixed assets* or *property, plant, and equipment*. This chapter examines the nature of plant assets, the accounting for their acquisition, use, and disposal, and some special records that may be kept for these assets.

## PART A NATURE OF PLANT ASSETS AND DEPRECIATION

The basic characteristics necessary for an asset to be classified as a plant asset are: (**1**) it is tangible (has physical properties); (**2**) it is long-lived (will last more than one year); (**3**) it is used in the operations of the business; and (**4**) it is not held for the purpose of resale.

A major distinction in determining if an asset is to be classified as a plant asset is whether it is to be used by the business in its operations. For example, a panel truck is a plant asset (equipment) to a florist, but a panel truck is an item of inventory, held for resale, to an automotive dealer. A typewriter is a plant asset (office equipment) to a law firm, but a typewriter is an item of inventory to an office equipment company.

### DETERMINING THE COST OF PLANT ASSETS

Plant assets should be recorded at cost. The cost of a plant asset consists of all expenditures incurred to acquire the asset and get it ready for use. This cost includes the purchase price of the asset (net of cash discount) plus delivery charges, sales taxes, insurance in transit, installation charges, and other costs incurred in getting the asset ready to use.

When an asset is constructed, its cost should include all items that can be identified with the construction. When a building is constructed, for example, its cost will include all construction costs, architect's fees, insurance during construction, interest paid on money borrowed during the construction period, and any other related costs, such as cleaning up and getting the building ready to use.

Costs incurred during an asset's life that add to the usefulness of the asset for more than one accounting period should be debited to the asset account. Charges that benefit only the current accounting period should be debited to an expense account. If a new engine is installed in a delivery truck, for example, the cost of the engine should be debited to Delivery Truck. If a tune-up is subsequently performed on the engine, the cost should be debited to Repairs and Maintenance Expense — Delivery Truck.

## DEPRECIATION

Although plant assets such as buildings, vehicles, machinery, and equipment will last for several years, they will all gradually wear out. Land is the only plant asset that does not "wear out" with the passage of time.

In accounting for a plant asset, one major objective is to charge the cost of the asset to the periods in which it is used. The systematic allocation of the cost of a plant asset over its useful life is known as *depreciation*.

### Accounting for Depreciation

When a plant asset is acquired, the asset account is debited and Cash or Accounts Payable is credited. For example, assume that an accounting machine (office equipment) was purchased at a cost of $3,800. The following entry, in general journal form, is required:

| | | | | |
|---|---|---|---|---|
| Jan. | 2 | Office Equipment | 3,800 | |
| | | Cash | | 3,800 |

The recording of depreciation of this machine is accomplished by the use of an adjusting entry at the end of the period, debiting Depreciation Expense — Office Equipment and crediting Accumulated Depreciation — Office Equipment. If it is estimated that the depreciation charge for the above machine is $600 per year, the adjusting entry is:

| | | | | | |
|---|---|---|---|---|---|
| Dec. | 31 | Depr. Exp. — Office Equip. | | 600 00 | |
| | | Accum. Depr. — Office Equip. | | | 600 00 |
| | | To record depr. for the year. | | | |

Depreciation Expense — Office Equipment is shown on the income statement as an operating expense. The account is closed to Income Summary at the end of the period.

Accumulated Depreciation — Office Equipment is shown on the balance sheet as a contra account, subtracted from Office Equipment in the plant asset section. Plant assets are shown as a major caption on the balance sheet below current assets. The office equipment and accumulated depreciation would appear as follows:

| | | | |
|---|---|---|---|
| Total current assets | | | 8 600 00 |
| Plant assets: | | | |
| Office equipment | 3 800 00 | | |
| Less accumulated depreciation | 600 00 | 3 200 00 | |

The original cost of the asset less accumulated depreciation represents the unexpired cost of the asset and is called the *book value*. The book value of the office equipment above is $3,200.

## Depreciation on Interim Statements

In the preceding example, the adjustment for depreciation was made at the end of the year. If the business prepares interim statements, it is necessary to record depreciation for the period covered by the statements. Assume that the company prepares interim financial statements on a quarterly basis. The adjusting entry at the end of March will be for three months or one fourth of a year, $150. The adjustment is recorded in the general journal as follows:

| | | | | | |
|---|---|---|---|---|---|
| Mar. | 31 | Depr. Exp. — Office Equip. | | 150 00 | |
| | | Accum. Depr. — Office Equip. | | | 150 00 |
| | | To record depreciation for the January–March quarter. | | | |

Office equipment is shown on the balance sheet at March 31, as follows:

| | | |
|---|---|---|
| Plant assets: | | |
| Office equipment | $3,800 | |
| Less accumulated depreciation | 150 | $3,650 |

Since the interim statements are prepared quarterly, the $150 adjustment for depreciation will also be made on June 30, September 30, and December 31. After the adjusting entries and the closing entry have been made for the year, the office equipment, accumulated depreciation — office equipment, and depreciation expense — office equipment accounts will appear as shown below and on the following page:

ACCOUNT **Office Equipment** ACCOUNT NO. **24**

| DATE | | ITEM | POST. REF. | DEBIT | CREDIT | BALANCE DEBIT | BALANCE CREDIT |
|---|---|---|---|---|---|---|---|
| 1982 Jan. | 2 | | J6 | 3 800 00 | | 3 800 00 | |

ACCOUNT **Accumulated Depreciation — Office Equipment** ACCOUNT NO. **24.1**

| DATE | | ITEM | POST. REF. | DEBIT | CREDIT | BALANCE DEBIT | BALANCE CREDIT |
|---|---|---|---|---|---|---|---|
| 1982 | | | | | | | |
| Mar. | 31 | Adjusting | J11 | | 150 00 | | 150 00 |
| June | 30 | Adjusting | J16 | | 150 00 | | 300 00 |
| Sept. | 30 | Adjusting | J22 | | 150 00 | | 450 00 |
| Dec. | 31 | Adjusting | J29 | | 150 00 | | 600 00 |

ACCOUNT **Depreciation Expense — Office Equipment** ACCOUNT NO. **54**

| DATE | | ITEM | POST. REF. | DEBIT | CREDIT | BALANCE DEBIT | BALANCE CREDIT |
|---|---|---|---|---|---|---|---|
| 1982 | | | | | | | |
| Mar. | 31 | Adjusting | J11 | 150 00 | | 150 00 | |
| June | 30 | Adjusting | J16 | 150 00 | | 300 00 | |
| Sept. | 30 | Adjusting | J22 | 150 00 | | 450 00 | |
| Dec. | 31 | Adjusting | J29 | 150 00 | | 600 00 | |
| Dec. | 31 | Closing | J30 | | 600 00 | — | — |

Many businesses make adjusting entries for interim statements only on the worksheet. If that were the case in the preceding example, there would be only one adjusting entry for $600 recorded in the ledger accounts.

### Depreciation on Asset Purchased During Period

When a plant asset is purchased during the period, depreciation at the end of the first year will be computed for the fraction of the year the asset is used. For example, if the office equipment in the preceding example had been purchased on November 1, the adjusting entry on December 31 of the first year would be for $100 (2/12 × $600) as follows:

| | | | | | |
|---|---|---|---|---|---|
| Dec. | 31 | Depr. Exp. — Office Equip. ................ | | 100 00 | |
| | | Accum. Depr. — Office Equip. ........ | | | 100 00 |
| | | To record depr. for 2 months. | | | |

The book value of the equipment at the end of the first year would then be $3,700 ($3,800 − $100).

## COMPUTING DEPRECIATION

The depreciable cost of an asset should be allocated over the number of periods the asset is expected to be used. *Depreciable cost* is defined as the original cost of the asset minus the residual or salvage value. The *residual value* or *salvage value* of a depreciable asset is the amount expected to be realized when the asset is disposed of. It is also called *scrap value* or *trade-in value*. If a plant asset is purchased at a cost of $3,800 and it is estimated that the residual value of the asset will be $800, the depreciable cost of the asset is $3,000 ($3,800 – $800).

## Estimating the Life of the Asset

Another major consideration in determining depreciation is to estimate the number of periods the asset will be used or how many units of service the asset will provide. If the asset is a vehicle to be used for delivery of merchandise and it is estimated that the vehicle will be operated for 60,000 miles, the depreciation charge per mile can readily be determined. Likewise, if it is estimated that the asset will be used for five years and will perform approximately the same service in each year, it is reasonable to allocate the depreciable cost equally to each of the years in which the asset will be used.

Generally, there is no way of knowing exactly how long an asset will last or exactly how many units of service it will provide. An estimate of these factors, as well as residual value, will be based on the best information available. Such information is normally provided by the company's past experience with similar assets, statistics supplied by government agencies or trade associations, or appraisals of engineers or architects.

Other factors to be considered in computing depreciation are inadequacy and obsolescence. The physical life of an asset may be much longer than its useful life to a business. If a delivery vehicle with an estimated five-year life was used for three years and by that time the business had grown to the point that the load capacity of the vehicle was too small, it might be traded in for a larger one. All of the above considerations emphasize the fact that the computation of depreciation is based on estimates.

## Methods of Computing Depreciation

Because of the many variables involved in estimating depreciation, several different methods of computing depreciation have been developed. The most common methods are: (1) *straight-line,* (2) *units-of-production,* (3) *sum-of-the-years-digits,* and (4) *declining-balance*.

**Straight-Line Method.** The *straight-line method* of computing depreciation assigns an equal charge to each period of the estimated useful life of the asset. The straight-line method is normally used when the asset is equally useful in each period. A building is a good example of an asset that performs the same service in each period and would be depreciated on the straight-line basis.

To illustrate the straight-line method, assume that an item of equipment is purchased for $6,500. The equipment has an estimated salvage value of $500 and an estimated useful life of 5 years. The depreciable cost of the asset is \$6,000 (\$6,500 − \$500). The annual depreciation would be \$1,200, computed as follows:

$$\frac{\$6{,}500 - \$500}{5 \text{ years}} = \frac{\$6{,}000}{5 \text{ years}} = \$1{,}200 \text{ per year}$$

Based on the five-year life, the depreciation rate would be 1/5 per year or 20% of depreciable cost.

A schedule showing the cost of the asset, depreciable cost, depreciation expense, accumulated depreciation, and book value of the equipment using the straight-line method is presented below. The entries in the table presume that the straight-line rate of 20% was applied each year to the depreciable cost of \$6,000.

If the equipment is used for five years, the book value at the end of the fifth year will be \$500, which is the estimated salvage value. The asset should not be depreciated below salvage value because this is the amount that is expected to be received when the asset is disposed of.

***Straight-Line Depreciation Schedule***

| Year | Cost | Depr. Cost | Depr. Expense | Accum. Depr. End of Year | Book Value End of Year |
|---|---|---|---|---|---|
| 1 | \$6,500 | \$6,000 | \$1,200 | \$1,200 | \$5,300 |
| 2 | 6,500 | 6,000 | 1,200 | 2,400 | 4,100 |
| 3 | 6,500 | 6,000 | 1,200 | 3,600 | 2,900 |
| 4 | 6,500 | 6,000 | 1,200 | 4,800 | 1,700 |
| 5 | 6,500 | 6,000 | 1,200 | 6,000 | 500 |

The principal advantage of the straight-line method of depreciation is its simplicity. When assets are equally useful from period to period, this method provides a reasonable allocation of costs to each period.

**Units-of-Production Method.** The *units-of-production method* of depreciation allocates the depreciable cost to the estimated number of units to be produced by the asset. For example, assume that the equipment previously mentioned will produce 120,000 units during its useful life. The depreciable cost of \$6,000 (\$6,500 − \$500) is divided by the estimated number of units to be produced, 120,000, to yield a depreciation cost per unit of \$.05:

$$\$6{,}000 \div 120{,}000 \text{ units} = \$.05 \text{ per unit}$$

If the machine produced 30,000 units during the first year of operation, the adjustment for depreciation expense at the end of the year would be \$1,500 (30,000 × \$.05).

Assuming that the units produced during the second through fifth years are 26,000, 23,000, 21,000, and 20,000 respectively, the schedule for depreciation expense, accumulated depreciation, and book value, using the units-of-production method, is shown below.

***Units-of-Production Depreciation Schedule***

| Year | Cost | Depr. Cost | Units Produced | Depr. Rate per Unit | Depr. Expense | Accum. Depr. End of Year | Book Value End of Year |
|---|---|---|---|---|---|---|---|
| 1 | \$6,500 | \$6,000 | 30,000 | .05 | \$1,500 | \$1,500 | \$5,000 |
| 2 | 6,500 | 6,000 | 26,000 | .05 | 1,300 | 2,800 | 3,700 |
| 3 | 6,500 | 6,000 | 23,000 | .05 | 1,150 | 3,950 | 2,550 |
| 4 | 6,500 | 6,000 | 21,000 | .05 | 1,050 | 5,000 | 1,500 |
| 5 | 6,500 | 6,000 | 20,000 | .05 | 1,000 | 6,000 | 500 |

The units-of-production method is advantageous when the use of a plant asset varies widely from period to period. This method is frequently used for recording depreciation on vehicles and is based on the number of miles driven.

## Accelerated Depreciation Methods

In some businesses and for certain types of assets it may be desirable to use a depreciation method that will charge a larger amount of depreciation expense to the early years of the asset life and a steadily declining amount to later years. The procedure of charging a greater amount to depreciation expense in the early years of the asset life and a successively lesser amount in each subsequent year is known as *accelerated depreciation*. Accelerated depreciation is a reasonable procedure for assets that will require increasing maintenance and repair expenses to keep them in good operating condition as they get older. The smaller depreciation charges in these later years will help equalize the annual cost (depreciation plus repairs and maintenance) of operating the asset over its useful life.

There also is an income tax advantage for a business using an accelerated depreciation method. By charging more depreciation in the early years, the business will report a lower taxable income and pay less income tax during these years. In later years the depreciation expense will be less and taxable income more. However, by delaying the payment of these taxes from the early years of the asset life to the later years, the business is able to have the use of this money in the early years.

The two most common types of accelerated depreciation are the sum-of-the-years-digits method and the declining-balance method.

**Sum-of-the-Years-Digits Method.** The depreciation rate used with the *sum-of-the-years-digits method* is a fraction that becomes progressively smaller each year. The numerator of the fraction, which decreases each year, is the number of years of remaining life of the asset at the beginning of the current year. The denominator, which remains the same, is the sum of the years representing the life of the asset. For example, if a machine has an estimated life of 5 years, the denominator (the-sum-of-the-years-digits) of the fraction would be determined by adding 5 + 4 + 3 + 2 + 1 to obtain 15. The fraction for depreciation for each year would be:

| Year | Fraction for Depreciation |
|---|---|
| 1 | 5/15 |
| 2 | 4/15 |
| 3 | 3/15 |
| 4 | 2/15 |
| 5 | 1/15 |
| 15 | |

For the first year the numerator would be 5, the number of years of life remaining at the beginning of the year. Therefore, the fraction for depreciation at the end of the first year would be 5/15, the fraction for depreciation for the second year would be 4/15, and so on. This fraction is applied to the depreciable cost of the asset.

Using the same $6,500 asset from preceding illustrations, the depreciation for the first year, applying the sum-of-the-years-digits method, will be 5/15 × $6,000, or $2,000. The depreciation for the second year will be 4/15 × $6,000, or $1,600.

A schedule showing the computation of depreciation, accumulated depreciation, and book value using the sum-of-the-years-digits method is shown below.

***Sum-of-the-Years-Digits Depreciation Schedule***

| Year | Cost | Depr. Cost | Fraction | Depr. Expense | Accum. Depr. End of Year | Book Value End of Year |
|---|---|---|---|---|---|---|
| 1 | $6,500 | $6,000 | 5/15 | **$2,000** | $2,000 | $4,500 |
| 2 | 6,500 | 6,000 | 4/15 | **1,600** | 3,600 | 2,900 |
| 3 | 6,500 | 6,000 | 3/15 | **1,200** | 4,800 | 1,700 |
| 4 | 6,500 | 6,000 | 2/15 | **800** | 5,600 | 900 |
| 5 | 6,500 | 6,000 | 1/15 | **400** | 6,000 | 500 |

**Declining-Balance Method.** A second method of accelerated depreciation is the *declining-balance method*. This method also provides a steadily decreasing charge for depreciation expense from period to period over the asset's estimated life. There are several different ways to apply this method, but the one most commonly used is to double the straight-line rate and multiply that rate by the declining book value of the asset. For example, if the estimated life of an item of equipment is 5 years, the straight-line rate of depreciation would be 1/5 per year, or 20%. The declining-balance rate of depreciation would therefore be 2/5, or 40%, per year, or twice the straight-line rate.

There are two important points to be noted about the declining-balance method: (**1**) this is the only method of depreciation that does not consider the salvage value when computing depreciation, and (**2**) the rate of depreciation determined (40% in the example) is applied to the asset's remaining book value at the end of each year.

Using the same $6,500 asset from preceding illustrations, the schedule of depreciation for the declining-balance method is shown below:

***Declining-Balance Depreciation Schedule***

| Year | Cost | Depr. Rate | Depr. Expense | Accum. Depr. End of Year | Book Value End of Year |
|---|---|---|---|---|---|
| 1 | $6,500 | 40% | **$2,600.00** | $2,600.00 | $3,900.00 |
| 2 | 6,500 | 40% | **1,560.00** | 4,160.00 | 2,340.00 |
| 3 | 6,500 | 40% | **936.00** | 5,096.00 | 1,404.00 |
| 4 | 6,500 | 40% | **561.60** | 5,657.60 | 842.40 |
| 5 | 6,500 | 40% | **336.96** | 5,994.56 | 505.44 |

The depreciation rate, 40%, is applied to the cost, $6,500, in the first year to determine the depreciation expense of $2,600. Note that the cost of $6,500 is also the first year's book value until depreciation is recorded at the end of the year. In the second and all following years the 40% rate is applied to the book value as of the end of the preceding year. For example, in the second year, the 40% rate was applied to the book value at the end of the first year, $3,900; therefore, the depreciation computed was $1,560 ($3,900 × 40%).

Although the salvage value of the asset is not considered in computing the annual depreciation for the declining-balance method, the asset should not be depreciated below the estimated salvage value.

As with the sum-of-the-years-digits method, the declining-balance method is most appropriately applied to assets whose productivity is greater in the early years of their lives. The accelerated methods are also desirable for assets that will probably become inadequate or obsolete before they physically wear out.

## QUESTIONS FOR DISCUSSION

1. What are the essential characteristics in the classification of plant assets?

2. Plant assets should be recorded on the books at cost. Name several items that might be included in the cost of: (a) a new air conditioning system for a factory; (b) a used delivery truck for a bakery.

3. Fox Storage Company installed an air conditioning unit in one section of its warehouse at a cost of $4,800. The normal life of the air conditioner is 10 years, but the company is planning a complete remodeling of the warehouse in four years, at which time the entire area will be centrally air conditioned. The estimated salvage value of a used air conditioner of this type is $800. (a) What would be the useful life of the air conditioner? (b) What would be the annual depreciation on the straight-line basis?

4. (a) Name two methods of accelerated depreciation. (b) What advantages are there to recording a higher depreciation expense in the early years of an asset's life?

5. Mooney recently purchased a large item of machinery and now must decide the depreciation method to use. If he uses the sum-of-the-years-digits method, his depreciation for the first year will be $4,500, and if he uses the straight-line method, it will be $2,350. Mooney's CPA advised him to take the sum-of-the-years-digits method and thereby reduce his taxable income by $2,150. The CPA also told Mooney that the total depreciation over the life of the machinery will be exactly the same; therefore Mooney cannot see any advantage to writing off a larger amount now, thereby reducing the amount he can charge off later. What is your advice to Mooney? Explain.

6. (a) What is the declining-balance method of depreciation? (b) What are the two important characteristics unique to the declining-balance method?

## EXERCISES

1. Indicate by placing a check mark in the columns provided which of the following expenditures should be debited to the Building Account:

| | Debit to Building YES | Debit to Building NO |
|---|---|---|
| a. Real estate acquired for building site | | |
| b. Payment of contractor for construction of building | | |
| c. Landscaping grounds | | |
| d. Architect's fee on building | | |
| e. Purchase of brick for outside wall of building | | |
| f. Interest paid on money borrowed during construction. | | |

2. On January 2, Dobbs Drilling Company purchased a piece of heavy machinery for $52,000. The machine has an expected life of 10 years and estimated salvage value of $2,000. Dobbs uses the straight-line method for computing depreciation.

   **Required:**

   (a) Compute the annual depreciation on the heavy machinery purchased by Dobbs.

   (b) Prepare the general journal entry to record depreciation at the end of the first year.

   (c) Show how the machinery and accumulated depreciation would be shown on the balance sheet at the end of the first year.

   (d) What is the book value of the machinery at the end of the first year? at the end of the third year?

3. The Mississippi Power Company purchased a large generator on January 2 of the current year for $38,500. The generator has an estimated useful life of 12 years, and an expected salvage value of $2,500. It is anticipated that the generator will operate effectively for 48,000 hours.

   **Required:** Determine the depreciation per year, the accumulated depreciation, and the book value of the generator at the end of each year for the first two years by the following depreciation methods:

   (a) straight-line

   (b) units-of-production (4,200 and 3,900 hours used in first two years respectively)

4. Broadway Meat Packers purchased a cutting machine for $6,000 with an estimated life of 10 years and a salvage value of $500.

   **Required:**

   (a) Determine the rate of depreciation using the declining-balance method at twice the straight-line rate.

   (b) Determine the depreciation expense for each of the first two years of the machine life using the declining-balance method.

   (c) Compute the book value of the machine at the end of the second year.

5. At the beginning of the year Green Yard Service purchased a tractor-mower at a cost of $3,500 with an estimated useful life of 5 years and a residual value of $500. Prepare the general journal entries to record depreciation on the mower at the end of Year 1 and Year 2 if Green uses the sum-of-the-years-digits method of recording depreciation.

## ASSIGNMENT 14-A

**Tear out pages 573–576 and complete Assignment 14-A. After submitting your papers for approval, continue with the following discussion until the next assignment is required.**

# PART B DISPOSAL OF PLANT ASSETS AND SPECIAL ASSET RECORDS

In Part A of this chapter, the cost of acquiring plant assets and their subsequent depreciation were discussed. As indicated, all plant assets except land will ultimately wear out or become inadequate or obsolete. When this occurs, the assets will be disposed of. Plant assets may be disposed of in one of the following ways: (1) sold, (2) retired or scrapped, or (3) traded in or exchanged for other plant assets. This part of the chapter is devoted to accounting for these disposals. The detailed records maintained for plant assets are also discussed.

## SALE OF PLANT ASSETS

When an asset is disposed of, the first step is to update the depreciation. When a plant asset is sold, this procedure is necessary in order to determine the book value of the asset at the date of sale. The next step is to record the cash received and write the asset off the books. This entry requires debits to Cash and Accumulated Depreciation and a credit to the asset account for its original cost. Any difference between the amount received for the asset and its book value is recognized as a gain or loss from the sale. For example, assume that store equipment purchased January 2, 1977, at a cost of $2,400 is being depreciated $300 per year. The equipment is sold for $900 on January 2, 1982, the beginning of the sixth year. The store equipment and accumulated depreciation accounts at the end of the fifth year immediately prior to the sale would appear as follows:

ACCOUNT **Store Equipment** ACCOUNT NO. **23**

| DATE | | ITEM | POST. REF. | DEBIT | CREDIT | BALANCE DEBIT | BALANCE CREDIT |
|---|---|---|---|---|---|---|---|
| 1977 Jan. | 2 | | P6 | 2 400 00 | | 2 400 00 | |

ACCOUNT **Accumulated Depreciation — Store Equipment** ACCOUNT NO. **23.1**

| DATE | | ITEM | POST. REF. | DEBIT | CREDIT | BALANCE DEBIT | BALANCE CREDIT |
|---|---|---|---|---|---|---|---|
| 1977 Dec. | 31 | Adjusting | J14 | | 300 00 | | 300 00 |
| 1978 Dec. | 31 | Adjusting | J26 | | 300 00 | | 600 00 |
| 1979 Dec. | 31 | Adjusting | J33 | | 300 00 | | 900 00 |
| 1980 Dec. | 31 | Adjusting | J39 | | 300 00 | | 1 200 00 |
| 1981 Dec. | 31 | Adjusting | J43 | | 300 00 | | 1 500 00 |

The book value of the store equipment at the date of sale is $900 (cost $2,400 – accumulated depreciation $1,500). Since the equipment is sold for $900, an amount equal to its book value, there is no gain or loss on the sale. The entry, in general journal form, to record the sale is:

| | | | | |
|---|---|---|---|---|
| Jan. | 2 | Cash | 900 | |
| | | Accumulated Depreciation — Store Equipment | 1,500 | |
| | | Store Equipment | | 2,400 |

## Gain or Loss on Sale of Plant Assets

When plant assets are sold, the amount realized from the sale is seldom equal to the book value of the asset. If the cash received is *greater* than book value, a profit is realized on the sale. This profit is called *gain on sale of plant assets*. If the cash received is *less* than the book value of the asset, a loss is realized on the sale. This loss is called *loss on sale of plant assets*. The gain or loss may be more specifically identified in the accounts, for example, as Gain on Sale of Machinery or Loss on Sale of Store Equipment.

If the equipment in the preceding example had been sold for $700, there would be a loss of $200 on the sale ($900 book value — $700 selling price). This transaction would be recorded as follows:

| | | | | |
|---|---|---|---|---|
| Jan. | 2 | Cash | 700 | |
| | | Accumulated Depreciation — Store Equipment | 1,500 | |
| | | Loss on Sale of Store Equipment | 200 | |
| | | Store Equipment | | 2,400 |

If the equipment had been sold for $1,150, there would be a gain of $250 on the sale ($1,150 selling price – $900 book value). This transaction would be recorded as follows:

| | | | | |
|---|---|---|---|---|
| Jan. | 2 | Cash | 1,150 | |
| | | Accumulated Depreciation — Store Equipment | 1,500 | |
| | | Store Equipment | | 2,400 |
| | | Gain on Sale of Store Equipment | | 250 |

**Plant Assets Sold During the Year.** Because the equipment was sold at the beginning of the period and the depreciation had been recorded at the end of the previous year, there was no entry required to update the accumulated depreciation. Assume, however, that the store equipment is sold on July 1, 1982, for $900. An adjusting entry, shown below, is required to record the depreciation of the asset from January 1, 1982, to July 1, 1982. The depreciation to be recorded for the six-month period at an annual rate of $300 is $150.

| | | | | | |
|---|---|---|---|---|---|
| July | 1 | Depr. Exp. — Store Equip. | | 150 00 | |
| | | Accum. Depr. — Store Equip. | | | 150 00 |
| | | To record depr. for 6 months. | | | |

Accumulated Depreciation — Store Equipment, page 311, now has a balance of $1,650. The book value of the equipment is $750 ($2,400 – $1,650); therefore, there is a gain on the sale of $150.

ACCOUNT **Accumulated Depreciation — Store Equipment** ACCOUNT NO. **23.1**

| DATE | | ITEM | POST. REF. | DEBIT | CREDIT | BALANCE DEBIT | BALANCE CREDIT |
|---|---|---|---|---|---|---|---|
| 1977 Dec. | 31 | Adjusting | J14 | | 300 00 | | 300 00 |
| 1978 Dec. | 31 | Adjusting | J26 | | 300 00 | | 600 00 |
| 1979 Dec. | 31 | Adjusting | J33 | | 300 00 | | 900 00 |
| 1980 Dec. | 31 | Adjusting | J39 | | 300 00 | | 1 200 00 |
| 1981 Dec. | 31 | Adjusting | J43 | | 300 00 | | 1 500 00 |
| 1982 July | 1 | Adjusting | J46 | | 150 00 | | 1 650 00 |

The entry to record the sale would be:

| | | | Debit | Credit |
|---|---|---|---|---|
| July | 1 | Cash | 900 | |
| | | Accumulated Depreciation — Store Equipment | 1,650 | |
| | | Store Equipment | | 2,400 |
| | | Gain on Sale of Store Equipment | | 150 |

**Gains and Losses on the Income Statement.** Gains and losses on the disposal of plant assets are not considered part of the normal operations of the business. They are therefore shown on the income statement as separate items below "Income from operations."

| | | |
|---|---|---|
| Income from operations | | $12,500 |
| Other income and expense: | | |
| Gain on sale of machinery | $430 | |
| Loss on sale of equipment | 180 | 250 |
| Net income | | $12,750 |

Gains (income) and losses (expense) are considered temporary accounts; thus they are closed to Income Summary at the end of the accounting period.

## RETIRING PLANT ASSETS

If a plant asset is no longer useful, it should be disposed of even though the asset has not been fully depreciated. If the asset cannot be sold, it should be retired.

### Retiring Fully Depreciated Assets

If a plant asset that has been fully depreciated is retired, there will be no gain or loss on its disposal. For example, if a machine that cost $2,200 with no estimated salvage value is retired after it has been fully depreciated, the following journal entry will be required:

| | | | Debit | Credit |
|---|---|---|---|---|
| Jan. | 4 | Accum. Depr. — Machinery | 2 200 00 | |
| | | Machinery | | 2 200 00 |
| | | To write off machinery retired. | | |

## Retiring Plant Assets at a Loss

If a plant asset is retired before it is fully depreciated and no salvage is realized, the asset is retired at a loss. For example, a typewriter that cost $500 on January 2 is being depreciated at $50 per year. If the typewriter is retired on June 30 of the eighth year of its life, the accumulated depreciation total for the first seven years would be $350 (7 years × $50). The office equipment and accumulated depreciation — office equipment accounts at the end of seven years will appear as follows:

ACCOUNT **Office Equipment** ACCOUNT NO. **24**

| DATE | | ITEM | POST. REF. | DEBIT | CREDIT | BALANCE DEBIT | BALANCE CREDIT |
|---|---|---|---|---|---|---|---|
| 1976 Jan. | 2 | | P6 | 500 00 | | 500 00 | |

ACCOUNT **Accumulated Depreciation — Office Equipment** ACCOUNT NO. **24.1**

| DATE | | ITEM | POST. REF. | DEBIT | CREDIT | BALANCE DEBIT | BALANCE CREDIT |
|---|---|---|---|---|---|---|---|
| 1982 Dec. | 31 | Adjusting | J60 | | 50 00 | | 350 00 |

Since the asset is retired during the year, the first step in writing it off is to update the depreciation. The depreciation is $50 per year, and because the asset is disposed of on June 30, the depreciation required will be for one-half year, or $25. The entry to bring the depreciation up to date is:

| | | | | | |
|---|---|---|---|---|---|
| June | 30 | Depr. Exp. — Office Equip. ................ | | 25 00 | |
| | | Accum. Depr. — Office Equip........ | | | 25 00 |
| | | To record depr. for 6 months. | | | |

After the adjusting entry is posted, Accumulated Depreciation — Office Equipment will show a balance of $375.

ACCOUNT **Accumulated Depreciation — Office Equipment** ACCOUNT NO. **24.1**

| DATE | | ITEM | POST. REF. | DEBIT | CREDIT | BALANCE DEBIT | BALANCE CREDIT |
|---|---|---|---|---|---|---|---|
| 1982 Dec. | 31 | Adjusting | J60 | | 50 00 | | 350 00 |
| 1983 June | 30 | Adjusting | J66 | | 25 00 | | 375 00 |

The book value of the typewriter at June 30 is $125 ($500 cost − $375 accumulated depreciation). If the machine is retired on this date, a loss of $125 is recognized. The entry to record the retirement of the asset is:

| | | | Debit | Credit |
|---|---|---|---|---|
| June | 30 | Accum. Depr. — Office Equip. | 375 00 | |
| | | Loss on Retirement of Office Equip. | 125 00 | |
| | | Office Equipment | | 500 00 |
| | | To write off equipment retired. | | |

Plant assets that have been fully depreciated but are still being used should not be written off. As long as the assets are being used, the cost and depreciation should be shown in the ledger.

## EXCHANGING PLANT ASSETS

When equipment or machinery becomes worn, it is often traded in for new equipment or machinery of a similar nature. The buyer will normally be given a trade-in allowance on the old asset which is deducted from the price of the new asset. The difference between the price of the new asset and the trade-in allowance is payable at the time of the transaction or as specified in the purchase agreement. When the trade-in allowance is more than the book value of the asset, there is a gain on the exchange; when the trade-in allowance is less than book value, there is a loss on the exchange.

### Gain on Exchange of Plant Assets

Recent accounting pronouncements require that the gain or loss on the exchange of plant assets be determined by the difference in the book value and fair market value of the asset being exchanged. All examples in this text will assume that the trade-in allowance for the asset is equal to its fair market value.

Assume that a delivery truck with a cost of $3,800 and accumulated depreciation to date of $3,100, is traded in on a new truck costing $4,100. The book value of the old truck is $700 ($3,800 − $3,100). If a trade-in allowance, representing the fair market value of the old truck, of $900 is allowed, there is a $200 gain on the exchange ($900 trade-in allowance − $700 book value). For financial reporting purposes, the gain on the exchange of plant assets cannot be recognized.

The balance to be paid ($3,200), also known as the *boot*, is determined by subtracting the trade-in allowance from the cost of the new truck ($4,100 − $900). The cost of the new asset ($3,900) is determined by adding the boot and the book value of the old asset ($3,200 + $700). The entry to record the transaction is as follows, assuming the balance is paid in cash.

| | | | Debit | Credit |
|---|---|---|---|---|
| Jan. | 4 | Delivery Equipment | 3,900 | |
| | | Accumulated Depreciation — Delivery Equip. | 3,100 | |
| | | Delivery Equipment | | 3,800 |
| | | Cash | | 3,200 |

## Loss on Exchange of Plant Assets

If the trade-in allowance is less than the book value of the asset, there is a loss on the exchange. For example, if a trade-in value of only $400 had been allowed on the delivery truck in the preceding example, a loss of $300 ($700 book value − $400 trade-in allowance) would result. Unlike the nonrecognition of gain on the exchange of a plant asset, the loss is recognized immediately. The balance to be paid, $3,700, is determined by subtracting the trade-in allowance from the cost of the new truck ($4,100 − $400). The entry to record this transaction, assuming that cash is paid, is shown below.

| | | | | |
|---|---|---|---|---|
| Jan. | 4 | Delivery Equipment | 4,100 | |
| | | Accumulated Depreciation — Delivery Equip. | 3,100 | |
| | | Loss on Exchange of Delivery Equipment | 300 | |
| | | Delivery Equipment | | 3,800 |
| | | Cash | | 3,700 |

In the above examples the trade-in was recorded at the beginning of the year, therefore the accumulated depreciation was up to date and no adjusting entry was required. If the trade-in had taken place during the year, the first step in recording the transaction would have been to update the depreciation. This adjustment must be made to determine the book value of the asset.

To illustrate, assume that a truck is traded for a new truck costing $4,100 on April 1. The cost of the old truck was $3,800 and the accumulated depreciation as of December 31 of last year was $3,100. The old truck has been depreciated at $600 per year. The entry to record depreciation for the 3-month period January 1–March 31, is:

| | | | | | |
|---|---|---|---|---|---|
| Apr. | 1 | Depr. Exp. — Delivery Equip. | | 150 00 | |
| | | Accum. Depr. — Delivery Equip. | | | 150 00 |
| | | To record depr. for 3 months. | | | |

Accumulated Depreciation — Delivery Equipment now has a $3,250 balance ($3,100 + $150). The book value of the truck is now $550 ($3,800 cost − $3,250 accumulated depreciation). If a trade-in allowance of $400 is granted, the entry to record the exchange is:

| | | | | |
|---|---|---|---|---|
| Apr. | 1 | Delivery Equipment | 4,100 | |
| | | Accumulated Depreciation — Delivery Equip. | 3,250 | |
| | | Loss on Exchange of Delivery Equipment | 150 | |
| | | Delivery Equipment | | 3,800 |
| | | Cash | | 3,700 |

## Recording Exchanges for Income Tax Purposes

Gains and losses resulting from the exchange of similar types of plant assets cannot be recognized for income tax purposes. Therefore, the treatment of a nonrecognized gain for income tax purposes is identical to the treatment for financial reporting purposes as illustrated on page 313. The cost of the new asset will be the book value of the old asset plus the cash paid.

Unlike the treatment of losses for financial reporting purposes where the loss is recognized immediately, losses resulting from the exchange of "like-kind" plant assets are not recognized for income tax purposes. For example, if a trade-in of $400 is allowed (illustration on page 314) on the old truck, the cost of the new truck, for income tax purposes, would be determined as follows:

| | |
|---|---|
| Cost of old truck | $3,800 |
| Less depreciation to date of sale | 3,100 |
| Book value of old truck | $ 700 |
| Cash to be paid ($4,100 − $400) | 3,700 |
| Cost of new truck | $4,400 |

The entry to record the exchange for income tax purposes would be:

| | | | | |
|---|---|---|---|---|
| Jan. | 4 | Delivery Equipment | 4,400 | |
| | | Accumulated Depreciation — Delivery Equip. | 3,100 | |
| | | Delivery Equipment | | 3,800 |
| | | Cash | | 3,700 |

Nonrecognition of gain or loss affects both the recorded cost of the asset acquired and the amount of depreciation expense to be taken on the new asset in subsequent years. In the illustration on page 314, the cost of the new truck was $4,100 when the loss was recognized. When the loss of $300 was not recognized, the cost of the new truck was recorded as $4,400. This cost of $4,400 will be depreciated over the life of the new truck; therefore, the total amount of depreciation expense will be increased by $300. The recognition of the loss becomes a matter of timing. If the loss is recognized, a $300 reduction in income is reported in the current period. If the loss is not recognized, the cost of the asset is increased by $300, and this amount reduces income reported in subsequent periods because the depreciation charges will be greater.

## CONTROL AND SUBSIDIARY ACCOUNTS FOR PLANT ASSETS

In a large company there are often many plant assets. As a result, it would not be practical to show each asset and its accumulated depreciation on the balance sheet. Under such circumstances, it is common to have general ledger control accounts for each class of plant asset with a subsidiary ledger for the individual items.

Common examples of plant asset control accounts are Buildings, Machinery, Office Equipment, Store Equipment, and Furniture and Fixtures. Each control account has a related accumulated depreciation account.

These control accounts are supported by an individual record for each asset in the group. These individual records provide information about the cost of the item, estimated life, salvage value, depreciation per year, accumulated depreciation, and book value. The format of the plant asset record varies depending on the needs of the individual firm. For illustration purposes, the store equipment control accounts and three related subsidiary ledger accounts are presented on the following pages.

**ACCOUNT** Store Equipment **ACCOUNT NO.** 23

| DATE | | ITEM | POST. REF. | DEBIT | CREDIT | BALANCE DEBIT | BALANCE CREDIT |
|---|---|---|---|---|---|---|---|
| 1979 Jan. | 2 | | CP2 | 450 00 | | 450 00 | |
| 1980 July | 3 | | P8 | 2 500 00 | | 2 950 00 | |
| 1982 Jan. | 6 | | CP17 | 275 00 | | 3 225 00 | |

**ACCOUNT** Accumulated Depreciation — Store Equipment **ACCOUNT NO.** 23.1

| DATE | | ITEM | POST. REF. | DEBIT | CREDIT | BALANCE DEBIT | BALANCE CREDIT |
|---|---|---|---|---|---|---|---|
| 1979 Dec. | 31 | Adjusting | J4 | | 40 00 | | 40 00 |
| 1980 Dec. | 31 | Adjusting | J6 | | 115 00 | | 155 00 |
| 1981 Dec. | 31 | Adjusting | J9 | | 190 00 | | 345 00 |
| 1982 Dec. | 31 | Adjusting | J11 | | 210 00 | | 555 00 |

**PLANT ASSET RECORD** Account No. 23-9

Item Display Case General Ledger Account Store Equipment
Serial No. 104-6615 Description Three-shelf glass
From Whom Purchased Denton Equipment and Office Supplies
Estimated Life 10 years Estimated Scrap or Trade-In Value $50 Depreciation Per Year $40

| DATE MO. | DAY | YR. | EXPLANATION | ASSET DEBIT | ASSET CREDIT | ASSET BALANCE | ACCUMULATED DEPRECIATION DEBIT | ACCUMULATED DEPRECIATION CREDIT | ACCUMULATED DEPRECIATION BALANCE | BOOK VALUE |
|---|---|---|---|---|---|---|---|---|---|---|
| 1 | 2 | 79 | | 450 | | 450 | | | | 450 |
| 12 | 31 | 79 | | | | | | 40 | 40 | 410 |
| 12 | 31 | 80 | | | | | | 40 | 80 | 370 |
| 12 | 31 | 81 | | | | | | 40 | 120 | 330 |
| 12 | 31 | 82 | | | | | | 40 | 160 | 290 |

**PLANT ASSET RECORD** Account No. 23-10

Item Cash Register General Ledger Account Store Equipment
Serial No. BB6-4321 Description NCR 4 drawer
From Whom Purchased Denton Equipment and Office Supplies
Estimated Life 15 years Estimated Scrap or Trade-In Value $250 Depreciation Per Year $150

| DATE MO. | DAY | YR. | EXPLANATION | ASSET DEBIT | ASSET CREDIT | ASSET BALANCE | ACCUMULATED DEPRECIATION DEBIT | ACCUMULATED DEPRECIATION CREDIT | ACCUMULATED DEPRECIATION BALANCE | BOOK VALUE |
|---|---|---|---|---|---|---|---|---|---|---|
| 7 | 3 | 80 | | 2,500 | | 2,500 | | | | 2,500 |
| 12 | 31 | 80 | One-half year | | | | | 75 | 75 | 2,425 |
| 12 | 31 | 81 | | | | | | 150 | 225 | 2,275 |
| 12 | 31 | 82 | | | | | | 150 | 375 | 2,125 |

**PLANT ASSET RECORD** Account No. 23-16

Item Adding Machine General Ledger Account Store Equipment
Serial No. A-16210 Description Monroe 10-key adder
From Whom Purchased Denton Equipment and Office Supplies
Estimated Life 12 years Estimated Scrap or Trade-In Value $35 Depreciation Per Year $20

| DATE MO. | DAY | YR. | EXPLANATION | ASSET DEBIT | ASSET CREDIT | ASSET BALANCE | ACCUMULATED DEPRECIATION DEBIT | ACCUMULATED DEPRECIATION CREDIT | ACCUMULATED DEPRECIATION BALANCE | BOOK VALUE |
|---|---|---|---|---|---|---|---|---|---|---|
| 1 | 6 | 82 | | 275 | | 275 | | | | 275 |
| 12 | 31 | 82 | | | | | | 20 | 20 | 255 |

It should be noted that the subsidiary ledger account numbers for plant assets are consistent with the numbering of the control account. The store equipment subsidiary accounts presented on page 316 and above are numbered 23-9, 23-10, and 23-16, clearly indicating that they are related to the store equipment control account, No. 23.

## Determination of Depreciation from Subsidiary Ledger

The adjustment for depreciation of store equipment at the end of each year is determined by adding the depreciation for each individual item in the subsidiary ledger. For example, the 1982 depreciation adjustment for the assets in the preceding illustration is computed as follows:

| | |
|---|---|
| Display case | $ 40 |
| Cash register | 150 |
| Adding machine | 20 |
| Total | $210 |

The adjusting entry to record the depreciation would be:

| | | | | |
|---|---|---|---|---|
| Dec. | 31 | Depr. Exp. — Store Equip. | 210 00 | |
| | | Accum. Depr. — Store Equip. | | 210 00 |
| | | To record depr. for year. | | |

The annual depreciation expense is recorded in each subsidiary account in the Accumulated Depreciation Credit column and the total accumulated depreciation to date is recorded in the Accumulated Depreciation Balance column.

The total of the balances in the subsidiary ledger accounts must equal the balances in the control accounts at the end of the year. A schedule of the balances in the store equipment subsidiary ledger as of December 31, 1982, is presented at the top of page 318.

| Item | Cost | Accumulated Depreciation | Book Value |
|---|---|---|---|
| Display case | $ 450 | $160 | $ 290 |
| Cash register | 2,500 | 375 | 2,125 |
| Adding machine | 275 | 20 | 255 |
| Total | $3,225 | $555 | $2,670 |

When a plant asset is disposed of, the asset cost is credited and the accumulated depreciation to date is debited in the appropriate subsidiary ledger account. The asset account is then removed from the subsidiary ledger and filed for future reference.

## PLANT ASSETS ON THE BALANCE SHEET

The presentation of plant assets on the balance sheet may take many forms. An arrangement often used is to show the cost, accumulated depreciation, and book value of each control account on a single line as illustrated below. This approach has the advantage of presenting all of the essential information in compact form.

*Plant Assets on the Balance Sheet*

| | Cost | Accumulated Depreciation | Book Value | |
|---|---|---|---|---|
| Total current assets | | | | $260,260 |
| Plant assets: | | | | |
| Store equipment | $ 60,630 | $ 20,150 | $ 40,480 | |
| Office equipment | 20,840 | 1,990 | 18,850 | |
| Buildings | 260,000 | 140,000 | 120,000 | |
| Land | 116,000 | — | 116,000 | |
| Total plant assets | $457,470 | $162,140 | $295,330 | 295,330 |

## QUESTIONS FOR DISCUSSION

1. (a) When a plant asset is disposed of, what is the first step in the accounting process? (b) Why is this procedure necessary?
2. How should gains and losses on the sale of plant assets be shown in the financial statements?
3. When should the cost and accumulated depreciation of a plant asset that is fully depreciated be removed from the ledger?
4. Explain the differences, if any, in recording the exchange of "like-kind" assets at a gain or loss for financial reporting purposes and for income tax purposes.
5. What is the purpose of using control accounts for plant assets?
6. In what ways is a control account for store equipment similar to the control account, Accounts Receivable?

## EXERCISES

1. A refrigerated display counter for meats in a butcher shop had a cost of $2,700. The display counter was sold on January 2 of the current year, when the accumulated depreciation was $2,400. Prepare the general journal entry to record the sale of the display counter for cash assuming it was sold for: (a) $300; (b) $500; (c) $150.

2. The Ralph Company retires an office desk which cost $750. Prepare the general journal entry to record this action assuming that the accumulated depreciation at the time of retirement was: (a) $750; (b) $675.

3. PDI has a copier that cost $1,200 with accumulated depreciation of $900 which is exchanged for a new copier with a cost of $2,000. A trade-in allowance, representing the fair market value of the old copier, $200, is granted on the exchange and the balance is paid in cash. (a) Will a gain or loss be recognized for financial reporting purposes, and, if so, how much? (b) Prepare the entry to record the exchange.

4. What will be the cost of the new copier in 3. above for income tax purposes? Explain your answer.

## ASSIGNMENT 14-B

**Tear out pages 577–584 and complete Assignment 14-B. Submit the papers to your instructor for approval.**

# INDEX

## A

## E



## F



## G



## I

## J



## L



## M



## N



## O



## P

## R



## S

## T



## U



## V



## W

# ASSIGNMENTS — OBJECTIVE QUESTIONS AND PROBLEMS

Assignment 1-A

**Perfect Score** 20 **Name** ______________________

**Student's Score** ____ **Date** ______________ **Class** ________

## PROPERTY AND RIGHTS TO PROPERTY

**Instructions.** Analyze each of the following statements carefully before writing your answer in the column at the right. Do not make any entries in the scoring column. It is provided for the use of your instructor.

| No. | Statement | Answer | For Scoring |
|---|---|---|---|
| 1 | Those from whom business people borrow money or buy on credit are known as | | 1 |
| 2 | The properties used in the operation of a business are called | | 2 |
| 3 | The property rights of creditors to a business are called | | 3 |
| 4 | The owner's claim to the business's assets is called | | 4 |
| 5 | Assets = (?) + Owner's Equity | | 5 |
| 6 | Liabilities = Assets − (?) | | 6 |
| 7 | The planning, summarizing, reporting, and interpreting of the bookkeeping records is known as | | 7 |
| 8 | The process of recording the transactions of a business is called | | 8 |
| 9 | Liabilities $1,400 + Owner's Equity $2,120 = Assets (?) | $ | 9 |
| 10 | Liabilities $1,090 = Assets $2,375 − Owner's Equity (?) | $ | 10 |
| 11 | Owner's Equity $1,660 = Assets $2,820 − Liabilities (?) | $ | 11 |
| 12 | The McKinney Company has assets of $75,000. The liabilities of the company are $45,000. The owner's equity is (?) | $ | 12 |
| 13 | Sue Lee, a kennel owner, has assets of $8,000 and owner's equity amounting to $5,500. The liabilities of the business are | $ | 13 |
| 14 | Ed Evans owns the building in which his business is located, $24,000, and equipment used in the business, $8,000. He owes his bank $4,000. His equity in the business is | $ | 14 |
| 15 | If a transaction results in an increase of $500 in the total assets and the liabilities remain unchanged, the owner's equity would be increased (decreased) by | | 15 |
| 16 | If a transaction results in a decrease of $700 in the total assets and the owner's equity remains unchanged, the liabilities would be increased (decreased) by | | 16 |
| 17 | Paul Bean, an automobile mechanic, owns a $100,000 building and $25,000 of equipment. He has no liabilities. His owner's equity is | $ | 17 |
| 18 | Marilyn Gunnels purchases a repair shop having the following assets and liabilities: cash, $1,200; equipment, $9,000; building, $80,000; a debt to a bank, $7,500; and a debt to another creditor, $750. The owner's equity is | $ | 18 |

*(Continued)*

| No. | Statement | Answer | For Scoring |
|---|---|---|---|
| 19 | Phil Lakota, a contractor, owns the building in which his business is located, $92,000; supplies which cost $24,000, one fourth of which has not yet been paid; and equipment, $5,600, of which he has paid $2,300. The owner's equity is ............ | $ | 19 |
| 20 | Anne Hooten has the following personal property: cash, $320; furniture, $2,800; and an automobile, $3,900, on which she has paid $1,500. Her personal equity is ............ | $ | 20 |

**1A-1.** Classify each of the following items as an asset, liability, or owner's equity.

| | *Asset* | *Liability* | *Owner's Equity* |
|---|---|---|---|
| 0. Cash | ✓ | | |
| 1. Building | | | |
| 2. Amount owed to Tres. Co. | | | |
| 3. Office supplies | | | |
| 4. Cletus Clark, capital | | | |
| 5. Mortgage payable on building | | | |
| 6. Merchandise | | | |
| 7. Owner's investment | | | |
| 8. Store equipment | | | |
| 9. Note payable to bank | | | |
| 10. Automobile | | | |
| 11. Cash in bank | | | |
| 12. Note payable on automobile | | | |

**1A-2.** Each of the following equations represents a transaction. Determine the amount missing in each equation.

| | *Assets* | = | *Liabilities* | + | *Owner's Equity* |
|---|---|---|---|---|---|
| 0. | $ 6,000 | = | $2,700 | + | $ *3,300* |
| 1. | 16,000 | = | ______ | + | 11,200 |
| 2. | ______ | = | 1,900 | + | 9,500 |
| 3. | 15,000 | = | –0– | + | ______ |
| 4. | ______ | = | 1,700 | + | 5,100 |
| 5. | 1,800 | = | ______ | + | 1,000 |

**1A-3.** Below are given the assets, liabilities, and owner's equity in equation form for Dominiques Painting Company. You are also given a series of transactions for the first month of operations. Show the effect of each transaction on the equation by recording your answers in the spaces provided. Be sure to enter all balances after recording each transaction. The first transaction is filled in as an example.

| ASSETS | | | = | LIABILITIES | + | OWNER'S EQUITY |
|---|---|---|---|---|---|---|
| Cash | + Painting Supplies | + Painting Equipment | = | Accounts Payable | + | Juan Dominiques, Capital |

0. Dominiques invested $8,000 cash in the business.

| | Cash | Painting Supplies | Painting Equipment | Accounts Payable | Juan Dominiques, Capital |
|---|---|---|---|---|---|
| | *+8,000* | | | | *+8,000* |
| Bal. | *8,000* | | | | *8,000* |

1. Purchased painting equipment from Todd Co. on account, $3,400.

| | | | | | |
|---|---|---|---|---|---|
| Bal. | | | | | |

2. Purchased painting supplies for $700 cash.

| | | | | | |
|---|---|---|---|---|---|
| Bal. | | | | | |

3. Paid $600 to Todd Co. on the equipment purchased in (1).

| | | | | | |
|---|---|---|---|---|---|
| Bal. | | | | | |

4. Received $1,300 cash for painting an office.

| | | | | | |
|---|---|---|---|---|---|
| Bal. | | | | | |

5. Purchased painting supplies from Richard's on account, $250.

| | | | | | |
|---|---|---|---|---|---|
| Bal. | | | | | |

6. Paid salaries owed to helpers for the month, $840.

| | | | | | |
|---|---|---|---|---|---|
| Bal. | | | | | |

7. Painted a small house and received cash, $700.

| | | | | | |
|---|---|---|---|---|---|
| Bal. | | | | | |

8. Paid for the supplies bought from Richard's in (5).

| | | | | | |
|---|---|---|---|---|---|
| Bal. | | | | | |

9. Paid utility bill, $390.

| | | | | | |
|---|---|---|---|---|---|
| Bal. | | | | | |

10. Dominiques withdrew $300 cash for personal use.

| | | | | | |
|---|---|---|---|---|---|
| Bal. | | | | | |

*(Page not used.)*

**Perfect Score** **50** **Name** ____________________

**Student's Score** ____ **Date** ____________ **Class** ________

## FINANCIAL STATEMENTS

**Instructions.** In Column 1, classify each of the following items as an asset, liability, revenue, expense, or drawing account. In Column 2, state whether each should be shown on the balance sheet, income statement, or capital statement.

| No. | Item | Classification | Financial Statement | For Scoring |
|---|---|---|---|---|
| 1–2 | Office equipment | | | 1–2 |
| 3–4 | Wages paid | | | 3–4 |
| 5–6 | Stationery and supplies on hand | | | 5–6 |
| 7–8 | Rent paid for office | | | 7–8 |
| 9–10 | Commissions received for services | | | 9–10 |
| 11–12 | Investment to begin business | | | 11–12 |
| 13–14 | Cost of heat and lights for office | | | 13–14 |
| 15–16 | Amount owed on a bank loan | | | 15–16 |
| 17–18 | Office supplies withdrawn for personal use | | | 17–18 |
| 19–20 | Fares collected by bus company | | | 19–20 |
| 21–22 | Cash in bank account | | | 21–22 |
| 23–24 | Postage paid | | | 23–24 |
| 25–26 | Panel truck used by florist | | | 25–26 |
| 27–28 | Gas and oil used in operating the truck | | | 27–28 |
| 29–30 | Note receivable | | | 29–30 |
| 31–32 | Monthly advertising paid | | | 31–32 |
| 33–34 | Amount owed to creditor | | | 33–34 |
| 35–36 | Additional investment of cash in business | | | 35–36 |
| 37–38 | Amount receivable from customer | | | 37–38 |
| 39–40 | Taxes paid for current period | | | 39–40 |

**Instructions.** Complete each of the following statements by writing in the correct answer in the space at the right.

| No. | Statement | Answer | For Scoring |
|---|---|---|---|
| 41 | The financial statement which shows the results of business operations for a specific period of time is the | | 41 |
| 42 | The financial statement which shows the amount and the nature of the assets, liabilities, and owner's equity as of a specific date is called the | | 42 |

*(Continued)*

| No. | Statement | Answer | For Scoring |
|---|---|---|---|
| 43 | Claims against a business by creditors for services rendered or merchandise sold are called.......... | | 43 |
| 44 | A twelve-month period covered by the income statement is known as a .......... | | 44 |
| 45 | The costs of goods and services consumed in the operations of the business are called .......... | | 45 |
| 46 | The gross increase in owner's equity resulting from business operations is called.......... | | 46 |
| 47 | The decrease in owner's equity resulting from the excess of expenses over revenues is called .......... | | 47 |
| 48 | If revenues for the period exceed expenses, the resulting increase in owner's equity is called.......... | | 48 |
| 49 | Withdrawals of assets by the owner in anticipation of a profit are called.......... | | 49 |
| 50 | The connecting link between the income statement and the balance sheet is the.......... | | 50 |

**1B-1.** The Lanier Music School is owned and operated by Gary Lanier. During the month of April of the current year, the business had the following revenue and expenses:

| | | | |
|---|---|---|---|
| Revenue | $3,860 | Salary expense | $1,160 |
| Utilities expense | 310 | Insurance expense | 45 |
| Rent expense | 220 | Supplies expense | 27 |
| Advertising expense | 100 | | |

**Required:**

(a) Prepare an income statement for Lanier Music School for the month of April, using the form below.

(b) Assuming that Lanier's capital on April 1 was $6,400 and that he withdrew $600 during the month, prepare a capital statement for the month of April using the form at the bottom of this page.

**1B-2.** On January 2 of the current year, Kathy Duncan invested $9,500 in the Duncan Company. She reported a net income of $11,500 on her income statement for the year. Duncan withdrew $400 per month during the year for personal living expenses. At December 31, the Duncan Company had the following assets and liabilities:

| | | | |
|---|---|---|---|
| Store equipment | $12,000 | Cash | $1,310 |
| Office equipment | 7,500 | Accounts payable — People Equipment Company | 3,000 |
| Store supplies | 400 | | |
| Office supplies | 260 | Accounts payable — Apex Suppliers | 2,270 |

**Required:** From the information given above, prepare a capital statement for the year and a balance sheet for the Duncan Company at December 31, using the ruled forms provided below.

**Perfect Score** 20 **Name** ____________________

**Student's Score** ____ **Date** ____________________ **Class** ________

## BALANCE SHEET ACCOUNTS

**Instructions.** Complete each of the following statements and answer each of the questions by writing your answer in the space at the right.

| No. | Statement | Answer | For Scoring |
|---|---|---|---|
| 1 | The individual record of each item appearing on the balance sheet is called a(an) .......... | | 1 |
| 2 | A group of accounts is called a.......... | | 2 |
| 3 | The right side of an account is called the .......... | | 3 |
| 4 | The left side of an account is called the.......... | | 4 |
| 5 | What effect (increase or decrease) does a *credit* have on an asset account?.......... | | 5 |
| 6 | What effect does a *credit* have on a liability account?.......... | | 6 |
| 7 | What effect does a *debit* have on an owner's equity account?.......... | | 7 |
| 8 | What effect does a *debit* have on an asset account?.......... | | 8 |
| 9 | What effect does a *debit* have on a liability account?.......... | | 9 |
| 10 | What effect does a *credit* have on an owner's equity account?.......... | | 10 |
| 11 | A schedule comparing the total debit balances with the total credit balances in the ledger to determine their equality is called a.......... | | 11 |
| 12 | The accounting system used to record and maintain the mathematical equality of the accounting equation is called the.......... | | 12 |
| 13 | The difference between the total debits to an account and the total credits to that account is called the.......... | | 13 |
| 14 | A skeleton form of ledger account frequently used for illustration purposes is called a.......... | | 14 |
| 15 | If the total amount of the debits in the ledger equals the total amount of the credits, the ledger is said to be.......... | | 15 |
| 16 | The procedure of totaling the debit and credit entries to each account and recording the total of each in small pencil figures below the last debit and credit entry is known as.......... | | 16 |

**Instructions.** In the answer column state the effect (increase, decrease, or no effect) on owner's equity of each transaction below.

| No. | Transaction | Answer | For Scoring |
|---|---|---|---|
| 17 | Total assets increase and total liabilities remain unchanged.......... | | 17 |
| 18 | Total assets increase and total liabilities increase by the same amount.. | | 18 |
| 19 | One asset increases and another decreases by the same amount.......... | | 19 |
| 20 | Total assets decrease and total liabilities remain the same.......... | | 20 |

**2A-1.**

| Account | Column 1<br>Normal Balance | Column 2<br>Effect of Debit | Column 3<br>Effect of Credit |
|---|---|---|---|
| 0. Cash | *Debit* | *Increase* | *Decrease* |
| 1. Automobiles | | | |
| 2. Owner's Equity | | | |
| 3. Store Supplies | | | |
| 4. Notes Payable | | | |
| 5. Accounts Receivable | | | |

**Required:**

(a) In Column 1 identify the normal balance (debit or credit) for each ledger account listed.
(b) In Column 2 state the effect a debit would have on the ledger account (increase or decrease).
(c) In Column 3 state the effect a credit would have on the ledger account (increase or decrease).

**2A-2.** Presented below is the ledger of the balance sheet accounts for the Teri Co. as of May 1, of the current year. The following are transactions completed by the Teri Co. during the month of May.

(a) Purchased store equipment on account from Ronnie Co., $600.
(b) Purchased store supplies for cash, $150.
(c) Teri made an additional investment in the business, $1,200.
(d) Sold equipment which was no longer needed in the business to an employee for cash at cost, $400.
(e) Paid for one half of the equipment purchased in transaction (a).
(f) Sold some store supplies for cash at cost to a neighborhood storekeeper, $40.

**Required:**

(a) Record the above transactions in the T-accounts provided below.
(b) Foot the T-accounts where necessary and enter the total of each column in small pencil figures just below the last debit or credit entry. If an account has entries on both sides, determine the balance and enter it in small pencil figures on the side with the larger total.
(c) Prepare a trial balance of the accounts as of May 31, using the ruled form on page 339.

**CASH**

| | | | |
|---|---|---|---|
| Bal. | 900 | | |

**BUILDINGS**

| | | | |
|---|---|---|---|
| Bal. | 36,000 | | |

**LAND**

| | | | |
|---|---|---|---|
| Bal. | 4,000 | | |

**STORE SUPPLIES**

| | | | |
|---|---|---|---|
| Bal. | 400 | | |

**ACCOUNTS PAYABLE — RONNIE CO.**

| | | | |
|---|---|---|---|
| | | Bal. | 4,400 |

**EQUIPMENT**

| | | | |
|---|---|---|---|
| Bal. | 3,200 | | |

**E. S. TERI, CAPITAL**

| | | | |
|---|---|---|---|
| | | Bal. | 40,100 |

**2A-2**

**2A-3.** The following accounts and transactions for the month of March of the current year appear in the ledger of the Lopez Company owned by Juan Lopez.

ACCOUNT *Cash* ACCOUNT NO.

| DATE | | ITEM | POST. REF. | DEBIT | DATE | | ITEM | POST. REF. | CREDIT |
|---|---|---|---|---|---|---|---|---|---|
| *19--* Mar. | 1 | *Balance* | | 700 00 | *19--* Mar. | 9 | | | 550 00 |
| | 4 | | | 1000 00 | | 19 | | | 50 00 |
| | 12 | | | 250 00 | | 27 | | | 450 00 |

ACCOUNT *Office Supplies* ACCOUNT NO.

| DATE | | ITEM | POST. REF. | DEBIT | DATE | | ITEM | POST. REF. | CREDIT |
|---|---|---|---|---|---|---|---|---|---|
| *19--* Mar. | 1 | *Balance* | | 140 00 | | | | | |
| | 19 | | | 50 00 | | | | | |
| | | | | | | | | | |

ACCOUNT *Office Equipment* ACCOUNT NO.

| DATE | | ITEM | POST. REF. | DEBIT | DATE | | ITEM | POST. REF. | CREDIT |
|---|---|---|---|---|---|---|---|---|---|
| *19--* Mar. | 1 | *Balance* | | 2600 00 | *19--* Mar. | 12 | | | 250 00 |
| | 9 | | | 550 00 | | | | | |
| | | | | | | | | | |

*(Continued)*

ACCOUNT *Accounts Payable — Gem Co.* ACCOUNT NO.

| DATE | | ITEM | POST. REF. | DEBIT | DATE | | ITEM | POST. REF. | CREDIT |
|---|---|---|---|---|---|---|---|---|---|
| 19-- Mar. | 27 | | | 450 00 | 19-- Mar. | 1 | Balance | | 950 00 |
| | | | | | | | | | |

ACCOUNT *Juan Lopez, Capital* ACCOUNT NO.

| DATE | | ITEM | POST. REF. | DEBIT | DATE | | ITEM | POST. REF. | CREDIT |
|---|---|---|---|---|---|---|---|---|---|
| | | | | | 19-- Mar. | 1 | Balance | | 2 490 00 |
| | | | | | | 4 | | | 1 000 00 |
| | | | | | | | | | |

**Required:**

(a) Answer the following questions.

1. What was the reason for each of the following cash receipts?

   March 4 ____________________

   March 12 ____________________

2. What was the reason for each of the following cash payments?

   March 9 ____________________

   March 19 ____________________

   March 27 ____________________

(b) Determine the balance of each ledger account by footing.

(c) Prepare a trial balance of the ledger as of March 31, using the ruled form below.

| | | |
|---|---|---|
| | | |
| | | |
| | | |
| | | |
| | | |
| | | |
| | | |
| | | |

| Perfect Score | 30 | Name ______________________ | |
|---|---|---|---|
| Student's Score | ____ | Date ______________ | Class ________ |

## INCOME STATEMENT ACCOUNTS

**Instructions.** Complete each statement below by writing your answer in the space at the right.

| No. | Statement | Answer | For Scoring |
|---|---|---|---|
| 1 | The costs of supplies or services used in the process of producing revenue are called........ | | 1 |
| 2 | The gross increase in owner's equity resulting from operations of the business is called........ | | 2 |
| 3 | Assets taken from the business by the owner in anticipation of profits are called........ | | 3 |
| 4 | The normal balance of an expense account is a........ | | 4 |
| 5 | The normal balance of the drawing account is a........ | | 5 |
| 6 | The normal balance of a revenue account is a........ | | 6 |
| 7 | The drawing account is increased by a (debit or credit)........ | | 7 |
| 8 | An expense account is increased by a........ | | 8 |
| 9 | A revenue account is decreased by a........ | | 9 |
| 10 | A revenue account is increased by a........ | | 10 |

**Instructions.** For each account listed below, indicate the financial statement (Income Statement, Capital Statement, or Balance Sheet) on which it would be shown. Also indicate the normal balance of the account (debit or credit).

| No. | Account | Financial Statement | Normal Balance | For Scoring |
|---|---|---|---|---|
| 0 | Cash........ | *Balance Sheet* | *Debit* | 0 |
| 11–12 | Buildings........ | | | 11–12 |
| 13–14 | Insurance Expense........ | | | 13–14 |
| 15–16 | Office Supplies........ | | | 15–16 |
| 17–18 | Revenue from Services........ | | | 17–18 |
| 19–20 | Land........ | | | 19–20 |
| 21–22 | Accounts Payable........ | | | 21–22 |
| 23–24 | Accounts Receivable........ | | | 23–24 |
| 25–26 | Commissions Earned........ | | | 25–26 |
| 27–28 | Drawing........ | | | 27–28 |
| 29–30 | Utilities Expense........ | | | 29–30 |

**2B-1.** The following selected ledger account balances are given for the Staggs Co. as of May 31 of the current year.

| | |
|---|---:|
| Nanette Staggs, Capital, May 1 | $2,200 |
| Nanette Staggs, Drawing | 200 |
| Revenue | 1,650 |
| Salary Expense | 400 |
| Rent Expense | 260 |
| Utilities Expense | 130 |
| Miscellaneous Expense | 45 |

**Required:**

(a) Prepare an income statement for the month ended May 31, using the form provided below.

(b) Prepare a capital statement for the month ended May 31, using the form provided at the bottom of this page.

**2B-2.** Scott Pedigo began a lawn maintenance business in December of the current year. The following transactions were completed during the first month of operation.

Dec. 1. Pedigo invested in the business $1,200 cash and equipment worth $1,600.
2. Purchased supplies from Bock Suppliers on account, $70.
4. Received cash for services, $220.
8. Purchased a used panel truck for $1,800 from Snow Co., $600 down and the balance on account.
8. Paid for ad in newspaper, $25.
13. Paid for gas and oil for truck, $16.
15. Received cash for services, $130.
18. Paid Bock Suppliers on account, $40.
18. Paid miscellaneous expenses, $30.
20. Paid salary to helper, $75.
22. Received cash for services, $165.
25. Pedigo withdrew cash for personal use, $90.
27. Paid utilities expense, $72.
28. Paid Snow Co. on account, $100.

**Required:**

(a) Record the transactions for Pedigo Lawn Maintenance Service in the following ledger accounts.

(b) Foot and determine the balance of each ledger account.

(c) Prepare a trial balance of the ledger accounts as of December 31, using the ruled form at the top of page 346.

(d) Prepare an income statement for the month of December, using the ruled form at the bottom of page 346.

## GENERAL LEDGER

ACCOUNT *Cash* ACCOUNT NO.

| DATE | ITEM | POST. REF. | DEBIT | DATE | ITEM | POST. REF. | CREDIT |
|---|---|---|---|---|---|---|---|
| | | | | | | | |

ACCOUNT *Lawn Supplies* ACCOUNT NO.

| DATE | ITEM | POST. REF. | DEBIT | DATE | ITEM | POST. REF. | CREDIT |
|---|---|---|---|---|---|---|---|
| | | | | | | | |

*(Continued)*

ACCOUNT *Lawn Maintenance Equipment* ACCOUNT NO.

| DATE | ITEM | POST. REF. | DEBIT | DATE | ITEM | POST. REF. | CREDIT |
|---|---|---|---|---|---|---|---|
| | | | | | | | |
| | | | | | | | |

ACCOUNT *Truck* ACCOUNT NO.

| DATE | ITEM | POST. REF. | DEBIT | DATE | ITEM | POST. REF. | CREDIT |
|---|---|---|---|---|---|---|---|
| | | | | | | | |
| | | | | | | | |

ACCOUNT *Accounts Payable — Bock Suppliers* ACCOUNT NO.

| DATE | ITEM | POST. REF. | DEBIT | DATE | ITEM | POST. REF. | CREDIT |
|---|---|---|---|---|---|---|---|
| | | | | | | | |
| | | | | | | | |
| | | | | | | | |

ACCOUNT *Accounts Payable — Snow Co.* ACCOUNT NO.

| DATE | ITEM | POST. REF. | DEBIT | DATE | ITEM | POST. REF. | CREDIT |
|---|---|---|---|---|---|---|---|
| | | | | | | | |
| | | | | | | | |
| | | | | | | | |

ACCOUNT *Scott Pedigo, Capital* ACCOUNT NO.

| DATE | ITEM | POST. REF. | DEBIT | DATE | ITEM | POST. REF. | CREDIT |
|---|---|---|---|---|---|---|---|
| | | | | | | | |
| | | | | | | | |
| | | | | | | | |

ACCOUNT *Scott Pedigo, Drawing* ACCOUNT NO.

| DATE | ITEM | POST. REF. | DEBIT | DATE | ITEM | POST. REF. | CREDIT |
|---|---|---|---|---|---|---|---|
| | | | | | | | |
| | | | | | | | |

ACCOUNT *Lawn Maintenance Revenue* ACCOUNT NO.

| DATE | | ITEM | POST. REF. | DEBIT | DATE | | ITEM | POST. REF. | CREDIT |
|---|---|---|---|---|---|---|---|---|---|
| | | | | | | | | | |
| | | | | | | | | | |
| | | | | | | | | | |
| | | | | | | | | | |

ACCOUNT *Advertising Expense* ACCOUNT NO.

| DATE | | ITEM | POST. REF. | DEBIT | DATE | | ITEM | POST. REF. | CREDIT |
|---|---|---|---|---|---|---|---|---|---|
| | | | | | | | | | |
| | | | | | | | | | |

ACCOUNT *Gas and Oil Expense* ACCOUNT NO.

| DATE | | ITEM | POST. REF. | DEBIT | DATE | | ITEM | POST. REF. | CREDIT |
|---|---|---|---|---|---|---|---|---|---|
| | | | | | | | | | |
| | | | | | | | | | |

ACCOUNT *Salary Expense* ACCOUNT NO.

| DATE | | ITEM | POST. REF. | DEBIT | DATE | | ITEM | POST. REF. | CREDIT |
|---|---|---|---|---|---|---|---|---|---|
| | | | | | | | | | |
| | | | | | | | | | |

ACCOUNT *Utilities Expense* ACCOUNT NO.

| DATE | | ITEM | POST. REF. | DEBIT | DATE | | ITEM | POST. REF. | CREDIT |
|---|---|---|---|---|---|---|---|---|---|
| | | | | | | | | | |
| | | | | | | | | | |

ACCOUNT *Miscellaneous Expense* ACCOUNT NO.

| DATE | | ITEM | POST. REF. | DEBIT | DATE | | ITEM | POST. REF. | CREDIT |
|---|---|---|---|---|---|---|---|---|---|
| | | | | | | | | | |
| | | | | | | | | | |

**2B-3.** Using the information in 2B-2 for Pedigo Lawn Maintenance Service, prepare:

(a) a capital statement for December on the ruled form below.

(b) a balance sheet as of December 31, on the ruled form at the bottom of this page.

*(Page not used.)*

Assignment 3-A

**Perfect Score** **20** **Name** ____________________

**Student's Score** ____ **Date** ________________ **Class** ________

**THE JOURNAL**

**Instructions.** A list of accounting terms is given in the left column. From this list, select the term that correctly completes each statement below and place the identifying letter in the Answer column.

| Terms | No. | Statements | Answer | For Scoring |
|---|---|---|---|---|
| A. Assets<br>B. Compound journal entry<br>C. Credit<br>D. Credited<br>E. Date column<br>F. Day<br>G. Debit<br>H. Debited<br>I. Description column<br>J. Financial statements<br>K. General journal<br>L. Journalizing<br>M. Ledger<br>N. Month<br>O. Original entry<br>P. Posting reference column<br>Q. Source documents | 1 | The record used to record the original transactions in their entirety is the ........ | | 1 |
| | 2 | The column used in the journal to record the titles of the accounts involved in the transaction is the ...................................... | | 2 |
| | 3 | An entry in the journal requiring more than one debit or credit is called a(n) ...... | | 3 |
| | 4 | The process of recording transactions in the journal is called ................................. | | 4 |
| | 5 | The original information concerning most transactions are sales tickets, invoices, contracts, checks, and various other business papers called.................... | | 5 |
| | 6 | The journal is often called the book of...... | | 6 |
| | 7 | The left amount column in the journal is used to record the (?) part of each transaction ........................................................ | | 7 |
| | 8 | The first column in the journal is the ........ | | 8 |
| | 9 | The left-hand side of the Date column is used to record the .................................... | | 9 |
| | 10 | The right-hand side of the Date column is used to record the ................................ | | 10 |
| | 11 | The right amount column in the journal is used to record the (?) of each transaction ........................................................ | | 11 |
| | 12 | The flow of information of business transactions in the accounting records is from the journal to the ledger to the ................ | | 12 |
| | 13 | When making a journal entry, the account being (?) is written on the first line of the Description column of the journal. | | 13 |
| | 14 | The name of the account being (?) is indented one-half inch in the Description column of the journal ............................... | | 14 |
| | 15 | The journal column in which the ledger account number is entered when information is transferred from the journal to the ledger is the....................................... | | 15 |

*(Continued)*

**Instructions.** Complete the statements or answer the questions below by writing your answer in the space at the right.

| No. | Statement | Answer | For Scoring |
|---|---|---|---|
| 16 | Ike purchased office equipment for $525 and office supplies for $90 from Dell Office Supplies on account. Which account(s) would be credited to record this transaction ........ | | 16 |
| 17 | What is the amount of the credit(s) in No. 16? ........ | | 17 |
| 18 | When Ike pays Dell for the items purchased in No. 16, what account(s) would be debited? ........ | | 18 |
| 19 | Which account is credited for the transaction described in No. 18? ....... | | 19 |
| 20 | What would be the amount of the credit in No. 18? ........ | | 20 |

**3A-1.** The following transactions were completed for the Hawkins Service Company for the month of June of the current year.

June 1. Frank Hawkins invested cash in the business, $2,700.
2. Purchased store supplies on account from Carla Supplies, $240.
6. Purchased store equipment from Massey Company on account, $2,600.
8. Received cash for services rendered, $800.
10. Paid advertising in local newspaper, $25.
13. Purchased store supplies for cash, $75.
16. Paid on account to Massey Company, $500.
20. Hawkins withdrew cash for personal expenses, $175.
24. Received cash for services rendered, $650.
27. Paid rent for month, $250.
30. Paid salary to assistant, $380.

**Required:** Record the transactions in the general journals provided below and on the following page, using the following accounts: Cash; Store Supplies; Store Equipment; Accounts Payable — Carla Supplies; Accounts Payable — Massey Company; Frank Hawkins, Capital; Frank Hawkins, Drawing; Service Revenue; Salary Expense; Rent Expense; Advertising Expense.

JOURNAL PAGE *1*

| | DATE | | DESCRIPTION | POST. REF. | DEBIT | CREDIT | |
|---|---|---|---|---|---|---|---|
| 1 | | | | | | | 1 |
| 2 | | | | | | | 2 |
| 3 | | | | | | | 3 |
| 4 | | | | | | | 4 |
| 5 | | | | | | | 5 |
| 6 | | | | | | | 6 |
| 7 | | | | | | | 7 |
| 8 | | | | | | | 8 |
| 9 | | | | | | | 9 |
| 10 | | | | | | | 10 |
| 11 | | | | | | | 11 |
| 12 | | | | | | | 12 |

JOURNAL PAGE 2

| DATE | | DESCRIPTION | POST. REF. | DEBIT | CREDIT |
|---|---|---|---|---|---|

Retain the solution to this problem for use in Problem 3B-1.

**3A-2.** The following transactions were completed by the Ford Cleaning Company during the first part of July of the current year.

July 1. Began operations by investing $900 cash and $750 cleaning equipment in the business.
6. Purchased cleaning supplies for $150, paying $80 cash with the balance on account from West Supply Co.
9. Purchased a typewriter for $400 and a vacuum cleaner for $270 from Barton Equipment Co. on account.
10. Completed a cleaning job for the First National Bank. The total fee for the job was $180. The bank paid Ford $50 cash with the balance on account.

**Required:** Record the compound journal entries for the above transactions, using the ruled form provided below. The Ford Cleaning Company has the following accounts in its ledger: Cash; Accounts Receivable — First National Bank; Cleaning Supplies; Cleaning Equipment; Office Equipment; Accounts Payable — West Supply Co.; Accounts Payable — Barton Equipment Co.; Cleaning Revenue; Mike Ford, Capital.

JOURNAL PAGE *1*

| DATE | | DESCRIPTION | POST. REF. | DEBIT | CREDIT |
|---|---|---|---|---|---|

**3A-3.** Katherine Fang owns and operates Fang Travel Agency. A trial balance of the accounts for Fang Travel Agency as of May 31 of the current year is shown at the top of page 353. The revenue and expense accounts represent the results of operations for the first five months of the year.

The transactions completed during June were as follows:

June 1. Purchased a typewriter from the Adams Co. on account, $320.
6. Received a commission on sale of tour package to Fantasyland, $530.
8. Paid Thomas Bros. the amount owed, $400.
9. Purchased office supplies for cash, $30.
10. Paid rent for the month of June, $250.
14. Received a commission on sale of cruise, $750.
16. Fang withdrew cash from her business for personal use, $200.
19. Paid advertising fees for June, $40.
20. Purchased additional furniture for the office from Thomas Bros. on account, $460.

26. Paid Adams Co. on amount owed them, $250.
28. Paid utilities for the month of June, $145.
30. Received monthly commissions for airline ticket sales, $910.
30. Paid office help for the month, $530.

FANG TRAVEL AGENCY
Trial Balance
May 31, 19--

| | | |
|---|---:|---:|
| Cash | 1,225 | |
| Office Supplies | 90 | |
| Furniture and Fixtures | 3,600 | |
| Office Equipment | 1,850 | |
| Accounts Payable — Adams Co. | | 350 |
| Accounts Payable — Thomas Bros | | 400 |
| Katherine Fang, Capital | | 2,810 |
| Katherine Fang, Drawing | 800 | |
| Commissions Revenue | | 8,210 |
| Advertising Expense | 280 | |
| Rent Expense | 1,250 | |
| Salary Expense | 2,560 | |
| Utilities Expense | 115 | |
| | 11,770 | 11,770 |

**Required:** Using the journal paper provided below and on page 354, journalize the June transactions.

JOURNAL PAGE *13*

| | DATE | | DESCRIPTION | POST. REF. | DEBIT | CREDIT | |
|---|---|---|---|---|---|---|---|
| 1 | | | | | | | 1 |
| 2 | | | | | | | 2 |
| 3 | | | | | | | 3 |
| 4 | | | | | | | 4 |
| 5 | | | | | | | 5 |
| 6 | | | | | | | 6 |
| 7 | | | | | | | 7 |
| 8 | | | | | | | 8 |
| 9 | | | | | | | 9 |
| 10 | | | | | | | 10 |
| 11 | | | | | | | 11 |
| 12 | | | | | | | 12 |
| 13 | | | | | | | 13 |
| 14 | | | | | | | 14 |
| 15 | | | | | | | 15 |
| 16 | | | | | | | 16 |
| 17 | | | | | | | 17 |
| 18 | | | | | | | 18 |
| 19 | | | | | | | 19 |
| 20 | | | | | | | 20 |

## JOURNAL

PAGE *14*

| DATE | | DESCRIPTION | POST. REF. | DEBIT | CREDIT |
|---|---|---|---|---|---|

**Retain the solution to this problem for use in Problem 3B-3.**

Perfect Score 20 Name ______________

Student's Score ____ Date ______________ Class ________

## THE CHART OF ACCOUNTS AND POSTING

**Instructions.** Complete the statements and answer the questions below by writing your answer in the space at the right.

| No. | Item | Answer | For Scoring |
|---|---|---|---|
| 1 | A coded listing of the accounts that are maintained in the ledger is called a | | 1 |
| 2 | The process of transferring the debits and credits from the journal to the ledger is called | | 2 |
| 3 | A posting reference number written next to an account recorded in the journal represents the | | 3 |
| 4 | The number written in the posting reference column of a ledger account represents the | | 4 |
| 5 | Credits in the journal are posted to the ledger as (debits or credits) | | 5 |
| 6 | After all the postings have been completed, the ledger accounts should be | | 6 |
| 7 | The schedule prepared to insure that the ledger accounts are in balance is the | | 7 |
| 8 | If the cash account had a $190 debit balance at the beginning of the month, and $240 in credits and $310 in debits were recorded during the period, the balance in the cash account at the end of the month would be | | 8 |
| 9 | Does a trial balance of the ledger accounts provide the information necessary to prepare the financial statements? | | 9 |
| 10 | The amount listed for Accounts Payable in the trial balance on June 30 represents the (beginning or ending) balance for the month of June | | 10 |

**Instructions.** Determine whether each of the following statements is true or false and place a check mark in the appropriate column.

| No. | Statement | True | False | For Scoring |
|---|---|---|---|---|
| 11 | The number of accounts to be kept in any one business should be about the same as in any other business | | | 11 |
| 12 | The account titles used on the balance sheet and the income statement should be the same as those appearing in the ledger | | | 12 |
| 13 | Once the postings have been completed, the information in the journal will be reflected in summary form in the ledger | | | 13 |
| 14 | A common system for numbering accounts using a two-digit code is to have all expense accounts begin with a 1 | | | 14 |
| 15 | In a two-digit coding system, the first digit indicates the major division of the ledger where an account has been placed | | | 15 |

*(Continued)*

| No. | Statement | True | False | For Scoring |
|---|---|---|---|---|
| 16 | An advantage of a multiple digit numbering system is that it allows the addition of new accounts when needed without disturbing the other account numbers ........ | | | 16 |
| 17 | The order of the accounts in the ledger should agree with the order of the account titles as they appear on all financial statements ........ | | | 17 |
| 18 | The posting reference column provides a cross-reference between the journal and ledger ........ | | | 18 |
| 19 | In many businesses today, posting is done by machines ........ | | | 19 |
| 20 | When the changes in owner's equity for the period are limited to net income and drawing, the information for the capital statement may be shown on the income statement ........ | | | 20 |

**3B-1.** The solution of Problem 3A-1 for Hawkins Service Company will be needed to solve this problem.

**Required:**

(a) Post to the ledger accounts below and on the following pages, the transactions for June which were recorded in the journal in Problem 3A-1. Be sure to use posting references in the journal and the ledger.

(b) Foot and determine the balances of the ledger accounts and prepare a trial balance as of June 30, using the ruled form on page 359.

## GENERAL LEDGER

ACCOUNT *Cash* ACCOUNT NO. *11*

| DATE | | ITEM | POST. REF. | DEBIT | DATE | | ITEM | POST. REF. | CREDIT |
|---|---|---|---|---|---|---|---|---|---|
| | | | | | | | | | |
| | | | | | | | | | |
| | | | | | | | | | |
| | | | | | | | | | |
| | | | | | | | | | |
| | | | | | | | | | |
| | | | | | | | | | |

ACCOUNT *Store Supplies* ACCOUNT NO. *12*

| DATE | | ITEM | POST. REF. | DEBIT | DATE | | ITEM | POST. REF. | CREDIT |
|---|---|---|---|---|---|---|---|---|---|
| | | | | | | | | | |
| | | | | | | | | | |
| | | | | | | | | | |

ACCOUNT *Store Equipment* ACCOUNT NO. *13*

| DATE | | ITEM | POST. REF. | DEBIT | DATE | | ITEM | POST. REF. | CREDIT |
|---|---|---|---|---|---|---|---|---|---|
| | | | | | | | | | |
| | | | | | | | | | |
| | | | | | | | | | |

ACCOUNT *Accounts Payable — Carla Supplies* ACCOUNT NO. *21*

| DATE | | ITEM | POST. REF. | DEBIT | DATE | | ITEM | POST. REF. | CREDIT |
|---|---|---|---|---|---|---|---|---|---|
| | | | | | | | | | |
| | | | | | | | | | |
| | | | | | | | | | |

*(Continued)*

ACCOUNT *Accounts Payable — Massey Company* ACCOUNT NO. *22*

| DATE | | ITEM | POST. REF. | DEBIT | DATE | | ITEM | POST. REF. | CREDIT |
|---|---|---|---|---|---|---|---|---|---|
| | | | | | | | | | |
| | | | | | | | | | |
| | | | | | | | | | |

ACCOUNT *Frank Hawkins, Capital* ACCOUNT NO. *31*

| DATE | | ITEM | POST. REF. | DEBIT | DATE | | ITEM | POST. REF. | CREDIT |
|---|---|---|---|---|---|---|---|---|---|
| | | | | | | | | | |
| | | | | | | | | | |
| | | | | | | | | | |

ACCOUNT *Frank Hawkins, Drawing* ACCOUNT NO. *32*

| DATE | | ITEM | POST. REF. | DEBIT | DATE | | ITEM | POST. REF. | CREDIT |
|---|---|---|---|---|---|---|---|---|---|
| | | | | | | | | | |
| | | | | | | | | | |
| | | | | | | | | | |

ACCOUNT *Service Revenue* ACCOUNT NO. *41*

| DATE | | ITEM | POST. REF. | DEBIT | DATE | | ITEM | POST. REF. | CREDIT |
|---|---|---|---|---|---|---|---|---|---|
| | | | | | | | | | |
| | | | | | | | | | |
| | | | | | | | | | |

ACCOUNT *Advertising Expense* ACCOUNT NO. *51*

| DATE | | ITEM | POST. REF. | DEBIT | DATE | | ITEM | POST. REF. | CREDIT |
|---|---|---|---|---|---|---|---|---|---|
| | | | | | | | | | |
| | | | | | | | | | |
| | | | | | | | | | |

ACCOUNT *Rent Expense* ACCOUNT NO. 52

| DATE | ITEM | POST. REF. | DEBIT | DATE | ITEM | POST. REF. | CREDIT |
|---|---|---|---|---|---|---|---|
| | | | | | | | |
| | | | | | | | |
| | | | | | | | |

ACCOUNT *Salary Expense* ACCOUNT NO. 53

| DATE | ITEM | POST. REF. | DEBIT | DATE | ITEM | POST. REF. | CREDIT |
|---|---|---|---|---|---|---|---|
| | | | | | | | |
| | | | | | | | |
| | | | | | | | |

**3B-2.** The ledger account postings of Mundy Typing Service after the first month of operations are given below and on page 361.

**Required:** Journalize the entries that were made, including an explanation of each transaction, using the journal form provided on page 362. Insert the appropriate posting references that would have been made in the journal and the ledger.

## GENERAL LEDGER

ACCOUNT *Cash* ACCOUNT NO. *11*

| DATE | | ITEM | POST. REF. | DEBIT | DATE | | ITEM | POST. REF. | CREDIT |
|---|---|---|---|---|---|---|---|---|---|
| 19-- Mar. | 1 | | | 1 000 00 | 19-- Mar. | 6 | | | 100 00 |
| | 5 | | | 250 00 | | 15 | | | 140 00 |
| | 17 | | | 275 00 | | 21 | | | 300 00 |
| | 29 | | | 300 00 | | 23 | | | 25 00 |
| | | | | | | 26 | | | 20 00 |
| | | | | | | 30 | | | 150 00 |

ACCOUNT *Typing Supplies* ACCOUNT NO. *12*

| DATE | | ITEM | POST. REF. | DEBIT | DATE | | ITEM | POST. REF. | CREDIT |
|---|---|---|---|---|---|---|---|---|---|
| 19-- Mar. | 6 | | | 100 00 | | | | | |

ACCOUNT *Office Equipment* ACCOUNT NO. *13*

| DATE | | ITEM | POST. REF. | DEBIT | DATE | | ITEM | POST. REF. | CREDIT |
|---|---|---|---|---|---|---|---|---|---|
| 19-- Mar. | 2 | | | 2 100 00 | | | | | |

ACCOUNT *Accounts Payable — Roden Company* ACCOUNT NO. *21*

| DATE | | ITEM | POST. REF. | DEBIT | DATE | | ITEM | POST. REF. | CREDIT |
|---|---|---|---|---|---|---|---|---|---|
| 19-- Mar. | 21 | | | 300 00 | 19-- Mar. | 2 | | | 2 100 00 |

ACCOUNT *Debra Mundy, Capital* ACCOUNT NO. 31

| DATE | | ITEM | POST. REF. | DEBIT | DATE | | ITEM | POST. REF. | CREDIT |
|---|---|---|---|---|---|---|---|---|---|
| | | | | | 19-- Mar. | 1 | | | 1 0 0 0 00 |

ACCOUNT *Debra Mundy, Drawing* ACCOUNT NO. 32

| DATE | | ITEM | POST. REF. | DEBIT | DATE | | ITEM | POST. REF. | CREDIT |
|---|---|---|---|---|---|---|---|---|---|
| 19-- Mar. | 30 | | | 1 5 0 00 | | | | | |

ACCOUNT *Typing Revenue* ACCOUNT NO. 41

| DATE | | ITEM | POST. REF. | DEBIT | DATE | | ITEM | POST. REF. | CREDIT |
|---|---|---|---|---|---|---|---|---|---|
| | | | | | 19-- Mar. | 5 | | | 2 5 0 00 |
| | | | | | | 17 | | | 2 7 5 00 |
| | | | | | | 29 | | | 3 0 0 00 |

ACCOUNT *Rent Expense* ACCOUNT NO. 51

| DATE | | ITEM | POST. REF. | DEBIT | DATE | | ITEM | POST. REF. | CREDIT |
|---|---|---|---|---|---|---|---|---|---|
| 19-- Mar. | 15 | | | 1 4 0 00 | | | | | |

ACCOUNT *Telephone Expense* ACCOUNT NO. 52

| DATE | | ITEM | POST. REF. | DEBIT | DATE | | ITEM | POST. REF. | CREDIT |
|---|---|---|---|---|---|---|---|---|---|
| 19-- Mar. | 23 | | | 2 5 00 | | | | | |

ACCOUNT *Miscellaneous Expense* ACCOUNT NO. 53

| DATE | | ITEM | POST. REF. | DEBIT | DATE | | ITEM | POST. REF. | CREDIT |
|---|---|---|---|---|---|---|---|---|---|
| 19-- Mar. | 26 | | | 2 0 00 | | | | | |

| DATE | | DESCRIPTION | POST. REF. | DEBIT | CREDIT |
|---|---|---|---|---|---|

**3B-3.** The May 31 trial balance and the June transactions of the Fang Travel Agency used in Problem 3A-3 are needed to solve this problem.

**Required:**

(a) In the following ledger, record the account balances given in the trial balance in Problem 3A-3. The June 1 balances which should be entered in the accounts are the same as those shown in the trial balance on page 353. (The June 1 balances *do not reflect* any June transactions; they represent balances *at the close of business* May 31.)

(b) Post the transactions for June that are recorded in the journal in Problem 3A-3 to the ledger accounts. Be sure to use posting references in the journal and the ledger.

(c) Foot and determine the balances of the ledger accounts and prepare a trial balance of the ledger as of June 30, using the ruled form provided at the top of page 366.

(d) Prepare an income statement for the six-month period ending June 30, using the ruled form on page 366.

(e) Prepare a capital statement for the six-month period ending June 30, using the ruled form on page 367.

(f) Prepare a balance sheet as of June 30, using the ruled form at the bottom of page 367.

## GENERAL LEDGER

ACCOUNT *Cash* ACCOUNT NO. *11*

| DATE | ITEM | POST. REF. | DEBIT | DATE | ITEM | POST. REF. | CREDIT |
|---|---|---|---|---|---|---|---|

ACCOUNT *Office Supplies* ACCOUNT NO. *12*

| DATE | ITEM | POST. REF. | DEBIT | DATE | ITEM | POST. REF. | CREDIT |
|---|---|---|---|---|---|---|---|

ACCOUNT *Furniture and Fixtures* ACCOUNT NO. *13*

| DATE | ITEM | POST. REF. | DEBIT | DATE | ITEM | POST. REF. | CREDIT |
|---|---|---|---|---|---|---|---|

*(Continued)*

ACCOUNT *Office Equipment* ACCOUNT NO. *14*

| DATE | | ITEM | POST. REF. | DEBIT | DATE | | ITEM | POST. REF. | CREDIT |
|---|---|---|---|---|---|---|---|---|---|
| | | | | | | | | | |
| | | | | | | | | | |
| | | | | | | | | | |
| | | | | | | | | | |

ACCOUNT *Accounts Payable — Adams Co.* ACCOUNT NO. *21*

| DATE | | ITEM | POST. REF. | DEBIT | DATE | | ITEM | POST. REF. | CREDIT |
|---|---|---|---|---|---|---|---|---|---|
| | | | | | | | | | |
| | | | | | | | | | |
| | | | | | | | | | |
| | | | | | | | | | |

ACCOUNT *Accounts Payable — Thomas Bros.* ACCOUNT NO. *22*

| DATE | | ITEM | POST. REF. | DEBIT | DATE | | ITEM | POST. REF. | CREDIT |
|---|---|---|---|---|---|---|---|---|---|
| | | | | | | | | | |
| | | | | | | | | | |
| | | | | | | | | | |
| | | | | | | | | | |

ACCOUNT *Katherine Fang, Capital* ACCOUNT NO. *31*

| DATE | | ITEM | POST. REF. | DEBIT | DATE | | ITEM | POST. REF. | CREDIT |
|---|---|---|---|---|---|---|---|---|---|
| | | | | | | | | | |
| | | | | | | | | | |
| | | | | | | | | | |
| | | | | | | | | | |

ACCOUNT *Katherine Fang, Drawing* ACCOUNT NO. *32*

| DATE | | ITEM | POST. REF. | DEBIT | DATE | | ITEM | POST. REF. | CREDIT |
|---|---|---|---|---|---|---|---|---|---|
| | | | | | | | | | |
| | | | | | | | | | |
| | | | | | | | | | |
| | | | | | | | | | |

ACCOUNT *Commissions Revenue* ACCOUNT NO. *41*

| DATE | ITEM | POST. REF. | DEBIT | DATE | ITEM | POST. REF. | CREDIT |
|---|---|---|---|---|---|---|---|

ACCOUNT *Advertising Expense* ACCOUNT NO. *51*

| DATE | ITEM | POST. REF. | DEBIT | DATE | ITEM | POST. REF. | CREDIT |
|---|---|---|---|---|---|---|---|

ACCOUNT *Rent Expense* ACCOUNT NO. *52*

| DATE | ITEM | POST. REF. | DEBIT | DATE | ITEM | POST. REF. | CREDIT |
|---|---|---|---|---|---|---|---|

ACCOUNT *Salary Expense* ACCOUNT NO. *53*

| DATE | ITEM | POST. REF. | DEBIT | DATE | ITEM | POST. REF. | CREDIT |
|---|---|---|---|---|---|---|---|

ACCOUNT *Utilities Expense* ACCOUNT NO. *54*

| DATE | ITEM | POST. REF. | DEBIT | DATE | ITEM | POST. REF. | CREDIT |
|---|---|---|---|---|---|---|---|

**3B-4.** The ledger accounts for Leander Roofing Company are given on pages 371–373 as of the beginning of the current year. The January 1 balances have been entered in the accounts where necessary. The following transactions were made during the month of January.

Jan. 4. Paid Wink Supplies on amount owed, $150.
6. Paid truck expenses, $45.
7. Received cash for services performed, $300.
9. Purchased supplies on account from Wink Supplies, $90.
11. Purchased equipment for cash $200.
14. Received cash for services performed, $260.
18. Paid rent for the month, $140.
20. Purchased supplies for cash, $50.
26. Received cash for services rendered, $390.
28. Paid cash for miscellaneous expenses, $45.
29. Paid utilities for the month, $125.
30. Paid salaries for the month, $350.
30. Paid truck expenses, $40.
31. Received revenue for services rendered, $175.
31. Leander withdrew cash for personal use, $250.

**Required:**

(a) Record the transactions for the month of January in the general journal on pages 369 and 370 using the account titles appearing in the ledger on pages 371–373.

(b) Post the transactions to the ledger accounts. Foot the accounts where necessary and enter the balances in small figures.

(c) Prepare a trial balance of the ledger, using the ruled form below.

(d) Prepare an income statement for the month of January, using the ruled form on page 373.

(e) Prepare a balance sheet as of January 31, including the changes in owner's equity for the period in the owner's equity section, using the ruled form on page 374.

JOURNAL PAGE *1*

| DATE | | DESCRIPTION | POST. REF. | DEBIT | CREDIT |
|---|---|---|---|---|---|
| | | | | | |

## JOURNAL

PAGE 2

| DATE | | DESCRIPTION | POST. REF. | DEBIT | CREDIT |
|---|---|---|---|---|---|
| | | | | | |

## GENERAL LEDGER

ACCOUNT *Cash* ACCOUNT NO. *11*

| DATE | | ITEM | POST. REF. | DEBIT | DATE | | ITEM | POST. REF. | CREDIT |
|---|---|---|---|---|---|---|---|---|---|
| 19-- Jan. | 1 | Balance | √ | 512 00 | | | | | |

ACCOUNT *Roofing Supplies* ACCOUNT NO. *12*

| DATE | | ITEM | POST. REF. | DEBIT | DATE | | ITEM | POST. REF. | CREDIT |
|---|---|---|---|---|---|---|---|---|---|
| 19-- Jan. | 1 | Balance | √ | 194 00 | | | | | |

ACCOUNT *Roofing Equipment* ACCOUNT NO. *13*

| DATE | | ITEM | POST. REF. | DEBIT | DATE | | ITEM | POST. REF. | CREDIT |
|---|---|---|---|---|---|---|---|---|---|
| 19-- Jan. | 1 | Balance | √ | 1540 00 | | | | | |

ACCOUNT *Truck* ACCOUNT NO. *14*

| DATE | | ITEM | POST. REF. | DEBIT | DATE | | ITEM | POST. REF. | CREDIT |
|---|---|---|---|---|---|---|---|---|---|
| 19-- Jan. | 1 | Balance | √ | 3200 00 | | | | | |

*(Continued)*

ACCOUNT *Accounts Payable — Wink Supplies* ACCOUNT NO. 21

| DATE | | ITEM | POST. REF. | DEBIT | DATE | | ITEM | POST. REF. | CREDIT |
|---|---|---|---|---|---|---|---|---|---|
| | | | | | 19-- Jan. | 1 | Balance | √ | 320 00 |
| | | | | | | | | | |
| | | | | | | | | | |

ACCOUNT *Dale Leander, Capital* ACCOUNT NO. 31

| DATE | | ITEM | POST. REF. | DEBIT | DATE | | ITEM | POST. REF. | CREDIT |
|---|---|---|---|---|---|---|---|---|---|
| | | | | | 19-- Jan. | 1 | Balance | √ | 5126 00 |
| | | | | | | | | | |

ACCOUNT *Dale Leander, Drawing* ACCOUNT NO. 32

| DATE | | ITEM | POST. REF. | DEBIT | DATE | | ITEM | POST. REF. | CREDIT |
|---|---|---|---|---|---|---|---|---|---|
| | | | | | | | | | |
| | | | | | | | | | |
| | | | | | | | | | |

ACCOUNT *Roofing Revenue* ACCOUNT NO. 41

| DATE | | ITEM | POST. REF. | DEBIT | DATE | | ITEM | POST. REF. | CREDIT |
|---|---|---|---|---|---|---|---|---|---|
| | | | | | | | | | |
| | | | | | | | | | |
| | | | | | | | | | |
| | | | | | | | | | |
| | | | | | | | | | |

ACCOUNT *Rent Expense* ACCOUNT NO. 51

| DATE | | ITEM | POST. REF. | DEBIT | DATE | | ITEM | POST. REF. | CREDIT |
|---|---|---|---|---|---|---|---|---|---|
| | | | | | | | | | |
| | | | | | | | | | |

ACCOUNT *Salary Expense* ACCOUNT NO. 52

| DATE | | ITEM | POST. REF. | DEBIT | DATE | | ITEM | POST. REF. | CREDIT |
|---|---|---|---|---|---|---|---|---|---|
| | | | | | | | | | |
| | | | | | | | | | |

ACCOUNT *Truck Expense* ACCOUNT NO. 53

| DATE | | ITEM | POST. REF. | DEBIT | DATE | | ITEM | POST. REF. | CREDIT |
|---|---|---|---|---|---|---|---|---|---|
| | | | | | | | | | |
| | | | | | | | | | |
| | | | | | | | | | |

ACCOUNT *Utilities Expense* ACCOUNT NO. 54

| DATE | | ITEM | POST. REF. | DEBIT | DATE | | ITEM | POST. REF. | CREDIT |
|---|---|---|---|---|---|---|---|---|---|
| | | | | | | | | | |
| | | | | | | | | | |

ACCOUNT *Miscellaneous Expense* ACCOUNT NO. 55

| DATE | | ITEM | POST. REF. | DEBIT | DATE | | ITEM | POST. REF. | CREDIT |
|---|---|---|---|---|---|---|---|---|---|
| | | | | | | | | | |
| | | | | | | | | | |

**Perfect Score** **20** **Name** ____________________

**Student's Score** ____ **Date** ____________________ **Class** ________

## LOCATING AND CORRECTING ERRORS

**Instructions.** Complete each statement and answer each question below by writing your answer in the space at the right.

| No. | Item | Answer | For Scoring |
|---|---|---|---|
| 1 | If the total debits and total credits of the trial balance are not equal, the trial balance is said to be........ | | 1 |
| 2 | What is the first step to be taken when the trial balance does not balance? ........ | | 2 |
| 3 | If a debit for $430 is recorded as $340, what type of error is this?.......... | | 3 |
| 4 | If the $430 debit is recorded as $43.00, what type of error is this?......... | | 4 |
| 5 | A journal entry had been recorded on May 8 for the purchase of equipment for cash, $400. When the entry was posted to the ledger, both the equipment account and cash account were credited for $400. Will this error cause the trial balance to be out of balance?...... | | 5 |
| 6 | By what amount will the trial balance in No. 5 be out of balance? ........ | $ | 6 |
| 7 | At the end of the accounting period, Marge Brooks discovered that a payment for supplies was erroneously debited to the equipment account. Will this error cause the trial balance to be out of balance?..... | | 7 |
| 8 | Bill Mack was in a hurry while posting the transactions for the month and failed to post the entry for the payment of monthly rent of $200. Will this cause the trial balance to be out of balance? ........ | | 8 |
| 9 | What effect will the error in No. 8 above have on income reported for the month?........ | | 9 |
| 10 | What would have been the effect on income if the transaction involving rent in No. 8 above had been posted twice?........ | | 10 |
| 11 | In a transaction involving the purchase of furniture on account for $360, the credit to Accounts Payable was erroneously posted as a debit in the ledger. How much will the trial balance be out of balance as a result of this error? | $ | 11 |

**Instructions.** The following errors in recording transactions were made during the month and posted to the ledger. For each transaction, indicate the account to be debited, the account to be credited, and the dollar amount needed to correct the error.

| No. | Transaction | Answer | For Scoring |
|---|---|---|---|
| 12–14 | The $175 rent payment for the month was debited to Utilities Expense and credited to Cash........ | | |
| | Debit | | 12 |
| | Credit | | 13 |
| | Amount | $ | 14 |

*(Continued)*

| No. | Transaction | Answer | For Scoring |
|---|---|---|---|
| 15–17 | Supplies purchased on account from Quan Supplies for $150 were entered as a debit to Supplies and a credit to Cash.............................. | | |
| | Debit | | 15 |
| | Credit | | 16 |
| | Amount | $ | 17 |
| 18–20 | A personal withdrawal of cash by Bill Cain, the owner, for $240 was recorded as a debit to Bill Cain, Drawing and a credit to Cash for $420........................................................................................... | | |
| | Debit | | 18 |
| | Credit | | 19 |
| | Amount | $ | 20 |

**3C-1.** The trial balance of the Delp Company presented below does not balance. In checking the ledger and other records, you discovered the following items.

(a) The balance of the store equipment account is $3,200.

(b) The debits in the store supplies account totaled $280 and the credits totaled $105.

(c) Payment of $140 owed to Garr Co. was recorded in the cash account but not in the accounts payable account.

(d) Receipt of $100 from Wish Co. as payment on its account had not been recorded at all.

DELP COMPANY
Trial Balance
April 30, 19--

| | | |
|---|---|---|
| Cash | 1,465 | |
| Accounts Receivable — Wish Company | 240 | |
| Store Supplies | 165 | |
| Store Equipment | 2,300 | |
| Accounts Payable — Garr Co. | | 380 |
| Jane Delp, Capital | | 4,840 |
| | 4,170 | 5,220 |

**Required:** From the information given above prepare a corrected trial balance for Delp Company using the form below.

**3C-2.** The following errors occurred in posting from a two-column journal:

(1) A credit of $50 to Accounts Receivable was not posted.
(2) A debit of $25 to Accounts Payable was posted as a credit.
(3) A debit of $100 to Office Supplies was posted twice.
(4) An entry debiting Cash and crediting Service Revenue was not posted.
(5) A credit of $80 to Accounts Payable was posted as $800.
(6) A debit of $820 to Accounts Receivable was posted as $280.

Considering each of the above transactions separately, indicate:

(a) whether the trial balance would be out of balance (yes or no).
(b) the amount by which the trial balance totals would differ.
(c) the trial balance column that would have the larger total.

Answers should be presented as follows using (1) above as an example:

| ERROR | OUT OF BALANCE | DIFFERENCE | LARGER TOTAL |
|---|---|---|---|
| *(1)* | *yes* | *$50* | *debit* |
| *(2)* | | | |
| *(3)* | | | |
| *(4)* | | | |
| *(5)* | | | |
| *(6)* | | | |

Assignment 4-A

Perfect Score 25 Name ______________________

Student's Score ___ Date ______________ Class ________

## ADJUSTING ENTRIES

**Instructions.** Complete the following statements by writing your answer in the space provided.

| No. | Statement | Answer | For Scoring |
|---|---|---|---|
| 1 | The accounts are brought up to date at the end of the accounting period by means of | | 1 |
| 2 | Assets that will be used for a number of years in the operation of the business are called | | 2 |
| 3 | The expired portion of a plant asset's cost is called | | 3 |
| 4 | The account used to record the expired cost of a plant asset is called | | 4 |
| 5 | All plant assets will wear out or become useless with the passage of time except | | 5 |
| 6 | A (?) account is used to partially or fully offset another account | | 6 |
| 7 | When depreciation is recorded, the reduction of the asset is credited to the (?) account | | 7 |
| 8 | The difference between the cost of an asset and the accumulated depreciation to date is called the | | 8 |
| 9 | An example of an expense that accumulates on an hourly or daily basis but is usually paid weekly or monthly is | | 9 |
| 10 | When insurance is paid for in advance, an asset account entitled (?) is debited | | 10 |

**Instructions.** In each of the following situations below you are given the data necessary to prepare the adjusting entry as of the end of the period. For each adjustment write the name of the account to be debited, the name of the account to be credited, and the amount.

| No. | Item | Answer | For Scoring |
|---|---|---|---|
| 11–13 | During April, paid $140 for store supplies. Supplies with a cost of $65 were on hand at the end of April | | |
| | Debit | | 11 |
| | Credit | | 12 |
| | Amount | | 13 |
| 14–16 | On October 1, paid a one-year insurance premium totaling $180 and debited the asset account, Prepaid Insurance. The books are adjusted at the end of the year, December 31 | | |
| | Debit | | 14 |
| | Credit | | 15 |
| | Amount | | 16 |

*(Continued)*

| No. | Item | Answer | For Scoring |
|---|---|---|---|
| 17–19 | The depreciation on an auto for the year ended December 31 was $300........ | | |
| | Debit | | 17 |
| | Credit | | 18 |
| | Amount | | 19 |
| 20–22 | Salaries owed for the last three days of the month amounted to $195.... | | |
| | Debit | | 20 |
| | Credit | | 21 |
| | Amount | | 22 |
| 23–25 | A four-month, $1,000 lease on an office was signed August 1; the transaction was recorded by debiting the asset account, Prepaid Rent. The accounts are adjusted on August 31........ | | |
| | Debit | | 23 |
| | Credit | | 24 |
| | Amount | | 25 |

**4A-1.** On the form below, prepare the following adjusting entries for the Roberta Company as of May 31.

(a) From the information found in the prepaid insurance account, prepare the adjusting entry required at the end of May of the current year.

ACCOUNT *Prepaid Insurance* ACCOUNT NO. *14*

| DATE | | ITEM | POST. REF. | DEBIT | DATE | | ITEM | POST. REF. | CREDIT |
|---|---|---|---|---|---|---|---|---|---|
| *19--* *May* | *1* | *(2-year policy)* | *J7* | *1 2 0 0 00* | | | | | |

(b) The weekly pay period ends on Friday and totals $2,500 for a five-day week. The last day of the month of May falls on a Tuesday. Prepare the adjusting entry for the salaries owed at the end of the month.

(c) On May 1, office supplies were purchased for $260 cash and no other supplies were purchased during May. A count of the supplies on hand at the end of the month totaled $150. Prepare the journal entry to make the necessary adjustment at the end of the month.

(d) Depreciation on a panel truck is $1,200 per year. Record the depreciation for the month of May.

JOURNAL PAGE *2*

| DATE | | DESCRIPTION | POST. REF. | DEBIT | CREDIT |
|---|---|---|---|---|---|

**4A-2.** The ledger account balances for Weldon Realty Company before adjustment at the end of the month of October of the current year are given below and on pages 383 and 384. The data needed to determine the month-end adjustments are presented below.

Adjustment data:

(a) Office supplies on hand at the end of the month, $190.
(b) The prepaid rent balance of $750 represents the remainder of the $1,500 prepayment made on July 1 for the six-month period July 1 to December 31.
(c) Salaries owed at the end of the month, $135.
(d) Depreciation on the office equipment for the month, $65.

**Required:**

(a) Prepare a trial balance of the ledger, using the ruled form at the bottom of page 385.
(b) From the adjustment data given above, record the adjusting entries in the general journal given on page 385.
(c) Post the adjusting entries to the ledger.
(d) Foot and determine the balances in the ledger accounts.

## GENERAL LEDGER

ACCOUNT *Cash* ACCOUNT NO. *11*

| DATE | | ITEM | POST. REF. | DEBIT | DATE | | ITEM | POST. REF. | CREDIT |
|---|---|---|---|---|---|---|---|---|---|
| 19-- Oct. | 31 | | ✓ | 1 1 5 0 00 | | | | | |
| | | | | | | | | | |
| | | | | | | | | | |

ACCOUNT *Office Supplies* ACCOUNT NO. *12*

| DATE | | ITEM | POST. REF. | DEBIT | DATE | | ITEM | POST. REF. | CREDIT |
|---|---|---|---|---|---|---|---|---|---|
| 19-- Oct. | 31 | | ✓ | 3 2 0 00 | | | | | |
| | | | | | | | | | |
| | | | | | | | | | |

ACCOUNT *Prepaid Rent* ACCOUNT NO. *13*

| DATE | | ITEM | POST. REF. | DEBIT | DATE | | ITEM | POST. REF. | CREDIT |
|---|---|---|---|---|---|---|---|---|---|
| 19-- Oct. | 31 | | ✓ | 7 5 0 00 | | | | | |
| | | | | | | | | | |
| | | | | | | | | | |

ACCOUNT *Office Equipment* ACCOUNT NO. *14*

| DATE | | ITEM | POST. REF. | DEBIT | DATE | | ITEM | POST. REF. | CREDIT |
|---|---|---|---|---|---|---|---|---|---|
| 19-- Oct. | 31 | | ✓ | 5 4 0 0 00 | | | | | |
| | | | | | | | | | |

ACCOUNT *Accumulated Depreciation — Office Equipment* ACCOUNT NO. *14.1*

| DATE | | ITEM | POST. REF. | DEBIT | DATE | | ITEM | POST. REF. | CREDIT |
|---|---|---|---|---|---|---|---|---|---|
| | | | | | 19-- Oct. | 31 | | √ | 1 800 00 |
| | | | | | | | | | |

ACCOUNT *Accounts Payable — King Company* ACCOUNT NO. *21*

| DATE | | ITEM | POST. REF. | DEBIT | DATE | | ITEM | POST. REF. | CREDIT |
|---|---|---|---|---|---|---|---|---|---|
| | | | | | 19-- Oct. | 31 | | √ | 580 00 |
| | | | | | | | | | |

ACCOUNT *Salaries Payable* ACCOUNT NO. *22*

| DATE | | ITEM | POST. REF. | DEBIT | DATE | | ITEM | POST. REF. | CREDIT |
|---|---|---|---|---|---|---|---|---|---|
| | | | | | | | | | |
| | | | | | | | | | |

ACCOUNT *Don Weldon, Capital* ACCOUNT NO. *31*

| DATE | | ITEM | POST. REF. | DEBIT | DATE | | ITEM | POST. REF. | CREDIT |
|---|---|---|---|---|---|---|---|---|---|
| | | | | | 19-- Oct. | 31 | | √ | 3 305 00 |
| | | | | | | | | | |

ACCOUNT *Don Weldon, Drawing* ACCOUNT NO. *32*

| DATE | | ITEM | POST. REF. | DEBIT | DATE | | ITEM | POST. REF. | CREDIT |
|---|---|---|---|---|---|---|---|---|---|
| 19-- Oct. | 31 | | √ | 350 00 | | | | | |
| | | | | | | | | | |

ACCOUNT *Commissions Revenue* ACCOUNT NO. *41*

| DATE | | ITEM | POST. REF. | DEBIT | DATE | | ITEM | POST. REF. | CREDIT |
|---|---|---|---|---|---|---|---|---|---|
| | | | | | 19-- Oct. | 31 | | √ | 4 370 00 |
| | | | | | | | | | |

*(Continued)*

ACCOUNT *Advertising Expense* ACCOUNT NO. *51*

| DATE | | ITEM | POST. REF. | DEBIT | DATE | | ITEM | POST. REF. | CREDIT |
|---|---|---|---|---|---|---|---|---|---|
| 19--<br>Oct. | 31 | | √ | 275 00 | | | | | |
| | | | | | | | | | |

ACCOUNT *Depreciation Expense — Office Equipment* ACCOUNT NO. *52*

| DATE | | ITEM | POST. REF. | DEBIT | DATE | | ITEM | POST. REF. | CREDIT |
|---|---|---|---|---|---|---|---|---|---|
| | | | | | | | | | |
| | | | | | | | | | |

ACCOUNT *Office Supplies Expense* ACCOUNT NO. *53*

| DATE | | ITEM | POST. REF. | DEBIT | DATE | | ITEM | POST. REF. | CREDIT |
|---|---|---|---|---|---|---|---|---|---|
| | | | | | | | | | |
| | | | | | | | | | |

ACCOUNT *Rent Expense* ACCOUNT NO. *54*

| DATE | | ITEM | POST. REF. | DEBIT | DATE | | ITEM | POST. REF. | CREDIT |
|---|---|---|---|---|---|---|---|---|---|
| | | | | | | | | | |
| | | | | | | | | | |

ACCOUNT *Salary Expense* ACCOUNT NO. *55*

| DATE | | ITEM | POST. REF. | DEBIT | DATE | | ITEM | POST. REF. | CREDIT |
|---|---|---|---|---|---|---|---|---|---|
| 19--<br>Oct. | 31 | | √ | 1810 00 | | | | | |
| | | | | | | | | | |
| | | | | | | | | | |

JOURNAL PAGE 22

| DATE | | DESCRIPTION | POST. REF. | DEBIT | CREDIT |
|---|---|---|---|---|---|
| | | | | | |
| | | | | | |
| | | | | | |
| | | | | | |
| | | | | | |
| | | | | | |
| | | | | | |
| | | | | | |
| | | | | | |
| | | | | | |
| | | | | | |
| | | | | | |
| | | | | | |

Retain the solution to this problem for use in Problem 4A-3.

**4A-3.** Using the information for Weldon Realty Company in 4A-2: (a) Prepare an income statement for the month of October in form A below; (b) Prepare a capital statement for the month of October in form B below.

A.

B.

Assignment 4-B

**Perfect Score** 20 **Name** ______________________

**Student's Score** ____ **Date** ________________ **Class** ________

## THE WORK SHEET AND FINANCIAL STATEMENTS

**Instructions.** Complete the statements and answer the questions by writing your answer in the space at the right.

| No. | Statement | Answer | For Scoring |
|---|---|---|---|
| 1 | The form prepared at the end of the accounting period which contains all the information necessary for completion of the end-of-period duties and the financial statements is called a.................................... | | 1 |
| 2 | When adjusting entries are recorded on a work sheet is it necessary to also record the adjustments in the journal?.......................................... | | 2 |
| 3 | The first two columns of a work sheet are used for the .......................... | | 3 |
| 4 | The second set of amount columns of a work sheet are for the.............. | | 4 |
| 5 | A debit to Salary Expense in the Adjustments column of the work sheet will require a credit to ............................................................... | | 5 |
| 6 | The amounts in the Income Statement and Balance Sheet columns represent the sum of the trial balance amounts and the __________ amounts.......................................................................................... | | 6 |
| 7 | Are all accounts on the work sheet trial balance adjusted?..................... | | 7 |
| 8 | The third set of amount columns in an eight-column work sheet are for the......................................................................................... | | 8 |
| 9 | The fourth set of amount columns in an eight-column work sheet are for the......................................................................................... | | 9 |
| 10 | The adjusted balances of the expense accounts are extended to the __________ columns in the work sheet............................................ | | 10 |
| 11 | The balance of the accounts payable account is extended to the __________ columns in the work sheet............................................ | | 11 |
| 12 | The balance of the capital account is extended to the __________ columns in the work sheet................................................................... | | 12 |
| 13 | If the debits of the Income Statement columns exceed the credits, the difference is called a............................................................................ | | 13 |
| 14 | If the credits of the Income Statement columns exceed the debits, the difference is called a............................................................................ | | 14 |
| 15 | A net income in the Income Statement columns is extended to the (debit or credit) side of the Balance Sheet columns............................ | | 15 |
| 16 | A net income in the Income Statement columns represents an increase in the __________ account on the balance sheet ................... | | 16 |
| 17 | An income statement for the period can easily be prepared from the __________ columns of the work sheet............................................ | | 17 |
| 18 | A balance sheet for the period can easily be prepared from the __________ columns of the work sheet............................................ | | 18 |

*(Continued)*

| No. | Statement | Answer | For Scoring |
|---|---|---|---|
| 19 | If the Income Statement debit column of the work sheet totals $5,050 and the credit column totals $6,220, what is the net income or net loss for the period? | | 19 |
| 20 | Kena Co.'s work sheet showed the following amounts in the Balance Sheet columns: Tod Kena, Capital, $3,980; Tod Kena, Drawing, $500; Net Income, $740. The amount of Kena's capital to be shown on the balance sheet, assuming he made no additional investments during the period would be | | 20 |

**4B-1.** Below is the trial balance for Susan Bishop, a free-lance writer, as of August 31 of the current year.

BISHOP COMPANY
Trial Balance
August 31, 19--

| | | |
|---|---|---|
| Cash | 570 | |
| Writing Supplies | 405 | |
| Prepaid Insurance | 290 | |
| Office Equipment | 6,100 | |
| Accumulated Depreciation — Office Equipment | | 1,200 |
| Accounts Payable — Keg Suppliers | | 925 |
| Susan Bishop, Capital | | 2,165 |
| Revenue from Publications | | 3,240 |
| Telephone Expense | 30 | |
| Utilities Expense | 135 | |
| | 7,530 | 7,530 |

Adjustment data:

(a) Writing supplies on hand, $280.
(b) Insurance expired during the month, $40.
(c) Depreciation on the office equipment for the month, $120.
(d) Rent owed at August 31, $175.

**Required:**

(a) The first four columns of an eight-column work sheet are provided on page 389. Record the trial balance for the Bishop Company in the Trial Balance columns of the work sheet for the month of August.

(b) Record the necessary adjustments in the Adjustments columns, cross-referencing each debit with the appropriate credit, and total the Adjustments columns.

(c) Using the information in the Adjustment columns, record the adjusting entries in a general journal, using the journal form provided at the bottom of page 389.

| | ACCOUNT TITLE | TRIAL BALANCE DEBIT (1) | TRIAL BALANCE CREDIT (2) | ADJUSTMENTS DEBIT (3) | ADJUSTMENTS CREDIT (4) | |
|---|---|---|---|---|---|---|
| 1 | | | | | | 1 |
| 2 | | | | | | 2 |
| 3 | | | | | | 3 |
| 4 | | | | | | 4 |
| 5 | | | | | | 5 |
| 6 | | | | | | 6 |
| 7 | | | | | | 7 |
| 8 | | | | | | 8 |
| 9 | | | | | | 9 |
| 10 | | | | | | 10 |
| 11 | | | | | | 11 |
| 12 | | | | | | 12 |
| 13 | | | | | | 13 |
| 14 | | | | | | 14 |
| 15 | | | | | | 15 |
| 16 | | | | | | 16 |
| 17 | | | | | | 17 |
| 18 | | | | | | 18 |
| 19 | | | | | | 19 |

## JOURNAL

PAGE *12*

| | DATE | | DESCRIPTION | POST. REF. | DEBIT | CREDIT | |
|---|---|---|---|---|---|---|---|
| 1 | | | | | | | 1 |
| 2 | | | | | | | 2 |
| 3 | | | | | | | 3 |
| 4 | | | | | | | 4 |
| 5 | | | | | | | 5 |
| 6 | | | | | | | 6 |
| 7 | | | | | | | 7 |
| 8 | | | | | | | 8 |
| 9 | | | | | | | 9 |
| 10 | | | | | | | 10 |
| 11 | | | | | | | 11 |

**4B-2.** The trial balance of Van's Barber Shop on December 31, the end of the current fiscal year, is recorded in the eight-column work sheet on the following page. Data for the adjustments as of the end of the year are as follows:

Adjustment data:

(a) Shop supplies on hand at December 31, $680.
(b) Depreciation on the shop equipment for the year, $800.
(c) Insurance expired during the year, $160.
(d) Salaries owed at December 31, $200.

**Required:** Complete the work sheet for Van's Barber Shop for the year ending December 31.

VAN'S BARBER SHOP

Work Sheet

For Year Ended December 31, 19--

| | ACCOUNT TITLE | 1 TRIAL BALANCE DEBIT | 2 TRIAL BALANCE CREDIT | 3 ADJUSTMENTS DEBIT | 4 ADJUSTMENTS CREDIT | 5 INCOME STATEMENT DEBIT | 6 INCOME STATEMENT CREDIT | 7 BALANCE SHEET DEBIT | 8 BALANCE SHEET CREDIT | |
|---|---|---|---|---|---|---|---|---|---|---|
| 1 | *Cash* | 780 00 | | | | | | | | 1 |
| 2 | *Shop Supplies* | 940 00 | | | | | | | | 2 |
| 3 | *Prepaid Insurance* | 480 00 | | | | | | | | 3 |
| 4 | *Shop Equipment* | 9200 00 | | | | | | | | 4 |
| 5 | *Accum. Depr. – Shop Equipment* | | 2400 00 | | | | | | | 5 |
| 6 | *Accounts Payable – Jud Co.* | | 900 00 | | | | | | | 6 |
| 7 | *Chris Van Dyke, Capital* | | 5240 00 | | | | | | | 7 |
| 8 | *Chris Van Dyke, Drawing* | 2700 00 | | | | | | | | 8 |
| 9 | *Revenue from Barber Shop* | | 10800 00 | | | | | | | 9 |
| 10 | *Rent Expense* | 1920 00 | | | | | | | | 10 |
| 11 | *Salary Expense* | 1400 00 | | | | | | | | 11 |
| 12 | *Utilities Expense* | 1360 00 | | | | | | | | 12 |
| 13 | *Miscellaneous Expense* | 560 00 | | | | | | | | 13 |
| 14 | | 19340 00 | 19340 00 | | | | | | | 14 |
| 15 | | | | | | | | | | 15 |
| 16 | | | | | | | | | | 16 |
| 17 | | | | | | | | | | 17 |
| 18 | | | | | | | | | | 18 |
| 19 | | | | | | | | | | 19 |
| 20 | | | | | | | | | | 20 |
| 21 | | | | | | | | | | 21 |
| 22 | | | | | | | | | | 22 |
| 23 | | | | | | | | | | 23 |
| 24 | | | | | | | | | | 24 |
| 25 | | | | | | | | | | 25 |
| 26 | | | | | | | | | | 26 |

**4B-3** The work sheet for the Laney Body Shop for the month of June of the current year is presented on page 393.

**Required:**

(a) Prepare an income statement for Laney for the month of June, using the ruled form below.

(b) Prepare a capital statement for Laney as of June 30, using the ruled form at the bottom of this page. Assume that no additional investments were made during the month.

(c) Prepare a report form balance sheet for Laney as of June 30, using the ruled form provided on page 394.

(d) Record the adjusting entries in the journal provided on page 394.

**LANEY BODY SHOP**

*Work Sheet*

*For Month Ended June 30, 19--*

| | Account Title | Trial Balance Debit (1) | Trial Balance Credit (2) | Adjustments Debit (3) | Adjustments Credit (4) | Income Statement Debit (5) | Income Statement Credit (6) | Balance Sheet Debit (7) | Balance Sheet Credit (8) | |
|---|---|---|---|---|---|---|---|---|---|---|
| 1 | Cash | 620 00 | | | | | | 620 00 | | 1 |
| 2 | Tools and Supplies | 1140 00 | | | (a) 550 00 | | | 590 00 | | 2 |
| 3 | Prepaid Insurance | 300 00 | | | (c) 100 00 | | | 200 00 | | 3 |
| 4 | Repair Equipment | 8800 00 | | | | | | 8800 00 | | 4 |
| 5 | Accum. Depr. – Repair Equip. | | 2400 00 | | (b) 200 00 | | | | 2600 00 | 5 |
| 6 | Accts. Pay. – Mercury Tool Co. | | 380 00 | | | | | | 380 00 | 6 |
| 7 | Mike Laney, Capital | | 6985 00 | | | | | | 6985 00 | 7 |
| 8 | Mike Laney, Drawing | 300 00 | | | | | | 300 00 | | 8 |
| 9 | Revenue from Repairs | | 2900 00 | | | | 2900 00 | | | 9 |
| 10 | Rent Expense | 260 00 | | | | 260 00 | | | | 10 |
| 11 | Salary Expense | 1150 00 | | (d) 150 00 | | 1300 00 | | | | 11 |
| 12 | Utilities Expense | 95 00 | | | | 95 00 | | | | 12 |
| 13 | | 12665 00 | 12665 00 | | | | | | | 13 |
| 14 | Tools and Supplies Expense | | | (a) 550 00 | | 550 00 | | | | 14 |
| 15 | Depr. Exp. – Repair Equip. | | | (b) 200 00 | | 200 00 | | | | 15 |
| 16 | Insurance Expense | | | (c) 100 00 | | 100 00 | | | | 16 |
| 17 | Salaries Payable | | | | (d) 150 00 | | | | 150 00 | 17 |
| 18 | | | | 1000 00 | 1000 00 | 2505 00 | 2900 00 | 10510 00 | 10115 00 | 18 |
| 19 | Net Income | | | | | 395 00 | | | 395 00 | 19 |
| 20 | | | | | | 2900 00 | 2900 00 | 10510 00 | 10510 00 | 20 |

JOURNAL PAGE

|  | DATE |  | DESCRIPTION | POST. REF. | DEBIT | CREDIT |  |
|---|---|---|---|---|---|---|---|
| 1 |  |  |  |  |  |  | 1 |
| 2 |  |  |  |  |  |  | 2 |
| 3 |  |  |  |  |  |  | 3 |
| 4 |  |  |  |  |  |  | 4 |
| 5 |  |  |  |  |  |  | 5 |
| 6 |  |  |  |  |  |  | 6 |
| 7 |  |  |  |  |  |  | 7 |
| 8 |  |  |  |  |  |  | 8 |
| 9 |  |  |  |  |  |  | 9 |
| 10 |  |  |  |  |  |  | 10 |

Retain the solution to this problem for use in Problem 4C-1.

Assignment 4-C

**Perfect Score** 20 **Name** ______________________

**Student's Score** ___ **Date** ______________ **Class** ________

## CLOSING ENTRIES, POST-CLOSING TRIAL BALANCE, AND SUMMARY OF ACCOUNTING CYCLE

**Instructions.** Complete each of the following statements by writing the missing word(s) in the space provided.

| No. | Statement | Answer | For Scoring |
|---|---|---|---|
| 1 | The revenue, expense, and drawing accounts which are closed at the end of the period are commonly called .............................................. | | 1 |
| 2 | The account used to facilitate the closing process is entitled................ | | 2 |
| 3 | The first step in the closing process is to close the __________ to Income Summary .................................................................................. | | 3 |
| 4 | The second step in the closing process is to close the __________ to Income Summary .................................................................................. | | 4 |
| 5 | Income Summary is closed to the __________ account........................ | | 5 |
| 6 | The revenue accounts are closed by crediting...................................... | | 6 |
| 7 | The revenue accounts are closed by debiting........................................ | | 7 |
| 8 | The drawing account is closed by crediting............................................ | | 8 |
| 9 | Expense accounts are closed by debiting.............................................. | | 9 |
| 10 | If after closing all revenue and expense accounts the income summary account has a debit balance, this balance represents a __________ for the period ................................................................ | | 10 |

**Instructions.** Indicate by placing a check mark in either the Yes or No columns at the right whether each of the following accounts would be closed at the end of the period.

| No. | Account | Yes | No | For Scoring |
|---|---|---|---|---|
| 11 | Utilities Expense .................................................................................. | | | 11 |
| 12 | Accumulated Depreciation — Truck...................................................... | | | 12 |
| 13 | Ray Moses, Drawing.............................................................................. | | | 13 |
| 14 | Salaries Payable .................................................................................. | | | 14 |
| 15 | Prepaid Rent ........................................................................................ | | | 15 |
| 16 | Ray Moses, Capital .............................................................................. | | | 16 |
| 17 | Revenue from Services.......................................................................... | | | 17 |
| 18 | Income Summary.................................................................................. | | | 18 |
| 19 | Accounts Payable.................................................................................. | | | 19 |
| 20 | Salary Expense...................................................................................... | | | 20 |

**4C-1.** This problem is based on the information given in Problem 4B-3. The information given in the Income Statement and Balance Sheet columns of the work sheet for Laney Body Shop will be needed to complete this problem.

**Required:** Record the general journal entries necessary to close the books at the end of June using the form below.

JOURNAL PAGE

| | DATE | | DESCRIPTION | POST. REF. | DEBIT | CREDIT | |
|---|---|---|---|---|---|---|---|
| 1 | | | | | | | 1 |
| 2 | | | | | | | 2 |
| 3 | | | | | | | 3 |
| 4 | | | | | | | 4 |
| 5 | | | | | | | 5 |
| 6 | | | | | | | 6 |
| 7 | | | | | | | 7 |
| 8 | | | | | | | 8 |
| 9 | | | | | | | 9 |
| 10 | | | | | | | 10 |
| 11 | | | | | | | 11 |
| 12 | | | | | | | 12 |
| 13 | | | | | | | 13 |
| 14 | | | | | | | 14 |
| 15 | | | | | | | 15 |
| 16 | | | | | | | 16 |
| 17 | | | | | | | 17 |
| 18 | | | | | | | 18 |
| 19 | | | | | | | 19 |
| 20 | | | | | | | 20 |
| 21 | | | | | | | 21 |
| 22 | | | | | | | 22 |
| 23 | | | | | | | 23 |
| 24 | | | | | | | 24 |
| 25 | | | | | | | 25 |
| 26 | | | | | | | 26 |
| 27 | | | | | | | 27 |
| 28 | | | | | | | 28 |
| 29 | | | | | | | 29 |
| 30 | | | | | | | 30 |

**4C-2.** The balances in the ledger accounts for Lewis Company at the end of the current year, after all adjustments have been made and posted, are presented below and on pages 398 and 399.

**Required:**

(a) Prepare the journal entries to close the books as of the end of the period, using the journal form on page 400.

(b) Post these entries to the ledger accounts.

(c) Prepare a post-closing trial balance using the ruled form on page 400.

## GENERAL LEDGER

ACCOUNT *Cash* ACCOUNT NO. *11*

| DATE | | ITEM | POST. REF. | DEBIT | CREDIT | BALANCE DEBIT | BALANCE CREDIT |
|---|---|---|---|---|---|---|---|
| *19--* *Dec.* | *31* | | √ | | | *1 9 0 0 00* | |
| | | | | | | | |

ACCOUNT *Office Supplies* ACCOUNT NO. *12*

| DATE | | ITEM | POST. REF. | DEBIT | CREDIT | BALANCE DEBIT | BALANCE CREDIT |
|---|---|---|---|---|---|---|---|
| *19--* *Dec.* | *31* | | √ | | | *1 0 4 0 00* | |
| | | | | | | | |

ACCOUNT *Prepaid Rent* ACCOUNT NO. *13*

| DATE | | ITEM | POST. REF. | DEBIT | CREDIT | BALANCE DEBIT | BALANCE CREDIT |
|---|---|---|---|---|---|---|---|
| *19--* *Dec.* | *31* | | √ | | | *5 1 0 00* | |
| | | | | | | | |

ACCOUNT *Office Equipment* ACCOUNT NO. *14*

| DATE | | ITEM | POST. REF. | DEBIT | CREDIT | BALANCE DEBIT | BALANCE CREDIT |
|---|---|---|---|---|---|---|---|
| *19--* *Dec.* | *31* | | √ | | | *13 1 4 0 00* | |
| | | | | | | | |

ACCOUNT *Accumulated Depreciation — Office Equipment* ACCOUNT NO. *14.1*

| DATE | | ITEM | POST. REF. | DEBIT | CREDIT | BALANCE DEBIT | BALANCE CREDIT |
|---|---|---|---|---|---|---|---|
| *19--* *Dec.* | *31* | | √ | | | | *4 1 5 0 00* |
| | | | | | | | |

ACCOUNT *Accounts Payable — Trumann Sales* ACCOUNT NO. *21*

| DATE | | ITEM | POST. REF. | DEBIT | CREDIT | BALANCE DEBIT | BALANCE CREDIT |
|---|---|---|---|---|---|---|---|
| *19--* *Dec.* | *31* | | √ | | | | *1 2 2 0 00* |
| | | | | | | | |

*(Continued)*

ACCOUNT *Accounts Payable — Cactus Co.* ACCOUNT NO. *22*

| DATE | | ITEM | POST. REF. | DEBIT | CREDIT | BALANCE DEBIT | BALANCE CREDIT |
|---|---|---|---|---|---|---|---|
| 19-- Dec. | 31 | | √ | | | | 740 00 |
| | | | | | | | |

ACCOUNT *Salaries Payable* ACCOUNT NO. *23*

| DATE | | ITEM | POST. REF. | DEBIT | CREDIT | BALANCE DEBIT | BALANCE CREDIT |
|---|---|---|---|---|---|---|---|
| 19-- Dec. | 31 | | √ | | | | 525 00 |
| | | | | | | | |

ACCOUNT *Rosa Lewis, Capital* ACCOUNT NO. *31*

| DATE | | ITEM | POST. REF. | DEBIT | CREDIT | BALANCE DEBIT | BALANCE CREDIT |
|---|---|---|---|---|---|---|---|
| 19-- Dec. | 31 | | √ | | | | 9825 00 |
| | | | | | | | |
| | | | | | | | |
| | | | | | | | |

ACCOUNT *Rosa Lewis, Drawing* ACCOUNT NO. *32*

| DATE | | ITEM | POST. REF. | DEBIT | CREDIT | BALANCE DEBIT | BALANCE CREDIT |
|---|---|---|---|---|---|---|---|
| 19-- Dec. | 31 | | √ | | | 3000 00 | |
| | | | | | | | |
| | | | | | | | |

ACCOUNT *Income Summary* ACCOUNT NO. *33*

| DATE | | ITEM | POST. REF. | DEBIT | CREDIT | BALANCE DEBIT | BALANCE CREDIT |
|---|---|---|---|---|---|---|---|
| | | | | | | | |
| | | | | | | | |
| | | | | | | | |
| | | | | | | | |

ACCOUNT *Service Revenue* ACCOUNT NO. *41*

| DATE | | ITEM | POST. REF. | DEBIT | CREDIT | BALANCE DEBIT | BALANCE CREDIT |
|---|---|---|---|---|---|---|---|
| 19-- Dec. | 31 | | √ | | | | 11400 00 |
| | | | | | | | |
| | | | | | | | |

ACCOUNT *Depreciation Expense — Office Equipment* ACCOUNT NO. 51

| DATE | | ITEM | POST. REF. | DEBIT | CREDIT | BALANCE DEBIT | BALANCE CREDIT |
|---|---|---|---|---|---|---|---|
| 19-- Dec. | 31 | | ✓ | | | 1 200 00 | |

ACCOUNT *Rent Expense* ACCOUNT NO. 52

| DATE | | ITEM | POST. REF. | DEBIT | CREDIT | BALANCE DEBIT | BALANCE CREDIT |
|---|---|---|---|---|---|---|---|
| 19-- Dec. | 31 | | ✓ | | | 1 350 00 | |

ACCOUNT *Salary Expense* ACCOUNT NO. 53

| DATE | | ITEM | POST. REF. | DEBIT | CREDIT | BALANCE DEBIT | BALANCE CREDIT |
|---|---|---|---|---|---|---|---|
| 19-- Dec. | 31 | | ✓ | | | 4 200 00 | |

ACCOUNT *Utilities Expense* ACCOUNT NO. 54

| DATE | | ITEM | POST. REF. | DEBIT | CREDIT | BALANCE DEBIT | BALANCE CREDIT |
|---|---|---|---|---|---|---|---|
| 19-- Dec. | 31 | | ✓ | | | 980 00 | |

ACCOUNT *Miscellaneous Expense* ACCOUNT NO. 55

| DATE | | ITEM | POST. REF. | DEBIT | CREDIT | BALANCE DEBIT | BALANCE CREDIT |
|---|---|---|---|---|---|---|---|
| 19-- Dec. | 31 | | ✓ | | | 540 00 | |

JOURNAL PAGE 24

| DATE | | DESCRIPTION | POST. REF. | DEBIT | CREDIT |
|---|---|---|---|---|---|

**4C-3.** Below you are given the Income Statement columns from the work sheet for the Moreno Modeling Agency for the month ended October 31 of the current year. Moreno's capital on October 1 was $9,300. She withdrew $540 during the month and made no additional investments.

**Required:**

(a) Prepare an income statement using the ruled form below and a capital statement for the month of October, using the ruled form on page 402.

(b) Prepare the entries to close the books as of October 31, using the journal form provided on page 402.

**MORENO MODELING AGENCY**
**Work Sheet**
**For Month Ended October 31, 19--**

| ACCOUNT TITLE | INCOME STATEMENT DEBIT | INCOME STATEMENT CREDIT |
|---|---|---|
| *Cash* | | |
| *Office Supplies* | | |
| *Prepaid Rent* | | |
| *Furniture and Fixtures* | | |
| *Accumulated Depreciation — Furniture & Fixtures* | | |
| *Accounts Payable — Vogue Co.* | | |
| *Sara Moreno, Capital* | | |
| *Sara Moreno, Drawing* | | |
| *Fees Earned* | | 5 600 00 |
| *Salary Expense* | 2 740 00 | |
| *Telephone Expense* | 26 00 | |
| *Utilities Expense* | 97 00 | |
| *Miscellaneous Expense* | 42 00 | |
| | | |
| *Rent Expense* | 180 00 | |
| *Depreciation Expense — Furniture & Fixtures* | 140 00 | |
| *Office Supplies Expense* | 112 00 | |
| *Salaries Payable* | | |
| | 3 337 00 | 5 600 00 |
| *Net Income* | 2 263 00 | |
| | 5 600 00 | 5 600 00 |

JOURNAL PAGE

| | DATE | | DESCRIPTION | POST. REF. | DEBIT | CREDIT | |
|---|---|---|---|---|---|---|---|
| 1 | | | | | | | 1 |
| 2 | | | | | | | 2 |
| 3 | | | | | | | 3 |
| 4 | | | | | | | 4 |
| 5 | | | | | | | 5 |
| 6 | | | | | | | 6 |
| 7 | | | | | | | 7 |
| 8 | | | | | | | 8 |
| 9 | | | | | | | 9 |
| 10 | | | | | | | 10 |
| 11 | | | | | | | 11 |
| 12 | | | | | | | 12 |
| 13 | | | | | | | 13 |
| 14 | | | | | | | 14 |
| 15 | | | | | | | 15 |
| 16 | | | | | | | 16 |
| 17 | | | | | | | 17 |
| 18 | | | | | | | 18 |

**Perfect Score** **20** **Name** ______________________

**Student's Score** ____ **Date** ______________ **Class** ________

## RECORDING CASH

**Instructions.** Complete each statement and answer each question below by writing your answer in the space at the right.

| No. | Statement | Answer | For Scoring |
|---|---|---|---|
| 1 | If a four-column journal is used, how many postings will be made to the cash account for a month? ........ | | 1 |
| 2 | Large businesses will often have two separate cash accounts, "Cash in Bank" and........ | | 2 |
| 3 | The journal designed to summarize the cash transactions by providing special columns to be used exclusively for cash debits and cash credits is the ........ | | 3 |
| 4 | The General columns of a four-column journal are posted ........ | | 4 |
| 5 | The Cash columns of a four-column journal are posted by ........ | | 5 |
| 6 | If the four-column journal is expanded to include other frequently used accounts, it is commonly called a........ | | 6 |
| 7 | A small sum of money kept on hand to make change and pay for small items is called........ | | 7 |
| 8 | All petty cash transactions are recorded in the........ | | 8 |
| 9 | When the petty cash fund is replenished, a check is made payable to .. | | 9 |
| 10 | When the petty cash account does not agree with the actual cash on hand, an account entitled __________ should be used ........ | | 10 |

**Instructions.** Determine whether each of the following statements is true or false and place a check mark in the appropriate column.

| No. | Statement | True | False | For Scoring |
|---|---|---|---|---|
| 11 | A petty cash fund is used by a business as part of a system of good internal control over cash ........ | | | 11 |
| 12 | Transactions recorded in a four-column general journal that do not involve cash are recorded in the same manner as they are in a two-column journal........ | | | 12 |
| 13 | Closing entries are recorded in the four-column journal below the column totals which have been ruled........ | | | 13 |
| 14 | The purpose of special columns in any journal is to simplify the recording and posting process ........ | | | 14 |
| 15 | The petty cash book is a book of original entry (journal)........ | | | 15 |
| 16 | When the petty cash fund is replenished, the account(s) debited are the individual expense accounts........ | | | 16 |

*(Continued)*

| No. | Statement | True | False | For Scoring |
|---|---|---|---|---|
| 17 | The petty cash fund should be replenished only at the end of an accounting period ........ | | | 17 |
| 18 | A constant balance is normally maintained in the petty cash account unless the size of the fund is permanently increased or decreased.... | | | 18 |
| 19 | Petty cash vouchers should be prenumbered and signed by the person receiving the cash........ | | | 19 |
| 20 | If the cash short and over account has a credit balance at the end of the fiscal period, it should be treated as an expense........ | | | 20 |

**5A-1.** During the month of May of the current year, Ron Redmond performed the following transactions:

May 2. Invested cash in a local moving company, $4,200.
4. Paid cash for a truck, $3,550.
7. Paid rent for the month, $180.
10. Received cash for movings to date, $560.
13. Purchased moving equipment on account from UHL Co., $1,500.
16. Received cash for moving an attorney's office, $450.
21. Paid UHL on account, $500.
24. Purchased office supplies, $50.
31. Paid monthly bill at local service station for truck expense, $123.
31. Paid helper for the month, $400.
31. Received cash for movings, $340.

**Required:**

(a) Record the above transactions in the four-column journal below.
(b) Foot the journal amount columns and prove these totals. Enter the totals and rule the columns.

## JOURNAL

PAGE

| | CASH | | DATE | DESCRIPTION | POST. REF. | GENERAL | | |
|---|---|---|---|---|---|---|---|---|
| | DEBIT | CREDIT | | | | DEBIT | CREDIT | |
| 1 | | | | | | | | 1 |
| 2 | | | | | | | | 2 |
| 3 | | | | | | | | 3 |
| 4 | | | | | | | | 4 |
| 5 | | | | | | | | 5 |
| 6 | | | | | | | | 6 |
| 7 | | | | | | | | 7 |
| 8 | | | | | | | | 8 |
| 9 | | | | | | | | 9 |
| 10 | | | | | | | | 10 |
| 11 | | | | | | | | 11 |
| 12 | | | | | | | | 12 |
| 13 | | | | | | | | 13 |
| 14 | | | | | | | | 14 |
| 15 | | | | | | | | 15 |

**5A-2.** The following petty cash transactions were completed by the petty cashier at the Municipal Zoo during August of the current year.

Aug. 1. Issued Check No. 761 to establish a petty cash fund of $50.
4. Recorded Voucher No. 501 for $9 to pay for stamps.
9. Recorded Voucher No. 502 for $4.50 to pay for miscellaneous expense.
15. Recorded Voucher No. 503 for $15.20 to pay for repairs.
17. Recorded Voucher No. 504 to pay for postage of $8.60.
20. Recorded Voucher No. 505 for $7.60 to pay for carbon paper.
21. Issued Check No. 794 to replenish the petty cash fund.
22. Recorded Voucher No. 506 for refreshments purchased for an office birthday party for one of the staff, $10.25 (Miscellaneous Expense).
24. Recorded Voucher No. 507 for $16 to pay a student to clean the office windows.
28. Recorded Voucher No. 508 for stamps, $6.
29. Recorded Voucher No. 509 for a telegram, $5.60 (Miscellaneous Expense).
30. Issued Check No. 821 to replenish the petty cash fund.
31. Issued Check No. 823 to increase the petty cash fund to $65.

**Required:**

(a) Record the transactions in the petty cash book provided on page 406.

(b) Using the journal paper provided below, prepare the entries to establish the petty cash fund on August 1, to replenish the fund on August 21 and 30, and to increase the fund on August 31.

JOURNAL PAGE

| DATE | | DESCRIPTION | POST. REF. | DEBIT | CREDIT |
|---|---|---|---|---|---|

PAGE *1* PETTY CASH DISBURSEMENTS FOR MONTH OF 19 PAGE *1*

| | DAY | DESCRIPTION | VOU. NO. | TOTAL AMOUNT | DISTRIBUTION OF CHARGES | | | | |
|---|---|---|---|---|---|---|---|---|---|
| | | | | | OFFICE SUP. EXP. | MISC. EXP. | ACCOUNT | AMOUNT | |
| 1 | | | | | | | | | 1 |
| 2 | | | | | | | | | 2 |
| 3 | | | | | | | | | 3 |
| 4 | | | | | | | | | 4 |
| 5 | | | | | | | | | 5 |
| 6 | | | | | | | | | 6 |
| 7 | | | | | | | | | 7 |
| 8 | | | | | | | | | 8 |
| 9 | | | | | | | | | 9 |
| 10 | | | | | | | | | 10 |
| 11 | | | | | | | | | 11 |
| 12 | | | | | | | | | 12 |
| 13 | | | | | | | | | 13 |
| 14 | | | | | | | | | 14 |
| 15 | | | | | | | | | 15 |
| 16 | | | | | | | | | 16 |
| 17 | | | | | | | | | 17 |
| 18 | | | | | | | | | 18 |
| 19 | | | | | | | | | 19 |
| 20 | | | | | | | | | 20 |
| 21 | | | | | | | | | 21 |
| 22 | | | | | | | | | 22 |

**5A-3.** Monica Boyett opened Boyett's Photography Studio and completed the following transactions during April of the current year.

Apr. 1. Invested cash in the business, $1,600.
1. Leased an office and paid the first month's rent, $150, Check No. 180.
3. Paid advertising expense, $42, Check No. 181.
3. Purchased camera supplies, $90, and camera, $600, from the Kodo Co. on account.
6. Received fee for photographing a wedding, $165.
7. Paid salary to part-time helper, $75, Check No. 182.
10. Paid miscellaneous expense, $27, Check No. 183.
12. Purchased camera supplies for cash, $60, Check No. 184.
13. Received fee for pictures taken at a bar mitzvah, $300.
14. Paid salary to helper, $75, Check No. 185.
17. Took publicity pictures for Bill Thompson on account, $80.
19. Paid miscellaneous expenses, $25, Check No. 186.
20. Received fee for pictures taken at a junior prom, $175.
21. Paid helper weekly salary, $75, Check No. 187.
24. Paid Kodo Co. on account, $80, Check No. 188.
25. Received cash from Bill Thompson for services completed on April 17, $40.
26. Paid utilities expense, $70, Check No. 189.
28. Paid helper weekly salary, $75, Check No. 190.
30. Purchased camera supplies for cash $150, Check No. 191.
30. Boyett withdrew cash for personal use, $150, Check No. 192.

**Required:**

(a) Record the transactions in the combined cash journal on pages 410 and 411.
(b) Foot the journal amount columns and prove these totals. Enter the totals and rule the columns.
(c) Post to the ledger accounts given below and on pages 408 and 409.
(d) Prepare a trial balance of the ledger, using the ruled form on page 412.

## GENERAL LEDGER

ACCOUNT *Cash* ACCOUNT NO. *11*

| DATE | | ITEM | POST. REF. | DEBIT | CREDIT | BALANCE DEBIT | BALANCE CREDIT |
|---|---|---|---|---|---|---|---|
| | | | | | | | |
| | | | | | | | |
| | | | | | | | |

ACCOUNT *Accounts Receivable — Bill Thompson* ACCOUNT NO. *12*

| DATE | | ITEM | POST. REF. | DEBIT | CREDIT | BALANCE DEBIT | BALANCE CREDIT |
|---|---|---|---|---|---|---|---|
| | | | | | | | |
| | | | | | | | |
| | | | | | | | |

ACCOUNT *Camera Supplies* ACCOUNT NO. *13*

| DATE | | ITEM | POST. REF. | DEBIT | CREDIT | BALANCE DEBIT | BALANCE CREDIT |
|---|---|---|---|---|---|---|---|
| | | | | | | | |
| | | | | | | | |
| | | | | | | | |

*(Continued)*

ACCOUNT *Camera Equipment* ACCOUNT NO. *14*

| DATE | | ITEM | POST. REF. | DEBIT | CREDIT | BALANCE | |
|---|---|---|---|---|---|---|---|
| | | | | | | DEBIT | CREDIT |
| | | | | | | | |
| | | | | | | | |
| | | | | | | | |
| | | | | | | | |

ACCOUNT *Accounts Payable — Kodo Co.* ACCOUNT NO. *21*

| DATE | | ITEM | POST. REF. | DEBIT | CREDIT | BALANCE | |
|---|---|---|---|---|---|---|---|
| | | | | | | DEBIT | CREDIT |
| | | | | | | | |
| | | | | | | | |
| | | | | | | | |
| | | | | | | | |

ACCOUNT *Monica Boyett, Capital* ACCOUNT NO. *31*

| DATE | | ITEM | POST. REF. | DEBIT | CREDIT | BALANCE | |
|---|---|---|---|---|---|---|---|
| | | | | | | DEBIT | CREDIT |
| | | | | | | | |
| | | | | | | | |
| | | | | | | | |

ACCOUNT *Monica Boyett, Drawing* ACCOUNT NO. *32*

| DATE | | ITEM | POST. REF. | DEBIT | CREDIT | BALANCE | |
|---|---|---|---|---|---|---|---|
| | | | | | | DEBIT | CREDIT |
| | | | | | | | |
| | | | | | | | |
| | | | | | | | |

ACCOUNT *Photography Revenue* ACCOUNT NO. *41*

| DATE | | ITEM | POST. REF. | DEBIT | CREDIT | BALANCE | |
|---|---|---|---|---|---|---|---|
| | | | | | | DEBIT | CREDIT |
| | | | | | | | |
| | | | | | | | |
| | | | | | | | |

ACCOUNT *Advertising Expense* ACCOUNT NO. 51

| DATE | | ITEM | POST. REF. | DEBIT | CREDIT | BALANCE | |
|---|---|---|---|---|---|---|---|
| | | | | | | DEBIT | CREDIT |
| | | | | | | | |
| | | | | | | | |
| | | | | | | | |

ACCOUNT *Rent Expense* ACCOUNT NO. 52

| DATE | | ITEM | POST. REF. | DEBIT | CREDIT | BALANCE | |
|---|---|---|---|---|---|---|---|
| | | | | | | DEBIT | CREDIT |
| | | | | | | | |
| | | | | | | | |
| | | | | | | | |

ACCOUNT *Salary Expense* ACCOUNT NO. 53

| DATE | | ITEM | POST. REF. | DEBIT | CREDIT | BALANCE | |
|---|---|---|---|---|---|---|---|
| | | | | | | DEBIT | CREDIT |
| | | | | | | | |
| | | | | | | | |
| | | | | | | | |
| | | | | | | | |

ACCOUNT *Utilities Expense* ACCOUNT NO. 54

| DATE | | ITEM | POST. REF. | DEBIT | CREDIT | BALANCE | |
|---|---|---|---|---|---|---|---|
| | | | | | | DEBIT | CREDIT |
| | | | | | | | |
| | | | | | | | |
| | | | | | | | |

ACCOUNT *Miscellaneous Expense* ACCOUNT NO. 55

| DATE | | ITEM | POST. REF. | DEBIT | CREDIT | BALANCE | |
|---|---|---|---|---|---|---|---|
| | | | | | | DEBIT | CREDIT |
| | | | | | | | |
| | | | | | | | |
| | | | | | | | |

# COMBINED CASH JOURNAL

| CASH | | CK. NO. | DAY | DESCRIPTION | POST. REF. |
|---|---|---|---|---|---|
| DEBIT 11 | CREDIT 11 | | | | |

FOR MONTH OF 19 PAGE 2

| | GENERAL | | PHOTOGRAPHY REVENUE 41 CR. | SALARY EXPENSE 56 DR. | |
|---|---|---|---|---|---|
| | DEBIT | CREDIT | | | |
| 1 | | | | | 1 |
| 2 | | | | | 2 |
| 3 | | | | | 3 |
| 4 | | | | | 4 |
| 5 | | | | | 5 |
| 6 | | | | | 6 |
| 7 | | | | | 7 |
| 8 | | | | | 8 |
| 9 | | | | | 9 |
| 10 | | | | | 10 |
| 11 | | | | | 11 |
| 12 | | | | | 12 |
| 13 | | | | | 13 |
| 14 | | | | | 14 |
| 15 | | | | | 15 |
| 16 | | | | | 16 |
| 17 | | | | | 17 |
| 18 | | | | | 18 |
| 19 | | | | | 19 |
| 20 | | | | | 20 |
| 21 | | | | | 21 |
| 22 | | | | | 22 |
| 23 | | | | | 23 |
| 24 | | | | | 24 |
| 25 | | | | | 25 |
| 26 | | | | | 26 |
| 27 | | | | | 27 |
| 28 | | | | | 28 |
| 29 | | | | | 29 |
| 30 | | | | | 30 |
| 31 | | | | | 31 |
| 32 | | | | | 32 |
| 33 | | | | | 33 |

**5A-4.** The Aquatic Swimming Center uses one cash register. The cash register is cleared and the cash counted and checked once each week. Below you are given the ledger account for Cash Short and Over with the balance as of July 1 of the current year, and the cash register tape totals and cash counted for each week in July.

| *Date* | *Cash Register Tape Total* | *Cash in Drawer* |
|---|---|---|
| July 7 | $485.00 | $483.25 |
| 14 | 376.50 | 371.00 |
| 21 | 402.75 | 406.40 |
| 28 | 395.60 | 389.10 |

**Required:**

(a) Prepare the entries to correct the cash account each week using the general journal form below.
(b) Post the entries to the cash short and over account below.
(c) Prepare the entry to close Cash Short and Over at July 31 using the form below.
(d) Post the closing entry to the cash short and over account.

ACCOUNT *Cash Short and Over* ACCOUNT NO. *68*

| DATE | | ITEM | POST. REF. | DEBIT | CREDIT | BALANCE DEBIT | BALANCE CREDIT |
|---|---|---|---|---|---|---|---|
| *19--* *July* | *1* | *Balance* | ✓ | | | *8 40* | |
| | | | | | | | |
| | | | | | | | |
| | | | | | | | |
| | | | | | | | |

JOURNAL PAGE *16*

| DATE | | DESCRIPTION | POST. REF. | DEBIT | CREDIT |
|---|---|---|---|---|---|
| | | | | | |

*(Page not used.)*

**Perfect Score** 20 **Name** ____________

**Student's Score** ____ **Date** ____________ **Class** ________

**BANKING PROCEDURES**

**Instructions.** Complete each of the statements below by writing your answer in the space at the right.

| No. | Statement | Answer | For Scoring |
|---|---|---|---|
| 1 | An overall system designed to meet the needs for control and safeguards within a business is called a system of.................................... | | 1 |
| 2 | The name of the business or individual which is written on the back of a check to transfer title of the check is called a(n).......................... | | 2 |
| 3 | An endorsement which specifies to whom the check is to be paid and such words as "For deposit only," is called a(n) ................................ | | 3 |
| 4 | A machine used to write and perforate the amount of a check in figures and in words is called a(n)............................................................ | | 4 |
| 5 | The process of proving the checkbook balance with the amount of cash shown on the bank statement is called ........................................ | | 5 |
| 6 | Checks written by the depositor that have not yet been processed by the bank at the time the bank statement is prepared are called.......... | | 6 |
| 7 | Deposits made too late to appear on the monthly bank statement are called...................................................................................... | | 7 |
| 8 | Customers' checks which have been deposited but which the bank has refused to pay are called ............................................................ | | 8 |
| 9 | The bank procedure of processing depositors' statements at various intervals during the month is known as ............................................ | | 9 |
| 10 | A bank service charge is normally charged to the ____________ expense account........................................................................... | | 10 |
| 11 | The term "NSF" means ................................................................ | | 11 |
| 12 | When a customer's NSF check is returned with the bank statement, the account debited on the depositor's books is.................................. | | 12 |
| 13 | The account credited on the depositor's books for an NSF check is...... | | 13 |

**Instructions.** Using the following classifications, indicate how each of the items listed below would be presented in a bank reconciliation by inserting the appropriate letter in the Answer column.

**A.** Added to bank statement balance
**B.** Deducted from bank statement balance
**C.** Added to checkbook balance
**D.** Deducted from checkbook balance

| No. | Item | Answer | For Scoring |
|---|---|---|---|
| 14 | Deposits in transit............................................................................ | | 14 |
| 15 | Check written for $120 erroneously recorded on check stub as $140 .... | | 15 |
| 16 | Check written by business and processed by bank but not recorded on check stub............................................................................ | | 16 |

*(Continued)*

| No. | Item | Answer | For Scoring |
|---|---|---|---|
| 17 | Bank service charges ........................................ | | 17 |
| 18 | Outstanding checks ........................................ | | 18 |
| 19 | Customer's NSF check returned by bank ........................................ | | 19 |
| 20 | Note receivable collected by the bank and appearing on the bank statement........................................ | | 20 |

**5B-1.** The following data are accumulated for use in reconciling the bank account of Zucconi Company for May of the current year.

| | |
|---|---|
| Balance per bank statement, May 31 | $932 |
| Note receivable collected by bank | 135 |
| Interest on note collected | 9 |
| Checks outstanding, May 31 | 184 |
| Bank service charge for May | 6 |
| Deposit in transit, May 31 | 110 |
| Balance per checkbook, May 31 | 720 |

**Required:** Prepare a bank reconciliation, using the ruled form provided below.

**5B-2.** The following information is taken from the checkbook stubs of Ajax Equipment Rentals for the month of April of the current year:

| *Date* | *Check No.* | *Amount* | *Deposit* | *Balance* |
|---|---|---|---|---|
| Apr. 1 | | | | $ 863.00 |
| 1 | 537 | $ 27.00 | | 836.00 |
| 2 | 538 | 41.50 | $210.00 | 1,004.50 |
| 4 | 539 | 32.00 | | 972.50 |
| 6 | 540 | 20.00 | | 952.50 |
| 9 | 541 | 50.00 | | 902.50 |
| 10 | 542 | 83.90 | 200.00 | 1,018.60 |
| 12 | 543 | 62.00 | | 956.60 |
| 14 | 544 | 15.00 | | 941.60 |
| 15 | 545 | 27.00 | | 914.60 |
| 18 | 546 | 39.00 | | 875.60 |
| 18 | 547 | 43.00 | 185.00 | 1,017.60 |
| 21 | 548 | VOID | | 1,017.60 |
| 21 | 549 | 100.00 | | 917.60 |
| 26 | 550 | 22.00 | | 895.60 |
| 30 | 551 | 37.50 | | 858.10 |
| 30 | 552 | 19.80 | 260.00 | 1,098.30 |

Ajax's bank statement for April is presented below. Checks which were outstanding on the March bank reconciliation are as follows: Check No. 510, $20.00; Check No. 513, $65.00; Check No. 533, $130.00.

ROCKY MOUNTAIN NATIONAL BANK

STATEMENT OF ACCOUNT

AJAX EQUIPMENT RENTALS
512 PERRY STREET
DENVER, COLORADO 80204-7631

ACCOUNT NUMBER: 141-53566

DATE OF STATEMENT: 4/30/--

| BALANCE FROM PREVIOUS STATEMENT | NUMBER OF DEBITS | AMOUNT OF CHECKS AND DEBITS | NUMBER OF CREDITS | AMOUNT OF DEPOSITS AND CREDITS | SERVICE CHARGE | STATEMENT BALANCE |
|---|---|---|---|---|---|---|
| 1,078.00 | 15 | 718.40 | 4 | 705.00 | 3.00 | 1,061.60 |

| DATE | CHECKS DEBITS | CHECKS DEBITS | DEPOSITS CREDITS | BALANCE |
|---|---|---|---|---|
| 4/01 | 20.00 | 65.00 | | 993.00 |
| 4/02 | 27.00 | | 210.00 | 1,176.00 |
| 4/05 | 130.00 | 32.00 | | 1,014.00 |
| 4/08 | 41.50 | 20.00 | MS 110.00 | 1,062.50 |
| 4/11 | 50.00 | 83.90 | 200.00 | 1,128.60 |
| 4/16 | 27.00 | | | 1,101.60 |
| 4/19 | 39.00 | 62.00 | | 1,000.60 |
| 4/20 | 43.00 | | 185.00 | 1,142.60 |
| 4/27 | 22.00 | | | 1,120.60 |
| 4/30 | 3.00 SC | 56.00 NSF | | 1,061.60 |

**PLEASE EXAMINE AT ONCE.** IF NO ERROR IS REPORTED WITHIN 10 DAYS THE ACCOUNT WILL BE CONSIDERED CORRECT AND VOUCHERS GENUINE. REFER ANY DISCREPANCY OR ERROR TO OUR BOOKKEEPING DEPT.

**EC-ERROR CORRECTION** **MS-MISCELLANEOUS** **SC-SERVICE CHARGE**
**NSF-NOT SUFFICIENT FUNDS** **OD-OVERDRAFT**

Checks returned by the bank with the April statement are rearranged in numerical sequence below:

| *Check No.* | *Amount* | *Check No.* | *Amount* |
|---|---|---|---|
| 510 | $ 20.00 | 541 | $50.00 |
| 513 | 65.00 | 542 | 83.90 |
| 533 | 130.00 | 543 | 62.00 |
| 537 | 27.00 | 545 | 27.00 |
| 538 | 41.50 | 546 | 39.00 |
| 539 | 32.00 | 547 | 43.00 |
| 540 | 20.00 | 550 | 22.00 |

The $110.00 collected by the bank was on a note receivable from a customer, Herman Haun. The note was non-interest bearing. The $56.00 NSF check was given to Ajax by Marge Freed as payment on her account and had been deposited in March.

**Required:**

(a) Prepare a bank reconciliation for Ajax Equipment Rentals for the month of April, using the ruled paper provided on page 420.

(b) Prepare any entries required to correct the cash account, using the two-column journal paper below.

JOURNAL PAGE

| DATE | | DESCRIPTION | POST. REF. | DEBIT | CREDIT |
|---|---|---|---|---|---|

Perfect Score 20 Name ____________________

Student's Score ____ Date ____________ Class ________

## SALES AND ACCOUNTS RECEIVABLE

**Instructions.** Complete each statement and answer each question below by writing your answer in the space at the right.

| No. | Statement | Answer | For Scoring |
|---|---|---|---|
| 1 | A business that buys and sells goods is a(n) | | 1 |
| 2 | The goods of a business which are purchased for resale are known as.. | | 2 |
| 3 | When merchandise is sold on account, the account debited is | | 3 |
| 4 | When a sale of merchandise is made, the revenue account credited is . | | 4 |
| 5 | A business document used to record all the detailed information pertaining to a retail sale is known as a(n) | | 5 |
| 6 | Sale of merchandise on account is recorded in a special journal called the | | 6 |
| 7 | The principal ledger containing all the balance sheet and income statement accounts is called the | | 7 |
| 8 | A separate ledger such as that used to record the individual customers' accounts is called a(n) | | 8 |
| 9 | The sales journal normally has only one amount column. This amount column is used to record credits to the account entitled | | 9 |
| 10 | The amount column in the sales journal is also used to record debits to the account entitled | | 10 |
| 11 | The accounts receivable account in the general ledger representing the total of the customers' accounts in the subsidiary ledger is called a(n) | | 11 |
| 12 | The balance in the control account should always be equal to the total of the individual accounts in the ________ ledger | | 12 |
| 13 | Lightfoot Dept. Store has 620 charge customers. If each of the customer accounts is kept in the general ledger rather than in a separate subsidiary ledger, how many *additional* items would appear on the trial balance and balance sheet? | | 13 |
| 14 | Are all sales of merchandise recorded in the sales journal? | | 14 |
| 15 | A convenient item used for identifying and approving charge customers in retailing is the | | 15 |

**Instructions.** For each type of business in Column A select the item in Column B that would be classified as inventory and write the letter corresponding to that item in the Answer column.

| No. | A | B | Answer | For Scoring |
|---|---|---|---|---|
| 16 | Men's shop | a. Cosmetics | | 16 |
| 17 | Service station | b. Shirts and ties | | 17 |
| 18 | Bakery shop | c. Table and chairs | | 18 |
| 19 | Furniture store | d. Bread | | 19 |
| 20 | Drugstore | e. Gasoline | | 20 |

**6A-1.** The following are the charge sales of Tanaka Company for the month of October:

Oct. 2. Sold merchandise on account to Curt Bowman for $130, Invoice No. 58.
5. Sold merchandise on account to Jane Dowl for $95, Invoice No. 59.
12. Sold merchandise on account to Kim Yee for $160, Invoice No. 60.
16. Sold merchandise on account to Walt Davis for $45, Invoice No. 61.
24. Sold merchandise on account to Sara Harp for $75, Invoice No. 62.
30. Sold merchandise on account to Ed Wilson for $142, Invoice No. 63.

**Required:**

(a) Record the transactions for Tanaka Company in the sales journal given below.
(b) Total and rule the journal.

## SALES JOURNAL

PAGE *6*

| DATE | | ACCOUNT DEBITED | SALE NO. | POST. REF. | ACCTS. REC. DR. SALES CR. |
|---|---|---|---|---|---|

**6A-2.** Transactions related to the sales on account completed by the Alpine Co. during January of the current year are described below. The general ledger accounts and the accounts receivable subsidiary ledger appear below and on page 424.

Jan. 3. Invoice No. 315 to Viki Farish, $90.
6. Invoice No. 316 to Doug Mann, $220.
10. Invoice No. 317 to Vu Phi, $125.
14. Invoice No. 318 to Sonia Cook, $148.
18. Invoice No. 319 to Robb Mink, $205.
24. Invoice No. 320 to Viki Farish, $105.
27. Invoice No. 321 to Robb Mink, $135.
30. Invoice No. 322 to Doug Mann, $185.

**Required:**

(a) Record the charge sales in the sales journal given below.

(b) Post the sales journal to the accounts receivable subsidiary ledger on page 424, and after totaling and ruling the journal, post to the general ledger accounts below.

## SALES JOURNAL

PAGE *19*

| | DATE | | ACCOUNT DEBITED | SALE NO. | POST. REF. | ACCTS. REC. DR. SALES CR. | |
|---|---|---|---|---|---|---|---|
| 1 | | | | | | | 1 |
| 2 | | | | | | | 2 |
| 3 | | | | | | | 3 |
| 4 | | | | | | | 4 |
| 5 | | | | | | | 5 |
| 6 | | | | | | | 6 |
| 7 | | | | | | | 7 |
| 8 | | | | | | | 8 |
| 9 | | | | | | | 9 |
| 10 | | | | | | | 10 |
| 11 | | | | | | | 11 |
| 12 | | | | | | | 12 |

ACCOUNT *Accounts Receivable* ACCOUNT NO. *12*

| DATE | | ITEM | POST. REF. | DEBIT | CREDIT | BALANCE | |
|---|---|---|---|---|---|---|---|
| | | | | | | DEBIT | CREDIT |
| | | | | | | | |
| | | | | | | | |

ACCOUNT *Sales* ACCOUNT NO. *41*

| DATE | | ITEM | POST. REF. | DEBIT | CREDIT | BALANCE | |
|---|---|---|---|---|---|---|---|
| | | | | | | DEBIT | CREDIT |
| | | | | | | | |
| | | | | | | | |

## ACCOUNTS RECEIVABLE LEDGER

**NAME** *Sonia Cook*

**ADDRESS** *1451 Hobart Drive, Philadelphia, PA 19136-7485*

| DATE | | ITEM | POST. REF. | DEBIT | CREDIT | BALANCE |
|---|---|---|---|---|---|---|
| | | | | | | |
| | | | | | | |

**NAME** *Viki Farish*

**ADDRESS** *19607 Jersey Blvd., Trenton, NJ 08638-2467*

| DATE | | ITEM | POST. REF. | DEBIT | CREDIT | BALANCE |
|---|---|---|---|---|---|---|
| | | | | | | |
| | | | | | | |
| | | | | | | |

**NAME** *Doug Mann*

**ADDRESS** *1212 Sycamore Rd., Philadelphia, PA 19140-7632*

| DATE | | ITEM | POST. REF. | DEBIT | CREDIT | BALANCE |
|---|---|---|---|---|---|---|
| | | | | | | |
| | | | | | | |

**NAME** *Robb Mink*

**ADDRESS** *5900 Westway, Harrisburg, PA 19140-4244*

| DATE | | ITEM | POST. REF. | DEBIT | CREDIT | BALANCE |
|---|---|---|---|---|---|---|
| | | | | | | |
| | | | | | | |
| | | | | | | |

**NAME** *Vu Phi*

**ADDRESS** *5105 Eastman Drive, Philadelphia, PA 19143-2954*

| DATE | | ITEM | POST. REF. | DEBIT | CREDIT | BALANCE |
|---|---|---|---|---|---|---|
| | | | | | | |
| | | | | | | |
| | | | | | | |

Assignment 6-B

Perfect Score 25 Name ______________________

Student's Score ____ Date ______________ Class ________

## CASH RECEIPTS

**Instructions.** Complete each statement and answer each question below by writing your answer in the space at the right.

| No. | Statement | Answer | For Scoring |
|---|---|---|---|
| 1 | All receipts of cash are recorded in the __________ journal | | 1 |
| 2 | The two most frequent sources of cash receipts in a mercantile business are collections on account and | | 2 |
| 3 | The sale of merchandise for cash is recorded in the __________ journal | | 3 |
| 4 | The Cash column in the cash receipts journal will have a __________ balance | | 4 |
| 5 | The Sales column in the cash receipts journal will have a __________ balance | | 5 |
| 6 | The Accounts Receivable column in the cash receipts journal will have a __________ balance | | 6 |
| 7 | The only column in the cash receipts journal that will not be posted by total is the | | 7 |
| 8 | How often should the special columns in the cash receipts journal be posted? | | 8 |
| 9 | How often should the subsidiary customers' accounts in the cash receipts journal be posted? | | 9 |
| 10 | The column in the cash receipts journal that will have an entry for every transaction recorded in this journal is the | | 10 |

**Instructions.** You are given the following selected transactions for Sandy Gale. For each transaction indicate the account(s) to be debited and the account(s) to be credited. Also indicate in which of the following journals each transaction will be recorded: Sales Journal (S), Cash Receipts Journal (CR), or General Journal (J).

| No. | Transaction | | Answer | For Scoring |
|---|---|---|---|---|
| 11–13 | Sold merchandise on account to Sam Book for $400 | Debit | | 11 |
| | | Credit | | 12 |
| | | Journal | | 13 |
| 14–16 | Gale invested an additional $500 in the business | Debit | | 14 |
| | | Credit | | 15 |
| | | Journal | | 16 |
| 17–19 | Purchased $300 of office supplies on account | Debit | | 17 |
| | | Credit | | 18 |
| | | Journal | | 19 |
| 20–22 | Received $150 from Sam Book on account | Debit | | 20 |
| | | Credit | | 21 |
| | | Journal | | 22 |
| 23–25 | Made a cash sale of $130 | Debit | | 23 |
| | | Credit | | 24 |
| | | Journal | | 25 |

**6B-1.** The following transactions relate to cash receipts of the Yamaguchi Tire Company. The company uses a cash receipts journal to record all cash received.

Nov. 3. Received cash from Howard Lowe on account, $150.
7. Received cash from Gayle Cotler in payment of her account in full, $240.
15. Recorded cash sales, $1,950.
19. Sold office supplies (not a merchandise item) for cash to the NRD Company as a convenience to them, $80.
25. Received cash from Bob Falls in payment of his account, $600.
27. Received cash as an additional investment from Jason Yamaguchi, the proprietor, $1,500.
30. Recorded cash sales, $2,025.

**Required:**

(a) Record the transactions in the cash receipts journal provided below.

(b) Foot the journal amount columns and prove these totals. Enter the totals and rule the columns. Prepare a schedule to prove the equality of the debit and credit totals, using the ruled form at the bottom of the page.

## CASH RECEIPTS JOURNAL

PAGE 29

| | DATE | | ACCOUNT CREDITED | POST. REF. | GENERAL ACCOUNTS CR. | SALES CR. | ACCOUNTS REC. CR. | CASH DR. | |
|---|---|---|---|---|---|---|---|---|---|
| 1 | | | | | | | | | 1 |
| 2 | | | | | | | | | 2 |
| 3 | | | | | | | | | 3 |
| 4 | | | | | | | | | 4 |
| 5 | | | | | | | | | 5 |
| 6 | | | | | | | | | 6 |
| 7 | | | | | | | | | 7 |
| 8 | | | | | | | | | 8 |
| 9 | | | | | | | | | 9 |
| 10 | | | | | | | | | 10 |
| 11 | | | | | | | | | 11 |
| 12 | | | | | | | | | 12 |
| 13 | | | | | | | | | 13 |

**6B-2.** Bud Hardy operates a general merchandise store under the name Hardy Merchandise. The general ledger and the subsidiary ledger reflect the balances of the accounts as of May 1 of the current year. The following transactions relate to the cash received by the shop during May.

May 3. Received cash from Jack Horrell in payment on his account, $200.
6. Received cash from Sue Jackson in payment of her account, $205.
9. Hardy invested additional cash in the business, $300.
10. Recorded cash sales, $900.
14. Received payment on account from Dick Metcalf, $160.
18. Sold store supplies (not a merchandise item) for cash to Biggers Co. as a convenience to them, $40.
20. Recorded cash sales, $643.
26. Received payment on account from Barbara McCord, $100.
30. Recorded cash sales, $710.

**Required:**

(a) Record the transactions for Hardy Merchandise in the cash receipts journal provided below, posting all subsidiary customers' accounts individually on a daily basis in the accounts receivable ledger on page 430.

(b) Post all items in the General Accounts column individually to the general ledger accounts on page 429.

(c) Foot the journal amount columns and prove these totals. Enter the totals and rule the columns. Prepare a schedule to prove the equality of the debit and credit totals, using the ruled form below.

(d) Post all special column totals to the general ledger.

(e) Prepare a schedule of accounts receivable using the form on page 428, and check the total against the balance in the accounts receivable control account.

## CASH RECEIPTS JOURNAL

PAGE 22

| | DATE | | ACCOUNT CREDITED | POST. REF. | GENERAL ACCOUNTS CR. | SALES CR. | ACCOUNTS REC. CR. | CASH DR. | |
|---|---|---|---|---|---|---|---|---|---|
| 1 | | | | | | | | | 1 |
| 2 | | | | | | | | | 2 |
| 3 | | | | | | | | | 3 |
| 4 | | | | | | | | | 4 |
| 5 | | | | | | | | | 5 |
| 6 | | | | | | | | | 6 |
| 7 | | | | | | | | | 7 |
| 8 | | | | | | | | | 8 |
| 9 | | | | | | | | | 9 |
| 10 | | | | | | | | | 10 |
| 11 | | | | | | | | | 11 |
| 12 | | | | | | | | | 12 |

# GENERAL LEDGER

ACCOUNT *Cash* ACCOUNT NO. *11*

| DATE | | ITEM | POST. REF. | DEBIT | CREDIT | BALANCE DEBIT | BALANCE CREDIT |
|---|---|---|---|---|---|---|---|
| 19-- May | 1 | Balance | √ | | | 530 00 | |
| | | | | | | | |
| | | | | | | | |

ACCOUNT *Accounts Receivable* ACCOUNT NO. *12*

| DATE | | ITEM | POST. REF. | DEBIT | CREDIT | BALANCE DEBIT | BALANCE CREDIT |
|---|---|---|---|---|---|---|---|
| 19-- May | 1 | Balance | √ | | | 1125 00 | |
| | | | | | | | |
| | | | | | | | |

ACCOUNT *Store Supplies* ACCOUNT NO. *13*

| DATE | | ITEM | POST. REF. | DEBIT | CREDIT | BALANCE DEBIT | BALANCE CREDIT |
|---|---|---|---|---|---|---|---|
| 19-- May | 1 | Balance | √ | | | 170 00 | |
| | | | | | | | |
| | | | | | | | |

ACCOUNT *Bud Hardy, Capital* ACCOUNT NO. *31*

| DATE | | ITEM | POST. REF. | DEBIT | CREDIT | BALANCE DEBIT | BALANCE CREDIT |
|---|---|---|---|---|---|---|---|
| 19-- May | 1 | Balance | √ | | | | 2260 00 |
| | | | | | | | |
| | | | | | | | |

ACCOUNT *Sales* ACCOUNT NO. *41*

| DATE | | ITEM | POST. REF. | DEBIT | CREDIT | BALANCE DEBIT | BALANCE CREDIT |
|---|---|---|---|---|---|---|---|
| | | | | | | | |
| | | | | | | | |
| | | | | | | | |

## ACCOUNTS RECEIVABLE

**NAME** *Jack Horrell*

**ADDRESS** *1006 Idaho Ave., Pocatello, ID 83201-5725*

| DATE | | ITEM | POST. REF. | DEBIT | CREDIT | BALANCE |
|---|---|---|---|---|---|---|
| 19-- May | 1 | Balance | ✓ | | | 200 00 |
| | | | | | | |
| | | | | | | |

**NAME** *Sue Jackson*

**ADDRESS** *1560 Woodland Drive, Twin Falls, ID 83301-7081*

| DATE | | ITEM | POST. REF. | DEBIT | CREDIT | BALANCE |
|---|---|---|---|---|---|---|
| 19-- May | 1 | Balance | ✓ | | | 340 00 |
| | | | | | | |
| | | | | | | |

**NAME** *Barbara McCord*

**ADDRESS** *2208 W. Hickory, Pocatello, ID 83201-2718*

| DATE | | ITEM | POST. REF. | DEBIT | CREDIT | BALANCE |
|---|---|---|---|---|---|---|
| 19-- May | 1 | Balance | ✓ | | | 300 00 |
| | | | | | | |

**NAME** *Dick Metcalf*

**ADDRESS** *217 Southridge, Blackfoot, ID 83221-1876*

| DATE | | ITEM | POST. REF. | DEBIT | CREDIT | BALANCE |
|---|---|---|---|---|---|---|
| 19-- May | 1 | Balance | ✓ | | | 160 00 |
| | | | | | | |
| | | | | | | |

**NAME** *Jim Spicer*

**ADDRESS** *7800 Canyon Creek, Idaho Falls, ID 83401-8811*

| DATE | | ITEM | POST. REF. | DEBIT | CREDIT | BALANCE |
|---|---|---|---|---|---|---|
| 19-- May | 1 | Balance | ✓ | | | 125 00 |
| | | | | | | |
| | | | | | | |

**6B-3.** The following incorrect entries were discovered after they had been posted.

(a) A cash receipt of $230, from Beth Morton on account, was recorded as $320.
(b) A charge sale to David Guam of $110 was recorded as a cash sale.
(c) A sale of merchandise on account for $160 to Judy Baker was recorded as a debit to the account of Jane Barker.

**Required:** Prepare the general journal entry necessary to correct each entry, assuming the errors are discovered on May 31 of the same fiscal period in which they occurred. (No explanation need be recorded.)

JOURNAL PAGE

| DATE | | DESCRIPTION | POST. REF. | DEBIT | CREDIT |
|---|---|---|---|---|---|

**6B-4.** Brant Boman owns and operates a clothing store in West Virginia where a 3% retail sales tax is imposed.

**Required:**

(a) Record the following sales invoices (all on account during April of the current year) in the sales journal given below:

| | | | |
|---|---|---|---|
| Apr. 3. | Invoice #826 | Byrle Roberts | \$50 plus sales tax |
| 7. | Invoice #827 | Sara Diaz | \$92 plus sales tax |
| 11. | Invoice #828 | Tim Woolsey | \$75 plus sales tax |
| 15. | Invoice #829 | Byrle Roberts | \$50 plus sales tax |
| 19. | Invoice #830 | Mickey Nix | \$100 plus sales tax |

(b) Post all subsidiary customers' accounts individually on a daily basis in the accounts receivable ledger on page 434.

(c) Foot the journal amount columns and prove these totals. Enter the totals and rule the columns. Prepare a schedule to prove the equality of the debit and credit totals, using the ruled form at the top of page 433.

(d) Post the column totals to the general ledger.

(e) Prepare, in general journal form, the entry to record receipt of payment of Invoice #826 from Roberts on May 4, using the form on page 435.

(f) Prepare, in general journal form, the entry on May 15 to pay the April sales tax liability to the state.

## SALES JOURNAL

PAGE *14*

| | DATE | INV. NO. | ACCOUNT DEBITED | POST. REF. | ACCOUNTS RECEIVABLE DR. | SALES TAX PAYABLE CR. | SALES CR. | |
|---|---|---|---|---|---|---|---|---|
| 1 | | | | | | | | 1 |
| 2 | | | | | | | | 2 |
| 3 | | | | | | | | 3 |
| 4 | | | | | | | | 4 |
| 5 | | | | | | | | 5 |
| 6 | | | | | | | | 6 |
| 7 | | | | | | | | 7 |
| 8 | | | | | | | | 8 |
| 9 | | | | | | | | 9 |
| 10 | | | | | | | | 10 |
| 11 | | | | | | | | 11 |
| 12 | | | | | | | | 12 |
| 13 | | | | | | | | 13 |
| 14 | | | | | | | | 14 |
| 15 | | | | | | | | 15 |
| 16 | | | | | | | | 16 |
| 17 | | | | | | | | 17 |
| 18 | | | | | | | | 18 |
| 19 | | | | | | | | 19 |
| 20 | | | | | | | | 20 |
| 21 | | | | | | | | 21 |
| 22 | | | | | | | | 22 |

## GENERAL LEDGER

ACCOUNT *Accounts Receivable* ACCOUNT NO. *12*

| DATE | | ITEM | POST. REF. | DEBIT | CREDIT | BALANCE | |
|---|---|---|---|---|---|---|---|
| | | | | | | DEBIT | CREDIT |
| | | | | | | | |
| | | | | | | | |
| | | | | | | | |

ACCOUNT *Sales Tax Payable* ACCOUNT NO. *21*

| DATE | | ITEM | POST. REF. | DEBIT | CREDIT | BALANCE | |
|---|---|---|---|---|---|---|---|
| | | | | | | DEBIT | CREDIT |
| | | | | | | | |
| | | | | | | | |

ACCOUNT *Sales* ACCOUNT NO. *41*

| DATE | | ITEM | POST. REF. | DEBIT | CREDIT | BALANCE | |
|---|---|---|---|---|---|---|---|
| | | | | | | DEBIT | CREDIT |
| | | | | | | | |
| | | | | | | | |
| | | | | | | | |

# ACCOUNTS RECEIVABLE LEDGER

NAME *Sara Diaz*

ADDRESS *302 Cardinal Lane, Charleston, WV 25309-1587*

| DATE | | ITEM | POST. REF. | DEBIT | CREDIT | BALANCE |
|---|---|---|---|---|---|---|
| | | | | | | |
| | | | | | | |
| | | | | | | |

NAME *Mickey Nix*

ADDRESS *1102 E. McKinney, Huntington, WV 25701-4811*

| DATE | | ITEM | POST. REF. | DEBIT | CREDIT | BALANCE |
|---|---|---|---|---|---|---|
| | | | | | | |
| | | | | | | |
| | | | | | | |

NAME *Byrle Roberts*

ADDRESS *1207 Bellemeade, Charleston, WV 25314-8688*

| DATE | | ITEM | POST. REF. | DEBIT | CREDIT | BALANCE |
|---|---|---|---|---|---|---|
| | | | | | | |
| | | | | | | |
| | | | | | | |
| | | | | | | |

NAME *Tim Woolsey*

ADDRESS *414 Mimosa Drive, St. Albans, WV 25117-7938*

| DATE | | ITEM | POST. REF. | DEBIT | CREDIT | BALANCE |
|---|---|---|---|---|---|---|
| | | | | | | |
| | | | | | | |
| | | | | | | |

JOURNAL PAGE

| DATE | | DESCRIPTION | POST. REF. | DEBIT | CREDIT |
|---|---|---|---|---|---|

*(Page not used.)*

Assignment 7-A

**Perfect Score** 20 **Name** ______________________

**Student's Score** ____ **Date** ______________ **Class** ________

## PURCHASES AND ACCOUNTS PAYABLE

**Instructions.** Complete each of the statements and answer each of the questions below by writing your answer in the space at the right.

| No. | Item | Answer | For Scoring |
|---|---|---|---|
| 1 | When goods are purchased on account for the purpose of resale, the account credited is ........ | | 1 |
| 2 | The account debited in (1) above is ........ | | 2 |
| 3 | The account Purchases is used only for the purchase of........ | | 3 |
| 4 | At the end of the fiscal period, the purchases and sales accounts will be closed to........ | | 4 |
| 5 | Goods on hand at the end of the period represent an asset and will be recorded in the account titled ........ | | 5 |
| 6 | A document mailed to the buyer at the time the goods are shipped which provides information about the goods purchased is called (from the viewpoint of the buyer) a(n)........ | | 6 |
| 7 | The document in No. 6 (from the viewpoint of the seller) is known as a ........ | | 7 |
| 8 | The individual totals on a purchase order arrived at by multiplying the quantity of each item by its unit price are called........ | | 8 |
| 9 | A special journal used to record only the purchases of *merchandise* on account is called a(n)........ | | 9 |
| 10 | If possible, all subsidiary ledger accounts should be posted........ | | 10 |
| 11 | The total of the single-column purchases journal is posted at the end of the month as a credit to ........ | | 11 |
| 12 | The total of the single-column purchases journal is posted at the end of the month as a debit to ........ | | 12 |
| 13 | The special journal designed to record *all* purchases on account is the | | 13 |
| 14 | Normally, the only credit column in the multicolumn purchases journal will be titled........ | | 14 |
| 15 | If a retailer buys merchandise for cash, the account that will be debited is........ | | 15 |
| 16 | The account that will be credited for the transaction in No. 15 above is ........ | | 16 |
| 17 | Would the transaction in No. 15 be recorded in the purchases journal? | | 17 |
| 18 | A local restaurant buys food supplies from a distributor on account. What will be the account debited in this transaction?........ | | 18 |
| 19 | What account will be credited in the transaction in No. 18?........ | | 19 |
| 20 | In which special journal will the transaction in No. 18 be recorded?.... | | 20 |

## PURCHASES JOURNAL

PAGE

| | DATE | | ACCOUNT CREDITED | POST. REF. | ACCOUNTS PAYABLE CR. | PURCHASES DR. | STORE SUPPLIES DR. | GENERAL ACCOUNTS DR. | | | |
|---|---|---|---|---|---|---|---|---|---|---|---|
| | | | | | | | | ACCOUNT | POST. REF. | AMOUNT | |
| 1 | | | | | | | | | | | 1 |
| 2 | | | | | | | | | | | 2 |
| 3 | | | | | | | | | | | 3 |
| 4 | | | | | | | | | | | 4 |
| 5 | | | | | | | | | | | 5 |
| 6 | | | | | | | | | | | 6 |
| 7 | | | | | | | | | | | 7 |
| 8 | | | | | | | | | | | 8 |
| 9 | | | | | | | | | | | 9 |
| 10 | | | | | | | | | | | 10 |
| 11 | | | | | | | | | | | 11 |
| 12 | | | | | | | | | | | 12 |
| 13 | | | | | | | | | | | 13 |
| 14 | | | | | | | | | | | 14 |
| 15 | | | | | | | | | | | 15 |
| 16 | | | | | | | | | | | 16 |
| 17 | | | | | | | | | | | 17 |
| 18 | | | | | | | | | | | 18 |
| 19 | | | | | | | | | | | 19 |
| 20 | | | | | | | | | | | 20 |
| 21 | | | | | | | | | | | 21 |
| 22 | | | | | | | | | | | 22 |
| 23 | | | | | | | | | | | 23 |

**7A-1.** On June 1 of the current year, Patti Corrales began operating the Frank-n-Stein, a fast-food operation specializing in various kinds of hot dogs. The books of original entry include a multicolumn purchases journal. The following purchases on account were made during the month of June:

June 1. Merchandise from Lucassi Distributors, 900 Steeler Drive, Pittsburgh, PA 19134-1581, $1,300.
5. Kitchen equipment from Medich Supplies, 10500 S. Jackson, Pittsburgh, PA 19148-2944, $900.
8. Merchandise from Ma Weaver Bakery, 12040 I-76 East, Pittsburgh, PA 19153-1214, $240.
10. Merchandise, $165, and store supplies, $140, from Jenkins Brothers, 1110 Ferguson Road, Pittsburgh, PA 19111-1293.
15. Merchandise from Pitt Meat Company, 5101 Madison Rd., Pittsburgh, PA 19111-7150, $420.
19. Store equipment, $300, and store supplies, $85, from Medich Supplies.
22. Merchandise from Ma Weaver Bakery, $107.
28. Store supplies from Jenkins Brothers, $55.

**Required:**

(a) Open general ledger accounts in the following order: Store Supplies, 14; Store Equipment, 17; Kitchen Equipment, 19; Accounts Payable, 21; Purchases, 51. The account forms are provided on page 440.

(b) Open an accounts payable subsidiary ledger with the following accounts: Jenkins Brothers, Lucassi Distributors, Ma Weaver Bakery, Medich Supplies, and Pitt Meat Company. The account forms are provided on page 441.

(c) Record the purchases in the multicolumn purchases journal on page 438, posting all subsidiary accounts individually on a daily basis to the accounts payable ledger.

(d) Post all items in the General Accounts column individually to the general ledger.

(e) Foot the journal amount columns and prove these totals. Enter the totals and rule the columns. Prepare a schedule to prove the equality of the debit and credit totals on the form below.

(f) Post all special columns to the general ledger.

ACCOUNT | ACCOUNT NO.

| DATE | | ITEM | POST. REF. | DEBIT | CREDIT | BALANCE | |
|---|---|---|---|---|---|---|---|
| | | | | | | DEBIT | CREDIT |
| | | | | | | | |
| | | | | | | | |

ACCOUNT | ACCOUNT NO.

| DATE | | ITEM | POST. REF. | DEBIT | CREDIT | BALANCE | |
|---|---|---|---|---|---|---|---|
| | | | | | | DEBIT | CREDIT |
| | | | | | | | |
| | | | | | | | |

ACCOUNT | ACCOUNT NO.

| DATE | | ITEM | POST. REF. | DEBIT | CREDIT | BALANCE | |
|---|---|---|---|---|---|---|---|
| | | | | | | DEBIT | CREDIT |
| | | | | | | | |
| | | | | | | | |
| | | | | | | | |

ACCOUNT | ACCOUNT NO.

| DATE | | ITEM | POST. REF. | DEBIT | CREDIT | BALANCE | |
|---|---|---|---|---|---|---|---|
| | | | | | | DEBIT | CREDIT |
| | | | | | | | |
| | | | | | | | |
| | | | | | | | |
| | | | | | | | |

ACCOUNT | ACCOUNT NO.

| DATE | | ITEM | POST. REF. | DEBIT | CREDIT | BALANCE | |
|---|---|---|---|---|---|---|---|
| | | | | | | DEBIT | CREDIT |
| | | | | | | | |
| | | | | | | | |
| | | | | | | | |

NAME

ADDRESS

| DATE | | ITEM | POST. REF. | DEBIT | CREDIT | BALANCE |
|---|---|---|---|---|---|---|
| | | | | | | |
| | | | | | | |
| | | | | | | |

NAME

ADDRESS

| DATE | | ITEM | POST. REF. | DEBIT | CREDIT | BALANCE |
|---|---|---|---|---|---|---|
| | | | | | | |
| | | | | | | |
| | | | | | | |

NAME

ADDRESS

| DATE | | ITEM | POST. REF. | DEBIT | CREDIT | BALANCE |
|---|---|---|---|---|---|---|
| | | | | | | |
| | | | | | | |
| | | | | | | |

NAME

ADDRESS

| DATE | | ITEM | POST. REF. | DEBIT | CREDIT | BALANCE |
|---|---|---|---|---|---|---|
| | | | | | | |
| | | | | | | |
| | | | | | | |

NAME

ADDRESS

| DATE | | ITEM | POST. REF. | DEBIT | CREDIT | BALANCE |
|---|---|---|---|---|---|---|
| | | | | | | |
| | | | | | | |
| | | | | | | |

**7A-2.** The Toshi Bookstore uses the purchase invoices as its purchases journal. At the end of September, the invoices were separated by the various kinds of purchases made on account and an adding machine tape run for each type of asset showed the following totals: purchases of merchandise, $11,710; office supplies, $145; store supplies, $303; store equipment, $520.

**Required:**

(a) Explain how and when postings are made to the subsidiary ledger accounts when this type of accounting system is utilized. Explain how and when journal entries are made when using this system.

(b) Prepare the general journal entry that would be required at the end of September.

JOURNAL PAGE

| | DATE | | DESCRIPTION | POST. REF. | DEBIT | CREDIT | |
|---|---|---|---|---|---|---|---|
| 1 | | | | | | | 1 |
| 2 | | | | | | | 2 |
| 3 | | | | | | | 3 |
| 4 | | | | | | | 4 |
| 5 | | | | | | | 5 |
| 6 | | | | | | | 6 |
| 7 | | | | | | | 7 |
| 8 | | | | | | | 8 |
| 9 | | | | | | | 9 |
| 10 | | | | | | | 10 |
| 11 | | | | | | | 11 |
| 12 | | | | | | | 12 |
| 13 | | | | | | | 13 |
| 14 | | | | | | | 14 |

**7A-3.** On May 3, Wallace Co. purchased $5,700 of merchandise on account from Jones Wholesalers. Wallace paid the invoice in full on May 21.

**Required:** Prepare the entries necessary to record the transactions on May 3 and May 21 (a) on the books of Wallace Co. and (b) on the books of Jones Wholesalers, using the journal forms below.

(a)

JOURNAL PAGE

| | DATE | DESCRIPTION | POST. REF. | DEBIT | CREDIT | |
|---|---|---|---|---|---|---|
| 1 | | | | | | 1 |
| 2 | | | | | | 2 |
| 3 | | | | | | 3 |
| 4 | | | | | | 4 |
| 5 | | | | | | 5 |
| 6 | | | | | | 6 |
| 7 | | | | | | 7 |
| 8 | | | | | | 8 |
| 9 | | | | | | 9 |
| 10 | | | | | | 10 |
| 11 | | | | | | 11 |
| 12 | | | | | | 12 |

(b)

JOURNAL PAGE

| | DATE | DESCRIPTION | POST. REF. | DEBIT | CREDIT | |
|---|---|---|---|---|---|---|
| 1 | | | | | | 1 |
| 2 | | | | | | 2 |
| 3 | | | | | | 3 |
| 4 | | | | | | 4 |
| 5 | | | | | | 5 |
| 6 | | | | | | 6 |
| 7 | | | | | | 7 |
| 8 | | | | | | 8 |
| 9 | | | | | | 9 |
| 10 | | | | | | 10 |
| 11 | | | | | | 11 |
| 12 | | | | | | 12 |

*(Page not used.)*

Perfect Score 20 Name ________________ **Assignment 7-B**

Student's Score ____ Date ________________ Class ________

## CASH PAYMENTS

**Instructions.** Complete each of the following statements by writing your answer in the space at the right.

| No. | Statement | Answer | For Scoring |
|---|---|---|---|
| 1 | The cash payments journal is used to record.......... | | 1 |
| 2 | The cash payments journal will always have a credit column for.......... | | 2 |
| 3 | In a merchandising enterprise, the most frequent payment of cash is to.......... | | 3 |
| 4 | The cash payments journal for a merchandising enterprise will always have a debit column for.......... | | 4 |
| 5 | An expense for which there is no special column in the cash payments journal would be recorded in the.......... | | 5 |

**Instructions.** When special journals are used, the Posting Reference column in the ledger accounts must reflect the source of the journal entry. Name the journal that each letter or letters listed below would indicate.

| No. | Item | Answer | For Scoring |
|---|---|---|---|
| 6 | CP.......... | | 6 |
| 7 | CR.......... | | 7 |
| 8 | J.......... | | 8 |
| 9 | P.......... | | 9 |
| 10 | S.......... | | 10 |

**Instructions.** Given below are the transactions for the Don Hancock Co. For each transaction state the account(s) to be debited (Column A) and account(s) to be credited (Column B). Indicate in Column C the journal in which each transaction should be recorded: Sales, Purchases, Cash Receipts, Cash Payments, or General.

| No. | Transaction | A Debit | B Credit | C Journal | For Scoring |
|---|---|---|---|---|---|
| 11 | Purchased merchandise on account.......... | | | | 11 |
| 12 | Received payment from a customer on account | | | | 12 |
| 13 | Paid utilities expense.......... | | | | 13 |
| 14 | Sold merchandise for cash.......... | | | | 14 |
| 15 | Purchased merchandise for cash.......... | | | | 15 |
| 16 | Hancock made a personal withdrawal of cash ... | | | | 16 |
| 17 | Recorded cash sales for the day.......... | | | | 17 |
| 18 | Sold merchandise on account.......... | | | | 18 |
| 19 | Purchased store equipment on account.......... | | | | 19 |
| 20 | Paid creditor for invoice due.......... | | | | 20 |

**7B-1.** Below you are given the cash payments journal of O'Rourke Imports Shop with the transactions recorded for the period, March 1–15 of the current year. The following transactions are for the last half of the month of March.

Mar. 16. Issued Check No. 949 to Kelley Company on amount owed, $200.
18. Issued Check No. 950 to pay for miscellaneous expenses, $54.
20. Issued Check No. 951 to Kay O'Rourke for personal withdrawal, $250.
23. Issued Check No. 952 to Asian Wholesalers on amount owed, $150.
25. Issued Check No. 953 for the purchase of merchandise, $120.
27. Issued Check No. 954 to Strum, Inc. on amount owed, $400.
29. Issued Check No. 955 for the purchase of office supplies, $45.
30. Issued Check No. 956 for salaries, $320.

**Required:**

(a) Using the accounts payable ledger on pages 448 and 449, post the transactions for March 1–15.

(b) Using the general ledger accounts on pages 447 and 448, post all items in the general accounts column for the transactions of March 1–15.

(c) Record the transactions for March 16–31 in the cash payments journal below posting all subsidiary accounts individually on a daily basis in the accounts payable ledger.

(d) Post all items in the General Accounts column individually to the general ledger accounts.

(e) Foot the journal amount columns and prove these totals. Enter the totals and rule the columns. Prepare a schedule to prove the equality of the debit and credit totals, using the ruled form at the top of page 447.

(f) Post the column totals to the general ledger on pages 447 and 448.

(g) Prepare a schedule of accounts payable using the ruled form provided on page 449 and check the total against the balance in the accounts payable control account.

## CASH PAYMENTS JOURNAL

PAGE *16*

| DATE | | CK. NO. | ACCOUNT DEBITED | POST. REF. | GENERAL ACCOUNTS DR. | ACCOUNTS PAYABLE DR. | CASH CR. |
|---|---|---|---|---|---|---|---|
| *19--* *Mar.* | *1* | *941* | *Asian Wholesalers* | | | *160 00* | *160 00* |
| | *3* | *942* | *Office Supplies* | | *35 00* | | *35 00* |
| | *6* | *943* | *Far East Suppliers* | | | *190 00* | *190 00* |
| | *7* | *944* | *Purchases* | | *125 00* | | *125 00* |
| | *9* | *945* | *Advertising Expense* | | *50 00* | | *50 00* |
| | *10* | *946* | *Yen Brothers* | | | *195 00* | *195 00* |
| | *12* | *947* | *Strum, Inc.* | | | *200 00* | *200 00* |
| | *14* | *948* | *Salary Expense* | | *325 00* | | *325 00* |

## GENERAL LEDGER

ACCOUNT *Cash* ACCOUNT NO. 11

| DATE | | ITEM | POST. REF. | DEBIT | CREDIT | BALANCE DEBIT | BALANCE CREDIT |
|---|---|---|---|---|---|---|---|
| 19-- Mar. | 1 | Balance | ✓ | | | 2 9 1 5 00 | |
| | | | | | | | |

ACCOUNT *Office Supplies* ACCOUNT NO. 12

| DATE | | ITEM | POST. REF. | DEBIT | CREDIT | BALANCE DEBIT | BALANCE CREDIT |
|---|---|---|---|---|---|---|---|
| 19-- Mar. | 1 | Balance | ✓ | | | 2 7 0 00 | |
| | | | | | | | |
| | | | | | | | |

ACCOUNT *Office Equipment* ACCOUNT NO. 13

| DATE | | ITEM | POST. REF. | DEBIT | CREDIT | BALANCE DEBIT | BALANCE CREDIT |
|---|---|---|---|---|---|---|---|
| 19-- Mar. | 1 | Balance | ✓ | | | 5 6 0 0 00 | |

ACCOUNT *Accounts Payable* ACCOUNT NO. 21

| DATE | | ITEM | POST. REF. | DEBIT | CREDIT | BALANCE DEBIT | BALANCE CREDIT |
|---|---|---|---|---|---|---|---|
| 19-- Mar. | 1 | Balance | ✓ | | | | 2 0 1 5 00 |
| | | | | | | | |

ACCOUNT *Kay O'Rourke, Capital* ACCOUNT NO. 31

| DATE | | ITEM | POST. REF. | DEBIT | CREDIT | BALANCE DEBIT | BALANCE CREDIT |
|---|---|---|---|---|---|---|---|
| 19-- Mar. | 1 | Balance | ✓ | | | | 6 7 7 0 00 |

(Continued)

ACCOUNT *Kay O'Rourke, Drawing* ACCOUNT NO. *32*

| DATE | | ITEM | POST. REF. | DEBIT | CREDIT | BALANCE | |
|---|---|---|---|---|---|---|---|
| | | | | | | DEBIT | CREDIT |
| | | | | | | | |
| | | | | | | | |

ACCOUNT *Purchases* ACCOUNT NO. *51*

| DATE | | ITEM | POST. REF. | DEBIT | CREDIT | BALANCE | |
|---|---|---|---|---|---|---|---|
| | | | | | | DEBIT | CREDIT |
| | | | | | | | |
| | | | | | | | |

ACCOUNT *Advertising Expense* ACCOUNT NO. *61*

| DATE | | ITEM | POST. REF. | DEBIT | CREDIT | BALANCE | |
|---|---|---|---|---|---|---|---|
| | | | | | | DEBIT | CREDIT |
| | | | | | | | |
| | | | | | | | |

ACCOUNT *Salary Expense* ACCOUNT NO. *62*

| DATE | | ITEM | POST. REF. | DEBIT | CREDIT | BALANCE | |
|---|---|---|---|---|---|---|---|
| | | | | | | DEBIT | CREDIT |
| | | | | | | | |
| | | | | | | | |

ACCOUNT *Miscellaneous Expense* ACCOUNT NO. *63*

| DATE | | ITEM | POST. REF. | DEBIT | CREDIT | BALANCE | |
|---|---|---|---|---|---|---|---|
| | | | | | | DEBIT | CREDIT |
| | | | | | | | |
| | | | | | | | |

## ACCOUNTS PAYABLE LEDGER

NAME *Asian Wholesalers*

ADDRESS *5170 W. 53rd St., New York, NY 10019-2272*

| DATE | | ITEM | POST. REF. | DEBIT | CREDIT | BALANCE |
|---|---|---|---|---|---|---|
| *19--* *Mar.* | *1* | *Balance* | ✓ | | | *410 00* |
| | | | | | | |
| | | | | | | |
| | | | | | | |

NAME *Far East Suppliers*

ADDRESS *5050 Broadway, New York, NY 10034-1918*

| DATE | | ITEM | POST. REF. | DEBIT | CREDIT | BALANCE |
|---|---|---|---|---|---|---|
| 19--<br>Mar. | 1 | Balance | ✓ | | | 290 00 |
| | | | | | | |

NAME *Kelley Company*

ADDRESS *12560 Front Street, New York, NY 10038-9610*

| DATE | | ITEM | POST. REF. | DEBIT | CREDIT | BALANCE |
|---|---|---|---|---|---|---|
| 19--<br>Mar. | 1 | Balance | ✓ | | | 370 00 |
| | | | | | | |

NAME *Strum, Inc.*

ADDRESS *1703 Southside, Buffalo, NY 14210-1181*

| DATE | | ITEM | POST. REF. | DEBIT | CREDIT | BALANCE |
|---|---|---|---|---|---|---|
| 19--<br>Mar. | 1 | Balance | ✓ | | | 750 00 |
| | | | | | | |
| | | | | | | |

NAME *Yen Brothers*

ADDRESS *2020 S. 40th St., New York, NY 10016-6351*

| DATE | | ITEM | POST. REF. | DEBIT | CREDIT | BALANCE |
|---|---|---|---|---|---|---|
| 19--<br>Mar. | 1 | Balance | ✓ | | | 195 00 |
| | | | | | | |

**7B-2.** During the month of January of the current year, Robertson's Auto Parts completed the transactions given below.

Jan. 2. Purchased merchandise from Portland Automotive on account, $180.
2. Purchased store supplies for cash, $90.
3. Purchased merchandise from Jason Distributors on account, $140.
6. Paid Portland Automotive on account, $125.
8. Purchased office supplies from ACE Suppliers on account, $75.
10. Paid miscellaneous expenses, $52.
11. Purchased store equipment from Maine Metals on account, $450.
12. Paid Carol Wholesale Parts on account, $45.
14. Purchased merchandise from Jason Distributors on account, $200.
16. Paid ACE Suppliers on account, $100.
19. Purchased store supplies from ACE Suppliers on account, $160.
20. Purchased merchandise for cash, $120.
23. Paid Maine Metals on account, $150.
25. Purchased merchandise from Carol Wholesale Parts on account, $175.
26. Paid salaries, $460.
28. Paid Jason Distributors on account, $140.
30. Ken Robertson withdrew cash for personal use, $180.
31. Purchased the following from Jason Distributors on account: merchandise, $110; office supplies, $35; and store supplies, $60.

**Required:**

(a) Record transactions for the month of January in the cash payments journal and purchases journal given below and on page 451. Begin with Check No. 707. Be sure to post the subsidiary accounts individually on a daily basis to the accounts payable ledger on pages 454 and 455.

(b) Post all items in the General Accounts column individually to the selected general ledger accounts on pages 452 and 453.

(c) Foot the journal amount columns and prove these totals. Enter the totals and rule the columns. Prepare schedules to prove the equality of the debit and credit totals, using the ruled form on page 455.

(d) Post all special column totals to the general ledger.

(e) Prepare a schedule of accounts payable, using the form at the bottom of page 455 and check the total against the balance in the accounts payable control account.

## CASH PAYMENTS JOURNAL

PAGE 4

| | DATE | CK. NO. | ACCOUNT DEBITED | POST. REF. | GENERAL ACCOUNTS DR. | ACCOUNTS PAYABLE DR. | CASH CR. | |
|---|---|---|---|---|---|---|---|---|
| 1 | | | | | | | | 1 |
| 2 | | | | | | | | 2 |
| 3 | | | | | | | | 3 |
| 4 | | | | | | | | 4 |
| 5 | | | | | | | | 5 |
| 6 | | | | | | | | 6 |
| 7 | | | | | | | | 7 |
| 8 | | | | | | | | 8 |
| 9 | | | | | | | | 9 |
| 10 | | | | | | | | 10 |
| 11 | | | | | | | | 11 |
| 12 | | | | | | | | 12 |
| 13 | | | | | | | | 13 |
| 14 | | | | | | | | 14 |
| 15 | | | | | | | | 15 |

## PURCHASES JOURNAL

PAGE 7

| | DATE | ACCOUNT CREDITED | POST. REF. | ACCOUNTS PAYABLE CR. | PURCHASES DR. | STORE SUPPLIES DR. | OFFICE SUPPLIES DR. | GENERAL ACCOUNTS DR. | | | |
|---|---|---|---|---|---|---|---|---|---|---|---|
| | | | | | | | | ACCOUNT | POST. REF. | AMOUNT | |
| 1 | | | | | | | | | | | 1 |
| 2 | | | | | | | | | | | 2 |
| 3 | | | | | | | | | | | 3 |
| 4 | | | | | | | | | | | 4 |
| 5 | | | | | | | | | | | 5 |
| 6 | | | | | | | | | | | 6 |
| 7 | | | | | | | | | | | 7 |
| 8 | | | | | | | | | | | 8 |
| 9 | | | | | | | | | | | 9 |
| 10 | | | | | | | | | | | 10 |
| 11 | | | | | | | | | | | 11 |
| 12 | | | | | | | | | | | 12 |
| 13 | | | | | | | | | | | 13 |
| 14 | | | | | | | | | | | 14 |
| 15 | | | | | | | | | | | 15 |
| 16 | | | | | | | | | | | 16 |
| 17 | | | | | | | | | | | 17 |
| 18 | | | | | | | | | | | 18 |
| 19 | | | | | | | | | | | 19 |
| 20 | | | | | | | | | | | 20 |
| 21 | | | | | | | | | | | 21 |
| 22 | | | | | | | | | | | 22 |
| 23 | | | | | | | | | | | 23 |

ACCOUNT *Cash* ACCOUNT NO. *11*

| DATE | | ITEM | POST. REF. | DEBIT | CREDIT | BALANCE DEBIT | BALANCE CREDIT |
|---|---|---|---|---|---|---|---|
| 19-- Jan. | 1 | Balance | ✓ | | | 5 1 2 0 00 | |
| | | | | | | | |
| | | | | | | | |

ACCOUNT *Office Supplies* ACCOUNT NO. *12*

| DATE | | ITEM | POST. REF. | DEBIT | CREDIT | BALANCE DEBIT | BALANCE CREDIT |
|---|---|---|---|---|---|---|---|
| 19-- Jan. | 1 | Balance | ✓ | | | 8 0 00 | |
| | | | | | | | |
| | | | | | | | |

ACCOUNT *Store Supplies* ACCOUNT NO. *13*

| DATE | | ITEM | POST. REF. | DEBIT | CREDIT | BALANCE DEBIT | BALANCE CREDIT |
|---|---|---|---|---|---|---|---|
| 19-- Jan. | 1 | Balance | ✓ | | | 2 1 0 00 | |
| | | | | | | | |
| | | | | | | | |
| | | | | | | | |

ACCOUNT *Store Equipment* ACCOUNT NO. *14*

| DATE | | ITEM | POST. REF. | DEBIT | CREDIT | BALANCE DEBIT | BALANCE CREDIT |
|---|---|---|---|---|---|---|---|
| 19-- Jan. | 1 | Balance | ✓ | | | 3 7 5 0 00 | |
| | | | | | | | |
| | | | | | | | |

ACCOUNT *Accounts Payable* ACCOUNT NO. *21*

| DATE | | ITEM | POST. REF. | DEBIT | CREDIT | BALANCE DEBIT | BALANCE CREDIT |
|---|---|---|---|---|---|---|---|
| 19-- Jan. | 1 | Balance | ✓ | | | | 5 7 0 00 |
| | | | | | | | |
| | | | | | | | |
| | | | | | | | |

ACCOUNT *Ken Robertson, Capital* ACCOUNT NO. *31*

| DATE | | ITEM | POST. REF. | DEBIT | CREDIT | BALANCE DEBIT | BALANCE CREDIT |
|---|---|---|---|---|---|---|---|
| 19-- Jan. | 1 | Balance | √ | | | | 8 3 1 0 00 |
| | | | | | | | |

ACCOUNT *Ken Robertson, Drawing* ACCOUNT NO. *32*

| DATE | | ITEM | POST. REF. | DEBIT | CREDIT | BALANCE DEBIT | BALANCE CREDIT |
|---|---|---|---|---|---|---|---|
| | | | | | | | |
| | | | | | | | |

ACCOUNT *Purchases* ACCOUNT NO. *51*

| DATE | | ITEM | POST. REF. | DEBIT | CREDIT | BALANCE DEBIT | BALANCE CREDIT |
|---|---|---|---|---|---|---|---|
| | | | | | | | |
| | | | | | | | |
| | | | | | | | |

ACCOUNT *Salary Expense* ACCOUNT NO. *61*

| DATE | | ITEM | POST. REF. | DEBIT | CREDIT | BALANCE DEBIT | BALANCE CREDIT |
|---|---|---|---|---|---|---|---|
| | | | | | | | |
| | | | | | | | |

ACCOUNT *Miscellaneous Expense* ACCOUNT NO. *62*

| DATE | | ITEM | POST. REF. | DEBIT | CREDIT | BALANCE DEBIT | BALANCE CREDIT |
|---|---|---|---|---|---|---|---|
| | | | | | | | |
| | | | | | | | |

## ACCOUNTS PAYABLE LEDGER

**NAME** *ACE Suppliers*

**ADDRESS** *601 N. Water St., Bangor, ME 04401-7467*

| DATE | | ITEM | POST. REF. | DEBIT | CREDIT | BALANCE |
|---|---|---|---|---|---|---|
| 19--<br>Jan. | 1 | Balance | ✓ | | | 250 00 |
| | | | | | | |
| | | | | | | |
| | | | | | | |
| | | | | | | |

**NAME** *Carol Wholesale Parts*

**ADDRESS** *200 Shackleford Rd., Bangor, ME 04401-6043*

| DATE | | ITEM | POST. REF. | DEBIT | CREDIT | BALANCE |
|---|---|---|---|---|---|---|
| 19--<br>Jan. | 1 | Balance | ✓ | | | 45 00 |
| | | | | | | |
| | | | | | | |
| | | | | | | |

**NAME** *Jason Distributors*

**ADDRESS** *2401 Airport Rd., Bangor, ME 04401-2432*

| DATE | | ITEM | POST. REF. | DEBIT | CREDIT | BALANCE |
|---|---|---|---|---|---|---|
| | | | | | | |
| | | | | | | |
| | | | | | | |
| | | | | | | |
| | | | | | | |

**NAME** *Maine Metals*

**ADDRESS** *300 S. Kingman, Portland, ME 04106-5693*

| DATE | | ITEM | POST. REF. | DEBIT | CREDIT | BALANCE |
|---|---|---|---|---|---|---|
| 19--<br>Jan. | 1 | Balance | ✓ | | | 150 00 |
| | | | | | | |
| | | | | | | |

NAME *Portland Automotive*

ADDRESS *5554 E. 12th St., Portland, ME 04102-3561*

| DATE | | ITEM | POST. REF. | DEBIT | CREDIT | BALANCE |
|---|---|---|---|---|---|---|
| 19--<br>Jan. | 1 | Balance | √ | | | 125 00 |
| | | | | | | |
| | | | | | | |

**7B-3.** The following selected transactions are given for the Zellner Specialty Shop during the month of June of the current year:

June 1. Purchased merchandise on account from Zack Co., $375.
3. Purchased office equipment on account from Sono Co., $500.
4. Paid advertising expense, $70.
6. Sold merchandise on account to Sam Yam, $200.
8. Paid miscellaneous expenses, $48.
9. Terri Zellner invests additional cash in the business, $400.
10. Sold merchandise to Laura Lilly on account, $50.
12. Purchased merchandise for cash, $150.
16. Recorded cash sales, $560.
19. Purchased the following from the Sono Co. on account: office supplies, $40; store supplies, $65.
20. Received payment from Lilly on her account, $50.
22. Paid utilities bill, $80.
23. Purchased office supplies from Timm Co. on account, $75.
24. Paid Sono Co. on account, $75.
25. Zellner withdrew $90 for personal use.
28. Paid salaries, $650.
30. Recorded depreciation expense on office equipment for the month, $125.
30. Recorded cash sales, $700.
30. Paid Zack Co. on account, $125.

**Required:**

(a) Record each transaction in a general journal, using the journal paper provided on pages 457 and 458.

(b) In the Posting Reference column indicate by the following letters, in which special journal each entry could have been recorded: Sales Journal (S); Multicolumn Purchases Journal (P); Cash Receipts Journal (CR); Cash Payments Journal (CP); General Journal (J).

JOURNAL PAGE *18*

| | DATE | | DESCRIPTION | POST. REF. | DEBIT | CREDIT | |
|---|---|---|---|---|---|---|---|
| 1 | | | | | | | 1 |
| 2 | | | | | | | 2 |
| 3 | | | | | | | 3 |
| 4 | | | | | | | 4 |
| 5 | | | | | | | 5 |
| 6 | | | | | | | 6 |
| 7 | | | | | | | 7 |
| 8 | | | | | | | 8 |
| 9 | | | | | | | 9 |
| 10 | | | | | | | 10 |
| 11 | | | | | | | 11 |
| 12 | | | | | | | 12 |
| 13 | | | | | | | 13 |
| 14 | | | | | | | 14 |
| 15 | | | | | | | 15 |
| 16 | | | | | | | 16 |
| 17 | | | | | | | 17 |
| 18 | | | | | | | 18 |
| 19 | | | | | | | 19 |
| 20 | | | | | | | 20 |
| 21 | | | | | | | 21 |
| 22 | | | | | | | 22 |
| 23 | | | | | | | 23 |
| 24 | | | | | | | 24 |
| 25 | | | | | | | 25 |
| 26 | | | | | | | 26 |
| 27 | | | | | | | 27 |
| 28 | | | | | | | 28 |
| 29 | | | | | | | 29 |
| 30 | | | | | | | 30 |
| 31 | | | | | | | 31 |
| 32 | | | | | | | 32 |
| 33 | | | | | | | 33 |
| 34 | | | | | | | 34 |

JOURNAL PAGE 19

| DATE | | DESCRIPTION | POST. REF. | DEBIT | CREDIT |
|---|---|---|---|---|---|

**Perfect Score** 20 **Name** ____________ Assignment 8-A

**Student's Score** ___ **Date** ____________ **Class** ________

## RETURNS AND ALLOWANCES

**Instructions.** Complete each statement and answer each question below by writing your answer in the space at the right.

| No. | Item | Answer | For Scoring |
|---|---|---|---|
| 1 | Sales of merchandise on account are recorded in the (?) journal........... | | 1 |
| 2 | If goods purchased from a supplier are found to be slightly damaged and the supplier grants a reduction in the invoice price, this is recorded on the books of the buyer as a(n)............................................ | | 2 |
| 3 | When merchandise purchased on account is returned, the buyer will notify the seller by issuing a(n)............................................ | | 3 |
| 4 | Transactions involving cash received are recorded in the (?) journal.... | | 4 |
| 5 | The total of the amount column in the sales returns and allowances journal is posted as a *debit* to............................................ | | 5 |
| 6 | The total of the amount column in the sales returns and allowances journal is posted as a *credit* to............................................ | | 6 |
| 7 | Cash purchases of merchandise are recorded in the (?) journal............. | | 7 |
| 8 | The total of the amount column in the purchases returns and allowances journal is posted as a *debit* to............................................ | | 8 |
| 9 | The total of the amount column in the purchases returns and allowances journal is posted as a *credit* to............................................ | | 9 |
| 10 | Purchases of merchandise on account are recorded in the (?) journal.... | | 10 |

Below are listed several books of original entry. Indicate the journal in which each transaction should be recorded by placing the letters representing the appropriate journal in the answer column:

CP Cash payments journal
CR Cash receipts journal
P Purchases journal (multicolumn)
S Sales journal
J General journal
PR Purchases returns and allowances journal
SR Sales returns and allowances journal

| No. | Item | Answer | For Scoring |
|---|---|---|---|
| 11 | Purchased merchandise on account............................................ | | 11 |
| 12 | Gave customer credit on account for merchandise returned.................. | | 12 |
| 13 | Owner invested additional cash in the business.................................. | | 13 |
| 14 | Sold merchandise on account............................................ | | 14 |
| 15 | Paid cash to customer for merchandise returned.................................. | | 15 |
| 16 | Purchased store equipment on account............................................ | | 16 |
| 17 | Received credit on account from supplier for allowance on merchandise damaged............................................ | | 17 |
| 18 | Owner withdrew cash for personal use............................................ | | 18 |
| 19 | Purchased office supplies for cash............................................ | | 19 |
| 20 | Sold merchandise for cash............................................ | | 20 |

**8A-1.** Wanda Chavez owns a boating supply company in Tampa, Florida, called Anchors Aweigh. Transactions involving sales of merchandise on account, cash receipts, and related returns and allowances during the month of May are described below.

May 2. Sold merchandise on account to Diane Trout, $170; Sales Invoice No. 52.
4. Sold merchandise on account to Betty Blue, $68; Sales Invoice No. 53.
7. Sold merchandise on account to Al Peeler, $145; Sales Invoice No. 54.
8. Issued Credit Memorandum No. 13 to Diane Trout for two life jackets returned from the sale on May 2, $42.
10. Sold merchandise to Dave Fitch on account, $163; Sales Invoice No. 55.
13. Received payment on account from Diane Trout, $128.
15. Recorded cash sales, $487.
19. Issued Credit Memorandum No. 14 to Al Peeler for merchandise returned from the sale on May 7, $20.
24. Sold merchandise on account to Dave Fitch, $65; Sales Invoice No. 56.
26. Received payment on account from Betty Blue, $68.
27. Issued Credit Memorandum No. 15 to Dave Fitch for an allowance on damaged merchandise sold on May 10, $33.
28. Sold merchandise on account to Diane Trout, $48; Sales Invoice No. 57.
29. Received payment on account from Al Peeler, $125.
31. Recorded cash sales, $507.

**Required:**

(a) Open accounts in the general ledger in the following order on the forms provided on page 463: Cash (11); Accounts Receivable (12); Sales (41); Sales Returns and Allowances (41.1). Open the following accounts in the accounts receivable ledger on the forms provided on pages 463 and 464: Betty Blue, 1916 Gulf Line Drive, Tampa, FL 33619-3619; Dave Fitch, 2719 Crestwood Place, St. Petersburg, FL 33713-2835; Al Peeler, 320 Mimosa, Clearwater, FL 33516-8687; Diane Trout, 936 Sailmaker, Tampa, FL 33618-4733.

(b) Record the transactions for the month in the proper journals provided on page 461, posting all subsidiary customers' accounts individually on a daily basis in the accounts receivable ledger.

(c) Foot the journal amount columns and prove these totals. Enter the totals and rule the columns. Prepare a schedule to prove the equality of the cash receipts journal debit and credit totals, using the ruled form below.

(d) Post all special column totals to the general ledger.

(e) Prepare a schedule of accounts receivable, using the form on page 464, and check the total against the balance in the accounts receivable control account.

## SALES JOURNAL

PAGE *1*

| | DATE | | ACCOUNT DEBITED | SALE NO. | POST. REF. | ACCTS. REC. DR. SALES CR. | |
|---|---|---|---|---|---|---|---|
| 1 | | | | | | | 1 |
| 2 | | | | | | | 2 |
| 3 | | | | | | | 3 |
| 4 | | | | | | | 4 |
| 5 | | | | | | | 5 |
| 6 | | | | | | | 6 |
| 7 | | | | | | | 7 |
| 8 | | | | | | | 8 |
| 9 | | | | | | | 9 |
| 10 | | | | | | | 10 |

## CASH RECEIPTS JOURNAL

PAGE *1*

| | DATE | | ACCOUNT CREDITED | POST. REF. | GENERAL ACCOUNTS CR. | SALES CR. | ACCOUNTS REC. CR. | CASH DR. | |
|---|---|---|---|---|---|---|---|---|---|
| 1 | | | | | | | | | 1 |
| 2 | | | | | | | | | 2 |
| 3 | | | | | | | | | 3 |
| 4 | | | | | | | | | 4 |
| 5 | | | | | | | | | 5 |
| 6 | | | | | | | | | 6 |
| 7 | | | | | | | | | 7 |
| 8 | | | | | | | | | 8 |

## SALES RETURNS AND ALLOWANCES JOURNAL

PAGE *1*

| | DATE | | CR. MEMO NO. | ACCOUNT CREDITED | POST. REF. | SALES RET. & ALLOW. DR. ACCTS. REC. CR. | |
|---|---|---|---|---|---|---|---|
| 1 | | | | | | | 1 |
| 2 | | | | | | | 2 |
| 3 | | | | | | | 3 |
| 4 | | | | | | | 4 |
| 5 | | | | | | | 5 |
| 6 | | | | | | | 6 |

*(Page not used.)*

## GENERAL LEDGER

ACCOUNT | ACCOUNT NO.

| DATE | | ITEM | POST. REF. | DEBIT | CREDIT | BALANCE | |
|---|---|---|---|---|---|---|---|
| | | | | | | DEBIT | CREDIT |
| | | | | | | | |
| | | | | | | | |

ACCOUNT | ACCOUNT NO.

| DATE | | ITEM | POST. REF. | DEBIT | CREDIT | BALANCE | |
|---|---|---|---|---|---|---|---|
| | | | | | | DEBIT | CREDIT |
| | | | | | | | |
| | | | | | | | |
| | | | | | | | |
| | | | | | | | |

ACCOUNT | ACCOUNT NO.

| DATE | | ITEM | POST. REF. | DEBIT | CREDIT | BALANCE | |
|---|---|---|---|---|---|---|---|
| | | | | | | DEBIT | CREDIT |
| | | | | | | | |
| | | | | | | | |
| | | | | | | | |

ACCOUNT | ACCOUNT NO.

| DATE | | ITEM | POST. REF. | DEBIT | CREDIT | BALANCE | |
|---|---|---|---|---|---|---|---|
| | | | | | | DEBIT | CREDIT |
| | | | | | | | |
| | | | | | | | |

## ACCOUNTS RECEIVABLE LEDGER

NAME

ADDRESS

| DATE | | ITEM | POST. REF. | DEBIT | CREDIT | BALANCE |
|---|---|---|---|---|---|---|
| | | | | | | |
| | | | | | | |
| | | | | | | |
| | | | | | | |

(Continued)

NAME

ADDRESS

| DATE | | ITEM | POST. REF. | DEBIT | CREDIT | BALANCE |
|---|---|---|---|---|---|---|
| | | | | | | |
| | | | | | | |
| | | | | | | |
| | | | | | | |
| | | | | | | |

NAME

ADDRESS

| DATE | | ITEM | POST. REF. | DEBIT | CREDIT | BALANCE |
|---|---|---|---|---|---|---|
| | | | | | | |
| | | | | | | |
| | | | | | | |
| | | | | | | |
| | | | | | | |

NAME

ADDRESS

| DATE | | ITEM | POST. REF. | DEBIT | CREDIT | BALANCE |
|---|---|---|---|---|---|---|
| | | | | | | |
| | | | | | | |
| | | | | | | |
| | | | | | | |
| | | | | | | |

**8A-2.** Carol Lewis owns and operates a drapery and curtain shop. Below are selected transactions related to purchases, cash payments, and purchases returns and allowances of Lewis Drapery Shop for the month of May of the current year.

May 1. Purchased merchandise from Tracy Mills on account, $1,200.
3. Purchased merchandise on account from Hana Curtain Co., $960.
5. Purchased store supplies for cash, $85; Check No. 933.
6. Paid rent expense for the month, $150; Check No. 934.
9. Purchased the following on account from Autry Supply Co.: store equipment, $400; store supplies, $92.
11. Returned merchandise to Hana Curtain Co. for credit, $40; Debit Memorandum No. 42.
14. Paid advertising expense, $40; Check No. 935.
15. Purchased merchandise from Triangle Company on account, $1,650.
15. Paid Hana Curtain Co. on account, $920; Check No. 936.
17. Returned store supplies to Autry Supply Co. for credit, $15; Debit Memorandum No. 43.
19. Purchased merchandise for cash, $400; Check No. 937.
20. Paid Tracy Mills on account, $600; Check No. 938.
22. Returned merchandise for credit on account to Triangle Company, $150; Debit Memo No. 44.
23. Paid Autry Supply Co. on account, $477; Check No. 939.
25. Purchased merchandise on account from Hana Curtain Co., $1,325.
26. Paid Triangle Company on account, $200; Check No. 940.
28. Purchased merchandise from Tracy Mills on account, $750.
30. Purchased store supplies from Autry Supply Co. on account, $150.
30. Lewis withdrew $200 for personal use; Check No. 941.

**Required:**

(a) Open the general ledger accounts in the following order on the forms provided below and on pages 466 and 467: Cash (11); Store Supplies (12); Store Equipment (13); Accounts Payable (21); Carol Lewis, Drawing (32); Purchases (51); Purchases Returns and Allowances (51.1); Advertising Expense (61); Rent Expense (62).

(b) Open the accounts payable ledger accounts in the following order on the forms provided on pages 467 and 468: Autry Supply Co., 1222 Pacific, Seattle, WA 98188-1725; Hana Curtain Co., 35700 I-5, Tacoma, WA 98444-8250; Tracy Mills, 5301 Loop 7, Seattle, WA 98122-1279; Triangle Company, 4036 Industrial Blvd., Seattle, WA 98144-3253.

(c) Record the transactions for the month in the proper journals provided on pages 469 and 470, posting all subsidiary accounts individually on a daily basis in the accounts payable ledger.

(d) Post all items in the General Accounts column individually to the general ledger accounts.

(e) Foot the proper journal amount columns and prove these totals. Enter the totals and rule the columns. Prepare a schedule to prove the equality of the debit and credit totals in both the cash payments journal and the purchases journal, using the ruled form on page 468.

(f) Post all special column totals to the general ledger.

(g) Prepare a schedule of accounts payable, using the form at the bottom of page 468 and check the total against the balance in the accounts payable control account.

## GENERAL LEDGER

ACCOUNT ACCOUNT NO.

| DATE | ITEM | POST. REF. | DEBIT | CREDIT | BALANCE | |
|---|---|---|---|---|---|---|
| | | | | | DEBIT | CREDIT |
| | | | | | | |
| | | | | | | |
| | | | | | | |

ACCOUNT ACCOUNT NO.

| DATE | ITEM | POST. REF. | DEBIT | CREDIT | BALANCE | |
|---|---|---|---|---|---|---|
| | | | | | DEBIT | CREDIT |
| | | | | | | |
| | | | | | | |
| | | | | | | |

*(Continued)*

ACCOUNT ACCOUNT NO.

| DATE | ITEM | POST. REF. | DEBIT | CREDIT | BALANCE | |
|---|---|---|---|---|---|---|
| | | | | | DEBIT | CREDIT |
| | | | | | | |
| | | | | | | |
| | | | | | | |

ACCOUNT ACCOUNT NO.

| DATE | ITEM | POST. REF. | DEBIT | CREDIT | BALANCE | |
|---|---|---|---|---|---|---|
| | | | | | DEBIT | CREDIT |
| | | | | | | |
| | | | | | | |
| | | | | | | |
| | | | | | | |
| | | | | | | |

ACCOUNT ACCOUNT NO.

| DATE | ITEM | POST. REF. | DEBIT | CREDIT | BALANCE | |
|---|---|---|---|---|---|---|
| | | | | | DEBIT | CREDIT |
| | | | | | | |
| | | | | | | |

ACCOUNT ACCOUNT NO.

| DATE | ITEM | POST. REF. | DEBIT | CREDIT | BALANCE | |
|---|---|---|---|---|---|---|
| | | | | | DEBIT | CREDIT |
| | | | | | | |
| | | | | | | |
| | | | | | | |

ACCOUNT ACCOUNT NO.

| DATE | ITEM | POST. REF. | DEBIT | CREDIT | BALANCE | |
|---|---|---|---|---|---|---|
| | | | | | DEBIT | CREDIT |
| | | | | | | |
| | | | | | | |

ACCOUNT ACCOUNT NO.

| DATE | ITEM | POST. REF. | DEBIT | CREDIT | BALANCE | |
|---|---|---|---|---|---|---|
| | | | | | DEBIT | CREDIT |
| | | | | | | |
| | | | | | | |

ACCOUNT ACCOUNT NO.

| DATE | | ITEM | POST. REF. | DEBIT | CREDIT | BALANCE | |
|---|---|---|---|---|---|---|---|
| | | | | | | DEBIT | CREDIT |
| | | | | | | | |
| | | | | | | | |

## ACCOUNTS PAYABLE LEDGER

NAME

ADDRESS

| DATE | | ITEM | POST. REF. | DEBIT | CREDIT | BALANCE |
|---|---|---|---|---|---|---|
| | | | | | | |
| | | | | | | |
| | | | | | | |
| | | | | | | |
| | | | | | | |

NAME

ADDRESS

| DATE | | ITEM | POST. REF. | DEBIT | CREDIT | BALANCE |
|---|---|---|---|---|---|---|
| | | | | | | |
| | | | | | | |
| | | | | | | |
| | | | | | | |
| | | | | | | |

NAME

ADDRESS

| DATE | | ITEM | POST. REF. | DEBIT | CREDIT | BALANCE |
|---|---|---|---|---|---|---|
| | | | | | | |
| | | | | | | |
| | | | | | | |
| | | | | | | |
| | | | | | | |

*(Continued)*

NAME

ADDRESS

| DATE | | ITEM | POST. REF. | DEBIT | CREDIT | BALANCE |
|---|---|---|---|---|---|---|
| | | | | | | |
| | | | | | | |
| | | | | | | |
| | | | | | | |

## CASH PAYMENTS JOURNAL

PAGE *18*

| | DATE | | CK. NO. | ACCOUNT DEBITED | POST. REF. | GENERAL ACCOUNTS DR. | ACCOUNTS PAYABLE DR. | CASH CR. | |
|---|---|---|---|---|---|---|---|---|---|
| 1 | | | | | | | | | 1 |
| 2 | | | | | | | | | 2 |
| 3 | | | | | | | | | 3 |
| 4 | | | | | | | | | 4 |
| 5 | | | | | | | | | 5 |
| 6 | | | | | | | | | 6 |
| 7 | | | | | | | | | 7 |
| 8 | | | | | | | | | 8 |
| 9 | | | | | | | | | 9 |
| 10 | | | | | | | | | 10 |
| 11 | | | | | | | | | 11 |
| 12 | | | | | | | | | 12 |
| 13 | | | | | | | | | 13 |
| 14 | | | | | | | | | 14 |

## PURCHASES RETURNS AND ALLOWANCES JOURNAL

PAGE *10*

| | DATE | | DEBIT MEMO. NO. | ACCOUNT DEBITED | POST. REF. | ACCTS. PAY. DR. PURCH. RET. & ALLOW. CR. | |
|---|---|---|---|---|---|---|---|
| 1 | | | | | | | 1 |
| 2 | | | | | | | 2 |
| 3 | | | | | | | 3 |
| 4 | | | | | | | 4 |
| 5 | | | | | | | 5 |
| 6 | | | | | | | 6 |
| 7 | | | | | | | 7 |

## JOURNAL

PAGE *23*

| | DATE | | DESCRIPTION | POST. REF. | DEBIT | CREDIT | |
|---|---|---|---|---|---|---|---|
| 1 | | | | | | | 1 |
| 2 | | | | | | | 2 |
| 3 | | | | | | | 3 |
| 4 | | | | | | | 4 |

# PURCHASES JOURNAL

PAGE *21*

| | DATE | | ACCOUNT CREDITED | POST. REF. | ACCOUNTS PAYABLE CR. | PURCHASES DR. | STORE SUPPLIES DR. | GENERAL ACCOUNTS DR. | | | |
|---|---|---|---|---|---|---|---|---|---|---|---|
| | | | | | | | | ACCOUNT | POST. REF. | AMOUNT | |
| 1 | | | | | | | | | | | 1 |
| 2 | | | | | | | | | | | 2 |
| 3 | | | | | | | | | | | 3 |
| 4 | | | | | | | | | | | 4 |
| 5 | | | | | | | | | | | 5 |
| 6 | | | | | | | | | | | 6 |
| 7 | | | | | | | | | | | 7 |
| 8 | | | | | | | | | | | 8 |
| 9 | | | | | | | | | | | 9 |
| 10 | | | | | | | | | | | 10 |
| 11 | | | | | | | | | | | 11 |
| 12 | | | | | | | | | | | 12 |
| 13 | | | | | | | | | | | 13 |
| 14 | | | | | | | | | | | 14 |
| 15 | | | | | | | | | | | 15 |
| 16 | | | | | | | | | | | 16 |
| 17 | | | | | | | | | | | 17 |
| 18 | | | | | | | | | | | 18 |
| 19 | | | | | | | | | | | 19 |
| 20 | | | | | | | | | | | 20 |
| 21 | | | | | | | | | | | 21 |
| 22 | | | | | | | | | | | 22 |
| 23 | | | | | | | | | | | 23 |

**8A-3.** Mark Mayo owns a sporting goods store in Madison, Wisconsin. During the month of November of the current year, Mayo completed the following selected transactions.

Nov. 1. Sold skis and poles to Bill Sample on account, $210.
2. Received $125 from Sherry Brown on account.
4. Borrowed $500 from First State Bank on a 60-day note payable.
5. Withdrew cash for personal use, $350.
8. Purchased caps, jackets, and gloves (merchandise) from Madison Industries on account, $400.
9. Paid rent expense for November, $230.
11. Issued Credit Memorandum No. 21 to Jon Robinson on account for snow boots returned because they did not fit properly, $105.
12. Received a check from Dana Stewart for $150 note receivable plus interest of $8.
14. Paid Marker Supplies for office supplies which had been purchased on account in October, $200.
15. Invested an additional $1,000 in the business.
16. Purchased office equipment on account from Home Equipment Company, $800.
18. Recorded cash sales, $1,135.
24. Returned one dozen gloves to Madison Industries for credit on account, $96.
26. Paid cash to T. M. Woolet, a customer, for tennis shoes returned due to defect in workmanship, $40.
29. Received cash from Humm Company for ski goggles returned for cash, $150.

**Required:** Record each transaction in the two-column general journals below and on page 472. On the line where the explanation is normally recorded, indicate in which special journal each entry would be recorded.

JOURNAL PAGE

| DATE | | DESCRIPTION | POST. REF. | DEBIT | CREDIT |
|---|---|---|---|---|---|

## JOURNAL

PAGE

| DATE | | DESCRIPTION | POST. REF. | DEBIT | CREDIT |
|---|---|---|---|---|---|

**Perfect Score** **20** **Name** ______________________

**Student's Score** ____ **Date** ______________ **Class** ________

**DISCOUNTS AND TRANSPORTATION COSTS**

**Instructions.** Complete each statement and answer each question below by writing your answer in the space at the right.

| No. | Item | Answer | For Scoring |
|---|---|---|---|
| 1 | The agreement between buyer and seller as to when payment for the goods will be made is called the ........ | | 1 |
| 2 | The deduction from the invoice price allowed for prompt payment is called a ........ | | 2 |
| 3 | A cash discount on the books of the buyer is called a(n) ........ | | 3 |
| 4 | A cash discount on the books of the seller is referred to as a(n) ........ | | 4 |
| 5 | When payment is required at the time the goods are delivered, the terms of the sale are said to be ........ | | 5 |
| 6 | If the purchaser is allowed a period of time in which to pay, this period is called the ........ | | 6 |
| 7 | A retail credit plan which allows the customer to pay a certain percentage of the bill plus a finance charge each month is called a(n) .... | | 7 |
| 8 | If payment is due 45 days from the invoice date without a discount, the terms would be shown on the invoice as ........ | | 8 |
| 9 | When the buyer is responsible for paying the transportation costs, the amount paid is debited to the account ........ | | 9 |
| 10 | On March 9, Bees Co. sells merchandise to Faye Dunn for $400 on account, terms 4/10, n/30. How much cash will be required to settle the account if it is paid on March 18? ........ | | 10 |
| 11 | How much cash will be required if the invoice in No. 10 is paid on March 25? ........ | | 11 |
| 12–14 | The following account of Lisa Glenn appears in the accounts receivable subsidiary ledger of Gideon Co. All sales made by Gideon are subject to terms of 3/10, n/30. (see ledger below) What amount should Gideon receive from Glenn if Glenn pays her account in full on: ........ April 16? | | 12 |
| | April 20? | | 13 |
| | April 25? | | 14 |
| 15 | A reduction from the list price quoted by some manufacturers and wholesalers, used as a convenient means of making price changes without printing new catalogs is called a(n) ........ | | 15 |
| 16 | The term COD means ........ | | 16 |

Ledger for items 12–14:

| Date | Post Ref. | Debit | Credit | Balance |
|---|---|---|---|---|
| Apr. 7 | S8 | 250 | | 250 |
| 11 | S8 | 100 | | 350 |
| 15 | S8 | 150 | | 500 |

*(Continued)*

| No. | Item | Answer | For Scoring |
|---|---|---|---|
| 17 | The term FOB means ........ | | 17 |
| 18 | If the terms are FOB destination, the freight charges will be paid by the........ | | 18 |
| 19 | If the terms are FOB shipping point, the freight charges will be paid by the ........ | | 19 |
| 20 | When the seller is responsible for paying the transportation costs, the amount paid is debited to the (?) account ........ | | 20 |

**8B-1.** The following is a list of the sales on account made by the Rainbow Company during May of the current year.

| *Date of Invoice* | *List Price* | *Trade Discount* | *Credit Terms* | *Date Paid* | *Selling Price* | *Sales Discount Allowed* | *Amount Received* |
|---|---|---|---|---|---|---|---|
| May 4 | $ 800 | 40% | 2/10 EOM | June 5 | | | |
| May 9 | 1,500 | 50% | 3/10, n/30 | May 20 | | | |
| May 16 | 450 | 30% | 2/10 EOM, n/60 | June 18 | | | |
| May 24 | 1,200 | 25% | 4/20, n/40 | June 12 | | | |
| May 28 | 500 | — | 5/10, n/30 | June 7 | | | |

**Required:**

(a) Compute the selling price, amount of the sales discount, and the amount to be received for each of the sales for Rainbow and record your answers in the appropriate columns above.

(b) Assuming the merchandise sold on May 24 above was sold to Ivan Hall, give the entries required for the Rainbow Co. to record the sale on May 24 and the receipt of payment on June 12, using the journal paper provided below.

JOURNAL PAGE

| | DATE | | DESCRIPTION | POST. REF. | DEBIT | CREDIT | |
|---|---|---|---|---|---|---|---|
| 1 | | | | | | | 1 |
| 2 | | | | | | | 2 |
| 3 | | | | | | | 3 |
| 4 | | | | | | | 4 |
| 5 | | | | | | | 5 |
| 6 | | | | | | | 6 |
| 7 | | | | | | | 7 |
| 8 | | | | | | | 8 |
| 9 | | | | | | | 9 |
| 10 | | | | | | | 10 |
| 11 | | | | | | | 11 |
| 12 | | | | | | | 12 |
| 13 | | | | | | | 13 |
| 14 | | | | | | | 14 |
| 15 | | | | | | | 15 |

**8B-2.** Transactions of the Mississippi Rice Mill related to sales and cash receipts during October of the current year are presented below. The terms of sales on account are 3/10, n/30. Selected general ledger accounts and their balances are given on pages 477 and 478. The accounts receivable subsidiary ledger accounts and their balances are given on pages 478 and 479.

Oct. 1. Sold merchandise to Pope's Restaurants on account, \$670, Invoice No. 603.
3. Jim Rupard, the owner, invested an additional \$950 in the business.
3. Merchandise of \$35 was returned by Pope's Restaurants on Invoice No. 603; Credit Memorandum No. 40.
6. Received payment from Delta Wholesalers for the Sept. 26 purchase.
7. Sold office supplies to the plant next door for cash as a convenience to them, \$25.
8. Received payment from Lucky's Markets for the purchase made on Sept. 28.
10. Received payment from Johnson Groceries for the purchase made on Sept. 30.
13. Sold merchandise on account to Delta Wholesalers for \$500; Invoice No. 604.
14. Sold merchandise on account to Lucky's Markets for \$440; Invoice No. 605.
15. Recorded cash sales, \$1,540.
16. Received payment from Pope's Restaurants for the purchase on Sept. 18.
17. Delta Wholesalers returned damaged goods purchased on Oct. 13 for credit on account, \$50; Credit Memorandum No. 41.
19. Sold merchandise on account to Johnson Groceries, \$910; Invoice No. 606.
22. Received payment from Delta Wholesalers for the purchase on Oct. 13.
24. Received payment from Lucky's Markets for the purchase on Oct. 14.
26. Johnson Groceries returned \$20 of merchandise for credit on account; Credit Memorandum No. 42.
27. Sold merchandise on account to Delta Wholesalers for \$640; Invoice No. 607.
29. Johnson Groceries paid for purchase made on Oct. 19.
30. Recorded cash sales, \$2,070.
31. Sold merchandise to Johnson Groceries on account, \$700; Invoice No. 608.

**Required:**

(a) Record the transactions for the month in the proper journals provided below and on page 476, posting all subsidiary accounts individually on a daily basis in the accounts receivable ledger on pages 478 and 479.

(b) Post all items in the General Accounts column individually to the general ledger accounts on pages 477 and 478.

(c) Foot the cash receipts journal amount columns and prove these totals. Enter the totals and rule the columns. Prepare a schedule to prove the equality of the debit and credit totals, using the ruled form on page 480.

(d) Post all special column totals to the general ledger.

(e) Prepare a schedule of accounts receivable, using the form on page 476 and check the total against the balance in the accounts receivable control account.

## SALES JOURNAL

PAGE 9

| | DATE | | ACCOUNT DEBITED | SALE NO. | POST. REF. | ACCTS. REC. DR. SALES CR. | |
|---|---|---|---|---|---|---|---|
| 1 | | | | | | | 1 |
| 2 | | | | | | | 2 |
| 3 | | | | | | | 3 |
| 4 | | | | | | | 4 |
| 5 | | | | | | | 5 |
| 6 | | | | | | | 6 |
| 7 | | | | | | | 7 |
| 8 | | | | | | | 8 |
| 9 | | | | | | | 9 |
| 10 | | | | | | | 10 |
| 11 | | | | | | | 11 |
| 12 | | | | | | | 12 |

## CASH RECEIPTS JOURNAL

PAGE 25

| | DATE | | ACCOUNT CREDITED | POST. REF. | GENERAL ACCOUNTS CR. | SALES CR. | ACCOUNTS REC. CR. | SALES DISCOUNT DR. | CASH DR. | |
|---|---|---|---|---|---|---|---|---|---|---|
| 1 | | | | | | | | | | 1 |
| 2 | | | | | | | | | | 2 |
| 3 | | | | | | | | | | 3 |
| 4 | | | | | | | | | | 4 |
| 5 | | | | | | | | | | 5 |
| 6 | | | | | | | | | | 6 |
| 7 | | | | | | | | | | 7 |
| 8 | | | | | | | | | | 8 |
| 9 | | | | | | | | | | 9 |
| 10 | | | | | | | | | | 10 |
| 11 | | | | | | | | | | 11 |
| 12 | | | | | | | | | | 12 |
| 13 | | | | | | | | | | 13 |
| 14 | | | | | | | | | | 14 |

## SALES RETURNS AND ALLOWANCES JOURNAL

PAGE 2

| | DATE | | CR. MEMO NO. | ACCOUNT CREDITED | POST. REF. | SALES RET. & ALLOW. DR. ACCTS. REC. CR. | |
|---|---|---|---|---|---|---|---|
| 1 | | | | | | | 1 |
| 2 | | | | | | | 2 |
| 3 | | | | | | | 3 |
| 4 | | | | | | | 4 |
| 5 | | | | | | | 5 |
| 6 | | | | | | | 6 |

# GENERAL LEDGER

ACCOUNT *Cash* ACCOUNT NO. *11*

| DATE | | ITEM | POST. REF. | DEBIT | CREDIT | BALANCE DEBIT | BALANCE CREDIT |
|---|---|---|---|---|---|---|---|
| 19-- Oct. | 1 | Balance | √ | | | 1 5 8 0 00 | |
| | | | | | | | |
| | | | | | | | |
| | | | | | | | |
| | | | | | | | |
| | | | | | | | |

ACCOUNT *Accounts Receivable* ACCOUNT NO. *12*

| DATE | | ITEM | POST. REF. | DEBIT | CREDIT | BALANCE DEBIT | BALANCE CREDIT |
|---|---|---|---|---|---|---|---|
| 19-- Oct. | 1 | Balance | √ | | | 2 7 9 0 00 | |
| | | | | | | | |
| | | | | | | | |
| | | | | | | | |
| | | | | | | | |
| | | | | | | | |

ACCOUNT *Office Supplies* ACCOUNT NO. *13*

| DATE | | ITEM | POST. REF. | DEBIT | CREDIT | BALANCE DEBIT | BALANCE CREDIT |
|---|---|---|---|---|---|---|---|
| 19-- Oct. | 1 | Balance | √ | | | 2 2 5 00 | |
| | | | | | | | |
| | | | | | | | |
| | | | | | | | |
| | | | | | | | |
| | | | | | | | |

ACCOUNT *Jim Rupard, Capital* ACCOUNT NO. *31*

| DATE | | ITEM | POST. REF. | DEBIT | CREDIT | BALANCE DEBIT | BALANCE CREDIT |
|---|---|---|---|---|---|---|---|
| 19-- Oct. | 1 | Balance | √ | | | | 4 5 9 5 00 |
| | | | | | | | |
| | | | | | | | |
| | | | | | | | |
| | | | | | | | |

*(Continued)*

ACCOUNT *Sales* ACCOUNT NO. *41*

| DATE | | ITEM | POST. REF. | DEBIT | CREDIT | BALANCE DEBIT | BALANCE CREDIT |
|---|---|---|---|---|---|---|---|
| | | | | | | | |
| | | | | | | | |
| | | | | | | | |
| | | | | | | | |
| | | | | | | | |

ACCOUNT *Sales Returns and Allowances* ACCOUNT NO. *41.1*

| DATE | | ITEM | POST. REF. | DEBIT | CREDIT | BALANCE DEBIT | BALANCE CREDIT |
|---|---|---|---|---|---|---|---|
| | | | | | | | |
| | | | | | | | |
| | | | | | | | |
| | | | | | | | |
| | | | | | | | |

ACCOUNT *Sales Discount* ACCOUNT NO. *41.2*

| DATE | | ITEM | POST. REF. | DEBIT | CREDIT | BALANCE DEBIT | BALANCE CREDIT |
|---|---|---|---|---|---|---|---|
| | | | | | | | |
| | | | | | | | |
| | | | | | | | |
| | | | | | | | |
| | | | | | | | |

## ACCOUNTS RECEIVABLE LEDGER

NAME *Delta Wholesalers*

ADDRESS *5119 Southmont Rd., Greenville, MS 38701-1123*

| DATE | | ITEM | POST. REF. | DEBIT | CREDIT | BALANCE |
|---|---|---|---|---|---|---|
| *19--* *Sept.* | *26* | | *S8* | *1 300 00* | | *1 300 00* |
| | | | | | | |
| | | | | | | |
| | | | | | | |
| | | | | | | |
| | | | | | | |
| | | | | | | |
| | | | | | | |

NAME *Johnson Groceries*

ADDRESS *500 N. Main, Jackson, MS 39213-7896*

| DATE | | ITEM | POST. REF. | DEBIT | CREDIT | BALANCE |
|---|---|---|---|---|---|---|
| 19-- Sept. | 30 | | S8 | 620 00 | | 620 00 |
| | | | | | | |
| | | | | | | |
| | | | | | | |
| | | | | | | |
| | | | | | | |
| | | | | | | |
| | | | | | | |

NAME *Lucky's Markets*

ADDRESS *1900 Crump Blvd., Memphis, TN 38128-1225*

| DATE | | ITEM | POST. REF. | DEBIT | CREDIT | BALANCE |
|---|---|---|---|---|---|---|
| 19-- Sept. | 28 | | S8 | 360 00 | | 360 00 |
| | | | | | | |
| | | | | | | |
| | | | | | | |
| | | | | | | |
| | | | | | | |
| | | | | | | |

NAME *Pope's Restaurants*

ADDRESS *211 Culberhouse, Jackson, MS 39209-7845*

| DATE | | ITEM | POST. REF. | DEBIT | CREDIT | BALANCE |
|---|---|---|---|---|---|---|
| 19-- Sept. | 18 | | S8 | 510 00 | | 510 00 |
| | | | | | | |
| | | | | | | |
| | | | | | | |
| | | | | | | |
| | | | | | | |
| | | | | | | |
| | | | | | | |

**8B-3.** On December 1, the Sandy Company purchased $800 of merchandise on account from the Philip Company, terms 4/10, n/30. The goods were shipped FOB shipping point. The freight charge of $36 was paid by Philip Company and added to the invoice mailed to Sandy Company.

**Required:**

(a) Prepare the entries on the books of Sandy Company, in the general journal form below, to record the following transactions:

Dec. 1. Purchased the goods from Philip Company, invoice includes the $36 freight charge.
10. Paid the invoice less discount.

JOURNAL PAGE

| | DATE | | DESCRIPTION | POST. REF. | DEBIT | CREDIT | |
|---|---|---|---|---|---|---|---|
| 1 | | | | | | | 1 |
| 2 | | | | | | | 2 |
| 3 | | | | | | | 3 |
| 4 | | | | | | | 4 |
| 5 | | | | | | | 5 |
| 6 | | | | | | | 6 |
| 7 | | | | | | | 7 |
| 8 | | | | | | | 8 |

(b) Assuming that the goods purchased by Sandy Company from Philip Company in (a) above were shipped FOB destination, prepare the following entries on the books of Philip Company, in the general journal form below.

Dec. 1. Sold $800 of merchandise to Sandy Company, on account, terms 4/10, n/30.
1. Paid Gibson Freight Company $36 for shipping merchandise to Sandy Company.
11. Received payment from Sandy Company for invoice of Dec. 1, less discount.

JOURNAL PAGE

| | DATE | | DESCRIPTION | POST. REF. | DEBIT | CREDIT | |
|---|---|---|---|---|---|---|---|
| 1 | | | | | | | 1 |
| 2 | | | | | | | 2 |
| 3 | | | | | | | 3 |
| 4 | | | | | | | 4 |
| 5 | | | | | | | 5 |
| 6 | | | | | | | 6 |
| 7 | | | | | | | 7 |
| 8 | | | | | | | 8 |
| 9 | | | | | | | 9 |
| 10 | | | | | | | 10 |
| 11 | | | | | | | 11 |

(c) Prepare the entries, in the general journal form below, to record the following transactions on the books of Sandy Company:

Dec. 1. Purchased $800 of merchandise from Philip Company, on account, FOB destination, terms 4/10, n/30.

10. Paid invoice to Philip Company, less discount.

JOURNAL PAGE

| DATE | DESCRIPTION | POST. REF. | DEBIT | CREDIT |
|---|---|---|---|---|

**Perfect Score** 25 **Name** ____________________

**Student's Score** ____ **Date** ____________ **Class** ________

## ACCOUNTING CYCLE FOR A MERCHANDISING ENTERPRISE

**Instructions.** Complete each of the following statements by writing the missing word(s) in the space at the right.

| No. | Statement | Answer | For Scoring |
|---|---|---|---|
| 1 | When merchandise is purchased during the accounting period, the account debited is | | 1 |
| 2 | The amount of inventory shown in the Trial Balance column of the work sheet represents the ________ inventory balance | | 2 |
| 3 | In the adjusting entries, ________ is transferred to the debit side of the income summary account | | 3 |
| 4 | Net sales minus ________ equals gross profit | | 4 |
| 5 | Gross sales less sales returns and allowances and sales discounts equals | | 5 |
| 6 | ________ plus net purchases of merchandise equals merchandise available for sale | | 6 |
| 7 | Cost of goods sold is determined by subtracting the ending inventory from the ________ | | 7 |
| 8 | The two accounts opposite to purchases are Purchases Discount and... | | 8 |
| 9 | Operating expenses directly related to the sale of merchandise are classified as | | 9 |
| 10 | Office supplies, insurance expense, and property taxes are all examples of ________ expenses | | 10 |

**Instructions.** Indicate whether each of the following expenses would normally be classified as a selling expense or a general expense by placing a check mark in the appropriate column.

| No. | Item | Selling | General | For Scoring |
|---|---|---|---|---|
| 11 | Office supplies | | | 11 |
| 12 | Sales salary expense | | | 12 |
| 13 | Insurance expense | | | 13 |
| 14 | Depreciation expense on office equipment | | | 14 |
| 15 | Postage expense | | | 15 |
| 16 | Miscellaneous selling expense | | | 16 |
| 17 | Advertising expense | | | 17 |
| 18 | Utilities expense | | | 18 |
| 19 | Depreciation expense on store equipment | | | 19 |
| 20 | Delivery expense | | | 20 |

*(Continued)*

**Instructions.** The Binka Co. had a beginning inventory of $17,300, purchases of $58,200, purchases returns and allowances of $1,450, purchases discounts of $2,170, and an ending inventory of $16,400. Based on this information, complete the following statements by writing your answer in the space at the right.

| No. | Statement | Answer | For Scoring |
|---|---|---|---|
| 21 | The amount of net purchases for the period is ........................................ | $ | 21 |
| 22 | The amount of merchandise available for sale for the period is ............ | $ | 22 |
| 23 | The cost of the goods sold is ........................................................................ | $ | 23 |
| 24 | In adjusting the merchandise inventory at the end of the period for the Binka Co., the amount of the debit to Income Summary is .......... | $ | 24 |
| 25 | The amount of the credit to Income Summary in the inventory adjustment is........................................................................................................ | $ | 25 |

**9A-1.** The following trial balance as of January 31 of the current year was prepared from the ledger of Sioux Leather Shop. The adjustment data needed are also presented below.

SIOUX LEATHER SHOP
Trial Balance
January 31, 19--

| Account | Debit | Credit |
|---|---|---|
| Cash | 2,270 | |
| Accounts Receivable | 4,700 | |
| Merchandise Inventory | 5,160 | |
| Store Supplies | 150 | |
| Prepaid Insurance | 336 | |
| Store Equipment | 16,000 | |
| Accumulated Depreciation — Store Equipment | | 5,160 |
| Accounts Payable | | 2,600 |
| Diana Sioux, Capital | | 19,601 |
| Sales | | 4,450 |
| Purchases | 2,760 | |
| Rent Expense | 205 | |
| Salary Expense | 230 | |
| | 31,811 | 31,811 |

Adjustment data:

(a) Merchandise inventory, January 31, $4,930.
(b) Store supplies on hand, January 31, $105.
(c) The balance in the prepaid insurance account represents a two-year policy which was paid on January 1 of this year.
(d) Depreciation on store equipment is 1% per month.
(e) Salaries owed at January 31, $78.

**Required:** Prepare the necessary adjusting entries for the Sioux Leather Shop for the month ended January 31 using the journal paper below.

JOURNAL PAGE

| DATE | | DESCRIPTION | POST. REF. | DEBIT | CREDIT |
|---|---|---|---|---|---|

**9A-2.** The trial balance for Watson Clock Shop as of December 31 of the current year is given below. The adjustment data needed for year-end adjustments are also presented below.

WATSON CLOCK SHOP
Trial Balance
December 31, 19--

| Account | Debit | Credit |
|---|---|---|
| Cash | 2,090 | |
| Accounts Receivable | 2,570 | |
| Merchandise Inventory | 8,340 | |
| Office Supplies | 215 | |
| Prepaid Rent | 1,800 | |
| Store Equipment | 4,200 | |
| Accumulated Depreciation — Store Equipment | | 1,150 |
| Accounts Payable | | 1,935 |
| Lucas Watson, Capital | | 12,090 |
| Lucas Watson, Drawing | 400 | |
| Sales | | 15,620 |
| Sales Returns and Allowances | 420 | |
| Purchases | 9,180 | |
| Purchases Discount | | 185 |
| Advertising Expense | 190 | |
| Salary Expense | 1,500 | |
| Miscellaneous Expense | 75 | |
| | 30,980 | 30,980 |

Adjustment data:

(a) Merchandise inventory, December 31, $8,600.
(b) Office supplies on hand, December 31, $60.
(c) Rent expired during the year, $1,200.
(d) Depreciation of store equipment, $175.
(e) Salaries owed on December 31, $90.

**Required:**

(a) Prepare a ten-column work sheet for the current year ended December 31 using the fold-out page at the back of this book.
(b) Record the adjusting entries in the general journal provided below.

JOURNAL PAGE

| | DATE | | DESCRIPTION | POST. REF. | DEBIT | CREDIT | |
|---|---|---|---|---|---|---|---|
| 1 | | | | | | | 1 |
| 2 | | | | | | | 2 |
| 3 | | | | | | | 3 |
| 4 | | | | | | | 4 |
| 5 | | | | | | | 5 |
| 6 | | | | | | | 6 |
| 7 | | | | | | | 7 |
| 8 | | | | | | | 8 |
| 9 | | | | | | | 9 |
| 10 | | | | | | | 10 |
| 11 | | | | | | | 11 |
| 12 | | | | | | | 12 |
| 13 | | | | | | | 13 |

**9A-3.** The accounting records of Selby Florist revealed the following information for the fiscal year ended December 31 of the current year.

| | |
|---|---|
| Steve Selby, capital, January 1 | $18,300 |
| Merchandise inventory, January 1 | 11,400 |
| Purchases discount | 2,600 |
| Purchases returns and allowances | 940 |
| Sales salary expense | 4,350 |
| Office salary expense | 1,950 |
| Property tax expense | 700 |
| Sales | 47,200 |
| Purchases | 22,730 |
| Store supplies expense | 180 |
| Office supplies expense | 100 |
| Insurance expense | 1,050 |
| Merchandise inventory, December 31 | 9,760 |
| Sales discount | 450 |
| Sales returns and allowances | 920 |
| Delivery expense | 220 |
| Depreciation expense — store equipment | 680 |
| Depreciation expense — office equipment | 920 |
| Steve Selby, drawing | 900 |

**Required:** Prepare a partial income statement up to and including the computation of gross profit for the year ended December 31, using the ruled form below.

*(Page not used.)*

| Perfect Score | 25 | Name ______________________ | |
|---|---|---|---|
| Student's Score | ____ | Date ______________ | Class ________ |

## FINANCIAL STATEMENTS AND COMPLETION OF THE ACCOUNTING CYCLE

**Instructions.** Complete each of the statements and answer each of the questions below by writing your answer in the space at the right.

| No. | Statement | Answer | For Scoring |
|---|---|---|---|
| 1 | Assets that may reasonably be expected to be converted into cash or consumed in normal business operations usually within one year are classified as........ | | 1 |
| 2 | Assets to be used in the business for a number of years are called........ | | 2 |
| 3 | Those debts of a business that are due within one year or less are classified as........ | | 3 |
| 4 | The portion of the cost of a plant asset which has been used up during the accounting period is known as........ | | 4 |
| 5 | The cost of a plant asset less its accumulated depreciation to date is called its........ | | 5 |
| 6 | Those obligations of a business that will not become due during the present accounting period are called........ | | 6 |
| 7 | Current assets divided by current liabilities is called the........ | | 7 |
| 8 | The excess of current assets over current liabilities is known as........ | | 8 |
| 9 | On October 1, Adam Page's assets were $30,000 and his liabilities were $16,000. One month later his assets were $33,000 and his liabilities were $18,300. What was his increase (or decrease) in capital during October?........ | $ | 9 |
| 10 | Janet West's capital on May 1 was $15,300 and on May 31 it was $11,500. If her drawings during May were $1,200, what was her profit or loss for the month?........ | $ | 10 |
| 11 | Alan Porter has current assets of $25,000 and current liabilities of $15,000. What is Porter's current ratio?........ | | 11 |
| 12 | Compute Porter's working capital using the information given in No. 11........ | $ | 12 |
| 13 | The Astec Co. had gross sales for the period of $105,000, sales returns and allowances of $2,700, sales discounts of $2,300, and a net income of $17,000. What was the percent of net income earned on sales for the period?........ | % | 13 |
| 14 | After closing all revenue and expense accounts for the Jana Co., the income summary account has a debit balance of $940. What does this balance represent?........ | | 14 |
| 15 | The entry to close Income Summary in No. 14 will require a debit to.. | | 15 |

*(Continued)*

**Instructions:** Indicate whether each of the following items would be classified as a current asset by placing a check mark in the appropriate column.

| No. | Item | Yes | No | For Scoring |
|---|---|---|---|---|
| 16 | Land | | | 16 |
| 17 | Office supplies | | | 17 |
| 18 | Prepaid insurance premiums | | | 18 |
| 19 | Cash on hand | | | 19 |
| 20 | Delivery truck | | | 20 |
| 21 | Merchandise inventory | | | 21 |
| 22 | Accounts receivable | | | 22 |
| 23 | Notes payable in two years | | | 23 |
| 24 | Notes receivable in six months | | | 24 |
| 25 | Store equipment | | | 25 |

**9B-1.** Give the normal balance (debit or credit) for each account listed below and indicate the financial statement (balance sheet or income statement) on which it would be shown. Specify the section of the balance sheet (current assets, current liabilities, etc.) or income statement (sales, cost of goods sold, or operating expenses) where the account would appear.

| Account | Normal Balance | Financial Statement | Section |
|---|---|---|---|
| 0. Cash | *Debit* | *Balance Sheet* | *Current Assets* |
| 1. Prepaid Rent | | | |
| 2. Mortgage Note Payable | | | |
| 3. Purchases Discount | | | |
| 4. Advertising Expense | | | |
| 5. Sales Returns and Allowances | | | |
| 6. Accounts Payable | | | |
| 7. Drawing | | | |
| 8. Accumulated Depreciation — Equipment | | | |
| 9. Store Supplies | | | |
| 10. Depreciation Expense — Equipment | | | |
| 11. Purchases | | | |
| 12. Accounts Receivable | | | |

**9B-2.** The following errors relate to (a) cost of goods sold, (b) net income, and (c) merchandise inventory on the balance sheet of the Klingstedt Company at the end of the period.

(1) During the counting of the inventory at the end of the period, $1,400 of inventory received but not yet unloaded from a truck was not counted.
(2) In taking the ending inventory, one area of the store containing $2,200 of inventory was counted twice.
(3) A purchase of $650 returned for credit on account was not recorded in the accounting records.
(4) A shipment of merchandise just received, costing $1,900, was not recorded as a purchase during the period and was not included in the ending inventory.

State the effect (Overstated, Understated, or No Effect) of each of the errors.

| Error | Effect on Cost of Goods Sold | Effect on Net Income | Effect on Merchandise Inventory on Balance Sheet |
|---|---|---|---|
| (1) | | | |
| (2) | | | |
| (3) | | | |
| (4) | | | |

**9B-3.** The trial balance below was taken from the books of Carlos' Designer T-Shirts at the end of September of the current year after the ledger was adjusted and all revenue and expense accounts were transferred to the income summary account.

CARLOS' DESIGNER T-SHIRTS
Trial Balance
September 30, 19--

| | | |
|---|---|---|
| Cash | 750 | |
| Accounts Receivable | 2,080 | |
| Merchandise Inventory | 1,800 | |
| Store Supplies | 40 | |
| Prepaid Insurance | 75 | |
| Store Equipment | 1,100 | |
| Accumulated Depreciation — Store Equipment | | 200 |
| Building | 3,200 | |
| Accumulated Depreciation — Building | | 600 |
| Land | 1,720 | |
| Accounts Payable | | 650 |
| Salaries Payable | | 140 |
| Taxes Payable | | 200 |
| Mortgage Notes Payable | | 1,600 |
| Juan Carlos, Capital | | 6,900 |
| Juan Carlos, Drawing | 550 | |
| Income Summary | | 1,025 |
| | 11,315 | 11,315 |

**Required:**

(a) Prepare a classified balance sheet including changes in owner's equity as of September 30 on the form provided on page 493.

(b) Determine the working capital and compute the current ratio for Carlos', using the ruled form provided below.

**9B-4.** The Income Statement and Balance Sheet columns from the work sheet of the Keel Supply Company for the year ended December 31 of the current year are shown below:

KEEL SUPPLY COMPANY
Work Sheet
For Year Ended December 31, 19--

| ACCOUNT TITLE | INCOME STATEMENT DEBIT | INCOME STATEMENT CREDIT | BALANCE SHEET DEBIT | BALANCE SHEET CREDIT |
|---|---|---|---|---|
| *Cash* | | | 7,500.00 | |
| *Accounts Receivable* | | | 20,800.00 | |
| *Merchandise Inventory* | | | 17,000.00 | |
| *Store Supplies* | | | 210.00 | |
| *Office Supplies* | | | 160.00 | |
| *Prepaid Insurance* | | | 480.00 | |
| *Store Equipment* | | | 11,000.00 | |
| *Accumulated Depreciation — Store Equipment* | | | | 2,000.00 |
| *Office Equipment* | | | 6,000.00 | |
| *Accumulated Depreciation — Office Equipment* | | | | 1,400.00 |
| *Accounts Payable* | | | | 6,500.00 |
| *Mortgage Note Payable (due 5 years)* | | | | 9,000.00 |
| *Margaret Keel, Capital* | | | | 41,775.00 |
| *Margaret Keel, Drawing* | | | 3,400.00 | |
| *Sales* | | 41,350.00 | | |
| *Sales Discount* | 625.00 | | | |
| *Purchases* | 24,700.00 | | | |
| *Purchases Discount* | | 420.00 | | |
| *Purchases Returns and Allowances* | | 680.00 | | |
| *Advertising Expense* | 300.00 | | | |
| *Sales Salary Expense* | 5,430.00 | | | |
| *Office Salary Expense* | 3,000.00 | | | |
| | | | | |
| *Income Summary* | 18,600.00 | 17,000.00 | | |
| *Store Supplies Expense* | 240.00 | | | |
| *Office Supplies Expense* | 190.00 | | | |
| *Insurance Expense* | 105.00 | | | |
| *Salaries Payable* | | | | 215.00 |
| *Depreciation Expense — Store Equipment* | 400.00 | | | |
| *Depreciation Expense — Office Equipment* | 200.00 | | | |
| | 53,790.00 | 59,450.00 | 66,550.00 | 60,890.00 |
| *Net Income* | 5,660.00 | | | 5,660.00 |
| | 59,450.00 | 59,450.00 | 66,550.00 | 66,550.00 |

**Required:**

(a) Prepare a classified income statement for the current fiscal year for Keel Supply Company, using the form provided on page 495.

(b) Prepare a classified balance sheet for the Keel Supply Company, including changes in owner's equity, using the form provided on page 496. No additional investments were made during the year.

(c) Prepare the entries necessary to adjust Merchandise Inventory, using the journal form provided on page 497.

(d) Prepare the closing entries using the journal form provided on page 498.

JOURNAL PAGE

| | DATE | | DESCRIPTION | POST. REF. | DEBIT | CREDIT | |
|---|---|---|---|---|---|---|---|
| 1 | | | | | | | 1 |
| 2 | | | | | | | 2 |
| 3 | | | | | | | 3 |
| 4 | | | | | | | 4 |
| 5 | | | | | | | 5 |
| 6 | | | | | | | 6 |
| 7 | | | | | | | 7 |
| 8 | | | | | | | 8 |
| 9 | | | | | | | 9 |
| 10 | | | | | | | 10 |
| 11 | | | | | | | 11 |
| 12 | | | | | | | 12 |
| 13 | | | | | | | 13 |
| 14 | | | | | | | 14 |
| 15 | | | | | | | 15 |
| 16 | | | | | | | 16 |
| 17 | | | | | | | 17 |
| 18 | | | | | | | 18 |
| 19 | | | | | | | 19 |
| 20 | | | | | | | 20 |
| 21 | | | | | | | 21 |
| 22 | | | | | | | 22 |
| 23 | | | | | | | 23 |
| 24 | | | | | | | 24 |
| 25 | | | | | | | 25 |
| 26 | | | | | | | 26 |
| 27 | | | | | | | 27 |
| 28 | | | | | | | 28 |
| 29 | | | | | | | 29 |
| 30 | | | | | | | 30 |
| 31 | | | | | | | 31 |
| 32 | | | | | | | 32 |
| 33 | | | | | | | 33 |
| 34 | | | | | | | 34 |

JOURNAL PAGE

| | DATE | | DESCRIPTION | POST. REF. | DEBIT | CREDIT | |
|---|---|---|---|---|---|---|---|
| 1 | | | | | | | 1 |
| 2 | | | | | | | 2 |
| 3 | | | | | | | 3 |
| 4 | | | | | | | 4 |
| 5 | | | | | | | 5 |
| 6 | | | | | | | 6 |
| 7 | | | | | | | 7 |
| 8 | | | | | | | 8 |
| 9 | | | | | | | 9 |
| 10 | | | | | | | 10 |
| 11 | | | | | | | 11 |
| 12 | | | | | | | 12 |
| 13 | | | | | | | 13 |
| 14 | | | | | | | 14 |
| 15 | | | | | | | 15 |
| 16 | | | | | | | 16 |
| 17 | | | | | | | 17 |
| 18 | | | | | | | 18 |
| 19 | | | | | | | 19 |
| 20 | | | | | | | 20 |
| 21 | | | | | | | 21 |
| 22 | | | | | | | 22 |
| 23 | | | | | | | 23 |
| 24 | | | | | | | 24 |
| 25 | | | | | | | 25 |
| 26 | | | | | | | 26 |
| 27 | | | | | | | 27 |
| 28 | | | | | | | 28 |
| 29 | | | | | | | 29 |
| 30 | | | | | | | 30 |
| 31 | | | | | | | 31 |
| 32 | | | | | | | 32 |
| 33 | | | | | | | 33 |
| 34 | | | | | | | 34 |

**Perfect Score** 20 **Name** ______________________

**Student's Score** ____ **Date** ______________ **Class** ________

## COMPUTING AND RECORDING THE PAYROLL

**Instructions.** Complete each of the following statements and answer each of the questions by writing your answer in the space provided.

| No. | Statement | Answer | For Scoring |
|---|---|---|---|
| 1 | The compensation paid to independent contractors, such as lawyers or architects, is called a(n) .......... | | 1 |
| 2 | An individual who performs services subject to the will and control of an employer is called an .......... | | 2 |
| 3 | The Wage and Hour Law requires that overtime be paid for all hours worked in excess of ________ per week .......... | | 3 |
| 4 | Businesses engaged in interstate commerce must pay their employees in conformance with the ________ Act .......... | | 4 |
| 5 | The FICA tax is commonly called the ________ tax .......... | | 5 |
| 6 | The initials FICA stand for .......... | | 6 |
| 7 | The system of requiring employers to withhold federal income taxes from wages paid to employees is referred to as the ________ system .......... | | 7 |
| 8 | The most common payroll deductions are federal income tax and.......... | | 8 |
| 9 | Compensation paid to an employee for management or administrative duties is commonly referred to as a(n) .......... | | 9 |
| 10 | Remuneration stated on an hourly or piecework basis, for skilled or unskilled labor, is normally referred to as a(n) .......... | | 10 |
| 11 | The FICA tax withheld from the employees' pay will be shown on the employer's balance sheet as a(n) ________ until paid .......... | | 11 |
| 12 | An employee's gross earnings less payroll deductions equals.......... | | 12 |
| 13 | The money actually received by the employee on payday is commonly called .......... | | 13 |
| 14 | Beth Sharp is employed in a local factory as a fabric cutter. Sharp is paid $5.60 per hour plus 1½ times the regular wage for all hours in excess of 40 worked each week. If Sharp worked 48 hours this week, how much would she make in overtime? .......... | $ | 14 |
| 15 | Sharp's gross earnings in No. 14 would be .......... | $ | 15 |
| 16 | If Sharp had earned $9,680 this year prior to the current week, what would be the amount of FICA tax deducted from her pay this week, using the tax rate and base assumed in the text? .......... | $ | 16 |
| 17 | Paul Berg is married and claims 4 withholding allowances for income tax purpose. If Berg earned $415 during the current week, how much federal income tax would be withheld from his pay? (Use tax table on page 206.) .......... | $ | 17 |

*(Continued)*

| No. | Statement | Answer | For Scoring |
|---|---|---|---|
| 18 | Li Chang earned $505 during the current week. How much FICA tax would be deducted from her pay if her total earnings for the year prior to this week had been $19,200, using the tax rate and base assumed in the text? | $ | 18 |
| 19 | How much FICA tax would be deducted from Chang's pay if her cumulative earnings prior to this week had been $24,700? | $ | 19 |
| 20 | How much FICA tax would be deducted in No. 18 if Chang's cumulative earnings prior to the current week had been $26,230? | $ | 20 |

**10A-1.** Jim George is employed at an hourly rate of $5.40 with 1½ times the regular rate for all hours worked over 40 each week. The information for George's payroll for the week ending April 23 of the current year is as follows:

| | |
|---|---|
| Hours worked | 56 |
| Earnings this year prior to this week | $7,880 |
| Deduction for health insurance | $8.40 |
| Deduction for U.S. Savings Bonds | $5.00 |

George is married and claims 5 allowances.

**Required:**

(a) Using the form below to show your computations, determine the following:

1. George's gross earnings for the week. ______________
2. Federal income tax to be withheld this week. ______________
3. The FICA tax to be withheld from his pay. ______________
4. George's net earnings for the week. ______________

(b) Using the general journal below, prepare the entry to record George's payroll on the books of his employer.

(c) Prepare the entry to record payment of the payroll to George on April 24.

JOURNAL PAGE

| DATE | | DESCRIPTION | POST. REF. | DEBIT | CREDIT |
|---|---|---|---|---|---|

**10A-2.** Shown on pages 502 and 503 is the Henton Hotel payroll register for the week ended December 6 of the current year. Pettit and Barger each authorized a U.S. Savings Bond deduction of $10 per week, and all employees authorized a $5 deduction for the United Fund except Cissell, who authorized $10. The overtime rate is 1½ times the regular rate for all hours over 40 a week. Deduct FICA tax at the rate given in the text. Federal income tax to be withheld can be computed from the table on page 206.

**Required:**

(a) Complete the payroll register. The first check number is 830.

(b) Prepare the entry to record the payroll in the general journal on the following page.

**PAYROLL FOR WEEK ENDING**

| EMPLOYEE | EARNINGS TO DATE | NO. OF ALLOWANCES | MARITAL STATUS | DAILY HOURS | | | | | | HOURLY RATE | REGULAR HOURS | OVERTIME HOURS | EARNINGS | | |
|---|---|---|---|---|---|---|---|---|---|---|---|---|---|---|---|
| | | | | M | T | W | T | F | S | | | | REGULAR | OVERTIME | TOTAL |
| *Barger, Clara* | *24,800.00* | *4* | *M* | *8* | *8* | *8* | *10* | *10* | *9* | *12.00* | *40* | *13* | | | |
| *Cissell, Anthony* | *8,100.00* | *2* | *M* | *10* | *8* | *8* | *8* | *8* | *8* | *5.50* | *40* | *10* | | | |
| *Pettit, Edward* | *27,840.00* | *5* | *M* | *10* | *8* | *8* | *7* | *8* | *10* | *12.50* | *40* | *11* | | | |
| *Tanaka, Anna* | *13,860.00* | *3* | *M* | *9* | *9* | *9* | *8* | *8* | *5* | *7.20* | *40* | *8* | | | |
| *Thornton, Bruce* | *12,600.00* | *7* | *M* | *8* | *9* | *8* | *8* | *7* | *9* | *6.20* | *40* | *9* | | | |
| | | | | | | | | | | | | | | | |

**JOURNAL** PAGE

| DATE | DESCRIPTION | POST. REF. | DEBIT | CREDIT |
|---|---|---|---|---|

| TAXABLE EARNINGS | | DEDUCTIONS | | | | | | NET PAID | | SALARY EXPENSE DR. |
|---|---|---|---|---|---|---|---|---|---|---|
| FICA | UNEMPLOYMENT COMP. | FEDERAL INCOME TAX | FICA | HEALTH INSUR. | U.S. BONDS | UNITED FUND | TOTAL | AMOUNT | CK. NO. | |
| | | | | *2.00* | | | | | | |
| | | | | *2.00* | | | | | | |
| | | | | *2.00* | | | | | | |
| | | | | *2.00* | | | | | | |
| | | | | *2.00* | | | | | | |
| | | | | | | | | | | |

**10A-3.** Below are the T-accounts for selected payroll items for the Hacienda Company for the month of May of the current fiscal year. Hacienda pays its employees twice a month.

**Salary Expense**

| Debit | | Credit | |
|---|---|---|---|
| Bal. | 2,960.00 | | |
| May 1 | 740.00 | | |
| 16 | 725.00 | | |

**Health Insurance Payable**

| Debit | | Credit | |
|---|---|---|---|
| May 10 | 24.00 | Bal. | 24.00 |
| | | May 1 | 12.00 |
| | | 16 | 12.00 |

**Employees' Income Tax Payable**

| Debit | | Credit | |
|---|---|---|---|
| | | May 1 | 90.62 |
| | | 16 | 88.80 |

**Union Dues Payable**

| Debit | | Credit | |
|---|---|---|---|
| May 3 | 32.00 | Bal. | 32.00 |
| | | May 1 | 16.00 |
| | | 16 | 16.00 |

**FICA Tax Payable**

| Debit | | Credit | |
|---|---|---|---|
| | | May 1 | 51.80 |
| | | 16 | 50.75 |

**Salaries Payable**

| Debit | | Credit | |
|---|---|---|---|
| May 2 | 569.58 | May 1 | 569.58 |
| 17 | 557.45 | 16 | 557.45 |

**Required:**

(a) From the information given in the T-accounts, reconstruct the following entries in the general journal on the following page for the Hacienda Company:

May 1 — Record the payroll.
May 2 — Pay the payroll.

(b) Using the journal on the following page, also prepare an entry on June 3 to record payment of the union dues collected during May.

JOURNAL PAGE

| DATE | | DESCRIPTION | POST. REF. | DEBIT | CREDIT |
|---|---|---|---|---|---|

Perfect Score 20 Name ______________________

Student's Score ____ Date ______________ Class ________

## EMPLOYER'S PAYROLL TAXES AND PAYROLL RECORDS

**Instructions.** Determine whether each of the following statements is true or false and place a check mark in the appropriate column.

| No. | Statement | True | False | For Scoring |
|---|---|---|---|---|
| 1 | The federal unemployment tax is paid by the employee only............... | | | 1 |
| 2 | The federal unemployment tax rate is 2.7% .......................................... | | | 2 |
| 3 | The federal unemployment tax is paid on the first $5,000 earned by the employee.......................................................................................... | | | 3 |
| 4 | All states have adopted state unemployment compensation taxes ........ | | | 4 |
| 5 | FICA taxes are paid by the employee and employer............................. | | | 5 |
| 6 | Employees are required to pay income taxes only on the first $25,000 earned ........................................................................................... | | | 6 |
| 7 | All payroll taxes levied against the employer under federal and state law are business expenses of the employer ....................................... | | | 7 |
| 8 | FICA tax deducted from employees' pay is carried on the employer's books as a current liability................................................................ | | | 8 |
| 9 | Payroll records must be maintained by the business for at least six years ............................................................................................ | | | 9 |
| 10 | The employer must provide each employee a statement of total earnings (Form W-2) on or before January 15 of the following year .......... | | | 10 |

**Instructions.** Based on the following information, complete each of the statements below by writing your answer in the space provided.

Sherrie Brown is a supervisor for the local water district. She is employed at an hourly rate of $6.20 with time and one half for all hours over 40 each week. The following payroll data are available for Brown for the week ended May 15.

Hours worked this week............................... 48
Earnings this year prior to current week... $5,800
Federal income tax withheld this week.... $43.20
Deduction for U.S. Savings Bond............. $15.00

Tax rates:
FICA — 7% on earnings up to $25,000.
Federal unemployment tax — .7% on earnings up to $6,000.
State unemployment tax — 2.7% on earnings up to $6,000.

| No. | Statement | Answer | For Scoring |
|---|---|---|---|
| 11 | The amount Brown earned in overtime this week was .......................... | $ | 11 |
| 12 | Brown's gross earnings for the week were ............................................ | $ | 12 |
| 13 | The FICA tax withheld from her pay was .............................................. | $ | 13 |
| 14 | The total deductions for Brown were...................................................... | $ | 14 |
| 15 | Brown's net earnings for the week were.................................................. | $ | 15 |

*(Continued)*

| No. | Statement | Answer | For Scoring |
|---|---|---|---|
| 16 | The amount of federal unemployment tax to be paid by the company on Brown's earnings was ............ | $ | 16 |
| 17 | The state unemployment tax on Brown's earnings was............ | $ | 17 |
| 18 | FICA tax on Brown's earnings paid by the employer was ............ | $ | 18 |
| 19 | The company's payroll taxes expense on Brown's earnings for the week was............ | $ | 19 |
| 20 | The federal unemployment tax is paid by the employer on all earnings of an employee up to............ | $ | 20 |

**10B-1.** Bono Insurance Agency has four employees. Cumulative earnings, wage rates, and hours worked for the week ending November 22 of the current year, are as follows:

| Employee | Earnings Prior to This Week | Hours Worked | Hourly Rate |
|---|---|---|---|
| A | $25,450 | 52 | $13.00 |
| B | 5,925 | 30 | 5.00 |
| C | 4,600 | 42 | 4.90 |
| D | 23,740 | 54 | 12.50 |

All employees are paid overtime at 1½ the hourly rate for hours worked in excess of 40.

**Required:**

(a) Make the following computations for the November 22 payroll:

| Employee | Earnings for Week | Earnings Subject to FICA Tax | Earnings Subject to Unemployment Taxes |
|---|---|---|---|
| A | | | |
| B | | | |
| C | | | |
| D | | | |

(b) Prepare the general journal entry to record the payroll taxes expense for Bono Insurance Agency for the week of November 22. The state unemployment, FICA, and federal unemployment tax rates are 2.7%, 7%, and .7%, respectively.

JOURNAL PAGE

| | DATE | | DESCRIPTION | POST. REF. | DEBIT | CREDIT | |
|---|---|---|---|---|---|---|---|
| 1 | | | | | | | 1 |
| 2 | | | | | | | 2 |
| 3 | | | | | | | 3 |
| 4 | | | | | | | 4 |
| 5 | | | | | | | 5 |
| 6 | | | | | | | 6 |
| 7 | | | | | | | 7 |
| 8 | | | | | | | 8 |
| 9 | | | | | | | 9 |
| 10 | | | | | | | 10 |
| 11 | | | | | | | 11 |
| 12 | | | | | | | 12 |

**10B-2.** On pages 508 and 509 is the payroll register for the Hoxie Camera Shop for the week ended June 19 of the current year. The overtime rate is 1½ times the regular rate for all hours worked in excess of 40 per week. Bond deductions and United Fund contributions are given on the payroll register. The payroll tax rates are the same as those used in Problem 10B-1, above. Income tax to be withheld should be determined from the table on page 206. All employees are married.

| EMPLOYEE | EARNINGS TO DATE | NO. OF ALLOWANCES | MARITAL STATUS | DAILY HOURS | | | | | | HOURLY RATE | REGULAR HOURS | OVERTIME HOURS | EARNINGS | | |
|---|---|---|---|---|---|---|---|---|---|---|---|---|---|---|---|
| | | | | M | T | W | T | F | S | | | | REGULAR | OVERTIME | TOTAL |
| *Adam, Gilbert* | *6,140.00* | *3* | *M* | *8* | *8* | *8* | *8* | *8* | *10* | *7.00* | *40* | *10* | | | |
| *Haggard, Susan* | *5,680.00* | *2* | *M* | *8* | *8* | *8* | *8* | *8* | *12* | *5.50* | *40* | *12* | | | |
| *Lou, George* | *2,040.00* | *5* | *M* | *9* | *8* | *8* | *9* | *8* | *10* | *5.50* | *40* | *12* | | | |
| *Thom, Melvin* | *3,290.00* | *4* | *M* | *8* | *9* | *9* | *8* | *8* | *8* | *6.00* | *40* | *10* | | | |
| *Wee, Wilma* | *5,910.00* | *1* | *M* | *8* | *8* | *8* | *10* | *8* | *6* | *7.00* | *40* | *8* | | | |
| | | | | | | | | | | | | | | | |

**Required:**

(a) Complete the payroll register for the week ended June 19. The first check number is 425.
(b) Using the journal below, prepare the entry to record the payroll.
(c) Prepare the entry to record the employer's payroll taxes expense for the week.
(d) Prepare the entry to record payment of the payroll on June 20.

**JOURNAL** PAGE

| DATE | | DESCRIPTION | POST. REF. | DEBIT | CREDIT |
|---|---|---|---|---|---|
| | | | | | |

**JUNE 19, 19--**

| TAXABLE EARNINGS | | DEDUCTIONS | | | | | NET PAID | | SALARY EXPENSE DR. |
|---|---|---|---|---|---|---|---|---|---|
| FICA | UNEMPLOYMENT COMP. | FEDERAL INCOME TAX | FICA | U.S. BONDS | UNITED FUND | TOTAL | AMOUNT | CK. NO. | |
| | | | | *3.00* | *5.00* | | | | |
| | | | | *6.00* | *2.00* | | | | |
| | | | | *3.00* | *5.00* | | | | |
| | | | | *6.00* | *8.00* | | | | |
| | | | | *6.00* | *6.00* | | | | |
| | | | | | | | | | |

**10B-3.** Selected totals from the payroll records of the New England Wholesale Seafood Co. for the month of October of the current year are given below:

| | | | |
|---|---|---|---|
| Warehouse salaries | $5,360 | Earnings subject to: | |
| Office salaries | 1,620 | FICA tax | $6,980 |
| Total salaries | $6,980 | Unemployment tax | 2,140 |

Deductions:

| | |
|---|---|
| Income tax | $839.60 |
| FICA tax | ? |
| Union dues | 40.00 |
| Health insurance | 28.50 |

Compute the amount of the FICA tax. The tax rates are the same as those used in Problem 10B-1.

**Required:**

Using the general journal below, prepare the following entries:

(a) The entry to record the payroll.

(b) The entry to record the employer's payroll taxes expense for the month.

JOURNAL PAGE

| | DATE | | DESCRIPTION | POST. REF. | DEBIT | CREDIT | |
|---|---|---|---|---|---|---|---|
| 1 | | | | | | | 1 |
| 2 | | | | | | | 2 |
| 3 | | | | | | | 3 |
| 4 | | | | | | | 4 |
| 5 | | | | | | | 5 |
| 6 | | | | | | | 6 |
| 7 | | | | | | | 7 |
| 8 | | | | | | | 8 |
| 9 | | | | | | | 9 |
| 10 | | | | | | | 10 |
| 11 | | | | | | | 11 |
| 12 | | | | | | | 12 |
| 13 | | | | | | | 13 |
| 14 | | | | | | | 14 |
| 15 | | | | | | | 15 |
| 16 | | | | | | | 16 |
| 17 | | | | | | | 17 |
| 18 | | | | | | | 18 |
| 19 | | | | | | | 19 |
| 20 | | | | | | | 20 |
| 21 | | | | | | | 21 |
| 22 | | | | | | | 22 |
| 23 | | | | | | | 23 |
| 24 | | | | | | | 24 |

**Perfect Score** 25 **Name** ____________________

**Student's Score** ____ **Date** ____________________ **Class** __________

**INTERNAL CONTROL; THE VOUCHER SYSTEM**

**Instructions.** Complete each of the following statements by writing the missing word(s) in the space provided.

| No. | Statement | Answer | For Scoring |
|---|---|---|---|
| 1 | The organization and procedures used to control business operations are called a system of.......... | | 1 |
| 2 | One basic feature of a good system of internal control of cash is the payment of all invoices by.......... | | 2 |
| 3 | An effective system used to control and coordinate the activities of purchasing, receiving, verifying, and paying for merchandise and other items purchased is a(n).......... | | 3 |
| 4 | The account credited in the voucher register will always be.......... | | 4 |
| 5 | The voucher register takes the place of the __________ journal.......... | | 5 |
| 6 | Unpaid vouchers should be filed in the.......... | | 6 |
| 7 | The __________ column is normally listed first in the voucher register.......... | | 7 |
| 8 | When a voucher system is used, all approved vouchers are paid by...... | | 8 |
| 9 | All payments are recorded in the __________ register.......... | | 9 |
| 10 | The check register takes the place of the.......... | | 10 |
| 11 | The account debited in the check register will always be.......... | | 11 |
| 12 | The only credit column in the check register besides Cash is.......... | | 12 |
| 13 | After vouchers are paid, they are normally filed in __________ order. | | 13 |
| 14 | The schedule of unpaid vouchers should always equal the balance in the __________ account.......... | | 14 |
| 15 | When a voucher is prepared incorrectly and cannot be used, the word __________ should be written in the payee column of the voucher register.......... | | 15 |
| | The Irene Company purchases merchandise for $200. If Irene Company uses a voucher system and pays the invoice immediately, two entries will be required. | | |
| 16 | The first entry will be recorded in the.......... | | 16 |
| 17 | The account debited will be.......... | | 17 |
| 18 | The account credited will be.......... | | 18 |
| 19 | The second entry will be recorded in the.......... | | 19 |
| 20 | The account debited will be.......... | | 20 |
| 21 | The account credited will be.......... | | 21 |
| 22 | If a 4% discount is allowed on the invoice above, an additional credit will be required in the __________ account.......... | | 22 |

*(Continued)*

| No. | Statement | Answer | For Scoring |
|---|---|---|---|
| 23 | The amount of the credit in No. 22 is........................................................ | $ | 23 |
| 24 | The amount of the debit to Accounts Payable for the transaction in No. 22 is ........................................................................................ | $ | 24 |
| 25 | The amount of the credit to Cash for No. 22 is........................................ | $ | 25 |

**10C-1.** You are given below and on the next page the voucher register for Wheeler Printing Co. for the month of July of the current year.

**Required:**

(a) Total and rule the columns. Prove the accuracy of the voucher register, using the form below.

PAGE *23* **VOUCHER**

| DATE | VOU. NO. | PAYEE | PAID DATE | PAID CK. NO. | ACCOUNTS PAYABLE CR. |
|---|---|---|---|---|---|
| *19--* | | | | | |
| *July 1* | *508* | *Spika Company*........................................ | *July 10* | 688 | *650.00* |
| *6* | *509* | *Dan Supply Co.*........................................ | *July 15* | 690 | *85.00* |
| *7* | *510* | *Wilson Paper Co.*........................................ | *July 17* | 691 | *220.00* |
| *12* | *511* | *Palmer Office Supply*........................................ | *July 14* | 689 | *42.00* |
| *16* | *512* | *Dan Supply Co.*........................................ | | | *50.00* |
| *21* | *513* | *Daily Gazette*........................................ | *July 21* | 692 | *95.00* |
| *24* | *514* | *Wilson Paper Co.*........................................ | | | *260.00* |
| *29* | *515* | *Palmer Office Supply*........................................ | | | *65.00* |

(b) Post from the voucher register to the accounts payable account below. Also post the payments on account for the month, which were the five vouchers paid this month plus the $200 beginning balance — total $1,292.

ACCOUNT *Accounts Payable* ACCOUNT NO. *21*

| DATE | | ITEM | POST. REF. | DEBIT | CREDIT | BALANCE DEBIT | BALANCE CREDIT |
|---|---|---|---|---|---|---|---|
| 19-- *July* | *1* | *Balance* | √ | | | | *200 00* |
| | | | | | | | |
| | | | | | | | |
| | | | | | | | |
| | | | | | | | |

(c) Prepare a schedule of unpaid vouchers and compare the total to the balance in Accounts Payable.

REGISTER PAGE *23*

| PURCHASES DR. | STORE SUPPLIES DR. | OFFICE SUPPLIES DR. | GENERAL ACCOUNTS DR. ACCOUNT | POST. REF. | AMOUNT |
|---|---|---|---|---|---|
| *650.00* | | | | | |
| | *85.00* | | | | |
| *220.00* | | | | | |
| | | *42.00* | | | |
| | *50.00* | | | | |
| | | | *Advertising Expense* | | *95.00* |
| *260.00* | | | | | |
| | | *65.00* | | | |

**10C-2.** You are given the transactions for the Chereé Fabric Shop for the month of August.

**Required:**

(a) Record each transaction in the Voucher Register given below and on the following page, numbering the vouchers consecutively beginning with No. 115.

Aug. 1. Purchased a display counter (store equipment) on account from Omaha Distributors, $500.
3. Purchased merchandise on account from Trey Milling Co., $250.
4. Purchased office supplies on account from Lincoln Supplies, $65.
7. Purchased merchandise on account from King Fabric Co., $475.
8. Prepared voucher payable to the Otto Company for maintenance on cooling and heating equipment, $140.
11. Purchased store supplies on account from Omaha Distributors, $35.
13. Prepared voucher for advertising expense, payable to radio station KWK, $25.
15. Purchased merchandise on account from King Fabric Co., $345.
18. Purchased merchandise on account from Trey Milling Co., $220.
20. Purchased on account from Lincoln Supplies, office supplies, $40, and store supplies, $90.
24. Prepared voucher payable to Zest Co. for miscellaneous expense, $60.
29. Purchased merchandise on account from King Fabric Co., $425.

(b) The following vouchers were paid on the dates indicated. Record this information in the voucher register.

| Vou. No. | Date Paid | Ck. No. | Amt. | Vou. No. | Date Paid | Ck. No. | Amt. |
|---|---|---|---|---|---|---|---|
| 115 | 8–12 | 202 | $500 | 119 | 8–19 | 207 | $140 |
| 116 | 8–18 | 206 | 250 | 120 | 8–21 | 208 | 35 |
| 117 | 8–12 | 203 | 65 | 121 | 8–13 | 204 | 25 |
| 118 | 8–17 | 205 | 475 | 123 | 8–28 | 209 | 220 |

PAGE *18*

## VOUCHER REGISTER

| | DATE | | Vou. No. | PAYEE | PAID DATE | | Ck. No. | ACCOUNTS PAYABLE CR. | |
|---|---|---|---|---|---|---|---|---|---|
| 1 | | | | | | | | | 1 |
| 2 | | | | | | | | | 2 |
| 3 | | | | | | | | | 3 |
| 4 | | | | | | | | | 4 |
| 5 | | | | | | | | | 5 |
| 6 | | | | | | | | | 6 |
| 7 | | | | | | | | | 7 |
| 8 | | | | | | | | | 8 |
| 9 | | | | | | | | | 9 |
| 10 | | | | | | | | | 10 |
| 11 | | | | | | | | | 11 |
| 12 | | | | | | | | | 12 |
| 13 | | | | | | | | | 13 |
| 14 | | | | | | | | | 14 |
| 15 | | | | | | | | | 15 |

(c) Total and rule the columns in the voucher register and prepare a schedule to prove the equality of the debits and credits in the register using the form below.

(d) Post the Accounts Payable column total to the ledger account below.
(e) Total the amount of the vouchers paid during the period and post this amount to Accounts Payable.

ACCOUNT *Accounts Payable* ACCOUNT NO. *21*

| DATE | ITEM | POST. REF. | DEBIT | CREDIT | BALANCE DEBIT | BALANCE CREDIT |
|---|---|---|---|---|---|---|
| | | | | | | |
| | | | | | | |

## VOUCHER REGISTER

PAGE *18*

| | PURCHASES DR. | STORE SUPPLIES DR. | OFFICE SUPPLIES DR. | GENERAL ACCOUNTS DR. ACCOUNT | POST. REF | AMOUNT | |
|---|---|---|---|---|---|---|---|
| 1 | | | | | | | 1 |
| 2 | | | | | | | 2 |
| 3 | | | | | | | 3 |
| 4 | | | | | | | 4 |
| 5 | | | | | | | 5 |
| 6 | | | | | | | 6 |
| 7 | | | | | | | 7 |
| 8 | | | | | | | 8 |
| 9 | | | | | | | 9 |
| 10 | | | | | | | 10 |
| 11 | | | | | | | 11 |
| 12 | | | | | | | 12 |
| 13 | | | | | | | 13 |
| 14 | | | | | | | 14 |
| 15 | | | | | | | 15 |

(f) Prepare a schedule of unpaid vouchers and compare the total with the balance in Accounts Payable.

**10C-3.** Teresa Moore is the inventory manager for the Rudd Tire Company. Her duties consist of ordering all goods needed by the company, receiving and inspecting the goods when they arrive, and approving the vouchers for payment. Moore also supervises the taking of the annual inventory and counts a great deal of the stock herself.

**Required:**

(a) What basic principle of internal control is being violated by the above system?

(b) Describe a better system to be used by the company.

**10C-4.** Below is the check register of Don Hancock for the month of February of the current year.

**Required:**

(a) Record the following transactions for February in the check register below.

Feb. 2. Issued Check No. 819 to Bob Conway in payment of Voucher No. 777, $250.
4. Issued Check No. 820 to H. H. Horn Co. in payment of Voucher No. 774, $400 less a 3% cash discount.
9. Issued Check No. 821 to Henry Supply in payment of Voucher No. 778, $90.
13. Issued Check No. 822 to Baker Garage in payment of Voucher No. 780, $52.
15. Issued Check No. 823 to Snow Co. in payment of Voucher No. 779, $160 less a 2% cash discount.
22. Issued Check No. 824 to H. H. Horn Co. in payment of Voucher No. 781, $900 less a 3% cash discount.
26. Issued Check No. 825 to Bob Conway in payment of Voucher No. 782, $65.

(b) Total and rule the columns and prove the accuracy of the check register using the ruled form below.

## CHECK REGISTER

PAGE *39*

| | DATE | | CK. NO. | PAYEE | VOU. NO. | ACCOUNTS PAYABLE DR. | PURCHASES DISCOUNT CR. | CASH CR. | |
|---|---|---|---|---|---|---|---|---|---|
| 1 | | | | | | | | | 1 |
| 2 | | | | | | | | | 2 |
| 3 | | | | | | | | | 3 |
| 4 | | | | | | | | | 4 |
| 5 | | | | | | | | | 5 |
| 6 | | | | | | | | | 6 |
| 7 | | | | | | | | | 7 |
| 8 | | | | | | | | | 8 |
| 9 | | | | | | | | | 9 |
| 10 | | | | | | | | | 10 |
| 11 | | | | | | | | | 11 |

**10C-5.** Gleeson Supermarket had the following unpaid vouchers at the end of October of the current year.

| Voucher No. | Payee | Amount |
|---|---|---|
| 216 | Reed Grocery Co. | $ 750 |
| 219 | Campbell Products | 440 |
| 220 | Morrison Mills | 630 |
| | | $1,820 |

The voucher register for Gleeson Supermarket for the month of November is given below and on the following page.

**Required:**

(a) Record the following checks in the check register on the following page, inserting the proper information in the voucher register.

| Ck. No. | Date Paid | Vou. No. | Disc. | Amt. |
|---|---|---|---|---|
| 191 | 11–2 | 216 | 2% | $735.00 |
| 192 | 11–6 | 219 | 2% | 431.20 |
| 193 | 11–9 | 223 | | 62.00 |
| 194 | 11–10 | 220 | 3% | 611.10 |
| 195 | 11–12 | 221 | | 100.00 |
| 196 | 11–15 | 222 | 2% | $441.00 |
| 197 | 11–21 | 227 | | 125.00 |
| 198 | 11–24 | 225 | 3% | 281.30 |
| 199 | 11–26 | 224 | | 260.00 |

PAGE *16*

## VOUCHER REGISTER

| | DATE | | VOU. NO. | PAYEE | PAID DATE | PAID CK. NO. | ACCOUNTS PAYABLE CR. | |
|---|---|---|---|---|---|---|---|---|
| | *19--* | | | | | | | |
| 1 | *Nov.* | *2* | *221* | *James Supply Co.* | | | *100 00* | 1 |
| 2 | | *5* | *222* | *Reed Grocery Co.* | | | *450 00* | 2 |
| 3 | | *9* | *223* | *Harold's Garage* | | | *62 00* | 3 |
| 4 | | *12* | *224* | *Campbell Products* | | | *260 00* | 4 |
| 5 | | *14* | *225* | *Morrison Mills* | | | *290 00* | 5 |
| 6 | | *17* | *226* | *Dayton Suppliers* | | | *75 00* | 6 |
| 7 | | *21* | *227* | *New Mexico Electric* | | | *125 00* | 7 |
| 8 | | *24* | *228* | *Reed Grocery Co.* | | | *710 00* | 8 |
| 9 | | *28* | *229* | *James Supply Co.* | | | *110 00* | 9 |
| 10 | | *30* | *230* | *Campbell Products* | | | *170 00* | 10 |
| 11 | | | | | | | | 11 |
| 12 | | | | | | | | 12 |
| 13 | | | | | | | | 13 |
| 14 | | | | | | | | 14 |
| 15 | | | | | | | | 15 |

## CHECK REGISTER

PAGE *11*

| | DATE | | CK. No. | PAYEE | VOU. No. | ACCOUNTS PAYABLE DR. | PURCHASES DISCOUNT CR. | CASH CR. | |
|---|---|---|---|---|---|---|---|---|---|
| 1 | | | | | | | | | 1 |
| 2 | | | | | | | | | 2 |
| 3 | | | | | | | | | 3 |
| 4 | | | | | | | | | 4 |
| 5 | | | | | | | | | 5 |
| 6 | | | | | | | | | 6 |
| 7 | | | | | | | | | 7 |
| 8 | | | | | | | | | 8 |
| 9 | | | | | | | | | 9 |
| 10 | | | | | | | | | 10 |
| 11 | | | | | | | | | 11 |
| 12 | | | | | | | | | 12 |

## VOUCHER REGISTER

PAGE *16*

| | PURCHASES DR. | STORE SUPPLIES DR. | OFFICE SUPPLIES DR. | GENERAL ACCOUNTS DR. | | | |
|---|---|---|---|---|---|---|---|
| | | | | ACCOUNT | POST. REF | AMOUNT | |
| 1 | | *60 00* | *40 00* | | | | 1 |
| 2 | *450 00* | | | | | | 2 |
| 3 | | | | *Repairs Expense* | | *62 00* | 3 |
| 4 | *260 00* | | | | | | 4 |
| 5 | *290 00* | | | | | | 5 |
| 6 | | *75 00* | | | | | 6 |
| 7 | | | | *Utilities Expense* | | *125 00* | 7 |
| 8 | *710 00* | | | | | | 8 |
| 9 | | *80 00* | *30 00* | | | | 9 |
| 10 | *170 00* | | | | | | 10 |
| 11 | | | | | | | 11 |
| 12 | | | | | | | 12 |
| 13 | | | | | | | 13 |
| 14 | | | | | | | 14 |
| 15 | | | | | | | 15 |

(b) Total and rule the columns in the voucher register and the check register. Using the ruled form below, prove the columns for both registers.

(c) Post the accounts payable total from the voucher register and check register to the accounts payable account below:

ACCOUNT *Accounts Payable* ACCOUNT NO. *26*

| DATE | | ITEM | POST. REF. | DEBIT | CREDIT | BALANCE DEBIT | BALANCE CREDIT |
|---|---|---|---|---|---|---|---|
| *19--* *Nov.* | *1* | *Balance* | √ | | | | *1 8 2 0 00* |
| | | | | | | | |
| | | | | | | | |
| | | | | | | | |
| | | | | | | | |
| | | | | | | | |
| | | | | | | | |
| | | | | | | | |
| | | | | | | | |

(d) Prepare a schedule of unpaid vouchers and compare the total with the balance in Accounts Payable.

*(Page not used.)*

| Perfect Score | 20 | Name ______________________ | |
|---|---|---|---|
| Student's Score | ____ | Date ______________ | Class ________ |

## ACCRUED EXPENSES AND REVENUE

**Instructions.** Complete each statement below by writing your answer in the space provided.

| No. | Statement | Answer | For Scoring |
|---|---|---|---|
| 1 | Expenses incurred in one fiscal period but not yet recorded at the end of the period are called | | 1 |
| 2 | Accrued interest payable at the end of the year will be shown on the balance sheet as a | | 2 |
| 3 | Accrued liabilities are also frequently called | | 3 |
| 4 | __________ are a convenient technique used at the beginning of the year which allows the recording of entries for items which have been affected by adjusting entries at the end of the preceding period | | 4 |
| 5 | A reversing entry is the exact reverse of the __________ entry | | 5 |
| 6 | Reversing entries are normally made on the __________ day of the new period | | 6 |
| 7 | Those revenues earned but not received at the end of the fiscal period are called | | 7 |
| 8 | Accrued revenue usually is not recorded until __________ | | 8 |
| 9 | The adjusting entry to record rent revenue which has accrued at the end of the period requires a debit to the __________ account | | 9 |
| 10 | The adjustment in No. 9 above requires a credit to the __________ account | | 10 |

**Instructions.** Determine whether each of the following statements is true or false and place a check mark in the appropriate column.

| No. | Statement | True | False | For Scoring |
|---|---|---|---|---|
| 11 | A good example of accrued expense is salaries to employees | | | 11 |
| 12 | When the adjusting entry is made for accrued salaries, the account credited is Salary Expense | | | 12 |
| 13 | The account debited in the adjusting entry in No. 12 is Accrued Salaries | | | 13 |
| 14 | The use of reversing entries makes closing entries unnecessary | | | 14 |
| 15 | If the adjusting entry for accrued salaries is reversed at the beginning of the following period, the balance in Salaries Payable would be zero | | | 15 |
| 16 | Immediately prior to the reversing entry for accrued salaries, Salary Expense will have a debit balance | | | 16 |

*(Continued)*

| No. | Statement | True | False | For Scoring |
|---|---|---|---|---|
| 17 | After the reversing entry is posted to Salary Expense, the account will have a credit balance representing a liability ..................................... | | | 17 |
| 18 | Accrued Advertising Receivable will be shown on the balance sheet as a current liability ......................................................................... | | | 18 |
| 19 | Reversing entries can be used for all accrued expenses......................... | | | 19 |
| 20 | The normal sequence of recording accrued expenses is adjusting entry, reversing entry, and closing entry............................................. | | | 20 |

**11A-1.** You are given the following ledger accounts before adjustments for Salary Expense and Salaries Payable for the Toyko Company on December 31, 1982. The Toyko Company's weekly payroll ends on Wednesday. On Friday, December 31, there was $370 of accrued salaries.

ACCOUNT *Salaries Payable* ACCOUNT NO. *27*

| DATE | | ITEM | POST. REF. | DEBIT | CREDIT | BALANCE DEBIT | BALANCE CREDIT |
|---|---|---|---|---|---|---|---|
| | | | | | | | |

ACCOUNT *Salary Expense* ACCOUNT NO. *27*

| DATE | | ITEM | POST. REF. | DEBIT | CREDIT | BALANCE DEBIT | BALANCE CREDIT |
|---|---|---|---|---|---|---|---|
| *1982* Dec. | *31* | *Balance* | √ | | | *40 6 7 0 00* | |

**Required:** Using the general journal below, prepare the following entries and post each entry to the accounts on page 524.

(a) The adjusting entry to record the accrued salaries.
(b) The closing entry on December 31.
(c) The reversing entry on January 1 of the following year.
(d) The entry to record the payment of the payroll on January 5 for $925.
(e) The entry to record the payment of the payroll for $925 on January 5 if a reversing entry is not made on January 1. (Do not post.)

JOURNAL PAGE *116*

| DATE | | DESCRIPTION | POST. REF. | DEBIT | CREDIT |
|---|---|---|---|---|---|
| | | | | | |

**11A-2.** On December 31, 1982, the Bullish Brokers had accrued commission income of $1,650 from Harvard Company. The ledger accounts for commissions receivable and commissions income for Bullish Brokers as of December 31 are presented below.

ACCOUNT *Commissions Receivable* ACCOUNT NO. *13*

| DATE | | ITEM | POST. REF. | DEBIT | CREDIT | BALANCE DEBIT | BALANCE CREDIT |
|---|---|---|---|---|---|---|---|
| | | | | | | | |
| | | | | | | | |
| | | | | | | | |
| | | | | | | | |

ACCOUNT *Commissions Income* ACCOUNT NO. *41*

| DATE | | ITEM | POST. REF. | DEBIT | CREDIT | BALANCE DEBIT | BALANCE CREDIT |
|---|---|---|---|---|---|---|---|
| *1982* Dec. | *31* | *Balance* | ✓ | | | | *25 4 0 0 00* |
| | | | | | | | |
| | | | | | | | |
| | | | | | | | |
| | | | | | | | |
| | | | | | | | |

**Required:** Using the journal on the following page, prepare the following entries and post those involving the above accounts.

(a) The adjusting entry for commissions accrued on December 31.
(b) The closing entry on December 31.
(c) The reversing entry on January 1, 1983.
(d) The entry on February 14, 1983, when Bullish receives payment of $2,250 in commissions from Harvard.
(e) The entry on February 14, when payment is received, if the reversing entry had not been made. (Do not post.)
(f) If the reversing entry technique is not used, will this change the amount of commissions income reported in the year in which the payment was received? Explain.

JOURNAL PAGE *71*

| DATE | | DESCRIPTION | POST. REF. | DEBIT | CREDIT |
|---|---|---|---|---|---|

**11A-3.** On November 1, 1982, William Wood agreed to rent enough space in his department store to Wanda Rufus to allow her to operate a cosmetics counter. Rufus will pay $300 per month, but Wood has agreed to allow her to delay the first payment until May 1, 1983, at which time the first six-months' rent will be due.

**Required:**

(a) Using the journal below, prepare the necessary entries to record the following transactions on Wood's books, assuming his fiscal year ends December 31.

1. December 31 adjusting entry.
2. December 31 closing entry.
3. January 1 reversing entry.
4. May 1 receipt of six-months' rent.

JOURNAL PAGE

| DATE | | DESCRIPTION | POST. REF. | DEBIT | CREDIT |
|---|---|---|---|---|---|

(b) Using the journal below, prepare the entries to record the following transactions on Rufus' books, assuming her fiscal year ends December 31.

1. December 31 adjusting entry.
2. December 31 closing entry.
3. January 1 reversing entry.
4. May 1 payment of six-months' rent.

JOURNAL PAGE

| DATE | | DESCRIPTION | POST. REF. | DEBIT | CREDIT |
|---|---|---|---|---|---|

**Perfect Score** **20** **Name** ________________

**Student's Score** ____ **Date** ________________ **Class** ________

## DEFERRED EXPENSES AND REVENUE

**Instructions.** Complete each statement and answer each question below by writing your answer in the space provided.

| No. | Item | Answer | For Scoring |
|---|---|---|---|
| 1 | The postponement of the recognition of an expense for which payment has already been made is called a ........ | | 1 |
| 2 | The postponement of the recognition of a revenue for which payment has been received is known as a ........ | | 2 |
| 3 | If the deferment of expenses is for a number of years, they should be shown on the balance sheet as ........ | | 3 |
| 4 | Expenses which have been prepaid for a period of one year or less are shown on the balance sheet as ........ | | 4 |
| 5 | When revenue from rental property is received in advance and the company follows the policy of crediting a revenue account, the account credited will be ........ | | 5 |
| 6 | If the company in No. 5 followed the policy of crediting a liability account, the account credited would be ........ | | 6 |
| 7 | On September 1, the Oda Company paid insurance premiums for the next 24 months totaling $480. If the company had debited the payment to an expense account, what would be the amount of the adjustment on December 31? ........ | $ | 7 |
| 8 | How much expense would be reported on the income statement at the end of the first year in No. 7 above? ........ | $ | 8 |
| 9 | If the Oda Company had debited the $480 payment to an asset account, what would be the amount of the adjustment on December 31? ........ | $ | 9 |
| 10 | How much expense would be reported by the Oda Company on the income statement at the end of the first year in No. 9 above? ........ | $ | 10 |

**Instructions.** Using the following classifications, determine how each of the items below would be classified by inserting the appropriate letter in the Answer column.

(A) Accrued expense (B) Accrued income (C) Prepaid expense (D) Unearned revenue

| No. | Statement | Answer | For Scoring |
|---|---|---|---|
| 11 | Receipts from sale of season tickets for baseball team ........ | | 11 |
| 12 | Property taxes owed at the end of the year, payable March 1 of the following year ........ | | 12 |
| 13 | Store supplies inventory at December 31 ........ | | 13 |
| 14 | Interest received in advance by bank for discounting a note ........ | | 14 |
| 15 | Interest owed on note payable due in the following year ........ | | 15 |

*(Continued)*

| No. | Statement | Answer | For Scoring |
|---|---|---|---|
| 16 | Insurance premiums received in advance by insurance company ......... | | 16 |
| 17 | Interest earned on note due next month .................................................. | | 17 |
| 18 | Rent receivable on office building owned .............................................. | | 18 |
| 19 | Property taxes paid in December for the following year ........................ | | 19 |
| 20 | Subscriptions collected in advance by *Daily News* ................................ | | 20 |

**11B-1.** On October 1, 1982, Maria Fashions paid $1,200 for ads to appear in the next 12 issues of *Women's Monthly*, a magazine.

**Required:**

(a) Prepare the following entries for Maria Fashions, assuming the $1,200 payment is debited originally to an asset account.

1982
Oct. 1. To record the payment.
Dec. 31. Adjusting entry.
31. Closing entry.
1983
Jan. 1. Reversing entry, if needed.
Dec. 31. Adjusting entry for 1983, if needed.

JOURNAL PAGE

| | DATE | | DESCRIPTION | POST. REF. | DEBIT | CREDIT | |
|---|---|---|---|---|---|---|---|
| 1 | | | | | | | 1 |
| 2 | | | | | | | 2 |
| 3 | | | | | | | 3 |
| 4 | | | | | | | 4 |
| 5 | | | | | | | 5 |
| 6 | | | | | | | 6 |
| 7 | | | | | | | 7 |
| 8 | | | | | | | 8 |
| 9 | | | | | | | 9 |
| 10 | | | | | | | 10 |
| 11 | | | | | | | 11 |
| 12 | | | | | | | 12 |
| 13 | | | | | | | 13 |

(b) Prepare the entries for Maria Fashions, assuming the $1,200 payment is debited originally to an expense account.

JOURNAL PAGE

| | DATE | | DESCRIPTION | POST. REF. | DEBIT | CREDIT | |
|---|---|---|---|---|---|---|---|
| 1 | | | | | | | 1 |
| 2 | | | | | | | 2 |
| 3 | | | | | | | 3 |
| 4 | | | | | | | 4 |
| 5 | | | | | | | 5 |
| 6 | | | | | | | 6 |
| 7 | | | | | | | 7 |
| 8 | | | | | | | 8 |
| 9 | | | | | | | 9 |
| 10 | | | | | | | 10 |
| 11 | | | | | | | 11 |
| 12 | | | | | | | 12 |
| 13 | | | | | | | 13 |

(c) What would be the difference in the amount of advertising expense and prepaid advertising shown in the financial statements at the end of the first year under the two methods used to record the payment in (a) and (b) above and on page 530?

**11B-2.** The entries in the subscriptions income ledger account shown below are identified by letters.

ACCOUNT *Subscriptions Income* ACCOUNT NO. *43*

| DATE | | ITEM | POST. REF. | DEBIT | CREDIT | BALANCE DEBIT | BALANCE CREDIT |
|---|---|---|---|---|---|---|---|
| *1982* *Aug.* | *1* | *(a) for 8 months* | | | *1 200 00* | | *1 200 00* |
| *Dec.* | *31* | *(b)* | | *450 00* | | | *750 00* |
| | *31* | *(c)* | | *750 00* | | — | — |
| *1983* *Jan.* | *1* | *(d)* | | | *450 00* | | *450 00* |

**Required:** On the form below, prepare the full journal entry that was made on each date in sequence and fully explain each entry.

JOURNAL PAGE

| DATE | | DESCRIPTION | POST. REF. | DEBIT | CREDIT |
|---|---|---|---|---|---|

**11B-3.** Each of the following five transactions relate to adjustments to the accounts of Hendrix Company on December 31, the end of the current fiscal year.

(a) The account Unearned Rent has a $4,800 credit balance, representing one year's rent beginning June 1 of the current year just ending.
(b) Store Supplies has a debit balance of $908. The supplies on hand, determined by actual count, totaled $183.
(c) The balance in Repairs Expense on December 31 includes a charge of $180 for advance payment for repairs and maintenance service on office machines for one year beginning September 1, of the current year just ending.
(d) On November 1, Hendrix paid for six monthly ads in the *Trade Journal* at a cost of $175 per ad. Advertising Expense was debited for $1,050 at that time.
(e) The balance in Prepaid Insurance, before adjustment is $880. Insurance expired during the year totaled $220.

**Required:** Prepare the adjusting entries necessary on December 31, using the general journal below.

JOURNAL PAGE

| | DATE | | DESCRIPTION | POST. REF. | DEBIT | CREDIT | |
|---|---|---|---|---|---|---|---|
| 1 | | | | | | | 1 |
| 2 | | | | | | | 2 |
| 3 | | | | | | | 3 |
| 4 | | | | | | | 4 |
| 5 | | | | | | | 5 |
| 6 | | | | | | | 6 |
| 7 | | | | | | | 7 |
| 8 | | | | | | | 8 |
| 9 | | | | | | | 9 |
| 10 | | | | | | | 10 |
| 11 | | | | | | | 11 |
| 12 | | | | | | | 12 |
| 13 | | | | | | | 13 |
| 14 | | | | | | | 14 |
| 15 | | | | | | | 15 |
| 16 | | | | | | | 16 |
| 17 | | | | | | | 17 |
| 18 | | | | | | | 18 |
| 19 | | | | | | | 19 |
| 20 | | | | | | | 20 |

(f) Which of the above entries should be reversed on January 1?

**11B-4.** The Jester Abstract Company has recently moved into new executive offices. Although the offices themselves are complete, the parking lot will not be completed for some time. Jester arranges with Epps Insurance Co. to lease parking space for six months beginning September 1, 1982, at a cost of $500 per month. Jester pays Epps Insurance Co. the full $3,000 on September 1. The fiscal year for both companies ends December 31.

**Required:**

(a) Using the general journal below, prepare the entries on the books of Jester Abstract Company to record:

1. The payment of the rent, assuming the payment was debited to Prepaid Rent.
2. The adjusting entry.
3. The closing entry.
4. The reversing entry if needed. Post each entry, as it is recorded, to the following accounts:

ACCOUNT *Prepaid Rent* ACCOUNT NO. *16*

| DATE | | ITEM | POST. REF. | DEBIT | CREDIT | BALANCE DEBIT | BALANCE CREDIT |
|---|---|---|---|---|---|---|---|
| | | | | | | | |
| | | | | | | | |
| | | | | | | | |

ACCOUNT *Rent Expense* ACCOUNT NO. *51*

| DATE | | ITEM | POST. REF. | DEBIT | CREDIT | BALANCE DEBIT | BALANCE CREDIT |
|---|---|---|---|---|---|---|---|
| | | | | | | | |
| | | | | | | | |
| | | | | | | | |

GENERAL JOURNAL PAGE *207*

| | DATE | | ACCOUNT TITLE | POST. REF. | DEBIT | CREDIT | |
|---|---|---|---|---|---|---|---|
| 1 | | | | | | | 1 |
| 2 | | | | | | | 2 |
| 3 | | | | | | | 3 |
| 4 | | | | | | | 4 |
| 5 | | | | | | | 5 |
| 6 | | | | | | | 6 |
| 7 | | | | | | | 7 |
| 8 | | | | | | | 8 |
| 9 | | | | | | | 9 |
| 10 | | | | | | | 10 |
| 11 | | | | | | | 11 |
| 12 | | | | | | | 12 |
| 13 | | | | | | | 13 |

(b) What additional entries, if any, will be required in the following fiscal year?

(c) Using the general journal below, prepare the same entries for the Jester Abstract Company as in (a) assuming the initial payment was debited to Rent Expense. Post each entry to the following accounts:

ACCOUNT *Prepaid Rent* ACCOUNT NO. *16*

| DATE | | ITEM | POST. REF. | DEBIT | CREDIT | BALANCE DEBIT | BALANCE CREDIT |
|---|---|---|---|---|---|---|---|
| | | | | | | | |
| | | | | | | | |
| | | | | | | | |

ACCOUNT *Rent Expense* ACCOUNT NO. *51*

| DATE | | ITEM | POST. REF. | DEBIT | CREDIT | BALANCE DEBIT | BALANCE CREDIT |
|---|---|---|---|---|---|---|---|
| | | | | | | | |
| | | | | | | | |
| | | | | | | | |
| | | | | | | | |

GENERAL JOURNAL PAGE *207*

| | DATE | | ACCOUNT TITLE | POST. REF. | DEBIT | CREDIT | |
|---|---|---|---|---|---|---|---|
| 1 | | | | | | | 1 |
| 2 | | | | | | | 2 |
| 3 | | | | | | | 3 |
| 4 | | | | | | | 4 |
| 5 | | | | | | | 5 |
| 6 | | | | | | | 6 |
| 7 | | | | | | | 7 |
| 8 | | | | | | | 8 |
| 9 | | | | | | | 9 |
| 10 | | | | | | | 10 |
| 11 | | | | | | | 11 |
| 12 | | | | | | | 12 |

(d) What additional entries, if any, will be required in the following fiscal year?

(e) Using the general journal below, prepare the entries on the books of the Epps Insurance Co. to record:

1. Receipt of the payment, assuming the receipt was credited to Unearned Rent.
2. The adjusting entry.
3. The closing entry.
4. The reversing entry if needed. Post each entry, as it is recorded, to the following accounts:

ACCOUNT *Unearned Rent* ACCOUNT NO. *24*

| DATE | | ITEM | POST. REF. | DEBIT | CREDIT | BALANCE DEBIT | BALANCE CREDIT |
|---|---|---|---|---|---|---|---|
| | | | | | | | |
| | | | | | | | |
| | | | | | | | |

ACCOUNT *Rent Income* ACCOUNT NO. *64*

| DATE | | ITEM | POST. REF. | DEBIT | CREDIT | BALANCE DEBIT | BALANCE CREDIT |
|---|---|---|---|---|---|---|---|
| | | | | | | | |
| | | | | | | | |
| | | | | | | | |

JOURNAL PAGE *77*

| | DATE | | DESCRIPTION | POST. REF. | DEBIT | CREDIT | |
|---|---|---|---|---|---|---|---|
| 1 | | | | | | | 1 |
| 2 | | | | | | | 2 |
| 3 | | | | | | | 3 |
| 4 | | | | | | | 4 |
| 5 | | | | | | | 5 |
| 6 | | | | | | | 6 |
| 7 | | | | | | | 7 |
| 8 | | | | | | | 8 |
| 9 | | | | | | | 9 |
| 10 | | | | | | | 10 |
| 11 | | | | | | | 11 |

(f) Prepare the same entries for the Epps Insurance Co. as in (e), assuming the receipt of payment was credited to Rent Income. Post each entry to the following accounts:

ACCOUNT *Unearned Rent* ACCOUNT NO. 24

| DATE | | ITEM | POST. REF. | DEBIT | CREDIT | BALANCE | |
|---|---|---|---|---|---|---|---|
| | | | | | | DEBIT | CREDIT |
| | | | | | | | |
| | | | | | | | |
| | | | | | | | |

ACCOUNT *Rent Income* ACCOUNT NO. 64

| DATE | | ITEM | POST. REF. | DEBIT | CREDIT | BALANCE | |
|---|---|---|---|---|---|---|---|
| | | | | | | DEBIT | CREDIT |
| | | | | | | | |
| | | | | | | | |
| | | | | | | | |
| | | | | | | | |
| | | | | | | | |

JOURNAL PAGE 77

| | DATE | | DESCRIPTION | POST. REF. | DEBIT | CREDIT | |
|---|---|---|---|---|---|---|---|
| 1 | | | | | | | 1 |
| 2 | | | | | | | 2 |
| 3 | | | | | | | 3 |
| 4 | | | | | | | 4 |
| 5 | | | | | | | 5 |
| 6 | | | | | | | 6 |
| 7 | | | | | | | 7 |
| 8 | | | | | | | 8 |
| 9 | | | | | | | 9 |
| 10 | | | | | | | 10 |
| 11 | | | | | | | 11 |
| 12 | | | | | | | 12 |
| 13 | | | | | | | 13 |
| 14 | | | | | | | 14 |
| 15 | | | | | | | 15 |
| 16 | | | | | | | 16 |
| 17 | | | | | | | 17 |

**11B-5.** The Shang Corporation prepares monthly financial statements and closes its accounts annually as of December 31. Local property taxes are assessed for the fiscal year beginning January 1. Tax statements are normally mailed in late January with payment due March 31.

**Required:**

(a) Prepare the journal entries to record the following selected transactions for Shang Corporation for the current year.

Jan. 26. Received tax statement for current year, $2,880. Record January accrual for property taxes.
Feb. 28. Record accrual for property taxes for February.
Mar. 29. Paid property taxes for year, $2,880.
Apr. 30. Record property taxes for April.

JOURNAL PAGE

| | DATE | | DESCRIPTION | POST. REF. | DEBIT | CREDIT | |
|---|---|---|---|---|---|---|---|
| 1 | | | | | | | 1 |
| 2 | | | | | | | 2 |
| 3 | | | | | | | 3 |
| 4 | | | | | | | 4 |
| 5 | | | | | | | 5 |
| 6 | | | | | | | 6 |
| 7 | | | | | | | 7 |
| 8 | | | | | | | 8 |
| 9 | | | | | | | 9 |
| 10 | | | | | | | 10 |
| 11 | | | | | | | 11 |
| 12 | | | | | | | 12 |
| 13 | | | | | | | 13 |
| 14 | | | | | | | 14 |
| 15 | | | | | | | 15 |
| 16 | | | | | | | 16 |
| 17 | | | | | | | 17 |
| 18 | | | | | | | 18 |
| 19 | | | | | | | 19 |
| 20 | | | | | | | 20 |

(b) Determine the balance in each of the following accounts related to property taxes for the Shang Corporation on the dates indicated:

| | April 30 | December 31 |
|---|---|---|
| Property Tax Expense | ________ | ________ |
| Prepaid Property Tax | ________ | ________ |
| Property Tax Payable | ________ | ________ |

Perfect Score 20 Name ______________________

Student's Score ___ Date ______________ Class ________

## ACCOUNTS RECEIVABLE AND UNCOLLECTIBLE ACCOUNTS

**Instructions:** Complete each of the following statements by writing the missing word(s) in the space provided.

| No. | Statement | Answer | For Scoring |
|---|---|---|---|
| 1. | The basis of accounting that recognizes revenue in the period it is earned is the | | 1. |
| 2. | When an entry is made to record sales on account, the account debited is | | 2. |
| 3. | When cash is received from the sale of merchandise on account, the credit is to | | 3. |
| 4. | The accounts receivable account in the general ledger is called a | | 4. |
| 5. | A separate ledger of the customers' accounts is called a | | 5. |
| 6. | Accounts receivable are reported on the balance sheet in the __________ section | | 6. |
| 7. | The method of recognizing a bad debt at the time the specific account is determined to be uncollectible is called the __________ method | | 7. |
| 8. | The method of estimating the losses from bad debts and recording them in the period the sales were made is called the | | 8. |
| 9. | Under the direct write-off method, when an account is considered uncollectible and written off, the debit is to | | 9. |
| 10. | The account credited for the write-off in No. 9 above is | | 10. |
| 11. | Under the allowance method, when an account is written off, the debit is to | | 11. |
| 12. | The account credited in No. 11 is | | 12. |
| 13. | The two widely recognized methods of estimating losses from bad debts are the percentage-of-sales method and the __________ method | | 13. |
| 14. | If a business does not have a record of its volume of charge sales, the percentage-of-sales method will have to be based on | | 14. |
| 15. | When the adjusting entries are made at the end of the year for uncollectible accounts, the account debited is | | 15. |
| 16. | When the percentage-of-sales method is used and an account is written off, the account debited is | | 16. |
| 17. | Gross sales minus sales discounts and sales returns and allowances equals | | 17. |
| 18. | When accounts receivable are analyzed in terms of their amount and how long they have been outstanding, the procedure is called | | 18. |
| 19. | The percentage-of-sales method is often known as the __________ approach | | 19. |
| 20. | The analysis-of-accounts-receivable method is often known as the __________ approach | | 20. |

**12A-1.** Stephen Rich is the owner of Rich Decorators. The following transactions relating to bad debts occurred over a two-year period. Rich Decorators uses the direct write-off method of recording bad debts.

1982

Aug. 6. Wrote off the account of Leslie Owen as uncollectible in the amount of $225.

Oct. 2. Learned of the bankruptcy of Charles Carr upon receipt of a check for $60 and a letter from his receiver in bankruptcy. Carr owed $135, but the letter stated that the enclosed check was in final settlement of the account.

Nov. 11. Wrote off the account of Mary Morris in the amount of $160 as uncollectible.

Dec. 15. Received $225 from Leslie Owen in full payment of account written off on August 6.

31. Closed the bad debts expense account.

1983

Jan. 17. Received $160 from Mary Morris in full payment of her account written off in November.

Feb. 4. Wrote off the account of Dick Meredith in the amount of $150 as uncollectible.

**Required:** Record the preceding transactions in the journal on the following page.

## JOURNAL

PAGE

| | DATE | | DESCRIPTION | POST. REF. | DEBIT | CREDIT | |
|---|---|---|---|---|---|---|---|
| 1 | | | | | | | 1 |
| 2 | | | | | | | 2 |
| 3 | | | | | | | 3 |
| 4 | | | | | | | 4 |
| 5 | | | | | | | 5 |
| 6 | | | | | | | 6 |
| 7 | | | | | | | 7 |
| 8 | | | | | | | 8 |
| 9 | | | | | | | 9 |
| 10 | | | | | | | 10 |
| 11 | | | | | | | 11 |
| 12 | | | | | | | 12 |
| 13 | | | | | | | 13 |
| 14 | | | | | | | 14 |
| 15 | | | | | | | 15 |
| 16 | | | | | | | 16 |
| 17 | | | | | | | 17 |
| 18 | | | | | | | 18 |
| 19 | | | | | | | 19 |
| 20 | | | | | | | 20 |
| 21 | | | | | | | 21 |
| 22 | | | | | | | 22 |
| 23 | | | | | | | 23 |
| 24 | | | | | | | 24 |
| 25 | | | | | | | 25 |
| 26 | | | | | | | 26 |
| 27 | | | | | | | 27 |
| 28 | | | | | | | 28 |
| 29 | | | | | | | 29 |
| 30 | | | | | | | 30 |
| 31 | | | | | | | 31 |
| 32 | | | | | | | 32 |
| 33 | | | | | | | 33 |

**12A-2.** The following transactions concern bad debts for Pearlman Jewelers. Pearlman Jewelers uses the allowance method of recording bad debts.

1982

Dec. 31. Bad debts are estimated at $475.

1983

Feb. 11. Wrote off the account of May Dunn as worthless, $85.

Apr. 23. Wrote off the account of John Ivers, $300, as uncollectible.

June 6. Received notice that Keith Knoles, a customer, had died. A check for $95 was enclosed as final payment on his account of $125. The balance of Knole's account is to be written off.

Sept. 26. Received a check for $85 from May Dunn in payment of her account written off in February.

Dec. 31. Bad debts are estimated at $360.

1984

Jan. 24. Received $300 from John Ivers in full payment of his account, which had been written off in April of last year.

**Required:** Using the journal below, record each of the above transactions.

JOURNAL PAGE

| DATE | | DESCRIPTION | POST. REF. | DEBIT | CREDIT |
|---|---|---|---|---|---|

**12A-3.** Below is given the subsidiary account of Luanne Curtis, a customer of the Ron Company. The company uses the allowance method for recording bad debts.

**NAME** *Luanne Curtis*

**ADDRESS** *731 Londonderry #22F, Wichita, KA 67207-1541*

| DATE | | ITEM | POST. REF. | DEBIT | CREDIT | BALANCE |
|---|---|---|---|---|---|---|
| *1982* Aug. | 9 | | S12 | 145 00 | | 145 00 |
| Nov. | 15 | Write off account | J7 | | 145 00 | — |
| *1983* Feb. | 3 | Reinstate account | J9 | 145 00 | | 145 00 |
| | 3 | | CR16 | | 145 00 | — |

**Required:** Prepare the entries, in general journal form, to record all transactions on the books of Ron indicated by Curtis' account.

JOURNAL PAGE

| | DATE | | DESCRIPTION | POST. REF. | DEBIT | CREDIT | |
|---|---|---|---|---|---|---|---|
| 1 | | | | | | | 1 |
| 2 | | | | | | | 2 |
| 3 | | | | | | | 3 |
| 4 | | | | | | | 4 |
| 5 | | | | | | | 5 |
| 6 | | | | | | | 6 |
| 7 | | | | | | | 7 |
| 8 | | | | | | | 8 |
| 9 | | | | | | | 9 |
| 10 | | | | | | | 10 |
| 11 | | | | | | | 11 |
| 12 | | | | | | | 12 |
| 13 | | | | | | | 13 |
| 14 | | | | | | | 14 |
| 15 | | | | | | | 15 |
| 16 | | | | | | | 16 |
| 17 | | | | | | | 17 |
| 18 | | | | | | | 18 |
| 19 | | | | | | | 19 |
| 20 | | | | | | | 20 |

**12A-4.** The following accounts for accounts receivable, allowance for bad debts, sales, sales returns and allowances, and bad debts expense before adjustment are given for Sipes Vacuum Center at the end of 1982, the first fiscal year of operations. The subsidiary account for Sue Simmons, a customer, is also given.

ACCOUNT *Accounts Receivable* ACCOUNT NO. *13*

| DATE | | ITEM | POST. REF. | DEBIT | CREDIT | BALANCE DEBIT | BALANCE CREDIT |
|---|---|---|---|---|---|---|---|
| 1982 Dec. | 31 | Balance | √ | | | 19 6 4 0 00 | |
| | | | | | | | |
| | | | | | | | |

ACCOUNT *Allowance for Bad Debts* ACCOUNT NO. *13.1*

| DATE | | ITEM | POST. REF. | DEBIT | CREDIT | BALANCE DEBIT | BALANCE CREDIT |
|---|---|---|---|---|---|---|---|
| | | | | | | | |
| | | | | | | | |
| | | | | | | | |

ACCOUNT *Sales* ACCOUNT NO. *51*

| DATE | | ITEM | POST. REF. | DEBIT | CREDIT | BALANCE DEBIT | BALANCE CREDIT |
|---|---|---|---|---|---|---|---|
| 1982 Dec. | 31 | Balance | √ | | | | 59 0 0 0 00 |
| | | | | | | | |

ACCOUNT *Sales Returns and Allowances* ACCOUNT NO. *51.1*

| DATE | | ITEM | POST. REF. | DEBIT | CREDIT | BALANCE DEBIT | BALANCE CREDIT |
|---|---|---|---|---|---|---|---|
| 1982 Dec. | 31 | Balance | √ | | | 1 8 0 0 00 | |
| | | | | | | | |

ACCOUNT *Bad Debts Expense* ACCOUNT NO. *62*

| DATE | | ITEM | POST. REF. | DEBIT | CREDIT | BALANCE DEBIT | BALANCE CREDIT |
|---|---|---|---|---|---|---|---|
| | | | | | | | |
| | | | | | | | |

NAME *Sue Simmons*

ADDRESS *4107 Argyle, Tacoma, WA 98466-6726*

| DATE | | ITEM | POST. REF. | DEBIT | CREDIT | BALANCE |
|---|---|---|---|---|---|---|
| 1982 Sept. | 5 | | S6 | 4 0 0 00 | | 4 0 0 00 |
| | | | | | | |
| | | | | | | |

**Required:**

(a) Prepare and post the adjusting entry for bad debts at December 31, 1982, if losses are estimated at 2% of net sales.

JOURNAL PAGE *12*

| | DATE | | DESCRIPTION | POST. REF. | DEBIT | CREDIT | |
|---|---|---|---|---|---|---|---|
| 1 | | | | | | | 1 |
| 2 | | | | | | | 2 |
| 3 | | | | | | | 3 |
| 4 | | | | | | | 4 |

(b) Show how the accounts receivable would be presented on the balance sheet at December 31.

(c) On March 6 of the following year Simmon's account is determined to be uncollectible. Prepare and post the entry to write off her account.

JOURNAL PAGE *15*

| | DATE | | DESCRIPTION | POST. REF. | DEBIT | CREDIT | |
|---|---|---|---|---|---|---|---|
| 1 | | | | | | | 1 |
| 2 | | | | | | | 2 |
| 3 | | | | | | | 3 |
| 4 | | | | | | | 4 |
| 5 | | | | | | | 5 |
| 6 | | | | | | | 6 |
| 7 | | | | | | | 7 |
| 8 | | | | | | | 8 |
| 9 | | | | | | | 9 |
| 10 | | | | | | | 10 |
| 11 | | | | | | | 11 |
| 12 | | | | | | | 12 |
| 13 | | | | | | | 13 |

**12A-5.** The Hawn Hardware Company had the following balances in Accounts Receivable and Allowance for Bad Debts, prior to adjustment, at December 31 of the current year.

| | |
|---|---|
| Accounts Receivable | $24,500 |
| Allowance for Bad Debts | 105 Dr. |

An analysis, by age, of the accounts receivable follows. The percentage of uncollectibility is also given.

| Age Interval | Amount of Receivables | Percent Uncollectible | Allowance for Bad Debts |
|---|---|---|---|
| Accounts not yet due | $15,600 | 2% | |
| 1–30 days past due | 5,300 | 4 | |
| 31–60 days past due | 1,840 | 10 | |
| 61–90 days past due | 960 | 20 | |
| Over 90 days past due | 800 | 50 | |
| | $24,500 | | |

**Required:**

(a) Using the aging method, complete the above analysis by writing the correct amounts in the Allowance for Bad Debts column.

(b) Using the form below, prepare the necessary adjusting entry for bad debts based on the above data.

(c) Prepare the necessary adjusting entry for bad debts assuming all the above data are the same except that the balance in the allowance for bad debts account is a $105 credit.

JOURNAL PAGE

| | DATE | DESCRIPTION | POST. REF. | DEBIT | CREDIT | |
|---|---|---|---|---|---|---|
| 1 | | | | | | 1 |
| 2 | | | | | | 2 |
| 3 | | | | | | 3 |
| 4 | | | | | | 4 |
| 5 | | | | | | 5 |
| 6 | | | | | | 6 |
| 7 | | | | | | 7 |
| 8 | | | | | | 8 |
| 9 | | | | | | 9 |
| 10 | | | | | | 10 |
| 11 | | | | | | 11 |
| 12 | | | | | | 12 |
| 13 | | | | | | 13 |
| 14 | | | | | | 14 |
| 15 | | | | | | 15 |
| 16 | | | | | | 16 |

**12A-6.** Following are transactions made by Tritt's Men's Shop during the current year. Given below are selected accounts and their balances as of January 1 of the current year.

Apr. 9. Wrote off the account of Jim Flint as uncollectible, $55.
May 12. Wrote off the account of Jean Giese as uncollectible, $78.
June 14. Wrote off the account of Mark Mann as uncollectible, $205.
Aug. 18. Wrote off the account of Helen Wang as uncollectible, $190.
Sept. 10. Received $55 from Flint in payment of his account written off on April 9.
Dec. 31. Record the following summary entries for accounts receivable for the current year:

| | |
|---|---|
| Net sales on account | $52,260 |
| Collection on accounts received in addition to those listed above | $49,880 |

31. Aged the accounts receivable and estimated that $560 would not be collected.
31. Closed the bad debts expense account.

ACCOUNT *Accounts Receivable* ACCOUNT NO. *14*

| DATE | | ITEM | POST. REF. | DEBIT | CREDIT | BALANCE DEBIT | BALANCE CREDIT |
|---|---|---|---|---|---|---|---|
| *19--* *Jan.* | *1* | *Balance* | √ | | | *9 2 1 0 00* | |
| | | | | | | | |
| | | | | | | | |
| | | | | | | | |
| | | | | | | | |
| | | | | | | | |
| | | | | | | | |
| | | | | | | | |

ACCOUNT *Allowance for Bad Debts* ACCOUNT NO. *14.1*

| DATE | | ITEM | POST. REF. | DEBIT | CREDIT | BALANCE DEBIT | BALANCE CREDIT |
|---|---|---|---|---|---|---|---|
| *19--* *Jan.* | *1* | *Balance* | √ | | | | *5 1 0 00* |
| | | | | | | | |
| | | | | | | | |
| | | | | | | | |
| | | | | | | | |
| | | | | | | | |

ACCOUNT *Income Summary* ACCOUNT NO. *33*

| DATE | | ITEM | POST. REF. | DEBIT | CREDIT | BALANCE DEBIT | BALANCE CREDIT |
|---|---|---|---|---|---|---|---|
| | | | | | | | |
| | | | | | | | |
| | | | | | | | |

*(Continued)*

ACCOUNT *Bad Debts Expense* ACCOUNT NO. *56*

| DATE | | ITEM | POST. REF. | DEBIT | CREDIT | BALANCE | |
|---|---|---|---|---|---|---|---|
| | | | | | | DEBIT | CREDIT |
| | | | | | | | |
| | | | | | | | |
| | | | | | | | |

**Required:**

(a) Record the transactions in the journal on the following page, and post to the proper accounts.
(b) Determine the net realizable value of accounts receivable at December 31.

(c) If Tritt's Men's Shop had used the percentage-of-sales method with the estimated loss from bad debts at 1.5% of net charge sales, determine the following, using the ruled form at the bottom of the page for your computations:

1. The adjusting entry on December 31.

| | | | | | | |
|---|---|---|---|---|---|---|
| 1 | | | | | | 1 |
| 2 | | | | | | 2 |
| 3 | | | | | | 3 |
| 4 | | | | | | 4 |

2. The balance in Allowance for Bad Debts after the adjusting entry. ______________

3. The net realizable value of accounts receivable on December 31. ______________

JOURNAL PAGE 9

| DATE | | DESCRIPTION | POST. REF. | DEBIT | CREDIT |
|---|---|---|---|---|---|

*(Page not used.)*

| Perfect Score | 25 | Name ______________________ | |
|---|---|---|---|
| Student's Score | ___ | Date ______________ | Class ________ |

## NOTES RECEIVABLE AND NOTES PAYABLE

**Instructions.** Complete the statements or answer the questions below by writing the missing word(s) in the space provided.

| No. | Statement | Answer | For Scoring |
|---|---|---|---|
| 1 | A written promise to pay a specified sum of money at a definite future date is a .......... | | 1 |
| 2 | The person who issues a note is referred to as the .......... | | 2 |
| 3 | The party receiving the note is called the .......... | | 3 |
| 4 | A 90-day note receivable would be shown on the balance sheet as a(n) .......... | | 4 |
| 5 | Notes receivable are always recorded at their __________ value .......... | | 5 |
| 6 | If a note does *not* require interest to be paid, it is said to be a __________ note .......... | | 6 |
| 7 | Interest received by a business on a note receivable is called .......... | | 7 |
| 8 | Interest rates are normally stated on a(n) __________ basis .......... | | 8 |
| 9 | For purposes of computing interest, a business year is normally considered to be __________ days .......... | | 9 |
| 10 | The face amount of the note is often referred to as the .......... | | 10 |
| 11 | When the term of a note is stated in months, the standard business practice is to consider each month as __________ days .......... | | 11 |
| 12 | If Chin received a 60-day note from a customer dated June 12, the note would be due on __________.......... | | 12 |
| 13 | If Chin received a 90-day note dated March 16, the note would be due on __________.......... | | 13 |
| 14 | If Chin received a three-month note dated March 16, the due date would be __________.......... | | 14 |
| 15 | The procedure whereby a bank loans money to a customer on a note and deducts the interest in advance is called .......... | | 15 |
| 16 | The rate used in computing the interest to be deducted in advance by the bank is called a.......... | | 16 |
| 17 | The interest deducted in advance by the bank is called .......... | | 17 |
| 18 | The difference between the maturity value of a note and the discount is known as the .......... | | 18 |
| 19 | The discount is always computed on the __________ of the note .......... | | 19 |
| 20 | When a customer's note is discounted, the period from the date the note is discounted to the day the note is due is called.......... | | 20 |
| 21 | Principal plus interest on a note equals .......... | | 21 |

*(Continued)*

| No. | Statement | Answer | For Scoring |
|---|---|---|---|
| 22 | Discounting a note receivable creates the possibility of a future liability called a ________ liability | | 22 |
| 23 | Roger discounted his own $400, 90 day, non-interest-bearing note at the bank at a discount rate of 6%. How much cash will Roger receive? | | 23 |
| 24 | Interest income is normally reported on the income statement as | | 24 |
| 25 | Would the account Interest Expense be included in "net income from operations," for a bank? | | 25 |

**12B-1.** Judy Jordan received a 60-day, 9% note from Harry Lucas dated April 9 of the current year, in payment of his account in the amount of $400. The note is payable at the First City Bank.

**Required:**

(a) Complete the following note for Lucas.

| | | |
|---|---|---|
| $__________ | AKRON, OHIO | ________________ 19____ |
| ________________ AFTER DATE ________________ PROMISE TO PAY TO | | |
| THE ORDER OF ________________________________ | | |
| ________________________________ DOLLARS | | |
| PAYABLE AT ________________________________ | | |
| WITH INTEREST AT __________ | | |
| NO. 29 | DUE ____________ | ________________ |

(b) Answer the following questions concerning the note:

1. Who is the payee? ____________________
2. Who is the maker? ____________________
3. What is the due date? ____________________
4. How much will the interest be? ____________________

(c) Prepare the entry to record the receipt of the note on Jordan's books.

| | | | | | | |
|---|---|---|---|---|---|---|
| 1 | | | | | | 1 |
| 2 | | | | | | 2 |
| 3 | | | | | | 3 |
| 4 | | | | | | 4 |
| 5 | | | | | | 5 |

(d) Prepare the entry to record the receipt of payment of the note plus interest on Jordan's books in the general journal below.

JOURNAL PAGE

| | DATE | | DESCRIPTION | POST. REF. | DEBIT | CREDIT | |
|---|---|---|---|---|---|---|---|
| 1 | | | | | | | 1 |
| 2 | | | | | | | 2 |
| 3 | | | | | | | 3 |
| 4 | | | | | | | 4 |
| 5 | | | | | | | 5 |

**12B-2.** Following are selected transactions, completed by Fitz Furniture and Appliances during the current year.

Jan. 9. Sold merchandise on account to Margie Horrell, $400.
21. Sold merchandise on account to Jan Paxton, $800.
Feb. 5. Received payment from Horrell for invoice of January 9, less a 3% cash discount.
Mar. 1. Accepted a 60-day, 9% note from Paxton in payment of invoice of January 21.
Apr. 3. Sold merchandise to Ed Hill for $500 and accepted his 90-day, 12% note for the amount of the invoice.
May 4. Loaned Horrell $300, accepting her 30-day, non-interest-bearing note for the debt.
28. Sold $95 of merchandise on account to Huggins Company.

**Required:** Record the above transactions in the general journal below.

JOURNAL PAGE

| | DATE | | DESCRIPTION | POST. REF. | DEBIT | CREDIT | |
|---|---|---|---|---|---|---|---|
| 1 | | | | | | | 1 |
| 2 | | | | | | | 2 |
| 3 | | | | | | | 3 |
| 4 | | | | | | | 4 |
| 5 | | | | | | | 5 |
| 6 | | | | | | | 6 |
| 7 | | | | | | | 7 |
| 8 | | | | | | | 8 |
| 9 | | | | | | | 9 |
| 10 | | | | | | | 10 |
| 11 | | | | | | | 11 |
| 12 | | | | | | | 12 |
| 13 | | | | | | | 13 |
| 14 | | | | | | | 14 |
| 15 | | | | | | | 15 |
| 16 | | | | | | | 16 |
| 17 | | | | | | | 17 |
| 18 | | | | | | | 18 |
| 19 | | | | | | | 19 |
| 20 | | | | | | | 20 |
| 21 | | | | | | | 21 |
| 22 | | | | | | | 22 |
| 23 | | | | | | | 23 |
| 24 | | | | | | | 24 |
| 25 | | | | | | | 25 |
| 26 | | | | | | | 26 |
| 27 | | | | | | | 27 |

**12B-3.** A. The Penley Dental Equipment Company received from customers the notes described below.

| | Date | Term | Interest Rate | Face Value | Due Date | Interest |
|---|---|---|---|---|---|---|
| No. 1. | April 10 | 2 months | 15% | $1,000 | ______ | ______ |
| No. 2. | June 17 | 60 days | 12% | 3,000 | ______ | ______ |
| No. 3. | June 21 | 90 days | 12% | 1,200 | ______ | ______ |
| No. 4. | July 6 | 90 days | none | 1,500 | ______ | ______ |
| No. 5. | August 1 | 75 days | 9% | 1,800 | ______ | ______ |

**Required:** Determine the due date and amount of interest due on each note at maturity and insert in the spaces provided.

B. Assume that note No. 3 was discounted on August 20 at the rate of 12% and that note No. 4 was discounted on August 5 at 12%.

**Required:**

(a) Determine the following for each note:

1. Maturity value.
2. Discount period.
3. Amount of discount.
4. Proceeds.

| Note | Maturity Value | Discount Period | Amount of Discount | Proceeds |
|---|---|---|---|---|
| No. 3. | ______ | ______ | ______ | ______ |
| No. 4. | ______ | ______ | ______ | ______ |

(b) Prepare the entries in the general journal of Penley to record the discounting of the notes.

JOURNAL PAGE

| | DATE | | DESCRIPTION | POST. REF. | DEBIT | CREDIT | |
|---|---|---|---|---|---|---|---|
| 1 | | | | | | | 1 |
| 2 | | | | | | | 2 |
| 3 | | | | | | | 3 |
| 4 | | | | | | | 4 |
| 5 | | | | | | | 5 |
| 6 | | | | | | | 6 |
| 7 | | | | | | | 7 |
| 8 | | | | | | | 8 |
| 9 | | | | | | | 9 |
| 10 | | | | | | | 10 |
| 11 | | | | | | | 11 |

**12B-4.** The Wooden Indian Construction Company frequently finances its operations by the use of short-term notes payable and discounting customers' notes receivable.

**Required:** Record in the general journal below and on pages 557 and 558 the following transactions for Wooden Indian Construction Company concerning the issuing, discounting, and paying of notes from May through October of the current year.

May 6. Issued a 90-day, 12 percent, $1,200 note to Rivera Cement Company to replace an open account.
20. Paid Andra Brick Company for a $400, 60-day, 15 percent note due today plus interest.
June 9. Issued a 60-day, 10 percent note to the Girdie Gravel Company for gravel delivered to a job site at a total cost of $720.
10. Received a $1,500, 90-day, non-interest-bearing note from John Houland as payment for merchandise purchased.
15. Discounted its own 30-day, non-interest-bearing note for $600 at the Cherokee National Bank at a discount rate of 12 percent.
22. Issued a 4-month, 9 percent note to Adkins Lumber Company in payment of its account due today in the amount of $2,000.
July 10. Discounted John Houland's $1,500, 90-day, non-interest-bearing note at the Cherokee National Bank. The discount rate was 12 percent.
12. Issued a 120-day, 11 percent note payable to the Mercantile Bank for cash in the amount of $4,000.
15. Paid Cherokee National Bank for the note discounted June 15, due today.
Aug. 4. Paid note payable to Rivera Cement Company due today. (Issued May 6.)
8. Paid note payable to Girdie Gravel Company due today. (Issued June 9.)
Sept. 8. The bank notified Wooden Indian that Houland had dishonored his note. Wooden Indian paid the amount due plus a $5 service charge.
Oct. 8. Received the amount due from Houland plus interest at 12 percent on the balance owed since the due date.

**JOURNAL** PAGE

| DATE | DESCRIPTION | POST. REF. | DEBIT | CREDIT |
|---|---|---|---|---|

## JOURNAL

PAGE

| DATE | | DESCRIPTION | POST. REF. | DEBIT | CREDIT |
|---|---|---|---|---|---|

(Continued)

JOURNAL PAGE

| DATE | | DESCRIPTION | POST. REF. | DEBIT | CREDIT |
|---|---|---|---|---|---|

| Perfect Score | 20 | Name ____________ | |
|---|---|---|---|
| Student's Score | ___ | Date ____________ | Class ________ |

## RECORDING AND COSTING INVENTORIES

**Instructions.** Complete each of the following statements by writing your answer in the space provided.

| No. | Statement | Answer | For Scoring |
|---|---|---|---|
| 1 | Goods purchased by a business specifically for resale are called........... | | 1 |
| 2 | Normally the largest single expense on the income statement of a mercantile enterprise is........... | | 2 |
| 3 | The inventory system whereby the acquisition of merchandise is shown as a debit to Purchases is called the........... | | 3 |
| 4 | The process of counting or otherwise measuring the quantity of goods on hand is known as........... | | 4 |
| 5 | On the inventory sheet the extensions are computed by multiplying the unit cost by the........... | | 5 |
| 6 | The form that provides columns to show the stock number of each item, description, unit cost, quantity, and extensions is called a(n)... | | 6 |
| 7 | The inventory method based on the assumption that the most recent unit costs of goods should be charged to cost of goods sold is........... | | 7 |
| 8 | The inventory method whereby the most recent unit costs of goods are charged to inventory is........... | | 8 |
| 9 | The inventory method that considers the number of units purchased as well as the unit costs is the........... | | 9 |
| 10 | The inventory method most consistent with the actual flow of the goods is........... | | 10 |

**Instructions.** Determine whether each of the following statements is true or false and place a check mark in the appropriate column.

| No. | Statement | True | False | For Scoring |
|---|---|---|---|---|
| 11 | In a mercantile enterprise the principal business activity is buying and selling merchandise........... | | | 11 |
| 12 | The best time to take a physical inventory is when the stock is at its lowest level........... | | | 12 |
| 13 | The extensions on the inventory sheet will normally be filled in before the counting starts........... | | | 13 |
| 14 | Under the lifo method the units on hand at the end of the period will be those purchased last........... | | | 14 |
| 15 | The fifo method assumes that the inventory is composed of the most recent purchases........... | | | 15 |
| 16 | A major advantage of the fifo method is that it matches the cost of the most recent purchases against current revenue........... | | | 16 |

*(Continued)*

| No. | Statement | True | False | For Scoring |
|---|---|---|---|---|
| 17 | Under the weighted average method, the units in cost of goods sold and the units still in the inventory would be valued at the same unit cost .......... | | | 17 |
| 18 | In a period of rising prices, the lifo method will yield the highest ending inventory .......... | | | 18 |
| 19 | In a period of rising prices, the fifo method will yield the highest net income .......... | | | 19 |
| 20 | If the cost of the units purchased during the period remains constant, all three methods will provide the same cost of goods sold .......... | | | 20 |

**13A-1.** There were 400 units of Mo on hand at the beginning of the period which cost $9.50 each. During the period three purchases of Mo were made in the following order: (1) 800 units at $9 per unit; (2) 400 units at $8 per unit, and (3) 500 units at $7.50 per unit.

**Required:**

(a) Compute the total cost of the 600 units on hand at the end of the period if the first-in, first-out method is used. (Show your computations.)

(b) Compute the cost of the 600 units in the inventory if the last-in, first-out method is used. (Show your computations.)

(c) Compute the cost of goods sold during the period using: (1) fifo and (2) lifo. (Show your computations.)

**13A-2.** The beginning inventory and purchases of Part TR-80 for the year are given below:

| | |
|---|---|
| Inventory, January 1 | 90 units @ $ 9.00 |
| March 10 purchase | 60 units @ 9.60 |
| June 3 purchase | 120 units @ 10.20 |
| September 9 purchase | 90 units @ 11.00 |

**Required:** Determine the cost of the 110 units on hand at the end of the year by the following methods. (Show your computations.)

(a) Fifo method.

(b) Lifo method.

(c) Weighted average method.

**13A-3.** Indicate the effect the errors in inventory listed below would have on (a) cost of goods sold, (b) net income, and (c) total assets, as shown on the financial statements at the end of the year using the following signs: overstated, +; understated, −; no effect, 0.

| | Cost of Goods Sold | Net Income | Total Assets |
|---|---|---|---|
| 1. Ending inventory understated | | | |
| 2. Beginning inventory understated | | | |
| 3. Goods in transit had been recorded as a purchase but not included in inventory | | | |
| 4. Goods shipped to customer on consignment were not included in inventory | | | |
| 5. Ending inventory overstated | | | |
| 6. A purchase invoice was recorded twice | | | |
| 7. One stack of goods was not counted in the ending inventory | | | |
| 8. Beginning inventory overstated | | | |

**13A-4.** Below is the subsidiary ledger account for Widgets, for the month of November.

WIDGETS

| | | | | |
|---|---|---|---|---|
| Nov. 1 | Bal. | 180 @ $40 | 7,200 | Sold during November — 550 units |
| 10 | | 190 @ $42 | 7,980 | |
| 15 | | 210 @ $44 | 9,240 | |
| 23 | | 170 @ $45 | 7,650 | |

**Required:**

(a) Determine the cost of the inventory at the end of November (and show your computations) by each of the following methods:

1. First-in, first-out.

2. Last-in, first-out.

3. Weighted average.

(b) Determine the cost of goods sold for November:

1. If the fifo method is used.

2. If the lifo method is used.

**13A-5.** The following income statement was presented by the Kailua Company for the fiscal year ended December of the current year.

KAILUA COMPANY

____________________

________________________

| | | | |
|---|---|---|---|
| Revenue: | | | |
| ________ | | $ ........ | |
| Less: Sales returns and allowances | $ 450 | | |
| ________ | ........ | 500 | |
| ________ | | | $ 39,300 |
| Cost of goods sold: | | | |
| ________ | | $ 14,000 | |
| Purchases | $ ........ | | |
| Less Purchases returns and allowances | 400 | | |
| ________ | | 17,600 | |
| ________ | | $ ........ | |
| Less Merchandise inventory, December 31, 19__ | | 12,700 | |
| ________ | | | ........ |
| ________ | | | $ ........ |
| ________: | | | |
| ________: | | | |
| Sales salary expense | $ 4,200 | | |
| Advertising expense | 1,150 | | |
| Store supplies expense | 400 | | |
| Total selling expenses | | $ ........ | |
| ________: | | | |
| Office salary expense | $ 1,900 | | |
| Office supplies expense | 400 | | |
| Insurance expense | 180 | | |
| Total general expenses | | ........ | |
| Total operating expense | | | ........ |
| ________ | | | $ ........ |

**Required:**

(a) Fill in the missing words and amounts in the spaces provided.

(b) Prepare the entries necessary to adjust the merchandise inventory at the end of the year, using the form on the following page.

JOURNAL PAGE

| DATE | | DESCRIPTION | POST. REF. | DEBIT | CREDIT |
|---|---|---|---|---|---|

*(Page not used.)*

| Perfect Score | 15 | Name ______ | |
|---|---|---|---|
| Student's Score | ___ | Date ______ | Class ______ |

## SPECIAL PROCEDURES IN INVENTORY VALUATION

**Instructions.** Complete each of the following statements by writing the missing word(s) in the space provided.

| No. | Statement | Answer | For Scoring |
|---|---|---|---|
| 1 | When the replacement cost of goods in the inventory has declined below original cost by a substantial amount, a procedure may be used for valuing the inventory called the.......... | | 1 |
| 2 | The lower of cost or market rule cannot be applied when the ______ method of costing the inventory is used.......... | | 2 |
| 3 | The financial statements prepared for a period shorter than a fiscal year are referred to as .......... | | 3 |
| 4 | A method of determining inventory value that utilizes the estimated percentage of gross profit realized on sales during previous periods is the.......... | | 4 |
| 5 | A method of estimating inventories that is widely used in retail businesses is the.......... | | 5 |
| 6 | The retail method of inventory valuation requires keeping records of purchases and ______ at both cost and retail prices .......... | | 6 |
| 7 | Under a ______ inventory system, a day-to-day record of inventory is maintained.......... | | 7 |
| 8 | When merchandise is purchased under the perpetual inventory system, the account debited is .......... | | 8 |
| 9 | When merchandise is sold under the perpetual inventory system, the reduction in inventory is recorded by a debit to .......... | | 9 |
| 10 | The account(s) credited in No. 9 is (are).......... | | 10 |

**Instructions.** Sedwick Shoe Store has engaged you to check the accuracy of its March 31 inventory. You have been given the following information as of March 31: inventory January 1, at cost, $6,075, at retail, $9,800; purchases January–March, at cost, $17,325, at retail, $26,200. Sales for the period January–March were $25,000. Complete each of the following statements by writing your answer in the space provided.

| No. | Statement | Answer | For Scoring |
|---|---|---|---|
| 11 | Merchandise available for sale at cost is.......... | $ | 11 |
| 12 | Merchandise available for sale at retail is.......... | $ | 12 |
| 13 | Cost to retail percentage is.......... | % | 13 |
| 14 | Inventory at March 31 at retail is.......... | $ | 14 |
| 15 | Inventory at March 31 at cost is.......... | $ | 15 |

**13B-1.** The Tampa Variety Shop had the following items in its ending inventory on December 31:

| Item | Quantity | Unit Cost | Unit Market |
|---|---|---|---|
| Dept. R | | | |
| R74 | 1,400 | $1.10 | $1.15 |
| R80 | 1,000 | 1.60 | 1.50 |
| R82 | 900 | .85 | .95 |
| Dept. T | | | |
| T143 | 820 | 2.20 | 2.30 |
| T151 | 700 | 3.10 | 3.00 |
| T157 | 500 | 2.70 | 2.60 |

**Required:** Using the form below, determine the value of the store's inventory using "cost or market, whichever is lower," assuming the valuation procedure is applied to:

(a) the individual item.
(b) each department.
(c) the inventory as a whole.

**13B-2.** The Redfern Wicker Shop's inventory was completely destroyed by fire on March 4. The safe was fireproof and the following information was obtained from the accounting records. Merchandise on hand, January 1, $8,200; purchases since January 1, $19,350; purchases returned, $550; purchase discounts taken, $400. Net retail sales for the quarter were $22,400. The store's average gross profit rate for the past several years had been 45%.

**Required:** On the form below, determine the cost of the inventory destroyed, using the gross profit method.

**13B-3.** Amos Jefferson owns a toy shop and has maintained a retail inventory system for several years. Jefferson has decided to prepare interim financial statements on September 30. You determined from the records of the store the following information: merchandise, January 1 at retail, $20,500, at cost $14,000; net purchases for the nine month period at retail, $89,500, at cost, $52,000; net sales for the nine-month period, $82,000; operating expenses for the nine month period, $19,400.

**Required:**

(a) On the form below, determine the estimated cost of inventory as of September 30, using the retail method.

(b) Prepare an income statement for Jefferson Toy Shop for the first nine months.

**13B-4.** An inventory stock record card for WUZ is presented below. The fifo method of inventory is used for WUZ, and all sales are at a retail price of $10 per unit.

INVENTORY STOCK RECORD CARD

Description *WUZ* Stock No. *W70*

Inventory Level: Maximum *20* Minimum *6*

Department *Finishing* Reorder Time *7 days*

| DATE | RECEIVED | | | ISSUED | | | BALANCE | | |
|---|---|---|---|---|---|---|---|---|---|
| | Pur. Order | Quantity | Unit Price | Sales Ticket No. | Quantity | Unit Price | Quantity | Unit Price | Total |
| *7-1* | | | | | | | *14* | *6.00* | *84.00* |
| *7-5* | | | | *1607* | *6* | | | | |
| *7-9* | *853* | *8* | *6.20* | | | | | | |
| *7-21* | | | | *1660* | *10* | | | | |
| *7-24* | *899* | *12* | *6.25* | | | | | | |

**Required:**

(a) Complete the inventory stock record card above.

(b) In the general journal below and on page 572, prepare all entries to record the purchases (on account) and sales (on account) if a perpetual inventory system is used.

JOURNAL PAGE

| | DATE | | DESCRIPTION | POST. REF. | DEBIT | CREDIT | |
|---|---|---|---|---|---|---|---|
| 1 | | | | | | | 1 |
| 2 | | | | | | | 2 |
| 3 | | | | | | | 3 |
| 4 | | | | | | | 4 |
| 5 | | | | | | | 5 |
| 6 | | | | | | | 6 |
| 7 | | | | | | | 7 |
| 8 | | | | | | | 8 |
| 9 | | | | | | | 9 |
| 10 | | | | | | | 10 |
| 11 | | | | | | | 11 |
| 12 | | | | | | | 12 |

*(Continued)*

## JOURNAL

PAGE

| DATE | | DESCRIPTION | POST. REF. | DEBIT | CREDIT |
|---|---|---|---|---|---|

Assignment 14-A

**Perfect Score** 25 **Name** ____________

**Student's Score** ___ **Date** ____________ **Class** ________

## NATURE OF PLANT ASSETS AND DEPRECIATION

**Instructions.** Complete each statement and answer each question below by writing your answer in the space at the right.

| No. | Statement | Answer | For Scoring |
|---|---|---|---|
| 1 | Plant assets should be recorded in the accounts at | | 1 |
| 2 | The systematic allocation of the cost of a plant asset over its useful life is called | | 2 |
| 3 | The plant asset that is not subject to depreciation is | | 3 |
| 4 | The normal balance in the depreciation expense account is a | | 4 |
| 5 | The cost of the asset less accumulated depreciation is called the | | 5 |
| 6 | When the adjusting entry for depreciation is made at the end of the period, the account credited is | | 6 |
| 7 | If a machine is purchased on April 1 and will be depreciated at the rate of $600 per year, how much depreciation will be recorded on December 31 of the first year? | $ | 7 |
| 8 | The amount expected to be realized for a plant asset when it is disposed of is called | | 8 |
| 9 | The original cost of an asset less the expected salvage value is the | | 9 |
| 10 | Two factors that contribute to the decline in usefulness of plant assets, besides physical wear, are inadequacy and | | 10 |
| 11 | The depreciation method that provides equal periodic charges to expense over the life of the asset is | | 11 |
| 12 | The principal advantage of the straight-line method of depreciation is | | 12 |
| 13 | The procedure that charges a larger amount of depreciation expense in the early years of the asset life and a successively smaller amount in later years is known as | | 13 |
| 14 | If a machine is purchased on January 2, at a cost of $7,000 and has an estimated life of 6 years and a salvage value of 10% of cost, what will be the depreciation charge for the first year by the straight-line method? | $ | 14 |
| 15 | What will be the depreciation charge for the fourth year in No. 14 above? | $ | 15 |
| 16 | If the machine above would produce an estimated 30,000 units during its life, what would be the depreciation charge per unit if the units-of-production method is used? | $ | 16 |
| 17 | If 6,000 units are produced in year two, what will be the depreciation expense for that year using the units-of-production method? | $ | 17 |
| 18 | What would be the sum-of-the-years-digits for the life of the machine in No. 14? | | 18 |

*(Continued)*

| No. | Statement | Answer | For Scoring |
|---|---|---|---|
| 19 | What would be the depreciation expense for the first year by the sum-of-the-years-digits method? | $ | 19 |
| 20 | What would be the depreciation expense for the third year by the sum-of-the-years-digits method? | $ | 20 |
| 21 | If equipment is purchased on January 2 at a cost of $24,000 with an estimated life of 8 years and a salvage value of $2,000, what will be the annual rate of depreciation using the declining-balance method at twice the straight-line rate? | % | 21 |
| 22 | What will be the depreciation expense for the first year in No. 21? | $ | 22 |
| 23 | What will be the book value of the equipment at the end of the first year? | $ | 23 |
| 24 | What will be the depreciation expense for the second year in No. 21? | $ | 24 |
| 25 | What will be the book value of the equipment at the end of the second year? | $ | 25 |

**14A-1.** Indicate in the columns given below which plant asset the following expenditures should be debited to; if none, check "Other."

| | Land | Building | Equipment | Other |
|---|---|---|---|---|
| 1. Insurance paid on office equipment during shipping | | | | |
| 2. Cost of typewriters to office equipment company for resale | | | | |
| 3. Freight charges on office equipment purchased | | | | |
| 4. Insurance paid during construction of building | | | | |
| 5. Maintenance contract on building | | | | |
| 6. Cost of repairing storm damage to building | | | | |
| 7. Fees paid abstract company for land title search | | | | |
| 8. Cost of carpet installed in new office building | | | | |
| 9. Insurance policy on new building | | | | |
| 10. Cost of typewriters to accounting firm | | | | |
| 11. State sales tax on equipment purchased | | | | |
| 12. Architect's fees on new building | | | | |
| 13. Installation charges on equipment | | | | |
| 14. Rebuilt engine on delivery truck | | | | |

**14A-2.** The Together Tee-Shirt Shop purchased a pressing machine to steam press decals on T-shirts. The pressing machine cost $2,200 and has an expected useful life of 10 years and estimated salvage value of $200.

**Required:**

(a) Compute the annual depreciation expense using the straight-line method.

(b) Prepare the journal entry to record the adjustment for depreciation at the end of the first year.

(c) Determine the book value of the asset at the end of the *fourth* year.

(d) Compute the rate of depreciation used if the above equipment were depreciated on the declining-balance method at twice the straight-line rate.

(e) Prepare the journal entries for Together Tee-Shirt Shop to record the adjustment for depreciation at the end of the first and second years if the declining-balance method at twice the straight-line rate is used.

**14A-3.** McMinn Ready-Mix Concrete Company purchased a concrete mixing truck at a cost of $40,000 at the beginning of the fiscal year. The truck has a useful life of 8 years and an estimated residual value of $4,000. McMinn anticipates driving this type of truck 120,000 miles.

**Required:** Determine for each of the first two years the depreciation expense per year, and the accumulated depreciation and book value at the end of each year for the following methods of depreciation:

| | | Depreciation Expense | Accumulated Depreciation | Book Value |
|---|---|---|---|---|
| (a) Straight-line | year 1 | | | |
| | year 2 | | | |
| (b) Units of production | year 1 (16,000 miles) | | | |
| | year 2 (17,000 miles) | | | |

*(Continued)*

| | | | | |
|---|---|---|---|---|
| (c) Sum-of-the-years-digits............year 1.................................. | ________ | ________ | ________ |
| year 2.................................. | ________ | ________ | ________ |
| (d) Declining-balance....................year 1.................................. | ________ | ________ | ________ |
| year 2.................................. | ________ | ________ | ________ |

**Retain the solution to this problem for use in Problem 14B-1.**

**14A-4.** The following is information for plant assets A, B, C, and D.

| Asset | Cost | Salvage Value | Estimated Life | Depreciation Method | Depreciation Yr. 1 | Depreciation Yr. 2 |
|---|---|---|---|---|---|---|
| A | $ 8,000 | $ 800 | 12 yrs. | Straight-line | ________ | ________ |
| B | 21,500 | 1,500 | 100,000 units | Units-of-production<br>Year 1 — 25,000 units<br>Year 2 — 20,000 units | ________ | ________ |
| C | 12,000 | 1,500 | 6 yrs. | Sum-of-the-years-digits | ________ | ________ |
| D | 20,000 | 1,200 | 10 yrs. | Declining-balance | ________ | ________ |

**Required:** Determine the depreciation expense for the first two years for each of the plant assets. Insert your answers in the spaces provided above.

**14A-5.** For each of the vehicles below, determine as of December 31, 1982, (1) the total accumulated depreciation to date, and (2) the book value. Enter the amounts in the appropriate columns.

| Vehicle | Date of Purchase | Cost | Salvage Value | Estimated Life | Depreciation Method | Accumulated Depreciation | Book Value |
|---|---|---|---|---|---|---|---|
| E | 4–1–79 | $ 9,800 | $800 | 6 yrs. | Straight-line | ________ | ________ |
| F | 6–30–80 | 9,000 | 600 | 12 yrs. | Straight-line | ________ | ________ |
| G | 1–4–81 | 6,000 | 400 | 7 yrs. | Sum-of-the-years-digits | ________ | ________ |
| H | 1–6–81 | 10,000 | 800 | 5 yrs. | Declining-balance | ________ | ________ |

Assignment 14-B

**Perfect Score** 20 Name ____________________

**Student's Score** ____ Date ____________ Class ________

## DISPOSAL OF PLANT ASSETS AND SPECIAL ASSET RECORDS

**Instructions.** Determine whether each of the following statements is true or false and place a check mark in the appropriate column.

| No. | Statement | True | False | For Scoring |
|---|---|---|---|---|
| 1 | When a plant asset is disposed of, the first step is to write-off the old asset | | | 1 |
| 2 | The difference between the amount received for the asset and its cost is the gain or loss from the sale | | | 2 |
| 3 | Gains and losses on the disposal of plant assets are shown on the income statement as separate items below "Income from operations" | | | 3 |
| 4 | When the trade-in allowance for a vehicle is larger than its book value, there will be a loss on the trade | | | 4 |
| 5 | Gains and losses on the exchange of similar types of plant assets are not recognized for income tax purposes | | | 5 |
| 6 | When the gain on an exchange is not recorded, the cost of the new asset will be the book value of the old asset plus the cash paid | | | 6 |
| 7 | It is not uncommon for a plant asset, such as equipment, to have a subsidiary ledger for recording the individual items | | | 7 |
| 8 | The depreciation will be recorded in each subsidiary asset account as a credit to Accumulated Depreciation | | | 8 |
| 9 | When equipment that has been fully depreciated is written off the books, the account credited is Accumulated Depreciation — Equipment | | | 9 |
| 10 | The equipment account in No. 9, would be debited for the cost of the asset minus the accumulated depreciation | | | 10 |

**Instructions.** Complete the statements and answer the questions below by writing your answer in the space provided.

| No. | Statement | Answer | For Scoring |
|---|---|---|---|
| 11 | If equipment with a book value of $1,200 is sold for $1,350, what will be the gain or loss on the sale? | $ | 11 |
| 12 | If equipment with a book value of $850 is sold for $500, what will be the gain or loss on the sale? | $ | 12 |
| 13 | Gains and losses on the disposal of plant assets are properly reported on the | | 13 |
| 14 | Furniture costing $2,600, which has been fully depreciated, is given to a junk dealer. What is the gain or loss on the disposal? | $ | 14 |

*(Continued)*

| No. | Statement | Answer | For Scoring |
|---|---|---|---|
| 15–17 | An automobile, used by the sales force, with a book value of $1,200 is traded in on a new model with a cost of $8,700. The trade-in allowance is $1,000 ........ | | |
| | What amount of cash will have to be paid? ........ | $ | 15 |
| | Will a gain or loss be recognized on the exchange for financial reporting purposes? ........ | $ | 16 |
| | What will be the recorded cost of the new car for financial reporting purposes? ........ | $ | 17 |
| 18–20 | If the trade-in allowance on the automobile in Nos. 15–17 above had been $1,500, determine the following: | | |
| | Cash to be paid ........ | $ | 18 |
| | Will a gain or loss on trade be recognized for financial reporting purposes? ........ | | 19 |
| | Recorded cost of the new car for income tax purposes ........ | $ | 20 |

**14B-1.** Using the data computed in Problem 14A-3, prepare the entries in general journal form for the following transactions for McMinn Ready-Mix Concrete Company.

(a) The truck was traded for a similar truck on January 1, 1983, the beginning of the third year. The new truck was priced at $42,500 and a trade-in of $20,000 was allowed on the old truck. (Sum-of-the-years-digits method.)

1. Entry to record the exchange for financial reporting purposes.

JOURNAL PAGE

| | DATE | | DESCRIPTION | POST. REF. | DEBIT | CREDIT | |
|---|---|---|---|---|---|---|---|
| 1 | | | | | | | 1 |
| 2 | | | | | | | 2 |
| 3 | | | | | | | 3 |
| 4 | | | | | | | 4 |
| 5 | | | | | | | 5 |
| 6 | | | | | | | 6 |

2. Entry to record the exchange for income tax purposes.

| | DATE | | DESCRIPTION | POST. REF. | DEBIT | CREDIT | |
|---|---|---|---|---|---|---|---|
| 7 | | | | | | | 7 |
| 8 | | | | | | | 8 |
| 9 | | | | | | | 9 |
| 10 | | | | | | | 10 |
| 11 | | | | | | | 11 |

(b) Assume the truck was traded on December 31, 1982, the end of the second year, for the new truck priced at $42,500 and a trade-in allowance of $24,000 was granted. (Declining-balance method.)

1. Entry to record the exchange for financial reporting purposes.

JOURNAL PAGE

| | DATE | | DESCRIPTION | POST. REF. | DEBIT | CREDIT | |
|---|---|---|---|---|---|---|---|
| 1 | | | | | | | 1 |
| 2 | | | | | | | 2 |
| 3 | | | | | | | 3 |
| 4 | | | | | | | 4 |
| 5 | | | | | | | 5 |

2. Entry to record the exchange for income tax purposes.

| | DATE | | DESCRIPTION | POST. REF. | DEBIT | CREDIT | |
|---|---|---|---|---|---|---|---|
| 6 | | | | | | | 6 |
| 7 | | | | | | | 7 |
| 8 | | | | | | | 8 |
| 9 | | | | | | | 9 |
| 10 | | | | | | | 10 |

**14B-2.** El Matamoras Bakery uses panel trucks for all local deliveries. The following transactions relating to these delivery trucks were made during the years 1981–1983.

1981

Jan. 10. Purchased a used panel truck for $3,600, paying $2,000 cash and giving a note payable for the balance.

12. Added an air conditioning unit to the truck, $400. (Debit Delivery Truck.)

May 5. Maintenance and minor repairs to truck $75.

Dec. 31. Recorded depreciation on the truck for the year. Estimated life is four years, with a trade-in value of $800, straight-line method is used.

31. Close all temporary accounts to Income Summary.

1982

Mar. 31. Traded in the panel truck on a new one priced at $8,000. Received a trade-in allowance of $2,700 and paid the balance in cash. (Bring depreciation up to date. The financial reporting method is to be used in recording the exchange.)

Nov. 5. New plugs and points and other minor repairs to the truck totaling $160 were paid.

Dec. 31. Record depreciation on the truck for the year. Estimated life is 90,000 miles, trade-in value $800. Miles driven this year, 12,000. (Use the unit-of-production method.)

31. Close all temporary accounts to Income Summary.

1983

Oct. 10. Sold the truck for $5,500, receiving cash. Miles driven during 1983, 14,000.

Dec. 31. Close all temporary accounts to Income Summary.

**Required:** Record the above transactions in the general journal forms provided on pages 582–583, posting after each entry only to the selected ledger accounts given below and on the following page. (Note: ledger accounts are not provided for every item.)

ACCOUNT *Delivery Truck* ACCOUNT NO. *14*

| DATE | | ITEM | POST. REF. | DEBIT | CREDIT | BALANCE | |
|---|---|---|---|---|---|---|---|
| | | | | | | DEBIT | CREDIT |
| | | | | | | | |
| | | | | | | | |
| | | | | | | | |
| | | | | | | | |
| | | | | | | | |
| | | | | | | | |

ACCOUNT *Accumulated Depreciation — Delivery Truck* ACCOUNT NO. *14.1*

| DATE | | ITEM | POST. REF. | DEBIT | CREDIT | BALANCE | |
|---|---|---|---|---|---|---|---|
| | | | | | | DEBIT | CREDIT |
| | | | | | | | |
| | | | | | | | |
| | | | | | | | |
| | | | | | | | |
| | | | | | | | |
| | | | | | | | |
| | | | | | | | |
| | | | | | | | |

ACCOUNT *Delivery Truck Repairs Expense* ACCOUNT NO. 51

| DATE | | ITEM | POST. REF. | DEBIT | CREDIT | BALANCE DEBIT | BALANCE CREDIT |
|---|---|---|---|---|---|---|---|
| | | | | | | | |
| | | | | | | | |
| | | | | | | | |
| | | | | | | | |
| | | | | | | | |
| | | | | | | | |

ACCOUNT *Depreciation Expense — Delivery Truck* ACCOUNT NO. 52

| DATE | | ITEM | POST. REF. | DEBIT | CREDIT | BALANCE DEBIT | BALANCE CREDIT |
|---|---|---|---|---|---|---|---|
| | | | | | | | |
| | | | | | | | |
| | | | | | | | |
| | | | | | | | |
| | | | | | | | |
| | | | | | | | |
| | | | | | | | |
| | | | | | | | |
| | | | | | | | |

ACCOUNT *Loss on Exchange of Delivery Truck* ACCOUNT NO. 79

| DATE | | ITEM | POST. REF. | DEBIT | CREDIT | BALANCE DEBIT | BALANCE CREDIT |
|---|---|---|---|---|---|---|---|
| | | | | | | | |
| | | | | | | | |
| | | | | | | | |

ACCOUNT *Loss on Sale of Delivery Truck* ACCOUNT NO. 82

| DATE | | ITEM | POST. REF. | DEBIT | CREDIT | BALANCE DEBIT | BALANCE CREDIT |
|---|---|---|---|---|---|---|---|
| | | | | | | | |
| | | | | | | | |
| | | | | | | | |
| | | | | | | | |

# JOURNAL

PAGE 9

| DATE | DESCRIPTION | POST. REF. | DEBIT | CREDIT |
|---|---|---|---|---|

## JOURNAL

PAGE *10*

| DATE | DESCRIPTION | POST. REF. | DEBIT | CREDIT |
|---|---|---|---|---|

**14B-3.** Westgate Hospital purchased a heavy duty floor buffer and cleaner (Cleaning Equipment) from Allied Equipment Company on January 5, 1977, at a cost of $1,800. The buffer had an estimated useful life of six years and no residual value.

**Required:**

(a) Fill in the plant asset record below for the buffer through December 31, 1981. The account number is 21-6. Westgate Hospital uses straight-line depreciation on all equipment.

**PLANT ASSET RECORD** Account No. ____________

Item ______________________ General Ledger Account ______________________

From Whom Purchased ____________________________________________

Estimated Life ____________ Estimated Scrap or Trade-In Value ____________ Depreciation Per Year ____________

| Date | | | Explanation | Asset | | | Accumulated Depreciation | | | Book Value |
|---|---|---|---|---|---|---|---|---|---|---|
| Mo. | Day | Yr. | | Debit | Credit | Balance | Debit | Credit | Balance | |
| | | | | | | | | | | |
| | | | | | | | | | | |
| | | | | | | | | | | |
| | | | | | | | | | | |
| | | | | | | | | | | |
| | | | | | | | | | | |
| | | | | | | | | | | |
| | | | | | | | | | | |
| | | | | | | | | | | |
| | | | | | | | | | | |
| | | | | | | | | | | |

(b) Assuming that the buffer is retired on June 30, 1982 with no salvage value being realized, prepare the general journal entries to (1) bring the depreciation up to date as of June 30, 1982, and (2) to retire the asset.

JOURNAL PAGE

| | DATE | | DESCRIPTION | POST. REF. | DEBIT | CREDIT | |
|---|---|---|---|---|---|---|---|
| 1 | | | | | | | 1 |
| 2 | | | | | | | 2 |
| 3 | | | | | | | 3 |
| 4 | | | | | | | 4 |
| 5 | | | | | | | 5 |
| 6 | | | | | | | 6 |
| 7 | | | | | | | 7 |
| 8 | | | | | | | 8 |
| 9 | | | | | | | 9 |

# SUPPLEMENTARY PROBLEMS

The following problems supplement those in Assignments 1-A through 14-B. These problems are designated to indicate the chapter part with which they correlate. For example, Problem 1S-2 (Part B) is the second supplementary problem for Chapter 1 and can only be completed after Part B of Chapter 1 has been studied. Looseleaf notebook paper can be used in solving these problems. Check with your instructor to determine whether notebook paper or accounting papers should be used in preparing these solutions.

## CHAPTER 1

**1S-1 (Part A).** The financial condition of Dulan Window Cleaning Company on January 1 is shown by the following equation:

| ASSETS | | | | | | | = | LIABILITIES | + | OWNER'S EQUITY |
|---|---|---|---|---|---|---|---|---|---|---|
| Cash | + | Cleaning Supplies | + | Cleaning Equipment | + | Building | = | Accounts Payable | + | Steve Dulan, Capital |
| $2,100 | | $1,700 | | $8,500 | | $20,000 | | $4,200 | | $28,100 |

The following transactions were completed by Dulan during January:

(a) Invested additional cash in the business, $450.
(b) Purchased cleaning supplies for cash, $100.
(c) Purchased cleaning equipment on credit, $650.
(d) Collected cash for services rendered, $450.
(e) Sold cleaning equipment at cost, receiving cash, $300.
(f) Paid on accounts payable, $400.
(g) Fire destroyed equipment that cost $700. This amount was a total loss as there was no insurance.
(h) Paid utilities for the month, $270.
(i) Used cleaning supplies costing $60.
(j) Collected cash for services rendered, $210.
(k) Withdrew cash from the business, $250.

**Instructions.** Prepare an equation stating the changes that each of the transactions produced in the assets, liabilities, and owner's equity of Dulan, indicating the new balance after each transaction.

**1S-2. (Part B).** Rita Morley, the proprietor of Morley Company, had a capital balance on October 1 of the current year of $14,100. During the month of October, Morley earned revenue of $5,700 and incurred the following expenses: salaries, $1,500; rent, $300; utilities, $210; insurance, $30; miscellaneous, $60. During the month, Morley withdrew $500 for personal living expenses.

**Instructions:**

(1) Prepare an income statement for the month ended October 31, using a form as shown on page 13.
(2) Prepare a capital statement for the month ended October 31, using a form as shown on page 13.

**1S-3 (Part B).** Harry Hall is the proprietor of Hall Laundry. On March 1 of the current year, the business had the following account balances:

| | |
|---|---|
| Cash | $ 950 |
| Laundry Supplies | 415 |
| Accounts Payable — TCU Suppliers | 730 |
| Notes Payable — Second National Bank | 20,000 |
| Land | 14,000 |
| Building | 45,000 |
| Fixtures | 2,400 |
| Laundry Equipment | 8,500 |
| Harry Hall, Capital | 50,775 |
| Accounts Receivable — Max Cole | 240 |

**Instructions:** Prepare a balance sheet in account form as of March 1, using a form as shown on page 8.

**1S-4 (Part B).** Ross Tatum, owner of Tatum Painting Company, completed the following transactions during June of the current year:

(a) Invested cash in the business, $10,000.
(b) Purchased brushes and supplies, paying cash, $250.
(c) Purchased 40 gallons of paint at $6 per gallon from Keith Co. on account.
(d) Bought a truck from LTD Co. for $8,000, paying $4,000 cash and the balance on account.
(e) Purchased ladders, spray-guns, and other painting equipment from Keith Co. on account, $975.
(f) Painted a house, receiving cash, $800.
(g) Paid LTD Co. on the truck purchased in (d), $500.
(h) Paid helper's salary, $140.
(i) Painted a warehouse damaged by fire, receiving cash, $1,200.
(j) Withdrew cash from the business for personal use, $300.
(k) Paid Keith Co. for paint purchased in (c).
(l) Paid the following expenses for the month: advertising, $45; insurance, $40; miscellaneous, $30.

**Instructions:**

(1) Using the following equation format, record the transactions for the month of June. Find the new account balances after each transaction.

| ASSETS | | | | = | LIABILITIES | | + | OWNER'S EQUITY |
|---|---|---|---|---|---|---|---|---|
| Cash | + Paints & Supplies | + Painting Equipment | + Truck | | Accts. Payable Keith Co. | + Accts. Payable LTD Co. | | Ross Tatum, Capital |

(2) Analyze the above transactions and prepare an income statement for the month of June. Be sure to list the individual expense items.
(3) Prepare a capital statement for the month of June.
(4) Prepare a report form balance sheet as of June 30.

## CHAPTER 2

**2S-1. (Part A).** The following trial balance was taken from the ledger accounts of Stone Company as of August 31 of the current year.

STONE COMPANY
Trial Balance
August 31, 19--

| | | |
|---|---|---|
| Cash | 825 | |
| Office Supplies | 220 | |
| Furniture and Fixtures | 2,400 | |
| Delivery Equipment | 4,000 | |
| Accounts Payable — Dim Co. | | 750 |
| Martha, Capital | | 6,695 |
| | 7,445 | 7,445 |

**Instructions:** Prepare a report form balance sheet for Stone Company as of August 31.

**2S-2. (Part A).** On February 1 of the current year, Bill Niekro was preparing to open Bill's Barber Shop. At that time he had the following assets: cash, $250; barber supplies, $175; barber equipment, $3,000; furniture and fixtures, $3,600. He owed the Lum Equipment Co. $900 for barber equipment purchased on account. Niekro completed the following transactions during February.

Feb. 2. Invested additional cash in the business, $1,000.
5. Purchased additional barber equipment from the Lum Equipment Co. on account, $500.
6. Purchased barber supplies for cash, $150.
9. Paid Lum Equipment Co. on account, $400.
12. Purchased barber supplies from LSL Co. on account, $100.
17. Sold some fixtures for cash at cost, $200.
24. Paid LSL Co. one half of the amount owed from the February 12 transaction.
28. Sold supplies to a neighborhood beauty shop for cash at the cost price, $30.

**Instructions:**

(1) Prepare a trial balance as of February 1, using a form as shown on page 24.
(2) Open a ledger account for each item on the trial balance, using forms as shown on page 23.
(3) Record the transactions for February in the accounts and open any new accounts that may be needed.
(4) Foot the accounts and enter the balances in the ledger. Prepare a trial balance as of the close of business on February 28, of the current year.

**2S-3 (Part A).** Barbara Chow is in the process of opening a lawn mower repair shop and completed the following transactions for the month of March of the current year.

Mar. 1. Invested in the business, $1,500.
3. Purchased repair equipment from Pryor Equipment on account, $2,000.
6. Purchased furniture and fixtures from Key Co. on account, $1,600.
8. Purchased repair supplies for cash, $200.
11. Borrowed from the Citizen's Bank (note payable) for use in the business, $1,000.
14. Paid Pryor Equipment Co. on account owed, $800.
20. Returned a table (Furniture and Fixtures) to Key Co. which was not satisfactory. Key gave Chow credit on the account for the cost of the table, $60.
22. Paid Key Co. on account owed, $840.
25. Purchased repair equipment for cash, $400.
28. Sold repair supplies to the business next door at cost, $45.
31. Invested additional cash in the business, $500.

**Instructions:**

(1) Prepare a ledger for Chow Lawn Mower Repairs, using the following account titles: Cash; Repair Supplies; Repair Equipment; Furniture and Fixtures; Accounts Payable — Pryor Equipment Co.; Accounts Payable — Key Co.; Notes Payable — Citizen's Bank; Barbara Chow, Capital.
(2) Record the March transactions in the account.
(3) Foot the accounts and enter the balances in the ledger. Prepare a trial balance as of March 31.
(4) Prepare a report form balance sheet as of the close of business, March 31.

**2S-4 (Part B).** The following selected ledger account balances are given for Welch Shoe Repairs as of April 30 of the current year.

| | |
|---|---|
| Joe Welch, Capital, April 1 | $2,160 |
| Joe Welch, Drawing | 200 |
| Revenue from Repairs | 1,210 |
| Salary Expense | 325 |
| Rent Expense | 150 |
| Utilities Expense | 90 |
| Supplies Expense | 55 |

**Instructions:**

(1) Prepare an income statement for Welch Shoe Repairs for the month of April.
(2) Prepare a capital statement for April.

**2S-5 (Part B).** Lynn Domino decided to open an office cleaning business known as Domino Cleaning Service. During the month of January, Domino completed the following transactions:

Jan. 2. Invested in the business $900 cash and a truck worth $2,100.
3. Purchased vacuum cleaners and other cleaning equipment from Aim Equipment Co. on account, $1,600.
3. Purchased cleaning supplies from Try Supplies on account, $180.
5. Received cash for cleaning jobs, $470.
7. Paid for advertising in a local paper, $25.

*(Continued)*

10. Paid garage bill for minor truck repairs, $95.
15. Paid Aim Equipment Co. on account, $300.
17. Received cash for cleaning office, $400.
18. Paid rent for the month, $180.
20. Paid service station for gas and oil for truck, $75.
22. Received cash for cleaning dentist's office, $190.
25. Domino withdrew cash for personal use, $75.
28. Paid salary to helper, $200.
29. Paid Try Supplies on account, $100.

**Instructions:**

(1) Open a ledger for Domino Cleaning Service, using the following accounts: Cash; Cleaning Supplies; Cleaning Equipment; Truck; Accounts Payable — Aim Equipment Co.; Accounts Payable — Try Supplies; Lynn Domino, Capital; Lynn Domino, Drawing; Cleaning Revenue; Salary Expense; Rent Expense; Truck Expense; Advertising Expense.
(2) Record the transactions for the month of January in the ledger.
(3) Foot the accounts and enter the balances in the ledger. Prepare a trial balance as of the close of business on January 31.
(4) Prepare an income statement for January.
(5) Prepare a capital statement for January.
(6) Prepare an account form balance sheet as of January 31.

## CHAPTER 3

**3S-1 (Part A).** Zane Wilson opened a television repair business on October 1 of the current year. Wilson completed the following transactions:

Oct. 1. Wilson invested $1,000 cash and repair equipment worth $2,500 in the business.
1. Paid rent for the month, $160.
3. Purchased repair supplies from T-V Co. on account, $140.
5. Purchased furniture and fixtures for cash, $600.
6. Received cash for repair jobs, $280.
8. Paid for ad in local newspaper, $25.
10. Purchased additional repair equipment from the Channel Equipment Co. on account, $400.
11. Received cash from repair jobs, $240.
14. Paid T-V Co. on amount owed, $100.
15. Purchased repair supplies from T-V Co. for cash, $75.
20. Received cash for repair jobs, $190.
22. Paid miscellaneous expenses, $40.
25. Paid Channel Equipment Co. on account, $200.
26. Paid salary to help for the month, $260.
28. Paid utilities for the month, $115.
30. Received cash for a repair job, $240.
31. Paid Channel Equipment Co. on account, $100.
31. Wilson withdrew cash for personal use, $150.

**Instructions:** Record the transactions for October in a general journal as shown on page 41, using the following account titles: Cash; Repair Supplies; Repair Equipment; Furniture and Fixtures; Accounts Payable — Channel Equipment Co.; Accounts Payable — T-V Co.; Zane Wilson, Capital; Zane Wilson, Drawing; Repair Revenue; Advertising Expense; Rent Expense; Utilities Expense; Salary Expense; Miscellaneous Expense.

**3S-2 (Part B).** The Ovard Company has the following list of accounts: Advertising Expense; Cash; Office Supplies; Miscellaneous Expense; Judy Ovard, Drawing; Service Revenue; Accounts Payable — Reed Wholesale; Accounts Payable — Garland Equipment Co.; Rent Expense; Judy Ovard, Capital; Salary Expense; Office Equipment; Furniture and Fixtures.

**Instructions:** Prepare a two-digit chart of accounts for the Ovard Company from the above list of accounts.

**3S-3 (Part B).** Bill Luker opened a dry cleaners known as Luker's Cleaners on March 1 of the current year. Luker's chart of accounts is given below.

**Assets**
- 11 Cash
- 12 Supplies
- 13 Furniture and Fixtures
- 14 Equipment

**Liabilities**
- 21 Accounts Payable — American Equip. Co.
- 22 Accounts Payable — Eco Supplies

**Owner's Equity**
- 31 Bill Luker, Capital
- 32 Bill Luker, Drawing

**Revenue**
- 41 Cleaning Revenue

**Expenses**
- 51 Rent Expense
- 52 Repairs Expense
- 53 Salary Expense
- 54 Utilities Expense

The following transactions were completed during March:

Mar. 1. Luker invested cash in the business, $5,000.
1. Paid rent expense for March, $190.
1. Purchased equipment from American Equipment Co. for $8,000, paying $2,000 in cash and the balance on account.
2. Purchased tables, chairs, light fixtures, and other furniture for the store, paying cash, $1,200.
4. Purchased various supplies from Eco Suppliers on account, $180.
10. Recorded cleaning revenue, $360.
14. Paid for minor repairs to equipment, $37.
16. Purchased supplies for cash, $25.
19. Recorded cleaning revenue, $150.
20. Paid American Equipment Co. on account, $200.
27. Paid utility bills: water, $42; electricity, $72; and gas, $15.
29. Paid to have machines repaired, $80.
30. Paid Eco Suppliers on account, $75.
31. Paid salary to helper for March, $330.
31. Luker withdrew cash for personal use, $60.
31. Recorded cleaning revenue, $210.

**Instructions:**
(1) Open ledger accounts for each item appearing in Luker's chart of accounts.
(2) Record the above transactions in a general journal.
(3) Post the transactions to the ledger accounts. Be sure to use posting references. Foot the accounts and enter the balances.
(4) Prepare a trial balance of the ledger as of March 31.
(5) Prepare an income statement for the month of March.
(6) Prepare a capital statement for the month of March.
(7) Prepare a report form balance sheet as of March 31.

**3S-4 (Part C).** Bellus Consulting Company is owned by Dan Bellus. Below you are given five transactions for the month of June and three examples of errors made in recording July transactions.

**Instructions:** Prepare the entries required for the June transactions and the correcting entries required for the July transactions (omit explanations). Correcting entries are made on July 31.

June transactions

June 4. Received fee for services performed, $250.
6. Paid office rent for month, $150.
10. Recorded fees earned from Ohio Co. on account, $300.
12. Purchased office supplies from Kern Suppliers on account, $65.
24. Received cash from Ohio Co. for amount owed, $300.

Errors made in July

July 2. Rent of $150 for July was recorded as a debit to Repairs Expense and a credit to Cash.
11. Bellus withdrew $50 for personal use. The entry was recorded as a debit to Wages Expense and a credit to Cash.
16. The purchase of office supplies from Lemon Office Supplies on account, $45, was recorded as a debit to Office Equipment and a credit to Cash.

**4S-1 (Part A).** The trial balance for the Englemann Racquet Club at the end of August is as follows:

ENGLEMAN RACQUET CLUB
Trial Balance
August 31, 19--

| | | |
|---|---|---|
| Cash | 2,500 | |
| Dues Receivable | 725 | |
| Supplies | 460 | |
| Prepaid Insurance | 875 | |
| Equipment | 7,200 | |
| Accumulated Depreciation — Equipment | | 1,140 |
| Accounts Payable — Kitty Court Cappers | | 1,900 |
| Accounts Payable — R & B Suppliers | | 565 |
| David Englemann, Capital | | 6,100 |
| David Englemann, Drawing | 310 | |
| Revenue from Dues | | 3,270 |
| Advertising Expense | 230 | |
| Salary Expense | 675 | |
| | 12,975 | 12,975 |

Adjustment data:

(a) Club members pay dues at the *end* of each month. Dues for the month of August total $340.
(b) A physical count showed that supplies costing $280 were on hand at the end of August.
(c) The balance in the Prepaid Insurance account is the remainder of a $2,100 one-year insurance premium paid on January 1.
(d) Depreciation on equipment is $720 per year.
(e) Wages of $315 for seven days are paid each Friday. August 31 falls on a Monday.

**Instructions:** Prepare all necessary adjusting entries on August 31 in general journal form.

**4S-2 (Part B).** The trial balance for Beddinger Consulting Service before adjustments at the end of September of the current year is presented below.

Data for end-of-month adjustments:

(a) Office supplies used during the month, $47.
(b) The prepaid insurance balance represents premium paid on September 1 for six months in advance.
(c) Depreciation on office equipment for the month, $65.
(d) Salaries owed, $45.

BEDDINGER CONSULTING SERVICE
Trial Balance
September 30, 19--

| | | |
|---|---|---|
| Cash | 740 | |
| Office Supplies | 215 | |
| Prepaid Insurance | 420 | |
| Office Equipment | 3,400 | |
| Accumulated Depreciation — Office Equipment | | 360 |
| Accounts Payable — Herron Co. | | 270 |
| Accounts Payable — Fisher Co. | | 320 |
| Dan Beddinger, Capital | | 1,690 |
| Dan Beddinger, Drawing | 400 | |
| Fees Earned | | 3,460 |
| Rent Expense | 160 | |
| Salary Expense | 670 | |
| Utilities Expense | 75 | |
| Miscellaneous Expense | 20 | |
| | 6,100 | 6,100 |

**Instructions:**

(1) Prepare an eight-column work sheet similar to that on page 65 for the month ended September 30.
(2) Prepare an income statement and a capital statement for the month of September and a report form balance sheet as of September 30.

**4S-3 (Part C).** The chart of accounts for Danny's Welding Shop is as follows:

**Assets**

| | |
|---|---|
| 11 | Cash |
| 12 | Welding Supplies |
| 13 | Prepaid Insurance |
| 14 | Shop Equipment |
| 14.1 | Accumulated Depreciation — Shop Equipment |

**Liabilities**

| | |
|---|---|
| 21 | Accounts Payable — WLD Suppliers |
| 22 | Accounts Payable — Mahoney Co. |
| 23 | Salaries Payable |

**Owner's Equity**

| | |
|---|---|
| 31 | Danny Casteneda, Capital |
| 32 | Danny Casteneda, Drawing |
| 33 | Income Summary |

**Revenue**

| | |
|---|---|
| 41 | Revenue from Welding |

**Expenses**

| | |
|---|---|
| 51 | Depreciation Expense — Shop Equipment |
| 52 | Insurance Expense |
| 53 | Rent Expense |
| 54 | Salary Expense |
| 55 | Utilities Expense |
| 56 | Welding Supplies Expense |
| 57 | Miscellaneous Expense |

The post-closing trial balance for Danny's Welding Shop as of March 31 of the current year is reproduced below.

DANNY'S WELDING SHOP
Post-Closing Trial Balance
March 31, 19--

| | | |
|---|---|---|
| Cash | 350 | |
| Welding Supplies | 220 | |
| Prepaid Insurance | 900 | |
| Shop Equipment | 5,800 | |
| Accumulated Depreciation — Shop Equipment | | 1,810 |
| Accounts Payable — WLD Suppliers | | 410 |
| Accounts Payable — Mahoney Co. | | 560 |
| Danny Casteneda, Capital | | 4,490 |
| | 7,270 | 7,270 |

The April transactions for Danny's Welding Shop are as follows:

Apr. 1. Purchased welding supplies from WLD Suppliers on account, $94.
1. Paid rent expense for April, $140.
4. Recorded revenue received for services, $260.
6. Paid Mahoney Co. on account, $100.
10. Recorded revenue received for services, $175.
14. Paid salary to assistant, $135.
16. Paid WLD Suppliers on amount owed, $95.
17. Purchased welding supplies for cash, $40.
20. Paid for postage and stamps, $15.
21. Recorded revenue received for services, $430.
22. Casteneda withdrew cash for personal use, $175.
25. Paid cash to have tree limbs and trash removed, $40.
26. Paid salary to assistant, $135.
28. Paid monthly utilities, $65.
29. Purchased additional shop equipment from Mahoney Co. on account, $600.
30. Paid to have leak in roof repaired, $35.
30. Casteneda withdrew cash from his savings account at the bank and invested it in the business, $470.

Adjustment data:

(a) Welding supplies on hand at the end of the month, $210.
(b) The prepaid insurance balance represents the balance of premiums paid in advance through December 31 of the current year.
(c) Salary owed, $55.
(d) Depreciation on shop equipment for the month, $85.

**Instructions:**

(1) Set up a four-column ledger which includes all of the accounts appearing in Danny Casteneda's chart of accounts.
(2) Record in the ledger the balances shown in the March 31 post-closing trial balance. Record the date as April 1, write the word "Balance" in the Description column, and place a check mark (√) in the Posting Reference column.

*(Continued)*

(3) Record the April transactions in a general journal inserting a journal page number.
(4) Post the transactions to the ledger accounts.
(5) Prepare a trial balance of the ledger, recording it on an eight-column work sheet.
(6) Complete the eight-column worksheet.
(7) Prepare an income statement, capital statement, and balance sheet.
(8) Record the adjusting entries in the general journal and post to the ledger.
(9) Record the closing entries in the general journal and post to the ledger.
(10) Prepare a post-closing trial balance.

## CHAPTER 5

**5S-1 (Part A).** Below you are given the four-column journal for the Preston Lawn Care Company for the month of November of the current year, the first month of operation for the business.

**Instructions:**

(1) Foot the journal amount columns and prove these totals. Enter the totals and rule the columns.
(2) Open the ledger accounts required by the transactions, assign account numbers to the accounts, and post the journal to these accounts.
(3) Prepare a trial balance of the ledger.
(4) If a combined cash journal had been used, what additional special columns would you recommend? Why?

### JOURNAL

PAGE *1*

| | CASH DEBIT | CASH CREDIT | DATE | | DESCRIPTION | POST. REF. | GENERAL DEBIT | GENERAL CREDIT | |
|---|---|---|---|---|---|---|---|---|---|
| | | | *19--* | | | | | | |
| 1 | *1100 00* | | *Nov.* | *1* | *Mike Preston, Capital* | | | *1100 00* | 1 |
| 2 | | *200 00* | | *1* | *Rent Expense* | | *200 00* | | 2 |
| 3 | | | | *2* | *Equipment* | | *1600 00* | | 3 |
| 4 | | | | | *Accounts Payable – Victor Co.* | | | *1600 00* | 4 |
| 5 | *510 00* | | | *6* | *Revenue* | | | *510 00* | 5 |
| 6 | | *190 00* | | *7* | *Salary Expense* | | *190 00* | | 6 |
| 7 | | *32 00* | | *10* | *Advertising Expense* | | *32 00* | | 7 |
| 8 | *475 00* | | | *14* | *Revenue* | | | *475 00* | 8 |
| 9 | | *190 00* | | *14* | *Salary Expense* | | *190 00* | | 9 |
| 10 | | *400 00* | | *18* | *Accounts Payable – Victor Co.* | | *400 00* | | 10 |
| 11 | *383 00* | | | *20* | *Revenue* | | | *383 00* | 11 |
| 12 | | *190 00* | | *21* | *Salary Expense* | | *190 00* | | 12 |
| 13 | | *27 00* | | *23* | *Miscellaneous Expense* | | *27 00* | | 13 |
| 14 | | *190 00* | | *28* | *Salary Expense* | | *190 00* | | 14 |
| 15 | *560 00* | | | *30* | *Revenue* | | | *560 00* | 15 |
| 16 | | *167 00* | | *30* | *Utilities Expense* | | *167 00* | | 16 |
| 17 | | | | | | | | | 17 |

**5S-2 (Part A).** On April 1 of the current year, Betty Scopes became a self-employed tour guide in New Orleans. Scopes completed the following transactions related to Scopes Guided Tours.

Apr. 1. Invested cash in the business, $2,000.
1. Paid office rent for the month, $150.
2. Purchased a used limousine from Rothburg Motors for $5,100, paying $1,000 down and the balance on account.
3. Ran an ad in the local newspaper, $60.
4. Paid service station for gas and oil, $75.

6. Revenue collected for the first week, $550.
8. Paid part-time driver, $46.50.
11. Paid phone bill for the month, $52.
12. Paid service station for gas, oil, and lubrication, $87.
14. Revenue collected for the week, $640.
15. Paid the part-time driver, $49.40.
18. Paid for advertising, $25.
20. Paid for miscellaneous expenses, $16.20.
22. Paid Rothburg Motors on account, $400.
22. Revenue collected for the week, $708.
22. Paid the part-time driver, $55.
24. Paid garage for having brakes relined and wheels balanced on limousine, $75.
26. Paid miscellaneous expenses, $16.
29. Revenue collected for week, $580.
29. Paid the part-time driver, $60.
30. Paid service station for gas, $74.30.
30. Paid utilities for the month, $86.
30. Scopes withdrew cash for personal use, $300.

**Adjustment data:**

(a) Depreciation on the limousine for the month, $150.
(b) Salaries owed, $32.

**Instructions:**

(1) From the April transactions, prepare a chart of accounts for Scopes Guided Tours and assign account numbers. All limousine repairs, gas, and oil should be charged to Limousine Expense.
(2) Set up a ledger from the chart of accounts.
(3) Using the headings shown below, record the transactions for the month of April in a combined cash journal as shown on pages 86 and 87.

**COMBINED CASH JOURNAL FOR MONTH OF** PAGE *1*

| Cash | | | | | General | | Tours Revenue | Salary Expense | Limousine Expense |
|---|---|---|---|---|---|---|---|---|---|
| Debit | Credit | Day | Description | Post. Ref. | Debit | Credit | Cr. | Dr. | Dr. |

(4) Foot the journal amount columns and prove these totals. Enter the totals and rule the columns.
(5) Post from the combined cash journal to the ledger.
(6) Prepare the necessary adjusting entries in the combined cash journal and post them to the ledger.
(7) Prepare a trial balance of the ledger.
(8) Prepare the three financial statements for the Scopes Guided Tours for the month of April.

**5S-3 (Part A).** The following entries relate to establishing, proving, and replenishing a petty cash fund for the Ten-Pin Bowling Lane.

May 1. Established a petty cash fund of $50.
16. Replenished the petty cash fund in the amount of $47.90 broken down as follows: Bowling Supplies Expense, $22.40; Office Supplies Expense, $11.90; Advertising Expense, $9.00; Miscellaneous Expense, $4.60.
31. Replenished the petty cash fund in the amount of $36.50 for the following; Store Supplies Expense, $15.80; Office Supplies Expense, $12.70; Miscellaneous Expense, $8.00.
June 1. Petty cash fund was increased to $75.

**Instructions:** Record the necessary entries in general journal form.

**5S-4 (Part B).** The following data are accumulated for use in reconciling the bank account of the Heidelberg Ski Resort for January of the current year.

| | |
|---|---|
| Checks outstanding, January 31 | $ 265 |
| Customer's check returned marked "NSF" — Check written by Don Manning | 30 |
| Bank service charge for the month | 7 |
| Note receivable (Jana Pruett) collected by bank. The note was non-interest bearing | 175 |
| Balance per checkbook, January 31 | 1,029 |
| Deposits in transit, January 31 | 200 |
| Balance per bank statement, January 31 | 1,232 |

**Instructions:**

(1) Prepare a bank reconciliation using a form as shown on page 105.
(2) Prepare the general journal entries necessary to correct the cash account.

**6S-1 (Part A).** Ross and Liz Grant own Grant Music Company, a retail store that sells musical instruments, sheet music, and supplies. In a two-column general journal, record in general journal form the following transactions completed by the company during the month of August:

Aug. 2. Sold sheet music and supplies to Paula Carpenter on account, \$140.
5. Sold a trumpet to Elmer Cummings on account, \$380.
7. Sold a piano bench, which had been special ordered, to Jean Manious for cash, \$190.
16. Paula Carpenter paid cash on the sale of August 2, \$70.
18. Sold music and tapes to Dick Baker on account, \$110.
20. Cummings paid cash on sale of August 5, \$100.
24. Sold saxophone case to Ken Fong for cash, \$65.
27. Carpenter paid the balance on her account for the items purchased on August 2, \$70.

**6S-2 (Part B).** Below are given the completed sales journal and cash receipts journal for Garza Co. for the month of April.

## SALES JOURNAL

PAGE *11*

| | DATE | | ACCOUNT DEBITED | SALE NO. | POST. REF. | ACCTS. REC. DR. SALES CR. | |
|---|---|---|---|---|---|---|---|
| 1 | *19--* *Apr.* | *3* | *Duke Gault* | *142* | | *120 00* | 1 |
| 2 | | *5* | *Charleen Humm* | *143* | | *65 00* | 2 |
| 3 | | *9* | *Max Cole* | *144* | | *70 00* | 3 |
| 4 | | *14* | *Al Calhoun* | *145* | | *150 00* | 4 |
| 5 | | *19* | *Duke Gault* | *146* | | *85 00* | 5 |
| 6 | | *25* | *Jane Lane* | *147* | | *60 00* | 6 |
| 7 | | *28* | *Marcia Ogbolu* | *148* | | *130 00* | 7 |
| 8 | | *30* | *Max Cole* | *149* | | *105 00* | 8 |
| 9 | | | | | | | 9 |
| 10 | | | | | | | 10 |

## CASH RECEIPTS JOURNAL

PAGE *9*

| | DATE | | ACCOUNT CREDITED | POST. REF. | GENERAL ACCOUNTS CR. | SALES CR. | ACCOUNTS REC. CR. | CASH DR. | |
|---|---|---|---|---|---|---|---|---|---|
| 1 | *19--* *Apr.* | *1* | *Jane Lane* | | | | *80 00* | *80 00* | 1 |
| 2 | | *4* | *Marcia Ogbolu* | | | | *60 00* | *60 00* | 2 |
| 3 | | *6* | *Office Supplies* | | *45 00* | | | *45 00* | 3 |
| 4 | | *9* | *Don Garza, Capital* | | *700 00* | | | *700 00* | 4 |
| 5 | | *12* | *Al Calhoun* | | | | *200 00* | *200 00* | 5 |
| 6 | | *15* | ✓ | | | *623 00* | | *623 00* | 6 |
| 7 | | *21* | *Marcia Ogbolu* | | | | *100 00* | *100 00* | 7 |
| 8 | | *24* | *Duke Gault* | | | | *90 00* | *90 00* | 8 |
| 9 | | *30* | ✓ | | | *712 00* | | *712 00* | 9 |
| 10 | | *30* | *Max Cole* | | | | *150 00* | *150 00* | 10 |
| 11 | | | | | | | | | 11 |

**Instructions:**

(1) Open the following selected general ledger accounts with their balances as of April 1 of the current year: Cash (11), \$462; Accounts Receivable (12), \$955; Office Supplies (13), \$130; Don Garza, Capital (31), \$1,140; Sales (41), no balance. (The complete general ledger is not given.)
(2) Open the following accounts receivable subsidiary ledger accounts with their balances as of April 1: Al Calhoun, \$300; Max Cole, \$150; Duke Gault, \$90; Charleen Humm, \$175; Jane Lane, \$80; Marcia Ogbolu, \$160.
(3) Post the transactions in the sales journal and cash receipts journal to the accounts receivable subsidiary ledger, using forms as shown on page 123. Post to the general ledger any accounts which will not be posted by column total.
(4) Foot the cash receipts journal amount columns and prove these totals. Enter the totals of both journals and rule the columns. Prepare a schedule to prove the equality of the debit and credit totals of the cash receipts journal.
(5) Post all special column totals to the general ledger.
(6) Prepare a schedule of accounts receivable and check the total against the balance in the accounts receivable control account.

**6S-3 (Part B).** Hogan Gift Shop completed the following transactions during the month of March.

Mar. 1. Sold merchandise on account to Vic Ashley, \$45.
2. Sold merchandise on account to Juna Caldwell, \$62.
4. Received cash from Bob Rogers in payment of his account, \$40.
8. Recorded cash sales, \$565.
10. Sold merchandise on account to Bill Booher, \$75.
14. Received cash from Juna Caldwell, \$140.
16. Holly Hogan invested additional cash in the business, \$600.
18. Sold merchandise on account to Mary Tang, \$80.
20. Recorded cash sales, \$402.
22. Sold merchandise on account to Bob Rogers, \$63.
23. Received cash from Vic Ashley on account, \$70.
24. Received cash from Bill Booher on account, \$90.
26. Sold merchandise on account to Juna Caldwell, \$50.
27. Sold a typewriter for cash, \$420.
28. Received payment on account from Mary Tang, \$80.
28. Sold merchandise on account to Vic Ashley, \$85.
30. Recorded cash sales, \$378.

**Instructions:**

(1) Set up general ledger accounts for the following and include their March 1 balances if given: Cash (11), \$470; Accounts Receivable (12), \$420; Office Equipment (13), \$1,460; Holly Hogan, Capital (31), \$1,600; Sales (41), no balance.
(2) Open the following accounts in the accounts receivable subsidiary ledger along with their balances: Vic Ashley, \$70; Bill Booher, \$90; Juna Caldwell, \$140; Bob Rogers, \$40; Mary Tang, \$80.
(3) Record the transactions for the month of March in a sales journal and in a cash receipts journal, using forms as shown on pages 114 and 120. For transactions involving the sale of merchandise, begin with Sales Invoice No. 736.
(4) Post to the accounts receivable subsidiary ledger on a daily basis. Also, post individually to the general ledger any accounts which will not be posted by column total.
(5) Foot the cash receipts journal amount columns and prove these totals. Enter the totals of both journals and rule the columns. Prepare a schedule to prove the equality of the debit and credit totals of the cash receipts journal.
(6) Post all special column totals to the general ledger.
(7) Prepare a schedule of accounts receivable and check the total against the balance in the accounts receivable control account.

**6S-4 (Part B).** Juan Trillo owns an appliance store in the state of Nebraska, where a 3% retail sales tax is imposed. Record in general journal form, the following selected transactions for Trillo during the month of July.

July 3. Sold refrigerator on account to Kathy Duncan totaling \$600 plus the 3% sales tax.
8. Cash sale of microwave oven to Tonny Harrah totaled \$400 plus 3% sales tax.
15. Paid to the state sales taxes for second quarter (April–June) totaling \$134.40.

## CHAPTER 7

**7S-1 (Part A).** The following transactions involve purchases on account by El Fenix Restaurant during May of the current year.

May 1. Purchased merchandise on account from Roddy Co., $500.
4. Purchased the following on account from Lajoie Supply Co.: office supplies, $105; kitchen supplies, $95.
9. Purchased merchandise on account from Dyer Distributors, $400.
13. Purchased kitchen equipment on account from Kirksey Equipment Co., $750.
16. Purchased kitchen supplies on account from Lajoie Supply Co., $150.
21. Purchased merchandise on account from Roddy Co., $160.
25. Purchased the following on account from Kirksey Equipment Co.: office supplies, $70; office equipment, $120.

**Instructions:**

(1) Record the transactions in a multicolumn purchases journal similar to that shown on page 135, using the following column headings: Accounts Payable Cr.; Purchases Dr.; Kitchen Supplies Dr.; Office Supplies Dr.; General Accounts Dr.
(2) Foot the journal amount columns and prove these totals. Enter the totals and rule the columns.
(3) Prepare a schedule proving the equality of debits and credits in the purchases journal.

**7S-2 (Part B).** The following payments were made by Henry Swimming Pool Supply Company for the month of June of the current year.

June 2. Paid rent expense for June, $180; Check No. 913.
4. Paid Elsie Co. for invoice of May 16, $290; Check No. 914.
7. Paid weekly salaries, $260; Check No. 915.
9. Paid for shop supplies purchased, $59; Check No. 916.
14. Paid Felix Suppliers on account, $300; Check No. 917.
15. Paid weekly salaries, $250; Check No. 918.
19. Paid for merchandise purchases, $140; Check No. 919.
19. Paid for office supplies purchased from Brian Co., $35; Check No. 920.
22. Paid Cruise Co. on account, $170; Check No. 921.
22. Paid weekly salaries, $250; Check No. 922.
26. Paid for store equipment purchased, $600; Check No. 923.
30. Paid monthly utilities, $137; Check No. 924.

**Instructions:**

(1) Record the transactions in a cash payments journal similar to that shown on page 141, using the following column headings: General Accounts Dr.; Accounts Payable Dr.; Salary Expense Dr.; Cash Cr.
(2) Foot the journal amount columns and prove these totals. Enter the totals and rule the columns.
(3) Prepare a schedule proving the equality of debits and credits in the cash payments journal.

**7S-3 (Part B).** Kris Smith owns Smith's Drapery Shop, which she operates with the help of two part-time sales clerks. Below are selected account balances for Smith's business as of April 1 of the current year. Since all of the general ledger accounts are not given, the ledger will not balance; however, the subsidiary ledgers are complete and they should reconcile with the control accounts in the general ledger. Smith's business records include the following special journals: sales, cash receipts, purchases, and cash payments.

**General Ledger**

| No. | Account | Balance | No. | Account | Balance |
|---|---|---|---|---|---|
| 11 | Cash | $514 | 31 | Kris Smith, Capital | $2,178 |
| 12 | Accounts Receivable | 333 | 32 | Kris Smith, Drawing | —0— |
| 13 | Store Supplies | 152 | 41 | Sales | —0— |
| 14 | Office Supplies | 78 | 51 | Purchases | —0— |
| 15 | Store Equipment | 1,140 | 61 | Interest Expense | —0— |
| 16 | Office Equipment | 935 | 62 | Rent Expense | —0— |
| 21 | Accounts Payable | 772 | 63 | Salary Expense | —0— |
| 22 | Notes Payable | 200 | 64 | Miscellaneous Expense | —0— |

**Accounts Receivable Ledger**

| | |
|---|---|
| Miles Anderson | $ 73 |
| Gloria Bailey | 60 |
| Roy Bushy | 45 |
| Tony Gonzalez | 117 |
| Cynthia Preston | 38 |

**Accounts Payable Ledger**

| | |
|---|---|
| Carolina Milling | $167 |
| Kuper Drapery Co. | 120 |
| Marcus Manufacturing | 250 |
| Rainbow Fabrics | 95 |
| Wilfong's | 140 |

The following transactions were completed by Smith's Drapery Shop:

Apr. 1. Issued Check No. 400 for rent expense for the month, $175.
1. Sold merchandise on account to Gloria Bailey, $63; Sales Invoice No. 615.
2. Received payment on account from Roy Bushy, $45.
3. Purchased merchandise on account from Carolina Milling, $160.
4. Sold merchandise on account to Cynthia Preston, $75; Sales Invoice No. 616.
4. Paid Rainbow Fabrics on account, $95; Check No. 401.
6. Received payment from Gloria Bailey on account, $60.
7. Purchased merchandise from Wilfong's on account, $120.
8. Sold merchandise on account to Roy Bushy, $110; Sales Invoice No. 617.
8. Purchased office equipment on account from Marcus Manufacturing, $180.
8. Paid Kuper Drapery Co. on account, $120; Check No. 402.
10. Paid Carolina Milling on account, $167; Check No. 403.
10. Purchased office supplies on account from Wilfong's, $43.
11. Sold office supplies to firm next door for cash, $20.
13. Paid Wilfong's on account, $140; Check No. 404.
13. Purchased the following on account from Marcus Manufacturing; store equipment, $200; store supplies, $50.
14. Sold merchandise on account to Miles Anderson, $50; Sales Invoice No. 618.
14. Paid salary expense, $400; Check No. 405.
15. Recorded cash sales, $960.
16. Paid note payable, $200, plus $20 interest expense; Check No. 406.
16. Smith invested additional cash in the business, $500.
17. Received payment from Cynthia Preston on account, $38.
18. Purchased the following on account from Marcus Manufacturing: store supplies, $40; office supplies, $30.
18. Paid for merchandise purchased, $150; Check No. 407.
20. Sold merchandise on account to Tony Gonzalez, $105; Sales Invoice No. 619.
21. Purchased merchandise on account from Rainbow Fabrics, $205.
22. Received payment on account from Gloria Bailey, $63.
22. Sold merchandise on account to Miles Anderson, $80; Sales Invoice No. 620.
23. Paid for miscellaneous expense, $25; Check No. 408.
24. Paid for store supplies purchased, $42; Check No. 409.
24. Purchased merchandise on account from Carolina Milling, $300.
25. Received payment on account from Miles Anderson, $73.
27. Paid Marcus Manufacturing on account, $250; Check No. 410.
28. Purchased merchandise on account from Kuper Drapery Co., $185.
28. Paid salary expense, $425; Check No. 411.
29. Sold merchandise on account to Roy Bushy, $65; Sales Invoice No. 621.
30. Smith withdrew cash for personal use, $190; Check No. 412.
30. Recorded cash sales, $850.

**Instructions:**

(1) Open the general ledger and subsidiary ledger accounts and enter the balances given.
(2) Prepare a schedule of accounts receivable and a schedule of accounts payable as of April 1, and check the totals with the control accounts in the general ledger.
(3) Record each transaction for the month of April in the proper journal. Post the subsidiary accounts and the accounts in the general columns individually on a daily basis.
(4) Foot the journal amount columns and prove these totals. Enter the totals and rule the columns.
(5) Post the appropriate column totals to the general ledger.
(6) Prepare a schedule of accounts receivable and a schedule of accounts payable at the end of the month and check the totals with the control accounts in the general ledger.

## CHAPTER 8

**8S-1 (Part A).** (a) On April 2, Spivey Dress Shop issued a credit memo to Gail Dann for $95 for a dress returned on account.

(b) Mort Cotlar owns an air conditioning company. On June 12 he returned an air conditioner to the Golden Co. for $740 credit, and on June 17 he returned $50 of office supplies to Gere Suppliers for credit.

**Instructions:**

(1) Prepare in general journal form the entries to record the April 2 transaction (a) on the books of Spivey and (b) on the books of Dann.
(2) Prepare in general journal form the entries required (a) on June 12 for both Cotlar and Golden Co.; and (b) on June 17 for both Cotlar and Gere Suppliers.

**8S-2 (Part B).** On January 16, Kathy Thompson purchased merchandise on account with a list price of $400 from Juan Jorge. The list price is subject to a 40% trade discount and the credit terms are 2/10, n/30. On January 21, Thompson returned damaged merchandise with a list price of $40 to Jorge. Thompson paid the balance of the invoice on January 25.

**Instructions:**

(1) Prepare the entries in general journal form to record the three transactions on Thompson's books.
(2) Prepare the entries in general journal form to record the three transactions on Jorge's books.

**8S-3 (Part B).** Below you are given two subsidiary accounts of Fuller Tie Rack as they appeared during the month of December:

NAME *Paisley Tie Co.*

ADDRESS *21407 Easterwood Circle, Chicago, IL 60653-2081*

| DATE | | ITEM | POST. REF. | DEBIT | CREDIT | BALANCE |
|---|---|---|---|---|---|---|
| *19--* Dec. | 9 | *4/10, n/EOM* | *P16* | | 1500 00 | 1500 00 |
| | 14 | | *PR2* | 300 00 | | 1200 00 |
| | 18 | | *CP11* | 1200 00 | | — |
| | | | | | | |
| | | | | | | |
| | | | | | | |

NAME *Dick Cooper*

ADDRESS *500 N. Akard, Rockford, IL 61102-2313*

| DATE | | ITEM | POST. REF. | DEBIT | CREDIT | BALANCE |
|---|---|---|---|---|---|---|
| *19--* Dec. | 2 | *2/20, n/40* | *S12* | 60 00 | | 60 00 |
| | 8 | | *SR3* | | 10 00 | 50 00 |
| | 12 | | *CR9* | | 50 00 | — |
| | | | | | | |
| | | | | | | |
| | | | | | | |

**Instructions:**

(1) Determine whether each account appears in the accounts receivable or accounts payable subsidiary ledger and explain how this determination was made.
(2) Prepare in general journal form all the entries that would have been recorded on Fuller's books for the transactions involving Paisley Tie Co.
(3) Prepare in general journal form all the entries that would have been recorded on Fuller's books for the transactions involving Dick Cooper.

**8S-4 (Part B).** You are given the following transactions for Mykoo Plumbing Supply Co. during the month of April of the current year. All sales on account have credit terms of 2/10, n/30. The company uses a purchases journal, a sales journal, a cash payments journal, a cash receipts journal, a purchases returns and allowances journal (as shown on page 154), a sales returns and allowances journal (as shown on page 151), and a general journal.

Apr. 1. Purchased merchandise from Tek Fittings on account, $600; terms 4/10, n/30.
2. Paid April rent, $200; Check No. 650.
4. Purchased store supplies on account from Corbin Supply Co., $70; terms n/30.
5. Sold merchandise on account to Hoe Company, $240; Sales Invoice No. 580.
8. Returned merchandise purchased from Tek Fittings on April 1 for credit on account, $100; Debit Memorandum No. 9.
9. Sold merchandise on account to Brim Builders, $300; Sales Invoice No. 581.
10. Paid Tek Fittings for merchandise purchased on April 1; Check No. 651.
11. Sold merchandise on account to Jobe Co. $175; Sales Invoice No. 582.
11. Returned supplies purchased from Corbin Supply Co. on April 4, $12; Debit Memorandum No. 10.
12. Received payment from the Hoe Company for sale of April 5.
15. Recorded cash sales, $925.
15. Brim Builders returned merchandise for credit from the sale of April 9, $40; Credit Memorandum No. 28.
16. Sold merchandise on account to Phi Co., $260; Sales Invoice No. 583.
17. Received payment from Brim Builders for sale of April 9.
17. Paid for office supplies purchased, $29; Check No. 652.
18. Received payment from Jobe Co. for sale of April 11.
18. Purchased merchandise on account from Fed Brass Co., $720; terms 3/15, n/30.
19. Sold store supplies at cost to Will Elliott for cash, $20.
19. Purchased the following on account from Corbin Supply Co.: store supplies, $62; store equipment, $307; terms n/30.
22. Paid for merchandise purchased, $125; Check No. 653.
22. Returned for credit $60 of bad fittings (merchandise) purchased from Fed Brass Co. on April 18; Debit Memorandum No. 11.
23. Paid Corbin Supply Co. for invoice of April 4; Check No. 654.
24. Sold merchandise on account to Brim Builders, $180; Sales Invoice No. 584.
25. Paid utilities expense for the month, $235; Check No. 655.
26. Received payment from Phi Co. for invoice of April 16.
26. Bill Mykoo withdrew $150 for personal use; Check No. 656.
29. Paid Fed Brass Co. for purchase made on April 18, less return; Check No. 657.
30. Recorded cash sales, $1,040.
30. Recorded salaries owed, $215.

**Instructions:**

(1) Record each transaction in the appropriate journal. The column headings to be used in the purchases journal are as follows: Accounts Payable Cr.; Purchases Dr.; Store Supplies Dr.; and General Accounts Dr.
(2) Foot the journal amount columns and prove these totals. Enter the totals and rule the columns.

## CHAPTER 9

**9S-1 (Part A).** The Atoka Luggage Company purchased $6,700 of merchandise during one fiscal period. Determine the cost of goods sold under each of the following conditions:

(1) There was no inventory on hand at the beginning or at the end of the fiscal period.
(2) There was no beginning inventory, but there was $900 of merchandise on hand at the end of the period.
(3) There was $2,100 of beginning inventory and $2,500 of ending inventory.
(4) There was $3,000 of beginning inventory and $4,200 of ending inventory.

**9S-2 (Part A).** On December 31, Silver's Lamp Shop reported the results of operations for the accounting period as shown below.

| | | | |
|---|---|---|---|
| Sales | $8,900 | Merchandise purchased | $5,750 |
| Beginning inventory | 1,400 | Operating expenses | 1,600 |
| Ending inventory | 1,700 | | |

**Instructions:** Determine the answer to each of the following questions:

(1) What was the amount of revenue of the business for the period?
(2) What was the amount of merchandise available for sale during the period?
(3) What was the cost of the goods sold for the period?
(4) What was the amount of gross profit?
(5) What was the amount of net income?
(6) What was the owner's equity at the end of the period if the capital at the beginning of the period was $6,000, drawings were $800, and there were no additional investments during the period?
(7) Give the adjusting entries for merchandise inventory.

**9S-3 (Part B).** The following trial balance and adjustment data for the Willett Company were obtained for the current fiscal year ending September 30.

WILLETT COMPANY
Trial Balance
September 30, 19--

| Account | Debit | Credit |
|---|---|---|
| Cash | 2,240 | |
| Accounts Receivable | 1,580 | |
| Merchandise Inventory | 7,650 | |
| Office Supplies | 148 | |
| Prepaid Insurance | 325 | |
| Office Equipment | 1,800 | |
| Accumulated Depreciation — Office Equipment | | 940 |
| Buildings | 14,000 | |
| Accumulated Depreciation — Buildings | | 5,100 |
| Land | 6,500 | |
| Accounts Payable | | 960 |
| Notes Payable (due in 3 years) | | 4,000 |
| Jim Willett, Capital | | 17,938 |
| Jim Willett, Drawing | 500 | |
| Sales | | 27,300 |
| Sales Returns and Allowances | 800 | |
| Purchases | 14,260 | |
| Purchases Returns and Allowances | | 490 |
| Advertising Expense | 410 | |
| Delivery Expense | 375 | |
| Sales Salary Expense | 2,800 | |
| Miscellaneous Selling Expense | 140 | |
| Office Salary Expense | 3,200 | |
| | 56,728 | 56,728 |

Adjustment data:

| | |
|---|---|
| (a) Merchandise inventory, September 30 | $5,100 |
| (b) Depreciation for the year: Buildings | 800 |
| Office equipment | 140 |
| (c) Office supplies on hand September 30 | 42 |
| (d) Insurance expired during the year | 25 |
| (e) Sales salaries owed | 180 |

**Instructions:**

(1) Set up the ledger accounts listed on the trial balance and record the September 30 balances.
(2) Prepare a ten-column work sheet as shown on page 176.
(3) Prepare a classified income statement for the year, using a form as shown on page 184.
(4) Prepare a classified balance sheet as of September 30, which includes the changes in owner's equity, using a form as shown on page 187.
(5) Record the adjusting and closing entries in a general journal.
(6) Post the adjusting and closing entries to the ledger accounts, setting up any additional accounts needed.

## CHAPTER 10

**10S-1 (Part A).** Max Cole is a maintenance supervisor for the Craighead Electric Corp. Cole earns $6.00 per hour plus 1½ times the regular rate for all hours over 40 and double time on Sundays and holidays. The following information is available for Cole's payroll for the week ending May 2 of the current year. Cole is married and claims 5 withholding allowances.

Hours worked:
Monday–Saturday — 48
Sunday — 6

| | |
|---|---|
| Earnings to date | $4,992.00 |
| Income tax (see table on page 206) | ? |
| Deduction for health insurance | 11.10 |
| Union dues | 7.25 |
| FICA tax rate | 7% |

**Instructions:**

(1) Determine the following, showing your computations in good form:
   (a) Cole's gross earnings for the week.
   (b) FICA tax.
   (c) Total deductions.
   (d) Take-home pay.
(2) Prepare the entry, in general journal form, to record Cole's payroll on the books of his employer.
(3) Prepare the entry, in general journal form, to record payment of the payroll to Cole.

**10S-2 (Part A).** Ace Swimming Pool Supply Company employed three salespersons and one office person. The office employee is paid a weekly salary and all salespeople are paid an hourly rate plus 1½ times the regular rate for all hours over 40 per week. The information necessary for the preparation of the payroll for the week ended June 12 of the current year is presented below; all of the employees are married.

| Employee | Number of Withholding Allowances | Earnings to Date | Hours Worked | Wage Rate | Deductions: Health Insurance | Deductions: U.S. Bonds |
|---|---|---|---|---|---|---|
| Office | | | | | | |
| Winters, Margaret | 2 | $5,500 | — | $305 | $3.60 | $5.00 |
| Sales | | | | | | |
| Bolin, Don | 4 | 5,930 | 48 | 7.00 | 4.50 | 8.00 |
| Finlay, Linda | 3 | 5,860 | 50 | 6.80 | 4.00 | 5.00 |
| Faught, Vincent | 6 | 4,986 | 50 | 6.40 | 5.00 | — |

Tax Rates

| | |
|---|---|
| FICA | 7% |
| Federal unemployment | .7% |
| State unemployment | 2.7% |

Withholding — see table on page 206.

**Instructions:**

(1) Prepare a payroll register following the form shown on pages 210–211 omitting the Daily Hours column and using the appropriate headings for deductions. Begin with Check No. 781.
(2) Prepare the entry in the general journal to record the weekly payroll.

**10S-3 (Part B).** The information determined in Problem 10S-2 is to be used in this problem.

**Instructions:**

(1) Compute the employer's payroll tax expense for Ace Swimming Pool Supply Company in Problem 10S-2 for each of the following taxes using tax rates of 7%, .7%, and 2.7% for the respective taxes: (a) FICA, (b) federal unemployment, and (c) state unemployment.
(2) Prepare the journal entry to record the employer's payroll taxes expense for the week.

**10S-4 (Part B).** A summary of payroll information for the Williford Meat Company is given below for the month of January of the current year.

| Salaries | | Deductions | |
|---|---|---|---|
| Sales salaries | $6,460 | Employees' income tax | $1,064 |
| Plant salaries | 4,215 | Union dues | 210 |
| Office salaries | 830 | Health insurance | 240 |
| | | Savings club | 500 |

Tax Rates

| | |
|---|---|
| FICA | 7% |
| Federal unemployment | .7% |
| State unemployment | 2.7% |

*(Continued)*

**Instructions:**

(1) Prepare the entry to record the payroll in the general journal.
(2) Prepare the entry to record the payroll taxes expense for the month. (All salaries are subject to these taxes this month.)
(3) Prepare the entry, in general journal form, to pay the union dues.
(4) If the above payroll is average for each month of the year, when will each of the following taxes be due for deposit, and what will be the period covered?
   (a) Employees' income tax
   (b) FICA taxes
   (c) Federal unemployment tax
   (d) State unemployment tax
(5) What will be the amount of the check to pay the income tax withheld and FICA taxes due for the first month?

**10S-5 (Part C).** Record the following selected transactions in a general journal and indicate in the Posting Reference column the name of the journal in which each entry would be recorded. Assume the use of a voucher register, VR, and check register, CP.

Aug. 2. Purchased merchandise on account from Anvel Co., $175.
4. Purchased office supplies on account from McKnight Inc., $85.
6. Received bill for advertising expense from News Magazine, $180.
10. Paid bill received from News Magazine.
18. Paid Anvel Co. for merchandise purchased on August 2, less a 4% cash discount.
24. Paid McKnight, Inc., for supplies purchased on August 4, less a 2% cash discount.
26. Purchased office equipment on account from Ace Co., $100.

**10S-6 (Part C).** Following are the transactions for the Spring River Gift Shop.

May 2. Purchased merchandise from E.T. Co., $160, on account.
4. Purchased merchandise from McPhearson Co., $185, on account.
5. Prepared voucher payable to Adams Trust Co., $210, for May rent expense.
7. Purchased office equipment from ASU Equipment Co., $215, on account.
9. Purchased office supplies from Ovid Co., $60, on account.
12. Purchased store supplies from Clark Supply Co., $75, on account.
15. Prepared voucher payable to Beck's Garage for repairs expense, $65.
17. Purchased office supplies from Ovid Co., $43, on account.
18. Purchased merchandise from McPhearson Co., $310, on account.
21. Purchased store supplies from Clark Supply Co., $65, on account.
24. Purchased office equipment for $170 and store equipment for $290 from ASU Equipment Co. on account.
26. Purchased merchandise on account from E.T. Co., $300.
30. Prepared voucher payable to City Utilities Dept. for $125 for utilities expense for month.

**Instructions:**

(1) Record the above transactions in a voucher register, beginning with Voucher No. 612. The voucher register will require special debit columns for Purchases, Store Supplies, and Office Supplies.
(2) Total and rule the columns in the voucher register and prepare a schedule to prove the equality of the debits and credits.

**10S-7 (Part C).** The Garcia Machine Shop uses a voucher system and a check register for approving and paying all bills. A schedule of unpaid vouchers for Garcia on March 1 of the current year is as follows:

| Voucher No. | Payee | Amount |
|---|---|---|
| 918 | T.B. Metals | $140 |
| 922 | Nelson Parts Co. | 54 |
| 924 | Kennedy Products | 96 |

The transactions relating to the voucher register and check register for the month of March are as follows:

Mar. 1. Paid Voucher No. 918 to T.B. Metals for $140 less a 5% discount, Check No. 880.
2. Purchased shop equipment on account from Pike Equipment Co. for $280, Voucher No. 925.
4. Paid Voucher No. 922 to Nelson Parts Co., $54, Check No. 881.
6. Prepared Voucher No. 926 to Hess Rental Co. for $190 for rent expense for the month.
6. Check No. 882 to Hess Rental Co. for Voucher No. 926.
8. Paid Voucher No. 924 to Kennedy Products, $96, Check No. 883.
10. Purchased merchandise on account from T.B. Metals, $290, Voucher No. 927.
12. Purchased merchandise on account from Kennedy Products, $450, Voucher No. 928.
12. Paid Pike Equipment Co. for Voucher No. 925 less a 2% discount, Check No. 884.

14. Purchased merchandise on account from Nelson Parts Co., $87, Voucher No. 929.
16. Prepared Voucher No. 930 to Northwest Electric Co., $105, for utilities for the month.
16. Check No. 885 for $105 for Voucher No. 930.
20. Check No. 886 to T.B. Metals for Voucher No. 927 less a 5% discount.
21. Purchased shop supplies, $85, and office supplies, $45, on account from Pike Equipment Co., Voucher No. 931.
22. Check No. 887 to Kennedy Products, $450, for Voucher No. 928.
24. Check No. 888 to Nelson Parts Co., $87, for Voucher No. 929.
26. Purchased merchandise on account from Kennedy Products for $240, Voucher No. 932.
28. Purchased shop supplies on account from Pike Equipment Co. for $60, Voucher No. 933.
29. Purchased merchandise on account from T.B. Metals, $410, Voucher No. 934.

**Instructions:**

(1) Record the transactions for March in a voucher register and check register. The voucher register will require special debit columns for Purchases and Shop Supplies *only*.
(2) Total and rule the columns in the voucher register and check register. Prove the equality of the debits and credits.
(3) Post from the voucher register and check register to the accounts payable account. Accounts Payable is Account No. 220, and had a credit balance of $290 at March 1.
(4) Prepare a schedule of unpaid vouchers and compare the total with the balance in Accounts Payable.

## CHAPTER 11

**11S-1 (Part A).** Below are the salary expense and salaries payable accounts of the Cleveland Company.

ACCOUNT *Salaries Payable* ACCOUNT NO. *26*

| DATE | | ITEM | POST. REF. | DEBIT | CREDIT | BALANCE DEBIT | BALANCE CREDIT |
|---|---|---|---|---|---|---|---|
| *1982* Dec. | 31 | | | | 520 00 | | 520 00 |
| *1983* Jan. | 1 | | | 520 00 | | — | — |

ACCOUNT *Salary Expense* ACCOUNT NO. *56*

| DATE | | ITEM | POST. REF. | DEBIT | CREDIT | BALANCE DEBIT | BALANCE CREDIT |
|---|---|---|---|---|---|---|---|
| *1982* Dec. | 26 | Balance | √ | | | 6,660 00 | |
| | 31 | | | 520 00 | | 7,180 00 | |
| | 31 | | | | 7,180 00 | — | — |
| *1983* Jan. | 1 | | | | 520 00 | | 520 00 |
| | 3 | | | 980 00 | | 460 00 | |

**Instructions:** Make all the journal entries indicated by the accounts and explain each entry.

**11S-2 (Part A).** Cynthia Preston owns the Preston Booking Agency. Below is the information necessary to prepare the adjusting entries required at December 31, the end of the current fiscal year.

Adjustment data:

(a) Salaries accrued to office personnel, $740.
(b) Depreciation on office equipment, $160.
(c) Commissions earned but not collected, $1,650.
(d) Rent on office is $430 per month payable quarterly. The next payment is due January 31 for the November–January quarter.
(e) Advertising in local newspaper is $20 per week. At December 31, two weeks of ads had not been paid.

**Instructions:** Prepare the adjusting entries required as of December 31.

**11S-3 (Part B).** On March 1, Apache Insurance Company received $900 for insurance premium from Philip's Cycle Shop covering the next twelve months.

**Instructions:**

(1) Prepare the general journal entries for the following transactions on the books of Apache Insurance Company, assuming the receipt of the $900 is credited to a liability account.
1982
Mar. 1. To record receipt of the premium.
Dec. 31. Adjusting entry.
31. Closing entry.
1983
Jan. 1. Reversing entry, if necessary.
Dec. 31. Adjusting entry for Year 2, if required.

(2) Prepare the entries above for the Apache Insurance Company, assuming the $900 was credited originally to a revenue account.

(3) Prepare the general journal entries for the following transactions on the books of Philip's Cycle Shop, assuming the payment of the $900 in insurance premiums is debited to an asset account.
1982
Mar. 1. To record payment of the premium.
Dec. 31. Adjusting entry.
31. Closing entry.
1983
Jan. 1. Reversing entry, if necessary.
Dec. 31. Adjusting entry for Year 2, if required.

(4) Prepare the entries above for Philip's Cycle Shop, assuming the $900 was debited originally to an expense account.

**11S-4 (Part B).** Anita Riney opened Riney's Antiques on June 1 of the current year. Riney will prepare interim monthly financial statements and close its books on December 31, the end of its fiscal year. The property taxes of the local school district are assessed for the fiscal year July 1–June 30. Tax statements are mailed in July, payable by November 30, without penalty.

**Instructions:**

(1) Prepare general journal entries to record the following selected transactions for property taxes:
July 24. Received tax statement from school district for tax year July 1–June 30 in the amount of $1,440. Record property taxes accrued in July.
Nov. 30. Paid property taxes for year, $1,440. Assume all intervening entries required for property taxes have been properly recorded.
Dec. 31. Record the adjusting entry for December property taxes.

(2) Determine the following account balances to be shown in Riney's financial statements as of December 31, the end of the fiscal year:
(a) Property Tax Expense
(b) Prepaid Property Tax
(c) Property Tax Payable

(3) Prepare the adjusting entry for property taxes for January of the following year.

## CHAPTER 12

**12S-1 (Part A).** Don Riggs owns a book store and uses the direct write-off method of recording bad debts. On October 13, Riggs determined the account of Jimmy Hunt for $60 to be worthless and wrote it off.

**Instructions:**

(1) Prepare the journal entry to record the write-off.
(2) If on December 20 of the same year Hunt paid Riggs $60 on his account which had been written off in October, prepare the entries necessary to reinstate his account and record the collection.
(3) If the payment of $60 by Hunt had been made on January 16 of the following year, prepare the entries necessary at that time to reinstate his account and record the collection.

**12S-2 (Part A).** Sara Latham owns Sara's Dress Shop. The following transactions relate to bad debts during 1982 and 1983. Latham uses the allowance method of recording bad debts.

1982
June 12. Wrote off the account of Zelda Cohen, $150, as uncollectible.
Sept. 19. Wrote off the account of Jackie West, $240, as uncollectible.
Nov. 4. Received a check for $50 and a letter from the attorney of Delbert Mahon stating that Mahon had been declared bankrupt and the check was in final settlement of his account, which totaled $150.
30. Received $65 from Zelda Cohen whose account was written off on June 12. Cohen indicated the balance of her account would be paid in January. Latham instructs you to reinstate to Cohen's account only the amount collected.
Dec. 31. Adjustment for bad debts is $850.
1983
Jan. 18. Wrote off the account of Jan Kleppe, $190, as uncollectible.
29. Received $85 from Zelda Cohen as final settlement of her account written off in June of 1982.

**Instructions:** Prepare the entries in general journal form to record these transactions for Sara's Dress Shop.

**12S-3 (Part A).** The following account balances are those of the Santoya's Department Store on March 31, the end of the fiscal year, prior to adjustments.

| | |
|---|---|
| Accounts Receivable | $24,620 |
| Allowance for Bad Debts | 160 cr. |
| Sales | 137,000 |
| Sales Returns and Allowances | 2,000 |

**Instructions:** Prepare the necessary adjusting entry to record bad debts in each of the following cases. Each case is to be considered independently of the others.

Case A Aging of accounts receivable indicates probable uncollectibility of $1,410.
Case B Losses are estimated at 2 percent of net sales.
Case C Assume the same facts as in Case A except that the balance in Allowance for Bad Debts is a $210 debit before adjustment.
Case D Assume the same facts as in Case B except that the balance in Allowance for Bad Debts is a $180 debit before adjustment.

**12S-4 (Part A).** The McPhearson Boot Company completed an analysis of its accounts receivable on December 31, the end of the first year of operations, as follows:

| | |
|---|---|
| Current accounts (not yet due) | $14,220 |
| 1–30 days past due | 4,450 |
| 31–60 days past due | 2,330 |
| Over 60 days past due | 900 |
| Total accounts receivable | $21,900 |

Based on industry averages, the following percentages of uncollectibility were determined.

| | |
|---|---|
| Current accounts | 2 percent |
| 1–30 days past due | 8 percent |
| 31–60 days past due | 15 percent |
| Over 60 days past due | 50 percent |

**Instructions:**

(1) Prepare a schedule of aging the accounts receivable.
(2) Prepare the adjusting entry to record the bad debts expense at the end of the year.
(3) Determine the net realizable value of the accounts receivable at December 31.

**12S-5 (Part B).** Hollenbeck Office Equipment Company received the following notes from its customers.

| Date | Term | Interest Rate | Face Value |
|---|---|---|---|
| (1) April 16 | 90 days | 10 percent | $1,600 |
| (2) May 12 | 6 months | 12 percent | 1,000 |
| (3) June 12 | 45 days | 12 percent | 1,500 |
| (4) July 21 | 120 days | None | 2,000 |
| (5) Aug. 17 | 60 days | 15 percent | 2,400 |

**Instructions:**

(a) Determine the due date and the amount of interest due on each note.
(b) Assuming that note (2) was discounted on September 12 at the rate of 12 percent and that note (4) was discounted on September 19 at the rate of 9 percent, prepare, in general journal form, the entries on Hollenbeck's books to record the discounting of the notes.
(c) Assuming that note (2) was dishonored at maturity, prepare the entry to record Hollenbeck's payment to the bank.

**12S-6 (Part B).** The following transactions were made by the Gulf Coast Boat Company concerning notes received from its customers during the current year.

Jan. 8. Received a 30-day, 12 percent note from Juan Diaz in the amount of $800 for payment of his account.
30. Received a 4-month, 11 percent note for $7,500 from Bryan Hundley for a used cabin cruiser.
Feb. 7. Received payment from Juan Diaz in payment of his note plus interest.
Mar. 28. Received a 90-day, 13 percent note from Jay Rosenfelt, a customer, for $700 cash loaned to him as a favor.

**Instructions:** Prepare the entries in general journal form to record the above transactions.

**12S-7 (Part B).** Pearl Crain has an opportunity to make a highly favorable purchase of merchandise but will have to borrow the cash to complete the deal. Crain has talked to two of her banker friends about borrowing $6,000 for 3 months. Banker A told Crain he would be happy to discount her non-interest-bearing note for $6,000 for 3 months at the rate of 12 percent. Banker B agreed to loan Crain $6,000 and accept a 3-month, 12 percent note for the face value.

**Instructions:** Which banker would you advise Crain to use? Why? Prepare computations to support your answer.

**12S-8 (Part B).** On May 4, Jamie Higgs purchased $600 of merchandise from Gary Reiman on account. On June 10, Higgs gave Reiman a 60-day, 12 percent note in payment of the goods purchased on May 4. On August 9, Higgs paid Reiman for the note due on that day plus interest.

**Instructions:**

(1) Prepare the entries to record the above transactions, in general journal form, on the books of Higgs.
(2) Prepare the entries in general journal form, necessary to record the transactions on the books of Reiman.

**12S-9 (Part B).** Following are sections of financial statements, each designated by a letter.

A — Current Asset
B — Current Liability
C — Operating Expense
D — Other Income
E — Other Expense

**Instructions:** Indicate in which section each of the following accounts would be shown in the financial statements.

0. *Insurance Expense — C*
1. Interest Expense
2. Prepaid Advertising
3. Accrued Salaries Payable
4. Unearned Subscriptions
5. Office Supplies
6. Accrued Interest Payable
7. Store Supplies Expense
8. Prepaid Insurance
9. Property Tax Payable
10. Commissions Receivable
11. Interest Income

**13S-1 (Part A).** Given below is the detailed information of the Tree House Specialty Shop's inventory for the current month.

| Stock No. | Inventory, January 1 | First Purchase | Second Purchase | Third Purchase | Units in inventory, January 31 |
|---|---|---|---|---|---|
| B214 | 4 @ $10.00 | 6 @ $11.00 | 5 @ $11.00 | 6 @ $12.00 | 8 |
| D199 | 10 @ 3.00 | 12 @ 3.25 | 15 @ 3.50 | 14 @ 4.00 | 18 |
| E307 | 60 @ .50 | 70 @ .55 | 95 @ .60 | 50 @ .65 | 80 |

**Instructions:** Compute the cost of the ending inventory by:

(1) The first-in, first-out method.
(2) The last-in, first-out method.

**13S-2 (Part A).** The cost of the merchandise inventory on hand for the Pocahontas Company at the end of the year is shown for each of the following methods:

| | |
|---|---|
| Fifo | $12,200 |
| Lifo | 10,800 |
| Weighted Average | 11,640 |

If the weighted average method is used, the net income for the year is $17,400.

**Instructions:** Based on the above information:

(1) Determine the net income if the fifo method is used.
(2) Determine the net income if the lifo method is used.

**13S-3 (Part B).** The merchandise inventory of the Kunimoto Company at the end of the fiscal period is composed of the following:

600 units of L; cost $3.00 per unit, market $2.50.
800 units of P; cost $3.20 per unit, market $3.50.
700 units of N; cost $2.10 per unit, market $1.80.

**Instructions:** Determine the value of the ending inventory at "cost or market, whichever is lower," if the valuation procedure is applied to:

(1) the individual items.
(2) the inventory as a whole.

**13S-4 (Part B).** Wayne Allison's Gift Shop was burglarized on August 7, and an undetermined amount of inventory was taken. You have been asked by Allison, to assist in preparing an estimate of the cost of the inventory stolen for the insurance claim. The accounting records of the company revealed the following:

| | |
|---|---|
| Merchandise inventory, January 1 | $ 31,000 |
| Net purchases since January 1 | 63,700 |
| Freight in | 1,900 |
| Sales for the period | 145,200 |
| Estimated gross profit percentage | 45% |

Allison determined by count that the merchandise still on hand cost $7,400.

**Instructions:** Determine the cost of inventory to be reported as stolen.

**13S-5 (Part B).** The following account balances were taken from the ledger of the Bomar Shirt Shop on June 30, of the current year.

| | |
|---|---|
| Merchandise inventory, January 1 | $ 8,060 |
| Net purchases | 29,900 |
| Sales | 45,200 |
| Sales returns | 1,200 |

The following data were also available: merchandise inventory, Janaury 1, at retail $10,600; net purchases at retail for the year were $47,800.

**Instructions:** Determine the inventory at June 30, using the retail method.

**13S-6 (Part B).** Manana Air Conditioning Sales and Service uses a perpetual inventory system on a fifo basis. Below you are given, in T-account form, the purchase and sales record of a 1.5 ton window unit, Model W1523, for the month of May. This model sells for $250 per unit.

Model W1523

| | | | | |
|---|---|---|---|---|
| Bal. May 1 | 2 @ 150 | May 3 | 1 unit to Ross Tate on account |
| 10 | 3 @ 160 | 12 | 2 units to Darrell Sams on account |
| 18 | 2 @ 160 | 26 | 1 unit to Wilson Jones for cash |

**Instructions:** Prepare the entries, in general journal form, for May to record the purchases and sales of Model W1523. All purchases are from the Dexter Co., on account.

## CHAPTER 14

**14S-1 (Part A).** Determine whether the following items would be recorded on the balance sheet as (a) plant assets, (b) inventory, or (c) some other classification.

1. Auto tires for Goodyear.
2. Auto tires for taxi cab company.
3. Installation costs of new equipment.
4. Current year property tax on land.
5. Microwave oven in restaurant.
6. Microwave oven in appliance store.
7. Realtor's fee on land purchased.
8. Cost to install new engine in delivery truck.
9. Shipping cost on merchandise purchased.
10. Sales tax on new typewriter for office.
11. Architect's fee on construction of building.
12. Delinquent property taxes paid on land purchased.

**14S-2 (Part A).** A bradding machine is purchased for use in the production process of a manufacturing company. The machine cost $17,500, and has an expected life of 8 years. It is estimated that the machine can brad 400,000 units during its life and will have a residual value of $1,500.

**Instructions:** Determine the depreciation expense on the machine for each of the first two years, assuming (a) that the straight-line method is used; (b) that the units-of-production method is used and that the number of units bradded are 60,000 and 45,000, in years 1 and 2 respectively.

**14S-3 (Part A).** A memory typewriter was purchased at a cost of $2,200 at the beginning of the current fiscal year. The typewriter has an expected life of 4 years and an estimated salvage value of $400.

**Instructions:** Determine for each of the first two years, the depreciation expense per year, and the accumulated depreciation and book value of the typewriter at the end of each year, using the sum-of-the-years-digits method.

**14S-4 (Part A).** The city utility department purchased a new street sweeper at a cost of $18,000. This type of sweeper has an expected useful life of 10 years and the normal salvage value is $2,000.

**Instructions:** Compute the depreciation expense per year, accumulated depreciation, and book value of the sweeper for the first three years of operation if the city uses the declining-balance method at twice the straight-line rate.

**14S-5 (Part B).** Peter Vogel, CPA, purchased a minicomputer for his office that cost $15,000, has an estimated useful life of 10 years, and no residual value.

**Instructions:** Record the journal entry for each situation below, using straight-line depreciation. (Use the account title "Office Equipment.")

(1) Retired the computer after its tenth year.
(2) Retired the computer after its seventh year.
(3) Sold the computer after 6 years for $4,000.
(4) Sold the computer after 4 years for $10,000.

**14S-6 (Part B).** A mag-card machine (Office Equipment) that had been purchased at a cost of $7,000 with a useful life of 8 years and estimated salvage of $1,000 was sold at the end of four and one-half years for $4,000.

**Instructions:** Prepare the entries to bring the depreciation up to date for the half-year using the straight-line method, and to record the sale of the mag-card machine.